THE
ART OF
RHETORIC

THE ART OF RHETORIC

FRANCIS CONNOLLY
Late of Fordham University

Edited and completed by
Gerald Levin
University of Akron

HARCOURT, BRACE & WORLD, INC.
New York / Chicago / San Francisco / Atlanta

The purposes of men are infinite in number, but for a treatise on Rhetoric we may reduce the motives which induce us to speak or write at any time to three general categories—to convey information, to induce others to act in a certain way, or thirdly, to give pleasure, to interest and delight by wit, feeling, or imagination.

Sir Herbert J. C. Grierson

Preface

THIS BOOK presents the substance of today's college composition courses. It introduces the student to the construction of the paragraph, the organization of the whole essay, and the types of discourse. But its approach is by way of traditional rhetoric as that rhetoric took shape through the teachings of Plato and Aristotle, was refined and further systematized by Cicero, and was modified and enriched by writers and teachers before and since the English Renaissance. This approach has the advantage of presenting reading and writing in such a way that the student can readily understand that they are counterparts, that reading is more than an aid to discussion or a resource of ideas, that invention and judgment are parts of a single process.

The book is organized to give the student first a brief introduction to the theory underlying that process, then to give him practice in the process. Specifically, the plan is as follows:

Part One, The Nature of Rhetoric, presents the theory of classical rhetoric with an emphasis on Cicero's contribution. The third chapter of this part traces the history of certain aspects of rhetoric from the early Middle Ages to the eighteenth century, ending with a discussion of the development of the English essay and of English prose style from Thomas More to Edmund Burke.

Part Two, The Practice of Rhetoric, is a reader of twenty-eight selections that contrasts essays by old and modern authors to illustrate both continuity and change in the rhetorical tradition in English. Its five sections—Description and Narration, Exposition, Argument and Persuasion, Expository Narrative, and Expository Argument—cover the traditional methods of development: the use of detail, examples and illustrations, definition, analysis, process, reasoning, logic, and so on. These methods of development are not presented as artificially isolated elements. Full headnotes and questions for discussion explore the rhetorical strategy of the particular writers and show how the chosen organization and rhetorical techniques have been used to realize an author's purpose in relation to his subject and his audience. The choices available to the writer are introduced systematically; in the Topics for Composition the student is encouraged to show his awareness of them. A feature of Part Two that may be of special interest to the instructor is the thorough treatment of argument and persuasion, beginning with a detailed analysis of Burke's speech *On Conciliation with the Colonies*.

Part Three, The Theory of Rhetoric, presents a series of readings in classical and modern rhetoric. The opening pages of Plato's *Republic* illustrate his dialectic in its beginning stage and suggest something of the way Socrates fits his argument to a particular audience without, however, altering the truth. The *Phaedrus*, which follows, explores the possibility of an ideal rhetoric and the problems of indifferent ones. The selection from Aristotle's *Rhetoric* includes his discussion of the province of rhetoric, its relation to dialectic, and the lines of argument. The three essays by modern writers explore problems of rhetoric of special interest to the student. Richard Weaver follows his penetrating analysis of the *Phaedrus* by examining the implications of the dialogue for an ideal rhetoric. Wayne C. Booth's "The Rhetorical Stance" discusses the importance of rhetoric to a literate, vigorous writing style and deals specifically with the student's chief writing problems. Kenneth Burke's "Rhetoric—Old and New" illustrates one of the new rhetorics that have arisen under the influence of the new social sciences. The headnotes and topics for discussion and composition in this part of the book provide a brief discussion of basic terms and ideas and offer suggestions for further study.

The late Francis Connolly completed the first two chapters of Part One and all of Part Two; he also selected most of the material included in Part Three.

My contribution has been the third chapter of Part
One and the editorial material for Part Three. In-
structors who have used Professor Connolly's previous books will find here his usual keen awareness
of the problems students face and the matters
about which they need to be informed.

GERALD LEVIN

❦ Contents

Contents

THE
ART OF
RHETORIC

Part One

THE NATURE OF RHETORIC

How Rhetoric Began

By the time the student of English begins college he knows a great deal about rhetoric. He knows that the term _rhetoric_ refers to the art of using language to influence the thought or action of others. Its usual synonym is _persuasion_, addressing others with the intention of inducing them to think, to feel, to believe, or to act in agreement with us. Hence, rhetoric implies _communication_, understood both as a system of verbal signals and as a mode of identification with others in a community. We form this community with persons to whom we have imparted our ideas and feelings and with whom, in consequence, we live in common understanding and with sympathy. In its largest sense rhetoric unites men through the exchange of thought and language. It is man's bond with society.

It does not surprise us, therefore, to discover that from earliest times man has studied the art of rhetoric. At first, he imitated the practice of the most effective speakers of his place and time. He learned good speech naturally by studying and imitating those who had succeeded in instructing, moving, and pleasing others.

In time, teachers of the art of speaking offered their services to citizens who, as democracy developed, could file a claim against their fellows, or defend themselves against the charge of crime, or propose that a law be enacted, or dispute the meaning of the law in the light of principle. How to argue a case logically, how to affect a jury, what kind of language to use and what to avoid, what modes of discourse to choose as appropriate to various subjects and audiences soon became matters of professional attention.

In Syracuse, Sicily, by the end of the fifth century B.C., Corax and his pupil Tisias had composed handbooks on rhetorical art. According to Aristotle, Corax divided the simple speech into three parts:

1. An exordium or introduction;
2. The arguments, those in favor of the proposition and those that had to be answered; and
3. An epilogue or conclusion.

The more elaborate speech included a narration of the facts of the case, which was placed after the introduction, and supplementary arguments or illustrations of the main argument. Thus, from very early times, the basic structure of oratory was firmly established in the natural pattern of beginning, middle, and end, with the middle containing both proof and refutation.

Corax's skills became available to the Athenians when his pupil Tisias and Tisias' pupil, Gorgias of Leontini, visited Athens as ambassadors from their city-state in Syracuse. Gorgias' discourses and his treatises on rhetorical art attracted imitators, so that soon Athens and other Greek cities witnessed a remarkable growth of professional orators and teachers of oratory. Some, concentrating only on the manner of speaking, by their indifference to matters of truth, gave to rhetoric a sophistic—that is, a clever but specious—turn and a reputation for triviality that endures to this day in the expression "mere rhetoric." Others, responding to the Greek quest for truth, harmonized the art of persuasion with ethical and philosophical ideals. A variety of styles flourished, some ornate, some severely plain, some moderate, so that many books of rhetoric were actually manuals of what their authors claimed to be the only correct style of addressing an audience. On the whole, the early development of rhetoric was marked by a practical concern with winning cases in court. The later emphasis on the relation of the art of rhetoric to the art of thinking—that is, to logic, politics, and psychology, and to the obligations imposed by one's duties to justice and truth—came with the critical analyses of Socrates and Plato and the brilliant synthesis of Aristotle.

In his dialogue *Gorgias,* Plato investigated the nature of rhetoric. Is rhetoric essentially devoted to the discovery of truth, or is it merely the art of plausibility, or even the perverse art of making the worse appear the better reason? Plato's spokesman, Socrates, doubted that in practice rhetoricians seek truth or that rhetoric itself is a true art. In *Phaedrus* (see Part Three) Socrates continued to attack rhetoric as an unsystematic science that tolerated absurdities and, if useful at all, trained young men to become facile speakers. It was a *paedeia,* a training for youth, rather than a *philosophia,* a search for wisdom. In *Phaedrus,* Plato dwelt emphatically on the relation of rhetoric to truth. In one place Socrates tells Phaedrus that no one should attempt to persuade others of a truth that he himself does not firmly possess. A true orator must know in advance

> the truth about each particular of which he speaks or writes. He must be able to define each one of them in itself. When he has defined them, he must, in turn, know how to subdivide them severally according to their species, to the point where a division cannot be carried further. By the same method of analysis, he must investigate the nature of the soul, and must discover what kind of argument is adapted to each nature. This done he must settle and order his discourse accordingly ... to be controlled by art for the purpose of instruction or persuasion.

As in other areas of knowledge, so too in the sphere of rhetoric, Aristotle developed and systematized the insights of his master Plato and those of many other predecessors. But he was not a mere imitator. He constantly displayed his original genius by giving a new turn to the work of others. Thus where Plato tended to make "true" rhetoric the equivalent of dialectic or logic, Aristotle made it a counterpart of logic; where Plato tended to depreciate the use of rhetoric to win a judgment in court, Aristotle applauded the skilled rhetorician who, he said, corrected the deficiencies of those unable to defend truth and justice.

Aristotle's main contribution, however, was not his correction of overemphasis or underemphasis in the work of other rhetoricians. Rather it was his comprehensive grasp of the nature and practice of rhetoric. He saw rhetoric from all sides: from the point of view of the speaker, the speech, and the audience. Moreover, he presented each of these elements in greater depth and perspective than did his rivals. In discussing the role of the speaker he stressed the importance of *ethos,* a man's natural character. Ethos referred primarily to moral character; the speaker's virtue and dignity gave authority to his proof. It also implied psychological insight into character, since the speaker's discrimination of the mental characteristics of his audience enabled him to stress the most appropriate proof, or to appeal to any emotion, or to express himself in a style appropriate to the occasion.

With similar acumen Aristotle perceived that each of the various kinds of speech required a different emphasis. His predecessors were chiefly concerned with forensic or legal oratory, where the issues were matters of fact or principles of justice and where the mode of proof was determined by court procedure. Aristotle directed equal attention to the deliberative oratory of the legislator, for whom the issues were the possibility of future actions, and to demonstrative (he called it *epideictic*) oratory, where the issues consisted of the reasons for praise or censure. He noted, too, in *Rhetoric* how each kind of oratory had its appropriate proof.

> Speaking generally, of the topics common to all rhetorical arguments, amplification [intensification by repetition, development, or heightened style] is most suitable for epideictic speakers, whose subject is actions not disputed.... Examples are most suitable for deliberative speakers, for it is by examination of the past that we divine and judge the future. Enthymemes [thoughts or arguments leading to probable proof] are most suitable for forensic speakers, because the past, by reasons of its obscurity, above all lends itself to the investigation of causes....

THE INFLUENCE OF ARISTOTLE'S "RHETORIC"

Comprehensive, penetrating, persuasive by virtue of its logic and its power of illustration, Aristotle's *Rhetoric* was destined to exert a permanent effect first on Greek oratory, then on Latin oratory, finally on the theory and practice of composition in all the languages that felt its influence. Some say, with British scholar Herbert J. C. Grierson, that although others have expanded or elaborated on his statements on rhetoric, "No one has added anything essential to Aristotle's treatment of the whole subject.... [Aristotle] composed a philosophical treatise on rhetoric of which it has been said that in it a science was at once begun and finished." Those responsive to the growth and development of thought and language still acknowledge a debt to Aristotle even when they feel compelled to modify his principles or to disassociate themselves from the philosophical assumptions that his *Rhetoric* contains.

Nor was the influence of *Rhetoric* confined merely to the composition of speeches. Aristotle himself had related poetry to rhetoric by referring the reader of his *Poetics* to his *Rhetoric* for a discussion of the important element of thought. In turn what Aristotle had to say about style in his *Rhetoric* was illustrated, more often than not, by poetry or verse. Poetry and rhetoric went hand in hand. As many scholars have noted, the Roman poet Horace was one of many commentators who boldly transferred elements of Aristotle's *Rhetoric* to the field of poetry. This fusion of rhetoric and poetics persisted from classical times, through the Middle Ages, and continued throughout the Renaissance to our own time, so that many join Renaissance scholar J. C. Scaliger in the belief that poetry and rhetoric have the same end, namely, persuasion. Thus Aristotle's *Rhetoric*, together with its companion piece, *Poetics*, has been, and is, a continuous influence on writing and on new theories of rhetoric.

ROMAN RHETORIC

Greek rhetoric was thoroughly assimilated by the Romans, thanks chiefly to Cicero (Marcus Tullius Cicero, 106–43 B.C.) and Quintilian (Marcus Fabius Quintilianus, A.D. 35?–97?), who developed an elaborate theory of rhetoric based on the principles and practice of Cicero. Although there are some important differences between Greek and Roman oratory, Roman rhetoric derived directly from Greek sources. It was not, however, unoriginal. Cicero and Quintilian systematized, explored, and extended the rhetorical theory of the Greeks and applied it shrewdly to their own Latin language. The Romans stressed, for instance, the importance of several studies in the training of an orator. Cicero's lifelong interest in philosophy, poetry, and history and Quintilian's references to these subjects as necessary elements in the education of the orator remind us how much these men helped to expand the concept of the orator from that of one skilled in the art of persuasion to that of the *bonus vir dicens,* the good man speaking. For the Romans the orator was not only the good man skilled in speaking; he was also the good speaker perfected by the study of all the liberal arts. The moral and intellectual virtues came to full flower in the ideal orator.

Hence, when we acknowledge that Roman rhetoric derives from the Greeks, we must also say that it passed down a new and valuable understanding of its Greek prototype. Moreover, by an accident of history most Western nations learned both literature and language from Rome rather than from Athens. Cicero and Quintilian rather than Demosthenes and Aristotle were the principal exemplars and teachers of the art of rhetoric to the nations of the West. The Latin influence on other literatures, consid-

The Nature of Rhetoric

ered in its full range and depth, is incalculable and, in its ultimate reaches, untraceable. Yet we may briefly describe our principal inheritance from the Roman theory of rhetoric under four topics—namely, the purpose of rhetoric in general, the various kinds of rhetoric, the elements common to all kinds of rhetoric, and later, in connection with Cicero's *Pro Archia,* the external form of the finished oratorical composition. At that point we shall demonstrate how Cicero exemplified rhetorical theory in practice in a speech that defends not only Archias the poet, but also the humane arts in general.

The Purpose of Rhetoric — to persuade, convince, + delight

Roman thinking corresponded to that of the Greeks in defining the general purpose of rhetoric as persuasion—that is, the presentation of reasonable motives for free action. The Romans pictured the orator as one who attempts to induce his hearers to judge the accused guilty or not guilty, to pass or reject a law, to join in praising an honorable man or action or in contemning a dishonorable one. Thus rhetoric was synonymous with persuasive speech in courts, in legislative assemblies, and on civic occasions. Later writers extended rhetoric to include poetry, letter-writing, history, and other modes of communication that, like the oration, presented to readers motives calculated to mold belief or lead to action.

Essentially, then, the purpose of rhetoric was to move (*movere*) the audience, that is, to bring about an action. But if the audience is free to act or not to act, the speaker must also convince his audience that the proposed action is reasonable. He does not command or exhort without explaining how or why it is reasonable, just, expedient, or appropriate for them to do what he invites them to do. To move an audience of reasonable men one must use reason by teaching (*docere*), informing, demonstrating, arguing, proving the propositions of the speech. Finally, the orator must not only appeal to will and reason but must also delight (*delectare*) by presenting his thought in harmonious proportions, in a style as pleasing as it is clear, and in a tone appropriate to his subject and audience. One delights his audience not by tacking on passages of purple prose but by making the language of the speech radiant with wit, grace, and variety, thus illuminating the subject. Hence the purpose of rhetoric was primarily to persuade but also, of necessity, to convince and to charm the listener. That purpose was unified since persuasion involved conviction and delight was conveyed by the way the orator achieved conviction and persuasion through the arrangement, style, and delivery of his speech. By giving parallel importance to the element of delight, the Romans tended to cultivate the esthetic qualities of an oration and thus to relate rhetoric to poetry whose purpose, according to Horace, was both to please and to instruct.

The Kinds of Rhetoric

The principles we have just discussed applied to rhetoric in general. All good speeches reflected a threefold appeal to the will, the intellect, and the esthetic sense. All sought to move the will, to convince the reason, and to capture the imagination. Just how they did this depended on the nature of the subject and the characteristics of the audience. As Quintilian remarked, "Rhetoric would be very easy and but a small matter, if it could be comprehended in one short set of rules, but rules must generally be altered in accordance with the nature of each individual case, the time, the occasion . . . " and so on. But there never was one set of rules because there were many kinds of oratory, each of which required its own kind of flexibility. We may observe this by a brief examination of the three kinds universally recognized throughout the Roman world—forensic, deliberative, and demonstrative.

Forensic Oratory

Forensic derives from the noun *forum,* a public square where official business was transacted. Forensic oratory was the kind of speech delivered in the courtroom either by the prosecutor of or by the defense counsel for a person accused of a crime or minor offense. It is also called judicial or legal oratory. Since forensic oratory concerned an act that was punishable according to the prescriptions of law, both the main purpose and the issues were predetermined. The speaker's purpose was to prove the guilt or innocence of the person accused. The relevant issue was a matter of fact, definition, or justification. Thus if a man was charged with bribing a senator, the possible issues could be stated in the following ways:

1. Whether *in fact* a bribe was offered and was accepted;
2. Whether, if a bribe was offered and accepted, the transaction could legally be *defined* as bribery;
3. Whether, presuming a bribe was offered and accepted and that bribery was admitted, the accused was *justified* in offering or accepting the bribe because of inculpable ignorance, the obscurity of the law, lack of evil intent, or extenuating circumstances.

Argument on any one of these issues limited the subject and, normally, called for certain prescribed methods of proof and refutation. To prove an issue of fact the speaker showed what happened and produced competent and credible witnesses and documents to support his view. To prove an issue of definition he attempted to show whether the alleged bribe was indeed a bribe according to legal definition. To prove an issue of justification he argued that the circumstances of the case and the reasons the accused person did what he did were sufficiently compelling to excuse him from the penalties of the law.

Deliberative Oratory — What ought to be done & why — "Congressional"—political

Forensic oratory dealt with past events and issues relating to justice. Deliberative oratory dealt with future events relating to issues such as the intrinsic worth or practical usefulness of proposed legislation. The deliberative speaker urged a choice among several possible actions. His topics were the good or evil effects or consequences of the action he sponsored or opposed. Thus in addressing the senate or a popular assembly, the deliberative orator debated issues like these:

1. Whether a proposed law or practice would benefit the Roman state;
2. Whether it would contribute to the glory and welfare of the citizens;
3. Whether it would be easy or difficult, expedient or inexpedient to put into effect.

Demonstrative Oratory — Ceremonial oratory — reasons for praise or blame

Demonstrative oratory (the epideictic oratory of the Greeks) had for its special purpose the praise or censure of a person or an institution. In this kind of speaking—by far the most comprehensive since it embraced ceremonial occasions like funerals, triumphs, dedications, anniversaries, and civic celebrations—the reasons for praise or blame were the predominent issues. Thus in the demonstrative section of the *Pro Archia* (p. 33) Cicero praises Archias for his learning and wit, while in his *Philippics* he castigates Mark Antony for rashness, ingratitude, and injustice. Similarly, in Shakespeare's *Julius Caesar* Mark Antony extolled Caesar's courage and generosity and insinuated that Brutus was ungrateful and treacherous (p. 57).

Thus the purposes of rhetoric were specifically directed to meet the needs of the court, the legislative body, and various civic audiences. In each instance the orator selected issues, developed arguments, fashioned a particular style not to persuade, inform, and delight an unspecified audience, but to convince a special kind of audience that a specific thesis was sound and that a specific decision was reasonable. A speech was good when it contributed directly to a specific purpose, even though for various reasons the orator failed to win his case or obtain passage of the law he sponsored.

This does not mean, however, that in either theory or practice Roman oratory was excessively rigid. Far from it. "My unusual manner of speaking," a phrase frequently used by Cicero, usually meant that he was about to employ the high style appropriate to a panegyric in a predominantly judicial speech like *Pro Archia* or that in the grave precincts of the Senate, where the plain style of explanation and reason was most becoming, he was about to express vehement indignation, as at the conspiracy of a Cataline. The Romans allowed for variations of style, mixed forms of discourse, even lengthy digressions, whenever the occasion demanded such departures from the usual manner of speaking.

The Elements of Rhetoric

While Roman orators and rhetoricians, like their Greek predecessors, gave much attention to the requirements of the special kinds of oratory we have just described, they also studied all the elements involved in the preparation of any kind of speech. They plotted the movement of the orator's mind from the moment he began to explore the subject, the occasion, and his prospective audience to that moment when the speech was given and the corrected manuscript was handed to a library slave for copying and distribution among friends and followers. Rhetorical study in general, they felt, consisted of five interrelated elements: invention or discovery, disposition or arrangement, elocution or style, memory, and delivery. Each of these elements depended on the other and each was equally important for the perfect speech.

Cicero showed how the foregoing elements were related when, in the person of Crassus, a character in the dialogue *De Oratore*, he wrote:

> And, since all the activity and ability of an orator falls into five divisions, I learned that he must first hit upon what to say; then manage and marshal his discoveries, not merely in orderly fashion, but with a discriminating eye for the exact weight as it were of each argument; next go on to array them in the adornments of style; after that keep them guarded in the memory; and in the end deliver them with effect and charm.

But we must not suppose that any orator could master each of these five elements all at once or even that he could eventually learn all that could be known about each one once and for all. The orator was constantly preparing himself for his task. He began with study under the *litterator*, who, in his analysis of Homer, pointed out the principles of a good style and exercised his young pupils in figures or unusual modes of phrase and sentence construction, in lines of argument and topics, and in the devices of memory or mnemonics. He continued in the second stage of Roman education under the *rhetor*, or teacher of rhetoric, who explained and analyzed difficult aspects of invention in the speeches and cases selected for study. He persisted throughout philosophical studies of his later years when the orator applied, so to speak, the modes of analyzing propositions and constructing arguments discovered in philosophy to the practical sphere of rhetoric.

Nor did his studies end with philosophy. For there was always need for the analysis of new cases, for the study of new situations, for a deeper penetration into the meaning of new subjects and new sets of relations between subjects. In short, the study of rhetoric extended from childhood to old age; it embraced both the simplest elements of style and the most searching elements of invention.

Invention or Discovery: Hitting upon what to say

To *invent* in its root sense meant to come upon, to find out, to discover, to learn. For the Roman schoolboy learning how to write speeches it meant, in effect, the methodical investigation of all the possible reasons he could find to support his thesis. The possible arguments might not be the most cogent, but they could provide a beginning for thought. Let us illustrate how that schoolboy might proceed in his search for something to say about a thesis set by his *rhetor*. Suppose that thesis, or proposition, to be "A good orator is a benefactor of the republic."

If the schoolboy followed the instructions learned from Cicero or later from Quintilian, he would begin to investigate the common topics, that is, the places where arguments could be found. These topics, distinguished and illustrated by Aristotle, were conventionally divided into extrinsic topics and intrinsic topics.

EXTRINSIC TOPICS - *using references, sources.*

An extrinsic or external topic was derived from sources outside the analysis of the proposition itself. Thus the student might begin looking for extrinsic proofs by recalling what he had heard or read about the contributions of a good orator to the welfare of the state. In short, he would find out what authorities—the famous rhetoricians and teachers, for example—had said on the subject. He could quote their views, as lawyers cited the testimony of authoritative witnesses, to show that orators had indeed benefited the republic. He could, and often did, cudgel his brain for famous maxims and proverbs that illustrated the truth of his proposition. Had not Cato once said . . . ? Was not Demosthenes the one who remarked . . . ? When he grew up and had obtained a wide acquaintance with the literature of oratory, he would merely consult his memory or that second memory, his library, for first-class authorities to support his view, as Cicero did in extolling the virtues of the poet in *Pro Archia*.

Later, as a lawyer, he would cite the law and precedents as sources of his arguments. His successors in our day would add to his sources a multitude of dictionaries, encyclopedias, and other reference books from a good research library.

INTRINSIC TOPICS *analyzing the argument.*

In addition to extrinsic topics, the student was trained to investigate the intrinsic sources of argument. A topic was called intrinsic when it derived from the analysis of the terms of the proposition. In a complete inventory of intrinsic topics most rhetoricians listed the following: *definition*, which was subdivided into genus or whole and species or parts; *comparison*, which was subdivided into points of similarity and difference, and degree; *essential relationship,* which was subdivided into cause and effect, antecedents and consequents, contraries, opposites, and contradictories; *circumstances,* or the facts surrounding the case. To these topics, or places where one looked for something to say about a proposition, some rhetoricians added two verbal topics: *derivation,* or analysis of the origin of a word; and *conjugates,* or analysis of words with the same root.

Although at one time or another the student might find any of these topics helpful, he normally concentrated on the principal ones—those pertaining to *definition, comparison,* and *essential relationship.*

We shall show how a few of these topics could help the student discover lines of thought that he could develop in a speech. Many of them, like definition, have been thoroughly assimilated into modern rhetoric. Others, like contraries and contradictories, are now studied in formal logic.

Under the heading of *definition,* the student could discover what the verbal terms of the thesis meant or implied. *Good orator* could certainly be taken to mean "a skillful speaker whose object was to give efficacy to truth." Thus, one could say that *good orator,* the subject of his thesis sentence, by definition implied the predicate, *a benefactor of the republic.* For if one assumed that the truth was always of benefit to the republic, then the man who made the truth prevail benefited the republic in numerous ways. Was not a man who used his skill in speaking to make the truth prevail a true benefactor of the republic? This line of argument did not constitute a proof but could lend support to one.

Further, each arm of the definition (the class or genus and the species or member of the class) pointed to new areas for more detailed investigation. A good orator belonged to the class or genus of one skilled in speaking. Here was a topic that the student could write about. What, precisely, constituted skill in speaking? What made that class of men ornaments of the state? Turning to the species of *good orator,* he could ask how specifically did an orator by his skill make reason and truth and justice prevail. There were several species of orators, some distinguished by the vigor of their appeal to emotions, some by the rigor of their argument, some by the grace and beauty of their language and delivery. Each type, in some proportion, benefited the state by inciting men to noble actions, by promoting justice, or by contributing to the glory of the Roman name. In addition, one could name individuals who constituted the class of good orators: Demosthenes and Socrates among the Greeks, Cato and Cicero among the Romans. Did they not demonstrably contribute to the welfare of the republic by arousing men to aid the officers of the state and to resist the enemies of the state?

A second topic, already suggested by the naming of individual orators, was *comparison.* The schoolboy needed no check list or table of topics to be told that he could also develop his subject by comparing the class *good orator* with the class *good poet,* or a specific oration with another in the same class, or an individual orator, Demosthenes, with another orator, Cicero. There were many points of likeness between the class *good orator* and the class *good poet*, between one good oration and another, between Demosthenes and Cicero. So too there were differences or contrasts. The good poet was unlike the good orator in that his aim was to give pleasure to his readers as he instructed them rather than to win a case in court or to bring about a specific action. Horace had said in *Ars Poetica:* "He has gained every vote who has mingled profit with pleasure by delighting the reader at once and instructing him." So too one Ciceronian speech differed from another, however similar their general character. Later generations of students, with their Plutarch before them, would draw from his *Parallel Lives* abundant examples of likeness and difference, examples that in turn furnished Shakespeare with characters of his Roman plays and many a poet with topics by which to praise kings, prelates, and warriors.

Comparison, too, was the source from which the young student drew the argument of degree. Thus, in supporting his thesis, "A good orator is a benefactor of the republic," he might develop either the how-much-more-so or the how-much-less-so comparison. If an honest trader were an acknowledged benefactor insofar as he increased the wealth of the state, how much more so was the good orator who protected the rights of the honest trader and increased his opportunities to add to his wealth? Or he might argue from the lesser to the greater in this manner: If the good orator who gave force to truth could not persuade the citizens, then how much less so could an ignorant and illiterate scoundrel?

Another intrinsic topic was *cause and effect*. The cause-effect relationship was radically connected with the most difficult problems of metaphysics. It was, in some respects, not far from mystery. Yet the young student did know that a cause was the reason something existed and that between a cause and its effect there was a necessary relationship. That is to say, where a cause was operative an effect followed; where an effect was observed a cause could be inferred.

According to these principles the student could examine his proposition by asking a series of questions. What made the good orator a benefactor of the state? This led the student to the discovery of what good orators had already accomplished. Had not Cicero exposed the plot of Cataline to seize the republic? An orator was good because he personally was responsible for good effects, as the statement of the student's proposed thesis implied. How was the orator responsible? By his moral character, by his ability as a thinker and a speaker, Cicero crushed the Cataline conspiracy and saved Rome from anarchy and destruction. Here indeed was a cause-effect argument. To pursue this topic further was to discover other reasons why the good orator was the cause of benefits to the state. He cooperated in establishing justice, in creating good laws, in promoting public order, in educating citizens, in elevating the tone of society by opposing his excellence of character and intellect to the ignorance and insolence of disorderly mobs.

Turning the topic around, the student could discover that the good orator himself was the product of a number of causes. His mind was developed through arduous studies, his character was fashioned by able teachers, his career was the result of a harmonious combination of his own efforts and the opportunities of his time and place. Surely this line of argument might serve to indicate how the orator benefited the state.

Closely related to the topic of cause and effect was that called *antecedent and consequent*. Whereas the cause-effect relationship was a necessary one, the antecedent-consequent relationship was a probable one. In cause and effect, if cause A was present, effect B necessarily followed. In antecedent and consequent, if antecedent A was present, consequent B normally or usually followed. Though the student knew that the topic of antecedent and consequent was logically less compelling than that of cause and effect, he also found that the former topic sometimes yielded an argument when the latter did not.

Similarly, the argument from circumstances, the familiar circumstantial evidence, which showed how the circumstances of time, place, person, and degree pointed to the possibility of an action, was often the only available argument. An "only" argument, he came to realize, might be the best argument, however low it was ranked in the table of topics.

Thus *invention*, the discovery of arguments by analysis of the terms of the proposition and of the relationship of those terms to each other, led the student to various possibilities. Depending on his own capacity and his own experience, he could find reasonable arguments to support a thesis and to test its consistency and its logic. His task, then, was to choose methods of analysis that best met his prospective needs. Some methods he would discard as irrelevant; others he would only touch upon because they demanded more dexterity in logic or more exact knowledge than he possessed. But the chances are that among the so-called external and internal topics he would find something to say, hopefully the exactly right thing to say, in support of the thesis, "A good orator is a benefactor of the republic."

Disposition or Arrangement: "Then manage and marshal his discoveries . . . with a discriminating eye . . ."

Invention or discovery was the most prominent element in the preparation of a speech. Embracing as it did all the possible ways of analyzing a proposition, it was equivalent to our modern term *research*. *Invention* meant both the study of subject matter and the various modes of analysis that give access to that subject matter, both knowledge as well as ways of examining knowledge. Small wonder that invention received by far the most attention in Roman and Greek rhetoric.

If invention seemed to be emphasized more than the other elements, it must be remembered that Roman and Greek rhetoric books were designed for beginners—young men of seventeen years or less—and not for experienced lawyers and rhetoricians. The skilled rhetoricians were most likely to choose swiftly from their abundance of expert knowledge the appropriate arguments to achieve a definite purpose, to meet the needs of an occasion, and to arrange those arguments in the most effective order. For them a flexible *ratio* or plan determined the arrangement of a speech. Just as the military general had a battle to fight, not on paper, but against a definite enemy in definite circumstances, so the orator met a particular problem on each new occasion. Hence the ideal order of the military manuals often gave way to emergency orders and improvised plans, divined intuitively rather than calculated beforehand in every detail. Logic might suggest the order of deduction from general to particular or the order of induction from particular to general as the mode of arranging arguments. But the needs of the particular situation might demand an emotional order rather than a logical one or the immediate display of the speaker's authority, his excellent intentions, and similar "ethical" arguments. As Cicero says in *De Oratore*, the two guiding principles of arrangement are "the orator's judgment and prudence," which enable him to choose freely the order of his arguments, and "the nature of the causes," which imposes a certain mode of procedure in judicial cases and another mode in deliberative cases.

Thus, the orator was theoretically free to choose among many orders: chronological order; logical order; an order of climax; an emergency order, wherein he used his best arguments first to meet the shock of a powerful opponent; and the time-honored Nestorian order of better-good-best. However, the most effective order was always that which was adapted to a particular speech. We shall touch on this again when we discuss the external form of the speech and Cicero's arrangement of arguments in *Pro Archia*.

Elocution or Style: "Language of power and elegance . . ."

The choice of a good style—that is, the words and the sentence structure adapted to the needs of the subject and the capacities of the audience—preoccupied Roman students as it does present-day young Americans. Although style was the principal concern of the grammar schools, it was reviewed, so to speak, at every stage of rhetorical study. The master rhetorician, no less than the beginning student, analyzed and perfected his use of language.

For Cicero elocution or style meant "language of power and elegance accommodated to the feelings and understanding of mankind." Cicero's concept of good style allowed both for firm standards and complete flexibility. Cardinal Newman perceived this double vision of Cicero when he wrote in

Essays and Sketches: ". . . it is by the invention of a style, which adapts itself with singular felicity to every class of subjects, whether lofty or familiar, philosophical or forensic, that Cicero answers even more exactly to his own definition of a perfect orator than by his plausibility, pathos, and brilliancy." [1] True, Cicero accepted the standard styles; the plain for clarity and logic, the grand for display of high passion, and the moderate for the exhibition of ornamental grace. But he recognized that these categories must be adjusted to the particular case and the particular audience. Similarly, Quintilian, after noting the three standard styles, immediately corrected the possible impression that these styles were as hard and fast as arithmetical addition, subtraction, and division. He wrote in his *Institutio Oratoria:*

> It is sheer folly which of these [styles] the orator should take as his model, since every species that is in itself correct has its use, and what is commonly called style of speaking does not depend on the orator. For he will use all styles, as circumstances may demand, and the choice will be determined not only by the case as a whole, but by the demands of the different portions of the case.

Further, he goes on to say, the choice of a style depends on whether he is defending a client on a serious charge or on a haggling matter of a loan, on whether he is addressing the senate or a cohort of soldiers. He will modify his style "to suit the different circumstances of time and place." Moreover, the orator, according to the Roman theorist, "in one and the same speech will use one style for stirring the emotions and another to conciliate the hearers." He will not use the same style in the various parts of an oration, but at various times will speak "gravely, severely, sharply, with vehemence, energy, fullness, bitterness or geniality, quietly, simply, flatteringly, gently, sweetly, briefly or wittily."

In stressing flexibility of style the Roman rhetoricians guarded against the cheap kind of accommodation that descended to vulgarity in the hope of being all things to all men. While addressing a popular audience in a popular way, the orator might not "always be like himself, but he will never be unworthy of himself." One might add, he would always be himself, the good and learned man speaking.

Memory: *"Keep arguments guarded in the memory."*

Memory was the power of the orator to recall the arguments that he had prepared for delivery. It was not, however, mere verbal memory, like that of the small child who recites by rote a poem in a language he does not

[1]Vol. 1 (London: Longmans, Green, 1948), p. 48.

understand. Memory was also the intellectual power, akin to awareness, whereby the speaker maintained possession of the process of his thought. What he intended to say, how and where he planned to make his several points, the particular arrangement of his language—all this called for the reflective mind trained in mnemonics.

A retentive memory was of course immensely more important in ancient times than it is in our day of the typescript, the teleprompter, and numerous other audio-visual aids. Hence the Roman orator had to train himself not to forget. He used various mnemonic devices to retain what he had arranged or written out beforehand. Moreover, he paid attention to the fact that, save in rare instances, his speech was not recorded or published. Hence he had to present his speech in a way that was easily remembered. Frequent repetitions, careful spelling out of divisions, markedly clear transitions—all these devices of arrangement and style were aids to the memory of both the speaker and the hearer.

Delivery: "In the end, deliver [the arguments] with effect and charm."

Although delivery is now often dismissed as the elocutionary phase of rhetoric—as part of public speaking rather than the intellectual preparation of a speech—Cicero among others regarded it as "the sole and supreme power." We may feel today that this view exaggerates the oral and auditory aspects of oratory. Yet the briefest exercise of our historical sense reminds us that delivery for the ancients meant in effect publication. What was the value of a well-written speech if it were not pronounced clearly and vigorously enough to be heard? Or why pronounce it in flat unvaried tones, without appropriate gestures to emphasize the main points or without modulations of pitch and rhythm to express the various feelings of the orator? Delivery was more than the sum of its parts. It included pronunciation and action, utterance and gesture. But its full meaning was *presence*, the total expression of the personality of the orator, a combination of his mind, character, and mode of being, his knowledge, wisdom, and wit, expressed by that most intimate and revealing organ, his voice.

Small wonder, then, that Roman rhetors trained their students in voice, diction or pronunciation, and action to insure the proper delivery of a speech. What the performance meant to the playwright and the actors, what the concert meant to the composer and musicians, the delivery meant to the orator. It was the ultimate test of his efforts, the *finis* or end that crowned the work. It remains for us now to examine an individual oration to see how Cicero, the greatest of the Roman orators, actually composed one of his most successful speeches.

✸ Cicero:
The Classical
Model of
Modern Rhetoric

Cicero raised rhetoric to plane of philosophy — combined lit. + phil. Cicero was peculiarly Roman proponent of liberal arts.

Cicero, who for many is the image of the ideal orator, was born on January 3, in 106 B.C., in Arpinum, a small city southeast of Rome, in the former land of the Volscians. His father, Marcus Tullius Cicero, senior, was a member of the equestrian order, the middle class that stood between the nobles—the descendants of men who had held high offices in government —and the commons—the so-called *plebs* or *populars*. The equestrian order engaged in trade and enjoyed the full rights of citizenship. Members of the middle class were also called *equites* or knights because the law required them to own the same amount of money that once entitled a man to serve in the cavalry. The knight had one great advantage. He could rise to the nobility by winning election to one of the higher offices, even to the Senate and the consulship, the highest offices in the Roman Republic. Cicero was to do just that. He advanced, at the swiftest pace allowed by law, from the lower ranks of *quaestor*, a financial office, of *aedile*, a police office, of *praetor*, a judicial office, to the consulship.

Cicero's rise and fall, his opposition first to Julius Caesar and then to the triumvirate of Mark Antony, Lepidus, and Octavius Caesar, and his death at the command of Antony, is itself an oft-told tale compounded of intrigues, wars, revolution, heroism, glory, and treachery. In his role as the defender of the Roman Republic and the opponent of the emerging Empire, Cicero tasted triumph during his consulship, when he destroyed Cataline, the great enemy of the Republic, and became for a while a popular hero. He knew too the bitter taste of ostracism and violence. After the sword of Antony's captain cut off his head, Cicero became a posthumous enemy of the state in the eyes of the new imperialists. Between his greatest triumph and his ignominious death, his career scudded uncertainly, but always gracefully, across the rough seas of an era of violent and sudden change. But, although Cicero's public and private life is both interesting and instructive, his influence on the art of rhetoric and of literature in general is perhaps his greatest legacy. Let us first briefly recall just what that influence was.

Cicero and his principal expositor, Quintilian, elevated the study of rhetoric from the level of the *litterator* (primary teacher), the *grammaticus* (secondary teacher), the *rhetor* (professional teacher), to that of the philosopher. The special character of Cicero's theory of rhetoric was its philosophical reach. For him a rhetorical education was not just the preliminary and professional training of the student but was a mature mastery of the liberal arts. Charles Norris Cochrane testifies to this in his *Christianity and Classical Culture,* where he approves Cicero's assertion in the *De Oratore* "that the combination of literature [grammar and rhetoric] and philosophy is peculiarly Roman, i.e., his own contribution to educational theory." Further, he goes on to say that, by imparting to classicism his literary and esthetic bias, Cicero "modified the whole complexion of Western culture, giving to it a rhetorical cast from which it was hardly to free itself even under the powerful stimulus of modern mathematical and physical science." [1]

As Mr. Cochrane suggests, many have acknowledged Cicero's influence without necessarily approving its predominance. Some indeed have deprecated that influence as excessive. But the fact remains that Cicero was one of the chief classical models of the Western literatures. In Michael Grant's words, ". . . the Renaissance became, above all else, a revival of Cicero, and only after him and through him of the rest of classical antiquity." Continental literature from the early Renaissance to the recent past derives its image of clear and elegant prose largely from Cicero. Grant goes on to say:

> Cicero's ideal of the whole man, combining mastery of language (including invective) with a sense of public responsibility and a cultivated employment of leisure, humanized philosophical studies and also became the basic education of the Renaissance upper class, through the colleges of Guarino at Ferrara and Vittorino da Feltre at Mantua. The former resembled a University department, but in the latter, with its pupils (drawn from a variety of classes) for whom knowledge of Cicero was the avenue to a political or diplomatic career, the roots of the English public-school system can be discerned.[2]

In England Cicero's influence was assured by the place of Latin in the curricula of the schools and by the prescribed study of his work, particularly the orations, at virtually every stage of education. What was established by authority was also confirmed by the free and deliberate choice of successive generations of England's great men of letters. Jonathan Swift, Samuel Johnson, Edward Gibbon, Edmund Burke, Lord Macaulay, and Cardinal Newman were among the many notable writers close to our time who, without falling into the idolatry of "Ciceronianism," consistently studied, admired, and imitated various works of the Roman orator. Through their influence many English and American writers, themselves unaware of the refinements of Latin, shared in the heritage of Cicero.

THE CICERONIAN HERITAGE — *Persuasive oratory*

Cicero's place in the English tradition has largely been determined by the persuasive example of his oratory. True, he was also a notable teacher and philosopher of rhetoric, as is evident in *On Invention (De Inventione)* 84 B.C., *On the Speaker (De Oratore)* 55 B.C., *The Topics (Topica)* 44 B.C., and other works. He wrote extensively on philosophy in *On the Greatest Degrees of Good and Evil, Tusculan Disputations, On the Nature of the Gods, On Divination, On Fate*—all in 45 B.C.—and *On Duties* and *On*

---

[1] (New York: Oxford Univ. Press, 1940), p. 146.
[2] *Cicero, Selected Works* (Baltimore: Penguin Books, 1960), pp. 26–27.

Virtues in 44 B.C. His letters, of which 864 survive, reveal him as a man of excellent wit and winning charm, whether he discoursed on business, the gossip of Rome, the nature of friendship, or the pleasures of society. "I do dearly love a dinner party," he once wrote to his well-to-do friend Atticus, "where I may talk on anything and everything." There are many facets to Cicero, not all of them immediately evident in the orations. Nevertheless, it is his fifty-eight surviving orations, slightly more than one half of his total recorded speeches, that have accounted for his enduring fame. His other work has been often admired for its lucidity, but the orations burn with incomparable brilliance. In *On the Sublime* Longinus compared Cicero to a spreading conflagration "which ranges and rolls over the whole field; the fire which burns is within him, plentiful and constant, distributed at his will now in one part, now in another.... " This fiery quality, so evident in his vivid and copious language, in his balanced and antithetical clauses, and in his sometimes scorching figures of speech and of thought, is clearly discernible in only Cicero's Latin. Even the best translations but faintly approximate Ciceronian ardor.

But if we can only indirectly feel the fire of Cicero's style we may more easily observe the light this fire has provided. Cicero's lucidity is the after-glow of his powerful feelings. It is also the result of his considerable logical power, nowhere displayed more successfully than in the external form of his speeches.

The form of the oration was defined probably at the end of the fifth century and the beginning of the fourth century B.C., though models of orations existed as early as Homer's *Iliad*. The great writer and teacher Isocrates (436–338 B.C.) refined and perfected in its written form the four-part structure (introduction, narration or discussion of past events that provided the occasion for debate, proof, and epilogue) that by his day had become fixed. The proof, it should be remembered, usually consisted of both the arguments supporting the speaker's position and the refutation of arguments opposing this position. Isocrates varied the form somewhat— separating the refutation from the proof in the forensic oration, adding where appropriate a proposition or brief summary statement of the issue, and sometimes combining the narration with the proof. The Ciceronian oration was a further refinement of the Isocratean, with a distribution and emphasis for the purpose of making the oration as clear as possible to the audience. The arrangement of these parts varied according to the occasion, and some might be omitted. The deliberative oration, as Aristotle indicated, might omit the narration—or at least have little to do with it—because of its concern not with the past but with the future.

Cicero's orations, in Cardinal Newman's words, "are generally laid out according to the plan proposed in rhetorical works," that is, in Aristotle's, his own, and Quintilian's studies of rhetoric. According to that plan, the complete speech might be outlined thus:

(handwritten in top left margin: Nov/26)

I. Introduction
    A. Exordium *(handwritten: (beginning) – win attention & good will ; short)*
    B. Narration or exposition of the case *(handwritten: – Thesis)*
    C. Division of the arguments in support of his proposition
II. Body of the Argument
    A. Proof: the presentation of the arguments in support of the proposition
    B. Refutation: the answer to arguments opposed to the proposition
III. Conclusion
    A. Summary of the arguments
    B. Peroration or emotional appeal for support of the proposition

I. The Introduction

Each part of the speech was carefully planned to serve the main purpose. Thus the *exordium,* which means simply *beginning,* normally included certain ethical proofs in which the speaker sought to win the good will, as well as the attention, of his audience by presenting himself and his subject in a most favorable light. In *Pro Archia,* paragraphs 1 and 2, notice Cicero's deference to the judges and the jury, his modest reference to his own accomplishments, his generous praise of Archias, whose position in Roman society was greatly inferior to his own. The exordium was, for the most part, direct, brief, and simple. At times, however, the orator began abruptly, as in Cicero's first oration against Cataline. Cicero starts out with an invective, "How long, O Cataline, will you continue to exhaust our patience!"

(handwritten in left margin: Use Antony's speech!)

More rarely, the exordium was insinuating or indirect—gradually revealing the purpose of the speech—because the audience was hostile either to the speaker or to his subject. According to Plutarch, Mark Antony employed this kind of exordium in his funeral oration for Julius Caesar. Shakespeare rendered it in that fashion in his play *Julius Caesar.* In the "Friends, Romans, countrymen" speech (Act III, scene 2; see pp. 56–62), Antony begins by pretending not to praise Caesar but to bury him, not to denounce Brutus for Caesar's assassination but to agree with its tragic necessity. Antony insinuates his actual intention to arouse sympathy for Caesar by the repeated irony of his "Brutus is an honorable man" and "They say Caesar was ambitious." Afterwards he appeals directly to the emotions of shame and pity.

The *narration* or *exposition* was usually the second part of the introduction, although it sometimes followed the statements of the proposition and the division of the proofs, as it does in *Pro Archia.* Here Cicero explained the relevant circumstances of the case—sometimes by telling what happened and by interpreting the law or principle or theory his proposition involves. Since the facts contained in this part of the speech were usually developed later in the proof, the narration or exposition was usually brief. The *division* was that part of the speech where the orator stated what he

The Nature of Rhetoric

intended to prove (his proposition) and his intended plan or arrangement of the arguments. Thus the introduction informed the audience of the orator's purpose, focused attention on the subject of the speech, and, by stimulating admiration for the speaker's purpose and by removing prejudices, disposed hearers to give the orator a favorable hearing.

II. THE BODY OF THE ARGUMENT

In the body of the speech the orator sought to convince his hearers of the truth or probability of his proposition. He presented the arguments for his proposition either deductively, in an enthymeme—that is, in the rhetorical form of the syllogism—or inductively through examples. "All orators," Aristotle said, "produce belief by employing as proofs either examples or enthymemes and nothing else." Thus, Cicero argued deductively in *Pro Archia,* paragraph 5:

1. Anyone who registered in compliance with the law was a citizen of Rome. (*major proposition implied*)
2. Archias enrolled at Heraclea in the presence of witnesses. (*minor proposition*)
3. Therefore Archias was a citizen. (*conclusion*)

Later, in paragraph 13, Cicero proved from the examples of Alexander the Great and Pompey the general truth of how literature exalted both "the nation whose high deeds it sings and those who stake their lives to fight in honor's cause."

In direct refutation of his opponent's case, the orator either denied his opponent's proposition outright and attempted to prove the opposite, or distinguished between its elements of truth and falsity, or retorted the argument—that is, turned it to his own advantage. In indirect refutation, the orator could reduce his opponent's argument to an absurdity by revealing contradictions or inconsistencies, or, if the facts warranted, he could attack the speaker's character and motives. Some speeches, of course, were developed as refutations of the charges made against a client. Thus the *Pro Archia* develops only a few positive arguments but shows that the prosecutor did not prove his case.

Although Cicero employed all the methods of proof and refutation at one time or another, he rarely found an opportunity to use them all in one speech. Rather he chose to expand the most telling points. Cardinal Newman observed and often imitated Cicero's tendency to amplify his favorite arguments. Thus he writes of Cicero's oratory:

> But it is not enough to have barely proved his point; he proceeds, either immediately, or towards the conclusion of his speech, to heighten the effect by amplification. Here he goes (as it were) round and round his object; surveys it in every light; examines it in all its parts; retires, and then advances; turns and re-turns it; compares and contrasts it; illustrates, confirms,

enforces his view of the question, till at last the hearer feels ashamed of doubting a position which seems built on a foundation so strictly argumentative.[3]

III. THE CONCLUSION

In effect, the conclusion was a reprise or summary of the main arguments developed throughout the speech and of the principal motives for consenting to the speaker's purpose. Often it rose to a hortatory climax, with an appeal to the feelings of the audience and an apostrophe to the immortal gods. If Cicero did follow, as Newman remarked, "the plan proposed in rhetorical works," he never did so slavishly. Whenever the occasion required, he modified his plan, nowhere more originally and successfully than in *Pro Archia*. We shall now study this speech in detail.

"PRO ARCHIA"

To understand Cicero's achievement in his speech for Archias we must recall that in 62 B.C., when he undertook the defense of the Greek poet, he was, in the popular view, the greatest man in Rome. Forty-five years old, at the height of his powers, he had just finished his term as consul, to which position he had been elected in 64 B.C., *suo anno*, in his own year—that is, the first year in which he was eligible for that office. His consulship was, in retrospect, the climax of republican glory in Rome. It witnessed Pompey's initial conquests in Syria after a prolonged campaign that had begun ten years before under the command of L. Licinius Lucullus. This foreign campaign coincided with Cicero's victory at home over Cataline, whom Cicero had denounced in three famous orations before the Senate.

Cicero's personal fortunes, too, were at their highest point. He was by far the most successful advocate in Rome. He owned a palace on the Palatine Hill and villas at Formiae and Tusculum. His brother Quintus Tullius Cicero was a praetor and Tullia, his daughter, was already married. Wherever Cicero traveled he was attended by a group of admiring clients. No man could have achieved more distinction or more popular acclaim. Nor could Cicero have foreseen the evil days ahead, when Julius Caesar would destroy Pompey in battle, when Caesar would fall victim to Brutus' vengeance, when Brutus would take his own life after his defeat by Mark Antony, when Mark Antony would commit suicide after his defeat by Octavius Caesar, and when Octavius Caesar would swallow up Cicero's sacred Republic in his new Empire. On the contrary, Cicero had every reason to hope that the Republic would survive under his watchful eyes and, with the Republic, those liberal ideals that he could cultivate for their own sakes.

It is not surprising, therefore, that Cicero was superbly prepared to make the most of his opportunities when he undertook the defense of Archias.

[3]John H. Newman, *Essays and Sketches,* Vol. 1 (London: Longman's Green, 1948), pp. 46–47.

Aware of his own prestige and power, he had the additional advantage of a strong brief and of sympathetic judges. Moreover, his case permitted him to defend not only the poet-friend of his friend Lucullus but also— what was closer to his heart—the place of the liberal arts in a civilized state. Cicero could at once advocate a worthy cause and could also defend a way of life—the liberal tradition that as time went on became his passionate concern. In short, in this speech Cicero presented the universal case for *humanitas*—the humanities, the arts of life that transform the merely human into the humane, that elevate politics and law to a philosophy of life.

Liberal Arts

If Cicero was prepared to make the most of his opportunity, opportunity itself cooperated with Cicero. In Archias he had a client who was a distinguished poet, a native of Antioch, the Rome of the East, who came to Rome in 102 B.C., where he was befriended by the Luculli. His poems in praise of Lucullus, together with an earlier work lauding the victories of Marius and Catulus over the Teutones and the Cimbri, were much admired, especially by the aristocratic party. Besides, Archias was planning to write a poem in praise of Cicero's defeat of Cataline. Gratius, who charged that Archias had claimed citizenship illegally, was an obvious cat's paw for Pompey, who was at that time a political opponent of Lucullus. At best Gratius' suit was a nuisance case. Thus, in defending the poet, Cicero could espouse a just cause and please the Luculli without directly attacking Pompey. On the contrary, he even found it possible to praise the conqueror of the east (paragraph 13) in terms reminiscent of his great speech in 66 B.C. supporting Pompey's appointment to the single command of the war against Mithridates.

The outline below reveals how prudently Cicero modified the classic plan in the light of his subject, his audience, and the opportunities the case presented. Instead of using the standard rhetorical plan set forth above, Cicero shaped *Pro Archia* into the following pattern.

  I. The Introduction
     A. Exordium
     B. Proposition and division
     C. Narration
  II. The Body of the Argument
     A. Confirmation
       1. Proof of the first part of the proposition
       2. Proof of the second part of the proposition
     B. Refutation—within the proof   (See notes on speech.)
  III. The Conclusion
     A. Summary
     B. Peroration

Let us now turn to the speech itself.

Cicero: The Classical Model of Modern Rhetoric   **25**

I. THE INTRODUCTION [1–4]

Exordium or Beginning

¶1   Cicero's acknowledgment that his talent, experience, and knowledge are derived from his studies with his old teacher simultaneously focuses on his own authority as a speaker and the admirable qualities of Archias the poet. In announcing his intention to defend the poet as a person he connects that cause with the defense of the arts and humanistic studies in general. Thus he informs the audience of the subject of his speech, excites interest by the promise of an unusual treatment of a forensic question, and elicits good will by his own attitude toward the legal defense of Archias, toward the poet himself, and toward the judges.

Aulus Licinius   Archias, whose name was Greek, adopted a Roman name in honor of his patron Lucullus, who belonged to the *gens* (clan) Licinius.

¶2   *Praetor*   The president of the court or chief judge. According to a persistent tradition, the presiding judge was Cicero's brother, Quintus, who was a poet and a friend of poets.

Jury of high dignity   The Roman jury was composed of one-third senators, one-third equestrians or knights, and one-third presidents of electoral districts. Cicero's tone of respect for their dignity is appropriate.

CICERO
The Speech on Behalf of Archias the Poet

(Delivered before a court of inquiry)

GENTLEMEN OF THE JURY:

Whatever talent I possess (and I realize its limitations), whatever be my [1] oratorical experience (and I do not deny that my practice herein has been not inconsiderable), whatever knowledge of the theoretical side of my profession I may have derived from a devoted literary apprenticeship (and I admit that at no period of my life has the acquisition of such knowledge been repellent to me),—to any advantage that may be derived from all these my friend Aulus Licinius has a pre-eminent claim, which belongs to him almost of right. For if I strain my mental vision far into the past, and strive to recall the most remote memories of my boyhood, the impression which such a survey leaves with me is that it was he who first fitted my back for its burden and my feet for their destined path. If this voice of mine, trained by his precepts and his exhortation, has on some few occasions proved of service, it is my client who has put into my hands the means of succouring others and perhaps saving some, and it is to his cause, therefore, that any power of help or protection, which it lies with me to exert, should be applied. My remarks may cause surprise; for it may be urged that the genius of the defendant is exercised in a sphere which bears no connexion with my own study and practice of oratory. But I would point out in reply that I myself have never concentrated my energies upon my professional interests to the exclusion of all others. Indeed, the subtle bond of a mutual relationship links together all arts which have any bearing upon the common life of mankind.

It may, however, be a matter for surprise in some quarters that in an in- [2] quiry dealing with statute law, in a public trial held before a specially selected praetor of the Roman people and a jury of high dignity, in the

---

THE SPEECH ON BEHALF OF ARCHIAS THE POET   Reprinted by permission of the publishers from N. H. Watts (trans.), Cicero, *Pro Archia Poeta* (Cambridge, Mass.: Harvard Univ. Press).

high praise,
tribute

My speech should be made in a style   The tone of Cicero's speech is that of the demonstrative speech or panegyric rather than that of legal orations. His subject is not only the point of law but, more importantly, the role of the poet in civilized society.

Proposition and Division

Let me but assure myself   The concluding sentence of the paragraph announces his two-fold proposition: Archias was indeed a citizen (the legal issue of fact); if he were not, he should be made one (partly an issue of justification, partly panegyric). Approximately one-sixth of the speech deals with the first part of the proposition.

Narration

¶3   Notice how Cicero's account of Archias' career leads directly to the proof of his citizenship.

Antioch   This famous capital of Syria was long regarded as a rival to Rome.

Marius and Catulus were consuls   Romans dated events by naming the consuls. The year was 102 B.C.

The garb of manhood   At seventeen, Roman youth exchanged the *toga praetexta* (a toga bordered with a purple stripe) for the *toga virilis*—the white garment of the young man.

Luculli, etc.   These families were leaders of Roman patrician society. Archias' friendship with them suggests that if he were not a citizen, he should be made one. Lucius Licinius Lucullus, a leader in the war against Mithridates, was at odds with Pompey, who succeeded him in command.

presence of a crowded audience of citizens, my speech should be made in a style out of keeping not merely with the conventions of the bar, but also with forensic language. But I crave your indulgence, an indulgence which will, I trust, cause you no inconvenience, and which is peculiarly applicable to the nature of my client's case; and I would ask you to allow me, speaking as I am on behalf of a distinguished poet and a consummate scholar, before a cultivated audience, an enlightened jury, and a praetor whom we see occupying the tribunal, to enlarge somewhat upon enlightened and cultivated pursuits, and to employ what is perhaps a novel and unconventional line of defence to suit the character of one whose studious seclusion has made him a stranger to the anxious perils of the courts. Let me but assure myself that you grant me this kind concession, and I will engage to convince you of the propriety, not only of refusing to exclude my client from the civic roll, since he is a citizen, but even of adding his name to that roll, supposing that he were not.

As soon as Archias had left behind him his boyhood, and those influences [3] which mould and elevate the boyish mind, he applied himself to the pursuit of a literary career. First at Antioch, where he had been born of gentle parents, a place which in those days was a renowned and populous city, the seat of brilliant scholarship and artistic refinement, his intellectual pre-eminence rapidly gained for him a commanding position among his contemporaries. During his subsequent travels through Greece and the rest of Asia, his arrival created such a stir that the hope of seeing him went beyond the rumour of his genius, and the hope was continually surpassed by the wonder of his actual presence. In Southern Italy at that time the arts and studies of Greece had great vogue, and excited more ardent interest in the towns of Latium also than even today; while here at Rome, too, owing to the rest from civil strife, they were not neglected. Accordingly, at Tarentum, at Rhegium, at Neapolis, he was presented with civic rights and other distinctions, and all that could discern true genius elected him to the circle of their acquaintance and hospitality. So, when the voice of fame had made him well known to men whom he had never met, he came to Rome, where Marius and Catulus were consuls. He was fortunate to find in the occupation of that office two men, one of whom could provide him with a magnificent theme for his pen, and another whose achievements could supply him with a theme, and who could also lend him an appreciative hearing. Immediately upon his arrival, and even before he had assumed the garb of manhood, the Luculli welcomed Archias to their home. Moreover, it speaks well for my client's inborn goodness, as well as for his genius as a poet, that the home, which was the earliest resort of his youth, has given an affectionate shelter to his declining years. He enjoyed at this time the warm friendship of Metellus, the hero of Numidia, and of his son Pius; he read his works to Marcus Aemilius; the doors of Quintus Catulus and his son were ever open to him; Lucius Crassus cultivated his acquaint-

¶4   *Heraclea*   A Greek city in Lucania, southern Italy, which was federated with Rome.

Law of Silvanus and Carbo   This was the *Lex Plautia Papiria* of 89 B.C.

II. THE BODY OF THE ARGUMENT [5-15]

Confirmation or Proof of the First Part of the Proposition

¶5   Cicero argues that Archias is indeed a citizen according to the law cited above. He points out first that Gratius, the prosecutor, upon whom the burden of proof rests, has not proved his charge. Then he refutes Gratius' argument that the defense lacked documentary evidence that Archias was a citizen of Heraclea by producing witnesses to the fact that Archias had registered as a citizen and by accounting for Archias' absence from the city during the last two valid registrations.

The validity of Archias' enfranchisement   Here Cicero begins his proof that Archias fulfilled the requirements of the *Lex Plautia Papiria* and is therefore a citizen.

Gratius   A relatively unknown political pawn of Pompey, he accused Archias to embarrass Pompey's rival, Lucullus.

Marcus Lucullus   The brother of Lucius Lucullus. Note the repetition and climactic arrangement of the sentences beginning, "We have been in court . . . ."

The Italian war   The Social War, 90–88 B.C., so-called because Rome's allies (*socii*) fought for the Republic against the rebellious forces of central Italy. It was a particularly destructive war.

It is absurd   Note how refutation is based on evidence presented in the form of rhetorical syllogism. Cicero's reasoning is the following: whatever contradicts known facts is absurd; Gratius' charges contradict known facts; hence his charges are absurd. Circumstances prove the impossibility of Gratius' charge.

Incorruptible corporation   Heraclea, represented by delegates at the trial.

Or did he fail to report himself   Note how this charge was anticipated in paragraph 4 above, "My client . . . reported himself duly to the praetor Quintus Metellus." Moreover, this was repeated in the official register of the praetors.

ance; he was bound by ties of close intimacy to the Luculli, Drusus, the Octavii, Cato, and the whole family of Hortensius; in a word, so honoured a position did he hold, that he was courted not only by those who wished to enjoy the elevating influences of hearing his poems, but also by those who perhaps feigned a desire for such enjoyment.

After a lapse of some few years he went to Sicily with Marcus Lucullus, [4] and, returning with him from that province, came to Heraclea. Full civic privileges had been accorded to this town by the terms of its treaty with Rome, and Archias expressed a wish to be enrolled among its burgesses. His personal qualities would have been sufficient recommendation, even had Lucullus not thrown the influence of his own popularity into the scale, and his wish was readily gratified by the inhabitants. He was granted the franchise by the terms of the law of Silvanus and Carbo, which enacts "that all who have been admitted to citizenship in federate townships must have been resident in Italy at the time of the passing of the law, and must have reported themselves to the praetor within sixty days." My client had for many years resided at Rome, and reported himself duly to the praetor Quintus Metellus, who was his personal friend.

If the validity of Archias' enfranchisement and his compliance with the [5] law are the only points at issue, I now close the case for the defence. For can you, Gratius, disprove either of these facts? Will you deny the enrolment at Heraclea at the time in question? We have here in court an influential witness of incorruptible honour, Marcus Lucullus, who is ready to state not that he thinks but that he knows, not that he heard but that he saw, not that he merely was present at the event but that he was the agent of it. We have here a distinguished body of representatives from Heraclea, who have come to Rome expressly for this trial to present their city's official evidence of my client's enrolment. And after all this my opponent asks that the archives of Heraclea should be brought into court, when it is a matter of universal knowledge that those archives were destroyed in the burning of the record-office during the Italian war. It is absurd to ignore the evidence which lies to our hand, and to demand evidence which cannot possibly be produced; to shut the ears to the record of living men, and to insist that a written record should be forthcoming. You have a statement of a noble gentleman, whose word is his bond. You have the sworn asseveration of an incorruptible corporation. There can be no tampering with these; yet you wave them aside, and demand documentary evidence, though in the same breath you admit its corruptibility. Or do you deny that my client resided at Rome, when for so many years before he was admitted to the franchise he had made Rome the depository of all his possessions and all his hopes? Or did he fail to report himself? No; he did report himself; and, what is more, out of all the declarations made at that time before the board of praetors, his alone was supported by documents which possess all the weight of official sanction.

¶6 *Appius* Appius Claudius Pulcher, father of Publius Claudius Pulcher, who later in the year 62 B.C. was attacked by Cicero.

Gabinius Publius Gabinius Capito, subsequently convicted of extortion.

Ancient Greek states The cities of Magna Graecia, such as those mentioned by Cicero further on.

Play-actors The argument from antecedent probability goes thus: if the city-states customarily bestowed citizenship on actors, who generally were not considered worthy of that dignity, it is highly unlikely they would have denied citizenship to Archias, a man held in highest esteem by the most estimable people.

Law of Papius This law, *Lex Papia*, enacted in 65 B.C., decreed that all persons who lacked a domicile in Italy would be expelled. Gratius prosecuted Archias according to the provisions of this law, since Archias' name did not appear on the Roman census rolls. But, as Cicero points out, he was registered at Heraclea, during the previous two censuses he had been serving with Lucullus in Asia, and the first census (89 B.C.) had never been taken.

Upon you lies Here Cicero concludes his legal argument in support of the first part of the proposition and introduces the proof of the second part—that is, if Archias were not a citizen, he should be made one.

Confirmation or Proof of the Second Part of the Proposition

¶7 This part is often designated *pars extra causam*, the part that lies outside the strictly legal issues. Whether it be a mere digression on the role of poetry and the poet in civilized society or whether it be relevant because it successfully joins the demonstrative kind of oratory with the strictly forensic has long been debated. History seems to have judged that Cicero, in his *pars extra causam*, artistically united the two kinds of oratory by citing relevant precedents for awarding citizenship to Archias.

For though the burgess-rolls of Appius, so it was alleged, had been care- [6]
lessly kept, and though the authenticity of all such documents had been
impaired by the frivolity of Gabinius, so long as his reputation survived,
and by his downfall, after his conviction, yet Metellus, that most conscientious and discreet of men, displayed in regard to them such scrupulous accuracy that he came to Lucius Lentulus the praetor, and a jury, and professed himself deeply embarrassed by the erasure of a single entry. These,
then, are the rolls; and here no erasure is to be seen in the entry of
Aulus Licinius' name. This being so, what grounds have you for questioning his enfranchisement, especially as his name is to be found on the rolls
of other cities as well as Heraclea? Citizens of the ancient Greek states
often went out of their way to associate with themselves in their civic privileges undistinguished men, of unimportant attainments, or of no attainments at all; and you would have me believe that the citizens of Rhegium
or Locri, Neapolis or Tarentum, withheld from a brilliant genius like my
client an honour which was commonly bestowed by them on play-actors.
Others have found some way of creeping into the rolls of the cities I have
mentioned, not merely after they had received the citizenship, but even
after the passing of the law of Papius; my client does not even avail himself of the presence of his name on these lists in which he is enrolled,
because he has always desired to belong to Heraclea; and shall he therefore be rejected? You say you look in vain for his name upon our census-
rolls. Yes; it is, I suppose, a close secret that at the time of the last census
he was with the army on the staff of the gallant general Lucius Lucullus;
at the time of the census before that he was again with Lucullus, who was
quaestor in Asia, while in the first year when censors, in the persons of
Julius and Crassus, were appointed after his admission to the franchise, no
census of any section of the people was held. But, since the census-roll is
no proof of a man's civil status, and since the appearance of his name there
does but indicate that when the census was taken he lived as a citizen, let
me further point out that at that time my client, whom you assert to have
had, even in his own view, no rights as a Roman citizen, had frequently
made his will according to Roman law, had entered upon legacies left to
him by Roman citizens, and had been recommended to the treasury for
reward by Lucius Lucullus as proconsul. Upon you lies the burden of proof,
if proof you can offer; for my client will never be refuted by an appeal to
any judgement which either he himself or his friends have passed upon
him.

You will no doubt ask me, Gratius, to account for the deep interest I [7]
feel in my friend. It is because he provides refreshment for my spirit after
the clamour of the courts, and repose for senses jaded by their vulgar
wrangling. Do you think that I could find inspiration for my daily speeches
on so manifold a variety of topics, did I not cultivate my mind with study,
or that my mind could endure so great a strain, did not study too provide

Thanks to the moral lessons Cicero had a wide acquaintance with Greek and Roman poets, philosophers, and historians.

Refutation—Within the Proof of the Second Part of the Proposition

¶8   Cicero considers a common objection that the great poets and writers themselves were not learned. He recognizes the distinction between natural gifts and acquired education but sees the ideal to be a union of the two. As examples of these ideals he cites Scipio Africanus (Minor) (189–129 B.C.), son of Hannibal's conqueror; Gaius Lalius, consul in 190 B.C.; and Lucius Furius Philus. They were all learned men, members of the circle of Scipio, and were devoted to uniting the culture of Greece with that of Rome.

it with relaxation? I am a votary of literature, and make the confession unashamed; shame belongs rather to the bookish recluse, who knows not how to apply his reading to the good of his fellows, or to manifest its fruits to the eyes of all. But what shame should be mine, gentlemen, who have made it a rule of my life for all these years never to allow the sweets of a cloistered ease or the seductions of pleasure or the enticements of repose to prevent me from aiding any man in the hour of his need? How then can I justly be blamed or censured, if it shall be found that I have devoted to literature a portion of my leisure hours no longer than others without blame devote to the pursuit of material gain, to the celebration of festivals or games, to pleasure and the repose of mind and body, to protracted banqueting, or perhaps to the gaming-board or to ball-playing? I have the better right to indulgence herein, because my devotion to letters strengthens my oratorical powers, and these, such as they are, have never failed my friends in their hour of peril. Yet insignificant though these powers may seem to be, I fully realize from what source I draw all that is highest in them. Had I not persuaded myself from my youth up, thanks to the moral lessons derived from a wide reading, that nothing is to be greatly sought after in this life save glory and honour, and that in their quest all bodily pains and all dangers of death or exile should be lightly accounted, I should never have borne for the safety of you all the brunt of many a bitter encounter, or bared my breast to the daily onsets of abandoned persons. All literature, all philosophy, all history, abounds with incentives to noble action, incentives which would be buried in black darkness were the light of the written word not flashed upon them. How many pictures of high endeavour the great authors of Greece and Rome have drawn for our use, and bequeathed to us, not only for our contemplation, but for our emulation! These I have held ever before my vision throughout my public career, and have guided the workings of my brain and my soul by meditating upon patterns of excellence.

"But," an objector may ask, "were these great men, whose virtues are [8] perpetuated in literature, themselves adepts in the learning which you describe in such fulsome terms?" It would be difficult to make a sweeping and categorical reply, but at the same time I have my answer ready. Many there have been, no doubt, exceptionally endowed in temperament and character, who, without any aid from culture, but only by a heaven-born light within their own souls, have been self-schooled in restraint and fortitude; I would even go so far as to say that natural gifts without education have more often attained to glory and virtue than education without natural gifts. Yet I do at the same time assert that when to a lofty and brilliant character is applied the moulding influence of abstract studies, the result is often inscrutably and unapproachably noble. Such a character our fathers were privileged to behold in the divine figure of Scipio Africanus; such were those patterns of continence and self-control, Gaius Laelius and

Marcus Cato   The censor, first opposed Greek culture but later became an apologist for it.

Other pursuits belong   This celebrated passage has been widely translated and frequently paraphrased.

¶9   *But it might happen*   This sentence is a transition to a new point: even if we ourselves are not practicing poets, we must admire the poetic ability of others.

Roscius   Quintus Roscius Gallus, who died in 62 B.C., was Rome's outstanding comic actor, a friend of Cicero, and the subject of Cicero's oration, *Pro Roscio Comoedo,* delivered about 77 B.C. The argument is again a *fortiori.* If we admire Roscius for his bodily gestures, how much more ought we admire Archias for his movement of soul and mind.

Ennius   Quintus Ennius (239–169 B.C.), the "father" of Roman poetry, was a native of Rudiae in Calabria. He wrote *Annales*—a history of Rome—as well as tragedies, comedies, and satires.

Savage beasts   According to Greek myth, Orpheus had "charms to soothe the savage beast."

Colophon   Here Cicero paraphrases the following Greek verse:

Seven cities claim him [Homer]: Smyrna,
Rhodes, Colophon, Salamis, Chios, Argos, and Athens.

Lucius Furius; such was the brave and venerable Marcus Cato, the most accomplished man of his day. These surely would never have devoted themselves to literary pursuits, had they not been aided thereby in the appreciation and pursuit of merit. But let us for the moment waive these solid advantages; let us assume that entertainment is the sole end of reading; even so, I think you would hold that no mental employment is so broadening to the sympathies or so enlightening to the understanding. Other pursuits belong not to all times, all ages, all conditions; but this gives stimulus to our youth and diversion to our old age; this adds a charm to success, and offers a haven of consolation to failure. In the home it delights, in the world it hampers not. Through the night-watches, on all our journeying, and in our hours of country ease, it is our unfailing companion.

But it might happen that we ourselves were without literary tastes or [9] attainments; yet even so, it would be incumbent upon us to reverence their manifestation in others. Was there a man among us so boorish or so insensible that the recent death of Roscius did not stir his deepest emotions? He died full of years, and yet we all felt that an artist of such grace and brilliance deserved immunity from our mortal lot. Merely by the motions of his body he had won all our hearts; and shall those hearts be insensible to the inscrutable motions of the soul and the agile play of genius? How often, gentlemen, have I seen my friend Archias—I shall presume upon your kindness, since I see you give so careful a hearing to my unconventional digression,—how often, I say, have I seen him, without writing a single letter, extemporizing quantities of excellent verse dealing with current topics! How often have I seen him, when recalled, repeat his original matter with an entire change of word and phrase! To his finished and studied work I have known such approval accorded that his glory rivalled that of the great writers of antiquity. Does not such a man deserve my affection and admiration? Should I not count it my duty to strain every nerve in his defence? And yet we have it on the highest and most learned authority that while other arts are matters of science and formula and technique, poetry depends solely upon an inborn faculty, is evoked by a purely mental activity, and is infused with a strange supernal inspiration. Rightly, then, did our great Ennius call poets "holy," for they seem recommended to us by the benign bestowal of God. Holy then, gentlemen, in your enlightened eyes let the name of poet be, inviolate hitherto by the most benighted of races! The very rocks of the wilderness give back a sympathetic echo to the voice; savage beasts have sometimes been charmed into stillness by song; and shall we, who are nurtured upon all that is highest, be deaf to the appeal of poetry? Colophon asserts that Homer is her citizen, Chios claims him for her own, Salamis appropriates him, while Smyrna is so confident that he belongs to her that she has even dedicated a shrine to him in her town; and many other cities besides engage in mutual strife for his possession.

¶10   *Shall a living poet*   The comparative argument again. If the Greeks honored a dead poet who was a foreigner, should we not honor a live one who is also a citizen? This argument leads into specific examples of Archias' services to Rome by his writings on the Cimbrian and Mithridatic wars.

Gaius Marius (157–80·B.C.)   Defeated the Cimbri in 102 B.C.

Themistocles (528–462 B.C.)   An Athenian statesman, noted as the architect of the naval victory over the Persians at Salamis.

Lucius Plotius   Teacher of rhetoric whom Cicero mentions as the first rhetorician to teach Romans how to declaim in Latin.

Pontus   The northeasternmost district of Asia Minor, along the coast of the Euxine. In A.D. 64, it was made a Roman province by Nero.

Tenedos   An island in the Aegean Sea, off the coast of Troas (Troy).

Ours, inalienably ours, are the trophies   Note how Cicero's praise of Archias is related to Archias' praise of the Roman people.

¶11   *Maximus*   Quintus Fabius Maximus Cunctator was a hero of the Second Punic War. The surname *Cunctator* (delayer) was earned by his delaying tactics in that war, which forced Hannibal to exhaust his army's energy and supplies.

Marcellus   Marcus Claudius Marcellus was another leader in the Second Punic War; he captured the city of Syracuse.

Fulvius   Marcus Fulvius Nobilior, consul in 189 B.C., was victor over the Aetolians. The poet Ennius, a witness of that campaign, owed his citizenship to Fulvius' son.

These peoples, then, are ambitious to claim, even after his death, one [10] who was an alien, merely because he was a poet; and shall a living poet be repudiated by us, though he is ours both by inclination and by the laws? Shall we do so, in spite of the fact that a short while ago he bent all the energies of his genius to celebrating the fame and glory of the Roman people? For in his youth he wrote on the Cimbrian compaign, thereby winning the approbation of the great Gaius Marius himself, who was generally considered to be insensible to such refinements. For indeed there is no man to whom the Muses are so distasteful that he will not be glad to entrust to poetry the eternal emblazonment of his achievements. It is related that the great Athenian hero, Themistocles, when asked what recital or what voice he loved best to hear, replied, "That which bears most eloquent testimony to my prowess." On a like foundation rested the deep attachment felt by Marius towards Lucius Plotius, whose genius he thought well qualified to perpetuate his exploits. Again, my client has treated in its entirety the great and difficult theme of the war with Mithridates, pursuing all its diverse operations by land and sea, and his work sheds lustre not only on the gallant and renowned Lucius Lucullus, but also upon the fame of the Roman people. For it was the Roman people who, with Lucullus at their head, opened up the Pontus, fortified as it was not only by the resources of its monarch, but also by an advantageous situation. It was an army of the Roman people, which, under the same commander, routed with a moderate force the innumerable hordes of Armenia. And it is to the Roman people, still under the directing skill of Lucullus, that the credit belongs of having torn away and saved the friendly city of Cyzicus from all the assaults of the king, and from being swallowed up in the ravaging jaws of war. To us shall it ever be imputed with praise that under Lucullus again we crushed a hostile fleet, slew its admirals, and fought that astonishing naval battle at Tenedos. Ours, inalienably ours, are the trophies, memorials, and triumphs of that campaign; and it is the glories of the Roman people which are sounded abroad by the genius of those who laud exploits such as these.

Our great Ennius enjoyed the close affection of the elder Africanus, and [11] so a marble statue of him is reputed to have been placed even in the tomb of the Scipios. Yet we may be sure that the panegyric he bestowed upon his patron lends adornment not only to its theme, but also to the name of the Roman people. He exalted to heaven the Cato whose great-grandson is now with us; and great glory is added thereby to the name of the Roman people. The rule holds good in every case; the glory of universal Rome borrows an added lustre from those works which distinguish the bearers of the great names of Maximus, Marcellus, or Fulvius.

For this reason our ancestors admitted their author, a citizen of Rudiae, [12] to the franchise; and shall we eject from our franchise one for whom

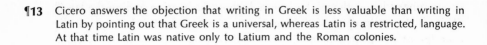

¶**13** Cicero answers the objection that writing in Greek is less valuable than writing in Latin by pointing out that Greek is a universal, whereas Latin is a restricted, language. At that time Latin was native only to Latium and the Roman colonies.

Sigeum The town on the south shore of the Straits of Bosphorus, northwest of Troy, the scene of the *Iliad*.

The title of Great Pompey.

Theophanes of Mytilene Pompey met Theophanes during the Mithridatic War, became his friend, and granted him citizenship in 62 B.C., either by a special law or by his own authority. This is a shrewd hit against the prosecutor, who was acting in Pompey's interests. How could Archias, a true citizen, be denied citizenship on a mere technicality, when Mytilene owed his citizenship to a special law or possibly to illegal privilege?

Sulla Lucius Sulla Felix (138–78 B.C.) the dictator.

Quintus Metellus Pius See page 31. Metellus had been proconsul in Spain during the period 79–71 B.C.

Corduba The chief Roman center in the province of Baetica, Spain; the modern Cordoba.

many states have striven, and whom Heraclea has gained, and constituted her citizen by due process of law?

For if anyone thinks that the glory won by the writing of Greek verse is [13] naturally less than that accorded to the poet who writes in Latin, he is entirely in the wrong. Greek literature is read in nearly every nation under heaven, while the vogue of Latin is confined to its own boundaries, and they are, we must grant, narrow. Seeing, therefore, that the activities of our race know no barrier save the limits of the round earth, we ought to be ambitious that whithersoever our arms have penetrated there also our fame and glory should extend; for the reason that literature exalts the nation whose high deeds it sings, and at the same time there can be no doubt that those who stake their lives to fight in honour's cause find therein a lofty incentive to peril and endeavour. We read that Alexander the Great carried in his train numbers of epic poets and historians. And yet, standing before the tomb of Achilles at Sigeum, he exclaimed,—"Fortunate youth, to have found in Homer an herald of thy valour!" Well might he so exclaim, for had the *Iliad* never existed, the same mound which covered Achilles' bones would also have overwhelmed his memory. Again, did not he to whom our own age has accorded the title of Great, whose successes have been commensurate with his high qualities, present with the citizenship before a mass meeting of his troops Theophanes of Mytilene, the historian of his campaigns? Were not our brave fellows, soldiers and peasants though they were, so smitten with the glamour of renown that they loudly applauded the act, feeling that they too had a share in the glory that had been shed upon their leader? Accordingly, if Archias were not legally a Roman citizen already, it would have been beyond his power, presumably, to win the gift of citizenship from some military commander. Sulla, no doubt, who gave it so freely to Spaniards and Gauls, would have refused it to the request of my client. It will be remembered that once at a public meeting some poetaster from the crowd handed up to that great man a paper containing an epigram upon him, improvised in somewhat unmetrical elegiacs. Sulla immediately ordered a reward to be paid him out of the proceeds of the sale which he was then holding, but added the stipulation that he should never write again. He accounted the diligent efforts of a poet worthy of some reward, bad though that poet was; and think you he would not have eagerly sought out my client, whose literary powers were so magnificent, and whose pen was so ready? Again, could not his own credit or the influence of the Luculli have gained him his desire from Quintus Metellus Pius, who was his intimate friend, and who had presented the citizenship to not a few? And it must be remembered that so ambitious was Metellus to have his deeds immortalized that he even deigned to lend a hearing to poets from Corduba, overladen and exotic though their style might be.

¶**14** *Ambition is an universal factor* Cicero picks up this theme from his preceding remarks, anticipating the possible objection that poets like Archias merely flatter their patrons. He anticipates, too, the objection that he favors Archias because the poet is composing a poem about Cicero's victory over the Cataline conspirators. (See page 19.)

Decimus Brutus Surnamed Gallaecus, for in the course of his conquest of Lusitania—modern Portugal—he defeated the Gallaeci.

Accius Lucius Accius, born 170? B.C., was a Roman tragic poet personally known to Cicero.

¶**15** *Magnanimity* Greatness of soul, the major virtue according to Aristotle and other classical writers. Since glory is the fruit of magnanimity, to be ambitious for glory is not a vice but a virtue.

III. THE CONCLUSION [16–18]

¶**16** *How much more anxious* Again the comparative, *a fortiori* argument: if men leave behind statues and so forth in their memory, how much more reasonable to leave behind the effigy of a noble mind and character—that is, the famous reputation that constitutes glory.

Ambition is an universal factor in life, and the nobler a man is, the more [14] susceptible is he to the sweets of fame. We should not disclaim this human weakness, which indeed is patent to all; we should rather admit it unabashed. Why, upon the very books in which they bid us scorn ambition philosophers inscribe their names! They seek advertisement and publicity for themselves on the very page whereon they pour contempt upon advertisement and publicity. That gallant officer and gentleman, Decimus Brutus, adorned the vestibules of the temples and monuments which he raised with the poems of his friend Accius; more, the great Fulvius, who took Ennius with him upon his Aetolian campaign, had no misgivings in dedicating to the Muses the spoils of the god of war. Surely, then, in a city where honour has been paid to the name of poet and the shrines of the Muses by generals who have scarce doffed the panoply of battle, it would ill befit a jury of peaceful citizens to disdain to pay respect to the Muses by extending protection to their bard.

And the more to incline you so to do, gentlemen of the jury, I will now [15] proceed to open to you my heart, and confess to you my own passion, if I may so describe it, for fame, a passion over-keen perhaps, but assuredly honourable. The measures which I, jointly with you, undertook in my consulship for the safety of the empire, the lives of our citizens, and the common weal of the state, have been taken by my client as the subject of a poem which he has begun; he read this to me, and the work struck me as at once so forcible and so interesting, that I encouraged him to complete it. For magnanimity looks for no other recognition of its toils and dangers save praise and glory; once rob it of that, gentlemen, and in this brief and transitory pilgrimage of life what further incentive have we to high endeavour? If the soul were haunted by no presage of futurity, if the scope of her imaginings were bounded by the limits set to human existence, surely never then would she break herself by bitter toil, rack herself by sleepless solicitude, or struggle so often for very life itself. But deep in every noble heart dwells a power which plies night and day the goad of glory, and bids us see to it that the remembrance of our names should not pass away with life, but should endure coeval with all the ages of the future.

Are we to show so poor a spirit to the world, we who are exposed to [16] all the perils and toils that beset a public career, as to think that, after having lived out our allotted span without ever drawing the breath of peace and repose, all is to die along with us? Many great men have been studious to leave behind them statues and portraits, likenesses not of the soul, but of the body; and how much more anxious should we be to bequeath an effigy of our minds and characters, wrought and elaborated by supreme talent? For my part, in the very enactment of my exploits, I felt that I was sowing broadcast to reap an undying memory throughout the whole world. It may be that after death I shall be insensible to it. It may be that, as philosophers have held, some part of my being shall yet be

Summary

¶17 *Wherefore gentlemen*   Cicero recapitulates his arguments in support of both parts of his proposition and appeals for Archias' acquittal.

Peroration

Note how the peroration, by referring to the fact that Archias "has shed glory upon you, upon your generals," appeals directly to the personal and patriotic emotions of the jurors.

¶18 *Who presides over the tribunal*   Cicero's brother Quintus. See *Praetor,* page 26.

conscious of it. Be that as it may, now at any rate I find satisfaction in the thought and in the hope.

Wherefore, gentlemen, protect, I beg of you, a man whose honour you [17] see to be attested both by the high position of his friends, and the durability of their friendship, whose genius you can estimate at its true worth by the fact that genius itself has set a premium upon it, and the righteousness of whose cause is established by the support of the law, the authority of a municipality, the evidence of Lucullus, and the burgess-rolls of Metellus. Throughout his career he has shed glory upon you, upon your generals, and upon the history of the Roman people; he is engaged upon a work which promises to be a glorious and undying testimony to those public perils which we have recently faced together; and he belongs to a profession which has been universally held inviolable, both in act and word. I implore you therefore, gentlemen, if such high talent deserves any commendation from men, nay more, from heaven, let him rest in the assurance of your protection, and let it be seen that so far from being assailed by your displeasure, he has been assisted by your humanity.

I am sure that my statement of the case, brief and straightforward as I, [18] true to my practice, have made it, has appealed to every one of you; and I hope that my departure from the practice and the conventions of the courts, and my digression upon the subject of my client's genius, and, in general terms, upon the art which he follows, has been welcomed by you in as generous a spirit as I am assured it has been welcomed by him who presides over this tribunal.

The Development of Rhetoric from the Middle Ages to the Eighteenth Century

RHETORIC IN THE MIDDLE AGES

In the early Middle Ages the conception of rhetoric began to change under the impact of Christian ideas. Christian thinkers began to reconsider rhetoric in relation to the discovery of truth. Cicero had joined wisdom to eloquence, arguing that the orator ought to be a virtuous man whose moral and intellectual character fitted him for the pursuit of truth. Wisdom for Cicero was a product of human reason, which was fit to discover the nature of things; proceeding from natural ideas about goodness and justice common to everyone, rhetoric could serve as a method of inquiry and not merely as the art of delivery.

This conception came into conflict with the early Christian emphasis on authority and biblical tradition as the basis of discovering truth. The early church father Augustine made an important distinction between divinely inspired eloquence and the eloquence of ordinary discourse. The province of rhetoric was by implication no longer a special kind of truth, informed by a wisdom inherent in the mind; for Augustine and his followers, rhetoric was chiefly an adaptation of Ciceronian invention to the clarifying and interpretation of Scripture and the expression of truths established by theology. However, Augustine did not ignore the art of rhetoric itself; his discussions in *De Doctrina Christiana* (A.D. 426–27) of great religious orators like Paul are concerned with style and persuasiveness.

The conception of rhetoric in the Middle Ages depended from one age to the next on what was thought to be its relation to logic. In general, logic was closely related to theology on the assumption that since truth, whether logic or theology, is a whole its methods are one; its method, moreover, owed much to Cicero and to other Latin rhetoricians, for the topics— the lines of argument—of Ciceronian invention had been given to logic. The application of both Ciceronian invention and disposition or judgment to general questions was called *dialectic*. Rhetoric was restricted to practical questions involving particular circumstances—hence its association with letter-writing; it was thus no longer an independent method of inquiry.

Dialectic in general refers to the art of examining assumptions and opinions, frequently through question and answer. Plato, in his dialogues, uses the word to describe the process by which opinions are compared for the purpose of reaching a consistent idea from which important conclusions can be drawn and, on a higher level, examined in relation to other ideas. On the beginning level of inquiry, the idea is shown to be noncontradictory —a just man cannot harm anyone because justice implies doing good only; therefore, justice cannot mean helping one's friends and harming one's enemies—and to be supported by everyday experience, on the basis of which opinions are formed. On the highest level of inquiry, ideas are examined without recourse to everyday sense experience. In the *Republic* Socrates says that reason on the highest level may be trained to intuit, by

Plato — knowledge is not acquired thru the senses. Dialectic moves from senses to pure reason.

Aristotle — Probable truth can be obtained thru senses. Dialectic - means of argumentation. Rhetoric became a method of inquiry

a kind of recollection or concentrated attention, forms or eternal models or ideas that exist apart from sensual reality. These forms are inherent in the mind and are not acquired through sense perception. Dialectic thus begins in sense experience but moves upward to a pure reason operating independently of the senses.

Aristotle, on the other hand, defined dialectic somewhat differently, in part because his theory of knowledge differs from Plato's. Knowledge based on sense experience may not be wholly reliable, Aristotle admitted, but certain less theoretical and more practical sciences, like politics, which cannot attain the precision of mathematics, can nevertheless attain highly probable truths. These truths are based on "opinions that are generally accepted." Dialectic for Aristotle is the part of logic that reasons from such opinions and beliefs and serves as the means of argumentation in these sciences. Its method, however, is much like the method of distinguishing demonstrable truths in the theoretical sciences like mathematics; in defining and testing the essential terms of these sciences, dialectic can serve as an adjunct to scientific reasoning.

For Aristotle, rhetoric, as the counterpart of dialectic, is concerned with generally accepted opinion—with highly probable truth; its chief aim is persuasion based on examination of choices. But, since it uses many tools of dialectic, it seemed that it might also be a method of inquiry into truth. The possibility of rhetoric as a method of inquiry was also implicit in Cicero's rhetoric, which derived from Aristotle. With the divorce of rhetoric from dialectic in the early Middle Ages, rhetoric became a repository of methods that could be applied in such activities as letter-writing and biblical exegesis. In medieval schools rhetoric, logic, and grammar constituted the *trivium*, one of the courses of study; in addition to the activities indicated, students learned to use rhetoric more for display than for persuasion, though they were trained to deliver discourses on historical and legal questions.

In the later Middle Ages, logic reemerged as a method separate from, though not inconsistent with, theology. In what was called New Logic, logic was identified with demonstrative reasoning—reasoning about certain and necessary truth; dialectic was identified with probable reasoning—reasoning about certain but, for the most part, not necessary truth. Rhetoric in some systems of the New Logic became a branch of dialectic. Thus it once again had become a method of inquiry.

Implicit in this redefinition was the elevation of reason to something like the importance it had held among classical thinkers. This crucial change occurred mainly through the influence of Peter Abelard (1079–1142), who sought to reconcile the many canons and doctrines, called "sentences," that had accumulated over the centuries from Scripture, church decrees, and authoritative writings. These sentences were discrete and noncontinuous, and Abelard wanted to sort them out and show their interrelationships and common assumptions. He sought to accomplish this reconciliation in part

48   The Nature of Rhetoric through the traditional rhetorical methods of comparison and examination of context and circumstances surrounding statements and, in the more advanced stages of inquiry, through the logical ordering of the sentences into a set of coherent propositions. Abelard was in effect applying reason as a test of truth. In his famous work *Sic et Non* (*Yes and No*), which dates from about 1120, he states: "The master key of knowledge is, indeed, a persistent and frequent questioning."

Though many thinkers in the later Middle Ages continued to subordinate rhetoric to theology, with some changes or modifications, others followed the direction of Abelard. The system of philosophy that evolved in the thirteenth century from his method was called Scholasticism. Thomas Aquinas (1225?–1274), a Dominican monk and the greatest of the Scholastic philosophers, systematized the connection of rhetoric and dialectic with probable reasoning. This connection was based on Aristotle, whose complete system of logic had been discovered through contact with the Arabic world and whose influence had become so enormous in the later Middle Ages that he was sometimes referred to as The Philosopher. For Aquinas the science of reasoning was of central concern because, though man's reason was limited and needed revelation and faith to complete it, the universe was rational and its laws were discoverable. In the *Summa Theologica*, his great synthesis of Scholastic philosophy, he states:

> The existence of God and other like truths about God, which can be known by natural reason, are not articles of Faith, but are preambles to the articles; for Faith presupposes natural knowledge, even as grace presupposes nature, and perfection something that can be perfected. Nevertheless, there is nothing to prevent a man, who cannot grasp its truth, from accepting, as a matter of Faith, something in itself capable of being known and demonstrated.

Scriptural wisdom and authority continued to be important; indeed, in Scholastic philosophy, invention was a way of drawing on such wisdom for inspiration. The important assumption, however, was that this wisdom was not ultimately inconsistent with natural reason—which cannot perceive God essentially or mystically but can know Him indirectly through the world, which reflects His unity and existence. In Aquinas' classification, based on the distinctions of Aristotle, rhetoric was that part of logic concerned with probable truth—more particularly, the discovery that leads not to conviction but to a tentative opinion simultaneously aware of contrary possibilities. ⁓

In addition to these two major conceptions of rhetoric—as a tool of theology and as an adjunct of dialectic—there was a conception devoted to figures and forms of words. The art of poetry itself was redefined by Geoffrey of Vinsauf in the early thirteenth century in terms of Cicero's rhetoric. In his *Poetria Nova* the poet's job is shown to comprise the five elements Cicero specified (See page 10) ; style is given the chief emphasis. There were other somewhat differing uses of Ciceronian rhetoric in works like the enormous encyclopedia of Vincent of Beauvais and, at the end of the Middle Ages, in the fifteenth century, the *Nova Rhetorica* of the Italian monk Lorenzo Traversagni—the first rhetoric printed in England (by William Caxton about 1479). This work discusses Cicero's five elements with respect to the three kinds of oratory—forensic, deliberative, and demonstrative.

A persistent concern, however, was whether rhetoric could deal with matters of truth as an independent method. In the English Renaissance of the sixteenth century, this concern continued, though the terms of discussion were to change in the light of new attitudes and needs, particularly with respect to logic.

RHETORIC IN THE ENGLISH RENAISSANCE

The English schoolboy of the sixteenth century was most certainly unaware of the controversies of previous centuries over the nature of rhetoric; like schoolboys of any age, he learned the rhetoric that was in fashion. In the sixteenth century the dominant rhetoric was Cicero's, which had been preserved in discussions of popular discourse. The five elements of Cicero's rhetoric had been introduced into English education by Alcuin, an Englishman who had set up for Charlemagne in the eighth century a court school modeled after the cathedral school at York. Sixteenth-century texts, among them the widely used *Arte of Rhetorique* (1553) of Thomas Wilson, followed the lead of such rhetoricians as Stephen Hawes, who, at the beginning of the century, had presented in English in his *Pastime of Pleasure* (1509) Cicero's rhetoric in relation to poetry, and Leonard Cox, whose *Rhetoryke* (1530?)—the first English textbook on the subject—treated Ciceronian invention systematically. The two classical works that Hawes and Cox drew upon were Cicero's *De Inventione* and *Rhetorica ad Herennium* (86? B.C.), the latter once thought to be by Cicero but now attributed by some to Cornificius; they could also draw upon influential works of the Middle Ages. Wilson's rhetoric was notable for its recognition of two kinds of invention—dialectic, used to prove and teach clearly, and rhetoric, used to persuade and ornament. However, Wilson did not pursue this distinction consistently in his treatment of disposition or arrangement.

Wilson's *The Rule of Reason* (1551) —the first study of logic written in English— presented to the English schoolboy the main ideas of Aristotle, filtered through the Scholastic logic of the late Middle Ages. The schoolboy was trained in logic before he undertook the primary subject, rhetoric. After mastering the essentials of Latin, he turned to simple logic; his chief

The Nature of Rhetoric

concern, however, was with the topics of invention—both intrinsic and extrinsic—which provided the material for amplifying or developing ideas through the accumulated wisdom common to educated people. Cicero was an important teacher, in part because he represented what was called the copious style, which emphasized amplification and ornamentation; the great early sixteenth-century Dutch scholar Erasmus, whose textbooks containing materials for amplification and instruction on the topics and schemes and tropes enormously influenced English education, reinvigorated the Ciceronian ideal by connecting amplification with the idea that traditional wisdom was essential to eloquence and by giving equal emphasis to thought and expression. Later in the sixteenth century, Roger Ascham, the teacher of Princess Elizabeth, expressed this idea in his *Toxophilus* (1545): "wisdom and eloquence, good matter and good utterance, were never or seldom asunder." The medieval ideal of two eloquences had dropped away. Other rhetorics in the sixteenth century, following the emphasis in Stephen Hawes, focused on style—on figures (unusual modes of expression and sentence construction) and tropes (metaphoric and ironic uses of language). The stress in these rhetorics—among them Henry Peacham's *The Garden of Eloquence* (1577)—depended on a number of assumptions, one of which being that ornamented language was appropriate to the aristocratic class with whom important communication took place. W. S. Howell states another of these assumptions in the following words:

> They conceived of wisdom and eloquence as the two forces which hold society together and maintain civilization. They conceived of oratory as the union of these two forces and as the organ of leadership. They conceived of wisdom as the force which man never elected to do without, whereas eloquence was the force which he might underrate and disparage in moments of pride and confidence. Thus eloquence had to be cultivated as a special power, and the study of eloquence became the study of the forms of speech, wisdom having already guaranteed that the substance of speech was present as raw material.[1]

Still other rhetorics—called "formulary"—focused on examples and models for imitation.

Insofar as the rhetoric of the sixteenth century concerned itself with invention, it served as a method of inquiry; as might be expected, this conception was to be attacked once again. This time the challenge came from French logician Petrus Ramus (1515–72), who argued that the topics of invention belonged exclusively to logic. Ramus insisted upon a strict division between rhetoric and logic. Good rhetoric adheres to strict logical argument, however, even though its province is style. Ramus made this

[1]*Logic and Rhetoric in England, 1500–1700* (New York: Russell & Russell, 1962), p. 134.

separation, in his *Dialectique* (1555), on the basis of three laws, through which he reformed Scholastic logic. The third of these—the *lex sapentiae* —argues that a proposition must place its subject in a proximate rather than in a remote class; for example, classifying the kangaroo with marsupials is more scientific than classifying it with mammals. On the same assumption, invention and arrangement could be said to belong to rhetoric only if they were classified unscientifically, in the following way:

> Method is arrangement, by which among many things the first in respect to conspicuousness is put in the first place, the second in the second, the third in the third, and so on. This term refers to every discipline and every dispute. Yet it commonly is taken in the sense of a direction sign and of a shortening of the highway. And by this metaphor it was practiced in school by the Greeks and the Latins, who, speaking also of rhetoric, called method arrangement, from the term for its genus. And under this term there is no doctrine, whether of proposition, or of syllogism, that is taught in rhetoric, except only so far as rhetoric makes mention of method.

The Ramist separation of rhetoric from methods of inquiry into truth continued into the seventeenth century, even when the traditional Ciceronian rhetoric—modified by the Ramist reforms—rose again in influence. Increasingly, rhetoric was becoming concerned with communication on all levels of discourse as well as with fact and research—with the discovery of what is, with accuracy of description and identification, with the eventual full disclosure of one's mind and thought. The older dependence on traditional wisdom and commonplaces as the matter of invention waned as the stress on observation and experimentation increased. This change in emphasis was paralleled and reinforced by the new logic of René Descartes, who stressed experience and experimentation rather than disputation and dialectic stressed by earlier centuries.

Other major intellectual influences of the seventeenth century reinforced this change in emphasis. The nature of the change in the conception of rhetoric can be illustrated in the work of Francis Bacon, who, in *The Advancement of Learning* (1605), referred to invention, judgment, memory, and elocution as the four important intellectual arts. These were basic to all the sciences and not merely to rhetoric, however; the scientist illuminates each of these arts in the light of his research. Bacon's contribution lay in his stress on rhetoric as the art by which reason and imagination could unite. In Bacon's words, "The duty and office of rhetoric is to apply Reason to Imagination for the better moving of the will." Rhetoric was needed in all kinds of discourse—whether directed to scholars or to the ordinary man—because of the constant influence of the passions. The choice of a rhetoric depended, however, on the purpose of the discourse; thus Bacon states in *The Advancement of Learning:*

For as knowledges are now delivered, there is a kind of contract of error between the deliverer and the receiver: for he that delivereth knowledge desireth to deliver it in such form as may be best believed, and not as may be best examined; and he that receiveth knowledge desireth rather present satisfaction than expectant inquiry; and so rather not to doubt than not to err: glory making the author not to lay open his weakness, and sloth making the disciple not to know his strength.

For Bacon rhetoric was an important means of making traditional wisdom available to all people. Indeed, its uses were changing with the rise of the middle class and the relatively decreasing importance of the aristocracy. As a result of this shift, the language of the ordinary man became increasingly favored over language full of figures and tropes; rhetorical theory became correspondingly simple. Thus the English philosopher Thomas Hobbes emphasized that an idea could not be expressed precisely unless it had been perceived clearly: one had to perfect his understanding as well as increase his knowledge. This ideal—consistent with the Ramist stress on the adherence to strict logic—was to be reflected in the new rhetorics, which stressed research. The Scholastic ideal was dying; the new rhetorics reflected new attitudes and approaches.

RHETORIC IN SHAKESPEARE

How deeply rooted traditional rhetoric was in the thought and art of the English Renaissance is evident in Shakespeare. Ben Jonson's famous statement that Shakespeare had "small Latin and less Greek" must be interpreted in the light of Jonson's own considerable learning and the probable extent of Shakespeare's grammar-school education, which Thomas W. Baldwin has amply documented. Sister Miriam Joseph and Milton B. Kennedy, in their important studies of Shakespeare's use of rhetoric, have shown that the plays provide a textbook of classical rhetoric in its many aspects.[2]

Rhetoric, these studies reveal, was especially important to Shakespeare as a means of articulating feeling with the greatest precision; it was not a dry discipline, devoid of use and abstract in interest. His use of rhetorical figures and tropes provides unusual insights into human character and motivation; thus the concept of essence in contrast to accidental characteristics— a distinction he most certainly drew from the topics of classical invention— becomes a major theme of the history plays: the difference between the individual king and the kingly state itself, as in these words of King Richard II (Act III, scene 3):

[2]See Sister Miriam Joseph, *Shakespeare's Use of the Arts of Language* (New York: Columbia Univ. Press, 1947); Milton B. Kennedy, *The Oration in Shakespeare* (Chapel Hill: Univ. of North Carolina Press, 1941).

What must the king do now? Must he submit?
The king shall do it: must he be deposed?
The king shall be contented: must he lose
The name of king? O' God's name, let it go.
I'll give my jewels for a set of beads,
My gorgeous palace for a hermitage,
My gay apparel for an almsman's gown,
My figured goblets for a dish of wood,
My scepter for a palmer's walking-staff,
My subjects for a pair of carvèd saints,
And my large kingdom for a little grave,
A little little grave, an obscure grave.

In *Julius Caesar,* Shakespeare gains precision through rhetorical devices
such as punning and what the Greeks called *paranomasia,* whereby words
similar but not identical in sound are repeated. Thus, in Act I, scene 1,
Cassius says of Julius Caesar, whom a mob is shouting for as king:

When went there by an age, since the great flood,
But it was famed with more than with one man?
When could they say till now that talked of Rome
That her wide walls encompassed but one man?
Nor is it *Rome* indeed, and *room* enough,
When there is in it but one only man.

The pun on *Rome* characterizes Cassius through his bitter, sharply ironic
view of Caesar implicit in the play of words; such irony suggests a man
who can believe that one can control his own destiny, that the fault, as he
says to Brutus early in the play, "is not in our stars, / But in ourselves, that
we are underlings," and that "Cassius from bondage will deliver Cassius."

The rhetoric of Shakespeare might consist of what were called schemes
or unusual patternings of words, as in the *hypallage* (a deliberate mis-
placing of words) of Antony's comment on the hole made by Brutus' stab
in Caesar's mantle: "This was the most *unkindest* cut of all." The application of *unkindest,* of course, calls attention not to the cut but to Brutus
who made it. Or rhetoric might consist of the topics of invention as in the
many disjunctions or alternative propositions, which indicate conflict, or
those distinctions between the general and particular through which Brutus
rationalizes and ultimately dignifies the murder of Caesar, as in Act II,
scene 1:

It must be by his death and for my part
I know no personal cause to spurn at him,
But for the general. He would be crown'd.
How that might change his nature, there's the question.

Or the rhetoric might take the form of argumentative devices such as *philophronesis* or the pacifying of one's enemies, as in Act III, scene 1, when Antony seeks to pacify the assassins through his servant, who says to Brutus:

> Thus, Brutus, did my master bid me kneel,
> Thus did Mark Antony bid me fall down,
> And, being prostrate, thus he bade me say:
> Brutus is noble, wise, valiant, and honest.

Another example is the use of *sarcasmus* or bitter taunting, as in Act V, scene 1, when Antony says to Brutus on the plains of Philippi:

> In your bad strokes, Brutus, you give good words.
> Witness the hole you made in Caesar's heart,
> Crying "Long live! Hail, Caesar!"

Shakespeare also makes highly skilled use of *enthymeme*, the equivalent of the syllogism in rhetoric—actually a compressed syllogism in which a premise or the conclusion is implied. Thus, in Act III, scene 2, Brutus says to the plebeians in his defense of Caesar's assassination: "Had you rather Caesar were living, and die all slaves, than that Caesar were dead, to live all freemen?" This enthymeme, Sister Miriam Joseph points out, is unusually effective because it compares two opposing arguments and joins these to an inference.

Shakespeare's orations exhibit his knowledge of classical rhetoric just as remarkably. All three kinds are to be found in plays of all periods—the forensic in Othello's apology to the Venetians for his secret marriage to Desdemona; the demonstrative in the speech of King Henry V to his soldiers before Harfleur, inspiring them to action; the deliberative in Henry's speech to the citizens of Harfleur persuading them to surrender. Milton B. Kennedy was able to distinguish more than eighty orations in the plays. The earliest, he suggests, were constructed according to the classical formula: proem or introduction, narration with division, proposition, confirmation, and conclusion. The form, of course, varies according to the needs of the dramatic action.

Mark Antony's funeral oration in *Julius Caesar* (Act III, scene 2) is perhaps the most famous and justly celebrated of Shakespeare's orations. In it Antony makes the three kinds of appeal distinguished by Aristotle—to *logos* or reason, *pathos* or emotion, and *ethos* or the respect for virtue. As Sister Miriam Joseph indicates, Antony first pretends to accept Brutus' argument that Caesar was driven by ambition: if this argument is true, Caesar has been punished for his fault. Then Antony appeals to *ethos:* the argument must be true because Brutus, who is an honorable man, says it is true. Antony then proceeds to attack the argument by comparing Brutus' statements with Caesar's actions. Increasingly Antony appeals to *pathos* by weeping and pretending to withhold the content of Caesar's will. Before reading the will he points to the stab holes in Caesar's mantle, at the same time persuading the people in the crowd that he himself is a good man whose concern is for them. These three appeals work together to turn the crowd against Brutus and the other conspirators; this was Antony's aim. Having aroused the crowd, he permits them to follow their course of burning and destruction. The speech supremely serves Shakespeare's dramatic purpose.

How carefully Shakespeare organized his oration may be seen in part through what he did with the materials he drew from Plutarch's *Parallel Lives*. The following passage is a relevant one from Plutarch's life of Antony:

> And therefore when Caesar's body was brought to the place where it should be buried, he made a funeral oration in commendation of Caesar, according to the ancient custom of praising noble men at their funerals. When he saw that the people were very glad and desirous also to hear Caesar spoken of, and his praises uttered, he mingled his oration with lamentable words, and by amplifying of matters did greatly move their hearts and affections unto pity and compassion. In fine to conclude his oration, he unfolded before the whole assembly the bloody garments of the dead, thrust through in many places with their swords, and called the malefactors cruel and cursed murderers. With these words he put the people into such a fury that they presently took Caesar's body, and burnt it in the market place, with such tables and forms as they could get together.

Plutarch provided the outline of the oration; in order to supply the particulars Shakespeare drew upon his knowledge of demonstrative rhetoric.

The oration as Shakespeare practiced it is based in all periods of his work on a three-part division—introduction, body or discussion, and epilogue—which is adapted to particular dramatic needs. In many orations—particularly the demonstrative, as in *Julius Caesar*—the body or discussion consists of a narration and proof. Antony's funeral oration exhibits this form and provides a remarkable example of the integration of rhetoric and poetic.

The first part, the proem or introduction, begins with his formal address to the crowd:

> Friends, Romans, countrymen, lend me your ears.
> I come to bury Caesar, not to praise him.

Antony then prepares the ground for arousing their resentment with a brief comment that ironically anticipates the reading of the will—a reading that will prove that the goodness of Caesar lives after him:

> The evil that men do lives after them,
> The good is oft interrèd with their bones.
> So let it be with Caesar.

He finishes his introduction by indicating the occasion for the oration, with attention to what Brutus has said and to the fact that he has been given permission to speak, and by insinuating his real purpose through his ironic emphasis on the presumed honor of the conspirators:

> The noble Brutus
> Hath told you Caesar was ambitious.
> If it were so, it was a grievous fault,
> And grievously hath Caesar answered it.
> Here, under leave of Brutus and the rest—
> For Brutus is an honorable man,
> So are they all, all honorable men—
> Come I to speak in Caesar's funeral.

This discussion of the occasion for the oration anticipates the narration —in the words of Wilson's *Arte of Rhetorique*, "a plain and manifest pointing of the matter, and an evident setting forth of all things that belong unto the same, with a brief rehearsal grounded upon some reason." The purpose of Antony's narration, following Aristotle's formula that the action is "considerably beyond the extent asserted," is to show that the facts are not as they were represented. Antony first underscores Caesar's absence of ambition and his value to the Romans whose coffers he filled:

> He was my friend, faithful and just to me.
> But Brutus says he was ambitious,
> And Brutus is an honorable man.
> He hath brought many captives home to Rome,
> Whose ransoms did the general coffers fill.
> Did this in Caesar seem ambitious?
> When that the poor have cried, Caesar hath wept—
> Ambition should be made of sterner stuff.
> Yet Brutus says he was ambitious,
> And Brutus is an honorable man.
> You all did see that on the Lupercal
> I thrice presented him a kingly crown,
> Which he did thrice refuse. Was this ambition?
> Yet Brutus says he was ambitious,

> And, sure, he is an honorable man.
> I speak not to disprove what Brutus spoke,
> But here I am to speak what I do know.

Implicit in these statements, it should be noted, is an attack on both the character and the arguments of the conspirators, which had been presented by Brutus in his preceding funeral oration. Shakespeare attacks the conspirators in this way instead of introducing a formal refutation following his proof that Caesar is a good man. The heavy irony serves to prepare the crowd, previously antagonistic to Caesar ("This Caesar was a tyrant"), for the direct appeals to their interest and self-esteem. Thus Antony indicates that Caesar has a claim to the love of people who formerly exhibited it:

> You all did love him once, not without cause.
> What cause withholds you then to mourn for him?
> O judgment, thou art fled to brutish beasts,
> And men have lost their reason! Bear with me,
> My heart is in the coffin there with Caesar,
> And I must pause till it come back to me.

After a brief interruption in which he weeps ("Poor soul! his eyes are red as fire with weeping," one onlooker observes) and in which the crowd begins to assent to the reason of his appeal, Antony returns to the same point—but with attention now to the role of Brutus and Cassius:

> But yesterday the word of Caesar might
> Have stood against the world. Now lies he there,
> And none so poor to do him reverence.
> O masters, if I were disposed to stir
> Your hearts and minds to mutiny and rage,
> I should do Brutus wrong and Cassius wrong,
> Who, you all know, are honorable men.
> I will not do them wrong; I rather choose
> To wrong the dead, to wrong myself and you,
> Than I will wrong such honorable men.

The renewed irony reinforces his attack, but it is now an irony that invites the crowd to join in the condemnation. Antony reiterates that he is appealing not just to their hearts but to their minds: men of reason must choose not to wrong the dead or themselves.

Antony immediately prepares for the proof by calling attention for the first time to the will and by arousing the crowd's interest in it:

> But here's a parchment with the seal of Caesar—
> I found it in his closet—'tis his will.

Let but the commons hear this testament—
Which, pardon me, I do not mean to read—
And they would go and kiss dead Caesar's wounds
And dip their napkins in his sacred blood,
Yea, beg a hair of him for memory,
And, dying, mention it within their wills,
Bequeathing it as a rich legacy
Unto their issue.

The implication that Caesar was more than a man—his blood is sacred—
and the reference to their own future legacies constitute a far more subtle
appeal than Antony has previously made, and the crowd accordingly interrupts and shouts to hear the will:

Have patience, gentle friends. I must not read it.
It is not meet you know how Caesar loved you.
You are not wood, you are not stones, but men;
And, being men, hearing the will of Caesar,
It will inflame you, it will make you mad.
'Tis good you know not that you are his heirs,
For if you should, oh, what would come of it!

The crowd interrupts again, and Antony continues:

Will you be patient? Will you stay a while?
I have o'ershot myself to tell you of it.
I fear I wrong the honorable men
Whose daggers have stabbed Caesar. I do fear it.

The frenzied crowd is now almost won over. As two of the plebeians proclaim the conspirators traitors and murderers, the rest of the crowd continues shouting for the will.

Following this preparation, the third part of the oration—the proof—
begins. This part contains a more direct appeal to the emotions of the
crowd—emotions that reinforce the logic of the narration. These appeals
have of course been simultaneous, though the emphasis has shifted, depending on what Antony has sensed to be the mood of the crowd. Sensing
their expectation, he now consents to read the will:

You will compel me then to read the will?
Then make a ring about the corpse of Caesar,
And let me show you him that made the will.
Shall I descend? And will you give me leave?

The crowd invites him to descend and forms a ring. Antony says: "Nay, press not so upon me. Stand far off." After the crowd has shouted for room, he proceeds to show the mantle and to recreate the circumstances of the assassination. His appeal to *pathos* becomes increasingly specific and concrete, because he wants the crowd to identify with Caesar as a person, to feel the pain and grief he felt, and not to see him merely as a fallen god:

> If you have tears, prepare to shed them now.
> You all do know this mantle. I remember
> The first time ever Caesar put it on.
> 'Twas on a summer's evening, in his tent,
> That day he overcame the Nervii.
> Look, in this place ran Cassius' dagger through.
> See what a rent the envious Casca made.
> Through this the well-belovèd Brutus stabbed,
> And as he plucked his cursèd steel away,
> Mark how the blood of Caesar followed it,
> As rushing out of doors, to be resolved
> If Brutus so unkindly knocked, or no.
> For Brutus, as you know, was Caesar's angel.
> Judge, O you gods, how dearly Caesar loved him!
> This was the most unkindest cut of all,
> For when the noble Caesar saw him stab,
> Ingratitude, more strong than traitors' arms,
> Quite vanquished him. Then burst his mighty heart,
> And, in his mantle muffling up his face,
> Even at the base of Pompey's statuë,
> Which all the while ran blood, great Caesar fell.
> Oh, what a fall was there, my countrymen!
> Then I, and you, and all of us fell down,
> Whilst bloody treason flourished over us.
> Oh, now you weep, and I perceive you feel
> The dint of pity. These are gracious drops.
> Kind souls, what weep you when you but behold
> Our Caesar's vesture wounded? Look you here—
> Here is himself, marred, as you see, with traitors.

Antony's descending from the pulpit to join the crowd has helped to reinforce the personal identification. The crowd's passions are now so thoroughly inflamed that it shouts for vengeance against the traitors who struck down Caesar. Antony now intensifies his attack by calling attention to his own presumed lack of eloquence, thus underscoring the emptiness and hypocrisy of Brutus' previous cold defense of the assassination. Indeed, the crux of his appeal here is that men without compassion or love can kill wantonly and coldly and can retain the wit to justify themselves, while men capable of compassion and love can speak only bluntly—without the kind of cleverness that steals the heart—and are bound to feel so strongly that they can be stirred to mutiny. Accordingly, after he interrupts the crowd with "Stay, countrymen," and after two plebeians call for quiet, Antony says:

> Good friends, sweet friends, let me not stir you up
> To such a sudden flood of mutiny.
> They that have done this deed are honorable.
> What private griefs they have, alas, I know not,
> That made them do it. They are wise and honorable,
> And will, no doubt, with reasons answer you.
> I come not, friends, to steal away your hearts.
> I am no orator, as Brutus is,
> But, as you know me all, a plain blunt man
> That love my friend; and that they know full well
> That gave me public leave to speak of him.
> For I have neither wit, nor words, nor worth,
> Action, nor utterance, nor the power of speech,
> To stir men's blood. I only speak right on,
> I tell you that which you yourselves do know,
> Show you sweet Caesar's wounds, poor poor dumb mouths,
> And bid them speak for me. But were I Brutus,
> And Brutus Antony, there were an Antony
> Would ruffle up your spirits, and put a tongue
> In every wound of Caesar that should move
> The stones of Rome to rise and mutiny.

If in the introduction irony was used to insinuate Antony's real purpose, in these lines it is used almost self-indulgently—suggesting that Antony is already savoring his success in shaping the crowd to his purposes. After the crowd calls again for mutiny, Antony clinches his proof by turning finally to the will:

> Why, friends, you go to do you know not what.
> Wherein hath Caesar thus deserved your loves?
> Alas, you know not. I must tell you, then—
> You have forgot the will I told you of.

The crowd shouts to hear the will, and Antony resumes:

> Here is the will, and under Caesar's seal.
> To every Roman citizen he gives,
> To every several man, seventy-five drachmas.

Some citizens shout that Caesar's death should be avenged. Antony continues describing the terms of the will:

Moreover, he hath left you all his walks,
His private arbors and new-planted orchards,
On this side Tiber. He hath left them you,
And to your heirs forever—common pleasures,
To walk abroad and recreate yourselves.

Antony's last statement to the crowd constitutes his epilogue—his final comment on the matter: "Here was a Caesar! When comes such another?" As the crowd scatters to burn and kill, Antony reveals his intention:

Now let it work. Mischief, thou art afoot,
Take thou what course thou wilt.

Julius Caesar reveals how important a role rhetoric plays in Shakespeare —and can play in all literature. Here the four-part oration has been adapted to the requirements of the dramatic action; the mounting intensity of the scene interrupts the oration so that we are hardly aware that Antony has moved from one part to another. And Antony is, of course, appealing directly to the emotions of the crowd; he does not want reason to prevail, though he pretends to be appealing to reason; his aim is anarchy, "mischief." The plain style Antony chooses for his oration is essential to his cunning plan, for it has the effect of identifying his interest with that of the crowd. By contrast, Brutus' oration in Act III, scene 2, is far more than plain, appeals to the abstract interest of the crowd—its desire for freedom —and keeps calling attention to Brutus himself:

Romans, countrymen, and lovers! Hear me for my cause, and be silent, that you may hear. Believe me for mine honor, and have respect to mine honor, that you may believe. Censure me in your wisdom, and awake your senses, that you may the better judge. If there be any in this assembly, any dear friend of Caesar's, to him I say that Brutus' love to Caesar was no less than his. If then that friend demand why Brutus rose against Caesar, this is my answer—not that I loved Caesar less, but that I loved Rome more. Had you rather Caesar were living, and die all slaves, than that Caesar were dead, to live all freemen? As Caesar loved me, I weep for him; as he was fortunate, I rejoice at it; as he was valiant, I honor him. But as he was ambitious, I slew him. There is tears for his love; joy for his fortune, honor for his valor, and death for his ambition. Who is here so base that would be a bondman? If any, speak, for him have I offended. Who is here so vile that will not love his country? If any, speak, for him have I offended. I pause for a reply.

The conception of rhetoric that Shakespeare drew upon in *Julius Caesar* included more than just a knowledge of the form of the oration; it involved a knowledge of styles suited to the occasion and audience. It consisted, in short, of a total theory of communication.

RHETORIC AND PROSE STYLE
IN THE ENGLISH RENAISSANCE

Like thought and art, English prose style during the sixteenth century was
rooted in traditional rhetoric. Intimately related to the forms and figures
of the oration were the three styles Cicero had distinguished: the plain for
clarity and logic, the grand for the display of intense passion, and the
moderate for ornamental grace. Quintilian, in his *Institutio Oratio,* distinguished the uses of these styles in the following words:

The higher the status of the person, the more elegant his language.

> The first [the plain] would seem best adapted for instructing, the second
> [the grand] for moving, and the third [the moderate or florid] (by which-
> ever name we call it) for charming or, as others would have it, conciliating
> the audience; for instruction the quality most needed is acumen, for concili-
> ation gentleness, and for stirring the emotions force. Consequently it is
> mainly in the plain style that we shall state our facts and advance our
> proofs .... The intermediate style will have more frequent recourse to met-
> aphor and will make more attractive use of figures, while it will introduce
> alluring digressions, will be neat in rhythm and pleasing in its reflec-
> tions .... But he whose eloquence is like to some great torrent that rolls
> down rocks and "disdains a bridge" and carves out its own banks for itself,
> will sweep the judge from his feet, struggle as he may, and force him to go
> whither he bears him.

Quintilian points out that there are many varieties of each style and recom-
mends moderation in their use:

> Thus the works of the orator will be great not extravagant, sublime not
> bombastic, bold not rash, severe but not gloomy, grave but not slow, rich
> but not luxuriant, pleasing but not effeminate, grand but not grandiose. It
> is the same with other qualities: the mean is safest, for the worst of all
> faults is to fly to extremes.

In the sixteenth and seventeenth centuries these styles became the focus of
discussion, though each style might be defined in a different way. Thus the
Spanish rhetorician and friend of Erasmus, Juan Luis Vives ("the second
Quintilian"), from whom Ben Jonson borrowed heavily in his work *Discoveries,* distinguished the high style, marked by sonorous diction and
swelling periods—that is, sentences swelling to a climactic idea; the middle
style, marked by plain diction and quietly moving sentences; and low style,
marked by simple, unadorned diction and sentences.

Cicero's grand style, exemplified in "The Dream of Scipio" in *De
Republica,* was marked by rhythmical units so proportioned that the prose
stands midway between the stricter metrical patterns of poetry and the
looser rhythms of speech. The concern, in other words, is with the naturally
proportioned rhythm of the whole sentence rather than with its parts:

Know then that you are divine, for that is divine which throbs with life, feels, remembers, foresees, which rules, controls, and makes to move the body over which it has been placed in charge; as over this universe rules that supreme God; so this mortal body is made to move by a deathless soul within.

Renaissance lofty style
Erasmus began trend
to plainer.

This grand style was popular with many English writers of the Renaissance. From the beginning of the sixteenth century, however, writers cultivated a looser prose—perhaps following the lead of Erasmus, who expressed his preference for the plain or Attic style, described by Cicero himself as "loose but not rambling" and consisting of short symmetrical clauses, unornamented yet illustrated with many maxims. This plainer style, George Williamson indicates in his definitive study of English prose style, was more typical of English prose, which had always been looser than the Ciceronian and close to, though not identical with, the patterns of speech—with loosely connected elements amplified by words and phrases similar in meaning and construction.

Loose prose in general depends heavily on conjunctions rather than on tight rhythm and structure; the chief idea comes early; modifying elements follow. Compare the following sentences from sixteenth- and seventeenth-century writers. The first is from Richard Hooker's *The Laws of Ecclesiastical Polity* (1593):

> What we do against our wills, or constrainedly, we are not properly said to do it, because the motive cause of doing it is not in ourselves, but carrieth us, as if the wind should drive a feather in the air, we no whit furthering that whereby we are driven.

Here the prose is loose; the modifying elements provide illustration; the chief idea opens the sentence; the reason follows.

The following two examples are from Philip Sidney's *An Apology for Poetry* (1595), which is an example of the classical oration.

> There is no art delivered to mankind that hath not the works of nature for his principal object, without which they could not consist, and on which they so depend, as they become actors and players, as it were, of what nature will have set forth.

Here the prose is loose; the dependent clauses provide additional but not essential information.

> But it is not the tragedy they do mislike; for it were too absurd to cast out so excellent a representation of whatsoever is most worthy to be learned.

Here the prose is looser than periodic; the clauses are of equal importance and depend on *for*.

The next two examples are from John Milton's *Aeropagitica* (1644).

> Lords and Commons of England, consider what nation it is whereof ye are, and whereof ye are the governors: a nation not slow and dull, but of a quick, ingenious and piercing spirit, acute to invent, subtle and sinewy to discourse, not beneath the reach of any point, the highest that human capacity can soar to.

This sentence is periodic: the meaning is not complete until the final element.

> The light which we have gained was given us, not to be ever staring on, but by it to discover onward things more remote from our knowledge.

This sentence is moderately periodic.

Hugh Blair, in the eighteenth century, distinguished between the periodic and the "coupé" or cut-up styles, marked by "short independent propositions, each complete within itself." But loose prose might give greater than normal attention to rhythm and parallelism; or might be extremely curt, with sharply separated elements, omitted conjunctions, and heavy parallelism—as in Bacon's aphoristic essays; or might be merely plain. There were, indeed, many kinds of ornate and plain style in the sixteenth and seventeenth centuries. The differences between these are extremely subtle, originating in different models and conceptions of the sentence. It may be helpful, however, to distinguish some of the important kinds.

One kind of ornate style was characterized by rhymed prose. George Williamson cites this passage from Thomas More, the sixteenth-century politician and humanist:

> Neither to the achieving of temperance in prosperity, nor to the purchasing of patience in adversity, nor to the despising of worldly vanity, nor to the desiring of heavenly felicity.

The balance here is moderate compared to the euphuistic style of John Lyly, the sixteenth-century dramatist and writer of the prose romance *Euphues* (1579)—an instance of rhymed prose carried to such an extreme that the style tends to dominate the matter:

> oftentimes delighted to hear discourses of love, but ever desirous to be instructed in learning; somewhat curious to keep her beauty, which made her comely, but more careful to increase her credit, which made her commendable: not adding the length of a hair to courtliness that might detract the breadth of a hair from chastity....

In the seventeenth century the ornate style increasingly reflected the interest of the age in ornamental, far-fetched figures and elaborate metaphors —called conceits—relating to abstract ideas. Compare the following examples. The first and third are from John Donne's *Devotions upon Emergent Occasions* (1624); the second and fourth are from *Hydriotaphia, Urn-Burial* (1658), by Thomas Browne.

> Honors, pleasures, possessions presented to us out of time, in our decrepit and distasted and unapprehensive age, lose their office and lose their name; they are not honors to us that shall never appear nor come abroad into the eyes of the people to receive honor from them who give it; nor pleasures to us who have lost our sense to taste them; nor possessions to us who are departing from the possession of them.

> If they fell by long and aged decay, yet wrapped up in the bundle of time, they fall into indistinction, and make but one blot with infants. If we begin to die when we live, and long life be but a prolongation of death, our life is a sad composition; we live with death, and die not in a moment.

> God employs several translators; some pieces are translated by age, some by sickness, some by war, some by justice; but God's hand is in every translation, and his hand shall bind up all our scattered leaves again for that library where every book shall lie open to one another.

> Life is a pure flame, and we live by an invisible sun within us. A small fire sufficeth for life, great flames seemed too little after death, while men vainly affected precious pyres....

The plain style, on the other hand, came into prominence in part through the influence of the Ramists' stress on simple, precise, logical argument and through the influence of classicists like Ben Jonson, who cultivated the concise Attic style of Seneca the Elder and of Quintilian. In *Timber* (1640), Jonson wrote:

> The congruent and harmonious fitting of parts in a sentence hath almost the fastening and force of knitting and connection; as in stones well squared, which will rise strong a great way without mortar. Periods are beautiful when they are not too long; for so they have their strength too, as in a pike or javelin.

The trend toward plain style was strengthened in the 1640's and in the years following by attacks on the ornate excesses of pulpit oratory and by the influence of the Royal Society, which in 1664 appointed, among others, John Dryden, John Evelyn, Thomas Sprat, and Edmund Waller to a committee to explore the possible improvement of the English language. In works of natural philosophy, J. W. H. Atkins indicates, the Society decreed a "rejection of all amplifications, digressions and swellings of style, and a return back to the primitive purity and shortness." The Society also sought "a close, naked, natural way of speaking, positive expressions, clear sense, a natural easiness, bringing all things as near to the Mathematical plainness as they can." [3]

Opinions about plain style differed somewhat, and leading writers and thinkers emphasized different problems. Thus Thomas Sprat, the historian of the Royal Society, attacked fantastic tropes and figures and "misty uncertainties"; Joseph Glanvill, a churchman and author of an influential book *The Vanity of Dogmatizing* (1661), attacked "bastard rhetoric" and recommended a plain style and the avoidance of "hard words," "deep and mysterious notions," "affected Rhetorications," and "Phantastical Phrases." Dryden, whose example was probably the major influence of the age, emphasized propriety, a language and style suited to the subject and audience, and rejected foreign and Latinate vocabularies when native English words could be used. Dryden's views were not always consistent, however; his ideal at least was "to write English as near as he could distinguish it from the tongue of pedants and that of affected travellers."

The character of English plain style was established for the eighteenth century at least by the example of Dryden and other influential writers, such as Jonathan Swift, who cited John Bunyan as a model and attacked curt prose and crude colloquialisms as well as ornamented style; and Joseph Addison, author of some of the essays in *The Spectator* and in other periodicals, who emphasized a style close to ordinary conversation but much more refined—"sentiments which are natural without being obvious."

A later eighteenth-century exponent of this conception was the Scottish philosopher and essayist David Hume, who applied to prose style the canon that "beauty lies in a medium." With Hume, however, we find evidence of a return in interest to something approximating the grand Ciceronian style, without excessive ornamentation. Hume argued that there was a place for sublime and noble eloquence, particularly in parlimentary and popular debate. This attitude is reflected in the speeches of the great Irish-born parliamentarian Edmund Burke, who was capable of the plain style and could rise to Ciceronian eloquence without becoming ornate or extravagant. The following sentence is from his *Reflections on the Revolution in France* (1790):

> We know that *we* have made no discoveries, and we think that no discoveries are to be made, in morality; nor many in the great principles of government, nor in the ideas of liberty, which were understood long before we were born, altogether as well as they will be after the grave has heaped its mould upon our presumption, and the silent tomb shall have imposed its law on our pert loquacity.

[3]*English Literary Criticism: Seventeenth and Eighteenth Centuries* (New York: Barnes and Noble, 1952), p. 44.

Hume represents a trend of thought given impetus by important thinkers at the beginning of the eighteenth century. His ideas had been anticipated in England by changes in attitude toward the passions and what
was commonly called "enthusiasm" ("Doth he think they knew it by
Enthusiasm or Revelation from Heaven?" one writer of the later seventeenth century asked). Alexander Pope, in his *Essay on Man,* pointed out
that the passions, "Modes of self-love," are basic to man and God:

> On life's vast ocean diversely we sail,
> Reason the card, but Passion is the gale;
> Nor God alone in the still calm we find,
> He mounts the storm, and walks upon the wind.

Happiness, Pope continues, depends on keeping the passions under rational
control, "to due bounds confin'd." And if reason cannot overthrow the
most powerful single passion, it must try to "rectify" it and put it to good
use.

A different emphasis appears in the works of the early eighteenth-century
critic John Dennis, who may have condemned enthusiasm in what he considered false religion but defended it in poetry and religion when it was
genuine in its inspiration. A contemporary of Dennis, the third Earl of
Shaftesbury, Anthony Ashley Cooper, wrote in *Characteristics* (1711):
"No poet ... can do anything great in his own way without the imagination or supposition of a divine presence, which may raise him to some degree of this passion [enthusiasm] we are speaking of." Later in the century
Edward Young, reflecting the influence of the third-century Greek critic
Longinus on the critical thought of many writers in the eighteenth century,
identified genius with enthusiasm. With the assumption that judgment
was a matter of instinct (particularly in the natural genius, who, Addison
suggested in *The Spectator,* No. 160, need not depend on rules), a theoretical justification was provided for the shift from the concern with figures
and tropes to the concern with delivery. Though many continued to defend the authority of the classical writers, a writer like Alexander Pope
could in his *Essay on Criticism* (1711) argue that the rules of the ancients
were important not because all things old were sacrosanct but because they
were "nature methodised."

Increasingly, then, the emphasis shifted to that orderly and supreme
model, Nature herself, and to emotion, which was associated with kinds
of experience Nature provided. Thus Hume's emphasis on emotion was
reflected in the rhetorical ideas of George Campbell, who, in his *Philosophy
of Rhetoric* (1776), tended to divorce deductive logic from rhetoric and to
place investigation with other disciplines. Campbell, more particularly,
considered rhetoric to be concerned with making ideas as vivid, individualized, and compelling as possible: the orator applies imagination to experience to state his conception concisely. Lord Kames, in his influential *Ele-*

ments of Criticism (1762), argued that "images, which are the life of poetry, cannot be raised in any perfection but by introducing particular objects" and that our perception of beauty is related to pleasure and of ugliness to pain. Finally, Hugh Blair, who, in his *Lectures on Rhetoric and Belles-Lettres* (1783), unites these ideas with the Ciceronian ideal that a man of eloquence must be a man of virtue, emphasized the natural instinct for beauty and the dominant role of feelings in art, particularly tragedy.

It was partly under the influence of these ideas that plain style could be modified or discarded for another style by an orator like Burke, whose critical writings are concerned with the emotions of the beautiful and the sublime—the overpowering force that produces awe and terror in the face of dark, vast, formless objects and experiences. How such a theory might affect language is apparent in Burke's comment in *Philosophical Inquiry into the Origin of Our Ideas of the Sublime and Beautiful* (1756) that passions can be produced by words for which we have no clear ideas: abstractions like *virtue* and *liberty* which are "in reality but mere sounds; but they are sounds, which being used on particular occasions, wherein we receive some good or suffer some evil . . . produce in the mind whenever they are afterwards mentioned, effects similar to those of their occasions."

RHETORIC AND THE ESSAY

Changing attitudes toward style are revealed in a new form of personal expression—the essay—which began in the English Renaissance and became especially important in the seventeenth and eighteenth centuries. Today, as Part Two of this book shows, the essay is one of the major forms of personal expression. Traditional rhetoric, as the repository of resources of style upon which writers could draw, contributed much to this form of writing.

The essay (from the Latin *exagium,* meaning a weighing or a balancing) in the sixteenth century was at first an extension of discourse, often a contrasting of opinions, and therefore resembled the argumentative form. Montaigne chose to call his essays by that name—*Essais*—because of this characteristic; Bacon referred to the contrasting of opposing opinions as *thesis,* following a type of school composition, directions for which were given in books like the *Progymnasmata* of Aphthonius, another ancient treatise carried into the Renaissance. The treatment in the essay was usually brief—briefer at least than a discourse of the length of Castiglione's *The Courtier* (1514), a treatise on the ideal gentleman of court written in the form of a dialogue—particularly when the subject did not offer many points of development, and the treatment was accepted as incomplete even when the materials had been amplified. The materials for amplification most frequently came from commonplace books such as Erasmus provided.

Bacon's early essays—constructed of aphorisms and other sententious materials—were presented in this form, sometimes with a markedly antithetical beginning, as in "Of Wisdom for a Man's Self" (1597):

> An ant is a wise creature for itself; but it is a shrewd thing in an orchard or garden. And certainly men that are great lovers of themselves waste the public. Divide with reason between self-love and society; and be so true to thyself, as thou be not false to others, especially to thy king and country.

Elementary school compositions, some resembling the thesis and others the simple amplification of an aphorism or other sententious matter, contributed to the growth of the essay. According to the American scholar W. G. Crane, schoolboys would elaborate a proverb into a theme through a process known as *chria*. This process consisted of the statement of the proverb; praise for or condemnation of the speaker if he could be identified; a restatement of the proverb; an indication of how it could be practically applied; a defense of arguments for it and refutation of arguments against it through the topics; and a concise epilogue. Some of these prototypes of the essay, like Montaigne's later essays, were demonstrative; others, deliberative. The essays might be introduced with a definition of logic or rhetoric, perhaps with the help of a simile or metaphor or a discussion of etymology. A descriptive essay might be introduced through a character speaking.

Of course, other forms of writing were cultivated during the English Renaissance. Treatises on letter-writing consisted of restatements of the rules of ancient treatises on the oration and the application of rhetorical figures intended to amplify and ornament these letters. Letters were sometimes classified as deliberative, demonstrative, and judicial; and to these Erasmus added the familiar letter. In addition, there were moral discourses and books of instruction of various kinds. All these contributed to the development of the essay, if only because they transmitted the resources of traditional rhetoric and showed how they could be used.

The course of the essay in the seventeenth century is illustrated by Francis Bacon, whose essays changed markedly in style. Those published in the *Essayes* of 1597 tended to be aphoristic, with sharply delineated observations, exact conclusions, and a plain to very curt style. These characteristics are seen in the following passage from "Of Studies":

> Studies serve for pastimes, for ornaments, for abilities; their chief use for pastimes is in privateness and retiring; for ornaments in discourse; and for ability in judgment; for expert men can execute, but learned men are more fit to judge and censure. To spend too much time in them is sloth; to use them too much for ornament is affectation; to make judgment wholly by their rules is the humor of a scholar; they perfect nature, and are themselves perfected by experience. . . .

In the 1612 edition there was a shift toward what Crane calls "methodical development and amplification," perhaps through proverbs, similes and examples. And in the 1625 edition there was to be further amplification and more attention to structure, as is shown in this passage from "Of Vain-Glory":

It was prettily devised of Aesop, "The fly sat upon the axle-tree of the chariot wheel, and said, What a dust do I raise!" So are there some vain persons, that whatsoever goeth alone or moveth upon greater means, if they have never so little hand in it, they think it is they that carry it. They that are glorious must needs be factious, for all bravery stands upon comparisons. They must needs be violent to make good their own vaunts. Neither can they be secret, and therefore not effectual; but according to the French proverb, *Beaucoup de bruit peu de fruit:* Much bruit, little fruit. Yet certainly there is use of this quality in civil affairs.

As in the previous century, definition might be aided by description, sometimes through a character; or the essay might be introduced by aphoristic or topical materials. In part through the influence of Isaac Casaubon's translation in 1592 of the *Characters* of the ancient Greek writer Theophrastus—these were sketches of character types portraying their typical actions—essays called "characters" became popular at the beginning of the seventeenth century. The "characters" of writers like Joseph Hall were used not only to satirize people who were under the influence of one of the humors—dominant passions arising from the over-abundance of one of the presumed four fluids or humors of the body—but to exhibit the wit of the writer. Thomas Overbury once said of the character: "To square out a character by our English level, it is a picture (real or personal) quaintly drawn, in various colors, all of them heightened by one shadowing." Certain other qualities, in other words, are blocked out to create a caricature. Thus Overbury describes the Puritan in the following way:

Where the gate stands open, he is ever seeking a stile; and where his learning ought to climb, he creeps through; give him advice, you run into *traditions*, and urge a modest course, he cries out *councils*.

Later in the seventeenth century, with the exhaustion of interest in the writing of characters, interest turned to biography and prose portraits. Some of the most celebrated works of this type came from Izaak Walton and Edward Hyde, Earl of Clarendon, whose *The History of the Rebellion*, which describes the civil war that led to the Puritan Interregnum, produced memorable portraits of the principals, including Oliver Cromwell. With this turn to individualized portraits, the writer was soon to portray himself —or at least impersonate himself or another character—as Addison did in the first issue of *The Spectator* on March 1, 1711. The fictional members of the Spectator Club, developed in succeeding issues, pointed the way to new kinds of character portrayal in the informal essay. And, of course, with the rising popularity of periodicals like *The Tatler* and *The Spectator* and, later in the eighteenth century, *The Rambler* and *The Idler*—to which Samuel Johnson contributed essays—the essay could be used for the expression of personal reflections and occasional thoughts of every kind, including literary criticism, such as Addison's series of essays on Milton's *Paradise Lost* in *The Spectator*.

By the end of the eighteenth century the essay had enlarged in conception so that it included series of rather disconnected reflections, critical prefaces like those of John Dryden, and philosophical treatises like John Locke's *Essay Concerning Human Understanding* (1690). Through the influence of Addison and Steele and Swift, among others, the plain style became associated with the essay. For one thing, the audience had been enlarged and was no longer restricted to the aristocracy; for another, the subject matter dealt more with ordinary experience and thought, though the lofty considerations of life and death of Browne's *Hydriotaphia, Urn-Burial* might be explored in a rather more modest way by Addison in the *Spectator* essay "Westminster Abbey."

All through this period, as up to the present, the English essay, though it differs from the classical oration in purpose and structure, drew upon the materials of invention and disposition and upon conceptions of style available to those writers educated in the classical tradition. Essay writers drew upon these materials much as the Renaissance schoolboy did, so that, instead of becoming a dead art, rhetoric was in all periods related to almost every kind of discourse and artistic form. Rhetoric was not, then, an accumulation of devices related to persuasion, existing apart from the everyday thought and expression of the Englishman.

Nor is it today merely an accumulation of devices. Traditional rhetoric exhibits its vitality in its contribution to every kind of discourse—from the humorous sketches of E. B. White and James Thurber to the oratory of Adlai Stevenson and Winston Churchill. The question of rhetoric as a method of inquiry has not been dormant in modern times. Indeed, some current discussions on the nature and scope of rhetoric are concerned with whether rhetoric is merely the art of persuasion with emphasis on style and delivery, or can be more than this, a science of investigation. Recent rhetoricians like I. A. Richards and Kenneth Burke (see Part Three) have developed new theories of rhetoric, drawing upon modern psychology, biology, and sociology. In so doing they have rejected the idea that rhetoric is nothing more than style and delivery. The history of rhetoric suggests that this question will continue to be debated.

Part Two

THE PRACTICE OF RHETORIC

Description and Narration

RICHARD STEELE

A Day's Ramble in London

RICHARD STEELE'S audience for this essay, which appeared in the August 11, 1712, issue of *The Spectator*, consisted chiefly of Londoners of the new middle class, which had been gaining political power for the past half-century. Although their chief interests were business and politics, these readers sought to be informed on cultural topics as well. They admired wit, elegance, and style, and they aspired to be recognized as gentlemen.

In *The Tatler* and *The Spectator*, Steele's principal aim was to meet these latter needs. He usually avoided the hot political disputes between Whigs and Tories, Jacobites and Hanoverians, and stressed instead the higher pleasures appropriate to polite society. "The present grandeur of the British nation," Steele wrote in an early essay, "might make us expect that we should rise in our public diversions, and the manner of enjoying life, in proportion to our advancement in glory and power."

Despite obvious differences in tone, sentence structure, and diction, Steele's writing closely resembles that of E. B. White (p. 8). Both writers show a common purpose: the civilized enjoyment derived from observing daily life in a great metropolis. Both evoke the genius of their time and place by lively descriptions of real events. Finally, in both we may observe the way in which persuasive purpose animates and unifies writing.

Sine me, vacivum tempus ne quod dem mihi Laboris.
TERENCE

It is an inexpressible Pleasure to know a little of the World, and be of no [1] Character or Significancy in it. To be ever unconcerned, and ever looking on new Objects with an endless Curiosity, is a Delight known only to those who are turned for Speculation: Nay, they who enjoy it, must value things only as they are the Objects of Speculation, without drawing any worldly Advantage to themselves from them, but just as they are what contribute to their Amusement, or the Improvement of the Mind. I lay one Night last Week at *Richmond*; and being restless, not out of Dissatisfaction, but a certain busie Inclination one sometimes has, I arose at Four in the Morning, and took Boat for *London*, with a Resolution to rove by Boat and Coach for the next Four and twenty Hours, till the many different Objects I must needs meet with should tire my Imagination, and give me an Inclination to a Repose more profound than I was at that time capable of. I beg People's Pardon for an odd Humour I am guilty of, and was often that

Day, which is saluting any Person whom I like, whether I know him or not. This is a Particularity would be tolerated in me, if they considered that the greatest Pleasure I know I receive at my Eyes, and that I am obliged to an agreeable Person for coming abroad into my View, as another is for a Visit of Conversation at their own Houses.

[2] The Hours of the Day and Night are taken up in the Cities of *London* and *Westminster* by People as different from each other as those who are Born in different Centuries. Men of Six-a-Clock give way to those of Nine, they of Nine to the Generation of Twelve, and they of Twelve disappear, and make Room for the fashionable World, who have made Two-a-Clock the Noon of the Day.

[3] When we first put off from Shoar, we soon fell in with a Fleet of Gardiners bound for the several Market-Ports of *London*; and it was the most pleasing Scene imaginable to see the Chearfulness with which those industrious People ply'd their Way to a certain Sale of their Goods. The Banks on each Side are as well Peopled, and beautified with as agreeable Plantations, as any Spot on the Earth; but the *Thames* itself, loaded with the Product of each Shoar, added very much to the Landskip. It was very easie to observe by their Sailing, and the Countenances of the ruddy Virgins, who were Supercargos, the Parts of the Town to which they were bound. There was an Air in the Purveyors for *Covent-Garden*, who frequently converse with Morning Rakes, very unlike the seemly Sobriety of those bound for *Stocks-Market*.

[4] Nothing remarkable happened in our Voyage; but I landed with Ten Sail of Apricock Boats at *Strand-Bridge*, after having put in at *Nine-Elmes*, and taken in Melons, consigned by Mr. *Cuffe* of that Place, to *Sarah Sewell* and Company, at their Stall in *Covent-Garden*. We arrived at *Strand-Bridge* at Six of the Clock, and were unloading; when the Hackney-Coachmen of the foregoing Night took their Leave of each other at the *Dark-House,* to go to Bed before the Day was too far spent. Chimney-Sweepers pass'd by us as we made up to the Market, and some Raillery happened between one of the Fruit-Wenches and those black Men, about the Devil and *Eve,* with Allusion to their several Professions. I could not believe any Place more entertaining than *Covent-Garden;* where I strolled from one Fruit-shop to another, with Crowds of agreeable young Women around me, who were purchasing Fruit for their respective Families. It was almost Eight of the Clock before I could leave that Variety of Objects. I took Coach and followed a young Lady, who tripped into another just before me, attended by her Maid. I saw immediately she was of the Family of the *Vainloves*. There are a Sett of these, who of all things affect the Play of *Blindman's-Buff*, and leading Men into Love for they know not whom, who are fled they know not where. This sort of Woman is usually a janty Slattern; she hangs on her Cloaths, plays her Head, varies her Posture, and changes place incessantly, and all with an Appearance of striving

at the same time to hide her self, and yet give you to understand she is in Humour to laugh at you. You must have often seen the Coachmen make Signs with their Fingers as they drive by each other, to intimate how much they have got that Day. They can carry on that Language to give Intelligence where they are driving. In an instant my Coachman took the Wink to pursue, and the Lady's Driver gave the Hint that he was going through *Long-Acre* towards St. *James's:* While he whipp'd up *James-Street,* we drove for *King Street,* to save the Pass at *St. Martin's-Lane.* The Coachmen took care to meet, justle, and threaten each other for Way, and be intangled at the End of *Newport-Street* and *Long-Acre.* The Fright, you must believe, brought down the Lady's Coach Door, and obliged her, with her Mask off, to enquire into the Bustle, when she sees the Man she would avoid. The Tackle of the Coach-Window is so bad she cannot draw it up again, and she drives on sometimes wholly discovered, and sometimes half-escaped, according to the Accident of Carriages in her Way. One of these Ladies keeps her Seat in a Hackney-Coach as well as the best Rider does on a managed Horse. The laced Shooe on her Left Foot, with a careless Gesture, just appearing on the opposite Cushion, held her both firm, and in a proper Attitude to receive the next Jolt.

As she was an excellent Coach-Woman, many were the Glances at each [5] other which we had for an Hour and an Half in all Parts of the Town by the Skill of our Drivers; till at last my Lady was conveniently lost with Notice from her Coachman to ours to make off, and he should hear where she went. This Chase was now at an End, and the Fellow who drove her came to us, and discovered that he was ordered to come again in an Hour, for that she was a Silk-Worm. I was surprised with this Phrase, but found it was a Cant among the Hackney Fraternity for their best Customers, Women who ramble twice or thrice a Week from Shop to Shop, to turn over all the Goods in Town without buying any thing. The Silk-Worms are, it seems, indulged by the Tradesmen; for tho' they never buy, they are ever talking of new Silks, Laces and Ribbands, and serve the Owners in getting them Customers, as their common Dunners do in making them pay.

The Day of People of Fashion began now to break, and Carts and Hacks [6] were mingled with Equipages of Show and Vanity; when I resolved to walk it out of Cheapness; but my unhappy Curiosity is such, that I find it always my Interest to take Coach, for some odd Adventure among Beggars, Ballad-Singers, or the like, detains and throws me into Expence. It happened so immediately; for at the Corner of *Warwick-Street,* as I was listening to a new Ballad, a ragged Rascal, a Beggar who knew me, came up to me, and began to turn the Eyes of the good Company upon me, by telling me he was extream Poor, and should die in the Streets for want of Drink, except I immediately would have the Charity to give him Sixpence to go into the next Ale-House and save his life. He urged, with a melancholy Face, that all his Family had died of Thirst. All the Mob have

Humour, and two or three began to take the Jest; by which Mr. *Sturdy* carried his point, and let me sneak off to a Coach. As I drove along it was a pleasing Reflection to see the World so prettily chequered since I left *Richmond*, and the Scene still filling with Children of a new Hour. This Satisfaction encreased as I moved toward the City; and gay Signs, well disposed Streets, magnificent publick Structures, and Wealthy Shops, adorned with contented Faces, made the Joy still rising till we came into the Centre of the City, and Centre of the World of Trade, the *Exchange* of *London*. As other Men in the Crowds about me were pleased with their Hopes and Bargains, I found my Account in observing them, in Attention to their several Interests. I, indeed, looked upon my self as the richest Man that walked the *Exchange* that Day; for my Benevolence made me share the Gains of every Bargain that was made. It was not the least of the Satisfactions in my Survey, to go up Stairs, and pass the Shops of agreeable Females; to observe so many pretty Hands busie in the Foldings of Ribbands, and the utmost Eagerness of agreeable Faces in the Sale of Patches, Pins, and Wires, on each Side the Counters, was an Amusement, in which I should longer have indulged my self, had not the dear Creatures called to me to ask what I wanted, when I could not answer, only *To look at you*. I went to one of the Windows which opened to the Area below, where all the several Voices lost their Distinction, and rose up in a confused Humming; which created in me a Reflection that could not come into the Mind of any but of one a little studious; for I said to my self, with a kind of Punn in thought, *What Nonsense is all the Hurry of this World to those who are above it?* In these, or not much wiser Thoughts, I had like to have lost my Place at the Chop-House; where every Man, according to the natural Bashfulness or Sullenness of our Nation, eats in a publick Room a Mess of Broth, or Chop of Meat, in dumb Silence, as if they had no Pretence to speak to each other on the Foot of being Men, except they were of each other's Acquaintance.

[7]   I went afterwards to *Robin's* and saw People who had dined with me at the Five-Penny Ordinary just before, give Bills for the Value of large Estates; and could not but behold with great Pleasure, Property lodged in, and transferred in a Moment from such as would never be Masters of half as much as is seemingly in them, and given from them every Day they live. But before Five in the Afternoon I left the City, came to my common Scene of *Covent-Garden*, and passed the Evening at *Will's* in attempting the Discourses of several Sets of People, who relieved each other within my Hearing on the Subjects of Cards, Dice, Love, Learning and Politicks. The last Subject kept me till I heard the Streets in the Possession of the Bell-man, who had now the World to himself, and cryed, *Past Two of Clock*. This rous'd me from my Seat, and I went to my Lodging, led by a Light, whom I put into the Discourse of his private Oeconomy, and made him give me an Account of the Charge, Hazard, Profit and Loss of a Family

that depended upon a Link, with a Design to end my trivial Day with the Generosity of Sixpence, instead of a third Part of that Sum. When I came to my Chambers I writ down these Minutes; but was at a Loss what Instruction I should propose to my Reader from the Enumeration of so many Insignificant Matters and Occurrences; and I thought it of great Use, if they could learn with me to keep their minds open to Gratification, and ready to receive it from any thing it meets with. This one Circumstance will make every Face you see give you the Satisfaction you now take in beholding that of a Friend; will make every Object a pleasing one; will make all the Good which arrives to any Man, an Encrease of Happiness to your self.

TOPICS FOR DISCUSSION

1. Show how Steele's theme or purpose is explicitly stated in paragraphs 1, 2, and 7. Where else is the theme stated or suggested? How is Steele's theme related to his own "odd Humour" and "Particularity" (paragraph 1)? What is the "Instruction" (paragraph 7) or moral of this essay? From what observations and experiences presented in the essay is the instruction clearly derived? Is the instruction, or moral, relevant to twentieth-century American readers? Explain.

2. The title "A Day's Ramble in London" suggests an unplanned adventure in which the writer informally records what occurred at various places at different times of the day. Steele regularly stresses the variety of the scenes and the spontaneity of the action. On the other hand, the essay seems carefully organized. The events follow a definite sequence in time. The reporter carefully shifts his focus from one place and person to another. He changes his tone in response to each changing situation, at one time applauding simplicity and good will, at another satirizing affectation and folly. In view of this careful literary strategy, may we say that Steele rambles according to a set plan? Does the formal structure aid or hinder the purpose of the essay? Explain why or why not.

3. The spelling, capitalization, punctuation, diction, sentence structure, and paragraphing of this essay naturally differ from twentieth-century usage. Note some of these differences in paragraphs 3 and 4. Shore is spelled *shoar*, gardeners is spelled *gardiners*, cheerfulness is *chearfulness*, landscape is *landskip*, set is *sett*, and so on. Nouns are capitalized; proper names and place names are in italics; semicolons are used where modern style prefers a period. Some words, such as *Plantations*, *Morning Rakes*, *Fruit-Wenches*, *janty Slattern*, are strange to modern British as well as to American speech. Compound and compound-complex sentences are as frequent as simple and complex ones. Paragraph 4 is considerably

longer than the paragraph in a modern essay. What other differences between eighteenth-century and twentieth-century style do you observe? Is the modern style preferable to the eighteenth-century style? Why? Rewrite paragraphs 3 and 4 in modern American English. Where necessary, substitute modern American equivalents for words like *janty Slattern*. Keep in mind the modern preference for relatively shorter sentences and paragraphs. After you have completed your revision, discuss what has been gained and what has been lost by the modernization. Point out some principles of rhetoric, particularly those pertaining to unity and coherence, that are present in both versions.

TOPICS FOR COMPOSITION

1. "A Day's Ramble in London" provides a useful model for original composition. Outline a composition on the topic "School Holiday," in which you recount your experiences on or off campus. As in Steele's essay, divide your composition according to time and place and persons encountered. Combine narrative and descriptive techniques to support a single dominant impression. Some alternate topics might be: "Learning to Use the Library," "My First Acquaintance with Registration," "Three Meals a Day with My Classmates," and "On Meeting a New Set of Teachers."

2. Explain why you agree or disagree with one of the following propositions. Support your view by citing evidence from the text of Steele's essay.

   a. Steele's central attitude is one of benevolence; for him riches consist in keeping an open mind and an open heart.

   b. Steele prefers the lower class to the upper class.

   c. The lady introduced in paragraph 4 is clearly the most successfully realized character in the essay.

   d. Steele advocates a kind of detachment that leads to enjoyment.

E. B. WHITE

Here Is New York

IN *The Tatler* Richard Steele wrote for his fellow Londoners and for those provincials who kept up with affairs at the capital. Over two hundred years later E. B. White addressed actual, potential, and arm-chair travelers in *Holiday,* a magazine devoted to the description of places and accounts of travel adventure. E. B. White is—as Steele was—one of the most celebrated literary journalists and essayists of his day. Like Steele, too, White stresses a kind of detachment, which he calls "the gift of privacy," and the pleasures, which he calls "the excitement of participation," that are the special gifts of a great and growing metropolis. Each writer describes what he saw and sensed and tells of those experiences that contribute to human enjoyment.

"A Day's Ramble in London" and "Here Is New York" are alike in their general purpose, in their common use of descriptive and narrative techniques. But E. B. White approaches his subject with a greater consciousness of its physical magnitude and with a greater awareness of the teeming possibilities New York contains for personal destruction and personal fulfillment. Moreover, White's attitude toward his readers is more intimate than Steele's, though Steele, for all his didactic intentions, is by no means impersonal or indifferent. White's fondness for concrete allusions to actual persons and places, his easy colloquial style, his tone of direct address sustained by the I-you relationship maintained throughout, his extended disclosure of his own personal anxieties—all testify to the greater stress in modern writing on the primacy of the individual, as opposed to the older stress on the primacy of a common human nature. Steele begins and ends his essay with philosophical observations; White begins and ends with intensely personal impressions.

On any person who desired such queer prizes, New York will bestow the [1] gift of loneliness and the gift of privacy. It is this largess that accounts for the presence within the city's walls of a considerable section of the population; for the residents of Manhattan are to a large extent strangers who have pulled up stakes somewhere and come to town, seeking sanctuary

HERE IS NEW YORK   From pages 9–26, 44–54 of *Here Is New York* by E. B. White. Copyright 1949 by the Curtis Publishing Company. Reprinted by permission of Harper & Row, publishers.

or fulfillment or some greater or lesser grail. The capacity to make such dubious gifts is a mysterious quality of New York. It can destroy an individual, or it can fulfill him, depending a good deal on luck. No one should come to New York to live unless he is willing to be lucky.

[2]   New York is the concentrate of art and commerce and sport and religion and entertainment and finance, bringing to a single compact arena the gladiator, the evangelist, the promoter, the actor, the trader, and the merchant. It carries on its lapel the unexpungeable odor of the long past, so that no matter where you sit in New York you feel the vibrations of great times and tall deeds, of queer people and events and undertakings. I am sitting at the moment in a stifling hotel room in 90-degree heat, halfway down an air shaft, in midtown. No air moves in or out of the room, yet I am curiously affected by emanations from the immediate surroundings. I am twenty-two blocks from where Rudolph Valentino lay in state, eight blocks from where Nathan Hale was executed, five blocks from the publisher's office where Ernest Hemingway hit Max Eastman on the nose, four miles from where Walt Whitman sat sweating out editorials for the *Brooklyn Eagle*, thirty-four blocks from the street Willa Cather lived in when she came to New York to write books about Nebraska, one block from where Marceline used to clown on the boards of the Hippodrome, thirty-six blocks from the spot where the historian Joe Gould kicked a radio to pieces in full view of the public; thirteen blocks from where Harry Thaw shot Stanford White, five blocks from where I used to usher at the Metropolitan Opera, and only a hundred and twelve blocks from the spot where Clarence Day the Elder was washed of his sins in the Church of the Epiphany (I could continue this list indefinitely); and for that matter I am probably occupying the very room that any number of exalted and somewise memorable characters sat in, some of them on hot, breathless afternoons, lonely and private and full of their own sense of emanations from without.

[3]   When I went down to lunch a few minutes ago I noticed that the man sitting next to me (about eighteen inches away along the wall) was Fred Stone, the actor. The eighteen inches were both the connection and the separation that New York provides for its inhabitants. My only connection with Fred Stone was that I saw him in *The Wizard of Oz* around the beginning of the century. But our waiter felt the same stimulus from being close to a man from Oz, and after Mr. Stone left the room the waiter told me that when he (the waiter) was a young man just arrived in this country and before he could understand a word of English, he had taken his girl for their first theater date to *The Wizard of Oz*. It was a wonderful show, the waiter recalled—a man of straw, a man of tin. Wonderful! (And still only eighteen inches away.) "Mr. Stone is a very hearty eater," said the waiter thoughtfully, content with this fragile participation in destiny, this link with Oz.

[4]   New York blends the gift of privacy with the excitement of participation;

and better than most dense communities it succeeds in insulating the individual (if he wants it, and almost everybody wants or needs it) against all enormous and violent and wonderful events that are taking place every minute. Since I have been sitting in this miasmic air shaft, a good many rather splashy events have occurred in town. A man shot and killed his wife in a fit of jealousy. It caused no stir outside his block and got only small mention in the papers. I did not attend. Since my arrival, the greatest air show ever staged in all the world took place in town. I didn't attend and neither did most of the eight million other inhabitants, although they say there was quite a crowd. I didn't even hear any planes except a couple of west-bound commercial airliners that habitually use this air shaft to fly over. The biggest ocean-going ships on the North Atlantic arrived and departed. I didn't notice them and neither did most other New Yorkers. I am told this is the greatest seaport in the world, with six hundred and fifty miles of water front, and ships calling here from many exotic lands, but the only boat I've happened to notice since my arrival was a small sloop tacking out of the East River night before last on the ebb tide when I was walking across the Brooklyn Bridge. I heard the *Queen Mary* blow one midnight, though, and the sound carried the whole history of departure and longing and loss. The Lions have been in convention. I've seen not one Lion. A friend of mine saw one and told me about him. (He was lame, and was wearing a bolero.) At the ballgrounds and horse parks the greatest sporting spectacles have been enacted. I saw no ballplayer, no race horse. The governor came to town. I heard the siren scream but that was all there was to that—an eighteen-inch margin again. A man was killed by a falling cornice. I was not a party to the tragedy, and again the inches counted heavily.

I mention these merely to show that New York is peculiarly constructed [5] to absorb almost anything that comes along (whether a thousand-foot liner out of the East or a twenty-thousand-man convention out of the West) without inflicting the event on its inhabitants; so that every event is, in a sense, optional, and the inhabitant is in the happy position of being able to choose his spectacle and so conserve his soul. In most metropolises, small and large, the choice is often not with the individual at all. He is thrown to the Lions. The Lions are overwhelming; the event is unavoidable. A cornice falls, and it hits every citizen on the head, every last man in town. I sometimes think that the only event that hits every New Yorker on the head is the annual St. Patrick's Day parade, which is fairly penetrating— the Irish are a hard race to tune out, there are 500,000 of them in residence, and they have the police force right in the family.

The quality in New York that insulates its inhabitants from life may [6] simply weaken them as individuals. Perhaps it is healthier to live in a community where, when a cornice falls, you feel the blow; where, when the governor passes, you see at any rate his hat.

E. B. White   **83**

[7]   I am not defending New York in this regard. Many of its settlers are probably here merely to escape, not face, reality. But whatever it means, it is a rather rare gift, and I believe it has a positive effect on the creative capacities of New Yorkers—for creation is in part merely the business of forgoing the great and small distractions.

[8]   Although New York often imparts a feeling of great forlornness or forsakenness, it seldom seems dead or unresourceful; and you always feel that either by shifting your location ten blocks or by reducing your fortune by five dollars you can experience rejuvenation. Many people who have no real independence of spirit depend on the city's tremendous variety and sources of excitement for spiritual sustenance and maintenance of morale. In the country there are a few chances of sudden rejuvenation—a shift in weather, perhaps, or something arriving in the mail. But in New York the chances are endless. I think that although many persons are here from some excess of spirit (which caused them to break away from their small town), some, too, are here from a deficiency of spirit, who find in New York a protection, or an easy substitution.

[9]   There are roughly three New Yorks. There is, first, the New York of the man or woman who was born here, who takes the city for granted and accepts its size and its turbulence as natural and inevitable. Second, there is the New York of the commuter—the city that is devoured by locusts each day and spat out each night. Third, there is the New York of the person who was born somewhere else and came to New York in quest of something. Of these three trembling cities the greatest is the last—the city of final destination, the city that is a goal. It is this third city that accounts for New York's high-strung disposition, its poetical deportment, its dedication to the arts, and its incomparable achievements. Commuters give the city its tidal restlessness; natives give it solidity and continuity; but the settlers give it passion. And whether it is a farmer arriving from Italy to set up a small grocery store in a slum, or a young girl arriving from a small town in Mississippi to escape the indignity of being observed by her neighbors, or a boy arriving from the Corn Belt with a manuscript in his suitcase and a pain in his heart, it makes no difference: each embraces New York with the intense excitement of first love, each absorbs New York with the fresh eyes of an adventurer, each generates heat and light to dwarf the Consolidated Edison Company.

[10]   The commuter is the queerest bird of all. The suburb he inhabits has no essential vitality of its own and is a mere roost where he comes at day's end to go to sleep. Except in rare cases, the man who lives in Mamaroneck or Little Neck or Teaneck, and works in New York, discovers nothing much about the city except the time of arrival and departure of trains and buses, and the path to a quick lunch. He is desk-bound, and has never, idly roaming in the gloaming, stumbled suddenly on Belvedere Tower in

the Park, seen the ramparts rise sheer from the water of the pond, and the boys along the shore fishing for minnows, girls stretched out negligently on the shelves of the rocks; he has never come suddenly on anything at all in New York as a loiterer, because he has had no time between trains. He has fished in Manhattan's wallet and dug out coins, but has never listened to Manhattan's breathing, never awakened to its morning, never dropped off to sleep in its night. About 400,000 men and women come charging onto the Island each week-day morning, out of the mouths of tubes and tunnels. Not many among them have ever spent a drowsy afternoon in the great rustling oaken silence of the reading room of the Public Library, with the book elevator (like an old water wheel) spewing out books onto the trays. They tend their furnaces in Westchester and in Jersey, but have never seen the furnaces of the Bowery, the fires that burn in oil drums on zero winter nights. They may work in the financial district downtown and never see the extravagant plantings of Rockefeller Center —the daffodils and grape hyacinths and birches and the flags trimmed to the wind on a fine morning in spring. Or they may work in a midtown office and may let a whole year swing round without sighting Governor's Island from the sea wall. The commuter dies with tremendous mileage to his credit, but he is no rover. His entrances and exits are more devious than those in a prairie-dog village; and he calmly plays bridge while his train is buried in the mud at the bottom of the East River. The Long Island Rail Road alone carried forty million commuters last year; but many of them were the same fellow retracing his steps.

The terrain of New York is such that a resident sometimes travels far- [11] ther, in the end, than a commuter. Irving Berlin's journey from Cherry Street in the lower East Side to an apartment uptown was through an alley and was only three or four miles in length; but it was like going three times around the world.

A poem compresses much in a small space and adds music, thus heighten- [12] ing its meaning. The city is like poetry: it compresses all life, all races and breeds, into a small island and adds music and the accompaniment of internal engines. The island of Manhattan is without any doubt the greatest human concentrate on earth, the poem whose magic is comprehensible to millions of permanent residents but whose full meaning will always remain elusive. At the feet of the tallest and plushiest offices lie the crummiest slums. The genteel mysteries housed in the Riverside Church are only a few blocks from the voodoo charms of Harlem. The merchant princes, riding to Wall Street in their limousines down the East River Drive, pass within a few hundred yards of the gypsy kings; but the princes do not know they are passing kings, and the kings are not up yet anyway—they live a more leisurely life than the princes and get drunk more consistently.

E. B. White   **85**

[13]   New York is nothing like Paris; it is nothing like London; and it is not Spokane multiplied by sixty, or Detroit multiplied by four. It is by all odds the loftiest of cities. It even managed to reach the highest point in the sky at the lowest moment of the depression. The Empire State Building shot twelve hundred and fifty feet into the air when it was madness to put out as much as six inches of new growth. (The building has a mooring mast that no dirigible has ever tied to; it employs a man to flush toilets in slack times; it has been hit by an airplane in a fog, struck countless times by lightning, and been jumped off of by so many unhappy people that pedestrians instinctively quicken step when passing Fifth Avenue and 34th Street.)

[14]   Manhattan has been compelled to expand skyward because of the absence of any other direction in which to grow. This, more than any other thing, is responsible for its physical majesty. It is to the nation what the white church spire is to the village—the visible symbol of aspiration and faith, the white plume saying that the way is up. The summer traveler swings in over Hell Gate Bridge and from the window of his sleeping car as it glides above the pigeon lofts and back yards of Queens looks southwest to where the morning light first strikes the steel peaks of mid-town, and he sees its upward thrust unmistakable: the great walls and towers rising, the smoke rising, the heat not yet rising, the hopes and ferments of so many awakening millions rising—this vigorous spear that presses heaven hard.

[15]   It is a miracle that New York works at all. The whole thing is implausible. Every time the residents brush their teeth, millions of gallons of water must be drawn from the Catskill mountains and the hills of Westchester. When a young man in Manhattan writes a letter to his girl in Brooklyn, the love message gets blown to her through a pneumatic tube—*pfft*—just like that. The subterranean system of telephone cables, power lines, steam pipes, gas mains, and sewer pipes is reason enough to abandon the island to the gods and the weevils. Every time an incision is made in the pavement, the noisy surgeons expose ganglia that are tangled beyond belief. By rights New York should have destroyed itself long ago, from panic or fire or rioting or failure of some vital supply line in its circulatory system or from some deep labyrinthine short circuit. Long ago the city should have experienced an insoluble traffic snarl at some impossible bottleneck. It should have perished of hunger when food lines failed for a few days. It should have been wiped out by a plague starting in its slums or carried in by ships' rats. It should have been overwhelmed by the sea that licks at it on every side. The workers in its myriad cells should have succumbed to nerves, from the fearful pall of smoke-fog that drifts over every few days from Jersey, blotting out all light at noon and leaving the high offices suspended, men groping and depressed, and the sense of world's end. It

should have been touched in the head by the August heat and gone off its rocker.

Mass hysteria is a terrible force, yet New Yorkers seem always to escape [16] it by some tiny margin: they sit in stalled subways without claustrophobia, they extricate themselves from panic situations by some lucky wisecrack, they meet confusion and congestion with patience and grit—a sort of perpetual muddling through. Every facility is inadequate—the hospitals and schools and playgrounds are overcrowded, the express highways are feverish, the unimproved highways and bridges are bottlenecks; there is not enough air and not enough light, and there is usually either too much heat or too little. But the city makes up for its hazards and its deficiencies by supplying its citizens with massive doses of a supplementary vitamin—the sense of belonging to something unique, cosmopolitan, mighty, and unparalleled.

. . .

To a New Yorker the city is both changeless and changing. In many re- [17] spects it neither looks nor feels the way it did twenty-five years ago. The elevated railways have been pulled down, all but the Third Avenue. An old-timer walking up Sixth past the Jefferson Market jail misses the railroad, misses its sound, its spotted shade, its little aerial stations, and the tremor of the thing. Broadway has changed in aspect. It used to have a discernible bony structure beneath its loud bright surface; but the signs are so enormous now, the buildings and shops and hotels have largely disappeared under the neon lights and letters and the frozen-custard façade. Broadway is a custard street with no frame supporting it. In Greenwich Village the light is thinning: big apartments have come in, bordering the Square, and the bars are mirrored and chromed. But there are still in the Village the lingering traces of poesy, Mexican glass, hammered brass, batik, lamps made of whisky bottles, first novels made of fresh memories—the old Village with its alleys and ratty one-room rents catering to the erratic needs of those whose hearts are young and gay.

Grand Central Terminal has become honky-tonk, with its extra-dimen- [18] sional advertising displays and its tendency to adopt the tactics of a travel broker. I practically lived in Grand Central at one period (it has all the conveniences and I had no other place to stay) and the great hall seemed to me one of the more inspiring interiors in New York, until advertisements for Lastex and Coca-Cola got into the temple.

All over town the great mansions are in decline. Schwab's house facing [19] the Hudson on Riverside is gone. Gould's house on Fifth Avenue is an antique shop. Morgan's house on Madison Avenue is a church administration office. What was once the Fahnestock house is now Random House.

Rich men nowadays don't live in houses; they live in the attics of big apartment buildings and plant trees on the setbacks, hundreds of feet above the street.

[20]   There are fewer newspapers than there used to be, thanks somewhat to the late Frank Munsey. One misses the *Globe,* the *Mail,* the *Herald;* and to many a New Yorker life has never seemed the same since the *World* took the count.

[21]   Police now ride in radio prowl cars instead of gumshoeing around the block swinging their sticks. A ride in the subway costs ten cents, and the seats are apt to be dark green instead of straw yellow. Men go to saloons to gaze at televised events instead of to think long thoughts. It is all very disconcerting. Even parades have changed some. The last triumphal military procession in Manhattan simply filled the city with an ominous and terrible rumble of heavy tanks.

[22]   The slums are gradually giving way to the lofty housing projects—high in stature, high in purpose, low in rent. There are a couple of dozen of these new developments scattered around; each is a city in itself (one of them in the Bronx accommodates twelve thousand families), sky acreage hitherto untilled, lifting people far above the street, standardizing their sanitary life, giving them some place to sit other than an orange crate. Federal money, state money, city money, and private money have flowed into these projects. Banks and insurance companies are in back of some of them. Architects have turned the buildings slightly on their bases, to catch more light. In some of them, rents are as low as eight dollars a month a room. Thousands of new units are still needed and will eventually be built, but New York never quite catches up with itself, is never in equilibrium. In flush times the population mushrooms and the new dwellings sprout from the rock. Come bad times and the population scatters and the lofts are abandoned and the landlord withers and dies.

[23]   New York has changed in tempo and in temper during the years I have known it. There is greater tension, increased irritability. You encounter it in many places, in many faces. The normal frustrations of modern life are here multiplied and amplified—a single run of a crosstown bus contains, for the driver, enough frustration and annoyance to carry him over the edge of sanity: the light that changes always an instant too soon, the passenger that bangs on the shut door, the truck that blocks the only opening, the coin that slips to the floor, the question asked at the wrong moment. There is greater tension and there is greater speed. Taxis roll faster than they rolled ten years ago—and they were rolling fast then. Hackmen used to drive with verve; now they sometimes seem to drive with desperation, toward the ultimate tip. On the West Side Highway, approaching the city, the motorist is swept along in a trance—a sort of fever of inescapable motion, goaded from behind, hemmed in on either side, a mere chip in a millrace.

The city has never been so uncomfortable, so crowded, so tense. Money [24]
has been plentiful and New York has responded. Restaurants are hard to
get into; businessmen stand in line for a Schrafft's luncheon as meekly as
idle men used to stand in soup lines. (Prosperity creates its bread lines, the
same as depression.) The lunch hour in Manhattan has been shoved ahead
half an hour, to 12:00 or 12:30, in the hopes of beating the crowd to a
table. Everyone is a little emptier at quitting time than he used to be.
Apartments are festooned with No Vacancy signs. There is standing-room-
only in Fifth Avenue buses, which once reserved a seat for every paying
guest. The old double-deckers are disappearing—people don't ride just for
the fun of it any more.

At certain hours on certain days it is almost impossible to find an empty [25]
taxi and there is a great deal of chasing around after them. You grab a
handle and open the door, and find that some other citizen is entering
from the other side. Doormen grow rich blowing their whistles for cabs;
and some doormen belong to no door at all—merely wander about through
the streets, opening cabs for people as they happen to find them. By comparison with other less hectic days, the city is uncomfortable and inconvenient; but New Yorkers temperamentally do not crave comfort and convenience—if they did they would live elsewhere.

The subtlest change in New York is something people don't speak much [26]
about but that is in everyone's mind. The city, for the first time in its
long history, is destructible. A single flight of planes no bigger than a
wedge of geese can quickly end this island fantasy, burn the towers, crum-
ble the bridges, turn the underground passages into lethal chambers,
cremate the millions. The intimation of mortality is part of New York
now; in the sound of jets overhead, in the black headlines of the latest
edition.

All dwellers in cities must live with the stubborn fact of annihilation; in [27]
New York the fact is somewhat more concentrated because of the concentration of the city itself, and because, of all targets, New York has a certain
clear priority. In the mind of whatever perverted dreamer might loose the
lightning, New York must hold a steady irresistible charm.

It used to be that the Statue of Liberty was the signpost that proclaimed [28]
New York and translated it for all the world. Today Liberty shares the
role with Death. Along the East River, from the razed slaughterhouses of
Turtle Bay, as though in a race with the spectral flight of planes, men are
carving out the permanent headquarters of the United Nations—the greatest housing project of them all. In its stride, New York takes on one more
interior city, to shelter, this time, all governments, and to clear the slum
called war. New York is not a capital city—it is not a national capital
or a state capital. But it is by way of becoming the capital of the world.
The building, as conceived by architects, will be cigar boxes set on end.

E. B. White

Traffic will flow in a new tunnel under First Avenue, Forty-seventh Street will be widened (and if my guess is any good), trucks will appear late at night to plant tall trees surreptitiously, their roots to mingle with the intestines of the town. Once again the city will absorb, almost without showing any sign of it, a congress of visitors. It has already shown itself capable of stashing away the United Nations—a great many of the delegates have been around town during the past couple of years, and the citizenry has hardly caught a glimpse of their coattails or their black Homburgs.

[29]   This race—this race between the destroying planes and the struggling Parliament of Man—it sticks in all our heads. The city at last perfectly illustrates both the universal dilemma and the general solution; this riddle in steel and stone is at once the perfect target and the perfect demonstration of nonviolence, of racial brotherhood, this lofty target scraping the skies and meeting the destroying planes halfway, home of all people and all nations, capital of everything, housing the deliberations by which the planes are to be stayed and their errand forestalled.

[30]   A block or two west of the new City of Man in Turtle Bay there is an old willow tree that presides over an interior garden. It is a battered tree, long suffering and much climbed, held together by strands of wire but beloved of those who know it. In a way it symbolizes the city: life under difficulties, growth against odds, sap-rise in the midst of concrete, and the steady reaching for the sun. Whenever I look at it nowadays, and feel the cold shadow of the planes, I think: "This must be saved, this particular thing, this very tree." If it were to go, all would go—this city, this mischievous and marvelous monument which not to look upon would be like death.

TOPICS FOR DISCUSSION

1. White begins his essay by speaking of New York's gifts to its residents of loneliness and privacy on the one hand (paragraph 1), and its residents' awareness of the "emanations from the immediate surroundings" (paragraph 2) and a sense of participation in the swarming activity of the city, on the other. Because of this paradoxical quality of the city, the sensitive New Yorker is aware of tensions, vibrations, excitements that can either charge or exhaust his energies. Thus the introduction clearly establishes the general point of view of White's essay—that is, the main impression he wishes to convey to his readers. This impression becomes, in effect, White's unifying purpose. Show how that purpose unifies the details of the incidents described

in paragraphs 2, 3, and 4. Show how paragraph 8 sums up that impression.

2. In paragraphs 1 through 8 White illustrates his point of view by describing his own immediate experiences. "I am sitting at the moment... yet I am curiously affected.... When I went down to lunch...I noticed...." In paragraphs 9 through 11 he draws upon the experiences of others. How does his distinction between the native New Yorker, the commuter, and the stranger "in quest of something" contribute to his main impression? With which of the three classes described in these paragraphs does White identify? How does he suggest this identification by his selection of details? By the tone of his language?

3. The concluding passage (paragraphs 17–31) develops the theme that New York is changeless and changing. Which of the three kinds of change (in physical appearance and activity, in tempo and temper, and in awareness of danger) is presented as the most significant? Why? Why is White confident that the city will survive?

4. In general the aim of description is to make the reader perceive through his senses the scene the writer has in mind. Objective or scientific description appeals directly to sight, hearing, touch, taste, and smell. List some words in paragraphs 1 through 4 that appeal to each of these senses. Artistic or evocative description is concerned with the sense of a whole scene, an impression that envelops individual sense perceptions in a unified emotional response. Show how in paragraphs 2 and 3 White evokes a mood of loneliness to which each individual detail contributes. Point out the successful use of contrast in these paragraphs.

5. In description, a clearly defined point of view is essential. We define a point of view by establishing our physical standpoint. The Empire State Building seems different to a man standing in the street below, to an elevator operator within, and to a pilot in a plane above. It seems different, too, when seen for the first time or for the hundredth time, when viewed by an architect, a mason, a real-estate operator and a cleaning man. Hence we also define our point of view by our mind's eye, that is, our habitual way of regarding a particular object. Show how White's mental attitude accounts for his generalized description of the commuters' day in paragraphs 10 and 11. Do you agree with the attitudes expressed in paragraph 11? If you do not, do you, or can you, respond sympathetically to the emotional thrust of the paragraph? Give reasons for your answer.

6. Most writers combine description with narration or other forms of discourse. In "Here Is New York," description serves the central idea and is intertwined with autobiographical narrative and with occasional expository passages. Test the accuracy of this statement by analyzing paragraph 10. Is it principally concerned with happenings in time (narration), objects in space (description), explanation of why "the commuter is the queerest bird of all" (exposition), reasons the "set-

tlers" are the most important elements of the population (argument)? Or does paragraph 10 consist of all forms of discourse? Does any one form of discourse predominate? Explain your answer.

TOPICS FOR COMPOSITION

1. Write a brief sketch about your own city, town, or neighborhood. Regard your present classmates as your audience. Remember that you give point to your writing if you adapt what Wayne Booth calls "a rhetorical stance." (See p. 434.) Decide beforehand what you really want your readers to believe, or what action—physical or mental—you wish them to take. Unify your composition by selecting incidents and details that will create a single dominant impression.

2. Write a personal letter to a foreign student of your age who plans to attend your school in the coming semester. Inform him of the general tone of the school, the kind of students, the expectations of the faculty, the curriculum, social life, and so on. Keep in mind that your reader has not visited this country and will require a full explanation of details you may be tempted to take for granted. Decide beforehand whether you intend to encourage him to come or to stay at home, what experiences you feel he should look for or avoid.

3. Reread Steele's "A Day's Ramble in London." Compare and contrast the style of that essay with that of "Here Is New York" with reference to their direct or indirect persuasive appeal, their use of informal and colloquial diction, their use of topic sentences.

4. Comment on one of the following statements:
   a. E. B. White's diction and sentence structure are simpler and hence more effective than Steele's.
   b. Steele's style is more economical than White's.
   c. To compare the style of Steele and White is as useful as comparing an apple with a grapefruit.

SHIRLEY JACKSON

The Night We All Had Grippe

SHIRLEY JACKSON'S opening paragraph presents an amusing domestic situation. Steele and White announce their chief ideas, but she proposes no thesis save that the common cold, commonly caught, has its comic as well as its physiological effects. Shirley Jackson is not here involved in a serious confrontation with her readers. She regards them with the same astringent affability she displays toward her family and includes them in the enjoyment of a family joke. Her purpose, in short, is entertainment.

Entertainment has a serious side. To make us laugh, the artist must make us perceive the ridiculous; to make us perceive the ridiculous requires wit, and wit involves both the candid recognition of our foibles and the successful mimicry of these foibles in language. Miss Jackson is a masterly mimic. She mimics herself best of all in her character of wife and mother. But she also makes us see, as in a film, the characteristic activities of her family. Her dramatic sense is also evident in the narrator's monologue, the basic English of the children's comments, and the amusing indirect discourse of her husband and the dog Toby.

My husband caught the grippe first, on a Friday, and snarled and shivered [1] and complained until I prevailed upon him to go to bed. By Friday night both Laurie and Sally were feverish, and on Saturday Jannie and I began to cough and sniffle. In our family we take ill in different manners; my husband is extremely annoyed at the whole procedure and is convinced that his being sick is somebody's fault, Laurie tends to become a little light-headed and strew handkerchiefs around his room. Jannie coughs and coughs and coughs, Sally turns bright red, and I suffer in stoical silence, so long as everyone knows clearly that I am sick. We are each of us privately convinced that our own ailment is far more severe than anyone else's. At any rate, on Saturday night I put all the children into their beds, gave each of them half an aspirin and the usual fruit juice, covered them warmly, and then settled my husband down for the night with his tumbler of water and his cigarettes and matches and ashtray; he had decided to sleep in the guest room because it was warmer. At about ten o'clock I checked to see that all the children were covered and asleep and that Toby was in his place on the bottom half of the double-decker. I then took two sleeping pills and went to sleep in my own bed in my own room. Because my husband was in the guest room I slept on his side of the bed, next to the bed table. I put my cigarettes and matches on the end table next to the ashtray, along with a small glass of brandy, which I find more efficacious than cough medicine.

[2]   I woke up some time later to find Jannie standing beside the bed. "Can't sleep," she said. "Want to come in *your* bed."

[3]   "Come along," I said. "Bring your own pillow."

[4]   She went and got her pillow and her small pink blanket and her glass of fruit juice, which she put on the floor next to the bed, since she had got the side without any end table. She put her pillow down, rolled herself in her pink blanket, and fell asleep. I went back to sleep, but sometime later Sally came in, asking sleepily, "Where's Jannie?"

[5]   "She's here," I said. "Are you coming in bed with us?"

[6]   "Yes," said Sally.

[7]   "Go and get your pillow, then," I said.

[8]   She returned with her pillow, her books, her doll, her suitcase, and her fruit juice, which she put on the floor next to Jannie's. Then she crowded in comfortably next to Jannie and fell asleep. Eventually the pressure of the two of them began to force me uneasily toward the edge of the bed, so I rolled out wearily, took my pillow and my small glass of brandy and my cigarettes and matches and my ashtray and went into the guest room, where my husband was asleep. I pushed at him and he snarled, but he finally moved over to the side next to the wall, and I put my cigarettes and matches and my brandy and my ashtray on the end table next to *his* cigarettes and matches and ashtray and tumbler of water and put my pillow on the bed and fell asleep. Shortly after this he woke me and asked me to let him get out of the bed since it was too hot in that room to sleep and he was going back to his own bed. He took his pillow and his cigarettes and matches and his ashtray and his aluminum glass of water and went padding off down the hall. In a few minutes Laurie came into the guest room where I had just fallen asleep again; he was carrying his pillow and his glass of fruit juice. "Too cold in my room," he said, and I moved out of the way and let him get into the bed on the side next to the wall. After a few minutes the dog came in, whining nervously, and came up onto the bed and curled himself up around Laurie and I had to get out or be smothered. I gathered together what of my possessions I could, and made my way into my own room, where my husband was asleep with Jannie on one side and the baby on the other. Jannie woke up when I came in and said, "Own bed," so I helped her carry her pillow and her fruit juice and her pink blanket back to her own bed.

[9]   The minute Jannie got out of our bed the baby rolled over and turned sideways, so there was no room for me. I could not get into the crib and I could not climb into the top half of the double-decker, so since the

dog was in the guest room I went and took the blanket off the crib and got into the bottom half of the double-decker, setting my brandy and my cigarettes and matches and my ashtray on the floor next to the bed. Shortly after that Jannie, who apparently felt left out, came in with her pillow and her pink blanket and her fruit juice and got up into the top half of the double-decker, leaving her fruit juice on the floor next to my brandy.

At about six in the morning the dog wanted to get out, or else he [10] wanted his bed back, because he came and stood next to me and howled. I got up and went downstairs, sneezing, and let him out, and then decided that since it had been so cold anyway in the bottom half of the double-decker I might as well stay downstairs and heat up some coffee and have that much warmth, at least. While I was waiting for the coffee to heat Jannie came to the top of the stairs and asked if I would bring *her* something hot, and I heard Laurie stirring in the guest room, so I heated some milk and put it into a jug and decided that while I was at it I might just as well give everybody something hot so I set out enough cups for everyone and brought out a coffee cake and put it on the tray and added some onion rolls for my husband, who does not eat coffee cake. When I brought the tray upstairs Laurie and Jannie were both in the guest room, giggling, so I set the tray down in there and heard Sally talking from our room in the front. I went to get her and she was sitting up in the bed talking to her father, who was only very slightly awake. "Play card?" she was asking brightly, and she opened her suitcase and dealt him, onto the pillow next to his nose, four diamonds to the ace jack and the seven of clubs.

I asked my husband if he would like some coffee, and he said it was [11] terribly cold. I suggested that he come down into the guest room, where it was warmer. He and the baby followed me down to the guest room, and my husband and Laurie got into the bed and the rest of us sat on the foot of the bed and I poured the coffee and the hot milk and gave the children coffee cake and my husband the onion rolls. Jannie decided to take her milk and coffee cake back into her own bed, and since she had mislaid her pillow she took one from the guest room bed. Sally of course followed her, going first back into our room to pick up *her* pillow. My husband fell asleep again while I was pouring his coffee, and Laurie set his hot milk precariously on the headboard of the bed and asked me to get his pillow from wherever it was, so I went into the double-decker and got him the pillow from the top, which turned out to be Jannie's, and her pink blanket was with it. I took my coffee cake and my coffee into my own bed and had just settled down when Laurie came in to say cloudily that Daddy had kicked him out of bed and could he stay in here. I said of course and he said he would get a pillow and he came back in a minute with the one from the bottom half of the double-decker which was mine. He went to sleep right away, and then the baby came in to get her books and her suitcase and decided to stay with her milk and her coffee cake, so I left and went into the guest room and made my husband move over and sat *there* and had my coffee. Meanwhile Jannie had moved into the top half of the double-decker, looking for her pillow, and had taken instead the pillow from Sally's bed and my glass of brandy and had settled down there to listen to Laurie's radio. I went downstairs to let the dog in and he came upstairs and got into his bed on the bottom half of the double-decker, and while I was gone my husband had moved back over onto the accessible side of the guest room bed so I went into Jannie's bed, which is rather too short, and I brought a pillow from the guest room, and my coffee.

[12] At about nine o'clock the Sunday papers came and I went down to get them, and at about nine-thirty everyone woke up. My husband had moved back into his own bed when Laurie and Sally vacated it for their own beds, Laurie driving Jannie into the guest room when he took back the top half of the double-decker, and my husband woke up at nine-thirty and found himself wrapped in Jannie's pink blanket, sleeping on Laurie's green pillow and with a piece of coffee cake and Sally's fruit juice glass, not to mention the four diamonds to the ace jack and the seven of clubs. Laurie, in the top half of the double-decker, had my glass of brandy and my cigarettes and matches and the baby's pink pillow. The dog had my white pillow and my ashtray. Jannie in the guest room had one white pillow and one blue pillow and two glasses of fruit juice and my husband's cigarettes and matches and ashtray and Laurie's hot milk, besides her own hot milk and coffee cake and her father's onion rolls. The baby in her crib had her father's aluminum tumbler of water and her suitcase and books and doll and a blue pillow from the guest room, but no blanket.

[13] The puzzle is, of course, what became of the blanket from Sally's bed? I took it off her crib and put it on the bottom half of the double-decker, but the dog did not have it when he woke up, and neither did any of the other beds. It was a blue-patterned patchwork quilt, and has not been seen since, and I would most particularly like to know where it got to. As I say, we are very short of blankets.

TOPICS FOR DISCUSSION

1. What references, allusions, and attitudes help to identify this piece as an autobiographical sketch? Point out how it also resembles fictional writing. What incidents in the story seem to be "arranged" for dramatic effect? Would you conclude that the techniques of factual narrative and fictional narrative are identical? Give reasons for your answer.

2. The main difference between this sketch and the two preceding essays

is greater emphasis on the narrative element—that is, on a sequence of events in time. Make an outline of each stage in the sequence of events. Show how interest and humor derive from the particular sequence of events. How is the narrative sequence related to the statement, "We are each of us privately convinced that our own ailment is far more severe than anyone else's." Is it also related to the statement, "The puzzle is, of course, what became of the blanket from Sally's bed?" Give reasons for your answers.

A narrative is said to be unified when all the incidents are so connected that they form a single predominant impression. In the light of this statement is "The Night We All Had Grippe" unified? In your own words give the predominant impression of the story.

3. Show how the use of the italicized expressions in the following paragraph helps to keep clear the sequence of events.

> She returned with her pillow, her books, her doll, her suitcase, and her fruit juice, which she put on the floor next to Jannie's. *Then* she crowded in comfortably next to Jannie and fell asleep. *Eventually* the pressure of the two of them began to force me uneasily toward the edge of the bed, so I rolled out wearily, took my pillow and my small glass of brandy and my cigarettes and matches and my ashtray and went into the guest room, where my husband was asleep. I pushed at him and he snarled, but he *finally* moved over to the side next to the wall, and I put my cigarettes and matches and my brandy and my ashtray on the end table next to his cigarettes and matches and ashtray and tumbler of water and put my pillow on the bed and fell asleep. *Shortly after this* he woke me and asked me to let him get out of bed since it was too hot in that room to sleep and he was going back to his own bed. He took his pillow and his cigarettes and matches and his ashtray and his aluminum glass of water and went padding off down the hall. *In a few minutes* Laurie came into the guest room where I *had just fallen asleep again*; he was carrying his pillow and his glass of fruit juice. "Too cold in my room," he said, and I moved out of the way and let him get into the bed on the side next to the wall. *After a few minutes* the dog came in, whining nervously, and came up onto the bed and curled himself up around Laurie and I had to get out or be smothered. I gathered together what of my possessions I could, and made my way into my own room, where my husband was asleep with Jannie on one side and the baby on the other. Jannie woke up when I came in and said, "Own bed," so I helped her carry her pillow and her fruit juice and her pink blanket back to her own bed.

Point out other expressions that make clear the time each action takes place. Note that all the verbs except one (*had fallen*) are in the past tense. Despite her use of the past tense, how does the author maintain a sense of continuing action?

4. Who tells the story and how it is told are just as important as the incidents. Why is the mother a believable narrator? What does she know and what qualities does she possess that give authority to her report? Could the father or one of the children have told the story as perceptively as the mother? Why or why not?

5. The narrator describes the appearance of her husband and children and her home in the course of the narrative sequence. Make a list of the descriptive details—that is, of physical appearances and mannerisms—that are important to the humor of this story. Show how repetition rather than amplification of these details contributes to the humor.

TOPICS FOR COMPOSITION

1. Write a humorous account of a family experience from the first-person point of view. Some possible titles are: "Camping Out," "The Pleasures of Sunday Driving," "Attending Some One Else's Graduation," "The Night the Plumbing Broke Down."

2. Comment on the statement below by analyzing evidence from the text: "This sketch succeeds partly because of a series of sudden, dramatic appearances, each of them ridiculously similar and ridiculously different."

DANIEL DEFOE

The Plague in London

WHEN the bubonic plague broke out in Marseilles, France, in 1721, all Europe trembled. Periodic scourges of the Black Death, hideous enough in fact, seemed especially appalling to the eighteenth-century reader because he regarded the plague as a divine chastisement. So too did Daniel Defoe, who by 1721 was already the author of countless pamphlets on politics, religion, business, and self-improvement. He quickly set about preparing still another, "Dire Preparations for the Plague," in which he gave practical advice for the care of soul and body.

Defoe was only five years old when the previous plague struck his native London in 1665, but as he was writing his pamphlet, he began to visualize, with a skill he had recently brought to perfection in *Robinson Crusoe* (1719) and *Moll Flanders* (1722), just how a contemporary might have experienced the plague. The pamphlet led to his celebrated *Journal of the Plague Year* (1722). In this semi-fictitious account Defoe chose as his narrator a saddler—perhaps in memory of his uncle, Henry Foe, who was of that trade. Besides searching his own memory he consulted many records for details. Defoe persuaded his generation to accept his account as authentic history. Our generation accepts the *Journal,* from which the following selection is taken, as an outstanding work of the historical imagination and one of Defoe's greatest masterpieces.

In these walks I had many dismal scenes before my eyes, as, particularly, of [1] persons falling dead in the streets, terrible shrieks and screechings of women, who in their agonies would throw open their chamber windows, and cry out in a dismal, surprising manner. It is impossible to describe the variety of postures in which the passions of the poor people would express themselves.

Passing through Token-House Yard in Lothbury, of a sudden a casement [2] violently opened just over my head, and a woman gave three frightful screeches, and then cried, "Oh! death, death, death!" in a most inimitable tone, and which struck me with horror, and a chillness in my very blood. There was nobody to be seen in the whole street, neither did any other window open, for people had no curiosity now in any case, nor could anybody help one another; so I went on to pass into Bell Alley.

Just in Bell Alley, on the right hand of the passage, there was a more [3] terrible cry than that, though it was not so directed out at the window. But the whole family was in a terrible fright, and I could hear women and children run screaming about the rooms like distracted, when a garret window opened, and somebody from a window on the other side the alley called and asked, "What is the matter?" Upon which from the first window it was answered, "O Lord, my old master has hanged himself!" The other asked again, "Is he quite dead?" and the first answered, "Ay, ay, quite dead; quite dead and cold!" This person was a merchant and a deputy alderman, and very rich. I care not to mention his name, though I knew his name too; but that would be an hardship to the family, which is now flourishing again.

[4]   But this is but one. It is scarce credible what dreadful cases happened in particular families every day,—people, in the rage of the distemper, or in the torment of their swellings, which was indeed intolerable, running out of their own government, raving and distracted, and oftentimes laying violent hands upon themselves, throwing themselves out at their windows, shooting themselves, etc.; mothers murdering their own children in their lunacy; some dying of mere grief as a passion, some of mere fright and surprise without any infection at all; others frighted into idiotism and foolish distractions, some into despair and lunacy, others into melancholy madness.

[5]   The pain of the swelling was in particular very violent, and to some intolerable. The physicians and surgeons may be said to have tortured many poor creatures even to death. The swellings in some grew hard, and they applied violent drawing plasters, or poultices, to break them; and, if these did not do, they cut and scarified them in a terrible manner. In some, those swellings were made hard, partly by the force of the distemper, and partly by their being too violently drawn, and were so hard that no instrument could cut them; and then they burned them with caustics, so that many died raving mad with the torment, and some in the very operation. In these distresses, some, for want of help to hold them down in their beds or to look to them, laid hands upon themselves as above; some broke out into the streets, perhaps naked, and would run directly down to the river, if they were not stopped by the watchman or other officers, and plunge themselves into the water wherever they found it.

[6]   It often pierced my very soul to hear the groans and cries of those who were thus tormented. But of the two, this was counted the most promising particular in the whole infection: for if these swellings could be brought to a head, and to break and run, or, as the surgeons call it, to "digest," the patient generally recovered; whereas those who, like the gentlewoman's daughter, were struck with death at the beginning, and had the tokens come out upon them, often went about indifferently easy till a little before they died, and some till the moment they dropped down, as in apoplexies and epilepsies is often the case. Such would be taken suddenly very sick, and would run to a bench or bulk, or any convenient place that offered itself, or to their own houses, if possible, as I mentioned before, and there

sit down, grow faint, and die. This kind of dying was much the same as it was with those who die of common mortifications, who die swooning, and, as it were, go away in a dream. Such as died thus had very little notice of their being infected at all till the gangrene was spread through their whole body; nor could physicians themselves know certainly how it was with them till they opened their breasts, or other parts of their body, and saw the tokens.

We had at this time a great many frightful stories told us of nurses and [7] watchmen who looked after the dying people, that is to say, hired nurses, who attended infected people, using them barbarously, starving them, smothering them, or by other wicked means hastening their end, that is to say, murdering of them: and watchmen being set to guard houses that were shut up, when there has been but one person left, and perhaps that one lying sick, that they have broke in and murdered that body, and immediately thrown them out into the dead-cart; and so they have gone scarce cold to the grave.

I cannot say but that some such murders were committed, and I think [8] two were sent to prison for it, but died before they could be tried; and I have heard that three others, at several times, were executed for murders of that kind. But I must say I believe nothing of its being so common a crime as some have since been pleased to say; nor did it seem to be so rational, where the people were brought so low as not to be able to help themselves; for such seldom recovered, and there was no temptation to commit a murder, at least not equal to the fact, where they were sure persons would die in so short a time, and could not live.

That there were a great many robberies and wicked practices committed [9] even in this dreadful time, I do not deny. The power of avarice was so strong in some that they would run any hazard to steal and to plunder; and, particularly in houses where all the families or inhabitants have been dead and carried out, they would break in at all hazards, and, without regard to the danger of infection, take even the clothes off the dead bodies, and the bedclothes from others where they lay dead.

This, I suppose, must be the case of a family in Houndsditch, where a [10] man and his daughter, the rest of the family being, as I suppose, carried away before by the dead-cart, were found stark naked, one in one chamber and one in another, lying dead on the floor, and the clothes of the beds, from whence 'tis supposed they were rolled off by thieves, stolen, and carried quite away.

It is indeed to be observed that the women were, in all this calamity, the [11] most rash, fearless, and desperate creatures; and, as there were vast numbers that went about as nurses to tend those that were sick, they committed a great many petty thieveries in the houses where they were employed; and some of them were publicly whipped for it, when perhaps they ought rather to have been hanged for examples, for numbers of houses were robbed on these occasions; till at length the parish officers were sent to recommend nurses to the sick, and always took an account who it was they sent, so as that they might call them to account if the house had been abused where they were placed.

[12] But these robberies extended chiefly to wearing-clothes, linen, and what rings or money they could come at, when the person died who was under their care, but not to a general plunder of the houses; and I could give you an account of one of these nurses, who several years after, being on her deathbed, confessed with the utmost horror the robberies she had committed at the time of her being a nurse, and by which she had enriched herself to a great degree. But as for murders, I do not find that there was ever any proofs of the fact in the manner as it has been reported, except as above.

[13] They did tell me, indeed, of a nurse in one place that laid a wet cloth upon the face of a dying patient whom she tended, and so put an end to his life, who was just expiring before; and another that smothered a young woman she was looking to, when she was in a fainting fit, and would have come to herself; some that killed them by giving them one thing, some another, and some starved them by giving them nothing at all. But these stories had two marks of suspicion that always attended them, which caused me always to slight them, and to look on them as mere stories that people continually frighted one another with. First—that wherever it was that we heard it, they always placed the scene at the farther end of the town, opposite or most remote from where you were to hear it. If you heard it in Whitechapel, it had happened at St. Giles's, or at Westminster, or Holborn, or that end of the town; if you heard of it at that end of the town, then it was done in Whitechapel, or in the Minories, or about Cripplegate Parish; if you heard of it in the city, why, then, it happened in Southwark; and, if you heard of it in Southwark, then it was done in the city, and the like.

[14] In the next place, of what part soever you heard the story, the particulars were always the same, especially that of laying a wet double clout on a dying man's face, and that of smothering a young gentlewoman: so that it was apparent, at least to my judgment, that there was more of tale than of truth in those things.

[15] However, I cannot say, but it had some effect upon the people; and particularly, that, as I said before, they grew more cautious who they took into their houses, and whom they trusted their lives with, and had them always recommended, if they could; and where they could not find such, for they were not very plenty, they applied to the parish officers.

[16] But here again, the misery of that time lay upon the poor, who, being infected, had neither food nor physic: neither physicians nor apothecary to assist them, nor nurse to attend them. Many of those died calling for help, and even for sustenance, out at their windows, in a most miserable

and deplorable manner; but it must be added that when ever the cases of such persons or families were represented to my Lord Mayor, they always were relieved.

It is true that in some houses where the people were not very poor, yet, [17] where they had sent perhaps their wives and children away, and if they had any servants, they had been dismissed; I say, it is true, that to save the expenses, many such as these shut themselves in, and, not having help, died alone.

A neighbor and acquaintance of mine, having some money owing to him [18] from a shopkeeper in Whitecross Street or thereabouts, sent his apprentice, a youth about eighteen years of age, to endeavor to get the money. He came to the door, and finding it shut, knocked pretty hard, and, as he thought, heard somebody answer within, but was not sure; so he waited, and after some stay knocked again, and then a third time, when he heard somebody coming downstairs.

At length the man of the house came to the door; he had on his breeches, [19] or drawers, and a yellow flannel waistcoat, no stockings, a pair of slipped-shoes, a white cap on his head, and, as the young man said, "death in his face."

When he opened the door, says he, "What do you disturb me thus for?" [20] The boy, though a little surprised, replied, "I come from such a one; and my master sent me for the money, which he says you know of." "Very well, child," returns the living ghost; "call, as you go by, at Cripplegate Church, and bid them ring the bell"; and with these words shut the door again, and went up again, and died the same day, nay, perhaps the same hour. This the young man told me himself, and I have reason to believe it. This was while the plague was not come to a height. I think it was in June, towards the latter end of the month. It must be before the dead-carts came about, and while they used the ceremony of ringing the bell for the dead, which was over for certain, in that parish at least, before the month of July; for by the 25th of July there died five hundred and fifty and upwards in a week, and then they could no more bury in form rich or poor.

TOPICS FOR DISCUSSION

1. In paragraphs 1 and 2 the narrator calls our attention to "many dismal scenes" that struck him "with horror, and a chillness in my very blood." Identify the principal scenes in this passage. Do they create the effect of horror? How? List all the words you can find in this passage that are synonyms for horror. How does the dialogue quoted in paragraphs 1, 2, and 20 support the dominant impression of horror?

Daniel Defoe

2. In general, the narrator tells a story (narrative) that includes his own and others' observations of the plague (description). In paragraphs 4 through 6 show how the narrative and descriptive elements are intermingled.

3. Paragraphs 7 through 15 report "frightful stories" about nurses and watchmen murdering and robbing their charges. At the same time, the narrator discounts these reports, as in paragraphs 12 and 15. What is his purpose in telling stories that he subsequently discounts? What solid advice does he give to his readers of 1722? What eventualities does he wish especially to prepare them to meet?

4. The spelling and capitalization of this passage have been modernized, but the diction, sentence structure, and some punctuation retain eighteenth-century characteristics. Rewrite paragraph 6 in modern idiomatic American English. Pay special attention to the expressions italicized below. Note, too, the special opportunities to break up longer sentences into shorter ones. When you have completed your assignment, compare and contrast the revision with the original version. Would it seem clearer, more coherent to a contemporary reader? Why or why not?

> It often pierced my very soul to hear the groans and cries of those who were thus *tormented*. But of the two, this was counted the most promising *particular* in the whole infection: for if these swellings could be brought to a head, and to break and run, or, as the surgeons call it, to *"digest,"* the patient generally recovered; whereas those who, like the gentlewoman's daughter, were struck with death at the beginning, and had the *tokens* come out upon them, often went about *indifferently easy* till a little before they died, and some till the moment they dropped down, as in apoplexies and epilepsies is often the case. Such would be taken suddenly very sick, and would run to a bench or bulk, or any convenient place that offered itself, or to their own houses, if possible, as I mentioned before, and there sit down, grow faint, and die. This kind of dying was much the same as it was with those who die of *common mortifications*, who die swooning, and, as it were, go away in a dream. Such as died thus had very little notice of their being infected at all till the gangrene was spread through their whole body; nor could physicians themselves know certainly how it was with them till they opened their breasts, or other parts of their body, and saw the *tokens*.

TOPICS FOR COMPOSITION

1. Write a first-person account of a past natural disaster, such as a flood, a hurricane, a tornado, or a drought. As in Defoe's *Journal*, warn your

readers of the physical and moral dangers attendant upon such disasters. Combine narrative and descriptive elements.

2. In common with other eighteenth-century writers Defoe frequently uses two or more words to convey the same idea. Note for example, *terrible shrieks and screechings, quite dead and cold, raving and distracted, idioticism and foolish distractions*. Study these and other doublets and repetitions. Then comment on the following statement: Defoe's repetitions are not necessarily careless; they often reflect an oral style acquired from speakers and preachers who used two words for one, first to give the listener a second chance to capture his meaning, and, second to reproduce, through parallel structure, the natural rhythm of speech.

JOHN HERSEY

A Noiseless Flash

WHEN atom bombs fell on Hiroshima and Nagasaki, John Hersey was a war correspondent in China. After the Japanese surrender he visited the stricken cities, interviewed some of the survivors, and wrote, in *The New Yorker* for August 31, 1946, his classic account *Hiroshima,* the first chapter of which appears below. Few war stories have evoked such an immediate, prolonged, and sickened response. Even now, long after the event, most readers read *Hiroshima* with a shudder of apprehension.

Any report of a catastrophic event is likely to interest readers who fear its repetition and hope for its prevention. But *Hiroshima* is more than a timely report. John Hersey brought to it a new kind of literary skill, one in which scrupulous accuracy, a concern for the testimony of witnesses drawn from different social ranks and professions, and a reliance upon objective evidence objectively presented all play an important role. To compare Hersey's *Hiroshima* with Defoe's *Journal* is to recognize the characteristics of this new approach. Defoe, for all his realistic detail, aims at arousing our feelings of horror and awe. For him feeling comes first, and details are presented as motives for feeling. Hersey, no less sensitive to the evil he describes, aims first at making us perceive. His report of detailed perceptions creates by slow stages a total impression of horrified awe. Hersey's is a consciously inductive mode of narrative; it allows the reader to accumulate impressions, to correct impressions as he goes on, and thus to derive his own general impression.

Hersey's tone of address and his narrative method reflect a habitual modern way of thinking and communicating. The influence of scientific method, with its stress on accurate observation and analysis and its suspicion of direct and overt persuasion, may be detected in Hersey's sustained detachment. He presents facts and lets them speak for themselves.

[1]   At exactly fifteen minutes past eight in the morning, on August 6, 1945, Japanese time, at the moment when the atomic bomb flashed above Hiroshima, Miss Toshiko Sasaki, a clerk in the personnel department of the

East Asia Tin Works, had just sat down at her place in the plant office and was turning her head to speak to the girl at the next desk. At that same moment, Dr. Masakazu Fujii was settling down cross-legged to read the Osaka *Asahi* on the porch of his private hospital, overhanging one of the seven deltaic rivers which divide Hiroshima; Mrs. Hatsuyo Nakamura, a tailor's widow, stood by the window of her kitchen, watching a neighbor tearing down his house because it lay in the path of an air-raid-defense fire lane; Father Wilhelm Kleinsorge, a German priest of the Society of Jesus, reclined in his underwear on a cot on the top floor of his order's three-story mission house, reading a Jesuit magazine, *Stimmen der Zeit;* Dr. Terufumi Sasaki, a young member of the surgical staff of the city's large, modern Red Cross Hospital, walked along one of the hospital corridors with a blood specimen for a Wassermann test in his hand; and the Reverend Mr. Kiyoshi Tanimoto, pastor of the Hiroshima Methodist Church, paused at the door of a rich man's house in Koi, the city's western suburb, and prepared to unload a handcart full of things he had evacuated from town in fear of the massive B-29 raid which everyone expected Hiroshima to suffer. A hundred thousand people were killed by the atomic bomb, and these six were among the survivors. They still wonder why they lived when so many others died. Each of them counts many small items of chance or volition—a step taken in time, a decision to go indoors, catching one streetcar instead of the next—that spared him. And now each knows that in the act of survival he lived a dozen lives and saw more death than he ever thought he would see. At the time, none of them knew anything.

The Reverend Mr. Tanimoto got up at five o'clock that morning. He was [2] alone in the parsonage, because for some time his wife had been commuting with their year-old baby to spend nights with a friend in Ushida, a suburb to the north. Of all the important cities of Japan, only two, Kyoto and Hiroshima, had not been visited in strength by *B-san,* or Mr. B., as the Japanese, with a mixture of respect and unhappy familiarity, called the B-29; and Mr. Tanimoto, like all his neighbors and friends, was almost sick with anxiety. He had heard uncomfortably detailed accounts of mass raids on Kure, Iwakuni, Tokuyama, and other nearby towns; he was sure Hiroshima's turn would come soon. He had slept badly the night before, because there had been several air-raid warnings. Hiroshima had been getting such warnings almost every night for weeks, for at that time the B-29s were using Lake Biwa, northeast of Hiroshima, as a rendezvous point, and no matter what city the Americans planned to hit, the Superfortresses streamed in over the coast near Hiroshima. The frequency of the warnings and the continued abstinence of Mr. B. with respect to Hiroshima had made its citizens jittery; a rumor was going around that the Americans were saving something special for the city

[3]   Mr. Tanimoto is a small man, quick to talk, laugh, and cry. He wears his black hair parted in the middle and rather long; the prominence of the frontal bones just above his eyebrows and the smallness of his mustache, mouth, and chin give him a strange, old-young look, boyish and yet wise, weak and yet fiery. He moves nervously and fast, but with a restraint which suggests that he is a cautious, thoughtful man. He showed, indeed, just those qualities in the uneasy days before the bomb fell. Besides having his wife spend the nights in Ushida, Mr. Tanimoto had been carrying all the portable things from his church, in the close-packed residential district called Nagaragawa, to a house that belonged to a rayon manufacturer in Koi, two miles from the center of town. The rayon man, a Mr. Matsui, had opened his then unoccupied estate to a large number of his friends and acquaintances, so that they might evacuate whatever they wished to a safe distance from the probable target area. Mr. Tanimoto had had no difficulty in moving chairs, hymnals, Bibles, altar gear, and church records by pushcart himself, but the organ console and an upright piano required some aid. A friend of his named Matsuo had, the day before, helped him get the piano out to Koi; in return, he had promised this day to assist Mr. Matsuo in hauling out a daughter's belongings. That is why he had risen so early.

[4]   Mr. Tanimoto cooked his own breakfast. He felt awfully tired. The effort of moving the piano the day before, a sleepless night, weeks of worry and unbalanced diet, the cares of his parish—all combined to make him feel hardly adequate to the new day's work. There was another thing, too: Mr. Tanimoto had studied theology at Emory College, in Atlanta, Georgia; he had graduated in 1940; he spoke excellent English; he dressed in American clothes; he had corresponded with many American friends right up to the time the war began; and among a people obsessed with a fear of being spied upon—perhaps almost obsessed himself—he found himself growing increasingly uneasy. The police had questioned him several times, and just a few days before, he had heard that an influential acquaintance, a Mr. Tanaka, a retired officer of the Toyo Kisen Kaisha steamship line, an anti-Christian, a man famous in Hiroshima for his showy philanthropies and notorious for his personal tyrannies, had been telling people that Tanimoto should not be trusted. In compensation, to show himself publicly a good Japanese, Mr. Tanimoto had taken on the chairmanship of his local *tonariguni*, or Neighborhood Association, and to his other duties and concerns this position had added the business of organizing air-raid defense for about twenty families.

[5]   Before six o'clock that morning, Mr. Tanimoto started for Mr. Matsuo's house. There he found that their burden was to be a *tansu*, a large Japanese cabinet, full of clothing and household goods. The two men set out. The morning was perfectly clear and so warm that the day promised to be uncomfortable. A few minutes after they started, the air-raid siren went off

—a minute-long blast that warned of approaching planes but indicated to the people of Hiroshima only a slight degree of danger, since it sounded every morning at this time, when an American weather plane came over. The two men pulled and pushed the handcart through the city streets. Hiroshima was a fan-shaped city, lying mostly on the six islands formed by the seven estuarial rivers that branch out from the Ota River; its main commercial and residential districts, covering about four square miles in the center of the city, contained three-quarters of its population, which had been reduced by several evacuation programs from a wartime peak of 380,000 to about 245,000. Factories and other residential districts, or suburbs, lay compactly around the edges of the city. To the south were the docks, an airport, and the island-studded Inland Sea. A rim of mountains runs around the other three sides of the delta. Mr. Tanimoto and Mr. Matsuo took their way through the shopping center, already full of people, and across two of the rivers to the sloping streets of Koi, and up them to the outskirts and foothills. As they started up a valley away from the tight-ranked houses, the all-clear sounded. (The Japanese radar operators, detecting only three planes, supposed that they comprised a reconnaissance.) Pushing the handcart up to the rayon man's house was tiring, and the men, after they had maneuvered their load into the driveway and to the front steps, paused to rest awhile. They stood with a wing of the house between them and the city. Like most homes in this part of Japan, the house consisted of a wooden frame and wooden walls supporting a heavy tile roof. Its front hall, packed with rolls of bedding and clothing, looked like a cool cave full of fat cushions. Opposite the house, to the right of the front door, there was a large, finicky rock garden. There was no sound of planes. The morning was still; the place was cool and pleasant.

Then a tremendous flash of light cut across the sky. Mr. Tanimoto has a [6] distinct recollection that it travelled from east to west, from the city toward the hills. It seemed a sheet of sun. Both he and Mr. Matsuo reacted in terror—and both had time to react (for they were 3,500 yards, or two miles, from the center of the explosion). Mr. Matsuo dashed up the front steps into the house and dived among the bedrolls and buried himself there. Mr. Tanimoto took four or five steps and threw himself between two big rocks in the garden. He bellied up very hard against one of them. As his face was against the stone, he did not see what happened. He felt a sudden pressure, and then splinters and pieces of board and fragments of tile fell on him. He heard no roar. (Almost no one in Hiroshima recalls hearing any noise of the bomb. But a fisherman in his sampan on the Inland Sea near Tsuzu, the man with whom Mr. Tanimoto's mother-in-law and sister-in-law were living, saw the flash and heard a tremendous explosion; he was nearly twenty miles from Hiroshima, but the thunder was greater than when the B-29's hit Iwakuni, only five miles away.)

When he dared, Mr. Tanimoto raised his head and saw that the rayon [7] man's house had collapsed. He thought a bomb had fallen directly on it. Such clouds of dust had risen that there was a sort of twilight around. In panic, not thinking for the moment of Mr. Matsuo under the ruins, he dashed out into the street. He noticed as he ran that the concrete wall of the estate had fallen over—toward the house rather than away from it. In the street, the first thing he saw was a squad of soldiers who had been burrowing into the hillside opposite, making one of the thousands of dug-outs in which the Japanese apparently intended to resist invasion, hill by hill, life for life; the soldiers were coming out of the hole, where they should have been safe, and blood was running from their heads, chests, and backs. They were silent and dazed.

[8]   Under what seemed to be a local dust cloud, the day grew darker and darker.

[9]   At nearly midnight, the night before the bomb was dropped, an announcer on the city's radio station said that about two hundred B-29's were approaching southern Honshu and advised the population of Hiroshima to evacuate to their designated "safe areas." Mrs. Hatsuyo Nakamura, the tailor's widow, who lived in the section called Nobori-cho and who had long had a habit of doing as she was told, got her three children—a ten-year-old boy, Toshio, an eight-year-old girl, Yaeko, and a five-year-old girl, Myeko—out of bed and dressed them and walked with them to the military area known as the East Parade Ground, on the northeast edge of the city. There she unrolled some mats and the children lay down on them. They slept until about two, when they were awakened by the roar of the planes going over Hiroshima.

[10]   As soon as the planes had passed, Mrs. Nakamura started back with her children. They reached home a little after two-thirty and she immediately turned on the radio, which, to her distress, was just then broadcasting a fresh warning. When she looked at the children and saw how tired they were, and when she thought of the number of trips they had made in the past weeks, all to no purpose, to the East Parade Ground, she decided that in spite of the instructions on the radio, she simply could not face starting out all over again. She put the children in their bedrolls on the floor, lay down herself at three o'clock, and fell asleep at once, so soundly that when planes passed over later, she did not waken to their sound.

[11]   The siren jarred her awake at about seven. She arose, dressed quickly, and hurried to the house of Mr. Nakamoto, the head of her Neighborhood Association, and asked him what she should do. He said that she should remain at home unless an urgent warning—a series of intermittent blasts of the siren—was sounded. She returned home, lit the stove in the kitchen, set some rice to cook, and sat down to read that morning's Hiroshima *Chugoku*. To her relief, the all-clear sounded at eight o'clock. She

heard the children stirring, so she went and gave each of them a handful of peanuts and told them to stay on their bedrolls, because they were tired from the night's walk. She had hoped that they would go back to sleep, but the man in the house directly to the south began to make a terrible hullabaloo of hammering, wedging, ripping, and splitting. The prefectural government, convinced, as everyone in Hiroshima was, that the city would be attacked soon, had begun to press with threats and warnings for the completion of wide fire lanes, which, it was hoped, might act in conjunction with the rivers to localize any fires started by an incendiary raid; and the neighbor was reluctantly sacrificing his home to the city's safety. Just the day before, the prefecture had ordered all able-bodied girls from the secondary schools to spend a few days helping to clear these lanes, and they started work soon after the all-clear sounded.

Mrs. Nakamura went back to the kitchen, looked at the rice, and began [12] watching the man next door. At first, she was annoyed with him for making so much noise, but then she was moved almost to tears by pity. Her emotion was specifically directed toward her neighbor, tearing down his home, board by board, at a time when there was so much unavoidable destruction, but undoubtedly she also felt a generalized, community pity, to say nothing of self-pity. She had not had an easy time. Her husband, Isawa, had gone into the Army just after Myeko was born, and she had heard nothing from or of him for a long time, until, on March 5, 1942, she received a seven-word telegram: "Isawa died an honorable death at Singapore." She learned later that he had died on February 15th, the day Singapore fell, and that he had been a corporal. Isawa had been a not particularly prosperous tailor, and his only capital was a Sankoku sewing machine. After his death, when his allotments stopped coming, Mrs. Nakamura got out the machine and began to take in piecework herself, and since then had supported the children, but poorly, by sewing.

As Mrs. Nakamura stood watching her neighbor, everything flashed [13] whiter than any white she had ever seen. She did not notice what happened to the man next door; the reflex of a mother set her in motion toward her children. She had taken a single step (the house was 1,350 yards, or three-quarters of a mile, from the center of the explosion) when something picked her up and she seemed to fly into the next room over the raised sleeping platform, pursued by parts of her house.

Timbers fell around her as she landed, and a shower of tiles pommelled [14] her; everything became dark, for she was buried. The debris did not cover her deeply. She rose up and freed herself. She heard a child cry, "Mother, help me!" and saw her youngest—Myeko, the five-year-old—buried up to her breast and unable to move. As Mrs. Nakamura started frantically to claw her way toward her baby, she could see or hear nothing of her other children.

[15] In the days right after the bombing, Dr. Masakazu Fujii, being prosperous, hedonistic, and at the time not too busy, had been allowing himself the luxury of sleeping until nine or nine-thirty, but fortunately he had to get up early the morning the bomb was dropped to see a house guest off on a train. He rose at six, and half an hour later walked with his friend to the station, not far away, across two of the rivers. He was back home by seven, just as the siren sounded its sustained warning. He ate breakfast and then, because the morning was already hot, undressed down to his underwear and went out on the porch to read the paper. This porch—in fact, the whole building—was curiously constructed. Dr. Fujii was the proprietor of a peculiarly Japanese institution: a private, single-doctor hospital. This building, perched beside and over the water of the Kyo River, and next to the bridge of the same name, contained thirty rooms for thirty patients and their kinfolk—for, according to Japanese custom, when a person falls sick and goes to a hospital, one or more members of his family go and live there with him, to cook for him, bathe, massage, and read to him, and to offer incessant familial sympathy, without which a Japanese patient would be miserable indeed. Dr. Fujii had no beds—only straw mats—for his patients. He did, however, have all sorts of modern equipment: an X-ray machine, diathermy apparatus, and a fine tiled laboratory. The structure rested two-thirds on the land, one-third on piles over the tidal waters of the Kyo. This overhang, the part of the building where Dr. Fujii lived, was queer-looking, but it was cool in summer and from the porch, which faced away from the center of the city, the prospect of the river, with pleasure boats drifting up and down it, was always refreshing. Dr. Fujii had occasionally had anxious moments when the Ota and its mouth branches rose to flood, but the piling was apparently firm enough and the house had always held.

[16] Dr. Fujii had been relatively idle for about a month because in July, as the number of untouched cities in Japan dwindled and as Hiroshima seemed more and more inevitably a target, he began turning patients away, on the ground that in case of a fire raid he would not be able to evacuate them. Now he had only two patients left—a woman from Yano, injured in the shoulder, and a young man of twenty-five recovering from burns he had suffered when the steel factory near Hiroshima in which he worked had been hit. Dr. Fujii had six nurses to tend his patients. His wife and children were safe; his wife and one son were living outside Osaka, and another son and two daughters were in the country on Kyushu. A niece was living with him, and a maid and a manservant. He had little to do and did not mind, for he had saved some money. At fifty, he was healthy, convivial, and calm, and he was pleased to pass the evenings drinking whiskey with friends, always sensibly and for the sake of conversation. Before the war, he had affected brands imported from Scotland and

America; now he was perfectly satisfied with the best Japanese brand, Suntory.

Dr. Fujii sat down cross-legged in his underwear on the spotless matting [17] of the porch, put on his glasses, and started reading the Osaka *Asahi*. He liked to read the Osaka news because his wife was there. He saw the flash. To him—faced away from the center and looking at his paper—it seemed a brilliant yellow. Startled, he began to rise to his feet. In that moment (he was 1,550 yards from the center), the hospital leaned behind his rising and, with a terrible ripping noise, toppled into the river. The Doctor, still in the act of getting to his feet was thrown forward and around and over; he was buffeted and gripped; he lost track of everything, because things were so speeded up; he felt the water.

Dr. Fujii hardly had time to think that he was dying before he realized [18] that he was alive, squeezed tightly by two long timbers in a V across his chest, like a morsel suspended between two huge chopsticks—held upright, so that he could not move, with his head miraculously above water and his torso and legs in it. The remains of his hospital were all around him in a mad assortment of splintered lumber and materials for the relief of pain. His left shoulder hurt terribly. His glasses were gone.

Father Wilhelm Kleinsorge, of the Society of Jesus, was, on the morning [19] of the explosion, in rather frail condition. The Japanese wartime diet had not sustained him, and he felt the strain of being a foreigner in an increasingly xenophobic Japan; even a German, since the defeat of the Fatherland, was unpopular. Father Kleinsorge had, at thirty-eight, the look of a boy growing too fast—thin in the face, with a prominent Adam's apple, a hollow chest, dangling hands, big feet. He walked clumsily, leaning forward a little. He was tired all the time. To make matters worse, he had suffered for two days, along with Father Cieslik, a fellow-priest, from a rather painful and urgent diarrhea, which they blamed on the beans and black ration bread they were obliged to eat. Two other priests then living in the mission compound, which was in the Nobori-cho section—Father Superior LaSalle and Father Schiffer—had happily escaped this affliction.

Father Kleinsorge woke up about six the morning the bomb was dropped, [20] and half an hour later—he was a bit tardy because of his sickness—he began to read Mass in the mission chapel, a small Japanese-style wooden building which was without pews, since its worshippers knelt on the usual Japanese matted floor, facing an altar graced with splendid silks, brass, silver, and heavy embroideries. This morning, a Monday, the only worshippers were Mr. Takemoto, a theological student living in the mission house; Mr. Fukai, the secretary of the diocese; Mrs. Murata, the mission's devoutly Christian housekeeper; and his fellow-priests. After Mass, while Father Kleinsorge was reading the Prayers of Thanksgiving, the siren sounded.

John Hersey

113

He stopped the service and the missionaries retired across the compound to the bigger building. There, in his room on the ground floor, to the right of the front door, Father Kleinsorge changed into a military uniform which he had acquired when he was teaching at the Rokko Middle School in Kobe and which he wore during air-raid alerts.

[21]   After an alarm, Father Kleinsorge always went out and scanned the sky, and in this instance, when he stepped outside, he was glad to see only the single weather plane that flew over Hiroshima each day about this time. Satisfied that nothing would happen, he went in and breakfasted with the other Fathers on substitute coffee and ration bread, which, under the circumstances, was especially repugnant to him. The Fathers sat and talked awhile, until, at eight, they heard the all-clear. They went then to various parts of the building. Father Schiffer retired to his room to do some writing. Father Cieslik sat in his room in a straight chair with a pillow over his stomach to ease his pain, and read. Father Superior LaSalle stood at the window of his room, thinking. Father Kleinsorge went up to a room on the third floor, took off all his clothes except his underwear, and stretched out on his right side on a cot and began reading his *Stimmen der Zeit*.

[22]   After the terrible flash—which, Father Kleinsorge later realized, reminded him of something he had read as a boy about a larger meteor colliding with the earth—he had time (since he was 1,400 yards from the center) for one thought: A bomb has fallen directly on us. Then, for a few seconds or minutes, he went out of his mind.

[23]   Father Kleinsorge never knew how he got out of the house. The next things he was conscious of were that he was wandering around in the mission's vegetable garden in his underwear, bleeding slightly from small cuts along his left flank; that all the buildings round about had fallen down except the Jesuits' mission house, which had long before been braced and double-braced by a priest named Gropper, who was terrified of earthquakes; that the day had turned dark; and that Murata-*san*, the housekeeper, was nearby, crying over and over, "*Shu Jesusu, awaremi tamai!* Our Lord Jesus, have pity on us!"

[24] On the train on the way into Hiroshima from the country, where he lived with his mother, Dr. Terufumi Sasaki, the Red Cross Hospital surgeon, thought over an unpleasant nightmare he had had the night before. His mother's house was in Mukaihara, thirty miles from the city, and it took him two hours by train and tram to reach the hospital. He had slept uneasily all night and had wakened an hour earlier than usual, and, feeling sluggish and slightly feverish, had debated whether to go to the hospital at all; his sense of duty finally forced him to go, and he had started out on an earlier train than he took most mornings. The dream had particu-

larly frightened him because it was so closely associated, on the surface at least, with a disturbing actuality. He was only twenty-five years old and had just completed his training at the Eastern Medical University, in Tsingtao, China. He was something of an idealist and was much distressed by the inadequacy of medical facilities in the country town where his mother lived. Quite on his own, and without a permit, he had begun visiting a few sick people out there in the evenings, after his eight hours at the hospital and four hours' commuting. He had recently learned that the penalty for practicing without a permit was severe; a fellow-doctor whom he had asked about it had given him a serious scolding. Nevertheless, he had continued to practice. In his dream, he had been at the bedside of a country patient when the police and the doctor he had consulted burst into the room, seized him, dragged him outside, and beat him up cruelly. On the train, he just about decided to give up the work in Mukaihara, since he felt it would be impossible to get a permit, because the authorities would hold that it would conflict with his duties at the Red Cross Hospital.

At the terminus, he caught a streetcar at once. (He later calculated that [25] if he had taken his customary train that morning, and if he had had to wait a few minutes for the streetcar, as often happened, he would have been close to the center at the time of the explosion and would surely have perished.) He arrived at the hospital at seven-forty and reported to the chief surgeon. A few minutes later, he went to a room on the first floor and drew blood from the arm of a man in order to perform a Wassermann test. The laboratory containing the incubators for the test was on the third floor. With the blood specimen in his left hand, walking in a kind of distraction he had felt all morning, probably because of the dream and his restless night, he started along the main corridor on his way toward the stairs. He was one step beyond an open window when the light of the bomb was reflected, like a gigantic photographic flash, in the corridor. He ducked down on one knee and said to himself, as only a Japanese would, "Sasaki, *gambare*! Be brave!" Just then (the building was 1,650 yards from the center), the blast ripped through the hospital. The glasses he was wearing flew off his face; the bottle of blood crashed against one wall; his Japanese slippers zipped out from under his feet—but otherwise, thanks to where he stood, he was untouched.

Dr. Sasaki shouted the name of the chief surgeon and rushed around to [26] the man's office and found him terribly cut by glass. The hospital was in horrible confusion: heavy partitions and ceilings had fallen on patients, beds had overturned, windows had blown in and cut people, blood was spattered on the walls and floors, instruments were everywhere, many of the patients were running about screaming, many more lay dead. (A colleague working in the laboratory to which Dr. Sasaki had been walking was dead; Dr. Sasaki's patient, whom he had just left and who a few moments before had been dreadfully afraid of syphilis, was also dead.) Dr. Sasaki found himself the only doctor in the hospital who was unhurt.

[27]   Dr. Sasaki, who believed that the enemy had hit only the building he was in, got bandages and began to bind the wounds of those inside the hospital; while outside, all over Hiroshima, maimed and dying citizens turned their unsteady steps toward the Red Cross Hospital to begin an invasion that was to make Dr. Sasaki forget his private nightmare for a long, long time.

[28]   Miss Toshiko Sasaki, the East Asia Tin Works clerk, who is not related to Dr. Sasaki, got up at three o'clock in the morning on the day the bomb fell. There was extra housework to do. Her eleven-month-old brother, Akio, had come down the day before with a serious stomach upset; her mother had taken him to the Tamura Pediatric Hospital and was staying there with him. Miss Sasaki, who was about twenty, had to cook breakfast for her father, a brother, a sister, and herself, and—since the hospital, because of the war, was unable to provide food—to prepare a whole day's meals for her mother and the baby, in time for her father, who worked in a factory making rubber earplugs for artillery crews, to take the food by on his way to the plant. When she had finished and had cleaned and put away the cooking things, it was nearly seven. The family lived in Koi, and she had a forty-five minute trip to the tin works, in the section of town called Kannonmachi. She was in charge of the personnel records in the factory. She left Koi at seven, and as soon as she reached the plant, she went with some of the other girls from the personnel department to the factory auditorium. A prominent local Navy man, a former employee, had committed suicide the day before by throwing himself under a train— a death considered honorable enough to warrant a memorial service, which was to be held at the tin works at ten o'clock that morning. In the large hall, Miss Sasaki and the others made suitable preparations for the meeting. This work took about twenty minutes.

[29]   Miss Sasaki went back to her office and sat down at her desk. She was quite far from the windows, which were off to her left, and behind her were a couple of tall bookcases containing all the books of the factory library, which the personnel department had organized. She settled herself at her desk, put some things in a drawer, and shifted papers. She thought that before she began to make entries in her lists of new employees, discharges, and departures for the Army, she would chat for a moment with the girl at her right. Just as she turned her head away from the windows, the room was filled with a blinding light. She was paralyzed by fear, fixed still in her chair for a long moment (the plant was 1,600 yards from the center).

[30]   Everything fell, and Miss Sasaki lost consciousness. The ceiling dropped

suddenly and the wooden floor above collapsed in splinters and the people up there came down and the roof above them gave way; but principally and first of all, the bookcases right behind her swooped forward and the contents threw her down, with her left leg horribly twisted and breaking underneath her. There, in the tin factory, in the first moment of the atomic age, a human being was crushed by books.

TOPICS FOR DISCUSSION

1. A successful narrative is said to answer for its readers the classic questions: Who? Where? When? What? How? Show where Hersey gives preliminary answers to these questions in paragraph 1. Where does he attempt to answer them more fully in the course of the passage as a whole? It is sometimes suggested that answers to all these questions contain the answer to the more elusive question: Why? Does Hersey attempt to answer that question in this essay? Explain.

2. Comment on the structure of this passage by pointing out how it is divided. What other divisions—according to time, place, action— would be possible? What is the advantage of the present division? Of other possible divisions?

3. In many respects a descriptive narrative resembles process-analysis. Through process-analysis we explore a subject—for example, the life cycle of a plant or animal, the functioning of a machine, or the experience of historical events—by tracing each essential step in the whole action or operation. Is this essay wholly or partly process-analysis? Explain.

4. "A Noiseless Flash" and "The Plague in London" deal with the effects of disaster. Point out several other similarities between them. How do they differ in subject matter? In the point of view of the narrator? Which has the more complex structure? Why? Which supplies more details? Show how "A Noiseless Flash" assumes a greater awareness of science on the part of the reader. Despite its objective tone, does "A Noiseless Flash" create an emotional impression upon the reader? How?

5. Throughout this passage, the author intertwines descriptive details with his narrative. Note, for example, the description of Mr. Tanimoto in (paragraph 3), of the city of Hiroshima (paragraph 5), of the explosion (paragraphs 6 and 7). Point out other paragraphs that contain similar descriptions. Show how these descriptions are both objective notations of what was seen, heard, and otherwise sensed, and personal or subjective responses to the explosion of the bomb. How do both kinds of de-

scription contribute to the imaginative and emotional appeal of the whole passage?

6. In the *Journal* Defoe presents his account from the point of view of a single narrator. In *Hiroshima* Hersey presents his from the point of view of six witnesses. What are the advantages and disadvantages of each approach? To what extent does the subject matter itself and the writer's access to his subject matter determine the appropriate point of view?

TOPICS FOR COMPOSITION

1. Write a descriptive narrative on one of the following subjects or on a similar subject. First summarize the whole action as Hersey does in "A Noiseless Flash"; then write separate accounts from the point of view of individual witnesses. You may choose to interview actual witnesses of a recent event, or you may investigate the documentary evidence of a past event. Suggested subjects are:

   a. the Battle of Gettysburg, or another battle, as seen by a general, a courier, a farmer in the vicinity, a medical corpsman, and a newspaper correspondent

   b. a student meeting protesting the abolition of football, or some restriction, as seen by a student leader, an experienced teacher, a college or high-school administrator, a chief of police, a parent of one of the student participants

   c. a report on the dangers of air or water pollution as seen by a public health officer, the president of a corporation accused of contributing to pollution, a sufferer from lung disease, a judge, a lover of nature.

2. In an article entitled "History by the Ounce" (*Harper's Magazine*, July 1965, pp. 64–75), Barbara W. Tuchman explains why "precise, factual" detail is valuable in the writing of narration.

   At a party given for its reopening last year, the Museum of Modern Art in New York served champagne to five thousand guests. An alert reporter for the *Times*, Charlotte Curtis, noted that there were eighty cases which, she informed her readers, amounted to 960 bottles or 7,680 three-ounce drinks. Somehow through this detail the Museum's party at once becomes alive; a fashionable New York occasion. One sees the crush, the women eyeing each other's clothes, the exchange of greetings, and feels the gratifying sense of elegance and importance imparted by champagne—even if, at one and a half drinks per person, it was not on an exactly riotous scale. All this is conveyed by Miss Curtis' detail. It is, I think, the way history as well as journalism should be written. It is what Pooh-Bah, in *The Mikado,* meant when, telling how the victim's head stood on its neck and bowed three times to him at the execution of Nanki-poo, he added that this was "corroborative detail intended to give artistic verisimilitude to an otherwise bald and unconvincing narrative." Not that Miss Curtis' narrative was either bald or unconvincing; on the contrary, it was precise, factual, and a model in every way. But what made it excel, made it vivid and memorable, was her use of corroborative detail.

Comment on the relevance of this statement to the success or failure of "A Noiseless Flash" or another selection in this section.

❦ Exposition

ABRAHAM
COWLEY

Of
Myself

A GOOD expository writer explains with clarity, conviction, and grace whatever subject his occasion or audience requires. His chief aim is clarity and the chief agent of clarity is definition, a mode of analysis by which we answer the question: What is it?

That question sometimes applies to words. Thus when we ask the meaning of *liberty* we find that, according to Funk and Wagnall's *Standard College Dictionary*, its principal meaning is: "Freedom from oppression, tyranny, or the domination of a government not freely chosen; political independence." The question also applies to the experience or reality that a word stands for, that is, to the particular meaning we attach to a word in a given context. Abraham Cowley, for instance, began an essay "Of Liberty" with these words:

The liberty of a people consists in being governed by laws which they have made themselves, under whatsoever form it be of government; the liberty of a private man, in being master of his own time and actions, as far as may consist with the laws of God and of his country. Of this latter only we are here to discourse, and to enquire what estate of life does best seat us in the possession of it.

This definition, logically accurate though it be, merely sufficed to introduce a developed definition in which Cowley cited many examples of liberty and its opposite. He described in great detail the way one achieves liberty and avoids servility. In short, he expanded his definition to suit his occasion and purpose.

Cowley wrote his essays, "Of Myself" among them, to justify his own withdrawal from active life, with its many dangers to personal freedom, to the true freedom of the country and the delights of the spirit. To define himself, he chose the only means adequate to that purpose, a brief narrative of his own life. It is a narrative, however, that explains his understanding of true liberty.

It is a hard and nice subject for a man to write of himself; it grates his [1] own heart to say any thing of disparagement, and the reader's ears to hear any thing of praise from him. There is no danger from me of offending him in this kind; neither my mind, nor my body, nor my fortune, allow me any materials for that vanity. It is sufficient for my own contentment, that they have preserved me from being scandalous, or remarkable on the defective side. But, besides that, I shall here speak of myself only in relation to the subject of these precedent discourses,[1] and shall be likelier thereby to fall into the contempt, than rise up to the estimation, of most people.

[2]   As far as my memory can return back into my past life, before I knew, or was capable of guessing, what the world, or the glories or business of it, were, the natural affections of my soul gave me a secret bent of aversion from them, as some plants are said to turn away from others, by an antipathy imperceptible to themselves, and inscrutable to man's understanding. Even when I was a very young boy at school, instead of running about on holy-days and playing with my fellows, I was wont to steal from them, and walk into the fields, either alone with a book, or with some one companion, if I could find any of the same temper. I was then, too, so much an enemy to all constraint, that my masters could never prevail on me, by any persuasions or encouragements, to learn without book the common rules of grammar; in which they dispensed with me alone, because they found I made a shift to do the usual exercise out of my own reading and observation. That I was then of the same mind as I am now (which, I confess, I wonder at, myself) may appear by the latter end of an ode, which I made when I was but thirteen years old, and which was then printed with many other verses.[2] The beginning of it is boyish; but of this part, which I here set down (if a very little were corrected), I should hardly now be much ashamed.

9

This only grant me, that my means may lie
Too low for envy, for contempt too high.
  Some honour I would have,
Not from great deeds, but good alone;
The unknown are better, than ill known:
  Rumour can ope the grave.
Acquaintance I would have, but when 't depends
Not on the number, but the choice of friends.

10

Books should, not business, entertain the light,
And sleep, as undisturb'd as death, the night.
  My house a cottage more
Than palace; and should fitting be

[1]This essay appeared in *Several Discourses by Way of Essays, in Verse and Prose* (1668). Among "the precedent discourses" were "Of Liberty," "Of Solitude," "Of Obscurity," "Of Greatness," "The Dangers of an Honest Man in Much Company." All these topics are applied to Cowley's own life in "Of Myself."

[2]The three stanzas at the end of the paragraph are from Cowley's *A Vote*, contained in his *Sylva* (1636).

For all my use, no luxury.
   My garden painted o'er
With nature's hand, not art's; and pleasures yield,
Horace might envy in his Sabin field.

11

Thus would I double my life's fading space;
For he, that runs it well, twice runs his race.
   And in this true delight,
These unbought sports, this happy state,
I would not fear, nor wish, my fate;
   But boldly say each night,
To-morrow let my sun his beams display,
Or, in clouds hide them; I have liv'd, to-day.

You may see by it, I was even then acquainted with the poets (for the   [3]
conclusion is taken out of Horace[3]); and perhaps it was the immature and
immoderate love of them, which stampt first, or rather engraved, these
characters in me: they were like letters cut into the bark of a young tree,
which with the tree still grow proportionably. But, how this love came to
be produced in me so early, is a hard question: I believe, I can tell the
particular little chance that filled my head first with such chimes of verse,
as have never since left ringing there: for I remember, when I began to
read, and to take some pleasure in it, there was wont to lie in my mother's
parlour (I know not by what accident, for she herself never in her life
read any book but of devotion) but there was wont to lie Spenser's works:
this I happened to fall upon, and was infinitely delighted with the stories
of the knights, and giants, and monsters, and brave houses, which I found
every where there (though my understanding had little to do with all
this); and, by degrees, with the tinkling of the rhyme and dance of the
numbers; so that, I think, I had read him all over before I was twelve
years old, and was thus made a poet as immediately as a child is made an
eunuch.

With these affections of mind, and my heart wholly set upon letters, I   [4]
went to the university; but was soon torn from thence by that violent public storm,[4] which would suffer nothing to stand where it did, but rooted
up every plant, even from the princely cedars to me the hyssop. Yet, I
had as good fortune as could have befallen me in such a tempest; for I
was cast by it into the family of one of the best persons,[5] and into the

---

[3]From *Odes* iii, 29, 41–45.
[4]The Civil War, which began in 1642. Cowley followed the royal family into exile in
  1646.
[5]Cowley was secretary to Lord Jermyn, later Earl of St. Albans.

court of one of the best princesses,[6] of the world. Now, though I was here engaged in ways most contrary to the original design of my life, that is, into much company, and no small business, and into a daily sight of greatness, both militant and triumphant (for that was the state then of the English and French courts); yet all this was so far from altering my opinion, that it only added the confirmation of reason to that which was before but natural inclination. I saw plainly all the paint of that kind of life, the nearer I came to it; and that beauty, which I did not fall in love with, when, for aught I knew, it was real, was not like to bewitch or entice me, when I saw that it was adulterate. I met with several great persons, whom I liked very well; but could not perceive that any part of their greatness was to be liked or desired, no more than I would be glad or content to be in a storm, though I saw many ships which rid safely and bravely in it: a storm would not agree with my stomach, if it did with my courage. Though I was in a crowd of as good company as could be found any where, though I was in business of great and honourable trust, though I ate at the best table, and enjoyed the best conveniences for present subsistence that ought to be desired by a man of my condition in banishment and public distresses; yet I could not abstain from renewing my old schoolboy's wish, in a copy of verses to the same effect:

Well then; I now do plainly see
This busy world and I shall ne'er agree, &c.[7]

And I never then proposed to myself any other advantage from his majesty's happy Restoration, but the getting into some moderately convenient retreat in the country; which I thought, in that case, I might easily have compassed, as well as some others, who with no greater probabilities or pretenses, have arrived to extraordinary fortune: but I had before written a shrewd prophecy against myself; and I think Apollo inspired me in the truth, though not in the elegance, of it:

Thou neither great at court, nor in the war,
Nor at th' exchange shall be, nor at the wrangling bar.
Content thyself with the small barren praise,
    Which neglected verse does raise.
  She spake; and all my years to come
    Took their unlucky doom.
Their several ways of life let others chuse,
  Their several pleasures let them use;
But I was born for Love, and for a Muse.

---

[6]Henrietta Maria, wife of Charles I. Cowley ciphered and deciphered the letters between the King and Queen.
[7]The verses are from Cowley's "Destiny" in *Pindaric Odes* (1656).

The Practice of Rhetoric

With Fate what boots it to contend?
Such I began, such am, and so must end.
  The star, that did my being frame,
  Was but a lambent flame,
  And some small light it did dispense,
  But neither heat nor influence.
No matter, Cowley; let proud Fortune see,
That thou canst her despise no less than she does thee.
  Let all her gifts the portion be
  Of folly, lust, and flattery,
  Fraud, extortion, calumny,
  Murder, infidelity,
  Rebellion and hypocrisy.
 Do thou nor grieve nor blush to be,
 As all th' inspired tuneful men,
And all thy great forefathers were, from Homer down to Ben.[8]

However, by the failing of the forces which I had expected, I did not [5]
quit the design which I had resolved on; I cast myself into it a *corps
perdu*,[9] without making capitulations, or taking counsel of fortune. But
God laughs at a man, who says to his soul, *Take thy ease:* I met presently
not only with many little incumbrances and impediments, but with so much
sickness (a new misfortune to me) as would have spoiled the happiness of
an emperor as well as mine: yet I do neither repent, nor alter my course.
"Non ego perfidum dixi sacramentum;" [10] nothing shall separate me from
a mistress, which I have loved so long, and have now at last married;
though she neither has brought me a rich portion, nor lived yet so quietly
with me as I hoped from her:

   Nor by me e'er shall you,
 You, of all names the sweetest, and the best,
 You, Muses, books, and liberty, and rest;
 You, gardens, fields, and woods, forsaken be,
 As long as life itself forsakes not me.[11]

But this is a very pretty ejaculation; because I have concluded all the [6]
other chapters with a copy of verses, I will maintain the humour to the last.

---

[8]The verses are from "Destiny."
[9]Literally, a lost body.
[10]The Latin means "I have not sworn a perfidious oath" and is from Horace, *Odes* ii, 17.
[11]Cowley's translation of his own Latin verse.

Since, dearest friend, 'tis your desire to see
A true receipt of happiness from me;
These are the chief ingredients, if not all:
Take an estate neither too great nor small,
Which *quantum sufficit* the doctors call.
Let this estate from parents' care descend;
The getting it too much of life does spend.
Take such a ground, whose gratitude may be
A fair encouragement for industry.
Let constant fires the winter's fury tame;
And let thy kitchen's be a vestal flame.
Thee to the town let never suit at law,
And rarely, very rarely, business draw.
Thy active mind in equal temper keep,
In undisturbed peace, yet not in sleep.
Let exercise a vigorous health maintain,
Without which all the composition's vain.
In the same weight prudence and innocence take,
Ana of each does the just mixture make.
But a few friendships wear, and let them be
By nature and by fortune fit for thee.
Instead of art and luxury in food,
Let mirth and freedom make thy table good.
If any cares into thy day-time creep,
At night, without wine's opium, let them sleep.
Let rest, which nature does to darkness wed,
And not lust, recommend to thee thy bed.
Be satisfied, and pleas'd with what thou art,
Act chearfully and well th' allotted part;
Enjoy the present hour, be thankful for the past,
And neither fear, nor wish, th' approaches of the last.

EPITAPH ON THE LIVING AUTHOR

1

Here, stranger, in this humble nest,
　Here, Cowley sleeps; here lies,
Scap'd all the toils, the life molest,
　And its superfluous joys.

2

Here, in no sordid poverty,
　And no inglorious ease,
He braves the world, and can defy
　Its frowns and flatteries.

3

The little earth, he asks, survey:
  Is he not dead, indeed?
"Light lye that earth," good stranger, pray,
  "Nor thorn upon it breed!"

4

With flow'rs, fit emblem of his fame,
  Compass your poet round;
With flow'rs of ev'ry fragrant name
  Be his warm ashes crown'd!

TOPICS FOR DISCUSSION

1. What are Cowley's professed motives for writing about himself? Are his apologies (paragraph 1) plausible? Why or why not?

2. Cowley's theme may be stated, in the language of Bishop Sprat his contemporary biographer, in the following way: true delight consists "of solitary studies, of temperate pleasures, and a moderate revenue below the malice and flatteries of fortune." Point out where Cowley states this theme for the first time. Point out restatements of the theme. To what extent may this essay be considered an extended definition of "true delight" or of "the good life"?

3. Insofar as "Of Myself" follows the chronological pattern of Cowley's life (see Headnote and Biography) the essay may be classified as a narrative. Indicate various stages in the narrative sequence by pointing out connective expressions.

4. Insofar as "Of Myself" explains and defends Cowley's ideas of a truly happy life it may also be classified as exposition. How does Cowley explain his idea of the good life? Do you think that, by telling us how he lived, he also defines what he lived for? Explain your answer.

5. How do the various verse quotations illustrate Cowley's idea of the good life? Do you admire his idea? Why or why not?

TOPICS FOR COMPOSITION

1. Write a brief autobiographical essay on the theme "How I Live and What I Live For."

2. Write a narrative about one of your important experiences. Show how that experience helped you define your idea of the good life.

3. Samuel Johnson sums up Cowley's character in his *Lives of the Poets* (1779–81) thus:

> He was buried with great pomp near Chaucer and Spenser [in Westminster Abbey]; and king Charles [II] pronounced, "That Mr. Cowley had not left a better man behind him in England." He is represented by Dr. Sprat as the most amiable of mankind; and this posthumous praise may be safely credited, as it has never been contradicted by envy or by faction.

Comment on Johnson's statement in the light of Cowley's self-revelation in "Of Myself."

J. B.
PRIESTLEY

All
About
Ourselves

AT FIRST glance J. B. Priestley's subject seems identical with that of Abraham Cowley. Both men address themselves to the same questions: Who am I? What do I stand for? Both men, aware of the difficulty of talking about themselves, approach their questions with humility and modesty. Both are candid and self-revealing. Despite these and other similarities, we become aware of decided differences. Cowley tells us of the details of his life and how he has responded to various ups and downs. J. B. Priestley reveals little about himself, but explores at some length the nature of self-knowledge. Cowley, believing that he has arrived at self-knowledge, expounds a definite philosophy of life. Priestley, believing himself to be still in the process of self-discovery, simply records what he has learned at successive stages of self-awareness.

These differences reflect not only the personalities of the two authors but the character of their times and the different expectations of their readers. The seventeenth century was an age of philosophical speculation, in which ultimate values were the subject of intense debate. Cowley addressed readers who knew the Latin and Greek classics and were familiar with the kind of meditative detachment with which he presented his life in "Of Myself." The twentieth century, on the other hand, while not without its great philosophers, has been preoccupied less with the ultimate *why* than with the scientific *how*. Priestley's concern with process, therefore, is appropriate not only to the theme inherent in his opening situation but also to a reading public disposed to study human nature in terms of psychological development. Note how, in his opening paragraph, Priestley not only tells us what he thinks but presents himself in the act of thinking.

"Now tell me," said the lady, "all about yourself." The effect was instantaneous, shattering. Up to that moment, I had been feeling expansive; I was self-confident, alert, ready to give a good account of myself in the skirmish of talk. If I had been asked my opinion of anything between here and Sirius, I would have given it at length, and I was quite prepared   [1]

ALL ABOUT OURSELVES Reprinted from *All About Ourselves and Other Essays* by J. B. Priestley, published by William Heinemann, Ltd., 1956. Copyright 1956 by J. B. Priestley.

to talk of places I had never seen and books I had never read; I was ready to lie, and to lie boldly and well. Had she not made that fatal demand, I would have roared like the sweet little lion she imagined me to be, roared as gently as any sucking dove or nightingale; for, unlike that haphazard impresario, Peter Quince, I had, you may say, "the lion's part written." [1] But to tell her all about myself. My expansive mood suddenly shrivelled to nothing; every richly-dyed shred of personality was stripped from me and there remained only my naked, shivering mortality. Nothing but a jumble of memorable old phrases haunted my mind: I was, like Socrates in the first syllogism, a man and therefore a mortal, such stuff as dreams are made on, born of a woman and full of trouble, one whose days are as grass.... What was there to be said? I stared at my sprightly companion, who was still smiling, half-playfully, half-expectantly, and I must have looked like a child peering from the ruins at the squadrons of an invading army. Then I mumbled something so unsatisfactory that, despairing of any intimate avowals, she passed on to some other topic, while I, donning my cloak and wig, my cap and bells, left the naked six feet of ground to which her demand had confined me, and made haste to follow her. Yorick was himself again. [2]

[2]   The request, so framed, was undoubtedly preposterous. Indeed, it was so obviously calculated to silence any normal human being that one may reasonably suspect the motive that lay behind it. To confess one's terror at meeting such a demand is not necessarily to hint at an engaging modesty. It was so all-embracing, so ultimate that only a megalomaniac or a great genius could have coped with it. A request to know what I had been doing for the past year or intended to do in the next twelve months, to know whether I approved of William Shakespeare or liked early rising, would have set my tongue wagging for an insufferable length of time. I am ready to talk about myself, that is, about my opinions, my likes and dislikes, my whims, my experiences, my hopes and fears, at any and every season. I have my own share of that windy, foolish, but, I hope, not too unpleasant vanity which is common to most people who do little tricks with words and pigments and fiddle-strings; I can fly my little coloured balloons of conceit with the next scribbler or chorus-girl or cabinet minister. But even if we only need the merest shadow of an excuse to talk about ourselves, there must be something interposed between the universe and our bare selves; there must be bounds assigned to our flow of egotism; we must be given some idea of ourselves to work upon, to build up or knock down. To tell *all* about ourselves in one vast breath is really to press the whole

[1]Peter Quince is a character in Shakespeare's *A Midsummer Night's Dream*. See Act I, scene 2, l. 67.
[2]See *Hamlet*, Act III, scene 1.

round world in the lemon-squeezer of our minds, to explain the sum total of things in terms of ourselves, to raise the ego to a monstrous height. The very thought of it flips the mind with "a three-man beetle" and stuns a man into humility.

Perhaps with most men there comes a time when they are able to give a [3] reasonable sort of account of themselves; but I, for one, am free to confess that I have not yet travelled so far. I am still busy trying, unsuccessfully as yet, to piece together the various impressions and opinions of myself I gather from other people to make up the fragments of my portrait. I am still noting, with amazement, the broken reflections and queer glimpses of myself that I catch sight of in other people's minds. This I conceive to be the third stage of one's progress in self-knowledge: how long it lasts and whether there is a fourth stage at all are questions that I cannot answer. But I can vouch for the two previous stages. When we are very young, not only has the earth and every common sight (to plunder Wordsworth[3]) the glory and the freshness of a dream, but we ourselves have something of the same glory and freshness; we gulp experience and do not question ourselves, and this golden age lasts until we realise, with something of a shock, that there are other selves who see us from the outside just as we see them. It is when we become conscious of other selves that we become self-conscious. Then we pass on to the second, most disquieting stage, which, for most people who are impressionable and imaginative, covers the whole period of their later teens and early twenties, and may even last considerably longer.

At this time we do nothing but question ourselves; rosy little Hamlets, [4] we are forever busy with self-communion. Never are we so anxious to discover what we are and never do we make so little of the matter as we do then. We examine ourselves in the light of everything we read, and become weathercocks swinging before the changing wind of ideas. An hour of Swinburne turns us into magnificent pagans and sensuous lovers, but before the day is out, a few pages of Carlyle have promptly transformed us into sturdy philosophers or roaring men of action. We can be Stoics before breakfast, Epicureans after lunch, and uncertain but hopeful Platonists before nightfall. Then gradually we lose heart, for though every philosophy attracts us and seems to have been almost designed to catch our eye, though we can always read so much of ourselves into every character we admire, yet there is always something essential wanting in us. We might be anything: we are nothing; nothing but a bundle of impulses, a rag-bag of discarded ideals and wavering loyalties. We are convinced that other people will never understand us, will never be subtle enough to ap-

[3]A paraphrase of lines 57–58 of Wordsworth's "Ode: Intimations of Immortality from Recollections of Early Childhood."

preciate that curious quality which, for all our wretched lack of anything like character, our instability of purpose, our wandering will, somehow makes us splendid and unique. Meanwhile, we can make nothing of ourselves, for we seem radically different from hour to hour, according to the company we are in. If we are with some great lout of a fellow, then we see ourselves dapper, fragile, precious, and, in a flash, decide the path we will take for the rest of our lives. But no sooner do we fall in with some little dandy than we hear our own voices, cutting through his mincing accents, and recognise in them the notes of strong determined men who will make their way in the world. So we go on, until we feel that we can show nothing to the world but this dance of shifting selves.

[5]   But we grow up, and then either we cast off introspection in engaging to do the world's work or we still try to puzzle it all out. Perhaps we begin to remark the figures we cut in the minds of our friends and acquaintances, and try to live up to the best of them; though how we discover which are the best of them is a question I am not prepared to answer. This may lead us into vanity, a swelling, eager sort of vanity, restless in pursuit of praise, a characteristic that is not so bad as it sounds. As some wiser men have already pointed out, vanity is at least warm, human, social, frankly dependent upon sympathy. There is an infinitely worse alternative, easy to fall into if we strongly approve of ourselves and yet shrink from soliciting other people's suffrages, and this is the solitary and desolating vice of pride. Many a man is praised for his reserve and so-called shyness when he is simply too proud to risk making a fool of himself. The vain man will cut capers in order to obtain notice and applause, the proud man asks for notice and applause without being willing to cut the capers, while the very proud man has such a miraculous self that he does not even want the applause. Some philosophies make this last state of complete self-satisfaction their goal, but one and all omit to mention the obvious advantages enjoyed by the oyster on such a plan of life. But unless we are victims of such icy folly, we discover, perhaps to our astonishment, that our greatest moments come when we find that we are not unique, when we come upon another self that is very like our own. The discovery of a continent is mere idle folly compared with this discovery of a sympathetic other-self, a friend or a lover. Where now is the sickly pleasure in not being understood, in being unique, miraculous, entirely self-satisfying, in shutting the painted doors and windows of the mind? Before this solid smashing happiness of thus being understood, all our walls go down and the sunlight comes streaming in. And then, and not until then, begins that endless tale which seems to be merely about this and that, but is really all about ourselves.

TOPICS FOR DISCUSSION

1. Despite its informal tone, this essay is carefully organized. It begins with a challenging question, explores the difficulty of that question, and then proposes a tentative answer by describing the stages of self-knowledge. What are these stages? Where precisely does Priestley discuss each stage? Show how each stage represents not simply change, but growth in self-awareness.

2. Like the essay as a whole, the paragraphs are clearly organized. Thus the topic of paragraph 1 is announced in sentence 2. Show how the details of the paragraph illustrate the effects of the lady's remark. Show how Priestley lends variety to his listing of effects by comparing and contrasting his role to that of Peter Quince, Socrates, and Yorick. Pick out the topic sentences in the remaining paragraphs. How is each topic sentence developed?

3. Presumably most college students are in the second stage of self-awareness, the one Priestley calls "most disquieting." Does this analysis of that stage correspond to your own experience? Comment particularly on the sentence in paragraph 4 beginning, "An hour of Swinburne. . . ."

4. Priestley's third stage of self-awareness, "the discovery of a sympathetic other-self," concludes his essay. Earlier he has speculated on a possible fourth stage of experience. What might that fourth stage be?

TOPICS FOR COMPOSITION

1. Write a brief essay on the topic, "Embarrassing Questions." If you wish, expand one of the following theme sentences:
   a. "Now tell me," said the Dean of Studies, "all about your reading of the Greek and Latin authors."
   b. "You go to college," said the mechanic. "Tell me what makes a turbo-engine work."
   c. In the midst of the class discussion our instructor said, "Now put your ideas in the form of a syllogism."
   d. If you don't know what you are studying for, why study?

2. Write a short essay commenting on the following statement: "We write our autobiography, whether we intend it or not, whenever we put any of our thoughts on paper. If you wish not to disclose yourself, be silent."

3. Compare and contrast Cowley's "Of Myself" and Priestley's "All About Ourselves" with reference to the following points: logical structure; relevance to a contemporary audience; disclosure of the writer's personality.

J. B. Priestley

SAMUEL JOHNSON

Biography

SAMUEL JOHNSON was forty-one and at the height of his literary and intellectual powers when, on October 13, 1750, he published "Biography" in *The Rambler*. Between 1750 and 1752 he would contribute two hundred essays to this magazine. Behind him were his apprenticeship as a hack writer, a translator, reporter, essayist, and editor. His satirical poems, *London* and *The Vanity of Human Wishes,* and his tragedy *Irene* had brought him literary fame. He was actively at work on his *Dictionary,* begun in 1747, to be completed in 1755.

Johnson's purpose in founding *The Rambler,* like that of Steele in *The Tatler* and *The Spectator,* was to present moral and religious truth in a rationally entertaining way. That Johnson was piously aware of this intention is evident from Boswell's records in his *Life* and Johnson's own motto for *The Rambler,* No. 7:

> From thee, great God, we spring, to thee we tend,
> Path, motive, guide, original and end.

Johnson's more immediate intention in writing "Biography" was to explain the value of a new and increasingly important type of literature. He had already discovered his affinity for biography when he wrote many short lives for *The Gentleman's Magazine.* In writing his long essay *The Life of Richard Savage* (1744) he learned even more about the importance of the biographical form. This preoccupation with biography foreshadowed the literary success of his *Lives of the Poets,* published during the years 1779–81.

In defining the art of biography, Johnson knew "that definitions are hazardous." Defining a subject is not only saying what a word means but also stating the genus and difference of the thing defined. In his Preface to his *Dictionary* (1755) he wrote: "I am not so lost in lexicography as to forget that words are the daughters of earth and that things are the sons of heaven." Accordingly, his brief essay defines not just a word but the biography as a particularly valuable form of literature. Note how he first defines literature as a genus or class and then assigns biography to that class. The true effects of literature, he goes on to say, are found above all "in narratives of the lives of particular persons; and therefore no species of writing seems more worthy of cultivation than biography. . . ."

Johnson does not rest with definition alone. He develops the definition informally by other methods of exposition. He compares and contrasts biography with history; he gives specific examples of the way a good biography tends to increase knowledge and provide motives for virtue. He describes what a good biography is not—negative definition—and what circumstances are favorable or unfavorable to the writing of biography. In short, Johnson illustrates many of the ways a subject may be explained. If he has not exhausted his subject, he has made it sufficiently clear; his readers understand what biography is and why Johnson regards it as preeminently useful and entertaining.

All joy or sorrow for the happiness or calamities of others is produced by [1] an act of the imagination that realizes the event, however fictitious, or approximates it, however remote, by placing us for a time in the condition of him whose fortune we contemplate; so that we feel, while the deception lasts, whatever motions would be excited by the same good or evil happening to ourselves.

Our passions are therefore more strongly moved, in proportion as we [2] can more readily adopt the pains or pleasure proposed to our minds, by recognizing them as once our own or considering them as naturally incident to our state of life. It is not easy for the most artful writer to give us an interest in happiness or misery, which we think ourselves never likely to feel, and with which we have never yet been made acquainted. Histories of the downfall of kingdoms and revolutions of empires are read with great tranquillity; the imperial tragedy pleases common auditors only by its pomp of ornament and grandeur of ideas; and the man whose faculties have been engrossed by business, and whose heart never fluttered but at the rise or fall of the stocks, wonders how the attention can be seized or the affection agitated by a tale of love.

Those parallel circumstances and kindred images to which we readily [3] conform our minds are, above all other writings, to be found in narratives of the lives of particular persons; and therefore no species of writing seems more worthy of cultivation than biography, since none can be more delightful or more useful, none can more certainly enchain the heart by irresistible interest, or more widely diffuse instruction to every diversity of condition.

The general and rapid narratives of history, which involve a thousand [4] fortunes in the business of a day and complicate innumerable incidents in one great transaction, afford few lessons applicable to private life, which derives its comforts and its wretchedness from the right or wrong management of things which nothing but their frequency makes considerable,

Parva si non fiunt quotidie,[1] says Pliny, and which can have no place in those relations which never descend below the consultation of senates, the motions of armies, and the schemes of conspirators.

[5] I have often thought that there has rarely passed a life of which a judicious and faithful narrative would not be useful. For, not only every man has, in the mighty mass of the world, great numbers in the same condition with himself, to whom his mistakes and miscarriages, escapes and expedients, would be of immediate and apparent use; but there is such an uniformity in the state of man, considered apart from adventitious and separable decorations and disguises, that there is scarce any possibility of good or ill but is common to human kind. A great part of the time of those who are placed at the greatest distance by fortune, or by temper, must unavoidably pass in the same manner; and though, when the claims of nature are satisfied, caprice and vanity and accident begin to produce discriminations and peculiarities, yet the eye is not very heedful or quick which cannot discover the same causes still terminating their influence in the same effects, though sometimes accelerated, sometimes retarded, or perplexed by multiplied combinations. We are all prompted by the same motives, all deceived by the same fallacies, all animated by hope, obstructed by danger, entangled by desire, and seduced by pleasure.

[6] It is frequently objected to relations of particular lives that they are not distinguished by any striking or wonderful vicissitudes. The scholar who passed his life among his books, the merchant who conducted only his own affairs, the priest whose sphere of action was not extended beyond that of his duty, are considered as no proper objects of public regard, however they might have excelled in their several stations, whatever might have been their learning, integrity, and piety. But this notion arises from false measures of excellence and dignity, and must be eradicated by considering that in the esteem of uncorrupted reason what is of most use is of most value.

[7] It is, indeed, not improper to take honest advantages of prejudice and to gain attention by a celebrated name; but the business of the biographer is often to pass slightly over those performances and incidents which produce vulgar greatness, to lead the thoughts into domestic privacies and display the minute details of daily life where exterior appendages are cast aside and men excel each other only by prudence and by virtue. The account of Thuanus[2] is, with great propriety, said by its author to have been written that it might lay open to posterity the private and familiar character of that man, *cuius ingenium et candorem ex ipsius scriptis sunt olim semper miraturi,*[3] whose candor and genius will to the end of time be by his writings preserved in admiration.

---

[1]Those events are trivial that do not occur daily.
[2]Jacques Auguste de Thou (1553–1617), author of *Historia Sui Temporis.*
[3]Johnson's translation appears immediately afterward.

There are many invisible circumstances which, whether we read as en- [8]
quirers after natural or moral knowledge, whether we intend to enlarge our
science or increase our virtue, are more important than public occurrences.
Thus Sallust, the great master of nature, has not forgot, in his account of
Catiline, to remark that "his walk was now quick, and again slow," as an
indication of a mind revolving something with violent commotion. Thus
the story of Melanchthon affords a striking lecture on the value of time by
informing us that when he made an appointment he expected not only the
hour but the minute to be fixed, that the day might not run out in the idle-
ness of suspense; and all the plans and enterprises of De Witt[4] are now of
less importance to the world than that part of his personal character which
represents him as "careful of his health and negligent of his life."

But biography has often been allotted to writers who seem very little [9]
acquainted with the nature of their task, or very negligent about the performance. They rarely afford any other account than might be collected
from public papers, but imagine themselves writing a life when they exhibit
a chronological series of actions or preferments; and so little regard the
manners or behavior of their heroes that more knowledge may be gained
of a man's real character by a short conversation with one of his servants
than from a formal and studied narrative begun with his pedigree and
ended with his funeral.

If now and then they condescend to inform the world of particular facts, [10]
they are not always so happy as to select the most important. I know not
well what advantage posterity can receive from the only circumstance by
which Tickell has distinguished Addison from the rest of mankind, "the
irregularity of his pulse"; nor can I think myself overpaid for the time
spent in reading the life of Malherb by being enabled to relate, after the
learned biographer, that Malherb had two predominant opinions: one,
that the looseness of a single woman might destroy all her boast of ancient
descent; the other, that the French beggars made use very improperly and
barbarously of the phrase "noble Gentleman," because either word included
the sense of both.

There are, indeed, some natural reasons why these narratives are often [11]
written by such as were not likely to give much instruction or delight, and
why most accounts of particular persons are barren and useless. If a life
be delayed till interest and envy are at an end, we may hope for im-
partiality, but must expect little intelligence; for the incidents which give
excellence to biography are of a volatile and evanescent kind, such as soon
escape the memory and are rarely transmitted by tradition. We know
how few can portray a living acquaintance, except by his most prominent
and observable particularities and the grosser features of his mind; and it

[4]Jan de Witt (1625–72), Dutch statesman and friend of the philosopher Spinoza; author
of *Memoirs* (1709).

may be easily imagined how much of this little knowledge may be lost in imparting it, and how soon a succession of copies will lose all resemblance of the original.

[12]   If the biographer writes from personal knowledge, and makes haste to gratify the public curiosity, there is danger lest his interest, his fear, his gratitude, or his tenderness, overpower his fidelity and tempt him to conceal if not to invent. There are many who think it an act of piety to hide the faults or failings of their friends, even when they can no longer suffer by their detection; we therefore see whole ranks of characters adorned with uniform panegyric, and not to be known from one another but by extrinsic and casual circumstances. "Let me remember," says Hale, "when I find myself inclined to pity a criminal, that there is likewise a pity due to the country."[5] If we owe regard to the memory of the dead, there is yet more respect to be paid to knowledge, to virtue, and to truth.

TOPICS FOR DISCUSSION

1. Johnson habitually employed definition even when he did not formally list the terms to be defined or label the defining words as genus and species. Show how *literature* is defined in paragraph 1 and *biography* in succeeding paragraphs. What other terms are defined throughout the essay? How do these definitions contribute to Johnson's main purpose?

2. Like other writers of his age, Johnson regularly developed a series of topic sentences. In the first sentence of paragraph 5 he asserts that a judicious and faithful account of any life is useful. How does he develop this assertion? In the first sentence of paragraph 8 he states that some "invisible circumstances .... are more important than public occurrences." How does he develop this assertion? Pick out topic sentences in several other paragraphs and show how they are developed. Show how each paragraph is related to Johnson's main purpose.

3. A characteristic of Johnson's sentence structure is his fondness for parallels, as in the last sentence of paragraph 5. Point out the parallel structure there. List several other sentences with a marked parallel structure. Show how this kind of structure helps achieve coherence and emphasis.

4. Johnson condemns ignorant or negligent biographers who furnish unimportant facts. Point out the kind of fact Johnson considers important. Do you agree with Johnson's view? Why or why not?

5. Does Violet Bonham Carter's "First Encounter" (p. 229) fulfill Johnson's standards of good biographical writing? Why or why not?

[5]Sir Mathew Hale (1609–76), English jurist and author of *Contributions, Moral and Divine*.

TOPICS FOR COMPOSITION

1. Write an extended definition of one of the terms italicized below. As Johnson does in his essay, develop a definition in the light of the theme stated in each sentence.

   a. True *poetry* contains more intense emotion than ordinary prose.

   b. An effective *composition* is not merely grammatically correct; it is as vivid and emphatic as the subject allows.

   c. *History* is both a record and an interpretation of public events.

   d. *Realistic writing* as illustrated by Defoe and Hersey (pp. 99, 106) succeeds in making you share the experience the author describes.

2. Johnson's remark that "definition is hazardous" assumes that, in addition to normal mistakes, misunderstandings, and changing meanings, some words are emotionally charged, particularly at certain places and times. Analyze the connotations—that is, the emotional suggestions— of one of the words listed below and then write a definition of what the word actually denotes: liberalism, conservatism, progressive, reactionary, new breed, beatnik, in-group. In your composition distinguish carefully between the connotations and the precise denotation you aim at.

GEORGE SAINTSBURY

Two Kinds of Biography

IN his essay on biography Samuel Johnson showed how a biography could be a true work of literature. An early student of the art of biography as well as one of the first successful biographers in English, Johnson's purpose was chiefly to define what was still an emerging literary form. By 1892, however, George Saintsbury was able to include in his survey many biographies that had already achieved the status of classics. The problem, as Saintsbury saw it, was no longer to identify biography as genuine literature, but to discriminate among various kinds of biography. To do this, Saintsbury wisely chose classification and division as his principal methods of analysis.

We use the terms *classification* and *division* to describe closely related modes of analysis. When we classify, we group individual objects under one heading because of common traits. Thus James Boswell's *Johnson*, J. G. Lockhart's *Scott*, Thomas Moore's *Byron*, and Violet Bonham Carter's *Winston Churchill* are grouped in the class of biography because each of them tells the story of an individual life. The basis of their common classification is their common attempt to tell the story of a single person. Division is the reverse of classification. When we divide, we distribute members of a class into smaller groups, again according to some common basis. Thus, Saintsbury first divides the general class biography into two principal kinds: artistic biography, or "biography pure and simple," and mixed biography, or one in which the writer reproduces various kinds of evidence, in the manner of a compiler, to which he adds his own interpretation. Later Saintsbury refers to a third and much inferior class—biography that is compiled without any effort on the part of the biographer to give form to his material.

Saintsbury's distinction supports his clearly stated desire to encourage the kind of biography in which all the evidence "is passed through the mind of a competent intelligent artist" to form "a finished picture, a real composition, not merely a bundle of details and data." The same division, however, might serve merely to clarify the field of biography or, employed by an author with a scientific point of view, to propose the merits of the "mixed" biography favored by Boswell, Moore, and Lockhart and many writers of our day.

All biography is obviously and naturally divided into two kinds. There is [1] the biography pure and simple, in which the whole of the materials is passed through the alembic of the biographer, and in which few if any of these materials appear except in an altered and digested condition. This, though apparently the oldest, is artistically the most perfect kind. Its shortest examples are always its best, and some of the best and shortest are among the best things in literature. The *Agricola* of Tacitus at one end of the list and Southey's *Nelson* almost at the other may save us the trouble of a long enumeration of the masterpieces; while nobody needs to be told that the list ranges from masterpieces like these down to those that *ego vel Cluvienus*[1] may write. There has always been a considerable demand for this sort of thing; but it is not quite the kind of biography which has been specially popular for the last century, and which has produced the famous books to which I have already alluded. This is the kind of "applied" or "mixed" biography, including letters from and to the hero, anecdotes about him, and the like, connected and wrought into a whole by narrative and comment of the author, or, as he sometimes calls himself, the editor. To this belong more or less wholly the great biographies which I shall take for texts, Boswell's *Johnson*, Moore's *Byron*, Lockhart's *Scott*, Carlyle's *Sterling* (much smaller than the others, for reasons, but distinctly on the same lines with them), and, of books more recent, Sir George Trevelyan's *Macaulay*. And to this class also, for reasons very easy to understand, belong almost all the biographies recently produced of men recently living. The reasons I say are easy to find. There is the great popularity of the great examples: there is the demand arising from this popularity; but most of all there is the fatal facility of the proceeding in appearance, and in appearance only.

There can of course be no doubt that to the inexperienced it looks easy [2] enough. In the first kind of biography the writer must to some extent master a considerable quantity of matter and subject it to some kind of intellectual or quasi-intellectual process of his own. At the very worst, the absolutely least, he must frame a sufficient number of sentences in his own head and (unless he dictates) write them with his own fingers—a number sufficient to fill the space between the covers of the book. And, unless he is a quite abnormally stupid or conceited man, he will be more or less conscious that he is doing this well or ill, sufficiently or insufficiently. He cannot to any great extent merely extract or quote. He must create, or at any

[1]Literally, I or Cluvienus, a phrase that concludes a long tirade of Juvenal in his first satire. Juvenal states that his anger at Rome will turn even the worst verse—written by him or even by a hack like Cluvienus—into poetry.

TWO KINDS OF BIOGRAPHY From "Some Great Biographies," *Macmillan's Magazine*, June 1892, pp. 97–107.

rate build, or do something that may at least cheat himself into the idea that he is building or creating.

[3]   The second path is in comparison quite a primrose one. In most cases the biographer by hypothesis finds himself in possession of a certain, often a considerable, stock of material in the way of diaries, letters, and what not. Even if he has struck out the notion of the book for himself and is not ready furnished with his materials by executorship, appointment of friends, and the like, his own unskilled labour or that of a few jackals at public and other libraries will generally stock him amply with all the stuff he wants. Very often this stuff is, in part at least, really interesting. What more simple than to calendar it; to omit whatever is more than is wanted to fill the one, two or three volumes ordered or accepted by the publisher; to string the rest together with a "John-a-Nokes was born on the ——th of ——. Of his earliest years we find" and so on; to insert here and there a reference, a reminiscence, a reflection, or a connecting narrative; and, if the operator be very conscientious, to wind up with an appreciation or summary, "We have thus followed a remarkable (or a painful, as the case may be) career to its close. Had this," and so forth? What, I repeat, more simple?

[4]   "It is not more stiff than that," says the engaging idiom of the Gaul. At any rate there is certainly a large and apparently an increasing number of persons, many of them educated, presumably not unintelligent, certainly not unacquainted with books, things, and men, who consider that there is no greater "stiffness" in it. Any competent critic, even any tolerably intelligent reader who dutifully studies or skims his new volumes from Mudie's,[2] could name books of this kind within the last few years, nay, within the last few months, some of which had no justification whatever for their existence; others which a really skilful hand would have reduced to a small volume or even to an ordinary quarterly essay; others which, though capable of having been made into books of the right sort by the right treatment, had only been made into books of the wrong sort by the wrong treatment. Anybody on the other hand who remembers many thoroughly satisfactory books of the kind for some years past must either be a much more fortunate or a much less fastidious reader and critic than I can pretend to be. . . .

[Saintsbury here analyzes the artistic merits of James Boswell's *Life of Johnson*, Lockhart's *Life of Sir Walter Scott*, Thomas Moore's *Life of Lord Byron*, George Trevelyan's *Life and Letters of Macaulay*, and Carlyle's *Life of John Sterling*.]

[5]   The examples I have taken are pretty well spread over the century (or

[2]Mudie's Circulating Library, founded in 1842 by Charles Edward Mudie.

rather less) in which they all appeared; and though the latest of them made its appearance so to speak yesterday, it is less satisfactory to remember that the subject of that life was born nearly at its beginning, and died very shortly after this nineteenth century had come to the end of its first half. It is quite possible that the materials for biography are not so promising as they used to be. Some persons pretend that the cry about the decay of letter-writing is nonsense. The cautious arguer will confine himself to replying that at any rate there are great temptations not to write letters. Telegrams, postcards, correspondence-cards, letter-cards—all of these things the truly good and wise detest and execrate; it is not quite so certain that they abstain from them. I believe that the habit of keeping a diary has really gone out to a great extent. Too often, moreover, nowadays the unauthorised person steps in with his privateering before the authorised person is ready for sea; and then the authorised person too often indulges in undignified chasings and cannonadings of his predecessor. Above all there seems to have been lost, in this and other things, the all-important sense of proportion in books, and we get "Lives" that would have been excellent in one volume watered out into two, "Lives" that would have been pleasant places in two, becoming pathless deserts in four. These things have had a bad effect on the class of persons who are likely to find biographers. One hears of their destroying materials with a "Please God, nobody shall deal with *me* as —— dealt with ——." Or else, as was the case with Cardinal Newman, they enjoin a method of dealing with their materials, which, though it permits any one of tolerable intelligence to construct a biography for himself with comparatively little difficulty, does not give him the biography actually made. For it cannot be too often repeated that a real biography ought to be something more than the presentation of mere materials, however excellently calendared, something more than Memoirs, Letters, Diary and so forth. The whole ought to be passed through the mind of a competent and intelligent artist, and to be presented to us, not indeed in such a way that we are bound to take his word for the details, but in such a way that we see a finished picture, a real composition, not merely a bundle of details and *data*.

TOPICS FOR DISCUSSION

1. Identify the kinds of biography described in this essay by referring to books other than those mentioned by Saintsbury. Are there kinds of biography besides those Saintsbury includes? If there are other kinds, why do they deserve a separate classification? How would you classify

the biographical essays on Prescott (p. 239) and on Churchill (p. 229)?
Give reasons for your answer.

2. In paragraphs 2 and 3 Saintsbury contrasts "pure" biography with
"mixed" biography. Although Saintsbury recognized that some mixed
biographies, such as Boswell's *Johnson*, are "wholly great," does he
appear to favor pure biography? Why? Saintsbury does not mention
the dangers of the pure biography. Does this mean that "pure biography" is necessarily successful? Or that this kind of biography is without
its own kind of danger? Explain.

3. Are the following sentences accurate statements of Saintsbury's ideas
on biography? Why or why not?
   a. Facts, data, details are relatively unimportant in the composition
   of a good biography.
   b. A pure biography contains many elements found in a mixed biography, while a mixed biography contains none of the elements found
   in a pure biography.
   c. The success of many mixed biographies has unfortunately encouraged inferior writers to imitate the documentation and to
   neglect the art of biography.

TOPICS FOR COMPOSITION

1. In the manner of Saintsbury write a short composition on one of the
following topics: "Two Kinds of Description: Objective and Subjective,"
"Arts and Sciences: Two Kinds of Knowledge," "New Breed and Old
Breed: Two Kinds of Men."

2. Use classification and division in an expository essay explaining your
college to a campus visitor. Begin with a geographical or physical
division of the campus, then proceed to discuss the various schools and
departments. Remember that division is effective when you make the
basis of the division clear and when you account for all the parts of the
subject you discuss.

JONATHAN SWIFT

The Spider and the Bee

"NO ONE shoots well without a target" is a proverb applicable to all writing and particularly to satire, the kind of writing most favored by Jonathan Swift. In his satires Swift's target was some aspect of human folly— political chicanery, religious extremism, human perversity, or, in this instance, a specific attitude toward literature that was based, according to Swift, on pride and ignorance.

Swift wrote *The Battle of the Books* (1697), which contains "The Spider and the Bee," to support the view of his patron, Sir William Temple. Temple's essay *Ancient and Modern Learning* (1690) accused the writers of his time of an exaggerated sense of their own achievements. He contrasted their reliance on the new science, their belief in automatic progress, their trust in the rightness of their own enthusiasms with the ancients' careful search for wisdom among other races and cultures and emphasis on moral, as opposed to scientific, truth. In short, Temple accused his contemporaries of undue intellectual pride.

In 1694 Rev. William Wotton, in his *Reflections on Ancient and Modern Learning,* pointed out that Temple's two principal illustrations of the wisdom of the ancients, Aesop's *Fables* and *The Epistles of Phalaris,* were taken from medieval documents. In a second edition of the *Reflections* the haughty and irascible scholar Richard Bentley, then royal librarian at St. James' Palace, supported Wotton in a brilliant dissertation. Bentley was immediately answered by Charles Boyle of Christ Church, Oxford. Soon the learned world was splitting hairs as to whether Temple, though mistaken on matters of fact, was right in principle, and Wotton and Bentley, though right on matters of fact, were wrong in principle.

Swift chose to defend his patron not by argument on specific issues but by an imaginative sally. In mock-heroic style, he arrayed the great ancients, Homer and Virgil, Aristotle and Plato, against moderns like Dryden and Bentley, Descartes and Milton. The books, surrogates for the men who wrote them, staged their quarrel in St. James' Library. The ancients, admired by Temple, were about to assault the moderns, admired by Wotton and Bentley, when Swift introduces the fable of the spider and the bee.

This fable serves as Swift's exposition of the nature of the quarrel. In the battle that follows, neither side wins, but Swift's sympathies are clearly with the ancients. Wotton and Bentley are portrayed as darlings of the goddess Criticism, herself the offspring of Pride and Ignorance. Though some moderns are spared, Bentley and Wotton are spitted on Boyle's lance. The final metaphor is at once funny and contemptuous:

As, when a skillful cook has trussed a brace of woodcocks, he, with iron skewer, pierces the tender sides of both, their legs and wings close pinioned to their ribs; so was this pair of friends transfixed, till down they fell, joined in their lives, joined in their deaths.

[1]   Things were at this crisis when a material accident fell out. For, upon the highest corner of a large window, there dwelt a certain spider, swollen up to the first magnitude by the destruction of infinite numbers of flies, whose spoils lay scattered before the gates of his palace, like human bones before the cave of some giant. The avenues to his castle were guarded with turn-pikes and palisadoes, all after the modern way of fortification. After you had passed several courts, you came to the centre, wherein you might be-hold the constable himself in his own lodgings, which had windows front-ing to each avenue, and ports to sally out, upon all occasions of prey or defence. In this mansion he had for some time dwelt in peace and plenty, without danger to his person by swallows from above, or to his palace, by brooms from below; when it was the pleasure of fortune to conduct thither a wandering bee, to whose curiosity a broken pane in the glass had dis-covered itself, and in he went; where, expatiating a while, he at last hap-pened to alight upon one of the outward walls of the spider's citadel; which, yielding to the unequal weight, sunk down to the very foundation. Thrice he endeavoured to force his passage, and thrice the centre shook. The spider within, feeling the terrible convulsion, supposed at first that nature was approaching to her final dissolution; or else, that Beelzebub,[1] with all his legions, was come to revenge the death of many thousands of his subjects, whom his enemy had slain and devoured. However, he at length valiantly resolved to issue forth, and meet his fate. Meanwhile the bee had acquitted himself of his toils, and, posted securely at some distance, was employed in cleansing his wings, and disengaging them from the ragged remnants of the cobweb. By this time the spider was adventured out, when, beholding the chasms, the ruins, and dilapidations of his for-tress, he was very near at his wit's end; he stormed and swore like a mad-man, and swelled till he was ready to burst. At length, casting his eye upon the bee, and wisely gathering causes from events (for they knew each other by sight) : "A plague split you," said he, "for a giddy son of a whore.

[1]A prince of devils, here represented as lord protector of the flies.

Is it you, with a vengeance, that have made this litter here? Could not you look before you, and be d—d? Do you think I have nothing else to do (in the devil's name) but to mend and repair after your arse?" "Good words, friend," said the bee (having now pruned himself, and being disposed to droll), "I'll give you my hand and word to come near your kennel no more; I was never in such a confounded pickle since I was born." "Sirrah," replied the spider, "if it were not for breaking an old custom in our family, never to stir abroad against an enemy, I should come and teach you better manners." "I pray have patience," said the bee, "or you'll spend your substance, and, for aught I see, you may stand in need of it all, toward the repair of your house." "Rogue, rogue," replied the spider, "yet, methinks you should have more respect to a person, whom all the world allows to be so much your betters. "By my troth," said the bee, "the comparison will amount to a very good jest, and you will do me a favour to let me know the reasons that all the world is pleased to use in so hopeful a dispute." At this the spider, having swelled himself into the size and posture of a disputant, began his argument in the true spirit of controversy, with a resolution to be heartily scurrilous and angry, to urge on his own reasons, without the least regard to the answers or objections of his opposite, and fully predetermined in his mind against all conviction.

"Not to disparage myself," said he, "by the comparison with such a [2] rascal, what art thou but a vagabond without house or home, without stock or inheritance, born to no possession of your own, but a pair of wings and a drone-pipe. Your livelihood is a universal plunder upon nature; a freebooter over fields and gardens; and, for the sake of stealing, will rob a nettle as easily as a violet. Whereas I am a domestic animal, furnished with a native stock within myself. This large castle (to shew my improvements in the mathematics[2]) is all built with my own hands, and the materials extracted altogether out of my own person."

"I am glad," answered the bee, "to hear you grant at least that I am [3] come honestly by my wings and my voice; for then, it seems, I am obliged to Heaven alone for my flights and my music; and Providence would never have bestowed on me two such gifts, without designing them for the noblest ends. I visit indeed all the flowers and blossoms of the field and garden; but whatever I collect thence enriches myself, without the least injury to their beauty, their smell, or their taste. Now, for you and your skill in architecture, and other mathematics, I have little to say. In that building of yours there might, for aught I know, have been labour and method enough; but, by woeful experience for us both, it is plain the materials are naught, and I hope you will henceforth take warning, and consider duration and matter, as well as method and art. You boast, indeed,

[2]The Moderns admired science, particularly mathematics, which they regarded as original.

Jonathan Swift

of being obliged to no other creature, but of drawing and spinning out all from yourself; that is to say, if we may judge of the liquor in the vessel by what issues out, you possess a good plentiful store of dirt and poison in your breast; and, though I would by no means lessen or disparage your genuine stock of either, yet I doubt you are somewhat obliged, for an increase of both, to a little foreign assistance. Your inherent portion of dirt does not fail of acquisitions, by sweepings exhaled from below; and one insect furnishes you with a share of poison to destroy another. So that, in short, the question comes all to this—whether is the nobler being of the two, that which, by a lazy contemplation of four inches round, by an overweening pride, feeding and engendering on itself, turns all into excrement and venom, producing nothing at all but flybane and a cobweb; or that which, by a universal range, with long search, much study, true judgment, and distinction of things, brings home honey and wax."

[4]   This dispute was managed with such eagerness, clamour, and warmth, that the two parties of books, in arms below, stood silent a while, waiting in suspense what would be the issue, which was not long undetermined. For the bee, grown impatient at so much loss of time, fled straight away to a bed of roses, without looking for a reply, and left the spider, like an orator, collected in himself, and just prepared to burst out.

[5]   It happened upon this emergency, that Aesop broke silence first. He had been of late most barbarously treated by a strange effect of the regent's humanity,[3] who had torn off his title-page, sorely defaced one half of his leaves, and chained him fast among a shelf of Moderns. Where, soon discovering how high the quarrel was like to proceed, he tried all his arts, and turned himself to a thousand forms. At length, in the borrowed shape of an ass, the regent mistook him for a Modern; by which means he had time and opportunity to escape to the Ancients, just when the spider and the bee were entering into their contest, to which he gave his attention with a world of pleasure; and when it was ended, swore in the loudest key that in all his life he had never known two cases so parallel and adapt to each other, as that in the window, and this upon the shelves. "The disputants," said he, "have admirably managed the dispute between them, have taken in the full strength of all that is to be said on both sides, and exhausted the substance of every argument *pro* and *con*. It is but to adjust the reasonings of both to the present quarrel, then to compare and apply the labours and fruits of each, as the bee has learnedly deduced them, and we shall find the conclusion fall plain and close upon the Moderns and us. For, pray, gentlemen, was ever anything so modern as the spider in his air, his turns, and his paradoxes? He argues in the behalf of you his brethren and himself, with many boastings of his native stock and great genius, that he

[3]The regent was Bentley. *Humanity* is used ironically.

spins and spits wholly from himself, and scorns to own any obligation or assistance from without. Then he displays to you his great skill in architecture, and improvement in the mathematics. To all this the bee, as an advocate retained by us the Ancients, thinks fit to answer, that, if one may judge of the great genius or inventions of the Moderns by what they have produced, you will hardly have countenance to bear you out, in boasting of either. Erect your schemes with as much method and skill as you please; yet if the materials be nothing but dirt, spun out of your own entrails (the guts of modern brains), the edifice will conclude at last in a cobweb, the duration of which, like that of other spiders' webs, may be imputed to their being forgotten, or neglected, or hid in a corner. For anything else of genuine that the Moderns may pretend to, I cannot recollect; unless it be a large vein of wrangling and satire, much of a nature and substance with the spider's poison; which, however they pretend to spit wholly out of themselves, is improved by the same arts, by feeding upon the insects and vermin of the age. As for us the Ancients, we are content, with the bee, to pretend to nothing of our own, beyond our wings and our voice, that is to say, our flights and our language. For the rest, whatever we have got has been by infinite labour and search, and ranging through every corner of nature; the difference is, that, instead of dirt and poison, we have rather chosen to fill our hives with honey and wax, thus furnishing mankind with the two noblest of things, which are sweetness and light."

TOPICS FOR DISCUSSION

1. How does the description of the palace help to identify the spider as a symbol of the "Modern"? How is the bee identified as a symbol of the Ancients? Point to passages that reveal whether Swift preferred the Ancients to the Moderns.

2. In paragraph 5, Aesop draws out the parallels between the spider and the Moderns and the bee and the Ancients. List all the many parallels you can find. In what sense are these parallels "exact"? Keep in mind that a parallel or comparison is said to be exact or strict when the two objects compared are of the same kind and when they are compared with reference to the same measure or standard.

3. In paragraph 5, Aesop also contrasts the spider and the bee; he points out the precise points of difference between them. In what respect is this contrast effective? In what respect could it be regarded as illogical?

4. Look up *allegory*. To what extent can this passage be considered allegorical? Which level of meaning—the concrete or the abstract—is the more important?

TOPICS FOR COMPOSITION

1. Many authors have presented their point of view through fables; George Orwell's *Animal Farm* (1954) is a modern example. Write a fable on a theme of your own choice. Make sure that you clearly identify your animal character with a person or with a human trait, and draw out the implication of your fable. Several typical situations are listed below:

   a. the grasshopper (merely spontaneous activity) and the ant (purposeful activity)

   b. the tortoise (sustained effort) and the hare (interrupted effort)

   c. the eagle (intellectual power) and the mole (common sense)

2. Write a satirical essay exposing some aspect of human folly or ignorance that you think particularly harmful at this time. Compare and contrast the trait you condemn with its opposite. Some possible subjects are: illogical advertisements, such as the identification of effective mouth wash with success in business; contradictory advice, such as advice to study for a degree to earn more money and to choose subjects for their intrinsic merit; absurd protests, such as a student strike for the right not to study.

3. Swift's contemporary readers derived part of their pleasure from his mock-heroic style—that is, his imitation of the ornate diction and elaborate rhetorical structure of epic and other heroic poems of his own period. Assuming that twentieth-century readers derive greater pleasure from a shorter, sharper exposition of the central idea, rewrite Swift's fable in idiomatic modern English. Wherever necessary substitute words in current usage for archaic expressions like *turnpikes, palisadoes, ports,* and *adventured out* in paragraph 1. Restructure the sentences and paragraphs to conform to current usage. Revise the punctuation when necessary.

PIERRE TEILHARD DE CHARDIN

Humanity in Progress

PIERRE TEILHARD DE CHARDIN, a French geologist and paleontologist, wrote extensively on science with particular attention to the evolution of animate matter. His scientific works, many of which are addressed to non-scientists, inspired him to speculations on the evolution of the universe. In the following passage, he explains the universe through comparisons. What is the world like? It is a process. In one negative comparison he tells what the process is not like. In a positive comparison, he points out the resemblance of the process to gestation and birth.

Clearly, in a scientific treatise these comparisons would require elaborate development and less poetic language. The *Hymn of the Universe* (1965), from which this passage is taken, is, however, a scientist's poetic reponse to his scientific knowledge. If the aim of scientific language, writes Simon Bartholomew, the translator of this passage, "is to provide exactly defined and unambiguous statements *about* reality, that of poetic language is to communicate reality itself, as experienced, by means of imagery. . . ." Hence the value of Teilhard's comparisons, as of those in Swift's fable, is their effectiveness in making the reader understand and share the writer's attitude and feeling toward his subject. (For strictly logical comparison, see p. 12.)

The world is a-building. This is the basic truth which must first be understood so thoroughly that it becomes an habitual and as it were natural springboard for our thinking. At first sight, beings and their destinies might seem to us to be scattered haphazard or at least in an arbitrary fashion over the face of the earth; we could very easily suppose that each of us might *equally well* have been born earlier or later, at this place or that, happier or more ill-starred, as though the universe from the beginning to end of its history formed in space-time a sort of vast flower-bed in which the flowers could be changed about at the whim of the gardener. But this idea is surely untenable. The more one reflects, with the help of all that science, philosophy and religion can teach us, each in its own field, the more one comes to realize that the world should be likened not to a bundle of elements artificially held together but rather to some organic system animated by a broad movement of development which is proper to

---

HUMANITY IN PROGRESS From *Hymn of the Universe* by Pierre Teilhard de Chardin. Reprinted by permission of Harper & Row, publishers.

itself. As the centuries go by it seems that a comprehensive plan is indeed being slowly carried out around us. A process is at work in the universe, an issue is at stake, which can best be compared to the processes of gestation and birth; the birth of that spiritual reality which is formed by souls and by such material reality as their existence involves. Laboriously, through and thanks to the activity of mankind, the new earth is being formed and purified and is taking on definition and clarity. No, we are not like the cut flowers that make up a bouquet: we are like the leaves and buds of a great tree on which everything appears at its proper time and place as required and determined by the good of the whole.

TOPICS FOR DISCUSSION

1. Explore the gardener–flower-bed explanation of the world. How does it imply that the world is governed by arbitrary laws? By whim? By artificial rules? Why does Teilhard appear to reject this explanation?
2. Explore the comparison between the process of the world's a-building and the process of gestation and birth. Show how this comparison implies an organic system. Does it also imply human activity that is somehow separate from the organic system of which it is a part? Explain your answer.
3. Show how Teilhard's vocabulary reflects his awareness of "science, philosophy, and religion" by picking out words and expressions proper to each field. Point out several expressions that have come into use in recent years.

TOPICS FOR COMPOSITION

1. Develop one of the subjects below by using two comparisons: one showing what the subject is not like, one showing what it is like.
   a. a nation—not like a country club, but like a family
   b. a liberally educated man—not like a cistern, but like a well
   c. a citizen—not like the audience at a play, but like an actor
   d. a true friend—not like a flatterer, but like a conscience
2. Write a short essay on "A Student in Progress" in which you develop as your basic truth the organic nature of learning. You might contrast merely departmentalized knowledge with interrelated knowledge.

HENRY FIELDING

The Character of a Novelist

FIELDING'S *Tom Jones* (1749) is praised chiefly because the deeds of its abundant, amusing, and boisterous characters are flumed through a brilliantly intricate plot and reported in an inimitably energetic style. The book bespeaks its author, a tall, handsome man, aristocratic by birth and intellectual formation, yet democratic in instinct and experience. Often studied as a dramatist, journalist, and novelist, Fielding is less often appreciated as a critic. Yet literary criticism was, in a sense, as important in stirring him to write as was his desire to entertain, to correct the follies and vices of his time, to set forth his own particular philosophy of rational benevolence, and to make a living.

Fielding's first novel, *Joseph Andrews* (1742), parodied Samuel Richardson's *Pamela* (1740), one of the best sellers of the day, exposing in the process what Fielding regarded as a grossly sentimental picture of life. His *Jonathan Wild* (1743) satirized another eighteenth-century fad, the romantic exaltation of the criminal. Indeed, it was not until he wrote *Tom Jones* that Fielding told a story directly for its own sake and not as an answer to, or a comment on, some specific novel or type of novel he regarded as contemptible. Even in *Tom Jones*, however, Fielding is criticizing manners and morals.

The whole conception of *Tom Jones* is antiromantic. Tom, the hero, is, euphemistically, not without blemish. Romantic love is presented, but in humble proportions. The romantic tendency to whiten the hero and blacken the villain is replaced by the realistic tendency to paint the warts on virtue and the rouge on vice. Fielding, in short, makes serious points about life in a deliberate way. What is implied in his plot and arrangement of characters is explicitly stated in his prefatory letter to George Lyttleton and in the essays that serve as prefaces to the individual parts of *Tom Jones*.

In these prefaces Fielding touches on virtually every problem he faced as a novelist: his effort to write a true yet fictitious history as opposed to a romance; his manner of achieving his moral purpose; the role of satire; the office of the critic; the justification for the realistic portrayal of human love and religious hypocrisy; the place of the marvelous in fiction.

The following essay appears in Book IX, Chapter 1, of *Tom Jones*. It sums up many points treated in Fielding's earlier critical essays.

[1]   To invent good stories, and to tell them well, are possibly very rare talents, and yet I have observed few persons who have scrupled to aim at both: and if we examine the romances and novels with which the world abounds, I think we may fairly conclude, that most of the authors would not have attempted to show their teeth (if the expression may be allowed me) in any other way of writing; nor could indeed have strung together a dozen sentences on any other subject whatever. *Scribimus indocti doctique passim,*[1] may be more truly said of the historian and biographer than of any other species of writing; for all the arts and sciences (even criticism itself) require some little degree of learning and knowledge. Poetry, indeed, may perhaps be thought an exception; but then it demands numbers, or something like numbers: whereas, to the composition of novels and romances, nothing is necessary but paper, pens, and ink, with the manual capacity of using them. This, I conceive, their productions show to be the opinion of the authors themselves: and this must be the opinion of their readers, if indeed there be any such.

[2]   Hence we are to derive that universal contempt which the world, who always denominate the whole from the majority, have cast on all historical writers who do not draw their materials from records. And it is the apprehension of this contempt that hath made us so cautiously avoid the term romance, a name with which we might otherwise have been well enough contented. Though, as we have good authority for all our characters, no less indeed than the vast authentic Doomsday-Book of Nature, as is elsewhere hinted, our labours have sufficient title to the name of history. Certainly they deserve some distinction from those works, which one of the wittiest of men regarded only as proceeding from a *pruritus,*[2] or indeed rather from a looseness of the brain.

[3]   But besides the dishonour which is thus cast on one of the most useful as well as entertaining of all kinds of writing, there is just reason to apprehend, that by encouraging such authors we shall propagate much dishonour of another kind; I mean to the characters of many good and valuable members of society; for the dullest writers, no more than the dullest companions, are always inoffensive. They have both enough of language to be indecent and abusive. And surely if the opinion just above cited be true, we cannot wonder that works so nastily derived should be nasty themselves, or have a tendency to make others so.

[4]   To prevent, therefore, for the future such intemperate abuses of leisure, of letters, and of the liberty of the press, especially as the world seems at

---

[1]Each desperate blockhead dares to write:
Verse is the trade of every living wight.
                    Francis
               [Fielding's note]
[2]Intense itching.

present to be more than usually threatened with them, I shall here venture to mention some qualifications, every one of which are in a pretty high degree necessary to this order of historians.

The first is, genius, without a full vein of which no study, says Horace, [5] can avail us. By genius I would understand that power, or rather those powers of the mind, which are capable of penetrating into all things within our reach and knowledge, and of distinguishing their essential differences. These are no other than invention and judgment; and they are both called by the collective name of genius, as they are of those gifts of nature which we bring with us into the world. Concerning each of which many seem to have fallen into very great errors; for by invention, I believe, is generally understood a creative faculty, which would indeed prove most romance writers to have the highest pretensions to it; whereas by invention is really meant no more (and so the word signifies) than discovery, or finding out; or to explain it at large, a quick and sagacious penetration into the true essence of all the objects of our contemplation. This, I think, can rarely exist without the concomitancy of judgment; for how we can be said to have discovered the true essence of two things, without discerning their difference, seems to me hard to conceive. Now this last is the undisputed province of judgment, and yet some few men of wit have agreed with all the dull fellows in the world in representing these two to have been seldom or never the property of one and the same person.

But though they should be so, they are not sufficient for our purpose, [6] without a good share of learning; for which I could again cite the authority of Horace, and of many others, if any was necessary to prove that tools are of no service to a workman, when they are not sharpened by art, or when he wants rules to direct him in his work, or hath no matter to work upon. All these uses are supplied by learning; for nature can only furnish us with capacity; or, as I have chose to illustrate it, with the tools of our profession; learning must fit them for use, must direct them in it, and, lastly, must contribute part at least of the materials. A competent knowledge of history and of the belles-lettres is here absolutely necessary; and without this share of knowledge at least, to affect the character of an historian, is as vain as to endeavour at building a house without timber or mortar, or brick or stone. Homer and Milton, who, though they added the ornament of numbers to their works, were both historians of our order, were masters of all the learning of their times.

Again, there is another sort of knowledge, beyond the power of learn- [7] ing to bestow, and this is to be had by conversation. So necessary is this to the understanding the characters of men, that none are more ignorant of them than those learned pedants whose lives have been entirely consumed in colleges and among books; for however exquisitely human nature may have been described by writers, the true practical system can be

Henry Fielding

learnt only in the world. Indeed the like happens in every other kind of knowledge. Neither physic nor law are to be practically known from books. Nay, the farmer, the planter, the gardener, must perfect by experience what he hath acquired the rudiments of by reading. How accurately soever the ingenious Mr. Miller[3] may have described the plant, he himself would advise his disciple to see it in the garden. As we must perceive, that after the nicest strokes of a Shakespeare or a Jonson, of a Wycherly or an Otway, some touches of nature will escape the reader, which the judicious action of a Garrick, of a Cibber, or a Clive,[4] can convey to him; so, on the real stage, the character shows himself in a stronger and bolder light than he can be described. And if this be the case in those fine and nervous descriptions which great authors themselves have taken from life, how much more strongly will it hold when the writer himself takes his lines not from nature, but from books? Such characters are only the faint copy of a copy, and can have neither the justness nor spirit of an original.

[8]   Now this conversation in our historian must be universal, that is, with all ranks and degrees of men; for the knowledge of what is called high life will not instruct him in low; nor, *é converso*,[5] will his being acquainted with the inferior part of mankind teach him the manners of the superior. And though it may be thought that the knowledge of either may sufficiently enable him to describe at least that in which he hath been conversant, yet he will ever here fall greatly short of perfection; for the follies of either rank do in reality illustrate each other. For instance, the affectation of high life appears more glaring and ridiculous from the simplicity of the low; and again, the rudeness and barbarity of this latter, strikes with much stronger ideas of absurdity when contrasted with, and opposed to, the politeness which controls the former. Besides, to say the truth, the manners of our historians will be improved by both these conversations; for in the one he will easily find examples of plainness, honesty, and sincerity; in the other of refinement, elegance, and a liberality of spirit; which last quality I myself have scarce ever seen in men of low birth and education.

[9]   Nor will all the qualities I have hitherto given my historian avail him, unless he have what is generally meant by a good heart, and be capable of feeling. The author who will make me weep, says Horace, must first weep himself. In reality, no man can paint a distress well which he doth not feel while he is painting it; nor do I doubt, but that the most pathetic and affecting scenes have been writ with tears. In the same manner it is with the ridiculous. I am convinced I never make my reader laugh heartily but where I have laughed before him; unless it should happen at any time,

[3]Philip Miller, author of *The Gardener's Dictionary* and foreman of the Chelsea Garden.
[4]David Garrick (1717–79) was the most celebrated actor of his day. *Cibber* probably refers to actress Susannah Maria Cibber, who worked with Garrick. Kitty Clive (1711–85) was a comic actress greatly praised by Garrick and Samuel Johnson as well as by Fielding.
[5]Literally, on the contrary.

that instead of laughing with me he should be inclined to laugh at me. Perhaps this may have been the case at some passages in this chapter, from which apprehension I will here put an end to it.

TOPICS FOR DISCUSSION

1. In paragraph 4, Fielding states his main purpose, to describe the qualifications of "this order of historian," namely the novelist. In each of the succeeding paragraphs he defines and explains those qualifications. Are the first three paragraphs necessary to clarify his main theme? Explain why or why not. Comment on his implied distinction between the novel and the romance. How does he distinguish between the historian or biographer and the novelist, whom he also calls a historian?

2. Show how Fielding's definition of *genius* involves definitions of *invention* and *judgment*. Why are all three terms linked? Why does Fielding appear to reject creativity as a genuine element of *invention?* In current usage, what do *invention* and *creativity* mean?

3. Fielding divides learning into (a) knowledge of history and literature and (b) conversation. What does *conversation* mean according to Fielding's usage? Why are both kinds of learning equally necessary?

4. Fielding explains what is meant by "a good heart" by describing the cause and effect relationship stated in the proverb, "No one gives what he has not got." Is Fielding's explanation convincing? Why or why not?

5. Fielding's emphasis on learning and his minimization of creativity are reminiscent of Swift's attitudes toward literature in "The Spider and the Bee." Show how the attitudes of both are similar in several important respects. Show how they differ in the manner of presenting their ideas. In what respect do you think each essay is effective? In what respect ineffective? Explain your answer.

TOPICS FOR COMPOSITION

1. Use Fielding's method of explaining the qualifications of a good novelist to set forth the qualifications of one of the following subjects: a good student, a successful teacher, a good actor, a worthy journalist. You will give point to your essay if you aim at popular misapprehensions about the subject you are attempting to explain.

2. Probably you have formed your own view of the qualifications of a good novelist. Compare and contrast your view with that of Fielding. Use some specific novelist as the basis of your comparison.

3. Write a review of a novel assigned by your instructor using the standards set forth by Fielding.

SAUL
BELLOW

Mind
over
Chatter

OVER two hundred years after Fielding told us who should write novels, Saul Bellow, an outstanding American writer, addressed himself to a similar subject. In his speech on the occasion of the presentation of the 1965 National Book Awards, he did not set out to tell his audience of writers, critics, and publishers how to write a good novel. To discuss the technicalities of plot and style or to name fashionable subjects and attitudes would have been talking down to his sophisticated audience and probably would have raised debatable issues peripheral to his main purpose.

That purpose was to speak about a special situation, the literary state of mind of this immediate generation. Along with many mature writers, Bellow was depressed by the tone of many current novels and poems—literature often rebellious without cause, dogmatically anti-social, offensively egotistic. He saw the tendency as self-defeating, one that cut off the writer from humanity and hence from access to the human truths without which the novel and the poem tend to become insignificant. The occasion, as well as Bellow's own experience as a novelist (see Biography), defined his purpose: to urge the writer to abandon his indifference and detachment and "to fight for justice and equality" and to begin by using his intelligence. Many of Bellow's attitudes resemble those of Fielding, suggesting once again that continuity as well as change is a constant in human experience.

[1] The fact that there are so many weak, poor, and boring stories and novels written and published in America has been ascribed by our rebels to the horrible squareness of our institutions, the idiocy of power, the debasement of sexual instincts, and the failure of writers to be alienated enough. The poems and novels of these same rebellious spirits, and their theoretical statements, are grimy and gritty and very boring too, besides being nonsensical, and it is evident by now that polymorphous sexuality and vehement declarations of alienation are not going to produce great works of art either.

[2] There is nothing left for us novelists to do but think. For unless we

think, unless we make a clearer estimate of our condition, we will continue to write kid stuff, to fail in our function, we will lack serious interests and become truly irrelevant. Here the critics must share the blame, for they too have failed to describe the situation. Literature has for several generations been its own source, its own province, has lived upon its own traditions, and accepted a romantic separation or estrangement from the common world. This estrangement, though it produced some masterpieces, has by now enfeebled the novel.

The separatism of writers is accompanied by the more or less conscious [3] acceptance of a theory of modern civilization. This theory says in effect that modern mass society is frightful, brutal, hostile to whatever is pure in the human spirit, a wasteland and a horror. To its ugliness, its bureau-cratic regimes, its thefts, its lies, its wars, and its unparalleled cruelties, the artist can never be reconciled. This is one of the traditions on which con-temporary literature has lived uncritically. But it is the task of artists and critics in their own day to look with their own eyes. Perhaps they will see evils even worse than those they have taken for granted, but they will at least be seeing for themselves. They will not, they can not, permit them-selves, generation after generation, to hold views they have not individu-ally examined. By refusing to look at civilization with our own eyes we lose the right to call ourselves artists; we have accepted what we ourselves condemn—received opinion, professionalism, snobbery and the formation of a caste. And unfortunately the postures of this caste, postures of libera-tion and independence and creativity, are attractive to poor souls dream-ing everywhere of a fuller, freer life.

The writer is admired, the writer is envied. But what has he to say for [4] himself? Why, he says, just as writers have said for more than a century, that he is cut off from the life of his own society, that he is despised by its overlords who are cynical about intellectuals and have nothing but con-tempt for the artist, and that he is without a true public, estranged. He dreams of ages when the poet or the painter expressed a perfect unit of time and place, had real acceptance, and enjoyed a vital harmony with his surroundings—he dreams of a golden age. In fact, without the golden age, there is no wasteland.

Well, this is no age of gold. It is only what it is. Can we do no more [5] than complain about it? We writers have better choices. We can either shut up because the times are too bad, or continue writing because we have an instinct for it, a talent to develop, which even in these disfigured times we cannot suppress. Isolated professionalism is death. Without the com-mon world the novelist is nothing but a curiosity and will find himself in a glass case along some dull museum corridor of the future.

Mechanization and bureaucracy are permanently with us. We cannot [6] pretend the technological revolution has not occurred. We are its beneficiaries; we may also become its slaves. The first necessity, therefore, is to fight for justice and equality. The artist, along with everyone else, must fight for his life, for his freedom. This is not to advise the novelist to rush immediately into the political sphere. But to begin with he must begin to use his intelligence, long unused. If he is to reject politics, he must understand what he is rejecting. He must begin to think, and to think not merely of his own narrower interests and needs, but of the common world he has for so long failed to see. If he thinks his alienation has much significance, he is wrong. It is nine-tenths cant. If he thinks his rebellion significant, he is wrong again because the world is far more revolutionary in being simply what it is. In their attempts to imitate power, *Realpolitik*,[1] by violence or vehemence, writers simply make themselves foolish. The "romantic criminal" or desperado cannot get within miles of the significant human truth. It is with this truth that the writer must be concerned.

TOPICS FOR DISCUSSION

1. What reasons do the "rebels" assign for the weakness of the contemporary American novel? What does Bellow think of these reasons? What principal reason does Bellow assign for the present state of fiction? What is his solution to the problem? Where does he state that solution at greatest length?

2. How is "isolated professionalism" (paragraph 5) related to "alienation" (paragraph 1), "estrangement" (paragraph 2), "separation" (paragraph 3), "dreams of a golden age" (paragraph 4) and "the romantic criminal" (paragraph 6)? Why does Bellow believe that isolated professionalism is death for the novelist?

3. Show how Bellow's emphasis on thought in this essay is related to Fielding's emphasis on genius. Point out other similarities between Bellow's idea of the noval and Fielding's ideas. In what respects do Bellow and Fielding differ?

4. What are some other qualifications for a good novelist besides those mentioned by Bellow and Fielding? Why are they important?

5. Bellow, in this passage, does not name authors and books to illustrate what he means by novelists who fight for justice and equality and novelists who are isolated professionals. Name some specific examples of each group. Discuss one novel in the light of Bellow's ultimate test—"significant human truth."

[1]Literally, realistic politics; the politics of violence.

TOPICS FOR COMPOSITION

1. Many writers explain their ideas by analysis of cause and effect as Bellow does in this essay. Note how Bellow begins by stating an effect—the fact that so many modern novels are weak. He then examines the alleged causes of that weakness, which he rejects. Afterwards he presents what he believes to be the true cause of the weakness—separatism, alienation, isolated professionalism, and so on. In like manner write a brief essay explaining the causes of one of the following situations:
   a. mediocre television programs
   b. the apathy of citizens toward civil rights
   c. the decline of reading for recreation
   d. the increasing public respect for the Peace Corps
   e. the respectability of informal dress
2. In consultation with your instructor, choose a novelist you regard as outstanding. Examine one of his works from the point of view of the standards developed through your study of Bellow and Fielding.

Argument and Persuasion

EDMUND BURKE

The Speech on Moving His Resolutions
for Conciliation with the Colonies

When Edmund Burke rose in the House of Commons on March 22, 1775, to present his resolutions for conciliation with the American colonies, he had been a Member of Parliament since 1765 and was England's foremost authority on the affairs of the American colonies. In 1757 he had helped write *An Account of the European Settlements in America,* a work largely devoted to the North American colonies. The next year, as editor of the *Annual Register,* he began his regular reports on the Seven Years War (1756–63), again concentrating on the affairs of the North American colonies. As private secretary to Lord Rockingham, who at that time was Prime Minister, Burke guided the repeal of the Stamp Act through Parliament. As relations between the colonies and the mother country continued to deteriorate under the administration of Rockingham's successor, Lord North, Burke became an increasingly important spokesman for reconciliation. In 1770, the year of the Boston Massacre, in *Thoughts on the Present Discontents,* Burke attacked the abuse of power and the failure to apply principles in the light of historical developments and changing circumstances.

After Burke was named agent for the New York colonial assembly in 1771, he became even more identified with the cause of the colonies. In his speech *On American Taxation* in 1774, he urged that Parliament, on the basis of English constitutional procedures, allow America to tax herself.

> Such, sir, is my idea of the Constitution of the British Empire, as distinguished from the Constitution of Britain; and on these grounds I think subordination and liberty may be sufficiently recognized throughout the whole—whether to serve a refining speculatist or a factious demogogue I know not, but enough surely for the ease and happiness of man.

His speech *On Conciliation with the Colonies,* delivered in 1775, shows that he had become a master of the facts. But he was also much more: he was a master political philosopher, balancing the equal claims of authority and liberty, justice and expediency, conservatism and progress. He gave to his *Conciliation* speech depth and solidity and insured its permanence as a classic of political thought.

Further, Burke added to his knowledge and thought superb powers of expression. He had made his reputation as a writer long before his entrance into politics. His *Vindication of Natural Society* (1757) was an exercise in irony comparable to that of his countryman Swift; his essay *Sublime and Beautiful,* published in the same year, showed him to be a practical stylist as well as a literary theorist. Regular contributions to the

Annual Register, as well as association with leading writers and actors of his day, sharpened his talent for speaking and writing. In addition, since his early days at Trinity College, Dublin, Burke had been a consistent student of the art of rhetoric. He read Cicero throughout his life, quoted him more often than any other author, and made use of his lucid yet complex style. To judge by unpublished manuscripts in the Fitzwilliam collection at Cambridge University, Burke may have planned to write a study of the art of rhetoric. His writings clearly embody a theory not unlike Cicero's, that the orator was *bonus vir dicens,* the good man speaking the whole truth of his mind.

Burke had two great advantages: his own genius and the presence of a brilliantly literate audience. Hence the high level of his language—reflected in its diction, its range of allusion, its lengthy and complex sentence structure—is at once a challenge and a reward to the modern reader.

I. THE INTRODUCTION [1–4]

Exordium or Beginning

Burke's introduction consists of the exordium, the history of the case, the statement of the proposition, the exposition of the principles relevant to the proposition, and the formal statement of the issues and the order of the proof to follow. The introduction is lengthy partly because the subject was complicated by parliamentary maneuvers, partly because emotions were intensified by American resistance, and partly because Burke's characteristic method was, in Oliver Goldsmith's language, "to wind into his subject like a serpent."

¶1   Burke clearly states his subject, attempts to arouse interest and to create a favorable attitude.

The grand penal bill   Burke makes clear his subject—the act in restraint of trade, which cut off all trade of the American colonies except with Great Britain.

Fortunate omens   He attempts to create a favorable atmosphere.

I look upon it   He arouses interest and cercern by reference to the gravity of the subject.

EDMUND BURKE

The Speech on Moving His Resolutions
for Conciliation with the Colonies

✝

I hope, Sir, that, notwithstanding the austerity of the Chair, your good-   [1]
nature will incline you to some degree of indulgence towards human frailty.
You will not think it unnatural, that those who have an object depending,
which strongly engages their hopes and fears, should be somewhat inclined
to superstition. As I came into the House, full of anxiety about the event
of my motion, I found, to my infinite surprise, that the grand penal bill by
which we had passed sentence on the trade and sustenance of America is
to be returned to us from the other House. I do confess, I could not help
looking on this event as a fortunate omen. I look upon it as a sort of
Providential favor by which we are put once more in possession of our
deliberative capacity, upon a business so very questionable in its nature, so
very uncertain in its issue. By the return of this bill, which seemed to have
taken its flight forever, we are at this very instant nearly as free to choose
a plan for our American government as we were on the first day of the

History of the Case

¶2 Burke relates the history of the American problem, beginning with his own entrance into Parliament in 1765. American affairs had long demanded Burke's attention. The rhetorical effect of this passage is to establish his authority to discuss the subject.

¶3 *Perfect concurrence* Burke refers here to the repeal of the Stamp Act on March 18, 1766, during the prime-ministership of Lord Rockingham, whom he served as secretary. Burke further establishes his authority by referring to his own consistency.

¶4 *Frequent changes* Parliament reverted to repressive measures against the colonies by passing the Townshend Acts (1767), the tea tax, and other restraints.

¶5 *A worthy member* Mr. Rose Fuller. In this paragraph, Burke explains how the political situation requires him to offer a plan for peace.

session. If, Sir, we incline to the side of conciliation, we are not at all embarrassed (unless we please to make ourselves so) by any incongruous mixture of coercion and restraint. We are therefore called upon, as it were by a superior warning voice, again to attend to America—to attend to the whole of it together,—and to review the subject with an unusual degree of care and calmness.

Surely it is an awful subject,—or there is none so on this side of the [2] grave. When I first had the honor of a seat in this House, the affairs of that continent pressed themselves upon us as the most important and most delicate object of Parliamentary attention. My little share in this great deliberation oppressed me. I found myself a partaker in a very high trust; and having no sort of reason to rely on the strength of my natural abilities for the proper execution of that trust, I was obliged to take more than common pains to instruct myself in everything which relates to our colonies. I was not less under the necessity of forming some fixed ideas concerning the general policy of the British empire. Something of this sort seemed to be indispensable, in order, amidst so vast a fluctuation of passions and opinions, to concentre my thoughts, to ballast my conduct, to preserve me from being blown about by every wind of fashionable doctrine. I really did not think it safe or manly to have fresh principles to seek upon every fresh mail which should arrive from America.

At that period I had the fortune to find myself in perfect concurrence [3] with a large majority in this House. Bowing under that high authority, and penetrated with the sharpness and strength of that early impression, I have continued ever since, without the least deviation, in my original sentiments. Whether this be owing to an obstinate perseverance in error, or to a religious adherence to what appears to me truth and reason, it is in your equity to judge.

Sir, Parliament, having an enlarged view of objects, made, during this [4] interval, more frequent changes in their sentiments and their conduct than could be justified in a particular person upon the contracted scale of private information. But though I do not hazard anything approaching to a censure on the motives of former Parliaments to all those alterations, one fact is undoubted,—that under them the state of America has been kept in continual agitation. Everything administered as remedy to the public complaint, if it did not produce, was at least followed by, an heightening of the distemper, until, by a variety of experiments, that important country has been brought into her present situation,—a situation which I will not miscall, which I dare not name, which I scarcely know how to comprehend in the terms of any description.

In this posture, Sir, things stood at the beginning of the session. About [5] that time, a worthy member, of great Parliamentary experience, who in the year 1766 filled the chair of the American Committee with much ability, took me aside, and, lamenting the present aspect of our politics, told me,

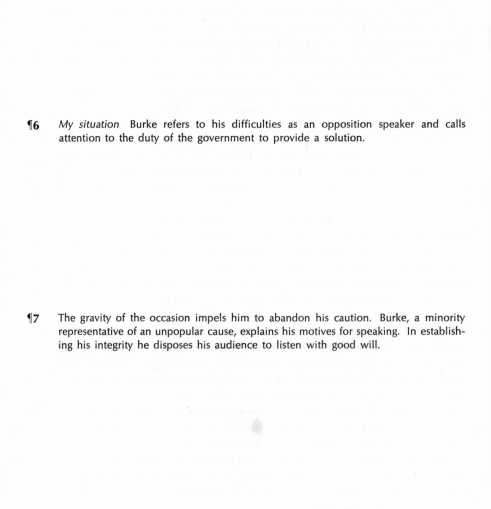

¶6   *My situation* Burke refers to his difficulties as an opposition speaker and calls attention to the duty of the government to provide a solution.

¶7   The gravity of the occasion impels him to abandon his caution. Burke, a minority representative of an unpopular cause, explains his motives for speaking. In establishing his integrity he disposes his audience to listen with good will.

¶8   The *you* addressed is the Chair, the personification of Parliament as a whole. While Burke explains his position logically, he also appeals to the sense of fair play.

things were come to such a pass that our former methods of proceeding in the House would be no longer tolerated,—that the public tribunal (never too indulgent to a long and unsuccessful opposition) would now scrutinize our conduct with unusual severity,—that the very vicissitudes and shiftings of ministerial measures, instead of convicting their authors of inconstancy and want of system, would be taken as an occasion of charging us with a predetermined discontent which nothing could satisfy, whilst we accused every measure of vigor as cruel and every proposal of lenity as weak and irresolute. The public, he said, would not have patience to see us play the game out with our adversaries; we must produce our hand. It would be expected that those who for many years had been active in such affairs should show that they had formed some clear and decided idea of the principles of colony government, and were capable of drawing out something like a platform of the ground which might be laid for future and permanent tranquillity.

I felt the truth of what my honorable friend represented; but I felt my [6] situation, too. His application might have been made with far greater propriety to many other gentlemen. No man was, indeed, ever better disposed, or worse qualified, for such an undertaking, than myself. Though I gave so far into his opinion, that I immediately threw my thoughts into a sort of Parliamentary form, I was by no means equally ready to produce them. It generally argues some degree of natural impotence of mind, or some want of knowledge of the world, to hazard plans of government, except from a seat of authority. Propositions are made, not only ineffectually, but somewhat disreputably, when the minds of men are not properly disposed for their reception; and for my part, I am not ambitious of ridicule, not absolutely a candidate for disgrace.

Besides, Sir, to speak the plain truth, I have in general no very exalted [7] opinion of the virtue of paper government, nor of any politics in which the plan is to be wholly separated from the execution. But when I saw that anger and violence prevailed every day more and more, and that things were hastening towards an incurable alienation of our colonies, I confess my caution gave way. I felt this as one of those few moments in which decorum yields to an higher duty. Public calamity is a mighty leveller; and there are occasions when any, even the slightest, chance of doing good must be laid hold on, even by the most inconsiderable person.

To restore order and repose to an empire so great and so distracted as [8] ours is, merely in the attempt, an undertaking that would ennoble the flights of the highest genius, and obtain pardon for the efforts of the meanest understanding. Struggling a good while with these thoughts, by degrees I felt myself more firm. I derived, at length, some confidence from what in other circumstances usually produces timidity. I grew less anxious, even from the idea of my own insignificance. For, judging of what you are by what you ought to be, I persuaded myself that you would not reject

Statement of the Proposition

¶9 Burke defines his proposition informally—first negatively, then positively—as the achievement of peace. Repetition of the word *peace* emphasizes as well as clarifies his thought. Burke formally states the proposition and division in paragraph 14.

¶10 *My idea*   The simplicity of Burke's proposition implies sincerity, in contrast to the complexity, confusion, and, by connotation, the insincerity of the plan of the Prime Minister.

Project   Lord North's project was his resolution of February 27, 1775, proposing to "conciliate the differences with America" by exempting from further taxation any colony that contributed voluntarily an amount satisfactory in proportion "to the condition, circumstances and situation of such colony." North's plan was to divide the colonial union already formed at the First Continental Congress and to compel each colony to bargain singly. Burke seized on North's offer of conciliation to propose his own more acceptable one.

Noble lord in the blue riband   Lord North, the Prime Minister from 1770–82, belonged to the Order of the Garter, one of whose insignia was a blue ribbon.

The interposition of your mace   A symbolic gesture by which the speaker directs the sergeant of arms to restore order.

Exposition of the Principles Relevant to the Proposition—Burke's Ideas of Conciliation

¶11 *The idea . . . is admissible*   In view of the passage of Lord North's resolution. See *Project* above.

Menacing front   The threats and penalties attracted to the Act in Restraint of Trade. See *The grand penal bill* (p. 164).

¶12 Burke states that conciliation has already been conceded in principle, and thus prepares for the formal statement of his proposition in paragraph 14.

a reasonable proposition because it had nothing but its reason to recommend it. On the other hand, being totally destitute of all shadow of influence, natural or adventitious, I was very sure, that, if my proposition were futile or dangerous, if it were weakly conceived or improperly timed, there was nothing exterior to it of power to awe, dazzle, or delude you. You will see it just as it is, and you will treat it just as it deserves.

The proposition is peace. Not peace through the medium of war; not [9] peace to be hunted through the labyrinth of intricate and endless negotiations; not peace to arise out of universal discord, fomented from principle, in all parts of the empire; not peace to depend on the juridical determination of perplexing questions, or the precise marking the shadowy boundaries of a complex government. It is simple peace, sought in its natural course and in its ordinary haunts. It is peace sought in the spirit of peace, and laid in principles purely pacific. I propose, by removing the ground of the difference, and by restoring the *former unsuspecting confidence of the colonies in the mother country,* to give permanent satisfaction to your people,—and (far from a scheme of ruling by discord) to reconcile them to each other in the same act and by the bond of the very same interest which reconciles them to British government.

My idea is nothing more. Refined policy ever has been the parent of [10] confusion,—and ever will be so, as long as the world endures. Plain good intention, which is as easily discovered at the first view as fraud is surely detected at last, is, let me say, of no mean force in the government of mankind. Genuine simplicity of heart is an healing and cementing principle. My plan, therefore, being formed upon the most simple grounds imaginable, may disappoint some people, when they hear it. It has nothing to recommend it to the pruriency of curious ears. There is nothing at all new and captivating in it. It has nothing of the splendor of the project which has been lately laid upon your table by the noble lord in the blue riband. It does not propose to fill your lobby with squabbling colony agents, who will require the interposition of your mace at every instant to keep the peace amongst them. It does not institute a magnificent auction of finance, where captivated provinces come to general ransom by bidding against each other, until you knock down the hammer, and determine a proportion of payments beyond all the powers of algebra to equalize and settle.

The plan which I shall presume to suggest derives, however, one great [11] advantage from the proposition and registry of that noble lord's project. The idea of conciliation is admissible. First, the House, in accepting the resolution moved by the noble lord, has admitted, notwithstanding the menacing front of our address, notwithstanding our heavy bill of pains and penalties, that we do not think ourselves precluded from all ideas of free grace and bounty.

The House has gone farther: it has declared conciliation admissible [12] *previous* to any submission on the part of America. It has even shot a good

¶13   Burke further defines the issue—the best means to achieve conciliation—and his idea of conciliation, by analysis of the duties of the superior power.

Formal Statement of the Issues and Order of the Proof to Follow

¶14   Burke has been leading up to this formal restatement of the proposition and announcement of the issues. In paragraph 9 and elsewhere, Burke advanced his proposition: we ought to seek peace with the colonies. The issues were implied in his history of the case. Here he states them as the chief questions to be debated. The last sentence of paragraph 14 announces that he is about to develop these issues.

II. DEVELOPMENT OR PROOF [15–47]

The First Issue

Several paragraphs, in which Burke develops his first issue—"whether you ought to concede"—have been omitted. Burke shows that the nature of the situation and the historical background demand concession. He points out that the population of the colonies is already one-third that of England and is constantly growing. He argues that the fact of population alone compels caution. He shows how the commerce of the colonies, their agriculture, and their fisheries are all flourishing, to England's advantage as well as to that of the colonies. All these circumstances favor prudent negotiation rather than the use of force, especially since force is temporary, uncertain, frustrating, and contrary to English experience. Burke proceeds to his third main reason for conciliating the colonies in paragraph 15.

¶15   Here and in the paragraphs that follow, Burke summarizes his preceding argument and makes a transition to the final argument on the issue "whether you ought to concede." The argument, based on the temper and character of the American peo-

deal beyond that mark, and has admitted that the complaints of our former mode of exerting the right of taxation were not wholly unfounded. That right thus exerted is allowed to have had something reprehensible in it,— something unwise, or something grievous; since, in the midst of our heat and resentment, we, of ourselves, have proposed a capital alteration, and, in order to get rid of what seemed so very exceptionable, have instituted a mode that is altogether new,—one that is, indeed, wholly alien from all the ancient methods and forms of Parliament.

The *principle* of this proceeding is large enough for my purpose. The [13] means proposed by the noble lord for carrying his ideas into execution, I think, indeed, are very indifferently suited to the end; and this I shall endeavor to show you before I sit down. But, for the present, I take my ground on the admitted principle. I mean to give peace. Peace implies reconciliation; and where there has been a material dispute, reconciliation does in a manner always imply concession on the one part or on the other. In this state of things I make no difficulty in affirming that the proposal ought to originate from us. Great and acknowledged force is not impaired, either in effect or in opinion, by an unwillingness to exert itself. The superior power may offer peace with honor and with safety. Such an offer from such a power will be attributed to magnanimity. But the concessions of the weak are the concessions of fear. When such a one is disarmed, he is wholly at the mercy of his superior; and he loses forever that time and those chances which, as they happen to all men, are the strength and resources of all inferior power.

The capital leading questions on which you must this day decide are [14] these two: First, whether you ought to concede; and secondly, what your concession ought to be. On the first of these questions we have gained (as I have just taken the liberty of observing to you) some ground. But I am sensible that a good deal more is still to be done. Indeed, Sir, to enable us to determine both on the one and the other of these great questions with a firm and precise judgment, I think it may be necessary to consider distinctly the true nature and the peculiar circumstances of the object which we have before us: because, after all our struggle, whether we will or not, we must govern America according to that nature and to those circumstances, and not according to our own imaginations, not according to abstract ideas of right, by no means according to mere general theories of government, the resort to which appears to me, in our present situation, no better than arrant trifling. I shall therefore endeavor, with your leave, to lay before you some of the most material of these circumstances in as full and as clear a manner as I am able to state them.

. . .

These, Sir, are my reasons for not entertaining that high opinion of untried [15] force by which many gentlemen, for whose sentiments in other particulars

ple, is developed on the basis of six characteristics: love of freedom, which is part of the colonists' English heritage (paragraphs 16–17); the habit of independence (paragraph 18); Protestant religious heritage in the northern colonies (paragraph 19); the haughty spirit of the southern colonies (paragraph 20); the prevalence of legal education among the colonists (paragraph 21); the physical remoteness of the colonies from England (paragraph 22). Burke argues that these six reasons make conciliation necessary (paragraphs 23–25).

¶16   *A love of freedom*   Burke analyzes the sources of the American spirit of liberty.

¶17   Burke traces love of liberty to English ideas and principles and, concretely, to questions of money and taxes.

Great contests for freedom   The struggle between the Crown and Parliament during the reign of the Stuarts.

English Constitution   This is not a single document but is a body of laws, precedents, and customs and the relationship developed through history among the various organs of the state and government.

I have great respect, seem to be so greatly captivated. But there is still behind a third consideration concerning this object, which serves to determine my opinion on the sort of policy which ought to be pursued in the management of America, even more than its population and its commerce: I mean its *temper and character*.

In this character of the Americans a love of freedom is the predominat- [16] ing feature which marks and distinguishes the whole: and as an ardent is always a jealous affection, your colonies become suspicious, restive, and un- tractable, whenever they see the least attempt to wrest from them by force, or shuffle from them by chicane, what they think the only advantage worth living for. This fierce spirit of liberty is stronger in the English colonies, probably, than in any other people of the earth, and this from a great variety of powerful causes; which, to understand the true temper of their minds, and the direction which this spirit takes, it will not be amiss to lay open somewhat more largely.

First, the people of the colonies are descendants of Englishmen. England, [17] Sir, is a nation which still, I hope, respects, and formerly adored, her free- dom. The colonists emigrated from you when this part of your character was most predominant; and they took this bias and direction the moment they parted from your hands. They are therefore not only devoted to liberty, but to liberty according to English ideas and on English principles. Abstract liberty, like other mere abstractions, is not to be found. Liberty inheres in some sensible object; and every nation has formed to itself some favorite point, which by way of eminence becomes the criterion of their happiness. It happened, you know, Sir, that the great contests for freedom in this country were from the earliest times chiefly upon the question of taxing. Most of the contests in the ancient commonwealths turned pri- marily on the right of election of magistrates, or on the balance among the several orders of the state. The question of money was not with them so immediate. But in England it was otherwise. On this point of taxes the ablest pens and most eloquent tongues have been exercised, the greatest spirits have acted and suffered. In order to give the fullest satisfaction con- cerning the importance of this point, it was not only necessary for those who in argument defended the excellence of the English Constitution to insist on this privilege of granting money as a dry point of fact, and to prove that the right had been acknowledged in ancient parchments and blind usages to reside in a certain body called an House of Commons: they went much further: they attempted to prove, and they succeeded, that in theory it ought to be so, from the particular nature of a House of Com- mons, as an immediate representative of the people, whether the old records had delivered this oracle or not. They took infinite pains to inculcate, as a fundamental principle, that in all monarchies the people must in effect themselves, mediately or immediately, possess the power of granting their own money, or no shadow of liberty could subsist. The colonies draw from

Edmund Burke

¶18   *Merely popular* Wholly democratic—that is, entirely elected by freemen, free-holders, or free inhabitants.

¶19   Burke traces love of liberty in the northern colonies to the fact of Protestantism, to the principles of Protestantism, and to the historical situation of Protestantism.

you, as with their life-blood, these ideas and principles. Their love of liberty, as with you, fixed and attached on this specific point of taxing. Liberty might be safe or might be endangered in twenty other particulars without their being much pleased or alarmed. Here they felt its pulse; and as they found that beat, they thought themselves sick or sound. I do not say whether they were right or wrong in applying your general arguments to their own case. It is not easy, indeed, to make a monopoly of theorems and corollaries. The fact is, that they did thus apply those general arguments; and your mode of governing them, whether through lenity or indolence, through wisdom or mistake, confirmed them in the imagination, that they, as well as you, had an interest in these common principles.

They were further confirmed in this pleasing error by the form of their [18] provincial legislative assemblies. Their governments are popular in an high degree: some are merely popular; in all, the popular representative is the most weighty; and this share of the people in their ordinary government never fails to inspire them with lofty sentiments, and with a strong aversion from whatever tends to deprive them of their chief importance.

If anything were wanting to this necessary operation of the form of gov- [19] ernment, religion would have given it a complete effect. Religion, always a principle of energy, in this new people is no way worn out or impaired; and their mode of professing it is also one main cause of this free spirit. The people are Protestants, and of that kind which is the most adverse to all implicit submission of mind and opinion. This is a persuasion not only favorable to liberty, but built upon it. I do not think, Sir, that the reason of this averseness in the dissenting churches from all that looks like absolute government is so much to be sought in their religious tenets as in their history. Every one knows that the Roman Catholic religion is at least coeval with most of the governments where it prevails, that it has generally gone hand in hand with them, and received great favor and every kind of support from authority. The Church of England, too, was formed from her cradle under the nursing care of regular government. But the dissenting interests have sprung up in direct opposition to all the ordinary powers of the world, and could justify that opposition only on a strong claim to natural liberty. Their very existence depended on the powerful and unremitted assertion of that claim. All Protestantism, even the most cold and passive, is a sort of dissent. But the religion most prevalent in our northern colonies is a refinement on the principle of resistance: it is the dissidence of dissent, and the protestantism of the Protestant religion. This religion, under a variety of denominations agreeing in nothing but in the communion of the spirit of liberty, is predominant in most of the northern provinces, where the Church of England, notwithstanding its legal rights, is in reality no more than a sort of private sect, not composing, most probably, the tenth of the people. The colonists left England when this spirit was high, and in the emigrants was the highest of all; and even that

¶20 Burke traces love of liberty in the southern colonies to the haughtiness of free men in a society that tolerates slavery.

Gothic ancestors The Anglo-Saxons and the Danes, who were jealous of their own freedom while they enslaved others.

¶21 Burke traces love of liberty to education in law.

Plantations Colonies.

Blackstone's "Commentaries" The classic *Commentaries on the Laws of England* by William Blackstone (1723–80) were published in 1765–69.

stream of foreigners which has been constantly flowing into these colonies has, for the greatest part, been composed of dissenters from the establishments of their several countries, and have brought with them a temper and character far from alien to that of the people with whom they mixed.

Sir, I can perceive, by their manner, that some gentlemen object to the [20] latitude of this description, because in the southern colonies the Church of England forms a large body, and has a regular establishment. It is certainly true. There is, however, a circumstance attending these colonies, which, in my opinion, fully counterbalances this difference, and makes the spirit of liberty still more high and haughty than in those to the northward. It is, that in Virginia and the Carolinas they have a vast multitude of slaves. Where this is the case in any part of the world, those who are free are by far the most proud and jealous of their freedom. Freedom is to them not only an enjoyment, but a kind of rank and privilege. Not seeing there, that freedom, as in countries where it is a common blessing, and as broad and general as the air, may be united with much abject toil, with great misery, with all the exterior of servitude, liberty looks, amongst them, like something that is more noble and liberal. I do not mean, Sir, to commend the superior morality of this sentiment, which has at least as much pride as virtue in it; but I cannot alter the nature of man. The fact is so; and these people of the southern colonies are much more strongly, and with an higher and more stubborn spirit, attached to liberty, than those to the northward. Such were all the ancient commonwealths; such were our Gothic ancestors; such in our days were the Poles; and such will be all masters of slaves, who are not slaves themselves. In such a people, the haughtiness of domination combines with the spirit of freedom, fortifies it, and renders it invincible.

Permit me, Sir, to add another circumstance in our colonies, which con- [21] tributes no mean part towards the growth and effect of this untractable spirit: I mean their education. In no country, perhaps, in the world is the law so general a study. The profession itself is numerous and powerful, and in most provinces it takes the lead. The greater number of the deputies sent to the Congress were lawyers. But all who read, and most do read, endeavor to obtain some smattering in that science. I have been told by an eminent bookseller, that in no branch of his business, after tracts of popular devotion, were so many books as those on the law exported to the plantations. The colonists have now fallen into the way of printing them for their own use. I hear that they have sold nearly as many of Blackstone's "Commentaries" in America as in England. General Gage marks out this disposition very particularly in a letter on your table. He states, that all the people in his government are lawyers, or smatterers in law,—and that in Boston they have been enabled, by successful chicane, wholly to evade many parts of one of your capital penal constitutions. The smartness of debate will say, that this knowledge ought to teach them

Edmund Burke 179

My honorable and learned friend   Edward Thurlow (1731–1806), then the Attorney General, later Lord Chancellor.

Abeunt studia in mores   Studies pass over into character. (Ovid *Heroides*, Ep. xv. 83.)

¶22   Burke traces America's love of liberty to remoteness from the source of authority.

Nature has said it   Burke supports the argument from the nature of things by specific examples from history.

¶23   Burke summarizes the six causes of the American spirit of liberty.

more clearly the rights of legislature, their obligations to obedience, and the penalties of rebellion. All this is mighty well. But my honorable and learned friend on the floor, who condescends to mark what I say for animadversion, will disdain that ground. He has heard, as well as I, that, when great honors and great emoluments do not win over this knowledge to the service of the state, it is a formidable adversary to government. If the spirit be not tamed and broken by these happy methods, it is stubborn and litigious. *Abeunt studia in mores.* This study renders men acute, inquisitive, dexterous, prompt in attack, ready in defence, full of resources. In other countries, the people, more simple, and of a less mercurial cast, judge of an ill principle in government only by an actual grievance; here they anticipate the evil, and judge of the pressure of the grievance by the badness of the principle. They augur misgovernment at a distance, and snuff the approach of tyranny in every tainted breeze.

The last cause of this disobedient spirit in the colonies is hardly less pow- [22] erful than the rest, as it is not merely moral, but laid deep in the natural constitution of things. Three thousand miles of ocean lie between you and them. No contrivance can prevent the effect of this distance in weakening government. Seas roll, and months pass, between the order and the execution; and the want of a speedy explanation of a single point is enough to defeat an whole system. You have, indeed, winged ministers of vengeance, who carry your bolts in their pounces to the remotest verge of the sea: but there a power steps in, that limits the arrogance of raging passions and furious elements, and says, "So far shalt thou go, and no farther." Who are you, that should fret and rage, and bite the chains of Nature? Nothing worse happens to you than does to all nations who have extensive empire; and it happens in all the forms into which empire can be thrown. In large bodies, the circulation of power must be less vigorous at the extremities. Nature has said it. The Turk cannot govern Egypt, and Arabia, and Kurdistan, as he governs Thrace; nor has he the same dominion in Crimea and Algiers which he has at Brusa and Smyrna. Despotism itself is obliged to truck and huckster. The Sultan gets such obedience as he can. He governs with a loose rein, that he may govern at all; and the whole of the force and vigor of his authority in his centre is derived from a prudent relaxation in all his borders. Spain, in her provinces, is perhaps not so well obeyed as you are in yours. She complies, too; she submits; she watches times. This is the immutable condition, the eternal law, of extensive and detached empire.

Then, Sir, from these six capital sources, of descent, of form of govern- [23] ment, of religion in the northern provinces, of manners in the southern, of education, of the remoteness of situation from the first mover of government,— from all these causes a fierce spirit of liberty has grown up. It has grown with the growth of the people in your colonies, and increased with the increase of their wealth: a spirit, that, unhappily meeting with an exercise of

Edmund Burke

¶24 Burke traces the effects of these causes in the present discontents.

Lord Dunmore John Murray, the fourth Earl of Dunmore (1732–1809), was governor of the colony of New York in 1770 and of Virginia in 1771. During his administration in Virginia, Lord Dunmore met with organized resistance and was forced to transfer his government to a British man-of-war. The colonial burgesses assumed his executive powers. Burke's reference to this well-known fact is a telling point in his general argument that obedience rather than force makes government.

power in England, which, however lawful, is not reconcilable to any ideas of liberty, much less with theirs, has kindled this flame that is ready to consume us.

I do not mean to commend either the spirit in this excess, or the moral [24] causes which produce it. Perhaps a more smooth and accommodating spirit of freedom in them would be more acceptable to us. Perhaps ideas of liberty might be desired more reconcilable with an arbitrary and boundless authority. Perhaps we might wish the colonists to be persuaded that their liberty is more secure when held in trust for them by us (as their guardians during a perpetual minority) than with any part of it in their own hands. But the question is not, whether their spirit deserves praise or blame,— what, in the name of God, shall we do with it? You have before you the object, such as it is,—with all its glories, with all its imperfections on its head. You see the magnitude, the importance, the temper, the habits, the disorders. By all these considerations we are strongly urged to determine something concerning it. We are called upon to fix some rule and line for our future conduct, which may give a little stability to our politics, and prevent the return of such unhappy deliberations as the present. Every such return will bring the matter before us in a still more untractable form. For what astonishing and incredible things have we not seen already! What monsters have not been generated from this unnatural contention! Whilst every principle of authority and resistance has been pushed, upon both sides, as far as it would go, there is nothing so solid and certain, either in reasoning or in practice, that has not been shaken. Until very lately, all authority in America seemed to be nothing but an emanation from yours. Even the popular part of the colony constitution derived all its activity, and its first vital movement, from the pleasure of the crown. We thought, Sir, that the utmost which the discontented colonists could do was to disturb authority; we never dreamt they could of themselves supply it, knowing in general what an operose business it is to establish a government absolutely new. But having, for our purposes in this contention, resolved that none but an obedient assembly should sit, the humors of the people there, finding all passage through the legal channel stopped, with great violence broke out another way. Some provinces have tried their experiment, as we have tried ours; and theirs has succeeded. They have formed a government sufficient for its purposes, without the bustle of a revolution, or the troublesome formality of an election. Evident necessity and tacit consent have done the business in an instant. So well they have done it, that Lord Dunmore (the account is among the fragments on your table) tells you that the new institution is infinitely better obeyed than the ancient government ever was in its most fortunate periods. Obedience is what makes government, and not the names by which it is called: not the name of Governor, as formerly, or Committee, as at present. This new government has originated directly from the people, and was not trans-

¶25 Burke draws a conclusion from the previous arguments: a new state of affairs requires a new approach to the problem. England suffers at home as well as abroad, because, by attacking freedom for America, England undercuts freedom for herself.

The Second Issue

Burke has developed his first issue—namely, that England ought to concede. He now proceeds to take up the second issue, the nature of the concession. He enumerates four possible ways of removing the causes of American discontent. He argues by denying three alternatives and affirming the last.

We may deal with America in four ways. We may give up the colonies, but this is mere peevishness (paragraph 26). We may try to change the spirit of the colonies, but this is impossible (paragraphs 27–36). We may prosecute criminality, but this is imprudent (paragraphs 37–42). Therefore, we must concede the justice of the American complaint against taxation without representation because such a concession is what "humanity, reason, and justice" demand (paragraphs 43–47).

¶26 Burke enumerates four solutions to the problem. He immediately rejects one solution—giving up the colonies.

mitted through any of the ordinary artificial media of a positive constitution. It was not a manufacture ready formed, and transmitted to them in that condition from England. The evil arising from hence is this: that the colonists having once found the possibility of enjoying the advantages of order in the midst of a struggle for liberty, such struggles will not henceforward seem so terrible to the settled and sober part of mankind as they had appeared before the trial.

Pursuing the same plan of punishing by the denial of the exercise of [25] government to still greater lengths, we wholly abrogated the ancient government of Massachusetts. We were confident that the first feeling, if not the very prospect of anarchy, would instantly enforce a complete submission. The experiment was tried. A new, strange, unexpected face of things appeared. Anarchy is found tolerable. A vast province has now subsisted, and subsisted in a considerable degree of health and vigor, for near a twelvemonth, without governor, without public council, without judges, without executive magistrates. How long it will continue in this state, or what may arise out of this unheard-of situation, how can the wisest of us conjecture? Our late experience has taught us that many of those fundamental principles formerly believed infallible are either not of the importance they were imagined to be, or that we have not at all adverted to some other far more important and far more powerful principles which entirely overrule those we had considered as omnipotent. I am much against any further experiments which tend to put to the proof any more of these allowed opinions which contribute so much to the public tranquillity. In effect, we suffer as much at home by this loosening of all ties, and this concussion of all established opinions, as we do abroad. For, in order to prove that the Americans have no right to their liberties, we are every day endeavoring to subvert the maxims which preserve the whole spirit of our own. To prove that the American ought not to be free, we are obliged to depreciate the value of freedom itself; and we never seem to gain a paltry advantage over them in debate, without attacking some of those principles, or deriding some of those feelings, for which our ancestors have shed their blood.

But, Sir, in wishing to put an end to pernicious experiments, I do not [26] mean to preclude the fullest inquiry. Far from it. Far from deciding on a sudden or partial view, I would patiently go round and round the subject, and survey it minutely in every possible aspect. Sir, if I were capable of engaging you to an equal attention, I would state, that, as far as I am capable of discerning, there are but three ways of proceeding relative to this stubborn spirit which prevails in your colonies and disturbs your government. These are,—to change that spirit, as inconvenient, by removing the causes,—to prosecute it, as criminal,—or to comply with it, as necessary. I would not be guilty of an imperfect enumeration; I can think of but these three. Another has, indeed been started,—that of giving up the

¶27 He takes up the first possible solution—changing the spirit of the colonies. He characterizes the plan as impossible.

¶28 He criticizes the specific scheme of stopping further grants of land. The effect of this plan would be to increase private monopoly and not to change the spirit of the population.

¶29 A second effect of this plan would be to make outlaws of the Americans. Burke projects recent American experiences into the future and links his argument from cause to effect with natural law and divine precept.

colonies; but it met so slight a reception that I do not think myself obliged to dwell a great while upon it. It is nothing but a little sally of anger, like the frowardness of peevish children, who, when they cannot get all they would have, are resolved to take nothing.

The first of these plans,—to change the spirit, as inconvenient, by removing the causes,—I think is the most like a systematic proceeding. It is radical in its principle; but it is attended with great difficulties: some of them little short, as I conceive, of impossibilities. This will appear by examining into the plans which have been proposed. [27]

As the growing population of the colonies is evidently one cause of their resistance, it was last session mentioned in both Houses, by men of weight, and received not without applause, that, in order to check this evil, it would be proper for the crown to make no further grants of land. But to this scheme there are two objections. The first, that there is already so much unsettled land in private hands as to afford room for an immense future population, although the crown not only withheld its grants, but annihilated its soil. If this be the case, then the only effect of this avarice of desolation, this hoarding of a royal wilderness, would be to raise the value of the possessions in the hands of the great private monopolists, without any adequate check to the growing and alarming mischief of population. [28]

But if you stopped your grants, what would be the consequence? The people would occupy without grants. They have already so occupied in many places. You cannot station garrisons in every part of these deserts. If you drive the people from one place, they will carry on their annual tillage, and remove with their flocks and herds to another. Many of the people in the back settlements are already little attached to particular situations. Already they have topped the Appalachian mountains. From thence they behold before them an immense plain, one vast, rich, level meadow: a square of five hundred miles. Over this they would wander without a possibility of restraint; they would change their manners with the habits of their life; would soon forget a government by which they were disowned; would become hordes of English Tartars, and, pouring down upon your unfortified frontiers a fierce and irresistible cavalry, become masters of your governors and your counsellors, your collectors and comptrollers, and of all the slaves that adhered to them. Such would, and in no long time, must be, the effect of attempting to forbid as a crime, and to suppress as an evil, the command and blessing of Providence, "Increase and multiply." Such would be the happy result of an endeavor to keep as a lair of wild beasts that earth which God by an express charter has given to the children of men. Far different, and surely much wiser, has been our policy hitherto. Hitherto we have invited our people, by every kind of bounty, to fixed establishments. We have invited the husbandman to look to authority for his title. We have taught him piously to believe in the [29]

¶30, Burke stresses the imprudence of the plan—that is, its contradictory character. An
31   impoverished colony will be of no help to England and may be of great harm.

Spoliatis arma supersunt "Arms still remain to the despoiled "(Juvenal *Satires* viii.
124).

¶32, Burke stresses the impracticality of the plan in view of the American character and
33   the changing mood of history.

mysterious virtue of wax and parchment. We have thrown each tract of land, as it was peopled, into districts, that the ruling power should never be wholly out of sight. We have settled all we could; and we have carefully attended every settlement with government.

Adhering, Sir, as I do, to this policy, as well as for the reasons I have [30] just given, I think this new project of hedging in population to be neither prudent nor practicable.

To impoverish the colonies in general, and in particular to arrest the [31] noble course of their marine enterprises, would be a more easy task. I freely confess it. We have shown a disposition to a system of this kind,— a disposition even to continue the restraint after the offence,—looking on ourselves as rivals to our colonies, and persuaded that of course we must gain all that they shall lose. Much mischief we may certainly do. The power inadequate to all other things is often more than sufficient for this. I do not look on the direct and immediate power of the colonies to resist our violence as very formidable. In this, however, I may be mistaken. But when I consider that we have colonies for no purpose but to be serviceable to us, it seems to my poor understanding a little preposterous to make them unserviceable, in order to keep them obedient. It is, in truth, nothing more than the old, and, as I thought, exploded problem of tyranny, which proposes to beggar its subjects into submission. But remember, when you have completed your system of impoverishment, that Nature still proceeds in her ordinary course; that discontent will increase with misery; and that there are critical moments in the fortune of all states, when they who are too weak to contribute to your prosperity may be strong enough to complete your ruin. *Spoliatis arma supersunt.*

The temper and character which prevail in our colonies are, I am afraid, [32] unalterable by any human art. We cannot, I fear, falsify the pedigree of this fierce people, and persuade them that they are not sprung from a nation in whose veins the blood of freedom circulates. The language in which they would hear you tell them this tale would detect the imposition; your speech would betray you. An Englishman is the unfittest person on earth to argue another Englishman into slavery.

I think it is nearly as little in our power to change their republican [33] religion as their free descent, or to substitute the Roman Catholic as a penalty, or the Church of England as an improvement. The mode of inquisition and dragooning is going out of fashion in the Old World, and I should not confide much to their efficacy in the New. The education of the Americans is also on the same unalterable bottom with their religion. You cannot persuade them to burn their books of curious science, to banish their lawyers from their courts of law, or to quench the lights of their assemblies by refusing to choose those persons who are best read in their privileges. It would be no less impracticable to think of wholly annihilating the popular assemblies in which these lawyers sit. The army, by which we

¶34, Even the enfranchisement of slaves is impracticable: some slaves are attached to
35 their masters; masters may free their slaves to help defend their own freedom;
slaves must suspect the offer of freedom from those who have sold them into
slavery.

¶36 The ocean renders the plan impracticable.

"Ye Gods!" Martinus Scriblerus, *The Art of Sinking in Poetry,* ch. xi. The use of
an example of bathos in poetry suggests that the plan under attack is equally silly.

¶37 Burke moves on the second plan proposed by government supporters—criminal
prosecution.

¶38 Burke characterizes this plan too as absurd because it treats a whole people as it
does a single individual.

must govern in their place, would be far more chargeable to us, not quite so effectual, and perhaps, in the end, full as difficult to be kept in obedience.

With regard to the high aristocratic spirit of Virginia and the southern [34] colonies, it has been proposed, I know, to reduce it by declaring a general enfranchisement of their slaves. This project has had its advocates and panegyrists; yet I never could argue myself into any opinion of it. Slaves are often much attached to their masters. A general wild offer of liberty would not always be accepted. History furnishes few instances of it. It is sometimes as hard to persuade slaves to be free as it is to compel freemen to be slaves; and in this auspicious scheme we should have both these pleasing tasks on our hands at once. But when we talk of enfranchisement, do we not perceive that the American master may enfranchise, too, and arm servile hands in defence of freedom?—a measure to which other people have had recourse more than once, and not without success, in a desperate situation of their affairs.

Slaves as these unfortunate black people are, and dull as all men are [35] from slavery, must they not a little suspect the offer of freedom from that very nation which has sold them to their present masters,—from that nation, one of whose causes of quarrel with those masters is their refusal to deal any more in that inhuman traffic? An offer of freedom from England would come rather oddly, shipped to them in an African vessel, which is refused an entry into the ports of Virginia or Carolina, with a cargo of three hundred Angola negroes. It would be curious to see the Guinea captain attempting at the same instant to publish his proclamation of liberty and to advertise his sale of slaves.

But let us suppose all these moral difficulties got over. The ocean re- [36] mains. You cannot pump this dry; and as long as it continues in its present bed, so long all the causes which weaken authority by distance will continue.

> Ye Gods! annihilate but space and time,
> And make two lovers happy,

was a pious and passionate prayer,—but just as reasonable as many of the serious wishes of very grave and solemn politicians.

If, then, Sir, it seems almost desperate to think of any alternative course [37] for changing the moral causes (and not quite easy to remove the natural) which produce prejudices irreconcilable to the late exercise of our authority, but that the spirit infallibly will continue, and, continuing, will produce such effects as now embarrass us,—the second mode under consideration is, to prosecute that spirit in its overt acts, as *criminal*.

At this proposition I must pause a moment. The thing seems a great deal [38] too big for my ideas of jurisprudence. It should seem, to my way of conceiving such matters, that there is a very wide difference, in reason and

Sir Edward Coke   Coke (1552–1634) was Attorney General in 1603 during the prosecution of Sir Walter Raleigh. His abuse of the accused was traditionally cited as a blot on English judicial procedure. Burke uses the reference to support a comparative (*a fortiori*) argument: if it be unjust to insult an individual, how much more unjust to insult a community.

¶39   *Local privileges and immunities*   Burke argues that it is absurd for a superior power to use its whole authority against subordinate powers.

Ex vi termini   By the very force of the expression.

¶40   Burke points out that in the criminal prosecution of America England is both judge and litigant—a situation that is inexpedient if not unjust.

policy, between the mode of proceeding on the irregular conduct of scattered individuals, or even of bands of men, who disturb order within the state, and the civil dissensions which may, from time to time, on great questions, agitate the several communities which compose a great empire. It looks to me to be narrow and pedantic to apply the ordinary ideas of criminal justice to this great public contest. I do not know the method of drawing up an indictment against an whole people. I cannot insult and ridicule the feelings of millions of my fellow-creatures as Sir Edward Coke insulted one excellent individual (Sir Walter Raleigh) at the bar. I am not ripe to pass sentence on the gravest public bodies, intrusted with magistracies of great authority and dignity, and charged with the safety of their fellow-citizens, upon the very same title that I am. I really think that for wise men this is not judicious, for sober men not decent, for minds tinctured with humanity not mild and merciful.

Perhaps, Sir, I am mistaken in my idea of an empire, as distinguished [39] from a single state or kingdom. But my idea of it is this: that an empire is the aggregate of many states under one common head, whether this head be a monarch or a presiding republic. It does, in such constitutions, frequently happen (and nothing but the dismal, cold, dead uniformity of servitude can prevent its happening) that the subordinate parts have many local privileges and immunities. Between these privileges and the supreme common authority the line may be extremely nice. Of course disputes, often, too, very bitter disputes, and much ill blood, will arise. But though every privilege is an exemption (in the case) from the ordinary exercise of the supreme authority, it is no denial of it. The claim of a privilege seems rather, *ex vi termini*, to imply a superior power: for to talk of the privileges of a state or of a person who has no superior is hardly any better than speaking nonsense. Now in such unfortunate quarrels among the component parts of a great political union of communities, I can scarcely conceive anything more completely imprudent than for the head of the empire to insist, that if any privilege is pleaded against his will or his acts, that his whole authority is denied,—instantly to proclaim rebellion, to beat to arms, and to put the offending provinces under the ban. Will not this, Sir, very soon teach the provinces to make no distinctions on their part? Will it not teach them that the government against which a claim of liberty is tantamount to high treason is a government to which submission is equivalent to slavery? It may not always be quite convenient to impress dependent communities with such an idea.

We are, indeed, in all disputes with the colonies, by the necessity of [40] things, the judge. It is true, Sir. But I confess that the character of judge in my own cause is a thing that frightens me. Instead of filling me with pride, I am exceedingly humbled by it. I cannot proceed with a stern, assured judicial confidence, until I find myself in something more like a judicial character. I must have these hesitations as long as I am compelled

¶41　Burke underlines the inconsistency of the plan by noting that its proponents formally petitioned the Crown to bring home American "traitors" for trial but then failed to take legal action.

¶42　Burke says that threats, force, and primitive laws have produced no results.

¶43　Since the first alternative is foolish and the second two are unworkable, Burke proposes the only remaining plan—conciliation.

¶44　Burke argues that the nature of the concession must be determined by the nature of the complaint. In this instance the colonists have complained that they are taxed without representation.

to recollect, that, in my little reading upon such contests as these, the sense of mankind has at least as often decided against the superior as the subordinate power. Sir, let me add, too, that the opinion of my having some abstract right in my favor would not put me much at my ease in passing sentence, unless I could be sure that there were no rights which, in their exercise under certain circumstances, were not the most odious of all wrongs and the most vexatious of all injustice. Sir, these considerations have great weight with me, when I find things so circumstanced that I see the same party at once a civil litigant against me in a point of right and a culprit before me, while I sit as criminal judge on acts of his whose moral quality is to be decided upon the merits of that very litigation. Men are every now and then put, by the complexity of human affairs, into strange situations; but justice is the same, let the judge be in what situation he will.

There is, Sir, also a circumstance which convinces me that this mode of [41] criminal proceeding is not (at least in the present stage of our contest) altogether expedient,—which is nothing less than the conduct of those very persons who have seemed to adopt that mode, by lately declaring a rebellion in Massachusetts Bay, as they had formerly addressed to have traitors brought hither, under an act of Henry the Eighth, for trial. For, though rebellion is declared, it is not proceeded against as such; nor have any steps been taken towards the apprehension or conviction of any individual offender, either on our late or our former address; but modes of public coercion have been adopted, and such as have much more resemblance to a sort of qualified hostility towards an independent power than the punishment of rebellious subjects. All this seems rather inconsistent; but it shows how difficult it is to apply these juridical ideas to our present case.

In this situation, let us seriously and coolly ponder. What is it we have [42] got by all our menaces, which have been many and ferocious? What advantage have we derived from the penal laws we have passed, and which, for the time, have been severe and numerous? What advances have we made towards our object, by the sending of a force, which, by land and sea, is no contemptible strength? Has the disorder abated? Nothing less.— When I see things in this situation, after such confident hopes, bold promises, and active exertions, I cannot, for my life, avoid a suspicion that the plan itself is not correctly right.

If, then, the removal of the causes of this spirit of American liberty be, [43] for the greater part, or rather entirely, impracticable,—if the ideas of criminal process be inapplicable, or, if applicable, are in the highest degree inexpedient, what way yet remains? No way is open, but the third and last,— to comply with the American spirit as necessary, or, if you please, to submit to it as a necessary evil.

If we adopt this mode, if we mean to conciliate and concede, let us see [44] of what nature the concession ought to be. To ascertain the nature of our concession, we must look at their complaint. The colonies complain that

¶45 *The policy of the question* The issue is what general assumptions should govern any specific exercise of the right of taxation. Below, Burke says that the governing assumption should be not mere legality but "claims of humanity, reason, and justice."

The great Serbonian bog Milton, *Paradise Lost,* II, lines 592–94.

¶46 Burke summarizes his belief that the people of the colonies must be governed by the principles of freedom.

they have not the characteristic mark and seal of British freedom. They complain that they are taxed in a Parliament in which they are not represented. If you mean to satisfy them at all, you must satisfy them with regard to this complaint. If you mean to please any people, you must give them the boon which they ask,—not what you may think better for them, but of a kind totally different. Such an act may be a wise regulation, but it is no concession; whereas our present theme is the mode of giving satisfaction

Sir, I think you must perceive that I am resolved this day to have nothing [45] at all to do with the question of the right of taxation. Some gentlemen startle,—but it is true: I put it totally out of the question. It is less than nothing in my consideration. I do not indeed wonder, nor will you, Sir, that gentlemen of profound learning are fond of displaying it on this profound subject. But my consideration is narrow, confined, and wholly limited to the policy of the question. I do not examine whether the giving away a man's money be a power excepted and reserved out of the general trust of government, and how far all mankind, in all forms of polity, are entitled to an exercise of that right by the charter of Nature,—or whether, on the contrary, a right of taxation is necessarily involved in the general principle of legislation, and inseparable from the ordinary supreme power. These are deep questions, where great names militate against each other, where reason is perplexed, and an appeal to authorities only thickens the confusion: for high and reverend authorities lift up their heads on both sides, and there is no sure footing in the middle. This point is the *great Serbonian bog, betwixt Damiata and Mount Casius old, where armies whole have sunk.* I do not intend to be overwhelmed in that bog, though in such respectable company. The question with me is, not whether you have a right to render your people miserable, but whether it is not your interest to make them happy. It is not what a lawyer tells me I *may* do, but what humanity, reason, and justice tell me I ought to do. Is a politic act the worse for being a generous one? Is no concession proper, but that which is made from your want of right to keep what you grant? Or does it lessen the grace or dignity of relaxing in the exercise of an odious claim, because you have your evidence-room full of titles, and your magazines stuffed with arms to enforce them? What signify all those titles and all those arms? Of what avail are they, when the reason of the thing tells me that the assertion of my title is the loss of my suit, and that I could do nothing but wound myself by the use of my own weapons?

Such is steadfastly my opinion of the absolute necessity of keeping up [46] the concord of this empire by a unity of spirit, though in a diversity of operations, that, if I were sure the colonists had, at their leaving this country, sealed a regular compact of servitude, that they had solemnly abjured all the rights of citizens, that they had made a vow to renounce all ideas of liberty for them and their posterity to all generations, yet I should hold

¶47 Burke asserts that the wise policy, in view of the general character and situation of the American people, is to extend to them the benefits of the British Constitution. The nature of the concessions is outlined in the note that follows the text.

myself obliged to conform to the temper I found universally prevalent in my own day, and to govern two million of men, impatient of servitude, on the principles of freedom. I am not determining a point of law; I am restoring tranquillity: and the general character and situation of a people must determine what sort of government is fitted for them. That point nothing else can or ought to determine.

My idea, therefore, without considering whether we yield as matter of [47] right or grant as matter of favor, is, *to admit the people of our colonies into an interest in the Constitution,* and, by recording that admission in the journals of Parliament, to give them as strong an assurance as the nature of the thing will admit that we mean forever to adhere to that solemn declaration of systematic indulgence.

.   .   .

In the remaining part of his speech, not included here, Burke attempts to show that concession to the American colonies accords with traditional English policy. He argues from "four capital examples," that of Ireland, to which England granted its own Parliament; that of Wales, to which England extended all the rights of English subjects; and those of the Palatine counties of Chester and Durham, which were granted legislative representation. The gist of Burke's argument is that the Americans are equally entitled to the freedom that the British Constitution granted to the Irish, the Welsh, and the citizens of Chester and Durham:

> I only wish you to recognize, for the theory, the ancient constitutional policy of this kingdom with regard to representation, as that policy has been declared in Acts of Parliament; and as to the practice, to return to that mode which a uniform experience has marked out to you as best, and in which you walked with security, advantage, and honor, until the year 1763.

Burke then proposes not new legislation—a gesture rendered impossible by his status as a minority member of Parliament—but a series of resolutions. These resolutions, if accepted by the House, would virtually force Lord North's government to prepare legislation in harmony with the principles of conciliation.

Although Burke's address was applauded for its learning and eloquence, the majority defeated his resolutions, not by a direct vote, but by invoking the parliamentary tactic of moving the previous question.

Edmund Burke

TOPICS FOR DISCUSSION

1. A successful exordium is said to render the audience well disposed to the speaker, attentive to what he has to say, and sufficiently informed about his subject and purpose to understand his discussion and arguments. How does Burke attempt to achieve these objectives in his opening paragraphs? Do you think he succeeded in his attempt? Why or why not?

2. Burke presents the historical background throughout the speech as well as in his introduction. Why are continued historical references relevant to his central purpose? Why does he choose from time to time—for example, paragraph 13—to explain principles of law and philosophy? How do these explanations contribute to his main theme?

3. Burke's argument against the use of force in American affairs and in favor of concession is based on the *temper and character* of the American people—that is, on their fierce spirit of liberty. This spirit of liberty is inevitable and must be dealt with, Burke argues, because it is an effect of the combined activity of six specific causes. Does Burke prove that these causes actually determined the fierce spirit of liberty in the colonies?

4. Burke states (paragraph 24) that he does not commend either the American spirit of liberty "in this excess" or the moral causes that produce it. What does Burke mean by *commend?* Does he imply that Parliament should yield to the demands of the colonies even though those demands may be thought unjust or excessive? Would the principles of conciliation stated in paragraph 45 and elsewhere support the view that twentieth-century Americans should have conciliated or appeased the North Koreans, the North Vietnamese, or the Chinese? Why or why not?

5. Burke's reasoning is presented in a rhetorical rather in than a severely logical style. Could his arguments be fairly presented in logical form? Discuss which of the following statements best approximates the essential thought of this speech as a guide to your answer.

   a. England should deal with her colonies according to her own Constitution and her own best interests.
   But conciliation in the form of giving the American colonies representation in the English Parliament is most in accord with the English Constitution and England's best interests.
   Therefore England should conciliate the American colonies.

   b. Whatever brings us peace with honor should be pursued.
   But conciliation can bring us peace with honor.
   Therefore conciliation should be pursued.

   c. If peace involves reconciliation, we must have reconciliation.
   But peace involves reconciliation.
   Therefore we must have reconciliation.

   d. Whatever is required by the principles of justice, expediency, and common humanity should be done in this dispute with the colonies.
   But conciliation in the light of the colonists' demand for representa-

tion in the Parliament is required by these principles.

Therefore we should resolve to enact laws promoting the colonies' representation in Parliament.

e. If the American colonies are fiercely independent and if we cannot change their spirit or prosecute them successfully, then we must accept them under the Constitution.

But the American colonies are fiercely independent, and we cannot change their spirit or prosecute them successfully.

Therefore we must accept them under the Constitution.

6. In *The Ethics of Rhetoric*, R. M. Weaver classifies Burke among those orators who relied chiefly on the argument from circumstances. Weaver defines that kind of argument thus:

> The argument from circumstance is, as the name suggests, the nearest of all arguments to purest expediency. This argument merely reads the circumstances—the "facts standing around"—and accepts them as coercive, or allows them to dictate the decision. If one should say, "The city must be surrendered because the besiegers are so numerous," one would be arguing not from genus, or similitude, but from a present circumstance. The expression "In view of the situation, what else are you going to do?" constitutes a sort of proposition-form for this type of argument. Such argument savors of urgency rather than of perspicacity; and it seems to be preferred by those who are easily impressed by existing tangibles. Whereas the argument from consequence attempts a forecast of results, the argument from circumstance attempts only an estimate of current conditions or pressures. By thus making present circumstance the overbearing consideration, it keeps from sight even the nexus of cause and effect. It is the least philosophical of all the sources of argument, since theoretically it stops at the level of perception of fact.[1]

That Weaver clearly regards Burke's *Conciliation* speech as an example of circumstantial argument appears in this analysis:

> The long recital is closed with an appeal which may be fitly regarded as the *locus classicus* of the argument from circumstance. For with this impressive review of the fierce spirit of the colonists before his audience, Burke declares: "The question is, not whether the spirit deserves praise or blame, but—what, in the name of God, shall we do with it?" The question then is not what is right or wrong, or what accords with our idea of justice or our scheme of duty; it is, how can we meet this circumstance? "I am not determining a point of law; I am restoring tranquility." The circumstance becomes the cue of the policy.

Do you agree that Burke had reduced his basic argument in his *Conciliation* speech to circumstances? Why or why not?

[1] (Chicago: Regnery, 1953), p. 57.

7. Traditionally the aims of the orator have been
   a. to move—that is, to propose and, if possible, to bring about some action on the part of the audience
   b. to prove—that is, to show the reasonableness of the action he proposes
   c. to delight—that is, to please his audience by the vividness, grace, and vigor of his thought and style

Point out where and how Burke achieves these aims. Analyze the style in paragraphs 5, 9, 29, and 45.

TOPICS FOR COMPOSITION

1. Develop one of the subjects listed below, or another of your own choice, in a brief speech designed to persuade a definite audience to perform a definite action:
   a. why we should or should not allow eighteen-year-olds to vote
   b. why we should or should not ban the atomic bomb
   c. why we should or should not abolish all personal income tax
   d. why students should or should not be paid to attend college
   e. why we should or should not expand the domestic Peace Corps
2. Many effective arguments are predominantly refutations of opposing points of view. Write a letter to a local newspaper refuting some statement you honestly regard as erroneous. Point to an error of fact, an error of principle, or a false or misleading definition. Be sure you prove, and not merely assert, the opposite of the point of view you are attacking.
3. Comment on one of the statements listed below by specific references to the text of the *Conciliation* speech.
   a. A passion for order and a passion for justice were the master-motives of Burke's thought.
   b. Burke's appeal lies, first, in what can only be called a generous capaciousness of mind, and, secondly, in his unrivalled power to distil creative principles of thought and action from the concrete, practical facts of a situation.
   c. In many of his paragraphs Burke achieves a master sentence, one that involves a thought, an image, a sentiment, all bearing on action.

ABRAHAM LINCOLN

Second Inaugural Address

IN his *Conciliation* speech, on March 22, 1775, Burke said that "the high aristocratic spirit of Virginia and the southern colonies" was one of the reasons why England could not hope to change the spirit of liberty in the colonies. In his *Second Inaugural Address,* on March 4, 1865, Abraham Lincoln showed how a new spirit of justice, charity, and hope could change the spirit of a divided unon.

Lincoln's speech was adjusted perfectly, many would say, to the circumstances of the time and occasion. The Civil War was in its fourth bitter year. Grant and Sheridan were pressing Lee against Richmond; Sherman had swept across Georgia to the sea. On February 3, Lincoln had met the Confederate Peace Commission aboard the *River Queen* at Hampton Roads, Virginia, in a fruitless conference. On February 6, General Robert E. Lee had requested a conference and been refused by General Grant. Only two days before Lincoln's inaugural speech, Confederate President Jefferson Davis had made Lee General-in-Chief of the Confederate Army in a last-minute effort to prolong the war. The great American tragedy was gasping to its end.

Thus the occasion of the second inauguration did not call for a crow of triumph or of recrimination. Lincoln's audience, we are told, was chastened and silent. They knew well enough that "little . . . new could be presented." They did not expect Lincoln to urge new laws; they had no heart for another debate on the legality, or morality, of the war. What they thirsted for was both victory and peace. Hence, while Lincoln explained how the war came about and why it was fought and while he adroitly used the arts of logic and language to persuade his audience, he rightly emphasized the ethics of his purpose. His best argument was his unfeigned expression of charity.

[Fellow Countrymen:] At this second appearing to take the oath of the [1] presidential office, there is less occasion for an extended address than there was at the first. Then a statement, somewhat in detail, of a course to be pursued, seemed fitting and proper. Now, at the expiration of four years, during which public declarations have been constantly called forth on every point and phase of the great contest which still absorbs the attention, and engrosses the energies of the nation, little that is new could be presented. The progress of our arms, upon which all else chiefly depends, is as well

203

known to the public as to myself; and it is, I trust, reasonably satisfactory and encouraging to all. With high hope for the future, no prediction in regard to it is ventured.

[2]   On the occasion corresponding to this four years ago, all thoughts were anxiously directed to an impending civil-war. All dreaded it—all sought to avert it. While the inaugural address was being delivered from this place, devoted altogether to *saving* the Union without war, insurgent agents were in the city seeking to *destroy* it without war—seeking to dissolve the Union, and divide effects, by negotiation. Both parties deprecated war; but one of them would *make* war rather than let the nation survive; and the other would *accept* war rather than let it perish. And the war came.

[3]   One eighth of the whole population were colored slaves, not distributed generally over the Union, but localized in the Southern part of it. These slaves constituted a peculiar and powerful interest. All knew that this interest was, somehow, the cause of the war. To strengthen, perpetuate, and extend this interest was the object for which the insurgents would rend the Union, even by war; while the government claimed no right to do more than to restrict the territorial enlargement of it. Neither party expected for the war, the magnitude, or the duration, which it has already attained. Neither anticipated that the *cause* of the conflict might cease with, or even before, the conflict itself should cease. Each looked for an easier triumph, and a result less fundamental and astounding. Both read the same Bible, and pray to the same God; and each invokes His aid against the other. It may seem strange that any men should dare to ask a just God's assistance in wringing their bread from the sweat of other men's faces; but let us judge not that we be not judged. The prayers of both could not be answered; that of neither has been answered fully. The Almighty has His own purposes. "Woe unto the world because of offences! for it must needs be that offences come; but woe to that man by whom the offence cometh!" If we shall suppose that American Slavery is one of those offences which, in the providence of God, must needs come, but which, having continued through His appointed time, He now wills to remove, and that He gives to both North and South, this terrible war, as the woe due to those by whom the offence came, shall we discern therein any departure from those divine attributes which the believers in a Living God always ascribe to Him? Fondly do we hope—fervently do we pray—that this mighty scourge of war may speedily pass away. Yet, if God wills that it continue, until all the wealth piled by the bond-man's two hundred and fifty years of unrequited toil shall be sunk, and until every drop of blood drawn with the lash shall be paid by another drawn with the sword, as was said three thousand years ago, so still it must be said "the judgments of the Lord are true and righteous altogether."

[4]   With malice toward none; with charity for all; with firmness in the right, as God gives us to see the right, let us strive on to finish the work we

are in; to bind up the nation's wounds; to care for him who shall have borne the battle, and for his widow, and his orphan—to do all which may achieve and cherish a just, and a lasting peace, among ourselves, and with all nations.

TOPICS FOR DISCUSSION

1. An inaugural speech derives its subject chiefly from the occasion. A new president or, in this case, a newly reelected president, upon taking the oath of office, reports past progress and reveals his future hopes and intentions. Is this the basic pattern of Lincoln's speech? If so, show how it is. If not, what pattern does he give it?

2. How is Lincoln's solemn tone expressed by the choice of diction? The rhythm of the sentences? His attitude toward his audience? His attitude toward the "enemy"? His references to God and the Bible? His use of climax? Since Lincoln knew the Union was on the verge of victory, what does his tone tell us about the purpose he wished to achieve in his speech?

3. Lincoln develops his speech chiefly by comparison and contrast and by causal analysis. How are the points of comparison and contrast between North and South rendered more emphatic by parallels and antitheses within one sentence and among several sentences? To what ultimate cause is analysis of the conflict traced?

4. Study the sentence structure in paragraph 3. How do the sentences vary in length, in kind, in beginnings and endings? Show how they are arranged in climactic order. Show how the climax is finally achieved in paragraph 4.

TOPICS FOR COMPOSITION

1. Write a brief speech on the occasion of the anniversary of the bombing of Hiroshima (see p. 106) or some other disaster, in which by comparison and contrast of the past and present you urge your audience to work for a lasting peace.

2. In the manner of Lincoln show how a war—World War II, Korea, Vietnam—began, what were its principal causes, and what attitude you think your fellow citizens should take toward the war.

3. Write an essay telling why Lincoln's style is memorable. If you wish, show how Lincoln combined the use of antithesis, inversion, and short and long, loose and periodic sentences.

T. S. ELIOT

Speeches of the Four Knights

WE usually think of argument and persuasion as direct, public discourse in which the speaker asks his audience to pass or defeat a proposed law, to judge a man innocent or guilty, or to praise or to condemn an act or proposal. Thus in his *Conciliation* speech Burke proposed resolutions and argued their merits in the interests of particular legislation. In his *Second Inaugural Address* Lincoln aimed at strengthening his audience's resolve to continue the war and to win the peace. So, too, in most other arguments and persuasions the speaker intends some real action, more or less specific, on the part of the audience, depending on the occasion of the speech and the speaker's relation with his hearers.

Argument and persuasion play another important role in fictional discourse. Here the speaker does not appear in his own person, but as an actor or character in a play or story. In this role he reenacts an attempted persuasion. If the most important kind of human action is that which influences the mind and will, the most important plays and fictions will be concerned with argument and persuasion. Small wonder that Sophocles, Shakespeare, Molière, Shaw—to mention only a few great dramatists—built their plays around the attempt to change the human mind and will. None has done so more effectively than T. S. Eliot in his *Murder in the Cathedral,* a play about Thomas à Becket's martyrdom in 1170.

The Four Knights speak just after they have murdered Thomas à Becket in Canterbury Cathedral. The audience has of course witnessed the event; if they respond to it in the usual manner, they are horrified at the brutality of the Four Knights. On their part, the Four Knights seek a public verdict of "Not Guilty." In addressing themselves to the ideas and prejudices of the audience, they brilliantly employ sophistries and rationalizations in the guise of realism and fair play.

[1]   FIRST KNIGHT We beg you to give us your attention for a few moments. We know that you may be disposed to judge unfavourably of our action. You are Englishmen, and therefore you believe in fair play: and

when you see one man being set upon by four, then your sympathies are all with the under dog. I respect such feelings, I share them. Nevertheless, I appeal to your sense of honour. You are Englishmen, and therefore will not judge anybody without hearing both sides of the case. That is in accordance with our long-established principle of Trial by Jury. I am not myself qualified to put our case to you. I am a man of action and not of words. For that reason I shall do no more than introduce the other speakers, who, with their various abilities, and different points of view, will be able to lay before you the merits of this extremely complex problem. I shall call upon our eldest member to speak first, my neighbour in the country: Baron William de Traci.

THIRD KNIGHT   I am afraid I am not anything like such an experienced [2] speaker as my old friend Reginald Fitz Urse would lead you to believe. But there is one thing I should like to say, and I might as well say it at once. It is this: in what we have done, and whatever you may think of it, we have been perfectly disinterested.

[*The other* KNIGHTS: 'Hear! hear!']

We are not getting anything out of this. We have much more to lose than to gain. We are four plain Englishmen who put our country first. I dare say that we didn't make a very good impression when we came in just now. The fact is that we knew we had taken on a pretty stiff job; I'll only speak for myself, but I had drunk a good deal— I am not a drinking man ordinarily—to brace myself up for it. When you come to the point, it does go against the grain to kill an Archbishop, especially when you have been brought up in good Church traditions. So if we seemed a bit rowdy, you will understand why it was; and for my part I am awfully sorry about it. We realised this was our duty, but all the same we had to work ourselves up to it. And, as I said, *we* are not getting a penny out of this. We know perfectly well how things will turn out. King Henry—God bless him— will have to say, for reasons of state, that he never meant this to happen; and there is going to be an awful row; and at the best we shall have to spend the rest of our lives abroad. And even when reasonable people come to see that the Archbishop *had* to be put out of the way— and personally I had a tremendous admiration for him—you must have noticed what a good show he put up at the end—they won't give *us* any glory. No, we have done for ourselves, there's no mistake about that. So, as I said at the beginning, please give us at least the credit for being completely disinterested in this business. I think that is about all I have to say.

FIRST KNIGHT   I think we will all agree that William de Traci has spoken [3] well and has made a very important point. The gist of his argument is this: that we have been completely disinterested. But our act itself needs more justification than that; and you must hear our other speakers. I shall next call upon Hugh de Morville, who has made a special study of statecraft and constitutional law. Sir Hugh de Morville.

[4] SECOND KNIGHT I should like first to recur to a point that was very well put by our leader, Reginald Fitz Urse: that you are Englishmen, and therefore your sympathies are always with the under dog. It is the English spirit of fair play. Now the worthy Archbishop, whose good qualities I very much admired, has throughout been presented as the under dog. But is this really the case? I am going to appeal not to your emotions but to your reason. You are hard-headed sensible people, as I can see, and not to be taken in by emotional clap-trap. I therefore ask you to consider soberly: what were the Archbishop's aims? And what are King Henry's aims? In the answer to these questions lies the key to the problem.

[5] The King's aim has been perfectly consistent. During the reign of the late Queen Matilda and the irruption of the unhappy usurper Stephen, the kingdom was very much divided. Our King saw that the one thing needful was to restore order: to curb the excessive powers of local government, which were usually exercised for selfish and often for seditious ends, and to reform the legal system. He therefore intended that Becket, who had proved himself an extremely able administrator—no one denies that—should unite the offices of Chancellor and Archbishop. Had Becket concurred with the King's wishes, we should have had an almost ideal State: a union of spiritual and temporal administration, under the central government. I knew Becket well, in various official relations; and I may say that I have never known a man so well qualified for the highest rank of the Civil Service. And what happened? The moment that Becket, at the King's instance, had been made Archbishop, he resigned the office of Chancellor, he became more priestly than the priests, he ostentatiously and offensively adopted an ascetic manner of life, he affirmed immediately that there was a higher order than that which our King, and he as the King's servant, had for so many years striven to establish; and that—God knows why—the two orders were incompatible.

[6] You will agree with me that such interference by an Archbishop offends the instincts of a people like ours. So far, I know that I have your approval: I read it in your faces. It is only with the measures we have had to adopt, in order to set matters to rights, that you take issue. No one regrets the necessity for violence more than we do. Unhappily, there are times when violence is the only way in which social justice can be secured. At another time, you would condemn an Archbishop by vote of Parliament and execute him formally as a traitor, and no one would have to bear the burden of being called murderer. And at a later time still, even such temperate measures as

The Practice of Rhetoric

these would become unnecessary. But, if you have now arrived at a just subordination of the pretensions of the Church to the welfare of the State, remember that it is we who took the first step. We have been instrumental in bringing about the state of affairs that you approve. We have served your interests; we merit your applause; and if there is any guilt whatever in the matter, you must share it with us.

FIRST KNIGHT   Morville has given us a great deal to think about. It seems   [7]
to me that he has said almost the last word, for those who have been able to follow his very subtle reasoning. We have, however, one more speaker, who has I think another point of view to express. If there are any who are still unconvinced, I think that Richard Brito, coming as he does of a family distinguished for its loyalty to the Church, will be able to convince them. Richard Brito.

FOURTH KNIGHT   The speakers who have preceded me, to say nothing of   [8]
our leader, Reginald Fitz Urse, have all spoken very much to the point. I have nothing to add along their particular lines of argument. What I have to say may be put in the form of a question: *Who killed the Archbishop?* As you have been eye-witnesses of this lamentable scene, you may feel some surprise at my putting it in this way. But consider the course of events. I am obliged, very briefly, to go over the ground traversed by the last speaker. While the late Archbishop was Chancellor, no one, under the King, did more to weld the country together, to give it the unity, the stability, order, tranquillity, and justice that it so badly needed. From the moment he became Archbishop, he completely reversed his policy; he showed himself to be utterly indifferent to the fate of the country, to be, in fact, a monster of egotism. This egotism grew upon him, until it became at last an undoubted mania. I have unimpeachable evidence to the effect that before he left France he clearly prophesied, in the presence of numerous witnesses, that he had not long to live, and that he would be killed in England. He used every means of provocation; from his conduct, step by step, there can be no inference except that he had determined upon a death by martyrdom. Even at the last, he could have given us reason: you have seen how he evaded our questions. And when he had deliberately exasperated us beyond human endurance, he could still have easily escaped; he could have kept himself from us long enough to allow our righteous anger to cool. That was just what he did not wish to happen; he insisted, while we were still inflamed with wrath, that the doors should be opened. Need I say more? I think, with these facts before you, you will unhesitatingly render a verdict of Suicide while of Unsound Mind. It is the only charitable verdict you can give, upon one who was, after all, a great man.

FIRST KNIGHT   Thank you, Brito, I think that there is no more to be said;   [9]
and I suggest that you now disperse quietly to your homes. Please be

careful not to loiter in groups at street corners, and do nothing that might provoke any public outbreak.

TOPICS FOR DISCUSSION

1. The First Knight, Reginald Fitz Urse, employs a classic opening by calling for attention and fair play. How does Eliot convey the irony of this speech?
2. How does William de Traci attempt to win favor from his audience? To what particular patriotic prejudice does he appeal? Point out the irony in the use of the word *disinterested*.
3. Analyze the arguments in the speech of the Second Knight, Hugh de Morville. Of what did Hugh de Morville hold Thomas à Becket guilty? Do you think the persuasive appeal in the concluding paragraph is effective? Why?
4. Richard Brito, the Fourth Knight, attempts to justify the death of Thomas à Becket. What is the basis of his argument?
5. The movement of the argument of the Four Knights may be called insinuating, that is, it begins with the bland admission of murder and concludes with a charge of suicide. First, there is the virtual admission of guilt and an appeal for a hearing. Second, the motives of the Knights are presented as "disinterested." Third, the Archbishop is said to have provoked his own murder. Fourth, the Archbishop is imputed to be guilty of suicide while of unsound mind. Thus, the argument proceeds from the virtual admission that the Knights are guilty of murder to the charge that the Archbishop is guilty of his own death. Show how the Four Knights reverse their position step by step. Show also how Eliot makes clear the irony of the reversal and how his tone and style point up the contemporary relevance of Thomas à Becket's murder.

TOPICS FOR COMPOSITION

1. Each of the Four Knights advances a plausible view in his own defense. Write a refutation of one of these views. Or discuss, in the context of the speeches, one of the statements listed below.
   a. "You are Englishmen and therefore will not judge anybody without hearing both sides of the case."—Reginald Fitz Urse
   b. "So, as I said at the beginning, please give us the credit for at least being completely disinterested in this business."—William de Traci

c. "Unhappily, there are times when violence is the only way in which social justice can be secured."—Hugh de Morville

d. "And when he had deliberately exasperated us beyond human endurance, he could still have easily escaped; he could have kept himself from us long enough to allow our righteous anger to cool. That was just what he did not wish to happen; he insisted, while we were still inflamed with wrath, that the doors should be opened. Need I say more?"—Richard Brito

2. Write an essay showing how T. S. Eliot characterizes one of the Four Knights by the arguments he uses and by the nature of his dialogue.

JOHN FITZGERALD KENNEDY

Inaugural Address

LINCOLN'S *Second Inaugural Address* (see p. 203) was delivered to a solemn, silent, war-weary audience. John F. Kennedy's *Inaugural Address* was delivered on January 20, 1961, to a new generation of Americans and to a world that eagerly awaited the disclosure of the new President's plans. President Kennedy spoke of the American commitments in the contemporary world, pledging cooperation to old allies, new states, poverty-stricken nations, the countries of Latin America, the world assembly of the United Nations, and, finally, to old adversaries of the United States. He identified the common task as a war against the common enemies of man: "tyranny, poverty, disease and war itself." With a plea for help to his fellow Americans and the citizens of the world, President Kennedy ended as he began—on a note of hope.

Many recall the excellent reception of the speech on inauguration day and for many months afterward. It bespoke the personality of the President—youthful, confident, aware of his country's history and present destiny in the world of nations. It presented essential truths with great literary skill, so that within a short time much of the world was quoting these notable sentences: "The rights of man come not from the generosity of the state but from the hand of God." "If a free society cannot help the many who are poor, it cannot save the few who are rich." "Let us never negotiate out of fear. But never let us fear to negotiate." "Ask not what your country can do for you—ask what you can do for your country."

The speech was as much a triumph of style as it was of energy, hope, and vision for the future. The sentences flowered into epigrams. Antitheses and parallelisms, repetitions, rhetorical questions, commands, and exhortations, occasional trumpeting metaphors helped make its relatively simple message not only memorable but persuasive. Like Lincoln's *Second Inaugural Address,* this brief speech has its own sinewy logic. It abounds in abridged syllogisms, or enthymemes, in sequences of propositions and brief illustrations sufficient to indicate the direction of arguments. President Kennedy is arguing, not merely stating, when he says: "And if a beachhead of cooperation may push back the jungles of suspicion, let both sides join in creating a new endeavor—not a new balance of power, but a new world of law, where the strong are just and the weak secure and the peace preserved."

We observe today not a victory of party but a celebration of freedom— [1]
symbolizing an end as well as a beginning—signifying renewal as well as
change. For I have sworn before you and Almighty God the same solemn
oath our forebears prescribed nearly a century and three-quarters ago.

The world is very different now. For man holds in his mortal hands the [2]
power to abolish all forms of human poverty and all forms of human life.
And yet the same revolutionary beliefs for which our forebears fought are
still at issue around the globe—the belief that the rights of man come not
from the generosity of the state but from the hand of God.

We dare not forget today that we are the heirs of that first revolution. [3]
Let the word go forth from this time and place, to friend and foe alike,
that the torch has been passed to a new generation of Americans—born in
this century, tempered by war, disciplined by a hard and bitter peace, proud
of our ancient heritage—and unwilling to witness or permit the slow
undoing of those human rights to which this nation has always been committed, and to which we are committed today at home and around the
world.

Let every nation know, whether it wishes us well or ill, that we shall pay [4]
any price, bear any burden, meet any hardship, support any friend, oppose
any foe to assure the survival and the success of liberty.

This much we pledge—and more. [5]

To those old allies whose cultural and spiritual origins we share, we [6]
pledge the loyalty of faithful friends. United, there is little we cannot do
in a host of new cooperative ventures. Divided, there is little we can do—
for we dare not meet a powerful challenge at odds and split asunder.

To those new states whom we welcome to the ranks of the free, we [7]
pledge our word that one form of colonial control shall not have passed
away merely to be replaced by a far more iron tyranny. We shall not always expect to find them supporting our view. But we shall always hope
to find them strongly supporting their own freedom—and to remember
that, in the past, those who foolishly sought power by riding the back of
the tiger ended up inside.

To those peoples in the huts and villages of half the globe, struggling to [8]
break the bonds of mass misery, we pledge our best efforts to help them
help themselves for whatever period is required—not because the Communists may be doing it, not because we seek their votes, but because it is
right. If a free society cannot help the many who are poor, it cannot
save the few who are rich.

To our sister republics south of our border, we offer a special pledge—to [9]
convert our good words into good deeds—in a new alliance for progress—
to assist free men and free governments in casting off the chains of poverty.
But this peaceful revolution of hope cannot become the prey of hostile

powers. Let all our neighbors know that we shall join with them to oppose aggression or subversion anywhere in the Americas. And let every other power know that this hemisphere intends to remain the master of its own house.

[10] To that world assembly of sovereign states, the United Nations, our last best hope in an age where the instruments of war have far outpaced the instruments of peace, we renew our pledge of support—to prevent it from becoming merely a forum for invective—to strengthen its shield of the new and the weak—and to enlarge the area in which its writ may run.

[11] Finally, to those nations who would make themselves our adversary, we offer not a pledge but a request: that both sides begin anew the quest for peace, before the dark powers of destruction unleashed by science engulf all humanity in planned or accidental self-destruction.

[12] We dare not tempt them with weakness. For only when our arms are sufficient beyond doubt can we be certain beyond doubt that they will never be employed.

[13] But neither can two great and powerful groups of nations take comfort from our present course—both sides overburdened by the cost of modern weapons, both rightly alarmed by the steady spread of the deadly atom, yet both racing to alter that uncertain balance of terror that stays the hand of mankind's final war.

[14] So let us begin anew—remembering on both sides that civility is not a sign of weakness, and sincerity is always subject to proof. Let us never negotiate out of fear. But let us never fear to negotiate.

[15] Let both sides explore what problems unite us instead of belaboring those problems which divide us.

[16] Let both sides, for the first time, formulate serious and precise proposals for the inspection and control of arms—and bring the absolute power to destroy other nations under the absolute control of all nations.

[17] Let both sides seek to invoke the wonders of science instead of its terrors. Together let us explore the stars, conquer the deserts, eradicate disease, tap the ocean depths and encourage the arts and commerce.

[18] Let both sides unite to heed in all corners of the earth the command of Isaiah—to "undo the heavy burdens . . . (and) let the oppressed go free."

[19] And if a beachhead of cooperation may push back the jungles of suspicion, let both sides join in creating a new endeavor—not a new balance of power, but a new world of law, where the strong are just and the weak secure and the peace preserved.

[20] All this will not be finished in the first one hundred days. Nor will it be finished in the first one thousand days, nor in the life of this Administration, nor even perhaps in our lifetime on this planet. But let us begin.

[21] In your hands, my fellow citizens, more than mine, will rest the final success or failure of our course. Since this country was founded, each gen-

eration of Americans has been summoned to give testimony to its national loyalty. The graves of young Americans who answered the call to service surround the globe.

Now the trumpet summons us again—not as a call to bear arms, though [22] arms we need—not as a call to battle, though embattled we are—but a call to bear the burden of a long twilight struggle year in and year out, "rejoicing in hope, patient in tribulation"—a struggle against the common enemies of man: tyranny, poverty, disease and war itself.

Can we forge against these enemies a grand and global alliance, north [23] and south, east and west, that can assure a more fruitful life for all mankind? Will you join in that historic effort?

In the long history of the world, only a few generations have been [24] granted the role of defending freedom in its hour of maximum danger. I do not shrink from this responsibility—I welcome it. I do not believe that any of us would exchange places with any other people or any other generation. The energy, the faith, the devotion which we bring to this endeavor will light our country and all who serve it—and the glow from that fire can truly light the world.

And so, my fellow Americans: ask not what your country can do for [25] you—ask what you can do for your country.

My fellow citizens of the world: ask not what America will do for you, [26] but what together we can do for the freedom of man.

Finally, whether you are citizens of America or citizens of the world, [27] ask of us here the same high standards of strength and sacrifice which we ask of you. With a good conscience our only sure reward, with history the final judge of our deeds, let us go forth to lead the land we love, asking His blessing and His help, but knowing that here on earth God's work must truly be our own.

THE NEW YORKER

The Rhetoric of the Kennedy Address

THE following editorial response to President Kennedy's inaugural address suggests something of the impact it had on Americans in 1961; the editorial suggests the nature of this impact by choosing to discuss not the ideas of the address, important as these are, but its rhetoric. The opening comment that rhetoric is becoming dispensable in the liberal arts would need revision today, in light of renewed interest in the role of rhetoric in all kinds of discourse; it indicates, however, why the address was considered unusual by many. Its careful attention to the elements of rhetoric was exceptional for its time, the editorial implies; it brought to public discussion a refinement not only of ideas but of expression too seldom encountered. The reference to such devices as *antithesis* (the balanced opposition of ideas), *anaphora* (the repetition of words at the beginning of succeeding clauses and sentences), and *paronomasia* (kinds of punning) suggests the extent of President Kennedy's training in these elements.

As rhetoric has become an increasingly dispensable member of the liberal arts, people have abandoned the idea, held so firmly by the ancient Greeks and Romans, that eloquence is indispensable to politics. Perhaps President Kennedy's achievements in both spheres will revive a taste for good oratory —a taste that has been alternately frustrated by inarticulateness and dulled by bombast. There have been a few notable orators in our day—most recently, Adlai Stevenson—but they have been the exceptions, and it has taken Mr. Kennedy's success as a politician to suggest that the power to "enchant souls through words" (Socrates) may soon be at a premium once more. Whatever the impact of the Inaugural Address on contemporary New Frontiersmen, we find it hard to believe that an Athenian or Roman citizen could have listened to it unmoved, or that Cicero, however jealous of his own reputation, would have found reason to object to it.

We are all familiar by now with the generally high praise the President received for his first speech, but before the responsibility for a final judgment is yielded to Time it would be a shame not to seek the opinion of a couple of true professionals. Both Aristotle and Cicero, the one a theorist and the other a theorizing orator, believed that rhetoric could be an art to the extent that the orator was, first, a logician, and, second, a psychologist with an appreciation and understanding of words. Cicero felt, further, that the ideal orator was the thoroughly educated man. (He would be pleased by Mr. Kennedy's background, with its strong emphasis on affairs of state: the philosopher-orator-statesman.) Of the three types of oratory defined by the ancients—political, forensic, and display (in which audience participation was limited to a judgment of style)—the political was esteemed most highly, because it dealt with the loftiest of issues: namely, the fate of peoples, rather than of individuals. ("Now the trumpet summons us again . . . against the common enemies of man . . . .") The ideal speech was thought to be one in which three kinds of persuasion were used by the speaker: logical, to present the facts of the case and construct an argument based on them; emotional, to reach the audience psychologically; and "ethical," to appeal to the audience by establishing one's own integrity and sincerity. The Inaugural Address, being a variation on the single theme of man's rights and obligations, is not primarily logical, although it contains no illogic; it is an appeal to men's souls rather than to their minds. During the Presidential campaign, Mr. Kennedy tested and patented an exercise in American psychology that proved to be all the emotional appeal he required for the inaugural speech: "And so, my fellow Americans, ask not what your country can do for you, ask what you can do for your country." His ethical persuasion, or indication of his personal probity, consisted of an extension of that appeal: ". . . ask of us here the same high standards of strength and sacrifice which we ask of you."

Aristotle recognized only one (good) style, while Cicero thought that there were three styles—the plain, the middle, and the grand. To Aristotle, who considered it sufficient for a style to be clear and appropriate, avoiding undue elevation (whence bombast) and excessive lowliness, it would have seemed that Mr. Kennedy had achieved the Golden Mean. The formality of the Inaugural Address ("To that world assembly of sovereign states, the United Nations . . .") is appropriate to the subject; the language ("In your hands, my fellow citizens, more than mine, will rest the final success or failure of our course") is clear and direct. Cicero's ideal orator was able to speak in all three styles, in accordance with the demands of his subject, and in that respect Mr. Kennedy filled the role by speaking plainly on the practical ("All this will not be finished in the first one hundred days"), by speaking formally but directly on the purpose of national defense ("For only when our arms are sufficient beyond doubt can we be certain beyond doubt that they will never be employed"), and by speaking grandly on the potential accomplishments of the movement toward the New Frontier ("The energy, the faith, the devotion which we bring to this endeavor will light our country and all who serve it—and the glow from that fire can truly light the world").

The address, however, is largely in the grand style, which is characterized by Cicero as the ultimate source of emotional persuasion, through figures of speech and a certain degree of dignified periodic rhythm, not iambic ("The world is very different now. For man holds in his mortal hands the power to abolish all forms of human poverty and all forms of human life"). The oration is so rich in figures of speech—the many metaphors include a torch, a beachhead, jungles, a trumpet, a tiger—that we can imagine students of the future studying it for examples of antithesis ("If a free society cannot help the many who are poor, it cannot save the few who are rich"), personification ("...the hand of mankind's final war"), and anaphora ("Not as a call to bear arms, though arms we need; not as a call to battle, though embattled we are..."). "Battle" and "embattled"—an excellent example of paronomasia.

And so we leave the speech to the students of rhetoric, having invoked for Mr. Kennedy the blessings of Aristotle and Cicero, and for ourself the hope that he has reestablished the tradition of political eloquence.

TOPICS FOR DISCUSSION

1. Discuss the purpose of the *Inaugural Address*. Show how it aims at bringing about some action on the part of the audience. Show also how the purpose is stressed in the last eight paragraphs.
2. Which of the following statements best approximates the central theme of the speech? Give reasons for your answer.
    a. America celebrates her new destiny.
    b. America pledges the survival and success of liberty.
    c. Let us begin a struggle against the common enemies of man: tyranny, poverty, disease, and war itself.
    d. America starts on a course of renewal as well as change.
3. Compare and contrast this speech with Burke's *Conciliation* speech. Show how the nature of the subject, the audience, and the occasion, as well as the place and the time, all demand a different kind of speech.
4. Is it impossible to judge a speech apart from its circumstances? Explain.
5. Several of President Kennedy's most quoted sentences are cited in the headnote. How does the President's use of parallels, antitheses, alliteration, and repetition of words and phrases help to make his ideas clear, interesting, and memorable?

The Practice of Rhetoric

TOPICS FOR COMPOSITION

1. Below are listed several ceremonial occasions frequently encountered by college students. For one of the occasions write a brief speech, embodying an apt purpose and a suitable style:

   a. a sports banquet at a popular restaurant in honor of a successful athlete

   b. an academic convocation at College Hall to induct new members of an honor society

   c. an introduction of the new Campus Queen to the student body at a Junior Promenade

   d. a justification of your class absences before the Faculty Committee on Academic Standards

   e. a plea to the Dean of Students for independent work under tutorial supervision instead of required classroom attendance

2. Write a brief critical essay on the *Inaugural Speech*, addressing yourself to the following questions:

   a. What are the standards of good political oratory asserted in the comments from *The New Yorker?*

   b. Are these standards in fact exemplified by President Kennedy in the *Inaugural Address?*

   c. Is President Kennedy's speech more or less vivid and moving in style in comparison with Lincoln's *Second Inaugural Address?*

SAMUEL ELIOT MORISON

Eulogy of John Fitzgerald Kennedy

A EULOGY is a speech or written composition in which we memorialize the dead who are worthy of praise. It expresses a common sorrow, offers a common thanks, and expresses a common hope. It is part ceremonial biography, part panegyric, part ritual. Since eulogy springs from powerful feelings, no form of writing is easier to attempt. And no form is easier to overdo. We do not always speak well when we speak of the dead unless, like Admiral Morison, we can render our thoughts as clearly as we feel them.

Like all good speeches, the effective eulogy is true to the character of the speaker, does justice to the subject, and respects the occasion. Here, Morison directly reveals his own mind and heart. The spiritual references, the allusions to historians, the basically historical cast of the speech, the deeply emotional tone—particularly of the concluding section—are all consistent with the speaker's character as a professional historian, as a military leader, and as a Christian humanist. The subject— John Fitzgerald Kennedy—is revealed not only by the presentation of facts, but by the communication of that kind of knowledge available only to those who add love to understanding. The occasion, a memorial service held November 22, 1964, in St. Brigid's Church, Lexington, Massachusetts, is reflected by the tone of reverence emphasized by the quotations from the Bible and by allusions to beliefs revered by the speaker, the subject, and the audience.

The purpose of a eulogy—praise of the worthy dead —suggests, if it does not prescribe, its structure and its style. One must talk of the dead man's career. Admiral Morison does just that when he illustrates the late President's constant growth in character, knowledge, and performance. One must explain why the subject of the eulogy is worthy of praise. Admiral Morison does that also when he illustrates how President Kennedy's administration resulted in the renewal of national ideals, the restoration of national unity, and the pursuit of excellence in national life. One must speak not only plainly and sincerely, but in an elevated tone. Admiral Morison does that too, especially in the concluding paragraphs where his tribute to his young leader is, like the poetic elegy, at once sorrowful and triumphant.

In the 44th chapter of the apocryphal Book of Ecclesiasticus it is written: [1]

> Let us now praise famous men, and our fathers that begat us. The Lord hath wrought great glory by them through his great power from the beginning. Such as did bear rule in their kingdoms . . . Leaders of the people by their counsels, and by their knowledge of learning meet for the people, wise and eloquent in their instructions . . . All these were honored in their generations, and were the glory of their times. There be of them, that have left a name behind them, that their praises might be reported. . . . Their bodies are buried in peace; but their name liveth for evermore.[1]

All the early years of John Fitzgerald Kennedy were preparation for the [2] Presidency. His political inheritance, then his education at school and college, residence at the American embassy in London, where he made sage observations of the failure of appeasement; at the London School of Economics which acquainted him with an ideology which would be a future challenge to him. And his naval career, brief but heroic, helped. Just as Edward Gibbon remarked of his youthful militia service, "The captain of the Hampshire grenadiers . . . has not been useless to the historian of the Roman empire," so Lieutenant John F. Kennedy, commanding officer of PT–109, was not useless to President Kennedy of the United States; since a naval vessel is a microcosm, teaching courage, decision, self-denial and the art of ruling men. But running through it all, supporting him in time of trial, was his religious faith, which taught him the fundamental truth that man is nothing, without the love of God.

Jack Kennedy showed a steady growth in knowledge, and in wisdom. [3] When not yet thirty years of age, he had the boldness to run for Congress from the Charlestown district, without having gone through the rough-and-tumble of ward and local politics. Some of you will remember how old-line Boston Democrats snorted, "What has he ever done to be elected? Did he ever get a man a job, or give a poor family a basket o' groceries?" That was the old Tammany system; but, as one of Edwin O'Connor's characters in *The Last Hurrah* pointed out, the New Deal made that sort of thing obsolete; and the Charlestown voters, far from being annoyed by Jack's wearing good clothes and never talking down to them, were complimented that one of their own looked and acted like a thoroughbred. The Kennedy and Fitzgerald inheritance doubtless helped, but Jack was really elected on the strength of his personality. After two terms in the House, the Massachusetts Democrats nominated him for the Senate in 1952, and in the election that fall, when the Bay State went heavily for General

---

[1]Ecclesiasticus 40 : 1–4, 7, 8, 14.

EULOGY OF JOHN FITZGERALD KENNEDY Reprinted by permission of Samuel Eliot Morison.

Samuel Eliot Morison **221**

Eisenhower and elected a Republican governor, she sent John F. Kennedy to the Senate.

[4]   Senator Kennedy bided his time. Elder statesmen told him, "The way to get along is to go along," and for about two years he did just about that. But a severe operation, followed by a long convalescence in 1954, raised his sights and gave him time to write *Profiles in Courage,* a series of thumbnail sketches of politicians who had exhibited that quality so far in politics. One of the remarkable things about John F. Kennedy was his constant *growth* in character, knowledge, and performance. And that quality makes his premature death seem even more tragic.

[5]   Then came the Democratic nomination for the presidency, and the election of 1960, in which Jack Kennedy proved to be the perfect candidate. His "Harvard accent" may have offended some; but his fine presence, youthful vigor, words well chosen and phrased, delivered in a strong, virile voice, appealed to voters who cared little for programs but appreciated personality and character. The religious aspect was by no means absent from the campaign. Maria Monk[2] and all the old standbys were trotted out once more, and countercharges were directed against "Protestant bigots." But how this actually affected the vote nobody knows. What is certain is that Jack's election, once for all, disproved the superstition that Protestant Americans would not vote for a Catholic for President of the United States.

[6]   Whatever the cause of this momentous election, we soon found that we had something fresh and new, yet in the pattern of American tradition. Millions of spectators and TV viewers felt just that on January 20, 1961, when they saw and heard venerable, white-haired Robert Frost read "The Gift Outright," and the young President—just half the age of the poet— fling out a challenging inaugural address. He opened with a promise that his administration meant "renewal" as well as change. In a very different world from the one that confronted Washington when he took the same oath of office in 1789, he said, "The same revolutionary beliefs for which our forebears fought are still at issue around the globe—the belief that the rights of man come not from the generosity of the state but from the hand of God.

[7]   "We dare not forget today that we are the heirs of that first revolution. Let the word go forth from this time and place, to friend and foe alike, that the torch has been passed to a new generation of Americans—born in this century, tempered by war, disciplined by a hard and bitter peace, proud

---

[2]Maria Monk (1817?–49) was a Canadian adventuress who made her appearance in New York in 1836. She claimed that she had escaped from a Montreal convent and wrote a book, *Awful Disclosures of the Hotel Dieu Nunnery of Montreal,* describing her experiences there. Two Protestant clergymen checked into the honesty of the book and discovered that she was an impostor. She was arrested in 1849 for theft and died shortly afterward in prison in New York.

of our ancient heritage—and unwilling to witness or permit the slow undoing of those human rights to which this nation has always been committed, and to which we are committed today at home and around the world."

To the world he said, "Let us begin anew—remembering on both sides [8] that civility is not a sign of weakness, and sincerity is always subject to proof. Let us never negotiate out of fear. But let us never fear to negotiate."

And to America he sounded a trumpet call, "a call to bear the burden of [9] a long twilight struggle year in and year out, 'rejoicing in hope, patient in tribulation'—a struggle against the common enemies of man: tyranny, poverty, disease and war itself.... And so, my fellow Americans, ask not what your country can do for you—ask what you can do for your country."

There had been no inaugural address like this since Abraham Lincoln's [10] second.

Note the recurrent theme—new, anew, renewal; recalling the motto on [11] our Great Seal, *Novus Ordo Seculorum*,[3] and Shelley's paraphrase of the Vergilian ode from which that motto came:

> The world's great age begins anew,
>   The golden years return
>
>   .   .   .
>
> Another Athens shall arise,
>   And to remoter time
> Bequeath, like sunset to the skies,
>   The splendor of its prime.

But observe, also, the solemn warning note of "the long twilight struggle year in and year out." And that was the note on which his life closed; in his last speech at Fort Worth, Texas, on November 21, 1963, President Kennedy said, "This is a dangerous and uncertain world.... No one expects our lives to be easy—not in this decade, not in this century." He heard from afar the thunder of the "chariot of Israel and the horsemen thereof."

Renewal was the one keynote of John Fitzgerald Kennedy's policy in his [12] short, too short, Presidency. The other notes in this tonic chord of the Kennedy administration were unity and excellence. He took to heart those lines in Lowell's *The Present Crisis,* written in the revolutionary decade of the 1840's:

> New occasions teach new duties,
> Time makes ancient good uncouth;
> They must upward still, and onward,
> Who would keep abreast of Truth.

[3]Literally, new order of the ages; from Vergil *Eclogues* iv. 5.

He realized that we are living in an era of profound, revolutionary changes in domestic affairs as in foreign relations, changes caused by the liberation of former colonies, by the burgeoning population, changes wrought by science and its applications, extending man's orbit into outer space, changes demanded by races formerly depressed and neglected, for their share of the good things in life. Almost everyone knows that we live in a quickly and vastly changing world for which old formulae are inadequate—the Vatican Ecumenical Congress knows it, the British government and people know it, the Latin American governments are painfully aware of it—all the big American corporations realize it. In fact, everyone seems to know that we live in a world of revolutionary change where problems cannot be met by nineteenth-century methods, except the Communists and the Goldwater wing of the Republican party. President Kennedy not only admitted the reality of changes, however disagreeable, that had come to stay, and also apprehended others that were in mid-course; he proposed to do something about them, to make the necessary adjustment in American domestic and foreign policy to meet these profound material and spiritual upheavals. Alas that he had so little time to do what so urgently needed to be done!

[13]   The second note of the President's tonic chord was *unity*. He aimed to restore our essential unity on basic American principles, as embodied in the Declaration of Independence, the Federal Constitution, and the Bill of Rights. In this effort he did his best to leach out the foul poison of hatred and suspicion that McCarthyism had left in the American commonwealth. In a message to the American Civil Liberties Union in 1962 he said: "It is in times such as these that many men, weak in courage and frail in nerve, develop the tendency to turn suspiciously on their neighbors and leaders. Unable to face up to the dangers from without, they become convinced that the real danger is from within. Our hard-won freedoms are frequently abandoned in an effort to escape the burdens of responsible citizenship."

[14]   A third note of his administration was struck by that line of Shelley's, "Another Athens shall arise," the note of *excellence*. He knew that mediocrity in performance, timidity in approaching issues, are as great enemies to the Republic as extremism on the left, or on the right. In pursuit of this goal of excellence, President Kennedy took the most important steps ever made by a President of the United States to foster literature and the arts. His admiration for accomplishment in every field led him to cultivate artists and writers. His establishment of the Medal of Freedom was but one of many ways in which he sought to reward talent and to impart to the public his respect for excellence and distaste for mediocrity. He made a good beginning of what John Quincy Adams tried to do and failed, the transplanting of high cultural values to the federal city where, if anywhere, a trans-Atlantic Athens should arise. Mrs. Jacqueline Kennedy, the President's fair partner in these enterprises, by her excellent taste and boundless

energy, transformed the White House into a residence worthy of the chief magistrate of a great republic. Pablo Casals was invited from Puerto Rico to give a cello recital at the White House, his first visit to Washington since Theodore Roosevelt's time. Not only did the Kennedys by their example enhance public respect for the arts, they surrounded themselves with gay, active, intelligent people who imparted a verve to Washington that it had not known in fifty years.

Note his repeated graciousness and consideration to Robert Frost, whom [15] he did not use simply to dress up the inauguration, but regarded as a valued friend and counselor. Nor did he forget other elderly people of distinction, even those overseas. Imagine the surprise and pleasure of the English historian George Peabody Gooch, receiving on his ninetieth birthday this message from President Kennedy: "For more than a half a century, as historian and as editor, you have maintained the noble traditions and high standards of liberal scholarship. You have seen history both as a reconstruction of the past and as an illumination of the present. I wish you many more years of continued health and activity." A typical example of his thoughtfulness.

In pursuit of this ideal of excellence, the American winners of Nobel [16] prizes, never before accorded official recognition in Washington, together with writers, scholars, and artists of many races, were given a dinner and reception in the White House, conducted with a good taste that no European court could have surpassed. And it was typical of the President that instead of greeting the distinguished guests with a solemn address, he set a gay note by announcing, "This is the most extraordinary collection of talent ... that has ever been gathered together at the White House—with the possible exception of when Thomas Jefferson dined alone!"

Truly it may be said of John F. Kennedy what Dr. Samuel Johnson wrote [17] in stately Latin of another great gentleman of Irish stock, Oliver Goldsmith, *Nullum quod tetigit non ornavit*, "He touched nothing that he did not adorn."

It is to President Kennedy's credit that he aroused the enmity of racial, [18] religious, and political bigots, one of whom committed the most abominable murder of the century. But this country, by and large, and the young and perceptive people worldwide, admired, even adored, the handsome presidential couple and their little children Caroline and "John-John," with whom the parents always found time to play and frolic. Everything that the Kennedys did was done with grace, elegance, style, and it all seemed natural, not forced; this was what Washington and the White House should always have been but almost never had been. John F. Kennedy was thorough, energetic, and perceptive in his handling of the myriad problems that beset a President. Yet during all the crises and complexities of those "thousand days," he found time for his family, time to greet both new and old friends, to whom he never appeared tense, but relaxed; never uncertain, but confident; never hurried, but calm, with that serenity which only those achieve to whom the Spirit speaketh.

[19]   Friday, November 22, 1963, *dies irae* for America and the free world, dawned. It was but a few months after his forty-sixth birthday. The President decided to visit first Florida and then Texas. His visit to Florida was a continual ovation. Thence he flew to Fort Worth, where he delivered his last speech. In the speech that he was to have given that afternoon but never delivered since the assassin's bullet stopped his breath, he begged his countrymen to exercise their strength "with wisdom and restraint—that we may achieve in our time and for all time the ancient vision of 'Peace on Earth, Good Will toward Men.'" For "As was written long ago, 'Except the Lord keep the city, the watchman waketh but in vain.'"

[20]   There was a gallantry and romance about the Kennedys in Washington which makes one think of some golden, legendary era of the world's history—Roland winding his horn at Roncesvalles, or the court of King Arthur and his Round Table at Camelot. Jack and Jacqueline may have felt it, too; for we know that their favorite musical recording, the one that they listened to almost nightly before retiring, was that of Lerner and Loewe's *Camelot*. Mrs. Kennedy's favorite lyric in that musical, I am told was "I loved you long in silence." And the President's favorite part was the finale, in which King Arthur, about to set forth to battle and certain death, enjoins a young squire to remember the "One brief shining moment that was known as Camelot."

> Ask every person if he's heard the story,
> And tell it strong and clear if he has not,
> That once there was a fleeting wisp of glory
>   Called Camelot.[4]

[21]   Alas, that our fleeting wisp of glory was so brief! But we who lived through it will never forget that one brief shining moment, the thousand days when the Presidency was occupied by a great gentleman whose every act and appearance appealed to our pride and gave us fresh confidence in ourselves and our country.

TOPICS FOR DISCUSSION

1. Does the quotation in paragraph 1 embody the general theme of the speech? Why or why not?

[4]Lyrics from the musical composition *Camelot*. Copyright © 1960 by Alan Jay Lerner and Frederick Loewe. Used by permission of Chappell & Co., Inc.

The Practice of Rhetoric

2. How does Morison develop the topic sentence (in paragraph 2) that "all the early years of John Fitzgerald Kennedy were preparation for the Presidency"?
3. Show how Morison supports the view that "Jack Kennedy showed a steady growth in knowledge, and in wisdom."
4. What facts support the statement that Kennedy was "something fresh and new, yet in the pattern of American tradition"?
5. What is the force of the one-sentence paragraph 10? Do you agree that the Kennedy address is comparable to Lincoln's *Second Inaugural Address?* In what specific ways are they comparable? Explain.
6. Reread President Kennedy's address on page 213. Do you agree with Morison's statement that the three tonic chords are renewal, unity, and excellence? Why or why not?
7. In most eulogies the final section sums up the life of the subject and expresses the speaker's feelings toward him. Does Morison follow this convention? Explain.

TOPICS FOR COMPOSITION

1. Write a eulogy on some public figure who has recently died. In giving an account of his life make sure you bring out the two or three main reasons why he is admired and why his death is regrettable. Possible subjects for a eulogy are: Albert Schweitzer, Winston Churchill, Pope John XXIII.
2. Closely related to eulogy is the panegyric, a public speech or writing in praise of someone. The classic panegyric, as Morison illustrates, normally shows how early life prepared the subject for his career, how he grew in intelligence and moral strength, and what his particular trait is. Write a panegyric in praise of someone you greatly admire. Make your praise discriminating.
3. After reviewing the speeches in this section, write a critical essay pointing out the differences among the various kinds of oratory. Show how these differences are determined in part by the purpose of the speaker, in part by the nature of the subject, and in part by the nature of the audience.

❀ Expository Narrative

VIOLET BONHAM CARTER

First Encounter

IN a brief preface to her biography of Winston Churchill, Violet Bonham Carter quotes Thomas Gray's remark that "any fool may write a most valuable book by chance, if he will only tell us what he heard and saw with veracity." With great modesty, she presents her *Winston Churchill* merely as her personal impressions and memories. To write such a book, she seems to suggest, one needs only what opportunity had supplied her, a life-long friendship with Winston Churchill.

Yet as one reads the brilliant introductory chapter entitled "First Encounter," one finds Gray's remark inappropriate. Anyone who can tell us what he heard and saw with veracity is hardly a fool. Under some circumstances, only a wise man has the sense to hear, to see, and to tell the truth. Truth cannot be turned on like a faucet. Under all circumstances it takes high talent, if not genius, to explain what kind of truth a genius reveals. And that is just what Violet Bonham Carter has done.

How she has done it may be described according to various vocabularies. One may speak of her narrative style, of her ability to sketch a scene, to introduce dialogue, to capture the Churchillian idiom and rhythms. One must note too the deftness with which she simultaneously records and explains Churchill's genius, as in her remark that "though he had vision he appeared to lack antennae—to ignore the need to feel his way about other minds." But these technical skills of narration and exposition are simply the intelligent and amiable servants of Violet Bonham Carter's own presiding vision—her affectionate understanding and admiration of a great man.

I first met Winston Churchill in the early summer of 1906 at a dinner party [1] to which I went as a very young girl. Our hostess was Lady Wemyss and I remember that Arthur Balfour, George Wyndham, Hilaire Belloc and Charles Whibley were among the guests.

The Liberal Party had just been swept back to power on the flood tide [2] of an overwhelming majority. Sir Henry Campbell-Bannerman was Prime Minister, my father, H. H. Asquith, Chancellor of the Exchequer and Win-

---

FIRST ENCOUNTER From *Winston Churchill: An Intimate Portrait* by Violet Bonham Carter. Copyright © 1965 by Violet Bonham Carter. Reprinted by permission of Harcourt, Brace & World, Inc., and Collins Publishers.

ston Churchill was holding his first office as Under-Secretary for the Colonies. With his dramatic South African exploits behind him and a political career in the making, he was already on the highroad to fame. His critics might have called it notoriety. For then as always he had critics. His unabashed confidence, unsquashable resilience, his push and dash and flair for taking short cuts through life, his contempt for humdrum conformity, always challenged stolid, stick-in-the-mud opinion here and elsewhere. No one knew better how to perform the public service known as putting the cat among the pigeons.

[3]   I found myself sitting next to this young man who seemed to me quite different from any other young man I had ever met. For a long time he remained sunk in abstraction. Then he appeared to become suddenly aware of my existence. He turned on me a lowering gaze and asked me abruptly how old I was. I replied that I was nineteen. "And I," he said almost despairingly, "am thirty-two already. Younger than anyone else who *counts*, though," he added, as if to comfort himself. Then savagely: "Curse ruthless time! Curse our mortality. How cruelly short is the allotted span for all we must cram into it!" And he burst forth into an eloquent diatribe on the shortness of human life, the immensity of possible human accomplishment—a theme so well exploited by the poets, prophets and philosophers of all ages that it might seem difficult to invest it with a new and startling significance. Yet for me he did so, in a torrent of magnificent language which appeared to be both effortless and inexhaustible and ended up with the words I shall always remember: "We are all worms. But I do believe that I am a glowworm."

[4]   By this time I was convinced of it—and my conviction remained unshaken throughout the years that followed.

[5]   Later on he asked me whether I thought that words had a magic and a music quite independent of their meaning. I said I certainly thought so, and I quoted as a classic though familiar instance the first lines that came into my head.

> Charm'd magic casements, opening on the foam
> Of perilous seas, in faery lands forlorn . . .

[6]   His eyes blazed with excitement. "Say that again," he said, "say it again —it is marvelous!" "But," I objected, "you know these lines. You know the 'Ode to a Nightingale.' " He had apparently never read it and never heard of it before. (I must, however, add that next time I met him he had learned not merely this but all the odes of Keats by heart—and he recited them quite mercilessly from start to finish, not sparing me a syllable.)

[7]   Finding that he liked poetry, I quoted to him from one of my own favorite poets, Blake. He listened avidly, repeating some lines to himself

The Practice of Rhetoric

with varying emphases and stresses, then added meditatively: "I never knew that that old Admiral had found time to write so much good poetry." I was astounded that he, with his acute susceptibility to words and power of using them, should have left such tracts of English literature entirely unexplored. But however it had happened he had lost nothing by it. As he himself put it, when he approached books it was "with a hungry, empty mind and with fairly strong jaws, and what I got I bit." And his ear for the beauty of language needed no tuning fork.

Until the end of dinner I listened to him spellbound. I can remember [8] thinking: *This is* what people mean when they talk of seeing stars. That is what I am doing now. I do not to this day know who was on my other side. Good manners, social obligation, duty—all had gone with the wind. I was transfixed, transported into a new element. I knew only that I had seen a great light. I recognized it as the light of genius.

Remembering my callow youth readers may well discount the indelible [9] impression I then received. But young and inexperienced as I was I had even then some standards of comparison. My lot happened to have been cast by Fortune in a context of rare and various minds. From earliest childhood my father had been my closest and most intimate friend. As I grew up I had met and listened with delight to many of his political colleagues and opponents, to Arthur Balfour, to John Morley, to Augustine Birrell, Lord Hugh Cecil and Edward Grey, to name a few. Among my own generation my friends were drawn from the contemporaries of my four Oxford brothers, who all belonged to vintage years. And yet, I knew that I had never met anyone before at all like Winston Churchill. What was it, I asked myself, which marked him out from all the rest? I might, if I had known them at the time, have answered my own question in the words of Dr. Johnson: "We all know what light is. But it is difficult to *tell* what it is."

I cannot attempt to analyze, still less to transmit, the light of genius. [10] But I will try to set down, as I remember them, some of the differences which struck me at the time between him and all the others, young and old, whom I had known.

First and foremost he was incalculable. He ran true to no form. There [11] lurked in every thought and word the ambush of the unexpected. I felt also that the impact of life, ideas and even words upon his mind was not only vivid and immediate, but *direct*. Between him and them there was no shock absorber of vicarious thought or precedent gleaned either from books or other minds. His relationship with all experience was firsthand.

My father and his friends were mostly scholars, steeped in the classical [12] tradition, deeply imbued with academic knowledge, erudition and experience. Their intellectual granaries held the harvests of the past. On many themes they knew most of the arguments and all the answers to them. In certain fields of thought there was to them "nothing new under the sun." But to Winston Churchill everything under the sun was new—seen and appraised as on the first day of Creation. His approach to life was full of ardor and surprise. Even the eternal verities appeared to him to be an exciting personal discovery. (He often seemed annoyed to find that some of them had occurred to other people long ago.) And because they were so new to him he made them shine for me with a new meaning. However familiar his conclusion it had not been reached by any beaten track. His mind had found its own way everywhere.

[13]   Again—unlike the scholars—he was intellectually quite uninhibited and unself-conscious. Nothing to him was trite. The whole world of thought was virgin soil. He did not seem to be the least ashamed of uttering truths so simple and eternal that on another's lips they would be truisms. (This was a precious gift he never lost.) Nor was he afraid of using splendid language. Even as I listened, glowing and vibrating to his words, I knew that many of my captious and astringent friends would label them as "bombast," "rhetoric," "heroics." But I also knew with certainty that if they did they would be wrong. There was nothing false, inflated, artificial in his eloquence. It was his natural idiom. His world was built and fashioned in heroic lines. He spoke its language.

[14]   One other, paradoxical impression I carried away from this, our first encounter. Although he had the ageless quality of greatness I felt that he was curiously young. In fact, in some pedestrian ways, he made me feel that I was older. I felt that, though armed to the teeth for life's encounter, he was also strangely vulnerable, that he would need protection from, interpretation· to, a humdrum world which would not easily apprehend or understand his genius. And in this last fear I was right.

[15]   It was my father's invariable habit to sit up reading in his bedroom for an hour or two before going to bed. I always went to say good night to him and share with him the adventures of my day. That night I burst into his room and poured out my experience, assuring him that for the first time in my life I had seen genius. I remember his amused response: "Well, Winston would certainly agree with you there—but I am not sure whether you will find many others of the same mind. Still, I know exactly what you mean. He is not only remarkable but unique. He will now have every chance to extend himself and show his paces."

[16]   I remember instinctively omitting from my story the fact that Winston had never read the "Ode to a Nightingale," fearing that it might lower him in my father's estimation. This unusual act of censorship was a proof that I had forged a new loyalty.

[17]   When I proclaimed to others my discovery, I found my father's warning fully justified. My estimate of Winston Churchill was not sympathetically received. In fact I was mocked by many. The attitude of the general public toward him at the time was, at best, one of expectant interest,

The Practice of Rhetoric

curiosity, and tolerant amusement; at worst, one of mistrust and acid reprobation. In Tory and social circles he had for some years past been a red rag which turned the mildest cows into infuriated bulls. He was an outsider, a pusher, thruster, and self-advertiser. After he crossed the Floor[1] he became, in addition, a rat, a turncoat, an *arriviste* and (worst crime of all) one who had certainly arrived. To take him down a peg or even several pegs was not only a pleasure but a duty—to society and to the nation.

The Liberals were naturally far more discerning. To their credit they [18] have never regarded intellect as a dangerous factor in a politician. They recognized Winston Churchill's quality and they gloried in their glittering catch. But even among Liberals there were certain reservations and suspicions. He was "sound" on Free Trade, on South Africa and on Retrenchment, but what about Reform—and Peace? He appeared to have found fighting a rather too congenial occupation in the past. Had he got Liberalism in his bones? Would he stay put?

In private life though he inspired devotion in his friends he did not [19] exercise on his contemporaries the fascination of his father, Lord Randolph Churchill. I remember asking my father, who as a young man in his early days in Parliament had known and loved Lord Randolph, which of the two he rated higher, and his reply: "You can't compare them. Randolph was irresistible. He had incomparably more charm, more wit. But— Winston is by far the better fellow of the two."

It is true I think that, though Winston Churchill impressed and often [20] dazzled, he did not charm or try to charm. He was as impervious to atmosphere as a diver in his bell. By a blessed fluke I found my way into the bell and never lost it. To me it was a far more exciting place than the watery elements it excluded. But for those outside it often seemed to be an impenetrable shell. He sometimes made a brilliant sortie, but in conversation he exhaled rather than inhaled and this was occasionally, and not unnaturally, resented by his interlocutor. I remember my stepmother, who enjoyed self-expression and indulged it to the full, complaining that he had "a noisy mind."

Hoping to provide a double treat I placed beside him at a luncheon party [21] one of the rarest and most remarkable women of her generation, Lady Horner, an intimate friend both of my father and of Lord Haldane, and before their day of Burne-Jones, Ruskin and the Pre-Raphaelites. Her conversational resources were unlimited, her human understanding flexible and deep. I noticed with anxiety that hardly a word had passed between them. In answer to my solicitous inquiries she told me that after an aeon of unbroken silence she made a frontal attack and said to him: "Do

[1]In the House of Commons the Government and Opposition sit facing each other. A member who changes his party, as Winston Churchill did, crosses the Floor and sits facing his former colleagues. [Bonham Carter's note.]

Violet Bonham Carter

tell me—what on earth *are* you thinking about?" He replied: "I am thinking of a diagram" and relapsed into complete absorption. She added: "I
don't like people who make me feel as though I wasn't there." In later
years they became fast friends.

[22]   When he was staying with us in Scotland the same fate overtook my
young stepcousin Diana Lister (now Lady Westmorland), who was so out-
raged by his neglect that she snatched up her plate and knife and fork
and finished her luncheon standing at the sideboard. He did not even
notice her flight till at the very end of luncheon, casually glancing at her
empty chair, he asked me innocently: "What happened to that jolly little
trout?" He was full of compunction when I told him what *had* happened
and explained the vital matter which had filled his mind to the exclusion
of all else. To me these trivial incidents were illustrations both of his
political weakness and his strength. William James once wrote that men
of genius differ from ordinary men not in any innate quality of the brain,
but in the aims and objects on which they concentrate and in the degree
of concentration they manage to achieve. Winston Churchill possessed a
power of concentration amounting almost to obsession. It gave his purpose a momentum which often proved irresistible. But the rock on which
that purpose sometimes foundered was the human element he had failed to
take into account. Though he was the most human of all human beings, he
was himself far too extraordinary to know how ordinary people "worked."

[23]   I take, as an illustration, the episode which wounded him more deeply
than any other in his whole career. The Dardanelles expedition, perhaps
the most imaginative strategic concept of the First World War, was first
frustrated by a monolithic soldier at the War Office and then defeated by
a megalomaniac sailor at the Admiralty. Winston had failed to recognize
that the essential condition of its success was to secure not the mere passive acquiescence but the active co-operation of Lord Kitchener. Again
the final breach with Fisher which hurled him from the Admiralty fell like
a thunderbolt. Their association had (in his own words) been "deep and
fiercely intimate." No two men had ever agreed and disagreed more often
and more passionately. No one knew better than he did just how invalu-
able and how impossible a colleague Fisher could be. And yet he seems
to have had no inkling that their relations had reached breaking point.

[24]   At the time of the Abdication his championship of Edward VIII was
inspired by a romantic loyalty. He would have been prepared to stand
alone beside his King against a world in arms. But he was also quite
oblivious to the state of mind of the ordinary men and women of this
country, who expected from their King a Queen and not a hole-and-corner
morganatic marriage.

[25]   Ordinary men and women were equally bewildered by his congenital
incapacity to be commonplace. The British people like seeing in their
statesmen a reflection of themselves, perhaps in slightly sublimated form.

Lord Baldwin recognized this taste and assuaged it to the full. He realized that the public loves to hear the tunes it knows and he played them with a masterly dexterity and skill.

I remember the old Duke of Devonshire of that day who suffered from [26] deafness once saying to my father of Lord Spencer: "I always hear *him* because I know exactly what he is going to say." The trouble with Winston Churchill was that no one ever knew what he was going to say—or do. The unpredictable is rarely popular. More often than not it is mistaken for the unreliable. The public likes getting what it expects. It resents surprises and prefers being lulled to being startled.

I am not of course suggesting that in that first summer of our early [27] friendship any of these reflections, forecasts, or analyses crossed my mind. But I knew that politics depends above all else upon the power of persuading others to accept ideas. I was disturbed to find among so many people a blank and blind refusal to recognize Winston Churchill's rare and dazzling quality. And I sometimes felt amazement and alarm at his own seeming unawareness of their reactions to himself. Though he had vision he appeared to lack antennae—to ignore the need to feel his way about other minds. I remembered, with some reassurance, the lines of Blake:

Does the Eagle know what is in the pit
Or wilt thou go ask the Mole?

What need was there for him to grope his way among the groundling [28] moles when he could soar above their heads? It was true that he never tempered the wind of his words or his opinions either to shorn or unshorn lambs. But how could he be expected to project himself into the mind or body of a sheep? Yet, as I had even then observed, the world was full of sheep, and sheep had votes.

It was he himself who had once quoted to me the words of one of his [29] great heroes, Napoleon Bonaparte: "I have always marched with the opinions of four or five millions of men." The day would come when he would need the support of millions to realize his aims. In his own words, "great numbers are at least an explanation of great changes." Armies are just as necessary in politics as in war. And they can only be recruited by persuasion.

Yet every time we met he exorcised in me any misgivings about his [30] future; by the impetus of his mind, by his unerring instinct for the living thought and word, above all by his imagination—"imagination, which, in truth, is but another name for absolute power." Although I knew he did not see the world we lived in as it was, I felt he had the latent power to make his world our own, to impose his shape and pattern on events.

And in spite of his dark moments of impatience and frustration some- [31]

times verging on despair, I was conscious of his own ultimate confidence in himself. He had no doubts about his star. He might have said with Keats: "There is an awful warmth about my heart like a load of immortality." Even in those early days he felt that he was walking with destiny and that he had been preserved from many perils to fulfill its purpose. And in this mystical conviction History has proved him right.

[32]   But in another instinctive certainty he proved wrong. He was convinced that he would die young, that he had only a short span of years in which to cover his appointed course, and this strange premonition filled him with a sense of burning urgency. Would he have time to do what Fate required of him? I was distressed and puzzled by this phantasy of early doom which had no root in facts or reason. I knew that he always traveled with cylinders of oxygen which he imbibed before speaking. Yet it was quite impossible to think of him as ill. His zest, vitality, activity and industry were inexhaustible. He seemed to have been endowed by Nature with a double charge of life. I probed for reasons. "Why should you die young? Why shouldn't you live till you are a hundred?" The only answer that I ever wrung from him was: "My father died when he was forty-six." And these words, though I so little understood their implication, held the key both to his entry into politics and to the course he followed throughout his early years. The mainspring of his thought and action was his hero worship of a father he had hardly known.

[33]   About his father's death he has written: "All my dreams of comradeship with him, of entering Parliament at his side and in his support were ended. There remained for me only to pursue his aims and vindicate his memory."

TOPICS FOR DISCUSSION

1. Violet Bonham Carter sums up her initial impression of Winston Churchill in paragraph 8. Do the preceding incidents justify her conclusion that Churchill was a genius? Explain.

2. According to what standards does Violet Bonham Carter call Churchill a genius? Why does she emphasize his differences from others? How did Churchill appear to differ from scholars? From Lord Randolph Churchill?

3. In paragraphs 21 through 28, the author gives several instances of Churchill's power of concentration. How do these illustrations support her view that Churchill was a genius?

4. Is the ultimate difference between Churchill and other men summed up in the word *imagination*? Explain.

5. Compare this biographical essay with Samuel Eliot Morison's "Eulogy of John Fitzgerald Kennedy" (p. 221), and "Prescott: The American Thucydides." What narrative and expository devices appear in all three essays? Are all three biographies excessively favorable? Give reasons for your answer.

TOPICS FOR COMPOSITION

1. Tell the story of your first encounter with an outstanding person. In telling the story, explain, as in this essay, just why you think him outstanding.
2. In his essay *Macaulay*, Lytton Strachey defines the qualities that make a good historian as "a capacity for absorbing facts, a capacity for stating them, and a point of view." Write an essay illustrating one of these qualities in the three essays in this section.

**WILLIAM H.
PRESCOTT**

**The March
to
Mexico**

EXPOSITORY narrative is a story that in the telling explains why or how something happened or someone achieved success or failure. When this kind of narrative deals primarily with public events, we call it history; when it deals primarily with an individual life, we call it biography. If we invent the story and plot the incidents to bring out general truths of human nature, our expository narrative becomes fiction.

"The March to Mexico" is a segment of a history, one long regarded as a classic both for its accuracy and its literary skill. It tells how Hernando Cortés leading a small band of Spaniards from Cuba, landed in Mexico in 1519, worked his way from Yucatán to what is now Vera Cruz. From Malinche, an outcast Indian girl, Cortés learned that the Aztec rule under Montezuma was bitterly resented. The Aztecs' enslavement of older native races, their large-scale ritualistic murders, and their reputation for treachery gave Cortés the opportunity to satisfy his ambition, his avarice, and his love of glory. He scuttled his ships, defied Aztec commands to stay away from the central valley, and led his men—not yet hardened into conquerors—up to the seat of the empire.

Cortés' march across the mountains, hazardous enough as a simple expedition, soon took on the character of a military campaign. Three battles with the Tlascalans ended with their defeat, capitulation, and alliance with Cortés. Cortés next defeated the Cholulans, who were conspiring with Montezuma. It is at this point in the book that the following selection begins.

Subsequent chapters of the *History of the Conquest of Mexico* recount Cortés' suppression of a private expedition in Vera Cruz and a large-scale revolution led by Chitlahua, Montezuma's brother.

Prescott's *History* has been widely praised for its vigorous narrative movement, its brilliant description, and its dramatic characterization of main figures such as Cortés, Malinche, Alvarado, and the various Aztec princes. Prescott's ability to explain how so great a victory was achieved over such incredible odds is as important as his power to inform and entertain. Though Prescott differed from the conquerors in race, temperament, education, and religion, he was able to see them as men of courage and common sense. Courage inspired Diego Ordaz and his companions to climb Popocatepetl, "which the natives declared no man could accomplish and live." Hard-headed prudence prompted Montaño's exploration of the same volcano in search of gunpowder. Practicality and romance, avarice and idealism mingled and became one in the hearts of Cortés and his men. "What wonder, then," writes Prescott, "if the Spaniard of that day, feeding his imagination with dreams of enchantment at home, and with its realities abroad, should have displayed a Quixotic enthusiasm—a romantic exaltation of character, not to be comprehended by the colder spirit of other lands!" Prescott's greatest achievement, however, is not that his story dazzles, but that it illuminates.[1]

Every thing being now restored to quiet in Cholula, the allied army of Spaniards and Tlascalans set forward in high spirits, and resumed the march on Mexico. The road lay through the beautiful savannas and luxuriant plantations that spread out for several leagues in every direction. On the march, they were met occasionally by embassies from the neighboring places, anxious to claim the protection of the white men, and to propitiate them by gifts, especially of gold, for which their appetite was generally known throughout the country. [1]

Some of these places were allies of the Tlascalans, and all showed much discontent with the oppressive rule of Montezuma. The natives cautioned the Spaniards against putting themselves in his power, by entering his capital; and they stated, as evidence of his hostile disposition, that he had caused the direct road to it to be blocked up, that the strangers might be compelled to choose another, which, from its narrow passes and strong positions, would enable him to take them at great disadvantage. [2]

The information was not lost on Cortés, who kept a strict eye on the movements of the Mexican envoys, and redoubled his own precautions against surprise. Cheerful and active, he was ever where his presence was needed, sometimes in the van, at others in the rear, encouraging the weak, stimulating the sluggish, and striving to kindle in the breasts of others the same courageous spirit which glowed in his own. At night he never omitted to go the rounds, to see that every man was at his post. On one occasion, his vigilance had well-nigh proved fatal to him. He approached so near a sentinel, that the man, unable to distinguish his person in the dark, levelled his crossbow at him, when fortunately an exclamation of the general, who gave the watchword of the night, arrested a movement, which might else have brought the campaign to a close, and given a respite for some time longer to the empire of Montezuma. [3]

The army came at length to the place mentioned by the friendly Indians, [4]

[1]Prescott's footnotes in the original text are here omitted.

William H. Prescott

where the road forked, and one arm of it was found, as they had fore-told, obstructed with large trunks of trees, and huge stones which had been strewn across it. Cortés inquired the meaning of this from the Mexican ambassadors. They said it was done by the emperor's orders, to prevent their taking a route which, after some distance, they would find nearly impracticable for the cavalry. They acknowledged, however, that it was the most direct road; and Cortés declaring that this was enough to decide him in favor of it, as the Spaniards made no account of obstacles, commanded the rubbish to be cleared away. Some of the timber might still be seen by the road-side, as Bernal Diaz tells us, many years after. The event left little doubt in the general's mind of the meditated treachery of the Mexicans. But he was too polite to betray his suspicions.

[5]   They were now leaving the pleasant champaign country, as the road wound up the bold sierra which separates the great plateaus of Mexico and Puebla. The air, as they ascended, became keen and piercing; and the blasts, sweeping down the frozen sides of the mountains, made the soldiers shiver in their thick harness of cotton, and benumbed the limbs of both men and horses.

[6]   They were passing between two of the highest mountains on the North American continent; Popocatepetl, "the hill that smokes," and Iztaccihuatl, or "white woman,"—a name suggested, doubtless, by the bright robe of snow spread over its broad and broken surface. A puerile superstition of the Indians regarded these celebrated mountains as gods, and Iztaccihuatl as the wife of her more formidable neighbor. A tradition of a higher character described the northern volcano, as the abode of the departed spirits of wicked rulers, whose fiery agonies, in their prisonhouse, caused the fearful bellowings and convulsions in times of eruption. It was the classic fable of Antiquity. These superstitious legends had invested the mountain with a mysterious horror, that made the natives shrink from attempting its ascent, which, indeed, was from natural causes a work of incredible difficulty.

[7]   The great *volcan*, as Popocatepetl was called, rose to the enormous height of 17,852 feet above the level of the sea; more than 2000 feet above the "monarch of mountains,"—the highest elevation in Europe.[1] During the present century, it has rarely given evidence of its volcanic origin, and "the hill that smokes" has almost forfeited its claim to the appellation. But at the time of the Conquest it was frequently in a state of activity, and raged with uncommon fury while the Spaniards were at Tlascala; an evil omen, it was thought, for the natives of Anahuac. Its head, gathered into a regular cone by the deposit of successive eruptions, wore the usual form of volcanic mountains, when not disturbed by the falling in of the crater. Soaring towards the skies, with its silver sheet of

[1]Mont Blanc.

everlasting snow, it was seen far and wide over the broad plains of Mexico and Puebla, the first object which the morning sun greeted in his rising, the last where his evening rays were seen to linger, shedding a glorious effulgence over its head, that contrasted strikingly with the ruinous waste of sand and lava immediately below, and the deep fringe of funereal pines that shrouded its base.

The mysterious terrors which hung over the spot, and the wild love of adventure, made some of the Spanish cavaliers desirous to attempt the ascent, which the natives declared no man could accomplish and live. Cortés encouraged them in the enterprise, willing to show the Indians that no achievement was above the dauntless daring of his followers. One of his captains, accordingly, Diego Ordaz, with nine Spaniards, and several Tlascalans, encouraged by their example, undertook the ascent. It was attended with more difficulty than had been anticipated. [8]

The lower region was clothed with a dense forest, so thickly matted, that in some places it was scarcely possible to penetrate it. It grew thinner, however, as they advanced, dwindling, by degrees, into a straggling, stunted vegetation, till, at the height of somewhat more than thirteen thousand feet, it faded away altogether. The Indians who had held on thus far, intimidated by the strange subterraneous sounds of the volcano, even then in a state of combustion, now left them. The track opened on a black surface of glazed volcanic sand and of lava, the broken fragments of which, arrested in its boiling progress in a thousand fantastic forms, opposed continual impediments to their advance. Amidst these, one huge rock, the *Pico del Fraile*, a conspicuous object from below, rose to the perpendicular height of a hundred and fifty feet, compelling them to take a wide circuit. They soon came to the limits of perpetual snow, where new difficulties presented themselves, as the treacherous ice gave an imperfect footing, and a false step might precipitate them into the frozen chasms that yawned around. To increase their distress, respiration in these aërial regions became so difficult, that every effort was attended with sharp pains in the head and limbs. Still they pressed on, till, drawing nearer the crater, such volumes of smoke, sparks and cinders were belched forth from its burning entrails, and driven down the sides of the mountain, as nearly suffocated and blinded them. It was too much even for their hardy frames to endure, and, however reluctantly, they were compelled to abandon the attempt on the eve of its completion. They brought back some huge icicles, —a curious sight in these tropical regions,—as a trophy of their achievement, which, however imperfect, was sufficient to strike the minds of the natives with wonder, by showing that with the Spaniards the most appalling and mysterious perils were only as pastimes. The undertaking was eminently characteristic of the bold spirit of the cavalier of that day, who, not content with the dangers that lay in his path, seems to court them from the mere Quixotic love of adventure. A report of the affair was [9] transmitted to the Emperor Charles the Fifth, and the family of Ordaz was allowed to commemorate the exploit by assuming a burning mountain on their escutcheon.

[10]   The general was not satisfied with the result. Two years after, he sent up another party, under Francisco Montaño, a cavalier of determined resolution. The object was to obtain sulphur to assist in making gunpowder for the army. The mountain was quiet at this time, and the expedition was attended with better success. The Spaniards, five in number, climbed to the very edge of the crater, which presented an irregular ellipse at its mouth, more than a league in circumference. Its depth might be from eight hundred to a thousand feet. A lurid flame burned gloomily at the bottom, sending up a sulphureous steam, which, cooling as it rose, was precipitated on the sides of the cavity. The party cast lots, and it fell on Montaño himself, to descend in a basket into this hideous abyss, into which he was lowered by his companions to the depth of four hundred feet! This was repeated several times, till the adventurous cavalier had collected a sufficient quantity of sulphur for the wants of the army. This doughty enterprise excited general admiration at the time. Cortés concludes his report of it, to the emperor, with the judicious reflection, that it would be less inconvenient, on the whole, to import their powder from Spain.

[11]   But it is time to return from our digression, which may, perhaps, be excused, as illustrating, in a remarkable manner, the chimerical spirit of enterprise,—not inferior to that in his own romances of chivalry,—which glowed in the breast of the Spanish cavalier in the sixteenth century.

[12]   The army held on its march through the intricate gorges of the sierra. The route was nearly the same as that pursued at the present day by the courier from the capital to Puebla, by the way of Mecameca. It was not that usually taken by travellers from Vera Cruz, who follow the more circuitous road round the northern base of Iztaccihuatl, as less fatiguing than the other, though inferior in picturesque scenery and romantic points of view. The icy winds, that now swept down the sides of the mountains, brought with them a tempest of arrowy sleet and snow, from which the Christians suffered even more than the Tlascalans, reared from infancy among the wild solitudes of their own native hills. As night came on, their sufferings would have been intolerable, but they luckily found a shelter in the commodious stone buildings which the Mexican government had placed at stated intervals along the roads for the accommodation of the traveller and their own couriers. It little dreamed it was providing a protection for its enemies.

[13]   The troops, refreshed by a night's rest, succeeded, early on the following day, in gaining the crest of the sierra of Ahualco, which stretches like a curtain between the two great mountains on the north and south. Their progress was now comparatively easy, and they marched forward with a buoyant step, as they felt they were treading the soil of Montezuma.

They had not advanced far, when, turning an angle of the sierra, they [14] suddenly came on a view which more than compensated the toils of the preceding day. It was that of the Valley of Mexico, or Tenochtitlan, as more commonly called by the natives; which, with its picturesque assemblage of water, woodland, and cultivated plains, its shining cities and shadowy hills, was spread out like some gay and gorgeous panorama before them. In the highly rarefied atmosphere of these upper regions, even remote objects have a brilliancy of coloring and a distinctness of outline which seem to annihilate distance. Stretching far away at their feet, were seen noble forests of oak, sycamore, and cedar, and beyond, yellow fields of maize and the towering maguey, intermingled with orchards and blooming gardens; for flowers, in such demand for their religious festivals, were even more abundant in this populous valley than in other parts of Anahuac. In the centre of the great basin were beheld the lakes, occupying then a much larger portion of its surface than at present; their borders thickly studded with towns and hamlets, and, in the midst,—like some Indian empress with her coronal of pearls,—the fair city of Mexico, with her white towers and pyramidal temples, reposing, as it were, on the bosom of the waters,—the far-famed "Venice of the Aztecs." High over all rose the royal hill of Chapoltepec, the residence of the Mexican monarchs, crowned with the same grove of gigantic cypresses, which at this day fling their broad shadows over the land. In the distance beyond the blue waters of the lake, and nearly screened by intervening foliage, was seen a shining speck, the rival capital of Tezcuco, and, still further on, the dark belt of porphyry, girdling the Valley around, like a rich setting which Nature had devised for the fairest of her jewels.

Such was the beautiful vision which broke on the eyes of the Conquerors. [15] And even now, when so sad a change has come over the scene; when the stately forests have been laid low, and the soil, unsheltered from the fierce radiance of a tropical sun, is in many places abandoned to sterility; when the waters have retired, leaving a broad and ghastly margin white with the incrustation of salts, while the cities and hamlets on their borders have mouldered into ruins,—even now that desolation broods over the landscape, so indestructible are the lines of beauty which Nature has traced on its features, that no traveller, however cold, can gaze on them with any other emotions than those of astonishment and rapture.

What, then, must have been the emotions of the Spaniards, when, after [16] working their toilsome way into the upper air, the cloudy tabernacle parted before their eyes, and they beheld these fair scenes in all their pristine magnificence and beauty! It was like the spectacle which greeted the eyes of Moses from the summit of Pisgah, and, in the warm glow of their feelings, they cried out, "It is the promised land!"

But these feelings of admiration were soon followed by others of a very [17] different complexion; as they saw in all this the evidences of a civilization and power far superior to any thing they had yet encountered. The more timid, disheartened by the prospect, shrunk from a contest so unequal, and demanded, as they had done on some former occasions, to be led back again to Vera Cruz. Such was not the effect produced on the sanguine spirit of the general. His avarice was sharpened by the display of the dazzling spoil at his feet; and, if he felt a natural anxiety at the formidable odds, his confidence was renewed, as he gazed on the lines of his veterans, whose weather-beaten visages and battered armor told of battles won and difficulties surmounted, while his bold barbarians, with appetites whetted by the view of their enemies' country, seemed like eagles on the mountains, ready to pounce upon their prey. By argument, entreaty, and menace, he endeavored to restore the faltering courage of the soldiers, urging them not to think of retreat, now that they had reached the goal for which they had panted, and the golden gates were opened to receive them. In these efforts, he was well seconded by the brave cavaliers, who held honor as dear to them as fortune; until the dullest spirits caught somewhat of the enthusiasm of their leaders, and the general had the satisfaction to see his hesitating columns, with their usual buoyant step, once more on their march down the slopes of the sierra.

[18]   With every step of their progress, the woods became thinner; patches of cultivated land more frequent; and hamlets were seen in the green and sheltered nooks, the inhabitants of which, coming out to meet them, gave the troops a kind reception. Everywhere they heard complaints of Montezuma, especially of the unfeeling manner in which he carried off their young men to recruit his armies, and their maidens for his harem. These symptoms of discontent were noticed with satisfaction by Cortés, who saw that Montezuma's "mountain-throne," as it was called, was, indeed, seated on a volcano, with the elements of combustion so active within, that it seemed as if any hour might witness an explosion. He encouraged the disaffected natives to rely on his protection, as he had come to redress their wrongs. He took advantage, moreover, of their favorable dispositions, to scatter among them such gleams of spiritual light as time and the preaching of father Olmedo could afford.

[19]   He advanced by easy stages, somewhat retarded by the crowd of curious inhabitants gathered on the highways to see the strangers, and halting at every spot of interest or importance. On the road, he was met by another embassy from the capital. It consisted of several Aztec lords, freighted, as usual, with a rich largess of gold, and robes of delicate furs and feathers. The message of the emperor was couched in the same deprecatory terms as before. He even condescended to bribe the return of the Spaniards, by promising, in that event, four loads of gold to the general, and one to each of the captains, with a yearly tribute to their sovereign. So effectually had the lofty and naturally courageous spirit of the barbarian monarch been subdued by the influence of superstition!

But the man, whom the hostile array of armies could not daunt, was not [20] to be turned from his purpose by a woman's prayers. He received the embassy with his usual courtesy, declaring, as before, that he could not answer it to his own sovereign, if he were now to return without visiting the emperor in his capital. It would be much easier to arrange matters by a personal interview than by distant negotiation. The Spaniards came in the spirit of peace. Montezuma would so find it, but, should their presence prove burdensome to him, it would be easy for them to relieve him of it.

The Aztec monarch, meanwhile, was a prey to the most dismal apprehensions. It was intended that the embassy above noticed should reach the [21] Spaniards before they crossed the mountains. When he learned that this was accomplished, and that the dread strangers were on their march across the Valley, the very threshold of his capital, the last spark of hope died away in his bosom. Like one who suddenly finds himself on the brink of some dark and yawning gulf, he was too much bewildered to be able to rally his thoughts, or even to comprehend his situation. He was the victim of an absolute destiny; against which no foresight or precautions could have availed. It was as if the strange beings, who had thus invaded his shores, had dropped from some distant planet, so different were they from all he had ever seen, in appearance and manners; so superior,—though a mere handful, in numbers,—to the banded nations of Anahuac in strength and science, and all the fearful accompaniments of war! They were now in the Valley. The huge mountain screen, which nature had so kindly drawn around it, for its defence, had been overleaped. The golden visions of security and repose, in which he had so long indulged, the lordly sway descended from his ancestors, his broad imperial domain, were all to pass away. It seemed like some terrible dream,—from which he was now, alas! to awake to a still more terrible reality.

In a paroxysm of despair, he shut himself up in his palace, refused food, [22] and sought relief in prayer and in sacrifice. But the oracles were dumb. He then adopted the more sensible expedient of calling a council of his principal and oldest nobles. Here was the same division of opinion which had before prevailed. Cacama, the young king of Tezcuco, his nephew, counselled him to receive the Spaniards courteously, as ambassadors, so styled by themselves of a foreign prince. Cuitlahua, Montezuma's more warlike brother, urged him to muster his forces on the instant, and drive back the invaders from his capital, or die in its defence. But the monarch found it difficult to rally his spirits for this final struggle. With downcast eye and dejected mien, he exclaimed, "Of what avail is resistance, when the gods have declared themselves against us! Yet I mourn most for the old and infirm, the women and children, too feeble to fight or to fly. For myself and the brave men around me, we must bare our breasts to the storm, and meet it as we may!" Such are the sorrowful and sympathetic tones in which the Aztec emperor is said to have uttered the bitterness of his grief. He would have acted a more glorious part, had he put his capital in a posture of defense, and prepared, like the last of the Palæologi, to bury himself under its ruins.

[23]   He straightway prepared to send a last embassy to the Spaniards, with his nephew, the lord of Tezcuco, at its head, to welcome them to Mexico.

[24]   The Christian army, meanwhile, had advanced as far as Amaquemecan, a well built town of several thousand inhabitants. They were kindly received by the cacique, lodged in large, commodious, stone buildings, and at their departure presented, among other things, with gold to the amount of three thousand *castellanos*. Having halted there a couple of days, they descended among flourishing plantations of maize, and of maguey, the latter of which might be called the Aztec vineyards, towards the lake of Chalco. Their first resting-place was Ajotzinco, a town of considerable size, with a great part of it then standing on piles in the water. It was the first specimen which the Spaniards had seen of this maritime architecture. The canals which intersected the city, instead of streets, presented an animated scene, from the number of barks which glided up and down freighted with provisions and other articles for the inhabitants. The Spaniards were particularly struck with the style and commodious structure of the houses, built chiefly of stone, and with the general aspect of wealth and even elegance which prevailed there.

[25]   Though received with the greatest show of hospitality, Cortés found some occasion for distrust in the eagerness manifested by the people to see and approach the Spaniards. Not content with gazing at them in the roads, some even made their way stealthily into their quarters, and fifteen or twenty unhappy Indians were shot down by the sentinels as spies. Yet there appears, as well as we can judge, at this distance of time, to have been no real ground for such suspicion. The undisguised jealousy of the Court, and the cautions he had received from his allies, while they very properly put the general on his guard, seem to have given an unnatural acuteness, at least in the present instance, to his perceptions of danger.

[26]   Early on the following morning, as the army was preparing to leave the place, a courier came, requesting the general to postpone his departure till after the arrival of the king of Tezcuco, who was advancing to meet him. It was not long before he appeared, borne in a palanquin or litter, richly decorated with plates of gold and precious stones, having pillars curiously wrought, supporting a canopy of green plumes, a favorite color with the Aztec princes. He was accompanied by a numerous suite of nobles and inferior attendants. As he came into the presence of Cortés, the lord of Tezcuco descended from his palanquin, and the obsequious officers swept the ground before him as he advanced. He appeared to be a young man of about twenty-five years of age, with a comely presence, erect and stately in his deportment. He made the Mexican salutation usually addressed to persons of high rank, touching the earth with his right hand,

and raising it to his head. Cortés embraced him as he rose, when the young prince informed him that he came as the representative of Montezuma, to bid the Spaniards welcome to his capital. He then presented the general with three pearls of uncommon size and lustre. Cortés, in return, threw over Cacama's neck a chain of cut glass, which, where glass was as rare as diamonds, might be admitted to have a value as real as the latter. After this interchange of courtesies, and the most friendly and respectful assurances on the part of Cortés, the Indian prince withdrew, leaving the Spaniards strongly impressed with the superiority of his state and bearing over any thing they had hitherto seen in the country.

Resuming its march, the army kept along the southern borders of the [27] lake of Chalco, overshadowed, at that time, by noble woods, and by orchards glowing with autumnal fruits, of unknown names, but rich and tempting hues. More frequently it passed through cultivated fields waving with the yellow harvest, and irrigated by canals introduced from the neighboring lake; the whole showing a careful and economical husbandry, essential to the maintenance of a crowded population.

Leaving the main land, the Spaniards came on the great dike or cause- [28] way, which stretches some four or five miles in length, and divides lake Chalco from Xochicalco on the west. It was a lance in breadth in the narrowest part, and in some places wide enough for eight horsemen to ride abreast. It was a solid structure of stone and lime, running directly through the lake, and struck the Spaniards as one of the most remarkable works which they had seen in the country.

As they passed along, they beheld the gay spectacle of multitudes of [29] Indians darting up and down in their light pirogues, eager to catch a glimpse of the strangers, or bearing the products of the country to the neighboring cities. They were amazed, also, by the sight of the *chinampas*, or floating gardens,—those wandering islands of verdure, to which we shall have occasion to return hereafter,—teeming with flowers and vegetables, and moving like rafts over the waters. All round the margin, and occasionally far in the lake, they beheld little towns and villages, which, half concealed by the foliage, and gathered in white clusters round the shore, looked in the distance like companies of wild swans riding quietly on the waves. A scene so new and wonderful filled their rude hearts with amazement. It seemed like enchantment; and they could find nothing to compare it with, but the magical pictures in the "Amadis de Gaula." Few pictures, indeed, in that or any other legend of chivalry, could surpass the realities of their own experience. The life of the adventurer in the New World was romance put into action. What wonder, then, if the Spaniard of that day, feeding his imagination with dreams of enchantment at home, and with its realities abroad, should have displayed a Quixotic enthusiasm, —a romantic exaltation of character, not to be comprehended by the colder spirits of other lands!

William H. Prescott

[30]   Midway across the lake the army halted at the town of Cuitlahuac, a place of moderate size, but distinguished by the beauty of the buildings,—the most beautiful, according to Cortés, that he had yet seen in the country. After taking some refreshment at this place, they continued their march along the dike. Though broader in this northern section, the troops found themselves much embarrassed by the throng of Indians, who, not content with gazing on them from the boats, climbed up the causeway, and lined the sides of the road. The general, afraid that his ranks might be disordered, and that too great familiarity might diminish a salutary awe in the natives, was obliged to resort not merely to command, but menace, to clear a passage. He now found, as he advanced, a considerable change in the feelings shown towards the government. He heard only of the pomp and magnificence, nothing of the oppressions, of Montezuma. Contrary to the usual fact, it seemed that the respect for the court was greatest in its immediate neighborhood.

[31]   From the causeway, the army descended on that narrow point of land which divides the waters of the Chalco from the Tezcucan lake, but which in those days was overflowed for many a mile now laid bare. Traversing this peninsula, they entered the royal residence of Iztapalapan, a place containing twelve or fifteen thousand houses, according to Cortés. It was governed by Cuitlahua, the emperor's brother, who, to do greater honor to the general, had invited the lords of some neighboring cities, of the royal house of Mexico, like himself, to be present at the interview. This was conducted with much ceremony, and, after the usual present of gold and delicate stuffs, a collation was served to the Spaniards in one of the great halls of the palace. The excellence of the architecture here, also, excited the admiration of the general, who does not hesitate, in the glow of his enthusiasm, to pronounce some of the buildings equal to the best in Spain. They were of stone, and the spacious apartments had roofs of odorous cedar-wood, while the walls were tapestried with fine cottons stained with brilliant colors.

[32]   But the pride of Iztapalapan, on which its lord had freely lavished his care and his revenues, was its celebrated gardens. They covered an immense tract of land; were laid out in regular squares, and the paths intersecting them were bordered with trellises, supporting creepers and aromatic shrubs that loaded the air with their perfumes. The gardens were stocked with fruit-trees, imported from distant places, and with the gaudy family of flowers which belong to the Mexican Flora, scientifically arranged, and growing luxuriant in the equable temperature of the tableland. The natural dryness of the atmosphere was counteracted by means of aqueducts and canals that carried water into all parts of the grounds.

[33]   In one quarter was an aviary, filled with numerous kinds of birds, remarkable in this region both for brilliancy of plumage and of song. The gardens were intersected by a canal communicating with the lake of Tez-

cuco, and of sufficient size for barges to enter from the latter. But the most elaborate piece of work was a huge reservoir of stone, filled to a considerable height with water well supplied with different sorts of fish. This basin was sixteen hundred paces in circumference, and was surrounded by a walk, made also of stone, wide enough for four persons to go abreast. The sides were curiously sculptured, and a flight of steps led to the water below, which fed the aqueducts above noticed, or, collected into fountains, diffused a perpetual moisture.

Such are the accounts transmitted of these celebrated gardens, at a period [34] when similar horticultural establishments were unknown in Europe; and we might well doubt their existence on this semi-civilized land, were it not a matter of such notoriety at the time, and so explicitly attested by the invaders. But a generation had scarcely passed after the Conquest, before a sad change came over these scenes so beautiful. The town itself was deserted, and the shore of the lake was strewed with the wreck of buildings which once were its ornament and its glory. The gardens shared the fate of the city. The retreating waters withdrew the means of nourishment, converting the flourishing plains into a foul and unsightly morass, the haunt of loathsome reptiles; and the water-fowl built her nest in what had once been the palaces of princes!

In the city of Iztapalapan, Cortés took up his quarters for the night. We [35] may imagine what a crowd of ideas must have pressed on the mind of the Conqueror, as, surrounded by these evidences of civilization, he prepared with his handful of followers to enter the capital of a monarch, who, as he had abundant reason to know, regarded him with distrust and aversion. This capital was now but a few miles distant, distinctly visible from Iztapalapan. And as its long lines of glittering edifices, struck by the rays of the evening sun, trembled on the dark-blue waters of the lake, it looked like a thing of fairy creation, rather than the work of mortal hands. Into this city of enchantment Cortés prepared to make his entry on the following morning.

TOPICS FOR DISCUSSION

1. Show how Prescott's history combines descriptive, narrative, and expository writing. Is each form of writing equally necessary to achieve Prescott's purpose? Why or why not? Analyze the natural interdependence of each kind of writing in a passage of your own choice from this selection.

2. How does Prescott illustrate the courage of Cortés? How does he

illustrate Cortés' qualities of leadership? Do you think Prescott exaggerates Cortés' spirit of chivalry? Why or why not?

3. In contrast to Cortés, Montezuma is represented as apprehensive, superstitious, and unenterprising. To what extent do these characteristics explain Cortés' conquest?

4. Discuss the point of view in this passage. Does the writer identify with Cortés and the Spaniards, with Montezuma and the Aztecs, or is he neutral? Give reasons for your answer.

TOPICS FOR COMPOSITION

1. Two passages—one recounting the climbing of Popocatepetl and the other the entrance into the Valley of Mexico—are particularly useful examples of expository narrative. Write a similar passage on one of the topics listed below. As in Prescott's history, make the account characterize the principal figures of the sketch:

    a. an inhabitant of a large American eastern city encounters the Grand Canyon

    b. a modern African explores an American city

    c. an astronaut conveys his impression of space

2. Write a historical account of an expedition or voyage of discovery in which you characterize the central figure. Choose for your subject a representative hero, for example: Lewis and Clark, Columbus, Daniel Boone, Magellan, Kit Carson, Sir Francis Drake, General John C. Frémont, Sir Walter Raleigh, Jim Bridger, Commodore Perry, Admiral Richard E. Byrd.

SAMUEL
ELIOT
MORISON

Prescott,
the American
Thucydides

BIOGRAPHY, as Samuel Johnson observed (p. 134), is useful, for every life bears on every other life, and we learn about ourselves from others. But an artistic biography, one that portrays a significant human life in a memorable way, is more than a useful lesson. Like a good portrait, it is at once a memorial and a pleasurable work of art. The artistic biographer, without distorting his subject, captures a distinctive personality, often with the vividness of the best novelist.

Virginia Woolf, herself a distinguished novelist, once wrote:

The biographer does more to stimulate the imagination than any poet or novelist save the very greatest. For few poets and novelists are capable of that high degree of tension which gives us reality. But almost any biographer, if he respects facts, can give us much more than another fact to add to our collection. He can give us the creative fact; the fertile fact; the fact that suggests and engenders.

It is just these creative and fertile facts that Samuel Eliot Morison provides about his fellow historian, W. H. Prescott. We meet Prescott, at the height of his fame, *in medias res* so to speak, as a man who has triumphed over grave physical disabilities. The biography then tells us how he achieved his triumph: his choice of a career, his years of preparation, his habits of work, his cultivation of scholarly ideals, his patriotic delight in proving to the learned world the integrity and maturity of American scholarship.

In 1774 Horace Walpole wrote to Sir Horace Mann, "The next Augustan [1] age will dawn on the other side of the Atlantic. There will perhaps be a Thucydides at Boston."

There was; and three quarters of a century later Walpole's friend Miss [2] Berry, then a venerable vestal of eighty-seven, had the satisfaction of meeting him in London. His name was William Hickling Prescott, and he was being received by political, social, and literary England in a manner that no American writer has experienced before or since. Macaulay gave him a breakfast party at the Albany; the Lyells took him to Royal Ascot; Oxford conferred on him an honorary D.C.L.; and the Earl of Carlisle entertained him and Queen Victoria at Castle Howard. Prescott sat next but one to her at dinner, and described her in a letter to his wife as "very plain, with fine eyes and teeth, but short and dumpy, with a skin that reddens easily with the heat of the room. I observed that the Queen did great justice to the bread and cheese."

[3]   This "American Thucydides," as people were beginning to call him, was then at the height of his fame. His three greatest works, *Ferdinand and Isabella*, *The Conquest of Mexico*, and *The Conquest of Peru*, had appeared, greeted with enthusiasm by the critics of both continents including even the snooty Scots reviewers, and they had been eagerly bought by the public. Prescott was then a tall, well-built gentleman of fifty-four, with an infectious smile and hearty laugh that charmed everyone. A pair of well-trimmed sideburns, in the fashion of the day, framed a strong, handsome countenance with a fine Roman nose, brown eyes, and a ruddy complexion. He was lively, agile, an excellent horseman, and a fast walker; few except his intimate friends suspected that for long intervals he was racked by rheumatism and that one of his eyes was artificial.

[4]   This was in 1850, when Prescott was reaping the fruits of thirty-five years of courageous struggle to overcome a grave physical disability. It is a curious coincidence that the only other American historian, Francis Parkman, to be mentioned in the same breath with Prescott, had to undergo a similar experience.

[5]   Let us take a look at him at almost the start of the struggle. It is the year 1817. Son of a Federalist lawyer and judge, grandson of Colonel William Prescott of Bunker Hill fame, young William had gone through Harvard College gaily and easily, but lost an eye as a result of a brawl in college commons. The infection had spread to the other eye and acute rheumatism set in. After the local physicians had almost killed him with "copious bleedings and other depletions," he had been sent to Europe in search of better medical aid than could be had in America. First he spent a winter with his maternal grandfather, Thomas Hickling, the United States consul at St. Michael's in the Azores, and there he became sensible of the beauty and mystery of the Old World. He then made an attenuated grand tour of Europe, consulted the best eye specialists in Paris, and returned to live in his parents' house, a big square mansion with a garden on Pearl Street, Boston. There the old malady returned. We may picture Prescott confined for days, sometimes weeks, to a dark room on the top story, a devoted sister reading aloud to him by lying on the floor where she could catch the light that came in over the threshold since any stronger light gave the young man excruciating pain.

[6]   Yet Prescott refused to admit defeat, and gave careful thought to what he should do for a profession. And he wooed and won a girl of his own social circle, Susan Amory. They were married on his twenty-fourth birthday, and for the next twenty-four years lived with the elder Prescotts. The Amorys were one of those American Loyalist families—more numerous

than is generally supposed—who managed to retain their property and social position through the turmoil of the American Revolution. Susan was a beautiful girl with a somewhat bovine character. "She didn't go out much—as an Amory she didn't have to," as a granddaughter remarked; she was content to rear a family and to watch tenderly over her husband's health and interests. He was completely and romantically devoted to her. She inherited the sword of her grandfather, who had served in the Royal Navy on board one of the British ships that supported the assault on Bunker Hill, and William inherited that of his grandfather, who commanded the provincial troops in that battle; so they had the two mounted and placed on the wall of the Prescott library. These were the famous "crossed swords" which Thackeray saw on his visit to Boston and which inspired *The Virginians*, as the opening paragraph of that novel relates.

Even before he married, Prescott decided to fit himself for what he called "the literary life," although as yet he had little inclination to any particular branch of that far-spreading tree. It was not really necessary that he do anything, considering his infirmity, his social position, and his father's generosity. But in Boston every young man was supposed to "make an effort," as the phrase went; Prescott himself later observed that an American who neither made money nor cultivated letters might "as well go hang himself; for as to a class of idle gentlemen, there is no such thing here." That was true in general; but even in Boston there were young men of means who did nothing in particular, and not too well at that, flitting about between New York, Newport, and London. Henry James has immortalized the type of American who rejected his native country as a hopeless Boeotia and moved to Paris or Rome to dabble in the arts or pursue some pallid branch of scholarship. Prescott was made of stouter stuff. [7]

As a scholar he had to start from scratch, having carried away from Harvard little more than a good knowledge of Latin and Greek. After many false starts and physical relapses, and with the guidance and advice of his older friend George Ticknor, he settled at the age of twenty-nine on a history of the reigns of Ferdinand and Isabella of Spain. [8]

There were two main reasons for this choice. He wished to show his compatriots that their history had a richer and more varied background than the Virginia Colony, the Pilgrim Fathers, and the Protestant Reformation. He wished to prove to the world that an American could produce a work at once scholarly and literary that would bear comparison with the best of England, France, Germany, and Spain. He was eager for the good opinion of European scholars. They might brush off anything he could write on United States history as inconsequential; but they would have to listen to a work which was the result of prolonged research, a nice weighing of conflicting authorities, and a thorough knowledge of classical and modern languages; especially if it were well presented. [9]

[10]   When Prescott made the great decision for Ferdinand and Isabella in 1826, ten years of almost unremitting labor were ahead of him. The material difficulties that he surmounted were even greater than his physical handicap. The way to perform the task with the greatest economy would have been to have settled in Madrid, as his friend the American minister there advised him to do. He could have worked there, or in London or Paris, far more effectively than in Boston, and have been nearer to specialists who could have kept his one good eye working. But Prescott was determined not to be an expatriate, even temporarily. He felt that he owed it to the memory of Colonel Prescott, and to his family and friends, to prove that an American could produce a literary and scholarly work of the highest quality right in Boston.

[11]   Yet how could that be done in Boston? There were no collections of old Spanish books there or anywhere else in the United States. Ticknor, blessed with ample means, imported the essential books as rapidly as he could find them and gave Prescott the run of his library; but Prescott was not content to "make new books, as apothecaries make new mixtures, by pouring out of one vessel into another," as Tristram Shandy once remarked. He must have the original sources, and with few exceptions these were still in manuscript. In those days there was no multi-volumed set of *Documentos Inéditos;* the Las Casas *Historia General de las Indias* had never been printed, nor the better part of Oviedo, nor Andres Bernaldez's chronicle of the Catholic Kings. These and hundreds of other manuscripts had to be copied for him in longhand. The cost was not excessive, since there were plenty of unemployed intellectuals in Europe who were glad to do such work for starvation wages; the trouble was to find responsible scholars to direct research in public and private archives and to supervise the copying. Therein the United States consuls and diplomatic officials gave indispensable aid, and Dr. Friedrich Lembke, a German who had written a history of Spain to the year 800, consented to carry on vicariously for Prescott in return for a modest retainer.

[12]   Eventually, books and copies of manuscripts began to pour in to the paternal mansion on Pearl Street, where they were placed on shelves in the son's attic study. And he managed to surmount his physical handicap by methodical living, by having most of the material read aloud to him by a secretary who learned to pronounce Spanish, and by a simple device called a noctograph, which had been invented in London to enable the blind to write. This was a sort of slate crossed by a grid of stout brass wires between which, with an ivory-pointed stylus, one could write on carbon paper, which made an indelible impression on another sheet of paper placed underneath.

[13]   When, after ten years of work, the manuscript of *Ferdinand and Isabella* was completed, it was set up in type at the author's expense and four

copies printed for his close friends to criticize. These privately printed copies were hawked about English and American publishing houses for months with slight success. Finally a short-lived firm called the American Stationers Company of Boston agreed, for a thousand dollars, to print 1250 copies of the three-volume set to be retailed at six dollars, if the author would foot the bills for the stereotype plates; and Richard Bentley agreed to publish a small edition in London.

Ferdinand and Isabella appeared in Boston on Christmas Day, 1837, [14] and in London a month or two later. It was an immediate and astounding success on both sides of the water, partly because it came as a complete surprise. The author's name was unknown in Europe; and so well had Prescott kept his secret in Boston, where everyone was supposed to know everyone else's business, and so gay and unrestrained had been his social life, that not more than six persons outside the immediate family knew what he had been doing. It was commonly supposed that he was reading for his own amusement. Only a week before *Ferdinand and Isabella* came out, an elderly relative stopped Prescott on the street to upbraid him for frittering away his life, and to tell him it was high time he amounted to something!

Prescott could have boasted, like Lord Byron, "I awoke one morning [15] and found myself famous." To a German who had called it folly to publish Spanish history in the United States, "where the taste was for nothing higher than a periodical," Prescott wrote that 3300 sets of *Ferdinand and Isabella* had been sold in the first sixteen months; "that is pretty well for 'Brother Jonathan,' is it not? ... The publishers indeed are quite as much surprised as I am."

He gained the favor of the critics by his vivid and spirited narrative [16] style, arresting as a historical novel, yet with each detail authenticated in a footnote. I shall not attempt to analyze his style, because it is to be enjoyed and admired, not plucked apart. Certain modern critics regard it as artificial (of course every style, even Hemingway's and Joyce's, is that); and certainly nobody would think of imitating it today. But he was a master of *narrative*, which history essentially is, a fact which too many modern historians have forgotten. And the quality which gave his works permanent value, and which appealed most to the more discriminating critics, was (as Roger B. Merriman wrote) "the scrupulous care and integrity with which he used his materials, and the pains that he took to find the exact truth. All his statements are supported by abundant references; if there is any possible doubt as to the interpretation of his authorities, it is fairly expressed in the footnotes; in short, one may be certain of the source for every fact which Prescott gives, though one may differ with him over the significance of it."

Before his first work appeared, Prescott had decided on the next two, [17] *The Conquest of Mexico* and *The Conquest of Peru*. Washington Irving, who had planned to do a *Mexico* himself, magnanimously dropped it in favor of the younger historian. Prescott's *Conquest of Mexico*, completed in 1843, was an even greater success than his first book, and has remained his best seller. Over 20,000 sets of it were sold during his lifetime; and as he had paid for the plates himself he collected substantial royalties. But the profits from each book were plowed into preparations for the next; into copying, salaries to secretaries and researchers, purchase of books and manuscripts. Only his inherited and invested income of somewhat over twelve thousand dollars a year enabled him to carry on.

[18]   Almost everyone who reads his works assumes that Prescott visited the scenes he wrote about, so vivid and convincing are his descriptions of scenery, battlefields, and the like. But, owing to his infirmities, he never went nearer South America than Washington, D.C. His lack of physical contact with these countries was compensated by a historical imagination, well controlled by the facts as related by Bernal Diaz and the early Spanish chronicles, and developed by correspondence with people who knew these countries at first hand. The most useful to him in that respect was Madame Calderón de la Barca, whose *Life in Mexico* has become a classic. She was Fanny Inglis, a charming and witty Scotswoman who had a private school in Boston and became a close friend of the Prescotts. After her marriage to the Spanish minister to the United States, who was later transferred to Mexico City, she continued to interchange letters with Prescott; and it is probably owing to her devotion that he was able to write his accurate and striking descriptions of Mexico City and Teotihuacan under the Aztecs.

[19]   It was also a subject of astonished praise that a Boston Protestant like Prescott could write so understandingly of Catholics and Catholicism, even asserting that there was something to be said for the Inquisition. He was the first English-speaking historian of Spanish lands whom a loyal Spaniard could read without disgust. For, Unitarian though he might be by conviction, Prescott judged historical characters by the standards of their day, not by those of nineteenth-century liberalism. He regarded the Catholic Church as one of the world's great religions, which was here to stay and not on the way out, as many liberals fondly imagined. And like other New Englanders who retained a "pious disbelief" after rejecting the Church, he found anticlericalism distasteful and the raillery of Voltaire disgusting.

[20]   Even more gratifying to Prescott than the acclaim of the critics was his popularity among all classes of American readers. When, shortly after the Mexican War, he visited Washington, he was delighted to hear from the Secretary of the Navy that the bluejackets of the *U.S.S. Delaware* had petitioned him to add *The Conquest of Mexico* to their ship's library; and that the secretary had not only done that, but ordered a set to be placed on board every ship of the United States Navy.

[21]   And there was one humble reader whom Prescott obtained many years

after his death, whose story would have gratified him immensely. That was Edward E. Ayer, a young Middle Westerner in the First California Cavalry, U.S. Army, who in 1862 was guarding the Cerro Colorado silver mine in Arizona against attacks by the Apache. Colonel Colt, of revolver fame, had given the mine a small library, and in it trooper Ayer discovered *The Conquest of Mexico*. He read it through twice, "and was astonished to find that history could be so interesting." After his discharge from the Army, Ayer was given by his father an interest in a country store in Illinois. On visiting Chicago to lay in a stock of goods he called at a bookshop and asked if they had a copy of this fascinating history. They had, and *The Conquest of Peru* as well, but the price was $17.50 for the set. Young Ayer—he was still only twenty-three years old—had only $3.50 to spare, but he offered to pay that for Volume I of the *Mexico*, and to buy a volume every month. The proprietor let him pay the $3.50 down and gave him the five volumes to take home. "My return was a triumphal procession," wrote Mr. Ayer almost fifty years later. "I was certainly the happiest boy in the world." And the world knows that Mr. Ayer became one of the greatest of American book collectors, to the ultimate benefit of the Newberry Library of Chicago. The place of honor in that library's Ayer Collection is given to these identical copies, which the owner eventually had sumptuously rebound in London at a cost over tenfold that of his original investment.

Prescott never wholly recovered from his physical disabilities, but he never [22] let them get him down. Fortunately one of his secretaries recorded in detail his regimen, a Spartan one which would have crushed the life out of a less valiant and buoyant man. The scene of it is the house still numbered 55 Beacon Street, Boston, which the historian bought after the death of his father and where he wrote most of *The Conquest of Peru*. His atelier, as he called his study, was on the third floor, rear; one viewing the outside of it today from the little street that runs behind Beacon would suppose that a recent owner had installed a picture window there, but the two large panes of plate glass were put in by Prescott in order to afford his weak eye maximum light.

The historian rose before seven, winter or summer, mounted one of his [23] saddle horses and rode for an hour and a half, to Jamaica Plain or Cambridge. This he called "winding himself up." After breakfast he shaved, bathed, and changed, while Mrs. Prescott read aloud to him from a novel by Scott, Dickens, or Dumas. Prescott not only enjoyed a good novel; he learned from them how to make his histories tridimensional by including chapters on manners and morals—social history, as it is now called. At ten o'clock he went out for a half-hour walk and at ten thirty started work in his atelier. After glancing at the headlines of the morning paper, he had the secretary read aloud items that he thought would be interesting—

but seldom found them so. Then came the correspondence. The secretary read letters that poured in from all parts of the world, and Prescott dictated the replies. Next came accounts. These were finished by noon, when the historian walked downtown to make purchases or talk to his friends; for all Boston, even the wharves, lay within twenty minutes' walk of his house.

[24]   Returning at one, he began the real business of the day. The secretary read aloud from memoirs and other documents pertaining to the book then being written, Prescott interrupting frequently to dictate notes or to discuss the persons and events described. After all sources for the chapter at hand had been gone through, the secretary read aloud repeatedly the notes he had taken, and was often called upon to reread some of the sources. This process went on for days. Prescott was then ready to compose. He outlined the entire chapter in his mind, sometimes while sitting silent in his study, but more often when walking or riding. He wrote the first draft very rapidly, on his noctograph. The secretary numbered each sheet as it was finished and copied it in a large, round hand so that Prescott could read it himself. His memory was so remarkable that he could commit a chapter of forty or fifty printed pages to memory, mull it over on horseback, and decide on alterations and improvements. He would then dictate to his secretary the changes to be made in the manuscript and have the whole reread to him. Finally he dictated the footnotes.

[25]   This same secretary, Robert Carter, wrote after the historian's death, "Mr. Prescott's cheerfulness and amiability were truly admirable. He had a finely-wrought, sensitive organization; he was high-spirited, courageous, resolute, independent; was free from cant or affectation of any sort.... He was always gay, good-humored and manly; most gentle and affectionate to his family, most kind and gracious to all around him.... Though not at all diffident, he was singularly modest and unassuming. He had not a particle of arrogance or haughtiness.... Praise did not elate him, nor censure disturb him.... He was totally free from the jealousy and envy so common among authors, and was always eager, in conversation, as in print, to point out the merits of the great contemporary historians, whom many men in his position would look upon as rivals."

[26]   Prescott dined at home at two thirty or, if with friends, at three o'clock, the then fashionable hour. He enjoyed good food, well cooked, and limited himself to exactly two and a half glasses of sherry or Madeira. At dinner he relaxed, drew out his family and friends in conversation, and never talked shop. After dinner he smoked one of the Havana cigars with which he was kept supplied by his Cuban admirers, while Mrs. Prescott read aloud again. Another half-hour solitary walk followed, and at six o'clock the secretary returned for a two-hour evening session in the study. At eight the family had supper, and at ten thirty the historian retired.

[27]   The evening session of work was omitted if Prescott attended one of his

The Practice of Rhetoric

club meetings or went to an evening party with his wife. The memory of one of these was preserved by President Charles W. Eliot of Harvard. "Prexy," in his old age, was asked by a young man whether he had ever heard Daniel Webster speak.

"Yes, once," said Dr. Eliot. "I was six or eight years old. My father [28] was entertaining him at dinner, and I hid in a corner of the hall on Beacon Street to catch a sight of the great man. In the procession to the dining room Mr. Webster led in Mrs. Prescott, a remarkably handsome lady; and just behind them were Mr. Prescott with Mrs. Webster, who was exceedingly plain. As they passed me, Mr. Webster, who had been talking with great animation to Mrs. Prescott, turned half around and said in his booming voice, 'Prescott, what do you say to our swapping wives for this evening?' "

Besides the Beacon Street mansion, Prescott maintained two other homes [29] —the ancestral farmhouse at Pepperell and a summer place at Nahant. At Pepperell he spent the spring and fall of each year, drawing strength from the soil that his ancestors had tilled for over a century; here the final chapter of *The Conquest of Peru* was composed. The house was rambling and unpretentious, but Prescott's friends and their children and his children's friends were often entertained there; life was free and easy, with riding, driving, and long walks, and charades and games in the evening. Prescott's favorite spot was a hill behind the house, with a superb view across the Nashua Valley to the rolling country of New Hampshire, dominated by the grand Monadnock. He had a seat built on the hill and used to sit there for hours, meditating and mentally composing; Monadnock had the same fascination for him as for Emerson and Thoreau. This mansion still stands.

The summer place was a flimsy wooden cottage, long since torn down, [30] on the rocky peninsula of Nahant, north of Boston. In the eighteen-thirties and forties Nahant was a leading American summer resort, where many of Prescott's friends such as Longfellow, Sumner, Eliot, and Appleton passed the season, together with hundreds of visitors from New York, Philadelphia, and the South. Life at Nahant was no unmixed blessing for Prescott. He was pestered by visitors in working hours. The cottage, which he named "Fitful Head" after the dwelling of Norna in Scott's *Pirate,* lay on a cliff overhanging Swallows' Cave and so near the water that the piazza was sprinkled with spray in every gale. "It is a wild spot," he wrote to his friend Fanny, "and the winds at this moment whistle an accompaniment to the breakers that might fill a poet's cranium with the sublime. But I am no poet. I imagine myself however in some such place as the bold headland in the Algarve, on which Prince Henry of Portugal established his residence when he sent out his voyages of discovery."

The Conquest of Peru was completed by the end of 1846. The reviews were [31] even more favorable than those of *Mexico*. But this historian was not one to rest on his laurels. He started promptly on *Philip the Second*. The work was interrupted by eye trouble and rheumatism, by tours to Albany, New York, and Washington, and by his visit to England in 1850. His English friends had long been urging him to come; but remembering the rigors of his early voyage to Europe in a sailing vessel, "bumping and thumping over the qualmish billows," he put it off until he could sail in a Cunarder, which made the voyage in only twelve days. One of his sons accompanied him, but Mrs. Prescott could not face an ocean voyage.

[32]   Prescott, like Irving and other American writers of his day, has been accused of being too deferential to the English by critics who mistake good manners for obsequiousness and regard a rude arrogance as the mark of sound Americanism. His letters are full of racy Americanisms like "OK," but for publication he tried to write the King's English, since he sought English-speaking readers all over the world. And to an English correspondent who sent him a long list of alleged Americanisms in *The Conquest of Peru* he replied, politely but firmly, that "realize" had become a verb, that "snarl" was a perfectly good noun for a tangle, and that "counterblast," to which his friend objected, had been taken from the famous tract of King James I against tobacco. Prescott was always sturdily American; if anyone doubts that, let him read in his collected *Miscellanies* his gently sarcastic remarks on Englishmen visiting America or his letters describing the scenery of England, which he thought "too tame." He longed to see "a ragged fence, or an old stump," as in his "own, dear, wild America."

[33]   In politics he was a steadfast liberal. His father had been a high Federalist, a member of the Hartford Convention; and the son, like almost everyone of his social standing in Boston, started as a Federalist and became a Whig. Boston society then took politics very hard and ostracized anyone who deviated from the accepted doctrine; George Bancroft, for example, was regarded as little better than a traitor after he joined the Democrats and accepted office under Polk, and Charles Sumner, until Brooks's assault made him a martyr, was generally looked upon as the most dangerous sort of radical. But Prescott always maintained an intimate friendship with both men. Instead of becoming a reactionary late in life, in 1856 he voted for the first Republican presidential candidate, John C. Frémont, and for Anson Burlingame for Congress, although his friend and neighbor Nathan Appleton was the Whig candidate. There is no doubt that he would have supported Lincoln in 1860 if he had lived.

[34]   The first two volumes of *Philip the Second*, published in 1855, met with the same favorable reception as did Prescott's earlier works. Work on the third volume was interrupted by a stroke, but it was finally published in 1858. He had started on the fourth and last when on January 27, 1859, he suffered a second stroke in his Beacon Street home and died within a few hours.

The Practice of Rhetoric

The entire community was moved by grief. Memorial meetings in Prescott's honor were held by the historical societies and academies of which he had been a member, as far West as Illinois and as far South as Maryland; all the noted orators, from Edward Everett down, held forth. He died "a man without an enemy; beloved by all and mourned by all," as Longfellow wrote in his diary. And Charles Sumner, writing from France, said, "There is a charm taken from Boston. Its east winds whistle more coldly around Park Street corner." [35]

Yet in Boston, where Prescott had so splendidly fulfilled Horace Walpole's prophecy of an American Thucydides, there is not now, almost a century after his death, a statue, a tablet, or even an inscription to tell the visitor that here lived and worked the greatest of American historians. [36]

TOPICS FOR DISCUSSION

1. Morison introduces us to Prescott at the height of the historian's career. What effect does Morison create by calling Prescott an American Thucydides? By the report of his reception in England in 1850? By the reference to his personal character?

2. How did Prescott prepare himself for his literary career? Why did he choose to concentrate on the Spanish Empire?

3. In telling the story of Prescott's career, Morison also explains how a historian works. According to Morison, what were Prescott's principal virtues as a historian? Can you indicate some of these virtues in his "The March to Mexico" (p. 239)? In paragraphs 22 through 31 Morison gives an account of Prescott's working habits. How does this account reveal his personal and scholarly character?

4. In the concluding paragraph Morison laments that one of the greatest of American historians is not honored in his death. Is this another way of saying that Prescott deserves honor? In your opinion has Morison shown him worthy of his honor? Explain.

5. Point out some similarities and differences in the style of Morison and Prescott.

TOPICS FOR COMPOSITION

1. Write a biographical account of some prominent American scholar, developing the theme that he is worthy of honor. Some suggested subjects are: Henry Adams, Van Wyck Brooks, William James, and Francis Parkman.

2. Write an essay explaining the value of biography in the formation of a national literature.

Expository
Argument

**JOHN HENRY
NEWMAN**

**What Is a
University?**

EXPOSITION, we have already observed, is a mode of
discourse in which we make our subject clear by various
kinds of analysis. The expositor defines his idea, classifies and divides it, gives examples of its various functions, compares and contrasts it to other subjects, and
so on. Argument is a mode of discourse in which we
attempt to prove a proposition by invoking the laws of
reason—those of deduction and induction. The arguer
aims at winning our assent, not simply at making his
own view clear. Expository argument aims at the clarification of a subject, but in the process of clarification
it provides the equivalent of argument and achieves the
effect of persuasion.

Expository argument was preeminently the mode of
discourse of many nineteenth-century prose writers.
Men like Thomas Carlyle, Cardinal Newman, Matthew
Arnold, and others, as John Holloway writes in his
The Victorian Sage, "persuade because they clarify."
True, they appeal to logical argument when logical
argument is relevant, but they are more concerned with
the whole man, his perceptions, his common sense, and
his inherited attitudes, as well as his pure reason. "What
he [the sage] has to say," writes Holloway, "is not a
matter just of 'content' or narrow paraphrasable meaning, but is transfused by the whole texture of his writing as it constitutes an experience for the reader." [1]

Cardinal Newman is frequently identified with expository argument because, though respectful of logical
inference, he placed much more emphasis upon the
material supports of argument than he did upon the
mechanical calculations of the syllogism or upon other
formulas of proof. For him, to express an insight fully
was to offer the grounds for proof. Thus, in "What Is
a University?" an article that appeared in the *Catholic
University Gazette* in June 1854, Newman begins simply
by stating that a university is a place where thought is
communicated by personal intercourse. He develops the
meaning of this term by contrasting the way thought is
communicated by books and by the personal influence
of the master. To these explanations he adds illustrations, "to explain my own language."

His illustrations of the young gentleman in the metropolis, of the statesman at Parliament, of the scientist
at the British Academy meeting, and the two analogies
he draws between the university and the metropolis and

[1] (London: Macmillan, 1953), pp. 10–11.

religious teaching and oral tradition are primarily for the faculty and students of the new university at Dublin and reflect Newman's awareness of their needs.

[1]   If I were asked to describe as briefly and popularly as I could, what a University was, I should draw my answer from its ancient designation of a *Studium Generale*, or "School of Universal Learning." This description implies the assemblage of strangers from all parts in one spot—*from all parts*; else, how will you find professors and students for every department of knowledge? and *in one spot*; else, how can there be any school at all? Accordingly, in its simple and rudimental form, it is a school of knowledge of every kind, consisting of teachers and learners from every quarter. Many things are requisite to complete and satisfy the idea embodied in this description; but such as this a University seems to be in its essence, a place for the communication and circulation of thought, by means of personal intercourse, through a wide extent of country.

[2]   There is nothing far-fetched or unreasonable in the idea thus presented to us; and if this be a University, then a University does but contemplate a necessity of our nature, and is but one specimen in a particular medium, out of many which might be adduced in others, of a provision for that necessity.   Mutual education, in a large sense of the word, is one of the great and incessant occupations of human society, carried on partly with set purpose, and partly not. One generation forms another; and the existing generation is ever acting and reacting upon itself in the persons of its individual members. Now, in this process, books, I need scarcely say, that is, the *litera scripta*, are one special instrument. It is true; and emphatically so in this age. Considering the prodigious powers of the press, and how they are developed at this time in the never-intermitting issue of periodicals, tracts, pamphlets, works in series, and light literature, we must allow there never was a time which promised fairer for dispensing with every other means of information and instruction. What can we want more, you will say, for the intellectual education of the whole man, and for every man, than so exuberant and diversified and persistent a promulgation of all kinds of knowledge? Why, you will ask, need we go up to knowledge, when knowledge comes down to us? The Sibyl wrote her prophecies upon the leaves of the forest, and wasted them; but here such careless profusion might be prudently indulged, for it can be afforded without loss, in consequence of the almost fabulous fecundity of the instrument which these latter ages have invented. We have sermons in stones, and books in the running brooks; works larger and more comprehensive than those which have gained for ancients an immortality, issue forth every morning, and

are projected onwards to the ends of the earth at the rate of hundreds of miles a day. Our seats are strewed, our pavements are powdered, with swarms of little tracts; and the very bricks of our city walls preach wisdom, by informing us by their placards where we can at once cheaply purchase it.

I allow all this, and much more; such certainly is our popular education, [3] and its effects are remarkable. Nevertheless, after all, even in this age, whenever men are really serious about getting what, in the language of trade, is called "a good article," when they aim at something precise, something refined, something really luminous, something really large, something choice, they go to another market; they avail themselves, in some shape or other, of the rival method, the ancient method, of oral instruction, of present communication between man and man, of teachers instead of learning, of the personal influence of a master, and the humble initiation of a disciple, and, in consequence, of great centres of pilgrimage and throng, which such a method of education necessarily involves. This, I think, will be found to hold good in all those departments or aspects of society, which possess an interest sufficient to bind men together, or to constitute what is called "a world." It holds in the political world, and in the high world, and in the religious world; and it holds also in the literary and scientific world.

If the actions of men may be taken as any test of their convictions, then [4] we have reason for saying this, viz., that the province and the inestimable benefit of the *litera scripta* is that of being a record of truth, and an authority of appeal, and an instrument of teaching in the hands of a teacher; but that, if we wish to become exact and fully furnished in any branch of knowledge which is diversified and complicated, we must consult the living man and listen to his living voice. I am not bound to investigate the cause of this, and anything I may say will, I am conscious, be short of its full analysis—perhaps we may suggest that no books can get through the number of minute questions which it is possible to ask on any extended subject, or can hit upon the very difficulties which are severally felt by each reader in succession. Or again, that no book can convey the special spirit and delicate peculiarities of its subject with that rapidity and certainty which attend on the sympathy of mind with mind, through the eyes, the look, the accent, and the manner, in casual expressions thrown off at the moment, and the unstudied turns of familiar conversation. But I am already dwelling too long on what is but an incidental portion of my main subject. Whatever be the cause, the fact is undeniable. The general principles of any study you may learn by books at home; but the detail, the colour, the tone, the air, the life which makes it live in us, you must catch all these from those in whom it lives already. You must imitate the student in French or German, who is not content with his grammar, but goes to Paris or Dresden; you must take example from the young artist, who aspires to visit the great masters in Florence and in Rome. Till we have discovered some intellectual daguerreotype, which takes off the course of thought, and the form, lineaments, and features of truth, as completely and minutely as the optical instrument reproduces the sensible object, we must come to the teachers of wisdom to learn wisdom, we must repair to the fountain and drink there. Portions of it may go from thence to the ends of the earth by means of books; but the fulness is in one place alone. It is in such assemblages and congregations of intellect that books themselves, the masterpieces of human genius, are written, or at least originated.

[5] The principle on which I have been insisting is so obvious, and instances in point are so ready, that I should think it tiresome to proceed with the subject, except that one or two illustrations may serve to explain my own language about it, which may not have done justice to the doctrine which it has been intended to enforce.

[6] For instance, the polished manners and high-bred bearing which are so difficult of attainment, and so strictly personal when attained, which are so much admired in society, from society are acquired. All that goes to constitute a gentleman—the carriage, gait, address, gestures, voice; the ease, the self-possession, the courtesy, the power of conversing, the talent of not offending; the lofty principle, the delicacy of thought, the happiness of expression, the taste and propriety, the generosity and forbearance, the candour and consideration, the openness of hand—these qualities, some of them come by nature, some of them may be found in any rank, some of them are a direct precept of Christianity; but the full assemblage of them, bound up in the unity of an individual character, do we expect they can be learned from books? are they not necessarily acquired, where they are to be found, in high society? The very nature of the case leads us to say so; you cannot fence without an antagonist, nor challenge all comers in disputation before you have supported a thesis; and in like manner, it stands to reason, you cannot learn to converse till you have the world to converse with; you cannot unlearn your natural bashfulness, or awkward-ness, or stiffness, or other besetting deformity, till you serve your time in some school of manners. Well, and is it not so in matter of fact? The metropolis, the court, the great houses of the land are the centres to which at stated times the country comes up, as to shrines of refinement and good taste; and then in due time the country goes back again home, enriched with a portion of the social accomplishments, which those very visits serve to call out and heighten in the gracious dispensers of them. We are un-able to conceive how the "gentlemanlike" can otherwise be maintained; and maintained in this way it is.

[7] And now a second instance; and here too I am going to speak without personal experience of the subject I am introducing. I admit I have not been in Parliament, any more than I have figured in the *beau monde;* yet I cannot but think that statesmanship, as well as high breeding, is learned,

The Practice of Rhetoric

not by books, but in certain centres of education. If it be not presumption to say so, Parliament puts a clever man *au courant* with politics and affairs of state in a way surprising to himself. A member of the Legislature, if tolerably observant, begins to see things with new eyes, even though his views undergo no change. Words have a meaning now, and ideas a reality, such as they had not before. He hears a vast deal in public speeches and private conversation, which is never put into print. The bearings of measures and events, the action of parties, and the persons of friends and enemies, are brought out to the man who is in the midst of them with a distinctness, which the most diligent perusal of newspapers will fail to impart to them. It is access to the fountain-heads of political wisdom and experience, it is daily intercourse, of one kind or another, with the multitude who go up to them, it is familiarity with business, it is access to the contributions of fact and opinion thrown together by many witnesses from many quarters, which does this for him. However, I need not account for a fact, to which it is sufficient to appeal: that the Houses of Parliament and the atmosphere around them are a sort of University of politics.

As regards the world of science, we find a remarkable instance of the [8] principle which I am illustrating in the periodical meetings for its advance, which have arisen in the course of the last twenty years, such as the British Association. Such gatherings would to many persons appear at first sight simply preposterous. Above all subjects of study, Science is conveyed, is propagated, by books, or by private teaching; experiments and investigations are conducted in silence; discoveries are made in solitude. What have philosophers to do with festive celebrities, and panegyrical solemnities with mathematical and physical truth? Yet on a closer attention to the subject, it is found that not even scientific thought can dispense with the suggestions, the instruction, the stimulus, the sympathy, the intercourse with mankind on a large scale, which such meetings secure. A fine time of year is chosen, when days are long, skies are bright, the earth smiles, and all nature rejoices; a city or town is taken by turns, of ancient name or modern opulence, where buildings are spacious and hospitality hearty. The novelty of place and circumstance, the excitement of strange, or the refreshment of well-known, faces, the majesty of rank or of genius, the amiable charities of men pleased both with themselves and with each other; the elevated spirits, the circulation of thought, the curiosity; the morning sections, the outdoor exercise, the well-furnished, well-earned board, the not ungraceful hilarity, the evening circle; the brilliant lecture, the discussions or collisions or guesses of great men one with another, the narratives of scientific processes, of hopes, disappointments, conflicts, and successes, the splendid eulogistic orations—these and the like constituents of the annual celebration are considered to do something real and substantial for the advance of knowledge which can be done in no other way. Of course they can but be occasional; they answer to the annual Act, or Commencement, or Commemoration of a University, not to its ordinary condition; but they are of a University nature; and I can well believe in their utility. They issue in the promotion of a certain living and, as it were, bodily communication of knowledge from one to another, of a general interchange of ideas, and a comparison and adjustment of science with science, of an enlargement of mind, intellectual and social, of an ardent love of the particular study, which may be chosen by each individual, and a noble devotion to its interests.

[9]   Such meetings, I repeat, are but periodical, and only partially represent the idea of a University. The bustle and whirl which are their usual concomitants are in ill keeping with the order and gravity of earnest intellectual education. We desiderate means of instruction which involve no interruption of our ordinary habits; nor need we seek it long, for the natural course of things brings it about, while we debate over it. In every great country, the metropolis itself becomes a sort of necessary University, whether we will or no. As the chief city is the seat of the court, of high society, of politics, and of law, so as a matter of course is it the seat of letters also; and at this time, for a long term of years, London and Paris are in fact and in operation Universities, though in Paris its famous University is no more, and in London a University scarcely exists except as a board of administration. The newspapers, magazines, reviews, journals, and periodicals of all kinds, the publishing trade, the libraries, museums, and academies there found, the learned and scientific societies, necessarily invest it with the functions of a University; and that atmosphere of intellect, which in a former age hung over Oxford or Bologna or Salamanca, has, with the change of times, moved away to the centre of civil government. Thither come up youths from all parts of the country, the students of law, medicine, and the fine arts, and the *employés* and *attachés* of literature. There they live, as chance determines; and they are satisfied with their temporary home, for they find in it all that was promised to them there. They have not come in vain, as far as their own object in coming is concerned. They have not learned any particular religion, but they have learned their own particular profession well. They have, moreover, become acquainted with the habits, manners, and opinions of their place of sojourn, and done their part in maintaining the tradition of them. We cannot then be without virtual Universities; a metropolis is such: the simple question is whether the education sought and given should be based on principle, formed upon rule, directed to the highest ends, or left to the random succession of masters and schools, one after another, with a melancholy waste of thought and an extreme hazard of truth.

[10]   Religious teaching itself affords us an illustration of our subject to a certain point. It does not indeed seat itself merely in centres of the world; this is impossible from the nature of the case. It is intended for the many, not the few; its subject matter is truth necessary for us, not truth recondite

and rare; but it concurs in the principle of a University so far as this, that its great instrument, or rather organ, has ever been that which nature prescribes in all education, the personal presence of a teacher, or, in theological language, Oral Tradition. It is the living voice, the breathing form, the expressive countenance, which preaches, which catechises. Truth, a subtle, invisible, manifold spirit, is poured into the mind of the scholar by his eyes and ears, through his affections, imagination, and reason; it is poured into his mind and is sealed up there in perpetuity, by propounding and repeating it, by questioning and requestioning, by correcting and explaining, by progressing and then recurring to first principles, by all those ways which are implied in the word "catechising." In the first ages, it was a work of long time; months, sometimes years, were devoted to the arduous task of disabusing the mind of the incipient Christian of its pagan errors, and of moulding it upon the Christian faith. The Scriptures indeed were at hand for the study of those who could avail themselves of them; but St. Irenæus does not hesitate to speak of whole races who had been converted to Christianity without being able to read them. To be unable to read or write was in those times no evidence of want of learning: the hermits of the deserts were, in this sense of the word, illiterate; yet the great St. Anthony, though he knew not letters, was a match in disputation for the learned philosophers who came to try him. Didymus again, the great Alexandrian theologian, was blind. The ancient discipline, called the *Disciplina Arcani,* involved the same principle. The more sacred doctrines of Revelation were not committed to books but passed on by successive tradition. The teaching on the Blessed Trinity and the Eucharist appears to have been so handed down for some hundred years; and when at length reduced to writing, it has filled many folios, yet has not been exhausted.

But I have said more than enough in illustration; I end as I began—a University is a place of concourse, whither students come from every quarter for every kind of knowledge. You cannot have the best of every kind everywhere; you must go to some great city or emporium for it. There you have all the choicest productions of nature and art all together, which you find each in its own separate place elsewhere. All the riches of the land, and of the earth, are carried up thither; there are the best markets, and there the best workmen. It is the centre of trade, the supreme court of fashion, the umpire of rival talents, and the standard of things rare and precious. It is the place for seeing galleries of first-rate pictures, and for hearing wonderful voices and performers of transcendent skill. It is the place for great preachers, great orators, great nobles, great statesmen. In the nature of things, greatness and unity go together; excellence implies a centre. And such, for the third or fourth time, is a University; I hope I do not weary out the reader by repeating it. It is the place to which a thousand schools make contributions; in which the intellect may safely range and speculate, sure to find its equal in some antagonist activity, and

[11]

its judge in the tribunal of truth. It is a place where inquiry is pushed forward, and discoveries verified and perfected, and rashness rendered innocuous, and error exposed, by the collision of mind with mind, and knowledge with knowledge. It is the place where the professor becomes eloquent, and is a missionary and a preacher, displaying his science in its most complete and most winning form, pouring it forth with the zeal of enthusiasm, and lighting up his own love of it in the breasts of his hearers. It is the place where the catechist makes good his ground as he goes, treading in the truth day by day into the ready memory, and wedging and tightening it into the expanding reason. It is a place which wins the admiration of the young by its celebrity, kindles the affections of the middle-aged by its beauty, and rivets the fidelity of the old by its associations. It is a seat of wisdom, a light of the world, a minister of the faith, an alma mater of the rising generation. It is this and a great deal more, and demands a somewhat better head and hand than mine to describe it well.

[12]   Such is a University in its idea and in its purpose; such in good measure has it before now been in fact. Shall it ever be again? We are going forward in the strength of the Cross, under the patronage of the Blessed Virgin, in the name of St. Patrick, to attempt it.

TOPICS FOR DISCUSSION

1. Newman defines a university "in its essence" as "a place for the communication and circulation of thought, by means of personal intercourse, through a wide extent of country." What elements in this definition are common to a metropolis, a Parliament, and a publishing center as well as to a university? What element applies only to a university? Is that element the most important one in the definition of a university? Why or why not?

2. What is the basis for Newman's distinction between a popular education and a university education? How does a university use *littera scripta* in a different way from other institutions?

3. Read the sentence in paragraph 4 that begins, "Till we have discovered some intellectual daguerreotype . . . . " Have we discovered that daguerreotype in educational television? If we have, must Newman's definition of a university be modified? Explain your answer.

4. Paragraph 11 has been widely praised for its eloquent description of a university "in its idea and its purpose." Does it also describe a present-day American university? If it does not, is Newman's eloquence "mere eloquence"? Explain your answer.

The Practice of Rhetoric

5. Analyze the rhetorical structure of paragraph 11 with respect to the unity, coherence, and the variety of the sentence structure. Point out how the rhythm of the sentences is established by repetition, parallel structure, and antithesis.

TOPICS FOR COMPOSITION

1. Develop one of the subjects listed below according to Newman's method of expository argument. After defining each term in your title carefully, clarify your meaning by three extended illustrations:
   a. what a modern American college is
   b. what we should not teach at college
   c. why we cannot be our own teachers
   d. how a metropolis is a university, and how it is not a university
2. Write an essay accounting for the important differences in organization and style between a formal oration like Burke's *Conciliation* speech (p. 165) and an expository argument like "What Is a University?"

WILLIAM D. TEMPLEMAN

Some Ideas of a University

TEMPLEMAN takes up his subject directly by recognizing the lively problem of American higher education. He accepts as a challenge the proposal by Clark Kerr, then president of the University of California, "that the most desirable and practical type of institution for higher education today" is the "multiversity." Kerr's proposal not only declares for the "multiversity," it rejects as a matter of course the liberal arts ideal identified with Cardinal Newman's writings on university education and the research ideal identified with Abraham Flexner's concept of a modern university.

Like Newman's "What Is a University?" Templeman's essay is an expository argument. Its exposition, clearly underlined by the documentation, presents various views on the purpose of higher education. As each view is unfolded, however, judgments begin to emerge, explanations tend to support one point of view, and the evidence converges to a conclusion that is more decisive than neutral explanation. The reader thus encounters argument not in a formal thesis and proof but in the content of the essay, not in explicit refutations but in indirect corrections and ripostes. Expository argument of this kind is particularly appropriate when, as in this instance, the writer cannot assume that his readers share his own feeling that "greatness and unity go together."

[1] Perhaps the time is appropriate for renewed thinking about what a university is and ought to be. The Commission on the Humanities, established by the American Council of Learned Societies, the Council of Graduate Schools in the United States, and the United Chapters of Phi Beta Kappa, has included in its report the following statement: "There is genuine doubt today whether the universities and colleges can insure that the purposes for which they were established and sometimes endowed will be fulfilled." [1]

[2] In April, 1963, as Godkin Lecturer at Harvard University, President Clark Kerr of the University of California talked about "The Uses of the University." The University of California has nine large campuses, widely

[1]*ACLS Newsletter*, Vol. XV, No. 5 (May 1964), p. 10. [Templeman's notes throughout.]

SOME IDEAS OF A UNIVERSITY Reprinted from *The Educational Forum*, Vol. 29, No. 3 (March 1965) by permission of Kappa Delta Pi, an honor society in education. Copyright 1965 by Kappa Delta Pi, West Lafayette, Indiana.

The Practice of Rhetoric

separated in a huge state. President Kerr indicated that America has developed a new kind of institution—the multiversity. But as he talked of "the multiversity" he referred repeatedly to "the university." [2] Also he referred again and again to John Henry Newman's *The Idea of a University.* The university of today, Kerr declared, derives from two "ideal types": one is "the academic cloister of Cardinal Newman"; the other is "the research organism of Abraham Flexner." [3] Newman's idea, he asserted, reflected "the beautiful ivory tower of Oxford as it once was." Elsewhere he stated that Newman's idea was of "a village with its priests"; that Flexner's idea of a modern university was of "a town—a one-industry town—with its intellectual oligarchy"; and that the idea of a multiversity is of "a city of infinite variety."

The students in the "city," Kerr contended, are "older, more likely to be   [3] married, more vocationally oriented, more drawn from all classes and races than the students in the village; and they find themselves in a most intensely competitive atmosphere." To be sure, he allowed that Newman's idea "still has its devotees—chiefly the humanists and the generalists and the undergraduates." He allowed also that Flexner's idea "still has it supporters—chiefly the scientists and the specialists and the graduate students." But the idea of a multiversity, said he, "has its practitioners—chiefly the administrators, who now number many of the faculty among them, and the leadership groups in society at large.... The university is so many things to so many different people that it must, of necessity, be partially at war with itself." Later he stated: "The multiversity is a confusing place for the student." However confusing and at war with itself the multiversity is, Kerr indicated that it is the most desirable and practical type of institution for higher education today. And he declared that the concept or idea urged by Newman for a university was outdated at the time Newman presented it.

Now Newman himself had declared that the characteristics of his ideal   [4] university had already become unacceptable to most people of his generation: "The majestic vision of the Middle Age, which grew steadily to perfection in the course of centuries, the University of Paris, or Bologna, or Oxford, has almost gone out in night. A philosophical comprehensiveness, an orderly expansiveness, an elastic constructiveness, men have lost them." Newman not only insisted that this had occurred; he also stated that men "cannot make out why" they have lost these characteristics from their vision

[2] See the published lectures in his *The Uses of the University* (Cambridge, Mass.: Harvard University Press, 1963), *passim.* For quotations from Kerr later in this paragraph, see pp. 126, 41, 8–9, 42.
[3] Abraham Flexner wrote concerning "The Idea of a Modern University" in his *Universities: American, English, German* (New York: Oxford University Press, 1930), pp. 3–36.

of a university. And then he asserted flatly: "This is why: because they have lost the idea of unity." [4]

[5]   Sir Arthur Quiller-Couch remarked at Cambridge University in 1913 that "no one knows when the great Universities [of Oxford and Cambridge] were founded, or precisely out of what schools they grew." He asserted that the term *universitas* simply means a society; it "has nothing to do with universality, whether of teaching or of frequenting"; the term *universitas* means "all of us." But he proceeded to say that though the word *universitas* or *university* originally meant merely an organized society composed of all its members, the word came to suggest something more. For the Cambridge university, or group of persons so called, was organized to promote learning; and so also was the Oxford university; and there has grown around those two great universities a connotation of splendid attractiveness, he indicated—so that they have seemed like huge flaming beacon-lights, and have attracted to them great numbers of young persons who move through life as migratory birds fly through the night. Although thousands of those attracted have been singed and even burned, many thousands

> have caught the sacred fire into their souls as they passed through and passed out, to carry it, to drop it, still as from wings, upon waste places of the world! Think of country vicarages, of Australian or Himalayan outposts, where men have nourished out lives of duty upon the fire of three transient, priceless years. Think of the generations of children to whom their fathers' lives, prosaic enough, could always be re-illumined if someone let fall the word "Oxford" or "Cambridge," so that they themselves came to surmise an aura about the name as of a land very far off; and then say if the ineffable spell of those two words do not lie somewhere in the conflux of generous youth with its rivalries and clash of minds, ere it disperses, generation after generation, to the duller business of life. [5]

[6]   "The conflux of generous youth with its rivalries and clash of minds"! There we have a superb phrase indicating part of what a university can and should mean, over and beyond a mere organized society of persons meeting in one place to promote learning. Quiller-Couch reminds us, moreover, that though we may analytically consider a university as a place of generous mental clash toward learning, vast numbers of alumni and alumnæ of universities in the world have indeed gained from their alma maters more than cold information and intellectual vigor; that in many

[4]Newman, *Discourses on the Scope and Nature of University Education* ... (Dublin, 1852), pp. 139–40, 142, as quoted in A. Dwight Culler, *The Imperial Intellect: A Study of Newman's Educational Ideal* (New Haven, Conn.: Yale University Press, 1955), p. 174.
[5]Sir Arthur Quiller-Couch, *On the Art of Writing* (New York: G. P. Putnam's Sons, 1916), pp. 246, 249, 269–70.

places universities have warmed thousands upon thousand with an exhilarating, inspiring, and continuing fire, enabling them to do their difficult subsequent jobs with a certain joy; that universities here and there have somehow made men and women feel almost enchanted, enabling them to see in memory one university or another as if it possessed a sort of group halo surrounding its people and also even its environmental buildings and grounds.

Notable nineteenth-century English men of letters gave much considera- [7] tion to what colleges and universities should be and do. One of them was Newman, whose famous 1873 volume with the title *The Idea of a University* included some essays he had delivered as lectures in Dublin in 1852, as part of a program to arouse interest in the formation of a university in Ireland. For the apparent source of the title we turn to Samuel Taylor Coleridge.

In 1803 Coleridge wrote to Robert Southey that [8]

> a strange use has been made of the word encyclopaedia. It signifies properly grammar, logic, rhetoric, and ethics, and metaphysics, which last, explaining the ultimate principle of grammar, logic, rhetoric, and ethics— formed a circle of knowledge.... To call a huge unconnected miscellany [of whatever is known], in an arrangement determined by the accident of initial letters, an encyclopaedia is ... impudent ignorance.

He referred to the alphabetical arrangement and lack of system in the [9] second and later editions of the *Encyclopaedia Britannica*. By 1817 Coleridge had planned a new encyclopedia. This was to be a voluminous publication entitled the *Encyclopaedia Metropolitana*. It was to be arranged "not according to the letters of the alphabet which happen to form the initials of the English *names* of the Treatises, but in agreement with a PHILOSOPHICAL SYSTEM, based on the *nature* of the subjects—a method which causes the entire work to become a rational exposition of the state of human knowledge, and the mutual dependence and relative importance of its different branches." Coleridge's plan provided an eight-volume "Chaos" at the end for miscellaneous material arranged alphabetically, because he realized that "a strictly *scientific* method" would not be practical. But in the *Encyclopaedia* proper, history and biography were to be presented chronologically, instead of alphabetically, and the various pure, mixed, and applied sciences were to be treated comprehensively and presented in a scale intended to show their derivation from a single master-thought. "The first pre-conception, or master-thought, on which our plan rests," wrote Coleridge, "is the *moral origin and tendency* of all true Science; in other words, our great objects are to exhibit the Arts and Sciences in their Philosophical harmony...."

For the *Encyclopaedia Metropolitana* Coleridge conceived the plan and [10] wrote only the general preface. But the younger faculty members at Oxford and Cambridge became greatly interested. Among others, Richard Whately of Oriel College, Oxford, took an active part in 1822—just when he was influential with the young Newman. He enlisted Newman's help with the composition of the article on logic. Newman later contributed other articles, and was asked for still more. When, early in the 1850's, Newman was faced with writing lectures on university education, part of his preparatory reading was Coleridge's preface to the *Encyclopaedia Metropolitana;* it was entitled "Preliminary Treatise on Method." Professor A. Dwight Culler, in his brilliant study of Newman, declares: "Without doubt he [Newman] regarded his own work as a kind of 'Preliminary Treatise on the Method of Education.'" And he points out that Coleridge had written on the *Idea of Church and State* and the "idea" of an encyclopedia, and that now Newman undertook to write on the "idea" of a university. And Culler adds: "[Newman] would do for the university what Coleridge had done for the encyclopedia, for the two institutions were not only parallel in themselves but were also confronted by parallel dangers. What the *Britannica* was to the *Metropolitana,* the University of London was to Oxford and Cambridge. And in Ireland the Queen's Colleges stood in the same relation to the proposed Catholic University of Ireland." [6]

[11]   Newman was aware of the etymological meaning of *universitas* as merely "an organization or society of people" taken collectively; but he declared that he was giving it its generally "recognized meaning, however it came to mean it, of *a place of universal knowledge*"—i.e., of knowledge composed of many parts turned into one and hence all-inclusive. Originally *universitas* had been followed by a defining phrase such as *magistrorum et scholarium* (so that *universitas magistrorum et scholarium* meant "a society —or university—of masters and scholars"). Later the defining phrase was assumed to be *scientiarum* (so that *universitas scientiarum* meant "a place —or university—of the sciences—i.e., of all the branches of knowledge"). Newman used the term "university" with this meaning, centuries old: "a place of all the sciences, of universal knowledge." He considered his ideal university to be a place of universal knowledge.

[12]   But of course he knew that knowledge is inescapably a matter of the actions of human beings. And involved with his *Encyclopaedia Metropolitana* concept of universal knowledge was the memory of his own activities as administrator, teacher, and scholar-student. In the 1850's he served actively as rector-elect for a university in Ireland. He had been student and faculty man at Oxford from 1817 to 1845. After undergraduate years in Trinity College he had become a Fellow of Oriel College in 1822. At Oriel, with other faculty members, he began to find in life some of the

---

[6]Culler, p. 178; for my next two paragraphs see Culler, especially pp. 180, 33–38; and see Culler, *passim,* for much of my material on Coleridge, Whately, etc.

characteristics that he had hoped for vainly as an undergraduate student. The provost of Oriel was Professor Edward Copleston, a great administrator and a great teacher who emphasized the question-answer technique. Copleston once wrote: "The more I think on it the more am I convinced that to *exercise* the mind of the student is the business of education, rather than to pour in knowledge."

Newman was concerned for students to teach one another through collision of student mind with student mind. But he was also concerned for students to be taught by formal studies, directed by teachers; and he thought that a proper university should offer a full-circle range of subjects, even though any one student can not study them all, for a student will gain, he declared, "by living among those and under those who represent the whole circle." He proceeded to indicate that his ideal student, in his ideal university, is a person who breathes a pure atmosphere of thought, even though he can be a formal student in only a few courses. Such an ideal student becomes part of an intellectual tradition that is independent of particular teachers. In Newman's words, [13]

> He apprehends the great outlines of knowledge, the principles on which it rests, the scale of its parts, its lights and its shades, its great points and its little, as he otherwise cannot apprehend them. Hence it is that his education is called "Liberal." A habit of mind is formed which lasts through life, of which the attributes are freedom, equitableness, calmness, moderation, and wisdom; or what in a former Discourse I have ventured to call a philosophical habit. This then I would assign as the special fruit of the education furnished at a University, as contrasted with other places of teaching or modes of teaching.[7]

Newman stated that "the scope of a University is to provide a liberal education, to give liberal knowledge. . . . Knowledge may be Useful Knowledge or Liberal Knowledge. . . . You see, then, here are two methods of Education; the end of the one is to be philosophical, of the other to be mechanical; the one rises towards general ideas, the other is exhausted upon what is particular and external." He insisted upon the *necessity* of Useful Knowledge, of mechanical and industrial and specialized professional knowledge, saying that we owe our daily welfare to it. But then he commented as follows: [14]

> I only say that knowledge, in proportion as it tends more and more to be particular [or, specialized], ceases to be Knowledge. . . . When I speak of Knowledge, I mean something intellectual, something which grasps what it perceives through the senses; something which takes a view of things;

[7] John Henry Newman, *The Idea of a University* . . . 9th ed. (London and New York: Longmans, Green, and Co., 1889), pp. 101–102.

which sees more than the senses convey; which reasons upon what it sees, and while it sees; which invests it with an idea ... it is more correct, as well as more usual, to speak of a University as a place of education, than of instruction.... We are instructed, for instance, in manual exercises, in the fine and useful arts, in trades, and in ways of business; for these are methods which have little or no effect upon the mind itself, are contained in rules committed to memory, to tradition, or to use, and bear upon an end external to themselves. But "education" is a higher word; it implies an action upon our mental nature, and the formation of a character; it is something individual and permanent....[8]

The University, Newman said further, "educates the intellect to reason well in all matters, to reach out towards truth, and to grasp it": this is the object of a University, "in its bare idea," considered by itself, and apart from the Church, and from the State, and from any other power that may use it.[9]

[15]   In a later Discourse Newman amplified his concept of the object of a University education. That object, he said, though basically concerned with training the intellect, is also and thereby concerned with training good members of society, for "that training of the intellect, which is best for the individual himself, best enables him to discharge his duties to society." He insisted that

a University is not a birthplace of poets or of immortal authors, of founders of schools, leaders of colonies, or conquerors of nations. It does not promise a generation of Aristotles or Newtons, of Napoleons or Washingtons, of Raphaels or Shakespeares, though such miracles of nature it has before now contained within its precincts. Nor is it content on the other hand with forming the critic or the expermentalist, the economist, or the engineer, though such too it includes within its scope. But a University training is the great ordinary means to a great but ordinary end; it aims at raising the intellectual tone of society, at cultivating the public mind, at purifying the national taste, at supplying true principles to popular enthusiasm and fixed aims to popular aspiration, at giving enlargement and sobriety to the ideas of the age, at facilitating the exercise of political power, and refining the intercourse of private life.[10]

[16]   Herbert Spencer wrote four tremendously influential essays on education that were published between 1854 and 1859. They had effect on university and college levels, as well as on the lower ones. He wrote of education generally, and insisted that the dominant place in the schools should be held by the new scientific studies. He helped greatly to popularize the theory of growth and of evolution, and the doctrine of the survival of the fittest. He showed clearly that a knowledge of science was very useful

[8]*Ibid.*, pp. 112–14.
[9]*Ibid.*, pp. 125, 126.
[10]*Ibid.*, pp. 177–78.

in the practical living of human beings. His famous essay (1859) on "What Knowledge Is of Most Worth?" contended that for discipline, as well as for guidance and information, scientific studies were of most worth. He urged that instruction should be made interesting and pleasurable; and that the laboratory method should be used for scientific studies. Education, according to Spencer, should prepare us for complete living. Professor Edgar W. Knight writes in his history of education that "with the development of state universities in the United States and of municipal universities in England ... [Spencer's] ideas gained widely." [11]

It is noteworthy that Thomas Carlyle's *Sartor Resartus* (1833–34), one [17] of the most influential publications of the century, presents a university professor as its chief character, and that this hero is a professor of "Things in General."

Matthew Arnold published in 1849 a poem indicating that as a young [18] university graduate in the "bad days" of the mid-century he felt especially indebted to Sophocles, "who saw life steadily and saw it whole." Arnold's praise of Sophocles' "view" of life as a unified whole, with component parts related, calls to mind such praise as Newman was giving, or was about to give, to the unified "system" of knowledge urged in Coleridge's prospectus for the *Encyclopaedia Metropolitana*. Arnold in 1853 published his famous poem "The Scholar-Gipsy." In it an Oxford University scholar who had joined the gipsies centuries ago is hailed as having had a unity in his way of living. Modern times are called diseased, largely because they have "divided aims." Arnold said that the centuries-old ghost of the admired scholar-gipsy shunned Oxford University in the mid-nineteenth century when he observed students participating in trivial festivity. Arnold in this way contended that Oxford was not giving to all of its students a sober sense of fundamental unity and harmony. A similar contention is conveyed by Arnold's 1866 poem "Thyrsis." But although he indicated dissatisfaction in some ways with Oxford, Arnold showed that at least a minority of students did receive from that university a vision, a "view" of a potentially unified and harmonious world.

Arnold's concept of an ideal university insisted that the students in it [19] would become aware of the potential unity and harmony of the world. They would see items steadily, and see them as parts of a whole. Arnold when a professor at Oxford urged upon students a certain inward condition of striving which he called "culture." This culture, he said, was an active pursuit of perfection by and in each individual student, a working toward well-rounded individual perfection (1) scientifically, with concern for *knowledge;* (2) aesthetically, with concern for *beauty,* for the fine arts and for the emotions that inspire them and are inspired by them; (3)

---

[11]Edgar W. Knight, *Twenty Centuries of Education* (Boston: Ginn and Co., 1940), p. 461; see also 3rd rev. ed. (Boston: Ginn and Co., 1951), p. 534.

morally, with concern for *right conduct* toward others—this, said Arnold, involved three-fourths of every person's life—; and (4) with concern for *social life and good manners.* Such striving, such continuous and conscious pursuit of unified and harmonious perfection, a pursuit wherein all phases of a person's life should be treated as interrelated and mutually dependent and supporting, Arnold urged for many years in numerous lectures delivered in England and America at various universities.

[20]   Thomas Henry Huxley, another professor, championed Darwin's theories of evolution, was sometimes called "Darwin's bull-dog," and was himself a great research scientist as well as a famous lecturer. He urged a university emphasis on the natural sciences. Arnold and Huxley actually were urging much the same sort of education—the difference being largely one of emphasis. Here is one of Huxley's pronouncements:

> education is the instruction of the intellect in the laws of nature, under which name I include not merely things and their forces, but men and their ways; and the fashioning of the affections and of the will into an earnest and loving desire to move in harmony with those laws.[12]

[21]   Still another great writer of the nineteenth century, Alfred Tennyson, told the story of a young man whose Soul went to an unsatisfactory "university"—a "Palace of Art." His Soul lived there in solitary pleasure, delighting in its sciences, music, literature, paintings, stained-glass windows, gardens, and landscapes. In the fourth year there his Soul became bitterly aware of a lack of human companionship and left the Palace in order to work helpfully with others, to involve his intellect with "men and their ways" as well as with the arts and sciences.

[22]   A university today may profitably come to have in larger degree the characteristics indicated below by Newman in 1854. This statement does *not* set forth a concept of a university as a place where people have "lost the idea of unity," or of a university as "a village with its priests."

> A University is a place of concourse, whither students come from every quarter for every kind of knowledge. You cannot have the best of every kind everywhere; you must go to some great city or emporium for it. . . . In the nature of things, greatness and unity go together; excellence implies a centre. And such . . . is a University. . . .[13]

[23]   Each individual student's experience in a college or a university should involve all phases of life, interrelatedly. This experience, furthermore, is

---

[12]Charles Frederick Harrold and William D. Templeman, eds., *English Prose of the Victorian Era* (New York: Oxford University Press, 1938), p. 1319.

[13]John Henry Newman, "What Is a University?" in *Catholic University Gazette* for June, 1854, as reprinted in Newman's *Essays and Sketches, Volume II,* ed. Charles Frederick Harrold (New York: Longmans, Green, and Co., 1948), p. 288.

ideally both self-centered and reaching out for other human beings—past, present, and future. To be sure, special schools at both undergraduate and graduate levels should offer specialized training; but both a separate "liberal arts" college and a college of liberal arts and sciences which is a component part of a university should give to a student the experience of an education "higher" and broader than a specialized education—an enlarging and harmonizing experience in which "greatness and *unity* go together."

TOPICS FOR DISCUSSION

1. We identify this essay as a research paper, a serious, objective, documented study of a lively current problem: What kind of university do we need in America today? In the course of his essay, Professor Templeman refers at some length to the views of Clark Kerr, John Henry Newman, Sir Arthur Quiller-Couch, Samuel Taylor Coleridge, Herbert Spencer, Matthew Arnold, Thomas H. Huxley, and Alfred, Lord Tennyson. Would you say his main purpose was:
   a. simply to survey the literature of higher education
   b. to argue against the views of Clark Kerr
   c. to point out the special relevance of Newman's ideas at the present time
   d. something else
   Give reasons for your answer.
2. How is Newman's *Idea of a University* related to Coleridge's plan for the *Encyclopaedia Metropolitana?* How are both related to the principle of the unity of knowledge?
3. In several places (see particularly paragraphs 5, 6, and 11) Templeman investigates various meanings of the term *university*. Why is the definition of university crucial in this discussion? Is it opposed to the term *multiversity?* How does the definition of *university* bear upon Templeman's conclusions in the last two paragraphs?
4. Of the various ideas of a university presented in this essay, which seems most acceptable to you? Which do you reject? Give reasons for your answer.

TOPICS FOR COMPOSITION

1. Write an expository argument in which you demonstrate how the various subjects you are presently studying are, or can be, interrelated.
2. Use the most effective illustrations at your command to make evident just what is meant by "The Pleasures of Knowledge."

William D. Templeman

**HOWARD
MUMFORD
JONES**

**On the Arts
and
Humanities**

THE more we know about the circumstances that prompted a speech, the more we are able to appreciate its strategy. The speaker in this instance was Howard Mumford Jones, appearing before the U.S. Senate Subcommittee on the Arts and Humanities as a representative of the Modern Language Association of America. The hearing, held on March 4, 1965, was devoted to two proposed bills aimed at the creation of a National Arts Foundation and a National Humanities Foundation. The senators wanted to know what Professor Jones, as the president of an important learned society, thought about the proposals. He was in favor of both of them. He chose, however, to speak specifically about the National Humanities Foundation and more narrowly about "two related ideas" contained in a section of the bill.

If you have read the two previous essays, you will have noted several useful arguments in favor of supporting the humanities and the liberal arts. Among these are the pursuit of truth for its own sake and the cultivation of pure research. Professor Jones did not dwell on these arguments. He stressed instead the bearing that research in the humanities has had on good teaching, its value in promoting a climate of political freedom, and its role in preparing Americans to exercise leadership in the contemporary world. Why did he choose to emphasize the practical values of humanistic culture? Were his illustrations shrewdly chosen?

We notice again a reliance on expository argument rather than on precise, formal debate. Although Professor Jones never loses sight of the action he is urging on his audience, he tends to be the witness, presenting what he has seen and experienced, rather than being the partisan advocate. As a witness, he testifies and explains rather than argues. And he avoids all quibbling and scoring of points, achieving thereby, you may agree, his mission of clarification.

[1]   As I understand it, there are two principal measures before the committee. One, S. 315, creates a National Arts Foundation. The other, S. 316, creates a National Humanities Foundation. These two projects are in a sense inter-

---

ON THE ARTS AND HUMANITIES   From *ACLS Newsletter*, Vol. 16, No. 3 (March 1965). Reprinted by permission of the American Council of Learned Societies and Howard Mumford Jones.

related. Section 5 of S. 316 carefully defines the area of the humanities and the area of the arts, and distinguishes between them. I think this distinction is a wise provision in the bill for the reason that many persons think that support given the arts is identical with support given the humanities. Certainly the arts and the humanities are interrelated, and each would be impoverished if the other should weaken or disappear. But the function of the artist is not the same as the function of the scholar. I think the arts deserve support, but as I am persuaded the arts will not lack for advocates, I shall confine myself to the humanities and address my remarks to the appropriate sections of S. 316.

Section 2 of this bill states with clarity and power the place, purpose, [2] and value of scholarly and cultural activities in and to the country and underlines the imbalance many of us have felt to exist between the support by government of science and technology, and the support of scholarly and cultural activities. It is not to be inferred that the government altogether neglects these activities, since the Library of Congress and museums like the National Museum are for some of the humanities what the laboratory is to the scientist. But this is indirect support. The present bill proposes more direct support. I shall not waste the time of the committee by saying over again what is excellently said of the situation in section 2 of the bill. I shall, instead, address myself to two important related ideas.

The language of the bill associates teaching and scholarship. This is as [3] it should be. It is sometimes argued, I think wrongly, that because federal aid, direct or indirect, goes towards education, since education includes teachers of the humanities, the federal government is already offering sufficient support to teachers of the humanities, and may offer more support in proportion as federal aid to education is extended. This is true as far as it goes but it does not go far enough. The training of teachers and the buying of school equipment are not the same thing as the support of humanistic scholarship.

The training of teachers becomes dry and dull unless the subjects they [4] teach are continually refreshed with new knowledge, new interpretations, new ideas, all resulting from competent investigation by professionally skilled research workers. This we take for granted in the sciences, but somehow we do not take it for granted in non-scientific subjects. Yet, just as in science there is an endless frontier that must be constantly patrolled, explored, and pushed back if science is to retain its vitality, so humane learning must be constantly revitalized along the endless frontier of knowledge in that great area of human life. Otherwise teaching becomes devitalized.

Let me take an illustration from European history. When I was an under- [5] graduate, I was taught as a matter of course that the Europe of the Holy Alliance—that is, the European balance of power established by statesmen after the fall of Napoleon—was an evil thing maintained through the cunning of cynical diplomats like Metternich. Looking back on European history today, looking at this period across the slaughter of two world wars and other tragic happenings of the twentieth century, the historian discovers that the period in Europe between 1815 and 1870 was a rather stable time. He inquires why. He reads and analyzes primary documents not available to the historians who taught my generation and discovers that the earlier view was too simple-minded, that the statesmen who created and long maintained the balance of power were not necessarily wicked men, that, indeed, they may have been wiser men than the books of 1910 described them as being. The relative calm in European affairs, among other things, permitted the United States to develop in its own way. In the contemporary world, where we are trying to make the United Nations an agency for permanent peace, this shift in the interpretation of the past, a shift based on new knowledge and better insight, may have considerable meaning for us. Certain it is that unless scholars are enabled to search out new facts and construct modern interpretations, teachers by and by are helpless to do more than teach by rote. This is not good education. We believe that on competent evidence Americans should learn to make their own judgments. Teachers, if they are to teach competently, must continually be refreshed by reports from the latest discoveries on the endless frontier of scholarship.

[6]   If the example be in any way persuasive, it is clear that we must do all we can to keep fresh winds of thought blowing across all the fields of humanistic activity. Let me cite another example. The English essayist, G. K. Chesterton, once said that if he were running a lodging house, he would be more interested in the philosophy of a prospective renter than he would be in his pocket book. I suppose this to mean that if the lodger clung to principles of honesty and integrity, he would pay the rent, but the mere fact that he had a bank account would be no proof that he intended to pay it. I am not a professional philosopher, but I believe one of the principal concerns of philosophers is continually to test the theories and the rules that govern belief as well as the language in which beliefs are cast. Nothing is more necessary to a nation than the general acceptance of principles of intellectual and moral integrity. Although at first glance nothing seems more remote from practical affairs than a philosopher brooding over some general idea, philosophy is central to the life of nations. For example, Thomas Jefferson was a philosopher who brooded a great deal over principles and he came up with what seem to us some right answers. Adolf Hitler was also a philosopher—at least he said he was— who brooded a great deal over principles and he came up with some wrong answers. The results in the one case were beneficial, in the other case abominable. Jefferson, in a celebrated statement, once said that he had sworn eternal hostility to every form of tyranny over the mind of man. Hitler, on the contrary, suppressed all inquiry except on preconceived lines.

Attempts to make everybody conform to an official philosophy as in the case of communist China seem to us the wrong way to go about it. We seek, instead, free inquiry; and free inquiry is the very essence of scholarly and scientific research.

I turn to the second proposition I wish to lay before the committee. The [7] language of the bill says that democracy demands wisdom and vision in its citizens and says also that American world leadership must be solidly founded upon worldwide respect and admiration for the Nation's high qualities as a leader in the realm of ideas and of the spirit. Alongside of this admirable ideal I wish now to state a second, equally practical concern. If the United States is to lead the world, it must understand the world it wants to lead. It cannot without danger assume as a matter of course that other nations are going to let themselves be led by the United States on the simple assumption that American values are inherently superior values and the values of other nations are inherently inferior values. It is essential to wise leadership that Americans shall understand not merely their own values but the value systems of other nations. By "values" in this context I mean something more than economic activity, health, politics, business, or military organization; I refer rather to the traditional notions that nations and cultures have of themselves.

Culture is an ambiguous word. To the anthropologist studying a rela- [8] tively primitive tribe it means patterns of behavior, patterns of tools, methods of burying the dead, familial and marriage customs and tabus, and so on. American anthropologists have contributed importantly to this branch of knowledge and will continue to do so. But there is another meaning to culture, as when one says of so-and-so that he is a cultured person. A national culture in this larger sense is a national or racial or religious tradition so long accepted that it has been transformed into some general form of value, usually spiritual in its connotations, which the nation accepts as deeply characteristic of what it has been, what it is, and what it wants to become. This culture, to be understood by an outsider, cannot be approached as if it were a question of tariff barriers or military bases or an alliance for progress. It can probably best be understood when it is approached through the art, the music, the literature, the philosophy, and the history of the country we are trying to understand. It is precisely in this area, I suggest, that our foreign relations are weakest and that support of humanistic research is needed.

Do North Americans, for example, really understand the pride of Latin [9] American republics in a cultural tradition older than our own? Do they understand that the concept of individualism means one thing in Argentina and a quite different thing in the United States? Do they sufficiently comprehend that the poetry of some of these nations is a better key to comprehension than problems about coffee or bananas? If the North American image among many such countries is that of a big bully, it is because we have too often tended to approach delicate problems of international relationship on a basis mainly materialistic. We do not have enough knowledge of the necessary foreign languages, we do not have enough knowledge of the literature, the philosophy, or the history of the countries south of us to approach their leading men in a tactful way. One of the great potentialities I see in this bill is that it makes possible a greater interplay among cultures. If we have vaguely felt that we were misunderstood by other nations, it is also possible that we have failed to try to understand them along the lines of their national values.

[10]   I have chosen this example from the New World. But the European countries also offer their instances of good intentions gone astray. Our generation has seen the dissolution of empires, including the Dutch empire. About the excellence or lack of excellence of Dutch rule in their former colonies I have no informed opinion. But the Dutch are a proud people. They resisted the mighty force of the Spanish Empire during their heroic age, a resistance narrated in the works of the great American historian John L. Motley. They were once mistress of the seas. They produced some of the greatest painters in Europe. They were so distinguished for philosophical and religious tolerance that the great Jewish philosopher, Spinoza, lived unmolested in Holland when his co-religionists threw him out, the Pilgrims fled there and were hospitably received before they decided to risk going to North America, and John Locke, the philosopher of the American Revolution and the idol of its leading thinkers, studied in the Low Countries. The Dutch have done distinguished work in astronomy, mathematics, physiology, mechanics, optics, and other branches of learning. I think they possibly may have been a little shocked when, assisting at the dissolution of their empire, the American attitude was simply: "Score another hit for democracy." The Dutch were tolerant long before the American colonies were tolerant, but I am under the impression that the remarkable history of this remarkable nation is only dimly known in the United States and that, in supporting humane studies and humanistic inquiry, this is the kind of knowledge that will help us to acquit ourselves more tactfully in the problems of leadership we are forced, as we think, to assume.

[11]   If my two illustrations of the need for greater understanding and greater tact in dealing with other nations are a little unusual, I confess that when we confront some of the great powers and some of the newer nations I find the same need for humanistic studies in depth. Russia, said Sir Winston Churchill, is an enigma wrapped in a riddle, and although Russian studies in the United States are better than they used to be, we still have a long way to go. Our ignorance of China is colossal. For most Americans Paris is a fun city and they are baffled by M. De Gaulle. Perhaps, however, a greater knowledge of French tradition, French literature, French individualism, and French art might enable us better to comprehend why

the doctrine of "la gloire" has its perennial appeal. Our ignorance of Canadian history and culture is equally fantastic.

But I do not wish to dwell unduly on our defects but rather to point [12] out the great and exciting implications of the bill before the committee. For virtually the first time in the nation's history it is proposed to throw the weight of the federal government behind a noble effort to increase our mastery of great fields of knowledge that, in the language of the proposed law, have been neglected because of our necessary interest in technology and defense. For the first time it is proposed that investigations into the arts, philosophy, the languages and literatures of the world, not to speak of the history of law, religion and science, archaeology, and other branches of humanistic learning are to receive federal support at least comparable to the support given to the so-called "practical" subjects. For the first time in American history inquiries into all past time and all cultures and nations, including our own, are thought to be financially relevant to the enrichment of American life.

I hope you will see why, as an American scholar long concerned about [13] the meaning of our own culture and about the interplay of life in the United States and life elsewhere on this planet, I am heartily in favor of S. 316. Doubtless weaknesses will appear in the organization and machinery of the organization proposed, but of these I am ignorant and these can be corrected by experience. Grover Cleveland once said that the way to resume specie payment is to resume. The way to begin supporting the humanistic scholarship and the humanities is to begin supporting them. Both in my private capacity as a scholar in the humanities and a teacher of humane learning, and in my official capacity as President of the Modern Language Association of America I urge upon the committee approval of the proposed legislation. Persons more experienced than I am in the operation of governmental offices may well have practical changes to offer in the bills I have read, but the general direction of the legislation seems to me to be good, the organization to be sound as a beginning measure, and the purpose one that I heartily applaud.

TOPICS FOR DISCUSSION

1. Why does Professor Jones confine his attention to two aspects of the National Humanities Foundation Bill? How are the two aspects he considers interrelated?
2. Summarize Jones' reasoning in paragraph 4. How is the reasoning supported by the examples developed in paragraphs 5 and 6? Are the examples particularly well chosen for the audience, a Senate subcommittee? Give reasons for your answer.

3. In paragraph 7, Jones states, "I turn to the second proposition I wish to lay before the Committee." What was the first proposition? Is the second proposition contained in any one sentence in paragraph 7, or is it distributed throughout several sentences? Discuss.
4. In what sense is the humanist definition of *culture* (paragraph 8) just as practical as the anthropological definition? How do the examples of Latin America and the Dutch point up the usefulness of humanistic culture? Why do you suppose Jones decided to develop those examples and not the examples of Russia, China, France, and Canada mentioned in paragraph 11?
5. In political discourse a good conclusion sums up the points favorable to the speaker's purpose and urges the audience to take a definite action. Evaluate the last two paragraphs in the light of this statement.

TOPICS FOR COMPOSITION

1. Write a brief essay explaining how the command of a foreign language or the knowledge of foreign history is of practical importance in modern life. Develop your essay by specific examples.
2. Write a letter to your newspaper expressing your own views on the proposed National Arts Foundation or the National Humanities Foundation. Stress the practical importance of the arts and humanities in today's world.
3. Write a critique of one of the ideas expressed in this essay. You might explore how free inquiry can be guaranteed in a National Humanities Foundation.

WALTER HORATIO PATER

Style

WALTER PATER'S "Style" appeared as the opening essay of *Appreciations* in 1889. Its impact was immediate and profound. Fifteen years later, in his *History of Criticism*, George Saintsbury acclaimed it as one of the great discourses on criticism, one that summed up older views and introduced new ones—notably those of Gustave Flaubert, now regarded as the classic theorist of modern style. Pater took for granted the fact that some old distinctions were no longer as relevant as they once had been. The lines that once divided literature, rhetoric, and poetry, for example, had become hard to trace. Objective literature of fact and subjective literature of vision had come closer together, and indeed, had commingled in the nineteenth century, so that there was no standard style for various forms of discourse.

In effect, then, Pater was arguing for a new understanding of style, one that placed the greatest stress on the writer's dedication to doing justice to his own vision: "the problem of style was there! the unique word, phrase, sentence, paragraph, essay, or song, absolutely proper to the single mental presentation or vision within."

Moreover, Pater's method of exposition is consistent with his theory of literary style. If the writer must do justice to a vision and if that vision be unique, then the principal feature of a good style is its conformity, within the bounds of good taste, to ideas deeply realized.

Pater, however, is no mere formalist. As he makes clear in his last paragraph, great literature, as opposed to good literature, is allied to great ends.

The distinction between great art and good art [depends] immediately, as regards literature at all events, not on its form, but on the matter.... It is on the quality of the matter it informs or controls, its compass, its variety, its alliance to great ends, or the depth of the note of revolt, or the largeness of hope in it, that the greatness of literary art depends ....

Like Newman and the other authors in this section, Pater explains his opinions without entering into formal argument. One may readily derive a coherent group of statements expressive of his philosophy of style, but the argument is implicit rather than explicit.

Since all progress of mind consists for the most part in differentiation, in   [1]
the resolution of an obscure and complex object into its component aspects,
it is surely the stupidest of losses to confuse things which right reason has

put asunder, to lose the sense of achieved distinctions, the distinction between poetry and prose, for instance, or, to speak more exactly, between the laws and characteristic excellences of verse and prose composition. On the other hand, those who have dwelt most emphatically on the distinction between prose and verse, prose and poetry, may sometimes have been tempted to limit the proper functions of prose too narrowly; and this again is at least false economy, as being, in effect, the renunciation of a certain means or faculty, in a world where after all we must needs make the most of things. Critical efforts to limit art *a priori,* by anticipations regarding the natural incapacity of the material with which this or that artist works, as the sculptor with solid form, or the prose-writer with the ordinary language of men, are always liable to be discredited by the facts of artistic production; and while prose is actually found to be a coloured thing with Bacon, picturesque with Livy and Carlyle, musical with Cicero and Newman, mystical and intimate with Plato and Michelet and Sir Thomas Browne, exalted or florid, it may be, with Milton and Taylor, it will be useless to protest that it can be nothing at all, except something very tamely and narrowly confined to mainly practical ends—a kind of "good round-hand"; as useless as the protest that poetry might not touch prosaic subjects as with Wordsworth, or an abstruse matter as with Browning, or treat contemporary life nobly as with Tennyson.[1] In subordination to one essential beauty in all good literary style, in all literature as a fine art, as there are many beauties of poetry so the beauties of prose are many, and it is the business of criticism to estimate them as such; as it is good in the criticism of verse to look for those hard, logical, and quasi-prosaic excellences which that too has, or needs. To find in the poem, amid the flowers, the allusions, the mixed perspectives, of *Lycidas*[2] for instance, the thought, the logical structure:—how wholesome! how delightful! as to identify in prose what we call the poetry, the imaginative power, not treating it as out of place and a kind of vagrant intruder, but by way of an estimate of its rights, that is, of its achieved powers, there.

[2]   Dryden, with the characteristic instinct of his age, loved to emphasise the distinction between poetry and prose, the protest against their confusion with each other, coming with somewhat diminished effect from one whose poetry was so prosaic. In truth, his sense of prosaic excellence affected his verse rather than his prose, which is not only fervid, richly figured, poetic, as we say, but vitiated, all unconsciously, by many a scanning line. Setting up correctness, that humble merit of prose, as the central literary excellence, he is really a less correct writer than he may seem, still with an imperfect

[1]The less familiar names in the sentence are French historian Jules Michelet (1798–1874) ; Sir Thomas Browne (1605–82), the author of *Religio Medici;* and Bishop Jeremy Taylor (1613–67), author of the celebrated *Holy Living* and *Holy Dying,* among many other works.
[2]An elegy written by John Milton in 1638.

The Practice of Rhetoric

mastery of the relative pronoun. It might have been foreseen that, in the rotations of mind, the province of poetry in prose would find its assertor; and, a century after Dryden, amid very different intellectual needs, and with the need therefore of great modifications in literary form, the range of the poetic force in literature was effectively enlarged by Wordsworth. The true distinction between prose and poetry he regarded as the almost technical or accidental one of the absence or presence of metrical beauty, or, say! metrical restraint; and for him the opposition came to be between verse and prose of course; but, as the essential dichotomy in this matter, between imaginative and unimaginative writing, parallel to De Quincey's distinction between "the literature of power and the literature of knowledge," in the former of which the composer gives us not fact, but his peculiar sense of fact, whether past or present.[3]

Dismissing then, under sanction of Wordsworth, that harsher opposition of poetry to prose, as savouring in fact of the arbitrary psychology of the last century, and with it the prejudice that there can be but one only beauty of prose style, I propose here to point out certain qualities of all literature as a fine art, which, if they apply to the literature of fact, apply still more to the literature of the imaginative sense of fact, while they apply indifferently to verse and prose, so far as either is really imaginative—certain conditions of true art in both alike, which conditions may also contain in them the secret of the proper discrimination and guardianship of the peculiar excellences of either. [3]

The line between fact and something quite different from external fact is, indeed, hard to draw. In Pascal,[4] for instance, in the persuasive writers generally, how difficult to define the point where, from time to time, argument which, if it is to be worth anything at all, must consist of facts or groups of facts, becomes a pleading—a theorem no longer, but essentially an appeal to the reader to catch the writer's spirit, to think with him, if one can or will—an expression no longer of fact but of his sense of it, his peculiar intuition of a world, prospective, or discerned below the faulty conditions of the present, in either case changed somewhat from the actual world. In science, on the other hand, in history so far as it conforms to scientific rule, we have a literary domain where the imagination may be thought to be always an intruder. And as, in all science, the functions of literature reduce themselves eventually to the transcribing of fact, so all the excellences of literary form in regard to science are reducible to various kinds of painstaking; this good quality being involved in all "skilled work" whatever, in the drafting of an act of parliament, as in sewing. Yet here again, the writer's sense of fact, in history especially, and in all those com- [4]

[3]Wordsworth offers the views cited here in his Preface to *Lyrical Ballads* (1798). De Quincey's distinction occurs in his essay *The Poetry of Pope* (1848).
[4]Blaise Pascal (1623–62) wrote the celebrated *Pensées*, in which scientific speculation is inextricably bound up with intuition.

plex subjects which do but lie on the borders of science, will still take the place of fact, in various degrees. Your historian, for instance, with absolutely truthful intention, amid the multitude of facts presented to him must needs select, and in selecting assert something of his own humour, something that comes not of the world without but of a vision within. So Gibbon moulds his unwieldy material to a preconceived view.[5] Livy, Tacitus, Michelet, moving full of poignant sensibility amid the records of the past, each, after his own sense, modifies—who can tell where and to what degree?—and becomes something else than a transcriber; each, as he thus modifies, passing into the domain of art proper. For just in proportion as the writer's aim, consciously or unconsciously, comes to be the transcribing, not of the world, not of mere fact, but of his sense of it, he becomes an artist, his work *fine* art; and good art (as I hope ultimately to show) in proportion to the truth of his presentment of that sense; as in those humbler or plainer functions of literature also, truth—truth to bare fact, there—is the essence of such artistic quality as they may have. Truth! there can be no merit, no craft at all, without that. And further, all beauty is in the long run only *fineness* of truth, or what we call expression, the finer accommodation of speech to that vision within.

[5]   —The transcript of his sense of fact rather than the fact, as being preferable, pleasanter, more beautiful to the writer himself. In literature, as in every other product of human skill, in the moulding of a bell or a platter, for instance, wherever this sense asserts itself, wherever the producer so modifies his work as, over and above its primary use or intention, to make it pleasing (to himself, of course, in the first instance) there, "fine" as opposed to merely serviceable art, exists. Literary art, that is, like all art which is in any way imitative or reproductive of fact—form, or colour, or incident—is the representation of such fact as connected with soul, of a specific personality, in its preferences, its volition and power.

[6]   Such is the matter of imaginative or artistic literature—this transcript, not of mere fact, but of fact in its infinite variety, as modified by human preference in all its infinitely varied forms. It will be good literary art not because it is brilliant or sober, or rich, or impulsive, or severe, but just in proportion as its representation of that sense, that soul-fact, is true, verse being only one department of such literature, and imaginative prose, it may be thought, being the special art of the modern world. That imaginative prose should be the special and opportune art of the modern world results from two important facts about the latter: first, the chaotic variety and complexity of its interests, making the intellectual issue, the really master currents of the present time incalculable—a condition of mind little susceptible of the restraint proper to verse form, so that the most char-

[5]Edward Gibbon (1737–94) was the author of *The Decline and Fall of the Roman Empire* (1776–88).

acteristic verse of the nineteenth century has been lawless verse; and secondly, an all-pervading naturalism, a curiosity about everything whatever as it really is, involving a certain humility of attitude, cognate to what must, after all, be the less ambitious form of literature. And prose thus asserting itself as the special and privileged artistic faculty of the present day, will be, however critics may try to narrow its scope, as varied in its excellence as humanity itself reflecting on the facts of its latest experience —an instrument of many stops, meditative, observant, descriptive, eloquent, analytic, plaintive, fervid. Its beauties will be not exclusively "pedestrian"; it will exert, in due measure, all the varied charms of poetry, down to the rhythm which, as in Cicero, or Michelet, or Newman, at their best, gives its musical value to every syllable.[6]

The literary artist is of necessity a scholar, and in what he proposes to [7] do will have in mind, first of all, the scholar and the scholarly conscience— the male conscience in this matter, as we must think it, under a system of education which still to so large an extent limits real scholarship to men. In his self-criticism, he supposes always that sort of reader who will go (full of eyes) warily, considerately, though without consideration for him, over the ground which the female conscience traverses so lightly, so amiably. For the material in which he works is no more a creation of his own than the sculptor's marble. Product of a myriad various minds and contending tongues, compact of obscure and minute association, a language has its own abundant and often recondite laws, in the habitual and summary recognition of which scholarship consists. A writer, full of a matter he is before all things anxious to express, may think of those laws, the limitations of vocabulary, structure, and the like, as a restriction, but if a real artist will find in them an opportunity. His punctilious observance of the proprieties of his medium will diffuse through all he writes a general air of sensibility, of refined usage. *Exclusiones debitae naturae*[7]—the exclusions, or rejections, which nature demands—we know how large a part these play, according to Bacon, in the science of nature. In a somewhat changed sense, we might say that the art of the scholar is summed up in the observance of those rejections demanded by the nature of his medium, the material he must use. Alive to the value of an atmosphere in which every term finds its utmost degree of expression, and with all the jealousy of a lover of words, he will resist a constant tendency on the part of the

---

[6]Mr. Saintsbury, in his *Specimens of English Prose, from Malory to Macaulay,* has succeeded in tracing, through successive English prose-writers, the tradition of that severer beauty in them, of which this admirable scholar of our literature is known to be a lover. *English Prose, from Mandeville to Thackeray,* more recently "chosen and edited" by a younger scholar, Mr. Arthur Galton, of New College, Oxford, a lover of our literature at once enthusiastic and discreet, aims at a more various illustration of the eloquent powers of English prose, and is a delightful companion. [Pater's note.]

[7]The Latin, translated in the text, is taken from Francis Bacon's *Novum Organum,* Book 2 of *Aphorisms,* No. 18.

majority of those who use them to efface the distinctions of language, the facility of writers often reinforcing in this respect the work of the vulgar. He will feel the obligation not of the laws only, but of those affinities, avoidances, those mere preferences, of his language, which through the associations of literary history have become a part of its nature, prescribing the rejection of many a neology, many a license, many a gipsy phrase which might present itself as actually expressive. His appeal, again, is to the scholar, who has great experience in literature, and will show no favour to short-cuts, or hackneyed illustration, or an affectation of learning designed for the unlearned. Hence a contention, a sense of self-restraint and renunciation, having for the susceptible reader the effect of a challenge for minute consideration; the attention of the writer, in every minutest detail, being a pledge that it is worth the reader's while to be attentive too, that the writer is dealing scrupulously with his instrument, and therefore, indirectly, with the reader himself also, but he has the science of the instrument he plays on, perhaps, after all, with a freedom which in such case will be the freedom of a master.

[8] For meanwhile, braced only by those restraints, he is really vindicating his liberty in the making of a vocabulary, an entire system of composition, for himself, his own true manner; and when we speak of the manner of a true master we mean what is essential in his art. Pedantry being only the scholarship of *le cuistre*[8] (we have no English equivalent) he is no pedant, and does but show his intelligence of the rules of language in his freedoms with it, addition or expansion, which like the spontaneities of matter in a well-bred person will still further illustrate good taste.—The right vocabulary! Translators have not invariably seen how all-important that is in the work of translation, driving for the most part at idiom or construction; whereas, if the original be first-rate, one's first care should be with its elementary particles, Plato, for instance, being often reproducible by an exact following, with no variation in structure, of word after word, as the pencil follows a drawing under tracing-paper, so only each word or syllable be not of false colour, to change my illustration a little.

[9] Well! that is because any writer worth translating at all has winnowed and searched through his vocabulary, is conscious of the words he would select in systematic reading of a dictionary, and still more of the words he would reject were the dictionary other than Johnson's; and doing this with his peculiar sense of the world ever in view, in search of an instrument for the adequate expression of that, he begets a vocabulary faithful to the colouring of his own spirit, and in the strictest sense original. That living authority which language needs lies, in truth, in its scholars, who recognising always that every language possesses a genius, a very fastidious genius, of its own, expand at once and purify its very elements, which must needs

8Literally, a college scout; hence, the allusion is to scholarship of a very narrow sort.

The Practice of Rhetoric

change along with the changing thoughts of living people. Ninety years ago, for instance, great mental force, certainly, was needed by Wordsworth, to break through the consecrated poetic associations of a century, and speak the language that was his, that was to become in a measure the language of the next generation.[9] But he did it with the tact of a scholar also. English, for a quarter of a century past, has been assimilating the phraseology of pictorial art; for half a century, the phraseology of the great German metaphysical movement of eighty years ago; in part also the language of mystical theology; and none but pedants will regret a great consequent increase of its resources. For many years to come its enterprise may well lie in the naturalisation of the vocabulary of science, so only it be under the eye of a sensitive scholarship—in a liberal naturalisation of the ideas of science too, for after all the chief stimulus of good style is to possess a full, rich, complex matter to grapple with. The literary artist, therefore, will be well aware of physical science; science also attaining, in its turn, its true literary ideal. And then, as the scholar is nothing without the historic sense, he will be apt to restore not really obsolete or really worn-out words, but the finer edge of words still in use: *ascertain, communicate, discover*—words like these it has been part of our "business" to misuse. And still, as language was made for man, he will be no authority for correctness which, limiting freedom of utterance, were yet but accidents in their origin; as if one vowed not to say *"its"* which ought to have been Shakespeare; *"his"* and *"hers,"* for inanimate objects, being but a barbarous and really inexpressive survival. Yet we have known many things like this. Racy Saxon monosyllables, close to us as touch and sight, he will intermix readily with those long, savoursome, Latin words, rich in "second intention." In this late day certainly, no critical process can be conducted reasonably without eclecticism. Of such eclecticism we have a justifying example in one of the first poets of our time. How illustrative of monosyllabic effect, of sonorous Latin, of the phraseology of science, of metaphysic, of colloquialism even, are the writings of Tennyson; yet with what a fine, fastidious scholarship throughout!

A scholar writing for the scholarly, he will of course leave something to [10] the willing intelligence of his reader. "To go preach to the first passer-by," says Montaigne, "to become tutor to the ignorance of the first I meet, is a thing I abhor"; a thing, in fact, naturally distressing to the scholar, who will therefore ever be shy of offering uncomplimentary assistance to the reader's wit. To really strenuous minds there is a pleasurable stimulus in the challenge for a continuous effort on their part, to be rewarded by securer and more intimate grasp of the author's sense. Self-restraint, a skilful economy of means, *ascêsis*,[10] that too has a beauty of its own; and

---

[9]The reference is to Wordsworth's Preface to *Lyrical Ballads*.
[10]Literally, exercise; its connotations are supplied in the passage that follows.

for the reader supposed there will be an æsthetic satisfaction in that frugal closeness of style which makes the most of a word, in the exaction from every sentence of a precise relief, in the just spacing out of word to thought, in the logically filled space connected always with the delightful sense of difficulty overcome.

[11]   Different classes of persons, at different times, make, of course, very various demands upon literature. Still, scholars, I suppose, and not only scholars, but all disinterested lovers of books, will always look to it, as to all other fine art, for a refuge, a sort of cloistral refuge, from a certain vulgarity in the actual world. A perfect poem like *Lycidas,* a perfect fiction like *Esmond,*[11] the perfect handling of a theory like Newman's *Idea of a University,* has for them something of the uses of a religious "retreat." Here, then, with a view to the central need of a select few, those "men of a finer thread" who have formed and maintain the literary ideal, everything, every component element, will have undergone exact trial, and, above all, there will be no uncharacteristic or tarnished or vulgar decoration, permissible ornament being for the most part structural, or necessary. As the painter in his picture, so the artist in his book, aims at the production by honourable artifice of a peculiar atmosphere. "The artist," says Schiller,[12] "may be known rather by what he *omits*"; and in literature, too, the true artist may be best recognised by his tact of omission. For to the grave reader words too are grave; and the ornamental word, the figure, the accessory form or colour or reference, is rarely content to die to thought precisely at the right moment, but will inevitably linger awhile stirring a long "brain-wave" behind it of perhaps quite alien associations.

[12]   Just there, it may be, is the detrimental tendency of the sort of scholarly attentiveness of mind I am recommending. But the true artist allows for it. He will remember that, as the very word ornament indicates what is in itself non-essential, so the "one beauty" of all literary style is of its very essence, and independent, in prose and verse alike, of all removable decoration; that it may exist in its fullest lustre, as in Flaubert's *Madame Bovary,* for instance, or in Stendhal's *Le Rouge et Le Noir,* in a composition utterly unadorned, with hardly a single suggestion of visibly beautiful things.[13] Parallel, allusion, the allusive way generally, the flowers in the garden:— he knows the narcotic force of these upon the negligent intelligence to which any *diversion,* literally, is welcome, any vagrant intruder, because one can go wandering away with it from the immediate subject. Jealous, if he have a really quickening motive within, of all that does not hold directly to that, of the facile, the otiose, he will never depart from the strictly pedestrian process, unless he gains a ponderable something there-

---

[11]*The History of Henry Esmond* (1852), a novel by William Makepeace Thackeray.

[12]Johann Christoph Friedrich von Schiller (1759–1805), German poet and dramatist.

[13]Gustave Flaubert's *Madame Bovary* appeared in 1857. Stendhal is the pseudonym of Marie Henri Beyle (1783–1842), whose *Le Rouge et Le Noir* was published in 1830.

The Practice of Rhetoric

by. Even assured of its congruity, he will still question its serviceableness. Is it worth while, can we afford, to attend to just that, to just that figure or literary reference, just then?—Surplusage! he will dread that, as the runner on his muscles. For in truth all art does but consist in the removal of surplusage, from the last finish of the gem-engraver blowing away the last particle of invisible dust, back to the earliest divination of the finished work to be, lying somewhere, according to Michelangelo's fancy, in the rough-hewn block of stone.

And what applies to figure or flower must be understood of all other [13] accidental or removable ornaments of writing whatever; and not of specific ornament only, but of all that latent colour and imagery which language as such carries in it. A lover of words for their own sake, to whom nothing about them is unimportant, a minute and constant observer of their physiognomy, he will be on the alert not only for obviously mixed metaphors of course, but for the metaphor that is mixed in all our speech, though a rapid use may involve no cognition of it. Currently recognising the incident, the colour, the physical elements of particles in words like *absorb, consider, extract,* to take the first that occur, he will avail himself of them, as further adding to the resources of expression. The elementary particles of language will be realised as colour and light and shade through his scholarly living in the full sense of them. Still opposing the constant degradation of language by those who use it carelessly, he will not treat coloured glass as if it were clear; and while half the world is using figure unconsciously, will be fully aware not only of all that latent figurative texture in speech, but of the vague, lazy, half-formed personification—a rhetoric, depressing, and worse than nothing, because it has no really rhetorical motive—which plays so large a part there, and, as in the case of more ostentatious ornament, scrupulously exact of it, from syllable to syllable, its precise value.

So far I have been speaking of certain conditions of the literary art aris- [14] ing out of the medium or material in or upon which it works, the essential qualities of language and its aptitudes for contingent ornamentation, matters which define scholarship as science and good taste respectively. They are both subservient to a more intimate quality of good style: more intimate, as coming nearer to the artist himself. The otiose, the facile, surplusage: why are these abhorrent to the true literary artist, except because in literary as in all other art, structure is all-important, felt, or painfully missed, everywhere?—that architectural conception of work, which foresees the end in the beginning and never loses sight of it, and in every part is conscious of all the rest, till the last sentence does but, with undiminished vigour, unfold and justify the first—a condition of literary art, which, in contradistinction to another quality of the artist himself, to be spoken of later, I shall call the necessity of *mind* in style.

[15]   An acute philosophical writer, the late Dean Mansel[14] (a writer whose works illustrate the literary beauty there may be in closeness, and with obvious repression or economy of a fine rhetorical gift) wrote a book, of fascinating precision in a very obscure subject, to show that all the technical laws of logic are but means of securing, in each and all of its apprehensions, the unity, the strict identity with itself, of the apprehending mind. All the' laws of good writing aim at a similar unity or identity of the mind in all the processes by which the word is associated to its import. The term is right, and has its essential beauty, when it becomes, in a manner, what it signifies, as with the names of simple sensations. To give the phrase, the sentence, the structural member, the entire composition, song, or essay, a similar unity with its subject and with itself:—style is in the right way when it tends towards that. All depends upon the original unity, the vital wholeness and identity, of the initiatory apprehension or view. So much is true of all art, which therefore requires always its logic, its comprehensive reason—insight, foresight, retrospect, in simultaneous action—true, most of all, of the literary art, as being of all the arts most closely cognate to the abstract intelligence. Such logical coherency may be evidenced not merely in the lines of composition as a whole, but in the choice of a single word, while it by no means interferes with, but may even prescribe, much variety, in the building of the sentence for instance, or in the manner, argumentative, descriptive, discursive, of this or that part or member of the entire design. The blithe, crisp sentence, decisive as a child's expression of its needs, may alternate with the long-contending, victoriously intricate sentence; the sentence, born with the integrity of a single word, relieving the sort of sentence in which, if you look closely, you can see much contrivance, much adjustment, to bring a highly qualified matter into compass at one view. For the literary architecture, if it is to be rich and expressive, involves not only foresight of the end in the beginning, but also development or growth of design, in the process of execution, with many irregularities, surprises, and afterthoughts; the contingent as well as the necessary being subsumed under the unity of the whole. As truly, to the lack of such architectural design, of a single, almost visual, image, vigorously informing an entire, perhaps very intricate, composition, which shall be austere, ornate, argumentative, fanciful, yet true from first to last to that vision within, may be attributed those weaknesses of conscious or unconscious repetition of word, phrase, motive, or member of the whole matter, indicating, as Flaubert was aware, an original structure in thought not organically complete. With such foresight, the actual conclusion will most often get itself written out of hand, before, in the more obvious sense, the work is finished. With some strong and leading sense of the world, the tight hold of which secures true *composition* and not mere loose accre-

[14]Henry L. Mansel (1820–71) became dean of St. Paul's Cathedral in 1869.

tion, the literary artist, I suppose, goes on considerately, setting joint to joint, sustained by yet restraining the productive ardour, retracing the negligences of his first sketch, repeating his steps only that he may give the reader a sense of secure and restful progress, readjusting mere assonances even, that they may soothe the reader, or at least not interrupt him on his way; and then, somewhat before the end comes, is burdened, inspired, with his conclusion, and betimes delivered of it, leaving off, not in weariness and because he finds *himself* at an end, but in all the freshness of volition. His work now structurally complete, with all the accumulating effect of secondary shades of meaning, he finishes the whole up to the just proportion of that ante-penultimate conclusion, and all becomes expressive. The house he has built is rather a body he has informed. And so it happens, to its greater credit, that the better interest even of a narrative to be recounted, a story to be told, will often be in its second reading. And though there are instances of great writers who have been no artists, an unconscious tact sometimes directing work in which we may detect, very pleasurably, many of the effects of conscious art, yet one of the greatest pleasures of really good prose literature is in the critical tracing out of that conscious artistic structure, and the pervading sense of it as we read. Yet of poetic literature too; for, in truth, the kind of constructive intelligence here supposed is one of the forms of the imagination.

That is the special function of mind, in style. Mind and soul:—hard to [16] ascertain philosophically, the distinction is real enough practically, for they often interfere, are sometimes in conflict, with each other. Blake, in the last century, is an instance of preponderating soul, embarrassed, at a loss, in an era of preponderating mind. As a quality of style, at all events, soul is a fact, in certain writers—the way they have of absorbing language, of attracting it into the peculiar spirit they are of, with a subtlety which makes the actual result seem like some inexplicable inspiration. By mind, the literary artist reaches us, through static and objective indications of design in his work, legible to all. By soul, he reaches us, somewhat capriciously perhaps, one and not another, through vagrant sympathy and a kind of immediate contact. Mind we cannot choose but approve where we recognise it; soul may repel us, not because we misunderstand it. The way in which theological interests sometimes avail themselves of language is perhaps the best illustration of the force I mean to indicate generally in literature, by the word *soul*. Ardent religious persuasion may exist, may make its way, without finding any equivalent heat in language: or, again, it may enkindle words to various degrees, and when it really takes hold of them doubles its force. Religious history presents many remarkable instances in which, through no mere phrase-worship, an unconscious literary tact has, for the sensitive, laid open a privileged pathway from one to another. "The altar-fire," people say, "has touched those lips!" The Vulgate, the English Bible, the English Prayer-Book, the writings of Swedenborg, the Tracts for the Times:[15]—there, we have instances of widely different and largely diffused phases of religious feeling in operation as soul in style. But something of the same kind acts with similar power in certain writers of quite other than theological literature, on behalf of some wholly personal and peculiar sense of theirs. Most easily illustrated by theological literature, this quality lends to profane writers a kind of religious influence. At their best, these writers become, as we say sometimes, "prophets"; such character depending on the effect not merely of their matter, but of their matter as allied to, in "electric affinity" with, peculiar form, and working in all cases by an immediate sympathetic contact, on which account it is that it may be called soul, as opposed to mind, in style. And this too is a faculty of choosing and rejecting what is congruous or otherwise, with a drift towards unity—unity of atmosphere here, as there of design—soul securing colour (or perfume, might we say?) as mind secures form, the latter being essentially finite, the former vague or infinite, as the influence of a living person is practically infinite. There are some to whom nothing has any real interest, or real meaning, except as operative in a given person; and it is they who best appreciate the quality of soul in literary art. They seem to know a *person*, in a book, and make way by intuition: yet, although they thus enjoy the completeness of a personal information, it is still a characteristic of soul, in this sense of the word, that it does but suggest what can never be uttered, not as being different from, or more obscure than, what actually gets said, but as containing that plenary substance of which there is only one phase or facet in what is there expressed.

[17]   If all high things have their martyrs, Gustave Flaubert might perhaps rank as the martyr of literary style. In his printed correspondence, a curious series of letters, written in his twenty-fifth year, records what seems to have been his one other passion—a series of letters which, with its fine casuistries, its firmly repressed anguish, its tone of harmonious grey, and the sense of disillusion in which the whole matter ends, might have been, a few slight changes supposed, one of his own fictions. Writing to Madame X.[16] certainly he does display, by "taking thought" mainly, by constant and delicate pondering, as in his love for literature, a heart really moved, but still more, and as the pledge of that emotion, a loyalty to his work. Madame X., too, is a literary artist, and the best gifts he can send her are

[15]The Vulgate is St. Jerome's Latin version of the Bible, translated between 383 and 405. Emanuel Swedenborg (1688–1772) was a Swedish religious leader. Tracts for the Times (1833–41) consisted of ninety pamphlets on the Oxford Movement; they were written by Newman, Keble, Pusey, Williams, and others.

[16]Madame X. was the poetess Louise Colet, with whom Flaubert was intimate between 1846 and 1854. The originals of the letters cited in the succeeding paragraphs may be found in Flaubert's *Oeuvres*, Vol. 2 (Paris, 1910), pp. 238–45. An excellent translation of many of these is *The Selected Letters of Gustave Flaubert*, edited and translated by Francis Steegmuller (New York: Farrar, Straus & Giroux, 1954).

precepts of perfection in art, counsels for the effectual pursuit of that better love. In his love-letters it is the pains and pleasures of art he insists on, its solaces: he communicates secrets, reproves, encourages, with a view to that. Whether the lady was dissatisfied with such divided or indirect service, the reader is not enabled to see; but sees that, on Flaubert's part at least, a living person could be no rival of what was, from first to last, his leading passion, a somewhat solitary and exclusive one.

I must scold you, he writes, for one thing, which shocks, scandalises me, the small concern, namely, you show for art just now. As regards glory be it so: there, I approve. But for art! —the one thing in life that is good and real—can you compare with it an earthly love? —prefer the adoration of a relative beauty to the *cultus* of the true beauty? Well! I tell you the truth. That is the one thing good in me: the one thing I have, to me estimable. For yourself, you blend with the beautiful a heap of alien things, the useful, the agreeable, what not?

The only way not to be unhappy is to shut yourself up in art, and count everything else as nothing. Pride takes the place of all beside when it is established on a large basis. Work! God wills it. That, it seems to me, is clear.

I am reading over again the *Æneid*, certain verses of which I repeat to myself to satiety. There are phrases there which stay in one's head, by which I find myself beset, as with those musical airs which are for ever returning, and cause you pain, you love them so much. I observe that I no longer laugh much, and am no longer depressed. I am ripe. You talk of my serenity, and envy me. It may well surprise you. Sick, irritated, the prey a thousand times a day of cruel pain, I continue my labour like a true working-man, who, with sleeves turned up, in the sweat of his brow, beats away at his anvil, never troubling himself whether it rains or blows, for hail or thunder. I was not like that formerly. The change has taken place naturally, though my will has counted for something in the matter.

Those who write in good style are sometimes accused of a neglect of ideas, and of the moral end, as if the end of the physician were something else than healing, of the painter than painting—as if the end of art were not, before all else, the beautiful.

What, then, did Flaubert understand by beauty, in the art he pursued with so much fervour, with so much self-command? Let us hear a sympathetic commentator: [18]

Possessed of an absolute belief that there exists but one way of expressing one thing, one word to call it by, one adjective to qualify, one verb to animate it, he gave himself to superhuman labour for the discovery, in every phrase, of that word, that verb, that epithet. In this way, he believed in some mysterious harmony of expression, and when a true word seemed to him to lack euphony still went on seeking another, with invincible patience, certain that he had not yet got hold of the *unique* word.... A thousand preoccupations would beset him at the same moment, always with this desperate certitude fixed in his spirit: Among all the expressions in the world, all forms and turns of expression, there is but *one*—one form, one mode—to express what I want to say.[17]

[19] The one word for the one thing,[18] the one thought, amid the multitude of words, terms, that might just do: the problem of style was there!—the unique word, phrase, sentence, paragraph, essay, or song, absolutely proper to the single mental presentation or vision within. In that perfect justice, over and above the many contingent and removable beauties with which beautiful style may charm us, but which it can exist without, independent of them yet dexterously availing itself of them, omnipresent in good work, in function at every point, from single epithets to the rhythm of a whole book, lay the specific, indispensable, very intellectual, beauty of literature, the possibility of which constitutes it a fine art.

[20] One seems to detect the influence of a philosophic idea there, the idea of a natural economy, of some pre-existent adaptation, between a relative, somewhere in the world of thought, and its correlative, somewhere in the world of language—both alike, rather, somewhere in the mind of the artist, desiderative, expectant, inventive—meeting each other with the readiness of "soul and body reunited," in Blake's rapturous design;[19] and, in fact, Flaubert was fond of giving his theory philosophical expression.

> There are no beautiful thoughts, he would say, without beautiful forms, and conversely. As it is impossible to extract from a physical body the qualities which really constitute it—colour, extension, and the like— without reducing it to a hollow abstraction, in a word, without destroying it; just so it is impossible to detach the form from the idea, for the idea only exists by virtue of the form.[20]

[21] All the recognised flowers, the removable ornaments of literature (including harmony and ease in reading aloud, very carefully considered by him) counted certainly; for these too are part of the actual value of what one says. But still, after all, with Flaubert, the search, the unwearied research, was not for the smooth, or winsome, or forcible word, as such, as with false Ciceronians, but quite simply and honestly, for the word's adjustment to its meaning. The first condition of this must be, of course, to know yourself, to have ascertained your own sense exactly. Then, if we

---

[17]The sympathetic commentator is Flaubert's friend and imitator Guy de Maupassant. The comment occurs in his introduction to *Lettres de Gustave Flaubert à George Sand* (Paris, 1884), pp. lxii–lxv.
[18]Pater is referring to *le mot juste*.
[19]Blake's design is his illustration of Robert Blair's *The Grave* (1808).
[20]*Oeuvres*, Vol. 2 (Paris, 1910), p. 244.

suppose an artist, he says to the reader,—I want you to see precisely what I see. Into the mind sensitive to "form," a flood of random sounds, colours, incidents, is ever penetrating from the world without, to become, by sympathetic selection, a part of its very structure, and, in turn, the visible vesture and expression of that other world it sees so steadily within, nay, already with a partial conformity thereto, to be refined, enlarged, corrected, at a hundred points; and it is just there, just at those doubtful points that the function of style, as tact or taste, intervenes. The unique term will come more quickly to one than another, at one time than another, according also to the kind of matter in question. Quickness and slowness, ease and closeness alike, have nothing to do with the artistic character of the true word found at last. As there is a charm of ease, so there is also a special charm in the signs of discovery, of effort and contention towards a due end, as so often with Flaubert himself—in the style which has been pliant, as only obstinate, durable metal can be, to the inherent perplexities and recusancy of a certain difficult thought.

If Flaubert had not told us, perhaps we should never have guessed how [22] tardy and painful his own procedure really was, and after reading his confession may think that his almost endless hesitation had much to do with diseased nerves. Often, perhaps, the felicity supposed will be the product of a happier, a more exuberant nature than Flaubert's. Aggravated, certainly, by a morbid physical condition, that anxiety in "seeking the phrase," which gathered all the other small *ennuis* of a really quiet existence into a kind of battle, was connected with his lifelong contention against facile poetry, facile art—art, facile and flimsy; and what constitutes the true artist is not the slowness or quickness of the process, but the absolute success of the result. As with those labourers in the parable,[21] the prize is independent of the mere length of the actual day's work. "You talk," he writes, odd, trying lover, to Madame X.

> You talk of the exclusiveness of my literary tastes. That might have enabled you to divine what kind of a person I am in the matter of love. I grow so hard to please as a literary artist, that I am driven to despair. I shall end by not writing another line.[22]

"Happy," he cries, in a moment of discouragement at that patient labour, [23] which for him, certainly, was the condition of a great success—

> Happy those who have no doubts of themselves! who lengthen out, as the pen runs on, all that flows forth from their brains. As for me, I hesitate, I disappoint myself, turn round upon myself in despite: my taste is

[21]The parable of the laborers in the vineyard appears in Matthew 20:1–16.
[22]The quotations from the letters to Louise Colet may be found on pages 213–14 of the work already cited in note 16.

augmented in proportion as my natural vigour decreases, and I afflict my soul over some dubious word out of all proportion to the pleasure I get from a whole page of good writing. One would have to live two centuries to attain a true idea of any matter whatever. What Buffon said is a big blasphemy: genius is not long-continued patience. Still, there is some truth in the statement, and more than people think, especially as regards our own day. Art! art! art! bitter deception! phantom that glows with light, only to lead one to destruction.

Again

I am growing so peevish about my writing. I am like a man whose ear is true but who plays falsely on the violin: his fingers refuse to reproduce precisely those sounds of which he has the inward sense. Then the tears come rolling down from the poor scraper's eyes and the bow falls from his hand.

[24]   Coming slowly or quickly, when it comes, as it came with so much labour of mind, but also with so much lustre, to Gustave Flaubert, this discovery of the word will be, like all artistic success and felicity, incapable of strict analysis: effect of an intuitive condition of mind, it must be recognised by like intuition on the part of the reader, and a sort of immediate sense. In every one of those masterly sentences of Flaubert there was, below all mere contrivance, shaping and afterthought, by some happy instantaneous concourse of the various faculties of the mind with each other, the exact apprehension of what was *needed* to carry the meaning. And that it fits with absolute justice will be a judgment of immediate sense in the appreciative reader. We all feel this in what may be called inspired translation. Well! all language involves translation from inward to outward. In literature, as in all forms of art, there are the absolute and the merely relative or accessory beauties; and precisely in that exact proportion of the term to its purpose is the absolute beauty of style, prose or verse. All the good qualities, the beauties, of verse also, are such, only as precise expression.

[25]   In the highest as in the lowliest literature, then, the one indispensable beauty is, after all, truth:—truth to bare fact in the latter, as to some personal sense of fact, diverted somewhat from men's ordinary sense of it, in the former; truth there as accuracy, truth here as expression, that finest and most intimate form of truth, the *vraie vérité*.[23] And what an eclectic principle this really is! employing for its one sole purpose—that absolute accordance of expression to idea—all other literary beauties and excellences whatever: how many kinds of style it covers, explains, justifies, and at the same time safeguards! Scott's facility, Flaubert's deeply pondered evoca-

[23]Literally, true truth or essential truth.

tion of "the phrase," are equally good art. Say what you have to say, what you have a will to say, in the simplest, the most direct and exact manner possible, with no surplusage:—there, is the justification of the sentence so fortunately born, "entire, smooth, and round," that it needs no punctuation, and also (that is the point!) of the most elaborate period, if it be right in its elaboration. Here is the office of ornament: here also the purpose of restraint in ornament. As the exponent of truth, that austerity (the beauty, the function, of which in literature Flaubert understood so well) becomes not the correctness or purism of the mere scholar, but a security against the otiose, a jealous exclusion of what does not really tell towards the pursuit of relief of life and vigour in the portraiture of one's sense. License again, the making free with rule, if it be indeed, as people fancy, a habit of genius, flinging aside or transforming all that opposes the liberty of beautiful production, will be but faith to one's own meaning. The seeming baldness of *Le Rouge et Le Noir* is nothing in itself; the wild ornament of *Les Misérables* is nothing in itself; and the restraint of Flaubert, amid a real natural opulence, only redoubled beauty—the phrase so large and so precise at the same time, hard as bronze, in service to the more perfect adaptation of words to their matter. Afterthoughts, retouchings, finish, will be of profit only so far as they too really serve to bring out the original, initiative, generative, sense in them.

In this way, according to the well-known saying, "The style is the man,"[24] [26] complex or simple, in his individuality, his plenary sense of what he really has to say, his sense of the world; all cautions regarding style arising out of so many natural scruples as to the medium through which alone he can expose that inward sense of things, the purity of this medium, its laws or tricks of refraction: nothing is to be left there which might give conveyance to any matter save that. Style in all its varieties, reserved or opulent, terse, abundant, musical, stimulant, academic, so long as each is really characteristic or expressive, finds thus its justification, the sumptuous good taste of Cicero being as truly the man himself, and not another, justified, yet insured inalienably to him, thereby, as would have been his portrait by Raphael, in full consular splendour, on his ivory chair.

A relegation, you may say perhaps—a relegation of style to the subjec- [27] tivity, the mere caprice, of the individual, which must soon transform it into mannerism. Not so! since there is, under the conditions supposed, for those elements of the man, for every lineament of the vision within, the one word, the one acceptable word, recognisable by the sensitive, by others "who have intelligence" in the matter, as absolutely as ever anything can be in the evanescent and delicate region of human language. The style, the manner, would be the man, not in his unreasoned and really unchar- acteristic caprices, involuntary or affected, but in absolutely sincere appre-

[24]A famous line from *Discours sur le Style*, delivered before the French Academy by Georges Louis Conte de Buffon in 1753.

hension of what is most real to him. But let us hear our French guide again.

> Styles, says Flaubert's commentator, *Styles,* as so many peculiar moulds, each of which bears the mark of a particular writer, who is to pour into it the whole content of his ideas, were no part of his theory. What he believed in was *Style:* that is to say, a certain absolute and unique manner of expressing a thing, in all its intensity and colour. For him the *form* was the work itself. As in living creatures, the blood, nourishing the body, determines its very contour and external aspect, just so, to his mind, the *matter,* the basis, in a work of art, imposed, necessarily, the unique, the just expression, the measure, the rhythm—the *form* in all its characteristics.[25]

[28]   If the style be the man, in all the colour and intensity of a veritable apprehension, it will be in a real sense "impersonal."

[29]   I said, thinking of books like Victor Hugo's *Les Misérables,* that prose literature was the characteristic art of the nineteenth century, as others, thinking of its triumphs since the youth of Bach, have assigned that place to music. Music and prose literature are, in one sense, the opposite terms of art; the art of literature presenting to the imagination, through the intelligence, a range of interests, as free and various as those which music presents to it through sense. And certainly the tendency of what has been here said is to bring literature too under those conditions, by conformity to which music takes rank as the typically perfect art. If music be the ideal of all art whatever, precisely because in music it is impossible to distinguish the form from the substance or matter, the subject from the expression, then, literature, by finding its specific excellence in the absolute correspondence of the term to its import, will be but fulfilling the condition of all artistic quality in things everywhere, of all good art.

[30]   Good art, but not necessarily great art; the distinction between great art and good art depending immediately, as regards literature at all events, not on its form, but on the matter. Thackeray's *Esmond,* surely, is greater art than *Vanity Fair,* by the greater dignity of its interests. It is on the quality of the matter it informs or controls, its compass, its variety, its alliance to great ends, or the depth of the note of revolt, or the largeness of hope in it, that the greatness of literary art depends, as *The Divine Comedy, Paradise Lost, Les Misérables, The English Bible,* are great art. Given the conditions I have tried to explain as constituting good art;— then, if it be devoted further to the increase of men's happiness, to the redemption of the oppressed, or the enlargement of our sympathies with each other, or to such presentment of new or old truth about ourselves and our relation to the world as may ennoble and fortify us in our sojourn here, or immediately, as with Dante, to the glory of God, it will be also

[25]Flaubert's commentator is again De Maupassant, from pages lxi–lxii of *Lettres.*

great art; if, over and above those qualities I summed up as mind and soul
—that colour and mystic perfume, and that reasonable structure, it has
something of the soul of humanity in it, and finds its logical, architectural
place, in the great structure of human life.

TOPICS FOR DISCUSSION

1. In paragraph 3, Pater proposes "to point out certain qualities of all
   literature as a fine art." What qualities does he point out throughout the
   essay?
2. Pater repeatedly stresses the "fineness of truth," "*vraie vérité,*" the soul
   of the work, and so on. Was Pater, therefore, opposed to the rational
   or logical aspects of literature? Explain.
3. In what sense does Pater regard Flaubert as "the martyr of literary
   style"?
4. Pater appears to identify literature with form, as in paragraphs 20 and
   21. Yet he explicitly states that the distinction of great literature depends not on the form but on the matter (paragraph 30). Is Pater's
   reasoning inconsistent? Why or why not?
5. How can a style reveal the man yet be impersonal, as Pater asserts in
   paragraphs 26 through 28?
6. In his introduction to *Prose of the Victorian Period* (1958), W. E.
   Buckler suggests that Pater's essay contains implicit criteria of imaginative prose. He presents those criteria in the form of the following questions (pp. xviii–xix): Has the author taken "a full, rich, complex
   matter to grapple with"? Has he achieved, in his language, balance
   between propriety and originality? Has he provided for the reader an
   intense intellectual challenge? Has he provided for the reader a worthwhile formal challenge? Has he given to his prose work his own (or its
   own) unique personality? Has he devoted his art to "great ends"?
   Where are these questions clearly implied or stated in the text of
   "Style"? Do you think these criteria are complete? Why or why not?

TOPICS FOR COMPOSITION

1. Write an analysis of Pater's prose style, illustrating your criteria of a
   good style by citing passages from essays contained in this book or in
   other sources.
2. Write an essay defining *fine* art. Defend your position by attacking
   merely useful or servile art. You may find paragraphs 4 and 5 useful
   springboards for your essay.

E. M. FORSTER

Art for Art's Sake

E. M. FORSTER'S aim, in this seemingly artless persuasion, is to induce the reader to accept the proposition suggested by his title in the exact sense that he understands it. That sense becomes apparent as Forster tells us first what art for art's sake does not mean, then what it does mean, by giving us two illustrations of internal order and internal life. What appears to be a digression on the unattainability of order in daily life and history, or in the social and political category, is a subtle contrast between the kind of harmony available in art and religion and the disharmony that has invaded the other orders of being. The remaining section of the essay pursues or, if that is too emphatic a word, then at least explores the possibilities of order in various categories.

That it is expository argument rather than argument in the formal sense is apparent partly from the personal or subjective tone of the opening statement. "I believe in art for art's sake" is at once challenging and disarming—challenging in its bluntness and candor, disarming in that the statement "I believe" makes less demands upon the reader than the flat assertion that art does exist for art's sake. The essay invites us to examine not so much the objective truth of a proposition as it does the truth of Forster's actual sentiments. Thus one may disagree with Forster's reasons yet admire the completeness and the accuracy with which he discloses them.

Pater's essay "Style" is one of the main sources of the art for art's sake theory that Forster has made his own. It is interesting to note how Pater devotes most of his efforts to unraveling the artistic qualities inherent in language. Forster, on the other hand, takes the importance of language for granted, pointing to it as an evident fact. Here perhaps is another illustration of how, in the continuous dialogue of literature, yesterday's novelty becomes today's commonplace.

[1]   I believe in art for art's sake. It is an unfashionable belief, and some of my statements must be of the nature of an apology. Fifty years ago I should have faced you with more confidence. A writer or a speaker who chose "Art for Art's Sake" for his theme fifty years ago could be sure of being in the swim, and could feel so confident of success that he sometimes dressed

---

himself in esthetic costumes suitable to the occasion—in an embroidered dressing-gown, perhaps, or a blue velvet suit with a Lord Fauntleroy collar; or a toga, or a kimono, and carried a poppy or a lily or a long peacock's feather in his mediaeval hand. Times have changed. Not thus can I present either myself or my theme today. My aim rather is to ask you quietly to reconsider for a few minutes a phrase which has been much misused and much abused, but which has, I believe, great importance for us —has, indeed, eternal importance.

Now we can easily dismiss those peacock's feathers and other affectations [2] —they are but trifles—but I want also to dismiss a more dangerous heresy, namely the silly idea that only art matters, an idea which has somehow got mixed up with the idea of art for art's sake, and has helped to discredit it. Many things, besides art, matter. It is merely one of the things that matter, and high though the claims are that I make for it, I want to keep them in proportion. No one can spend his or her life entirely in the creation or the appreciation of masterpieces. Man lives, and ought to live, in a complex world, full of conflicting claims, and if we simplified them down into the esthetic he would be sterilised. Art for art's sake does not mean that only art matters, and I would also like to rule out such phrases as "The Life of Art," "Living for Art," and "Art's High Mission." They confuse and mislead.

What does the phrase mean? Instead of generalising, let us take a specific [3] instance—Shakespeare's *Macbeth*, for example, and pronounce the words, *"Macbeth* for *Macbeth's* sake." What does that mean? Well, the play has several aspects—it is educational, it teaches us something about legendary Scotland, something about Jacobean England, and a good deal about human nature and its perils. We can study its origins, and study and enjoy its dramatic technique and the music of its diction. All that is true. But *Macbeth* is furthermore a world of its own, created by Shakespeare and existing in virtue of its own poetry. It is in this aspect *Macbeth* for *Macbeth's* sake, and that is what I intend by the phrase "art for art's sake." A work of art—whatever else it may be—is a self-contained entity, with a life of its own imposed on it by its creator. It has internal order. It may have external form. That is how we recognise it.

Take for another example that picture of Seurat's which I saw two years [4] ago in Chicago—*"La Grande Jatte."* [1] Here again there is much to study and to enjoy: the pointillism, the charming face of the seated girl, the nineteenth-century Parisian Sunday sunlight, the sense of motion in immobility. But here again there is something more; *"La Grande Jatte"* forms a world of its own, created by Seurat and existing by virtue of its own poetry: *"La Grande Jatte" pour "La Grande Jatte": l'art pour l'art.* Like Macbeth it has internal order and internal life.

[1] Literally, the great bowl.

[5]   It is to the conception of order that I would now turn. This is important to my argument, and I want to make a digression, and glance at order in daily life, before I come to order in art.

[6]   In the world of daily life, the world which we perforce inhabit, there is much talk about order, particularly from statesmen and politicians. They tend, however, to confuse order with orders, just as they confuse creation with regulations: Order, I suggest, is something evolved from within, not something imposed from without; it is an internal stability, a vital harmony, and in the social and political category it has never existed except for the convenience of historians. Viewed realistically, the past is really a series of *dis*orders, succeeding one another by discoverable laws, no doubt, and certainly marked by an increasing growth of human interference, but disorders all the same. So that, speaking as a writer, what I hope for today is a disorder which will be more favourable to artists than is the present one, and which will provide them with fuller inspirations and better material conditions. It will not last—nothing lasts—but there have been some advantageous disorders in the past—for instance, in ancient Athens, in Renaissance Italy, eighteenth-century France, periods in China and Persia—and we may do something to accelerate the next one. But let us not again fix our hearts where true joys are not to be found. We were promised a new order after the first world war through the League of Nations. It did not come, nor have I faith in present promises, by whomsoever endorsed. The implacable offensive of Science forbids. We cannot reach social and political stability for the reason that we continue to make scientific discoveries and to apply them, and thus to destroy the arrangements which were based on more elementary discoveries. If Science would discover rather than apply—if, in other words, men were more interested in knowledge than in power—mankind would be in a far safer position, the stability statesmen talk about would be a possibility, there could be a new order based on vital harmony, and the earthly millennium might approach. But Science shows no signs of doing this: she gave us the internal combustion engine, and before we had digested and assimilated it with terrible pains into our social system, she harnessed the atom, and destroyed any new order that seemed to be evolving. How can man get into harmony with his surroundings when he is constantly altering them? The future of our race is, in this direction, more unpleasant than we care to admit, and it has sometimes seemed to me that its best chance lies through apathy, uninventiveness, and inertia. Universal exhaustion might promote that Change of Heart which is at present so briskly recommended from a thousand pulpits. Universal exhaustion would certainly be a new experience. The human race has never undergone it, and is still too perky to admit that it may be coming and might result in a sprouting of new growth through the decay.

[7]   I must not pursue these speculations any further—they lead me too far

from my terms of reference and maybe from yours. But I do want to emphasize that order in daily life and in history, order in the social and political category, is unattainable under our present psychology.

Where is it attainable? Not in the astronomical category, where it was [8] for many years enthroned. The heavens and the earth have become terribly alike since Einstein. No longer can we find a reassuring contrast to chaos in the night sky and look up with George Meredith to the stars, the army of unalterable law, or listen for the music of the spheres. Order is not there. In the entire universe there seem to be only two possibilities for it. The first of them—which again lies outside my terms of reference— is the divine order, the mystic harmony, which according to all religions is available for those who can contemplate it. We must admit its possibility, on the evidence of the adepts, and we must believe them when they say that it is attained, if attainable, by prayer. "O thou who changest not, abide with me," said one of its poets. *"Ordina questo amor, o tu che m'ami,"* said another: "Set love in order, thou who lovest me." The existence of a divine order, though it cannot be tested, has never been disproved.

The second possibility for order lies in the esthetic category, which is [9] my subject here: the order which an artist can create in his own work, and to that we must now return. A work of art, we are all agreed, is a unique product. But why? It is unique not because it is clever or noble or beautiful or enlightened or original or sincere or idealistic or useful or educational—it may embody any of those qualities—but because it is the only material object in the universe which may possess internal harmony. All the others have been pressed into shape from outside, and when their mould is removed they collapse. The work of art stands up by itself, and nothing else does. It achieves something which has often been promised by society, but always delusively. Ancient Athens made a mess—but the *Antigone* stands up. Renaissance Rome made a mess—but the ceiling of the Sistine got painted. James I made a mess—but there was *Macbeth*. Louis XIV—but there was *Phèdre*. Art for art's sake? I should just think so, and more so than ever at the present time. It is the one orderly product which our muddling race has produced. It is the cry of a thousand sentinels, the echo from a thousand labyrinths; it is the lighthouse which cannot be hidden: *c'est le meilleur témoignage que nous puissions donner de notre dignité.*[2] *Antigone* for *Antigone's* sake, *Macbeth* for *Macbeth's*, "La Grande Jatte" pour "La Grande Jatte."

If this line of argument is correct, it follows that the artist will tend to [10] be an outsider in the society to which he has been born, and that the nineteenth-century conception of him as a Bohemian was not inaccurate. The conception erred in three particulars: it postulated an economic system

[2]Literally, it is the best evidence we can give of our dignity.

where art could be a full-time job, it introduced the fallacy that only art matters, and it overstressed idiosyncrasy and waywardness—the peacock-feather aspect—rather than order. But it is a truer conception than the one which prevails in official circles on my side of the Atlantic—I don't know about yours: the conception which treats the artist as if he were a particularly bright government advertiser and encourages him to be friendly and matey with his fellow citizens, and not to give himself airs.

[11]   Estimable is mateyness, and the man who achieves it gives many a pleasant little drink to himself and to others. But it has no traceable connection with the creative impulse, and probably acts as an inhibition on it. The artist who is seduced by mateyness may stop himself from doing the one thing which he, and he alone, can do—the making of something out of words or sounds or paint or clay or marble or steel or film which has internal harmony and presents order to a permanently disarranged planet. This seems worth doing, even at the risk of being called uppish by journalists. I have in mind an article which was published some years ago in the London *Times,* an article called "The Eclipse of the Highbrow," in which the "Average Man" was exalted, and all contemporary literature was censured if it did not toe the line, the precise position of the line being naturally known to the writer of the article. Sir Kenneth Clark, who was at that time director of our National Gallery, commented on this pernicious doctrine in a letter which cannot be too often quoted. "The poet and the artist," wrote Clark, "are important precisely because they are not average men; because in sensibility, intelligence, and power of invention they far exceed the average." These memorable words, and particularly the words "power of invention," are the Bohemian's passport. Furnished with it, he slinks about society, saluted now by a brickbat and now by a penny, and accepting either of them with equanimity. He does not consider too anxiously what his relations with society may be, for he is aware of something more important than that—namely the invitation to invent, to create order, and he believes he will be better placed for doing this if he attempts detachment. So round and round he slouches, with his hat pulled over his eyes, and maybe a louse in his beard, and—if he really wants one—with a peacock's feather in his hand.

[12]   If our present society should disintegrate—and who dare prophesy that it won't?—this old-fashioned and démodé figure will become clearer: the Bohemian, the outsider, the parasite, the rat—one of those figures which have at present no function either in a warring or a peaceful world. It may not be dignified to be a rat, but many of the ships are sinking, which is not dignified either—the officials did not build them properly. Myself, I would sooner be a swimming rat than a sinking ship—at all events I can look around me for a little longer—and I remember how one of us, a rat with particularly bright eyes called Shelley, squeaked out, "Poets are the

unacknowledged legislators of the world," before he vanished into the waters of the Mediterranean.

What laws did Shelley propose to pass? None. The legislation of the [13] artist is never formulated at the time, though it is sometimes discerned by future generations. He legislates through creating. And he creates through his sensitiveness and his power to impose form. Without form the sensitiveness vanishes. And form is as important today, when the human race is trying to ride the whirlwind, as it ever was in those less agitating days of the past, when the earth seemed solid and the stars fixed, and the discoveries of science were made slowly, slowly. Form is not tradition. It alters from generation to generation. Artists always seek a new technique, and will continue to do so as long as their work excites them. But form of some kind is imperative. It is the surface crust of the internal harmony, it is the outward evidence of order.

My remarks about society may have seemed too pessimistic, but I believe [14] that society can only represent a fragment of the human spirit, and that another fragment can only get expressed through art. And I wanted to take this opportunity, this vantage ground, to assert not only the existence of art, but its pertinacity. Looking back into the past, it seems to me that that is all there has ever been: vantage grounds for discussion and creation, little vantage grounds in the changing chaos, where bubbles have been blown and webs spun, and the desire to create order has found temporary gratification, and the sentinels have managed to utter their challenges, and the huntsmen, though lost individually, have heard each other's calls through the impenetrable wood, and the lighthouses have never ceased sweeping the thankless seas. In this pertinacity there seems to me, as I grow older, something more and more profound, something which does in fact concern people who do not care about art at all.

In conclusion, let me summarise the various categories that have laid [15] claim to the possession of Order.

(1) The social and political category. Claim disallowed on the evidence of history and of our own experience. If man altered psychologically, order here might be attainable; not otherwise.

(2) The astronomical category. Claim allowed up to the present century, but now disallowed on the evidence of the physicists.

(3) The religious category. Claim allowed on the evidence of the mystics.

(4) The esthetic category. Claim allowed on the evidence of various works of art, and on the evidence of our own creative impulses, however weak these may be, or however imperfectly they may function. Works of art, in my opinion, are the only objects in the material universe to possess internal order, and that is why, though I don't believe that only art matters, I do believe in Art for Art's Sake.

TOPICS FOR DISCUSSION

1. Forster attacks as silly the idea that "only art matters." Why does he feel that this idea is silly?
2. *Macbeth* and *"La Grande Jatte"* are offered as examples of internal order and internal life. As Forster presents these examples, do they actually illustrate the principles of internal order and internal life or are they merely said to illustrate these principles? Explain.
3. Do you agree with Forster's view that "order in daily life and in history, order in the social and political category, is unattainable under our present psychology?" Why or why not?
4. "The work of art stands up by itself, and nothing else does." In the context of the explanations developed in paragraphs 8 and 9, is that statement (a) evident in itself, (b) proved to be true, (c) merely asserted, (d) probably true, (e) a mere speculation? Give reasons for your answer.
5. Forster posits, particularly in paragraphs 11 and 13, an antagonism between the artist and other members of society. Do you think this antagonism in fact exists? If it does, is the antagonism necessary or inevitable, or the result of historical accidents? Give reasons for your answer.
6. In his concluding paragraph, Forster allows the claim of religion to the possession of order and then asserts that "Works of art, in my opinion, are the only objects in the material universe to possess internal order." Is he inconsistent here? Explain.

TOPICS FOR COMPOSITION

1. Write an essay defending your belief in a currently unfashionable idea like the art for art's sake doctrine. Indicate clearly why the idea is not considered fashionable.
2. Expand Forster's assertion that a work of art has a life of its own by illustrating in detail the order that characterizes a specific work of art of your own choice.
3. Compare and contrast the implications of the art for art's sake doctrine in Pater's "Style" and in Forster's essay.

**C. S.
LEWIS**

**Christianity
and
Literature**

IN their essays in this volume, Walter Pater, E. M. Forster and C. S. Lewis all address themselves to the central problem of literary values. The term *literary values* involves two interrelated questions: What makes a piece of writing literature? What makes a piece of literature worthwhile? Literature is literature because it is finely expressed, and fine expression may be explained by various formulas. All of them, however, focus on the literary standards of structure and style. But, as T. S. Eliot remarks in his essay "Religion and Literature," "The 'greatness' of literature cannot be determined solely by literary standards; though we must remember that whether it is literature or not can be determined only by literary standards." What makes a piece of writing literature does not make it valuable literature. Other standards—of philosophy, culture, and religion—determine whether literature is great. These other standards, as Eliot writes in "A Dialogue on Dramatic Poetry," are inseparable from literary standards: "You can never draw the line between aesthetic criticism and moral and social criticism; you cannot draw a line between criticism and metaphysics; you start with literary criticism, and however rigorous an aesthete you may be, you are over the frontier into something else sooner or later."

We have observed how Pater crossed the frontier in the final paragraph of his essay and how Forster crossed it at one point but jumped back quickly to more familiar territory. Lewis does not hesitate about crossing frontiers, particularly because he is a citizen of both the republic of letters and Christendom. Possessing this dual citizenship, he can freely explore the two spheres of literature: modern literature, which he sees as informed by ideals described by the words *creativity, spontaneity,* and *freedom;* and Christian literature, informed by ideals summed up by *imitation, reflection,* and *assimilation.*

Lewis' essay is the most complex of the three essays, although that does not mean the most complicated. It is most complex because it considers more problems together; hence it presents more paradoxes—the one, for instance, that regards literature as essentially serious and important but also as comically intense. Lewis is always aware that "The real frivolity, the solemn vacuity is all with those who make literature a self-distinct thing to be valued for its own sake. Pater prepared for pleasure as if it were martyrdom."

Like Pater and Forster, Lewis also accents the argu-

mentative element. His explanations of the characteristics of Christian literature introduce challenging points,
among them, the apparent devaluation of creativity,
spontaneity, and freedom in favor of the derivative, the
conventional, and the normal.

[1]   When I was asked to address this society,[1] I was at first tempted to refuse
because the subject proposed to me, that of Christianity and Literature, did
not seem to admit of any discussion. I knew, of course, that Christian story
and sentiment were among the things on which literature could be written,
and, conversely, that literature was one of the ways in which Christian
sentiment could be expressed and Christian story told; but there seemed
nothing more to be said of Christianity in this connexion than of any of
the hundred and one other things that men make books about. We are
familiar, no doubt, with the expression "Christian Art," by which people
usually mean Art that represents Biblical or hagiological scenes, and there
is, in this sense, a fair amount of "Christian Literature." But I question
whether it has any literary qualities peculiar to itself. The rules for writing a good passion play or a good devotional lyric are simply the rules for
writing tragedy or lyric in general: success in sacred literature depends on
the same qualities of structure, suspense, variety, diction, and the like which
secure success in secular literature. And if we enlarge the idea of Christian
Literature to include not only literature on sacred themes but all that is
written by Christians for Christians to read, then, I think, Christian Literature can exist only in the same sense in which Christian cookery might
exist. It would be possible, and it might be edifying, to write a Christian
cookery book. Such a book would exclude dishes whose preparation involves unnecessary human labour or animal suffering, and dishes excessively luxurious. That is to say, its choice of dishes would be Christian.
But there could be nothing specifically Christian about the actual cooking
of the dishes included. Boiling an egg is the same process whether you are
a Christian or a Pagan. In the same way, literature written by Christians
for Christians would have to avoid mendacity, cruelty, blasphemy, por-
nography, and the like, and it would aim at edification in so far as edification was proper to the kind of work in hand. But whatever it chose to do
would have to be done by the means common to all literature; it could
succeed or fail only by the same excellences and the same faults as all

[1]A religious society at Oxford.

CHRISTIANITY AND LITERATURE Reprinted from *Rehabilitation and Other Essays* by
C. S. Lewis by permission of Oxford University Press and W. H. Lewis.

The Practice of Rhetoric

literature; and its literary success or failure would never be the same thing as its obedience or disobedience to Christian principles.

I have been speaking so far of Christian Literature *proprement dite*[2]— [2] that is, of writing which is intended to affect us as literature, by its appeal to imagination. But in the visible arts I think we can make a distinction between sacred art, however sacred in theme, and pure iconography—between that which is intended, in the first instance, to affect the imagination and the aesthetic appetite, and that which is meant merely as the starting-point for devotion and meditation. If I were treating the visible arts I should have to work out here a full distinction of the work of art from the icon on the one hand and the toy on the other. The icon and the toy have this in common that their value depends very little on their perfection as artefacts—a shapeless rag may give as much pleasure as the costliest doll, and two sticks tied crosswise may kindle as much devotion as the work of Leonardo. And to make matters more complicated the very same object could often be used in all three ways. But I do not think the icon and the work of art can be so sharply distinguished in literature. I question whether the badness of a really bad hymn can ordinarily be so irrelevant to devotion as the badness of a bad devotional picture. Because the hymn uses words, its badness will, to some degree, consist in confused or erroneous thought and unworthy sentiment. But I mention this difficult question here only to say that I do not propose to treat it. If any literary works exist which have a purely iconographic value and no literary value, they are not what I am talking about. Indeed I could not, for I have not met them.

Of Christian Literature, then, in the sense of "work aiming at literary [3] value and written by Christians for Christians," you see that I have really nothing to say and believe that nothing can be said. But I think I have something to say about what may be called the Christian approach to literature: about the principles, if you will, of Christian literary theory and criticism. For while I was thinking over the subject you gave me I made what seemed to me a discovery. It is not an easy one to put into words. The nearest I can come to it is to say that I have found a disquieting contrast between the whole circle of ideas used in modern criticism and certain ideas recurrent in the New Testament. Let me say at once that it is hardly a question of logical contradiction between clearly defined concepts. It is too vague for that. It is more a repugnance of atmospheres, a discordance of notes, an incompatibility of temperaments.

What are the key-words of modern criticism? *Creative*, with its opposite [4] *derivative; spontaneity*, with its opposite *convention; freedom*, contrasted with *rules*. Great authors are innovators, pioneers, explorers; bad authors bunch in schools and follow models. Or again, great authors are always

²Literally, properly called or properly so called.

"breaking fetters" and "bursting bonds." They have personality, they "are themselves." I do not know whether we often think out the implication of such language into a consistent philosophy; but we certainly have a general picture of bad work flowing from conformity and discipleship, and of good work bursting out from certain centres of explosive force—apparently self-originating force—which we call men of genius.

[5] Now the New Testament has nothing at all to tell us of literature. I know that there are some who like to think of Our Lord Himself as a poet and cite the parables to support their view. I admit freely that to believe in the Incarnation at all is to believe that every mode of human excellence is implicit in His historical human character: poethood, of course, included. But if all had been developed, the limitations of a single human life would have been transcended and He would not have been a man; therefore all excellences save the spiritual remained in varying degrees implicit. If it is claimed that the poetic excellence is more developed than others—say, the intellectual—I think I deny the claim. Some of the parables do work like poetic similes; but then others work like philosophic illustrations. Thus the Unjust Judge[3] is not emotionally or imaginatively like God: he corresponds to God as the terms in a proportion correspond, because he is to the Widow (in one highly specialized respect) as God is to man. In that parable Our Lord, if we may so express it, is much more like Socrates than Shakespere. And I dread an overemphasis on the poetical element in His words because I think it tends to obscure that quality in His human character which is, in fact, so visible in His irony, His *argumenta ad homines*,[4] and His use of the *a fortiori*,[5] and which I would call the homely, peasant shrewdness. Donne points out that we are never told He laughed; it is difficult in reading the Gospels not to believe, and to tremble in believing, that He smiled.

[6] I repeat, the New Testament has nothing to say of literature; but what it says on other subjects is quite sufficient to strike that note which I find out of tune with the language of modern criticism. . . . The answer always seems to be something like imitation, reflection, assimilation. Thus in Gal. IV : 19 Christ is to be "formed" inside each believer—the verb here used (μορφωθῇ) meaning to shape, to figure, or even to draw a sketch. In First Thessalonians (1 : 6) Christians are told to imitate St. Paul and the Lord, and elsewhere (1 Cor. x : 33) to imitate St. Paul as he in turn imitates Christ—thus giving us another stage of progressive imitation. Changing the metaphor we find that believers are to acquire the fragrance of Christ, *redolere Christum* (2 Cor. II : 16): that the glory of God has

---

[3]See Luke 18:1–8.

[4]Literally, arguments to the man—that is, appealing to personal feelings—as opposed to arguments directed *ad rem*—to the point.

[5]Literally, for a still stronger reason. In this context, *a fortiori* means that if an unjust judge will listen to prayer, how much more will the just God.

appeared in the face of Christ as, at the creation, light appeared in the universe (2 Cor. IV : 6); and, finally, if my reading of a much disputed passage is correct, that a Christian is to Christ as a mirror to an object (2 Cor. III : 18).

These passages, you will notice, are all Pauline; but there is a place in [7] the Fourth Gospel which goes much farther—so far that if it were not a Dominical utterance we would not venture to think along such lines. There (v:19) we are told that the Son does only what He sees the Father doing. He watches the Father's operations and does the same (ʿομοιος ποιεῖ) or "copies." The Father, because of His love for the Son, shows Him all that He does. I have already explained that I am not a theologian. What aspect of the Trinitarian reality Our Lord, as God, saw while He spoke these words, I do not venture to define; but I think we have a right and even a duty to notice carefully the earthly image by which He expressed it—to see clearly the picture He puts before us. It is a picture of a boy learning to do things by watching a man at work. I think we may even guess what memory, humanly speaking, was in His mind. It is hard not to imagine that He remembered His boyhood, that He saw Himself as a boy in a carpenter's shop, a boy learning how to do things by watching while St. Joseph did them. So taken, the passage does not seem to me to conflict with anything I have learned from the creeds, but greatly to enrich my conception of the Divine sonship.

Now it may be that there is no absolute logical contradiction between [8] the passages I have quoted and the assumptions of modern criticism: but I think there is so great a difference of temper that a man whose mind was at one with the mind of the New Testament would not, and indeed could not, fall into the language which most critics now adopt. In the New Testament the art of life itself is an art of imitation: can we, believing this, believe that literature, which must derive from real life, is to aim at being "creative," "original," and "spontaneous." "Originality" in the New Testament is quite plainly the prerogative of God alone; even within the triune being of God it seems to be confined to the Father. The duty and happiness of every other being is placed in being derivative, in reflecting like a mirror. Nothing could be more foreign to the tone of scripture than the language of those who describe a saint as a "moral genius" or a "spiritual genius" thus insinuating that his virtue or spirituality is "creative" or "original." If I have read the New Testament aright, it leaves no room for "creativeness" even in a modified or metaphorical sense. Our whole destiny seems to lie in the opposite direction, in being as little as possible ourselves, in acquiring a fragrance that is not our own but borrowed, in becoming clean mirrors filled with the image of a face that is not ours. I am not here supporting the doctrine of total depravity, and I do not say that the New Testament supports it; I am saying only that the highest good of a creature must be creaturely—that is, derivative or reflective—

C. S. Lewis

good. In other words, as St. Augustine makes plain (*De Civitate Dei,* XII, cap. 1), pride does not only go before a fall but is a fall—a fall of the creature's attention from what is better, God, to what is worse, itself.

[9]   Applying this principle to literature, in its greatest generality, we should get as the basis of all critical theory the maxim that an author should never conceive himself as bringing into existence beauty or wisdom which did not exist before, but simply and solely as trying to embody in terms of his own art some reflection of eternal Beauty and Wisdom. Our criticism would therefore from the beginning group itself with some existing theories of poetry against others. It would have affinities with the Homeric theory in which the poet is the mere pensioner of the Muse. It would have affinities with the Platonic doctrine of a transcendent Form partly imitable on earth; and remoter affinities with the Aristotelian doctrine of mimesis and the Augustan doctrine about the imitation of Nature and the Ancients. It would be opposed to the theory of genius as, perhaps, generally understood; and above all it would be opposed to the idea that literature is self-expression.

[10]   But here some distinctions must be made. I spoke just now of the ancient idea that the poet was merely the servant of some god, of Apollo, or the Muse; but let us not forget the highly paradoxical words in which Homer's Phemius asserts his claim to be a poet—"I am self-taught; a god has inspired me with all manner of songs." (*Odes,* XXII, 347.) It sounds like a direct contradiction. How can he be self-taught if the god has taught him all he knows? Doubtless because the god's instruction is given internally, not through the senses, and is therefore regarded as part of the Self, to be contrasted with such external aids as, say, the example of other poets. And this seems to blur the distinction I am trying to draw between Christian imitation and the "originality" praised by modern critics. Phemius obviously claims to be original, in the sense of being no other poet's disciple, and in the same breath admits his complete dependence on a supernatural teacher. Does not this let in "originality" and "creativeness" of the only kind that have ever been claimed?

[11]   If you said "the only kind that ought to have been claimed," I would agree; but as things are, I think the distinction remains, though it becomes finer than our first glance suggested. A Christian and an unbelieving poet may both be equally original in the sense they neglect the example of their poetic forbears and draw on resources peculiar to themselves, but with this difference. The unbeliever may take his own temperament and experience, just as they happen to stand, and consider them worth communicating simply because they are facts or, worse still, because they are his. To the Christian his own temperament and experience, as mere fact, and as merely his, are of no value or importance whatsoever: he will deal with them, if at all, only because they are the medium through which, or the position from which, something universally profitable appeared to him. We can

imagine two men seated in different parts of a church or theatre. Both, when they come out, may tell us their experiences, and both may use the first person. But the one is interested in his seat only because it was his—"I was most uncomfortable," he will say. "You would hardly believe what a draught comes in from the door in that corner. And the people! I had to speak pretty sharply to the woman in front of me." The other will tell us what could be seen from his seat, choosing to describe this because this is what he knows, and because every seat must give the best view of something. "Do you know," he will begin, "the moulding on those pillars goes on round at the back. It looks, too, as if the design on the back were the older of the two." Here we have the expressionist and the Christian attitudes towards the self or temperament. Thus St. Augustine and Rousseau both write *Confessions;* but to the one his own temperament is a kind of absolute *(au moins je suis autre*[6]*)*, to the other it is "a narrow house, too narrow for Thee to enter—oh make it wide. It is in ruins—oh rebuild it." And Wordsworth, the romantic who made a good end, has a foot in either world and though he practises both, distinguishes well the two ways in which a man may be said to write about himself. On the one hand he says:

I must tread on shadowy ground, must sink
Deep, and aloft ascending breathe in worlds
To which the heaven of heavens is but a veil.

On the other he craves indulgence if

                        with this
I mix more lowly matter; with the thing
Contemplated, describe the Mind and Man
Contemplating; and who and what he was—
The transitory being that beheld
This vision.

    In this sense, then, the Christian writer may be self-taught or original. [12] He may base his work on the "transitory being" that he is, not because he thinks it valuable (for he knows that in his flesh dwells no good thing), but solely because of the "vision" that appeared to it. But he will have no preference for doing this. He will do it if it happens to be the thing he can do best; but if his talents are such that he can produce good work by writing in an established form and dealing with experiences common to all his race, he will do so just as gladly. I even think he will do so more gladly. It is to him an argument not of strength but of weakness that he should respond fully to the vision only "in his own way." And always, of every idea and of every method he will ask not "Is it mine?" but "Is it good?"

[6]Literally, at least I am another—that is, I am not the same as everyone else.

C. S. Lewis

[13] This seems to me the most fundamental difference between the Christian and the unbeliever in their approach to literature. But I think there is another. The Christian will take literature a little less seriously than the cultured Pagan: he will feel less uneasy with a purely hedonistic standard for at least many kinds of work. The unbeliever is always apt to make a kind of religion of his aesthetic experiences; he feels ethically irresponsible, perhaps, but he braces his strength to receive responsibilities of another kind which seem to the Christian quite illusory. He has to be "creative"; he has to obey a mystical amoral law called his artistic conscience; and he commonly wishes to maintain his superiority to the great mass of mankind who turn to books for mere recreation. But the Christian knows from the outset that the salvation of a single soul is more important than the pro-duction or preservation of all the epics and tragedies in the world: and as for superiority, he knows that the vulgar since they include most of the poor probably include most of his superiors. He has no objection to comedies that merely amuse and tales that merely refresh; for he thinks like St. Thomas Aquinas *ipsa ratio hoc habet ut quandoque rationis usus intercipiatur.*[7] We can play, as we can eat, to the glory of God. It thus may come about that Christian views on literature will strike the world as shallow and flippant; but the world must not misunderstand. When Christian work is done on a serious subject there is no gravity and no sublimity it cannot attain. But they will belong to the theme. That is why they will be real and lasting—mighty nouns with which literature, an adjectival thing, is here united, far over-topping the fussy and ridiculous claims of literature that tries to be important simply as literature. And *a posteriori*[8] it is not hard to argue that all the greatest poems have been made by men who valued something else more than poetry. The real frivolity, the solemn vacuity, is all with those who make literature a self-existent thing to be valued for its own sake. Pater prepared for pleasure as if it were martyrdom.

[14] Now that I see where I have arrived a doubt assails me. It all sounds conspicuously like things I have said before, starting from very different premises. Is it King Charles's Head?[9] Have I mistaken for the "vision" the same old "transitory being" who, in some ways, is not nearly transitory enough? It may be so: or I may, after all, be right. I would rather be right if I could; but if not, if I have only been once more following my own footprints, it is the sort of tragi-comedy which, on my own principles, I must try to enjoy. I find a beautiful example proposed in the *Paradiso* (XXVIII) where poor Pope Gregory, arrived in Heaven, discovered that his

[7]Literally, reason itself demands that from time to time the use of reason be suspended.
[8]From effect to cause based on actual observation or experience.
[9]King Charles I of England was beheaded in 1649. In Dickens' *David Copperfield,* Mr. Dick, the lunatic, believes that the reason he cannot complete a memorial of his affairs is that the trouble that was in King Charles's head has been put into his head.

322

theory of the hierarchies, on which presumably he had taken pains, was quite wrong. We are told how the redeemed soul behaved; *"di sè medesmo rise."* [10] It was the funniest thing he'd ever heard.

TOPICS FOR DISCUSSION

1. In what sense does Lewis think the subject Christianity and literature admits of no discussion? Do you agree or disagree with his view? Why or why not?
2. What is the difference between Christian literature and Christian literary theory and criticism? Do you agree that modern criticism emphasizes creativity, spontaneity, and freedom? Give reasons for your answer. Do you agree that the theory of Christian literature emphasizes the opposite qualities? Why or why not?
3. In several passages, notably in paragraph 8, Lewis notes that the opposition between the Christian theory of literature and the modern theory is not absolute or logical, but a matter of temperament or tone. May temperament or tone represent a decisive difference? Why or why not?
4. Discuss the contrasting theories of originality presented in paragraphs 11 and 12. What is the main point of difference between the modern theory of originality and the Christian theory? Why is Wordsworth said to illustrate both theories?
5. Why is the artistic conscience called "a mystical amoral law"? Is there a sense in which it can be otherwise described? How would you describe it?
6. Why may some Christian views on literature "strike the world as shallow and flippant"? If they do, is it because the world misunderstands? In what sense does the world misunderstand?

TOPICS FOR COMPOSITION

1. As literature has important relations with Christianity, so too does it have connections with other subjects. Write an essay exploring the relationship of literature with some aspect of philosophy, history, psychology, or science. Give point to your essay by discussing a debatable proposition such as one of the following: "Art as Psychological Use of Language," "Art for the Sake of Human Progress," "Art as a Promoter of Personal Happiness," "Art as a Mode of Immortality."

[10]Literally, he smiled at himself, from *Paradiso* xxviii. 135.

C. S. Lewis

2. Following the suggestions implied in the quotations from T. S. Eliot cited in the headnote, write an essay explaining the literary qualities that make a composition literature and the moral, social, and philosophical qualities that make a literary composition great.
3. Show how, by explaining his point of view on Christianity and literature, C. S. Lewis directly or indirectly argues for one interpretation.

Part Three

THE THEORY OF RHETORIC

☙ Classical
Theorists

PLATO

FROM

The Republic

THE opening pages of Plato's *Republic* exhibit the method of question and answer and comparison of ideas that Plato calls *dialectic*. This word has several meanings; the method exhibited here illustrates the dialectic associated with argumentation in its initial stages. Ideas drawn from sense experience are examined for consistency in themselves and with other related ideas and experiences.

The chief concern of the *Republic* is the idea of justice—the justice that is found in the properly ordered individual and society. The opening discussion of Book One, reprinted here, is a preparation for the complex distinctions of the later pages. In the course of the dialogue, Socrates leads his partners in the discussion to the idea that the soul has three parts —the rational, the appetitive or irrational, and the spirited, which, says Socrates, is distinct from the appetitive because when reason and appetite are divided, the spirited part of the soul takes the side of reason. Corresponding to these divisions in the state are the legislators or counsellors, representing reason; the businessmen, representing appetite; and the soldiers, representing spirit. In both the perfect individual and the perfect state, reason rules appetite, with the help of spirit. Justice is the quality that orders these elements: it is not merely a measure of our actions with regard to others. Socrates summarizes his argument as follows:

The just man does not allow the several elements in his soul to usurp one another's functions; he is indeed one who sets his house in order, by self-mastery and discipline coming to be at peace with himself, and bringing into tune those three parts, like the terms in the proportion of a musical scale, the highest and lowest notes and the mean between them, with all the intermediate intervals.

But before he can approach these absolute distinctions, Socrates must convince his partners that their ordinary ideas of justice are so vague and inadequate that they lead to contradiction. The dialectic on this level serves to reach a more certain conclusion that will be free of contradiction and can be used to reach other more certain conclusions, and serves to lead the auditors, who are likely to think well of their ordinary ideas, to change their assumptions when these are shown to be faulty. Dialectic is thus, on this level, a kind of logic and rhetoric.

On the higher level of discourse, it should be noted, dialectic becomes the accounting of the essential form of each thing; in some passages of the dialogues it is defined as the ratio between mathematical and geometrical proportions—a ratio to be apprehended through the reason. In the *Republic* Socrates states:

> This, then, is the class of things that I spoke of as intelligible, but with two qualifications: first, that the mind, in studying them, is compelled to employ assumptions, and, because it cannot rise above these, does not travel upwards to a first principle; and second, that it uses as images those actual things which have images of their own in the section below them and which, in comparison with those shadows and reflections, are reputed to be more palpable and valued accordingly.

On the higher level, the unaided reason moves to the absolute,

> by the power of dialectic, when it treats its assumptions, not as first principles, but as *hypotheses* in the literal sense, things "laid down" like a flight of steps up which it may mount all the way to something that is not hypothetical, the first principle of all; and having grasped this, may turn back and, holding on to the consequences which depend upon it, descend at last to a conclusion, never making use of any sensible object, but only of Forms, moving through Forms from one to another, and ending with Forms.

The personality of Socrates and his relation to his auditors are of interest to the student of rhetoric. Socrates treats Cephalus one way and Cephalus' son another way; he is at moments playfully ironic with Polemarchus, but he is more deliberately ironic with Thrasymachus, who angrily interrupts the discussion to demand that Socrates define *justice*, instead of merely asking questions and attacking the answers. When Socrates answers that he and Polemarchus are searching earnestly for justice but that the enterprise may be too difficult for them, Thrasymachus responds: "Good Lord . . . Socrates at his old trick of shamming ignorance! I knew it; I told the others you would refuse to commit yourself and do anything sooner than answer a question." Thrasymachus is partly right; but he misses the intention. Socrates begins with the experience of his auditors; he ends with an idea that transcends that experience. The purpose of his irony is to make his auditors begin to doubt ideas that seem indisputable so that they will examine new ideas in earnest. Even the irascible Thrasymachus is forced to do this.

We see in this selection, then, not only Socrates' characteristic approach to large questions such as the meaning of justice, but also the application of one idea of rhetoric developed in the *Phaedrus*—the dialogue that follows this selection—the fitting of truth to the requirements of particular situations without altering the truth or improvising for mere advantage in argument.

I went down yesterday to the Piraeus with Glaucon, the son of Ariston, to pay my devotions to the goddess, and also because I wished to see how they would conduct the festival, since this was its inauguration.

I thought the procession of the citizens very fine, but it was no better than the show made by the marching of the Thracian contingent.

After we had said our prayers and seen the spectacle we were starting for town when Polemarchus, the son of Cephalus, caught sight of us from a distance as we were hastening homeward and ordered his boy run and bid us to wait for him, and the boy caught hold of my himation from behind and said, Polemarchus wants you to wait.

And I turned around and asked where his master was.

There he is, he said, behind you, coming this way. Wait for him.

So we will, said Glaucon. And shortly after Polemarchus came up and Adimantus, the brother of Glaucon, and Niceratus, the son of Nicias, and a few others apparently from the procession.

Whereupon Polemarchus said, Socrates, you appear to have turned your faces townward and to be going to leave us.

Not a bad guess, said I.

But you see how many we are? he said.

Surely.

You must either then prove yourselves the better men or stay here.

Why, is there not left, said I, the alternative of our persuading you that you ought to let us go?

But *could* you persuade us, said he, if we refused to listen?

Nohow, said Glaucon.

Well, we won't listen, and you might as well make up your minds to it.

Do you mean to say, interposed Adimantus, that you haven't heard that there is to be a torchlight race this evening on horseback in honor of the goddess?

On horseback? said I. That is a new idea. Will they carry torches and pass them along to one another as they race with the horses, or how do you mean?

That's the way of it, said Polemarchus, and, besides, there is to be a night festival which will be worth seeing. For after dinner we will get up and go out and see the sights and meet a lot of the lads there and have good talk. So stay and do as we ask.

It looks as if we should have to stay, said Glaucon.

Well, said I, if it so be, so be it.

So we went with them to Polemarchus' house, and there we found Lysias and Euthydemus, the brothers of Polemarchus, yes, and Thrasymachus,

THE REPUBLIC Reprinted by permission of the publishers and the Loeb Classical Library. Paul Shorey (trans.), Plato, *Republic* (Cambridge, Mass.: Harvard Univ. Press).

too, of Chalcedon, and Charmantides of the deme of Paeania, and Clito-
phon the son of Aristonymus. And the father of Polemarchus, Cephalus,
was also at home.

And I thought him much aged, for it was a long time since I had seen
him. He was sitting on a sort of chair with cushions and he had a chaplet
on his head, for he had just finished sacrificing in the court. So we went
and sat down beside him, for there were seats there disposed in a circle.

As soon as he saw me Cephalus greeted me and said, You are not a
very frequent visitor, Socrates. You don't often come down to the Piraeus
to see us. That is not right. For if I were still able to make the journey
up to town easily there would be no need of your resorting hither, but
we would go to visit you. But as it is you should not space too widely
your visits here. For I would have you know that, for my part, as the
satisfactions of the body decay, in the same measure my desire for the
pleasures of good talk and my delight in them increase. Don't refuse then,
but be yourself a companion to these lads and make our house your resort
and regard us as your very good friends and intimates.

Why, yes, Cephalus, said I, and I enjoy talking with the very aged. For
to my thinking we have to learn of them as it were from wayfarers who
have preceded us on a road on which we too, it may be, must sometime
fare—what it is like. Is it rough and hard-going or easy and pleasant to
travel? And so now I would fain learn of you what you think of this
thing, now that your time has come to it, the thing that the poets call
'the threshold of old age.' Is it a hard part of life to bear or what report
have you to make of it?

Yes, indeed, Socrates, he said, I will tell you my own feeling about it.
For it often happens that some of us elders of about the same age come
together and verify the old saw of like to like. At these reunions most
of us make lament, longing for the lost joys of youth and recalling to
mind the pleasures of wine, women, and feasts, and other things thereto
appertaining, and they repine in the belief that the greatest things have
been taken from them and that then they lived well and now it is no life
at all. And some of them complain of the indignities that friends and
kinsmen put upon old age and thereto recite a doleful litany of all the
miseries for which they blame old age. But in my opinion, Socrates, they
do not put the blame on the real cause. For if it were the cause I too
should have had the same experience so far as old age is concerned, and
so would all others who have come to this time of life. But in fact I have
ere now met with others who do not feel in this way, and in particular I
remember hearing Sophocles the poet greeted by a fellow who asked, How
about your service of Aphrodite, Sophocles—is your natural force still
unabated? And he replied, Hush, man, most gladly have I escaped this
thing you talk of, as if I had run away from a raging and savage beast

of a master. I thought it a good answer then and now I think so still more. For in very truth there comes to old age a great tranquility in such matters and a blessed release. When the fierce tensions of the passions and desires relax, then is the word of Sophocles approved, and we are rid of many and mad masters. But indeed, in respect of these complaints and in the matter of our relations with kinsmen and friends there is just one cause, Socrates—not old age, but the character of the man. For if men are temperate and cheerful even old age is only moderately burdensome. But if the reverse, old age, Socrates, and youth are hard for such dispositions.

And I was filled with admiration for the man by these words, and desirous of hearing more I tried to draw him out and said, I fancy, Cephalus, that most people, when they hear you talk in this way, are not convinced but think that you bear old age lightly not because of your character but because of your wealth, for the rich, they say, have many consolations.

You are right, he said. They don't accept my view and there is something in their objection, though not so much as they suppose. But the retort of Themistocles comes in pat here, who, when a man from the little island of Seriphus grew abusive and told him that he owed his fame not to himself but to the city from which he came, replied that neither would he himself ever have made a name if he had been born in Seriphus nor the other if he had been an Athenian. And the same principle applies excellently to those who not being rich take old age hard, for neither would the reasonable man find it altogether easy to endure old age conjoined with poverty, nor would the unreasonable man by the attainment of riches ever attain to self-contentment and a cheerful temper.

May I ask, Cephalus, said I, whether you inherited most of your possessions or acquired them yourself?

Acquired, quotha? he said. As a money-maker, I hold a place somewhere halfway between my grandfather and my father. For my grandfather and namesake inherited about as much property as I now possess and multiplied it many times, my father Lysanias reduced it below the present amount, and I am content if I shall leave the estate to these boys not less but by some slight measure more than my inheritance.

The reason I asked, I said, is that you appear to me not to be overfond of money. And that is generally the case with those who have not earned it themselves. But those who have themselves acquired it have a double reason in comparison with other men for loving it. For just as poets feel complacency about their own poems and fathers about their own sons, so men who have made money take this money seriously as their own creation and they also value it for its uses as other people do. So they are hard to talk to since they are unwilling to commend anything except wealth.

You are right, he replied.

I assuredly am, said I. But tell me further this. What do you regard as the greatest benefit you have enjoyed from the possession of property?

Something, he said, which I might not easily bring many to believe if I told them. For let me tell you, Socrates, he said, that when a man begins to realize that he is going to die, he is filled with apprehensions and concern about matters that before did not occur to him. The tales that are told of the world below and how the men who have done wrong here must pay the penalty there, though he may have laughed them down hitherto, then begin to torture his soul with the doubt that there may be some truth in them. And apart from that the man himself either from the weakness of old age or possibly as being now nearer to the things beyond has a somewhat clearer view of them. Be that as it may, he is filled with doubt, surmises, and alarms and begins to reckon up and consider whether he has ever wronged anyone. Now he to whom the ledger of his life shows an account of many evil deeds starts up even from his dreams like a child again and again in affright and his days are haunted by anticipations of worse to come. But on him who is conscious of no wrong that he has done a sweet hope ever attends and a goodly, to be nurse of his old age, as Pindar too says. For a beautiful saying it is, Socrates, of the poet that when a man lives out his days in justice and piety, 'sweet companion with him, to cheer his heart and nurse his old age, accompanieth hope, who chiefly ruleth the changeful mind of mortals.' That is a fine saying and an admirable. It is for this, then, that I affirm that the possession of wealth is of most value, not it may be to every man but to the good man. Not to cheat any man even unintentionally or play him false, not remaining in debt to a god for some sacrifice or to a man for money, so to depart in fear to that other world—to this result the possession of property contributes not a little. It has also many other uses. But, setting one thing against another, I would lay it down, Socrates, that for a man of sense this is the chief service of wealth.

An admirable sentiment, Cephalus, said I. But speaking of this very thing, justice, are we to affirm thus without qualification that it is truthtelling and paying back what one has received from anyone, or may these very actions sometimes be just and sometimes unjust? I mean, for example, as everyone I presume would admit, if one took over weapons from a friend who was in his right mind and then the lender should go mad and demand them back, that we ought not to return them in that case and that he who did so return them would not be acting justly—nor yet would he who chose to speak nothing but the truth to one who was in that state.

You are right, he replied.

Then this is not the definition of justice—to tell the truth and return what one has received.

Nay, but it is, Socrates, said Polemarchus breaking in, if indeed we are to put any faith in Simonides.

Very well, said Cephalus, indeed I make over the whole argument to you. For it is time for me to attend the sacrifices.

Well, said I, is not Polemarchus the heir of everything that is yours?

Certainly, said he with a laugh, and at the same time went out to the sacred rites.

Tell me, then, you the inheritor of the argument, what it is that you affirm that Simonides says and rightly says about justice.

That it is just, he replied, to render to each his due. In saying this I think he speaks well.

I must admit, said I, that it is not easy to disbelieve Simonides. For he is a wise and inspired man. But just what he may mean by this you, Polemarchus, doubtless know, but I do not. Obviously he does not mean what we were just speaking of, this return of a deposit of anyone whatsoever even if he asks it back when not in his right mind. And yet what the man deposited is due to him in a sense, is it not?

Yes.

But rendered to him it ought not to be by any manner of means when he demands it not being in his right mind.

True, said he.

It is then something other than this that Simonides must, as it seems, mean by the saying that it is just to render back what is due.

Something else in very deed, he replied, for he believes that friends owe it to friends to do them some good and no evil.

I see, said I. You mean that he does not render what is due or owing who returns a deposit of gold if this return and the acceptance prove harmful and the returner and the recipient are friends. Isn't that what you say Simonides means?

Quite so.

But how about this—should one not render to enemies what is their due?

By all means, he said, what is due and owing to them, and there is due and owing from an enemy to an enemy what also is proper for him, some evil.

It was a riddling definition of justice, then, that Simonides gave after the manner of poets, for while his meaning, it seems, was that justice is rendering to each what befits him, the name that he gave to this was 'the due.'

What else do you suppose? said he.

In heaven's name! said I. Suppose someone had questioned him thus. Tell me, Simonides, the art that renders what that is due and befitting to what is called the art of medicine? What do you take it would have been his answer?

Obviously, he said, the art that renders to bodies drugs, foods, and drinks.

And the art that renders to what things what that is due and befitting is called the culinary art?

Seasoning to meats.

Good. In the same way tell me the art that renders what to whom would be denominated justice.

If we are to follow the previous examples, Socrates, it is that which renders benefits and harms to friends and enemies.

To do good to friends and evil to enemies, then, is justice in his meaning?

I think so.

Who then is the most able when they are ill to benefit friends and harm enemies in respect to disease and health?

The physician.

And who navigators in respect of the perils of the sea?

The pilot.

Well then, the just man, in what action and for what work is he the most competent to benefit friends and harm enemies?

In making war and as an ally, I should say.

Very well. But now if they are not sick, friend Polemarchus, the physician is useless to them.

True.

And so to those who are not at sea the pilot.

Yes.

Shall we also say this, that for those who are not at war the just man is useless?

By no means.

There is a use then even in peace for justice?

Yes, it is useful.

But so is agriculture, isn't it?

Yes.

Namely, for the getting of a harvest?

Yes.

But likewise the cobbler's art?

Yes.

Namely, I presume you would say, for the getting of shoes.

Certainly.

Then tell me, for the service and getting of what would you say that justice is useful in time of peace?

In engagements and dealings, Socrates.

And by dealings do you mean associations, partnerships, or something else?

Associations, of course.

Is it the just man, then, who is a good and useful associate and partner in the placing of draughts or the draughts player?

The player.

And in the placing of bricks and stones is the just man a more useful and better associate than the builder?

By no means.

Then what is the association in which the just man is a better partner than the harpist as a harpist is better than the just man for striking the chords?

For money dealings, I think.

Except, I presume, Polemarchus, for the use of money when there is occasion to buy in common or sell a horse. Then, I take it, the man who knows horses, isn't it so?

Apparently.

And again, if it is a vessel, the shipwright or the pilot.

It would seem so.

What then is the use of money in common for which a just man is the better partner?

When it is to be deposited and kept safe, Socrates.

You mean when it is to be put to no use but is to lie idle?

Quite so.

Then it is when money is useless that justice is useful in relation to it?

It looks that way.

And similarly when a scythe is to be kept safe, then justice is useful both in public and private. But when it is to be used, the vinedresser's art is useful?

Apparently.

And so you will have to say that when a shield and a lyre are to be kept and put to no use, justice is useful, but when they are to be made use of, the military art and music.

Necessarily.

And so in all other cases, in the use of each thing, justice is useless but in its uselessness useful?

It looks that way.

Then, my friend, justice cannot be a thing of much worth if it is useful only for things out of use and useless. But let us consider this point. Is not the man who is most skillful to strike or inflict a blow in a fight, whether as a boxer or elsewhere, also the most wary to guard against a blow?

Assuredly.

Is it not also true that he who best knows how to guard against disease is also most cunning to communicate it and escape detection?

I think so.

But again, the very same man is a good guardian of an army who is good at stealing a march upon the enemy in respect of their designs and proceedings generally.

Certainly.

Of whatsoever, then, anyone is a skillful guardian, of that he is also a skillful thief?

It seems so.

If then the just man is an expert in guarding money he is an expert in stealing it.

The argument certainly points that way.

A kind of thief then the just man it seems has turned out to be, and it is likely that you acquired this idea from Homer. For he regards with complacency Autolycus, the maternal uncle of Odysseus, and says, 'he was gifted beyond all men in thievery and perjury.' So justice, according to you and Homer and Simonides, seems to be a kind of stealing, with the qualification that it is for the benefit of friends and the harm of enemies. Isn't that what you meant?

No, by Zeus, he replied. I no longer know what I did mean. Yet this I still believe, that justice benefits friends and harms enemies.

May I ask whether by friends you mean those who seem to a man to be worthy or those who really are so, even if they do not seem, and similarly of enemies?

It is likely, he said, that men will love those whom they suppose to be good and dislike those whom they deem bad.

Do not men make mistakes in this matter so that many seem good to them who are not and the reverse?

They do.

For those, then, who thus err the good are their enemies and the bad their friends?

Certainly.

But all the same it is then just for them to benefit the bad and injure the good?

It would seem so.

But again, the good are just and incapable of injustice.

True.

On your reasoning then it is just to wrong those who do no injustice.

Nay, nay, Socrates, he said, the reasoning can't be right.

Then, said I, it is just to harm the unjust and benefit the just.

That seems a better conclusion than the other.

It will work out, then, for many, Polemarchus, who have misjudged men that it is just to harm their friends, for they have got bad ones, and to benefit their enemies, for they are good. And so we shall find ourselves saying the very opposite of what we affirmed Simonides to mean.

Most certainly, he said, it does work out so. But let us change our ground, for it looks as if we were wrong in the notion we took up about the friend and the enemy.

What notion, Polemarchus?

That the man who seems to us good is the friend.

And to what shall we change it now? said I.

That the man who both seems and is good is the friend, but that he who seems but is not really so seems but is not really the friend. And there will be the same assumption about the enemy.

Then on this view it appears the friend will be the good man and the bad the enemy.

Yes.

So you would have us qualify our former notion of the just man by an addition. We then said it was just to do good to a friend and evil to an enemy, but now we are to add that it is just to benefit the friend if he is good and harm the enemy if he is bad?

By all means, he said, that, I think, would be the right way to put it.

Is it then, said I, the part of a good man to harm anybody whatsoever?

Certainly it is, he replied. A man ought to harm those who are both bad and his enemies.

When horses are harmed does it make them better or worse?

Worse.

In respect of the excellence or virtue of dogs or that of horses?

Of horses.

And do not also dogs when harmed become worse in respect of canine and not of equine virtue?

Necessarily.

And men, my dear fellow, must we not say that when they are harmed it is in respect of the distinctive excellence or virtue of man that they become worse?

Assuredly.

And is not justice the specific virtue of man?

That too must be granted.

Then it must also be admitted, my friend, that men who are harmed become more unjust.

It seems so.

Do musicians then make men unmusical by the art of music?

Impossible.

Well, do horsemen by horsemanship unfit men for dealing with horses?

No.

By justice then do the just make men unjust, or in sum do the good by virtue make men bad?

Nay, it is impossible.

It is not, I take it, the function of heat to chill but of its opposite.

Yes.

Nor of dryness to moisten but of its opposite.

Assuredly.

Nor yet of the good to harm but of its opposite.

So it appears.

But the just man is good?

Certainly.

It is not then the function of the just man, Polemarchus, to harm either friend or anyone else, but of his opposite, the unjust.

I think you are altogether right, Socrates.

If, then, anyone affirms that it is just to render to each his due and he means by this that injury and harm is what is due to his enemies from the just man and benefits to his friends, he was no truly wise man who said it. For what he meant was not true. For it has been made clear to us that in no case is it just to harm anyone.

I concede it, he said.

We will take up arms against him, then, said I, you and I together, if anyone affirms that either Simonides or Bias or Pittacus or any other of the wise and blessed said such a thing.

I, for my part, he said, am ready to join in the battle with you.

Do you know, said I, to whom I think the saying belongs—this statement that it is just to benefit friends and harm enemies?

To whom? he said.

I think it was the saying of Periander or Perdiccas or Xerxes or Ismenias the Theban or some other rich man who had great power in his own conceit.

That is most true, he replied.

Very well, said I, since it has been made clear that this too is not justice and the just, what else is there that we might say justice to be?

TOPICS FOR DISCUSSION

1. What can you determine about Socrates' reputation among the young Athenians from the way he is greeted by Polemarchus and is persuaded to stay? Is he serious when he says he may have to convince Polemarchus to let him and his companions depart?

2. Why is Socrates interested in the question of the greatest advantage of wealth? Is the chief reason that Cephalus, given his years of experience, is likely to be wise in such matters? Does the discussion turn by chance to proper conduct, or has Socrates guided the discussion in this direction?

3. What is the attitude of Polemarchus toward the saying of Simonides that justice is to give each man his due? What is the tone of Socrates' response that it is difficult to disbelieve a "wise and inspired man" like Simonides? How is his true attitude toward Simonides revealed in the course of the dialogue?
4. By what analogies does Socrates lead Polemarchus to the conclusion that the just man has turned out to be a kind of thief? How does he reveal the defects of Simonides' definition?
5. Is the chief defect to be found in the conception of justice or in its application—in the uses to which people like Simonides put it?
6. Polemarchus is not at first willing to give up his definition. Why is he willing to do so after Socrates has explored whether justice means doing good to friends and harming the evil man? Why did Socrates not begin with this consideration?
7. Socrates might have given an exposition of his view of the conception of justice under discussion. What did he gain by not doing so? How has he fitted the argument to his audience? Would he have chosen different analogies if he had questioned Cephalus on his conception of justice?

TOPICS FOR COMPOSITION

1. On the basis of the detail provided in these opening pages of the *Republic*, characterize Socrates. Give particular attention to his use of irony—reflected here in the discrepancy between what he says and what he means.
2. In the pages that follow this excerpt Socrates explores the idea that justice represents the interests of the stronger in society. Write two paragraphs, one defending this idea, the other criticizing it. Then write a brief Socratic dialogue exploring this conception.
3. Write a summary of what you consider to be the most prevalent conception of justice in your community. Explain why you consider it to be the most prevalent.
4. Analyze the rhetoric of Socrates in refuting Simonides' idea of justice. Comment on Socrates' approach to his particular audience—both the old and young—his use of irony, and the method by which he exposes the defects of Simonides' idea.

PLATO

Phaedrus

PHAEDRUS begins with an exploration of the nature of love and ends with a discourse on true rhetoric. Phaedrus begins by delivering a speech of Lysias—the brother of Polemarchus, with whom Socrates debated in the *Republic*—extolling the nonlover over the lover. Phaedrus thinks the speech clever because it seems to make a good case for a position difficult to defend. Socrates presents a less repetitious defense of the non-lover, proceeding in a different way; then repenting because of his impiety to the god of Love, he presents a defense of the lover, showing that there is such a thing as gentle love that ennobles rather than degrades the loved one. Following this second speech, Socrates and Phaedrus discourse on the nature of rhetoric. True rhetoric, Socrates insists, proceeds from the love of truth and not from calculation of what will best convince a particular audience; the rhetorician must know the parts of the soul and the kind of argument best fitted to each, for men differ according to these parts. In conclusion Socrates extols the spoken over the written word.

At first reading, the exploration of love may seem only remotely connected to the discourse on rhetoric; that is, the three speeches may seem merely to illustrate the problems of rhetoric. Actually, however, the two considerations are directly connected, for both are related to the nature of truth. The divine, says Socrates, is "fair, wise, and good, and possessed of all other such excellences"; furthermore, "the soul that hath seen the most of being shall enter into the human babe that shall grow into a seeker after wisdom or beauty, a follower of the Muses and a lover."

The true rhetorician is also a lover of truth; indeed his attention to proportion and proper construction—qualities lacking in the speech of Lysias—reflects his love of beauty. However ironic Socrates may have been with Phaedrus, his own rhetoric would have been specious had it not been animated and nourished by the truth. His concluding prayer to Pan—"grant that I may become fair within, and that such outward things as I have may not war against the spirit within me"—is not made in jest.

Phaedrus indicates that for Plato a true rhetoric is possible, even though rhetoric is often a matter of calculation. Absolute and unchanging though the truth is, it can be explained in different ways to accommodate different people. In this lies the superiority of speech over writing: the speaker has more control over the meaning and application of his words and he is more in control of the course of the discussion as it is shaped by the assumptions and interests of his partners.

SOCRATES   Where do you come from, Phaedrus my friend, and where are you going?

PHAEDRUS   I've been with Lysias, Socrates, the son of Cephalus, and I'm off for a walk outside the wall, after a long morning's sitting there. On the instructions of our common friend Acumenus I take my walks on the open roads; he tells me that is more invigorating than walking in the colonnades.

SOCRATES   Yes, he's right in saying so. But Lysias, I take it, was in town.

PHAEDRUS   Yes, staying with Epicrates, in that house where Morychus used to live, close to the temple of Olympian Zeus.

SOCRATES   Well, how were you occupied? No doubt Lysias was giving the company a feast of eloquence.

PHAEDRUS   I'll tell you, if you can spare time to come along with me and listen.

SOCRATES   What? Don't you realize that I should account it, in Pindar's words, 'above all business' to hear how you and Lysias passed your time?

PHAEDRUS   Lead on then.

SOCRATES   Please tell me.

PHAEDRUS   As a matter of fact the topic is appropriate for your ears, Socrates, for the discussion that engaged us may be said to have concerned love. Lysias, you must know, has described how a handsome boy was tempted, but not by a lover—that's the clever part of it. He maintains that surrender should be to one who is not in love rather than to one who is.

SOCRATES   Splendid! I wish he would add that it should be to a poor man rather than a rich one, an elderly man rather than a young one, and, in general, to ordinary folk like myself. What an attractive democratic theory that would be! However, I'm so eager to hear about it that I vow I won't leave you even if you extend your walk as far as Megara, up to the walls and back again as recommended by Herodicus.

PHAEDRUS   What do you mean, my good man? Do you expect an amateur like me to repeat by heart, without disgracing its author, the work of the ablest writer of our day, which it took him weeks to compose at his leisure? That is far beyond me, though I'd rather have had the ability than come into a fortune.

PHAEDRUS   Reprinted from *Collected Dialogues of Plato*, R. Hackforth (trans.), by permission of Cambridge Univ. Press.

SOCRATES   I know my Phaedrus. Yes indeed, I'm as sure of him as of my own identity. I'm certain that the said Phaedrus didn't listen just once to Lysias' speech; time after time he asked him to repeat it to him, and Lysias was very ready to comply. Even that would not content him. In the end he secured the script and began poring over the parts that specially attracted him, and thus engaged he sat there the whole morning, until he grew weary and went for a walk. Upon my word, I believe he had learned the whole speech by heart, unless it was a very long one, and he was going into the country to practice declaiming it. Then he fell in with one who has a passion for listening to discourses, and when he saw him he was delighted to think he would have someone to share his frenzied enthusiasm; so he asked him to join him on his way. But when the lover of discourses begged him to discourse, he became difficult, pretending he didn't want to, though he meant to do so ultimately, even if he had to force himself on a reluctant listener. So beg him, Phaedrus, to do straightway what he will soon do in any case.

PHAEDRUS   Doubtless it will be much my best course to deliver myself to the best of my ability, for I fancy you will never let me go until I have given you some sort of a speech.

SOCRATES   You are quite right about my intention.

PHAEDRUS   Then here's what I will do. It really is perfectly true, Socrates, that I have not got the words by heart, but I will sketch the general purport of the several points in which the lover and the nonlover were contrasted, taking them in order one by one, and beginning at the beginning.

SOCRATES   Very well, my dear fellow, but you must first show me what it is that you have in your left hand under your cloak, for I surmise that it is the actual discourse. If that is so, let me assure you of this, that much as I love you I am not altogether inclined to let you practice your oratory on me when Lysias himself is here present. Come now, show it me.

PHAEDRUS   Say no more, Socrates; you have dashed my hope of trying out my powers on you. Well, where would you like us to sit for our reading?

SOCRATES   Let us turn off here and walk along the Ilissus; then we can sit down in any quiet spot you choose.

PHAEDRUS   It's convenient, isn't it, that I chance to be barefoot; you of course always are so. There will be no trouble in wading in the stream, which is especially delightful at this hour of a summer's day.

SOCRATES   Lead on then, and look out for a place to sit down.

PHAEDRUS   You see that tall plane tree over there?

SOCRATES   To be sure.

The Theory of Rhetoric

PHAEDRUS   There's some shade, and a little breeze, and grass to sit down on, or lie down if we like.

SOCRATES   Then make for it.

PHAEDRUS   Tell me, Socrates, isn't it somewhere about here that they say Boreas seized Orithyia from the river?

SOCRATES   Yes, that is the story.

PHAEDRUS   Was this the actual spot? Certainly the water looks charmingly pure and clear; it's just the place for girls to be playing beside the stream.

SOCRATES   No, it was about a quarter of a mile lower down, where you cross to the sanctuary of Agra; there is, I believe, an altar dedicated to Boreas close by.

PHAEDRUS   I have never really noticed it, but pray tell me, Socrates, do you believe that story to be true?

SOCRATES   I should be quite in the fashion if I disbelieved it, as the men of science do. I might proceed to give a scientific account of how the maiden, while at play with Pharmacia, was blown by a gust of Boreas down from the rocks hard by, and having thus met her death was said to have been seized by Boreas, though it may have happened on the Areopagus, according to another version of the occurrence. For my part, Phaedrus, I regard such theories as no doubt attractive, but as the invention of clever, industrious people who are not exactly to be envied, for the simple reason that they must then go on and tell us the real truth about the appearance of centaurs and the Chimera, not to mention a whole host of such creatures, Gorgons and Pegasuses and countless other remarkable monsters of legend flocking in on them. If our skeptic, with his somewhat crude science, means to reduce every one of them to the standard of probability, he'll need a deal of time for it. I myself have certainly no time for the business, and I'll tell you why, my friend. I can't as yet 'know myself,' as the inscription at Delphi enjoins, and so long as that ignorance remains it seems to me ridiculous to inquire into extraneous matters. Consequently I don't bother about such things, but accept the current beliefs about them, and direct my inquiries, as I have just said, rather to myself, to discover whether I really am a more complex creature and more puffed up with pride than Typhon, or a simpler, gentler being whom heaven has blessed with a quiet, un-Typhonic nature. By the way, isn't this the tree we were making for?

PHAEDRUS   Yes, that's the one.

SOCRATES   Upon my word, a delightful resting place, with this tall, spreading plane, and a lovely shade from the high branches of the *agnos*. Now that it's in full flower, it will make the place ever so fragrant. And what a lovely stream under the plane tree, and how cool to the

Plato

feet! Judging by the statuettes and images I should say it's consecrated to Achelous and some of the nymphs. And then too, isn't the
freshness of the air most welcome and pleasant, and the shrill sum-
mery music of the cicada choir! And as crowning delight the grass,
thick enough on a gentle slope to rest your head on most comfortably.
In fact, my dear Phaedrus, you have been the stranger's perfect guide.

PHAEDRUS Whereas you, my excellent friend, strike me as the oddest of
men. Anyone would take you, as you say, for a stranger being shown
the country by a guide instead of a native—never leaving town to
cross the frontier nor even, I believe, so much as setting foot outside
the walls.

SOCRATES You must forgive me, dear friend; I'm a lover of learning, and
trees and open country won't teach me anything, whereas men in the
town do. Yet you seem to have discovered a recipe for getting me out.
A hungry animal can be driven by dangling a carrot or a bit of
greenstuff in front of it; similarly if you proffer me volumes of
speeches I don't doubt you can cart me all round Attica, and anywhere
else you please. Anyhow, now that we've got here I propose for the
time being to lie down, and you can choose whatever posture you
think most convenient for reading, and proceed.

PHAEDRUS Here you are then.

You know how I am situated, and I have told you that I think it to
our advantage that this should happen. Now I claim that I should not
be refused what I ask simply because I am not your lover. Lovers,
when their craving is at an end, repent of such benefits as they have
conferred, but for the other sort no occasion arises for regretting what
has passed. For being free agents under no constraint, they regulate
their services by the scale of their means, with an eye to their own
personal interest. Again, lovers weigh up profit and loss accruing to
their account by reason of their passion, and with the extra item of
labor expended decide that they have long since made full payment
for favors received, whereas the nonlovers cannot allege any conse-
quential neglect of their personal affairs, nor record any past exertions
on the debit side, nor yet complain of having quarreled with their
relatives; hence, with all these troubles removed, all they have left to
do is to devote their energies to such conduct as they conceive likely
to gratify the other party.

Again, it is argued that a lover ought to be highly valued because
he professes to be especially kind toward the loved one, and ready to
gratify him in words and deeds while arousing the dislike of everyone
else. If this is true, however, it is obvious that he will set greater
store by the loved one of tomorrow than by that of today, and will
doubtless do any injury to the old love if required by the new.

And really, what sense is there in lavishing what is so precious upon

The Practice of Rhetoric

one laboring under an affliction which nobody who knew anything of it would even attempt to remove? Why, the man himself admits that he is not sound, but sick, that he is aware of his folly, but cannot control himself. How then, when he comes to his senses, is he likely to approve of the intentions that he formed in his aberration?

And observe this. If you are to choose the best of a number of lovers, your choice will be only among a few, whereas a general choice of the person who most commends himself to you gives you a wide field, so that in that wide field you have a much better prospect of finding someone worthy of your friendship.

Now maybe you respect established conventions, and anticipate odium if people get to hear about you; if so, it may be expected that a lover, conceiving that everyone will admire him as he admires himself, will be proud to talk about it and flatter his vanity by declaring to all and sundry that his enterprise has been successful, whereas the other type, who can control themselves, will prefer to do what is best rather than shine in the eyes of their neighbors.

Again, a lover is bound to be heard about and seen by many people, consorting with his beloved and caring about little else, so that when they are observed talking to one another, the meeting is taken to imply the satisfaction, actual or prospective, of their desires, whereas, with the other sort, no one ever thinks of putting a bad construction on their association, realizing that a man must have someone to talk to by way of friendship or gratification of one sort or another.

And observe this. Perhaps you feel troubled by the reflection that it is hard for friendship to be preserved, and that whereas a quarrel arising from other sources will be a calamity shared by both parties, one that follows the sacrifice of your all will involve a grievous hurt to yourself; in that case it is doubtless the lover who should cause you the more alarm, for he is very ready to take offense, and thinks the whole affair is to his own hurt. Hence he discourages his beloved from consorting with anyone else, fearing that a wealthy rival may overreach him with his money, or a cultured one outdo him with his intelligence, and he is perpetually on guard against the influence of those who possess other advantages. So by persuading you to become estranged from such rivals he leaves you without a friend in the world; alternatively, if you look to your own interest and show more good sense than your lover, you will find yourself quarreling with him. On the other hand, one who is not a lover, but has achieved what he asked of you by reason of his merit, will not be jealous of others who seek your society, but will rather detest those who avoid it, in the belief that the latter look down on him, whereas the former are serving his turn. Consequently the object of his attentions is far more likely to make friends than enemies out of the affair.

And observe this. A lover more often than not wants to possess you before he has come to know your character or become familiar with your general personality, and that makes it uncertain whether he will still want to be your friend when his desires have waned, whereas in the other case, the fact that the pair were already friends before the affair took place makes it probable that instead of friendship diminishing as the result of favors received, these favors will abide as a memory and promise of more to come.

And observe this. It ought to be for your betterment to listen to me rather than to a lover, for a lover commends anything you say or do even when it is amiss, partly from fear that he may offend you, partly because his passion impairs his own judgment. For the record of Love's achievement is, first, that when things go badly, he makes a man count that an affliction which normally causes no distress; secondly, that when things go well, he compels his subjects to extol things that ought not to gratify them, which makes it fitting that they should be pitied far more than admired by the objects of their passion. On the other hand, if you listen to me, my intercourse with you will be a matter of ministering not to your immediate pleasure but to your future advantage, for I am the master of myself, rather than the victim of love; I do not bring bitter enmity upon myself by resenting trifling offenses. On the contrary, it is only on account of serious wrongs that I am moved, and that but slowly, to mild indignation, pardoning what is done unintentionally, and endeavoring to hinder what is done of intent, for these are the tokens of lasting friendship. If however you are disposed to think that there can be no firm friendship save with a lover, you should reflect that in that case we should not set store by sons, or fathers, or mothers, nor should we possess any trustworthy friends. No, it is not to erotic passion that we owe these, but to conduct of a different order.

Again, if we ought to favor those who press us most strongly, then in other matters too we should give our good offices not to the worthiest people but to the most destitute, for since their distress is the greatest, they will be the most thankful to us for relieving them. And observe this further consequence. When we give private banquets, the right people to invite will be not our friends but beggars and those in need of a good meal, for it is they that will be fond of us and attend upon us and flock to our doors; it is they that will be most delighted and most grateful and call down blessings on our heads. No, the proper course, surely, is to show favor not to the most importunate but to those most able to make us a return—not to mere beggars, but to the deserving; not to those who will regale themselves with your youthful beauty, but to those who will let you share their prosperity when you are older; not to those who, when they have had their will of you, will flatter their vanity by telling the world, but to those who will keep a strict and modest silence; not to those who are devoted to you for a brief period, but to those who will continue to be your friends as long as you live; not to those who, when their passion is spent, will look for an excuse to turn against you, but to those who, when your beauty is past, will make that the time for displaying their own goodness.

Do you therefore be mindful of what I have said and reflect that, while lovers are admonished by their friends and relatives for the wrongness of their conduct, the other sort have never been reproached by one of their family on the score of behaving to the detriment of their own interest.

Perhaps you will ask me whether I recommend you to accord your favors to all and sundry of this sort. Well, I do not suppose that even a lover would bid you to be favorable toward all and sundry lovers; in the first place a recipient would not regard it as meriting so much gratitude, and in the second you would find it more difficult if you wished to keep your affairs concealed, and what is wanted is that the business should involve no harm, but mutual advantage.

And now I think I have said all that is needed; if you think I have neglected anything, and want more, let me know.

What do you think of the speech, Socrates? Isn't it extraordinarily fine, especially in point of language?

SOCRATES Amazingly fine indeed, my friend. I was thrilled by it. And it was you, Phaedrus, that made me feel as I did. I watched your apparent delight in the words as you read. And as I'm sure that you understand such matters better than I do, I took my cue from you, and therefore joined in the ecstasy of my right worshipful companion.

PHAEDRUS Come, come! Do you mean to make a joke of it?

SOCRATES Do you think I am joking, and don't mean it seriously?

PHAEDRUS No more of that, Socrates. Tell me truly, as one friend to another, do you think there is anyone in Greece who could make a finer and more exhaustive speech on the same subject?

SOCRATES What? Are you and I required to extol the speech not merely on the score of its author's lucidity and terseness of expression, and his consistently precise and well-polished vocabulary, but also for his having said what he ought? If we are, we shall have to allow it only on your account, for my feeble intelligence failed to appreciate it; I was only attending to it as a piece of rhetoric, and as such I couldn't think that even Lysias himself would deem it adequate. Perhaps you won't agree with me, Phaedrus, but really it seemed to me that he said the same things several times over. Maybe he's not very clever at expatiating at length on a single theme, or possibly he has no interest in such topics. In fact it struck me as an extravagant performance, to demonstrate his ability to say the same thing twice, in different words but with equal success.

PHAEDRUS Not a bit of it, Socrates. The outstanding feature of the discourse is just this, that it has not overlooked any important aspect of the subject, so making it impossible for anyone else to outdo what he has said with a fuller or more satisfactory oration.

SOCRATES If you go as far as that I shall find it impossible to agree with you; if I were to assent out of politeness, I should be confuted by the wise men and women who in past ages have spoken and written on this theme.

PHAEDRUS To whom do you refer? Where have you heard anything better than this?

SOCRATES I can't tell you offhand, but I'm sure I have heard something better, from the fair Sappho maybe, or the wise Anacreon, or perhaps some prose writer. What ground, you may ask, have I for saying so? Good sir, there is something welling up within my breast, which makes me feel that I could find something different, and something better, to say. I am of course well aware it can't be anything originating in my own mind, for I know my own ignorance; so I suppose it can only be that it has been poured into me, through my ears, as into a vessel, from some external source, though in my stupid fashion I have actually forgotten how, and from whom, I heard it.

PHAEDRUS Well said! You move me to admiration. I don't mind your not telling me, even though I should press you, from whom and how you heard it, provided you do just what you say. You have undertaken to make a better speech than that in the book here and one of not less length which shall owe nothing to it; I in my turn undertake like the nine Archons to set up at Delphi a golden life-sized statue, not only of myself but of you also.

SOCRATES How kind you are, Phaedrus, and what a pattern of golden-age simplicity, in supposing me to mean that Lysias has wholly missed the mark and that another speech could avoid all his points! Surely that couldn't be so even with the most worthless of writers. Thus, as regards the subject of the speech, do you imagine that anybody could argue that the nonlover should be favored, rather than the lover, without praising the wisdom of the one and censuring the folly of the other? That he could dispense with these essential points, and then bring up something different? No, no, surely we must allow such arguments, and forgive the orator for using them, and in that sort of field what merits praise is not invention, but arrangement; but when it comes to nonessential points, that are difficult to invent, we should praise arrangement and invention too.

PHAEDRUS I agree. What you say seems fair enough. For my part, this is what I will do. I will allow you to take it for granted that the

The Theory of Rhetoric

lover is less sane than the nonlover, and for the rest, if you can replace what we have here by a fuller speech of superior merit, up with your statue in wrought gold beside the offering of the Cypselids at Olympia.

SOCRATES Have you taken me seriously, Phaedrus, for teasing you with an attack on your darling Lysias? Can you possibly suppose that I shall make a real attempt to rival his cleverness with something more ornate?

PHAEDRUS As to that, my friend, I've got you where I can return your fire. Assuredly you must do what you can in the way of a speech, or else we shall be driven, like vulgar comedians, to capping each other's remarks. Beware. Do not deliberately compel me to utter the words. 'Don't I know my Socrates? If not, I've forgotten my own identity,' or 'He wanted to speak, but made difficulties about it.' No, make up your mind that we're not going to leave this spot until you have delivered yourself of what you told me you had within your breast. We are by ourselves in a lonely place, and I am stronger and younger than you, for all which reasons 'mistake not thou my bidding' and please don't make me use force to open your lips.

SOCRATES But, my dear good Phaedrus, it will be courting ridicule for an amateur like me to improvise on the same theme as an accomplished writer.

PHAEDRUS Look here, I'll have no more of this affectation, for I'm pretty sure I have something to say which will compel you to speak.

SOCRATES Then please don't say it.

PHAEDRUS Oh, but I shall, here and now, and what I say will be on oath. I swear to you by—but by whom, by what god? Or shall it be by this plane tree? I swear that unless you deliver your speech here in its very presence, I will assuredly never again declaim nor report any other speech by any author whatsoever.

SOCRATES Aha, you rogue! How clever of you to discover the means of compelling a lover of discourse to do your bidding!

PHAEDRUS Then why all this twisting?

SOCRATES I give it up, in view of what you've sworn. For how could I possibly do without such entertainment?

PHAEDRUS Then proceed.

SOCRATES Well, do you know what I'm going to do?

PHAEDRUS Do about what?

SOCRATES I shall cover my head before I begin; then I can rush through my speech at top speed without looking at you and breaking down for shame.

PHAEDRUS You can do anything else you like, provided you make your speech.

SOCRATES Come then, ye clear-voiced Muses, whether it be from the nature of your song, or from the musical people of Liguria that ye came to be so styled, 'assist the tale I tell' under compulsion by my good friend here, to the end that he may think yet more highly of one dear to him, whom he already accounts a man of wisdom.

Well then, once upon a time there was a very handsome boy, or rather young man, who had a host of lovers, and one of them was wily, and had persuaded the boy that he was not in love with him, though really he was, quite as much as the others. And on one occasion, in pressing his suit he actually sought to convince him that he ought to favor a nonlover rather than a lover. And this is the purport of what he said.

My boy, if anyone means to deliberate successfully about anything, there is one thing he must do at the outset. He must know what it is he is deliberating about; otherwise he is bound to go utterly astray. Now most people fail to realize that they don't know what this or that really is; consequently when they start discussing something, they dispense with any agreed definition, assuming that they know the thing; then later on they naturally find, to their cost, that they agree neither with each other nor with themselves. That being so, you and I would do well to avoid what we charge against other people, and as the question before us is whether one should preferably consort with a lover or a nonlover, we ought to agree upon a definition of love which shows its nature and its effects, so that we may have it before our minds as something to refer to while we discuss whether love is beneficial or injurious.

Well now, it is plain to everyone that love is some sort of desire, and further we know that men desire that which is fair without being lovers. How then are we to distinguish one who loves from one who does not? We must go on to observe that within each one of us there are two sorts of ruling or guiding principle that we follow. One is an innate desire for pleasure, the other an acquired judgment that aims at what is best. Sometimes these internal guides are in accord, sometimes at variance; now one gains the mastery, now the other. And when judgment guides us rationally toward what is best, and has the mastery, that mastery is called temperance, but when desire drags us irrationally toward pleasure, and has come to rule within us, the name given to that rule is wantonness. But in truth wantonness itself has many names, as it has many branches or forms, and when one of these forms is conspicuously present in a man it makes that man bear its name, a name that it is no credit or distinction to possess. If it be in the matter of food that desire has the mastery over judgment of what is for the best, and over all other desires, it is called gluttony, and the person in question will be called a glutton, or again if desire has achieved domination in the matter of drink, it is plain what term we shall apply to its subject who is led down that path, and no less plain what are the appropriate names in the case of other such persons and of other such desires, according as this one or that holds sway.

Now the reason for saying all this can hardly remain in doubt; yet even so a statement of it will be illuminating. When irrational desire, pursuing the enjoyment of beauty, has gained the mastery over judgment that prompts to right conduct, and has acquired from other desires, akin to it, fresh strength to strain toward bodily beauty, that very strength provides it with its name—it is the strong passion called love.

Well, Phaedrus my friend, do you think, as I do, that I am divinely inspired?

PHAEDRUS Undoubtedly, Socrates, you have been vouchsafed a quite unusual eloquence.

SOCRATES Then listen to me in silence. For truly there seems to be a divine presence in this spot, so that you must not be surprised if, as my speech proceeds, I become as one possessed; already my style is not far from dithyrambic.

PHAEDRUS Very true.

SOCRATES But for that you are responsible. Still, let me continue; possibly the menace may be averted. However, that must be as God wills; our business is to resume our address to the boy.

Very well then, my good friend, the true nature of that on which we have to deliberate has been stated and defined, and so, with that definition in mind, we may go on to say what advantage or detriment may be expected to result to one who accords his favor to a lover and a nonlover, respectively.

Now a man who is dominated by desire and enslaved to pleasure is of course bound to aim at getting the greatest possible pleasure out of his beloved, and what pleases a sick man is anything that does not thwart him, whereas anything that is as strong as, or stronger than, himself gives him offense. Hence he will not, if he can avoid it, put up with a favorite that matches or outdoes him in strength, but will always seek to make him weaker and feebler, and weakness is found in the ignorant, the cowardly, the poor speaker, the slow thinker, as against the wise, the brave, the eloquent, the quick-minded. All these defects of mind and more in the beloved are bound to be a source of pleasure to the lover; if they do not exist already as innate qualities, he will cultivate them, for not to do so means depriving himself of immediate pleasure. And of course he is bound to be jealous, constantly debarring the boy not only, to his great injury, from the advantages of consorting with others, which would make a real man of him, but, greatest injury of all, from consorting with that which would most increase his wisdom—by which I mean divine philosophy.

No access to that can possibly be permitted by the lover, for he dreads becoming thereby an object of contempt. And in general he must aim at making the boy totally ignorant and totally dependent on his lover, by way of securing the maximum of pleasure for himself, and the maximum of damage to the other.

Hence in respect of the boy's mind it is anything but a profitable investment to have as guardian or partner a man in love.

After the mind, the body; we must see what sort of physical condition will be fostered, and how it will be fostered, in the boy that has become the possession of one who is under compulsion to pursue pleasure instead of goodness. We shall find him, of course, pursuing a weakling rather than a sturdy boy, one who has had a cozy, sheltered upbringing instead of being exposed to the open air, who has given himself up to a soft unmanly life instead of the toil and sweat of manly exercise, who for lack of natural charm tricks himself out with artificial cosmetics, and resorts to all sorts of other similar practices which are too obvious to need further enumeration. Yet before leaving the topic we may sum it up in a sentence. The boy will be of that physical type which in wartime, and other times that try a man's mettle, inspires confidence in his enemies and alarm in his friends, aye and in his very lovers too.

And now let us pass from these obvious considerations and raise the next question. What advantage or detriment in respect of property and possessions shall we find resulting from the society and guardianship of a lover? Well, one thing is plain enough to anyone, and especially to the lover, namely that his foremost wish will be for the boy to be bereft of his dearest possessions, his treasury of kindness and ideal affection—father and mother, kinsmen and friends— he will want him to be robbed of them all, as likely to make difficulties and raise objections to the intercourse which he finds so pleasant. If however the boy possesses property, in money or whatever it may be, he will reckon that he will not be so easy to capture, or if captured to manage; hence a lover is bound to nurse a grudge against one who possesses property, and to rejoice when he loses it. Furthermore he will want his beloved to remain as long as possible without wife or child or home, so as to enjoy for as long as may be his own delights.

There are, to be sure, other evils in life, but with most of them heaven has mixed some momentary pleasure. Thus in the parasite, a fearsome and most pernicious creature, nature has mingled a dash of pleasing wit or charm; a courtesan may well be branded as pernicious, not to mention many other similar creatures with their respective callings; yet in everyday life they can be very agreeable, but a lover, besides being pernicious, is the most disagreeable of all men for a boy to spend his days with. There's an old saying about 'not match-ing May with December,' based, I suppose, on the idea that similarity of age tends to similarity of pleasures and consequently makes a cou-ple good friends; still even with such a couple the association is apt to pall. Then again, in addition to the dissimilarity of age, there is that compulsion which is burdensome for anybody in any circum-stances, but especially so in the relations of such a pair.

The elderly lover will not, if he can help it, suffer any desertion by his beloved by day or by night; he is driven on by a compelling, goading power, lured by the continual promise of pleasure in the sight, hearing, touching, or other physical experience of the beloved; to minister unfailingly to the boy's needs is his delight. But what pleasure or what solace will he have to offer to the beloved? How will he save him from experiencing the extremity of discomfort in those long hours at his lover's side, as he looks upon a face which years have robbed of its beauty, together with other consequences which it is unpleasant even to hear mentioned, let alone to have continually to cope with in stark reality. And what of the suspicious precautions with which he is incessantly guarded, with whomsoever he associates, the unseasonable fulsome compliments to which he has to listen, al-ternating with reproaches which when uttered in soberness are hard to endure, but coming from one in his cups, in language of unlimited, undisguised coarseness, are both intolerable and disgusting?

To continue, if while his love lasts he is harmful and offensive, in later days, when it is spent, he will show his bad faith. He was lavish with promises, interspersed among his vows and entreaties, re-garding those later days, contriving with some difficulty to secure his partner's endurance of an intercourse which even then was bur-densome, by holding out hopes of benefits to come. But when the time comes for fulfilling the promises, a new authority takes the place within him of the former ruler; love and passion are replaced by wis-dom and temperance; he has become a different person. But the boy does not realize it, and demands a return for what he gave in the past, reminding him of what had been done and said, as though he were talking to the same person, while the erstwhile lover, who has now acquired wisdom and temperance, cannot for very shame bring him-self to declare that he has become a new man, nor yet see his way to redeeming the solemn assurances and promises made under the old regime of folly; he fears that if he were to go on acting as before he would revert to his old character, his former self. So he runs away from his obligations as one compelled to default; it's 'tails' this time instead of 'heads,' and he has to turn tail and rush away. But the boy must needs run after him, crying indignantly to high heaven, though from start to finish he has never understood that he ought not to have yielded to a lover inevitably devoid of reason, but far rather to one possessed of reason and not in love. He should have known that the wrong choice must mean surrendering himself to a faithless, peevish, jealous, and offensive captor, to one who would ruin his property, ruin his physique, and above all ruin his spiritual development, which is assuredly and ever will be of supreme value in the sight of gods and men alike.

Let that then, my boy, be your lesson. Be sure that the attentions of a lover carry no good will; they are no more than a glutting of his appetite, for 'As wolf to lamb, so lover to his lad.'

There, I knew I should [break out into verse], Phaedrus. Not a word more shall you have from me; let that be the end of my discourse.

PHAEDRUS Why, I thought you were only halfway through and would have an equal amount to say about the nonlover, enumerating his good points and showing that he should be the favored suitor. Why is it, Socrates, that instead of that you break off?

SOCRATES My dear good man, haven't you noticed that I've got beyond dithyramb, and am breaking out into epic verse, despite my faultfinding? What do you suppose I shall do if I start extolling the other type? Don't you see that I shall clearly be possessed by those nymphs into whose clutches you deliberately threw me? I therefore tell you, in one short sentence, that to each evil for which I have abused the one party there is a corresponding good belonging to the other. So why waste words? All has been said that needs saying about them both. And that being so, my story can be left to the fate appropriate to it, and I will take myself off across the river here before you drive me to greater lengths.

PHAEDRUS Oh, but you must wait until it gets cooler, Socrates. Don't you realize that it's just about the hour of 'scorching noonday,' as the phrase goes? Let us wait and discuss what we've heard; when it has got cool perhaps we will go.

SOCRATES Phaedrus, your enthusiasm for discourse is sublime, and really moves me to admiration. Of the discourses pronounced during your lifetime no one, I fancy, has been responsible for more than you, whether by delivering them yourself or by compelling others to do so by one means or another—with one exception, Simmias of Thebes; you are well ahead of all the rest. And now it seems that once more you are the cause of my having to deliver myself.

PHAEDRUS It might be a lot worse! But how so? To what do you refer?

SOCRATES At the moment when I was about to cross the river, dear friend, there came to me my familiar divine sign—which always checks me when on the point of doing something or other—and all at once I seemed to hear a voice, forbidding me to leave the spot until I had made atonement for some offense to heaven. Now, you must know, I am a seer—not a very good one, it's true, but, like a poor scholar, good enough for my own purposes—hence I understand already well enough what my offense was. The fact is, you know, Phaedrus, the mind itself has a kind of divining power, for I felt disturbed some while ago as I was delivering that speech, and had a misgiving lest I might, in the words of Ibycus, 'By sinning in the sight of God win high renown from man.' But now I realize my sin.

PHAEDRUS   And what is it?

SOCRATES   That was a terrible theory, Phaedrus, a terrible theory that you introduced and compelled me to expound.

PHAEDRUS   How so?

SOCRATES   It was foolish, and somewhat blasphemous, and what could be more terrible that that?

PHAEDRUS   I agree, if it merits your description.

SOCRATES   Well, do you not hold Love to be a god, the child of Aphrodite?

PHAEDRUS   He is certainly said to be.

SOCRATES   But not according to Lysias, and not according to that discourse of yours which you caused my lips to utter by putting a spell on them. If Love is, as he is indeed, a god or a divine being, he cannot be an evil thing; yet this pair of speeches treated him as evil. That then was their offense toward Love, to which was added the most exquisite folly of parading their pernicious rubbish as though it were good sense because it might deceive a few miserable people and win their applause.

And so, my friend, I have to purify myself. Now for such as offend in speaking of gods and heroes there is an ancient mode of purification, which was known to Stesichorus, though not to Homer. When Stesichorus lost the sight of his eyes because of his defamation of Helen, he was not, like Homer, at a loss to know why. As a true artist he understood the reason, and promptly wrote the lines:

> False, false the tale.
> Thou never didst sail in the well-decked ships
> Nor come to the towers of Troy.

And after finishing the composition of his so-called palinode he straightway recovered his sight. Now it's here that I shall show greater wisdom than these poets. I shall attempt to make my due palinode to Love before any harm comes to me for my defamation of him, and no longer veiling my head for shame, but uncovered.

PHAEDRUS   Nothing you could say, Socrates, would please me more.

SOCRATES   Yes, dear Phaedrus, you understand how irreverent the two speeches were, the one in the book and that which followed. Suppose

we were being listened to by a man of generous and humane character, who loved or had once loved another such as himself. Suppose
he heard us saying that for some trifling cause lovers conceive bitter
hatred and a spirit of malice and injury toward their loved ones.
Wouldn't he be sure to think that we had been brought up among
the scum of the people and had never seen a case of noble love?
Wouldn't he utterly refuse to accept our vilification of Love?

PHAEDRUS Indeed, Socrates, he well might.

SOCRATES Then out of respect for him, and in awe of Love himself, I
should like to wash the bitter taste out of my mouth with a draught
of wholesome discourse, and my advice to Lysias is that he should
lose no time in telling us that, other things being equal, favor should
be accorded to the lover rather than to the nonlover.

PHAEDRUS Rest assured; that will be done. When you have delivered
your encomium of the lover, I shall most certainly make Lysias compose a new speech to the same purport.

SOCRATES I'm sure of that, so long as you continue to be the man you are.

PHAEDRUS Then you may confidently proceed.

SOCRATES Where is that boy I was talking to? He must listen to me
once more, and not rush off to yield to his nonlover before he hears
what I have to say.

PHAEDRUS Here he is, quite close beside you, whenever you want him.

SOCRATES Now you must understand, fair boy, that whereas the preceding discourse was by Phaedrus, son of Pythocles, of Myrrhinus, that
which I shall now pronounce is by Stesichorus, son of Euphemus, of
Himera. This then is how it must run.

'False is the tale' that when a lover is at hand favor ought rather
to be accorded to one who does not love, on the ground that the
former is mad, and the latter sound of mind. That would be right
if it were an invariable truth that madness is an evil, but in reality,
the greatest blessings come by way of madness, indeed of madness
that is heaven-sent. It was when they were mad that the prophetess
at Delphi and the priestesses at Dodona achieved so much for which
both states and individuals in Greece are thankful; when sane they did
little or nothing. As for the Sibyl and others who by the power of
inspired prophecy have so often foretold the future to so many, and
guided them aright, I need not dwell on what is obvious to everyone.
Yet it is in place to appeal to the fact that madness was accounted no
shame nor disgrace by the men of old who gave things their names;
otherwise they would not have connected that greatest of arts,
whereby the future is discerned, with this very word 'madness,' and
named it accordingly. No, it was because they held madness to be a
valuable gift, when due to divine dispensation, that they named that
art as they did, though the men of today, having no sense of values,

have put in an extra letter, making it not *manic* but *mantic*. That is borne out by the name they gave to the art of those sane prophets who inquire into the future by means of birds and other signs; the name was '*oionoistic*,' which by its components indicated that the prophet attained understanding and information by a purely human activity of thought belonging to his own intelligence, though a younger generation has come to call it '*oionistic*,' lengthening the quantity of the *o* to make it sound impressive. You see then what this ancient evidence attests. Corresponding to the superior perfection and value of the prophecy of inspiration over that of omen reading, both in name and in fact, is the superiority of heaven-sent madness over man-made sanity.

And in the second place, when grievous maladies and afflictions have beset certain families by reason of some ancient sin, madness has appeared among them, and breaking out into prophecy has secured relief by finding the means thereto, namely by recourse to prayer and worship, and in consequence thereof rites and means of purification were established, and the sufferer was brought out of danger, alike for the present and for the future. Thus did madness secure, for him that was maddened aright and possessed, deliverance from his troubles.

There is a third form of possession or madness, of which the Muses are the source. This seizes a tender, virgin soul and stimulates it to rapt passionate expression, especially in lyric poetry, glorifying the countless mighty deeds of ancient times for the instruction of posterity. But if any man come to the gates of poetry without the madness of the Muses, persuaded that skill alone will make him a good poet, then shall he and his works of sanity with him be brought to nought by the poetry of madness, and behold, their place is nowhere to be found.

Such then is the tale, though I have not told it fully, of the achievements wrought by madness that comes from the gods. So let us have no fears simply on that score; let us not be disturbed by an argument that seeks to scare us into preferring the friendship of the sane to that of the passionate. For there is something more that it must prove if it is to carry the day, namely that love is not a thing sent from heaven for the advantage both of lover and beloved. What we have to prove is the opposite, namely that this sort of madness is a gift of the gods, fraught with the highest bliss. And our proof assuredly will prevail with the wise, though not with the learned.

Now our first step toward attaining the truth of the matter is to discern the nature of soul, divine and human, its experiences, and its activities. Here then our proof begins.

All soul is immortal, for that which is ever in motion is immortal.

But that which while imparting motion is itself moved by something else can cease to be in motion, and therefore can cease to live; it is only that which moves itself that never intermits its motion, inasmuch as it cannot abandon its own nature; moreover this self-mover is the source and first principle of motion for all other things that are moved. Now a first principle cannot come into being, for while anything that comes to be must come to be from a first principle, the latter itself cannot come to be from anything whatsoever; if it did, it would cease any longer to be a first principle. Furthermore, since it does not come into being, it must be imperishable, for assuredly if a first principle were to be destroyed, nothing could come to be out of it, nor could anything bring the principle itself back into existence, seeing that a first principle is needed for anything to come into being.

The self-mover, then, is the first principle of motion, and it is as impossible that it should be destroyed as that it should come into being; were it otherwise, the whole universe, the whole of that which comes to be, would collapse into immobility, and never find another source of motion to bring it back into being.

And now that we have seen that that which is moved by itself is immortal, we shall feel no scruple in affirming that precisely that is the essence and definition of soul, to wit, self-motion. Any body that has an external source of motion is soulless, but a body deriving its motion from a source within itself is animate or *besouled*, which implies that the nature of soul is what has been said.

And if this last assertion is correct, namely that 'that which moves itself' is precisely identifiable with soul, it must follow that soul is not born and does not die.

As to soul's immortality then we have said enough, but as to its nature there is this that must be said. What manner of thing it is would be a long tale to tell, and most assuredly a god alone could tell it, but what it resembles, that a man might tell in briefer compass. Let this therefore be our manner of discourse. Let it be likened to the union of powers in a team of winged steeds and their winged charioteer. Now all the gods' steeds and all their charioteers are good, and of good stock, but with other beings it is not wholly so. With us men, in the first place, it is a pair of steeds that the charioteer controls; moreover one of them is noble and good, and of good stock, while the other has the opposite character, and his stock is opposite. Hence the task of our charioteer is difficult and troublesome.

And now we must essay to tell how it is that living beings are called mortal and immortal. All soul has the care of all that is inanimate, and traverses the whole universe, though in ever-changing forms. Thus when it is perfect and winged it journeys on high and controls the whole world, but one that has shed its wings sinks down

The Theory of Rhetoric

until it can fasten on something solid, and settling there it takes to itself an earthy body which seems by reason of the soul's power to move itself. This composite structure of soul and body is called a living being, and is further termed 'mortal'; 'immortal' is a term applied on no basis of reasoned argument at all, but our fancy pictures the god whom we have never seen, nor fully conceived, as an immortal living being, possessed of a soul and a body united for all time. Howbeit, let these matters, and our account thereof, be as God pleases; what we must understand is the reason why the soul's wings fall from it, and are lost. It is on this wise.

The natural property of a wing is to raise that which is heavy and carry it aloft to the region where the gods dwell, and more than any other bodily part it shares in the divine nature, which is fair, wise, and good, and possessed of all other such excellences. Now by these excellences especially is the soul's plumage nourished and fostered, while by their opposites, even by ugliness and evil, it is wasted and destroyed. And behold, there in the heaven Zeus, mighty leader, drives his winged team. First of the host of gods and daemons he proceeds, ordering all things and caring therefor, and the host follows after him, marshaled in eleven companies. For Hestia abides alone in the gods' dwelling place, but for the rest, all such as are ranked in the number of the twelve as ruler gods lead their several companies, each according to his rank.

Now within the heavens are many spectacles of bliss upon the highways whereon the blessed gods pass to and fro, each doing his own work, and with them are all such as will and can follow them, for jealousy has no place in the choir divine. But at such times as they go to their feasting and banquet, behold they climb the steep ascent even unto the summit of the arch that supports the heavens, and easy is that ascent for the chariots of the gods, for they are well balanced and readily guided. But for the others it is hard, by reason of the heaviness of the steed of wickedness, which pulls down his driver with his weight, except that driver have schooled him well.

And now there awaits the soul the extreme of her toil and struggling. For the souls that are called immortal, so soon as they are at the summit, come forth and stand upon the back of the world, and straightway the revolving heaven carries them round, and they look upon the regions without.

Of that place beyond the heavens none of our earthly poets has yet sung, and none shall sing worthily. But this is the manner of it, for assuredly we must be bold to speak what is true, above all when our discourse is upon truth. It is there that true being dwells, without color or shape, that cannot be touched; reason alone, the soul's pilot, can behold it, and all true knowledge is knowledge thereof. Now even as the mind of a god is nourished by reason and knowledge, so also is it with every soul that has a care to receive her proper food; wherefore when at last she has beheld being she is well content, and contemplating truth she is nourished and prospers, until the heaven's revolution brings her back full circle. And while she is borne round she discerns justice, its very self, and likewise temperance, and knowledge, not the knowledge that is neighbor to becoming and varies with the various objects to which we commonly ascribe being, but the veritable knowledge of being that veritably is. And when she has contemplated likewise and feasted upon all else that has true being, she descends again within the heavens and comes back home. And having so come, her charioteer sets his steeds at their manger, and puts ambrosia before them and draught of nectar to drink withal.

Such is the life of gods. Of the other souls that which best follows a god and becomes most like thereunto raises her charioteer's head into the outer region, and is carried round with the gods in the revolution, but being confounded by her steeds she has much ado to discern the things that are; another now rises, and now sinks, and by reason of her unruly steeds sees in part, but in part sees not. As for the rest, though all are eager to reach the heights and seek to follow, they are not able; sucked down as they travel they trample and tread upon one another, this one striving to outstrip that. Thus confusion ensues, and conflict and grievous sweat. Whereupon, with their charioteers powerless, many are lamed, and many have their wings all broken, and for all their toiling they are balked, every one, of the full vision of being, and departing therefrom, they feed upon the food of semblance.

Now the reason wherefore the souls are fain and eager to behold the plain of Truth, and discover it, lies herein—to wit, that the pasturage that is proper to their noblest part comes from that meadow, and the plumage by which they are borne aloft is nourished thereby.

Hear now the ordinance of Necessity. Whatsoever soul has followed in the train of a god, and discerned something of truth, shall be kept from sorrow until a new revolution shall begin, and if she can do this always, she shall remain always free from hurt. But when she is not able so to follow, and sees none of it, but meeting with some mischance comes to be burdened with a load of forgetfulness and wrongdoing, and because of that burden sheds her wings and falls to the earth, then thus runs the law. In her first birth she shall not be planted in any brute beast, but the soul that hath seen the most of being shall enter into the human babe that shall grow into a seeker after wisdom or beauty, a follower of the Muses and a lover; the next, having seen less, shall dwell in a king that abides by law, or a warrior and ruler; the third in a statesman, a man of business, or a trader; the

fourth in an athlete, or physical trainer, or physician; the fifth shall
have the life of a prophet or a Mystery priest; to the sixth that of a
poet or other imitative artist shall be fittingly given; the seventh shall
live in an artisan or farmer; the eighth in a Sophist or demagogue;
the ninth in a tyrant.

Now in all these incarnations he who lives righteously has a better
lot for his portion, and he who lives unrighteously a worse. For a
soul does not return to the place whence she came for ten thousand
years, since in no lesser time can she regain her wings, save only his
soul who has sought after wisdom unfeignedly, or has conjoined his
passion for a loved one with that seeking. Such a soul, if with three
revolutions of a thousand years she has thrice chosen this philosophical life, regains thereby her wings, and speeds away after three thousand years; but the rest, when they have accomplished their first life,
are brought to judgment, and after the judgment some are taken to be
punished in places of chastisement beneath the earth, while others are
borne aloft by Justice to a certain region of the heavens, there to live
in such manner as is merited by their past life in the flesh. And after
a thousand years these and those alike come to the allotment and
choice of their second life, each choosing according to her will; then
does the soul of a man enter into the life of a beast, and the beast's
soul that was aforetime in a man goes back to a man again. For only
the soul that has beheld truth may enter into this our human form—
seeing that man must needs understand the language of forms, passing from a plurality of perceptions to a unity gathered together by
reasoning—and such understanding is a recollection of those things
which our souls beheld aforetime as they journeyed with their god,
looking down upon the things which now we suppose to be, and gazing up to that which truly is.

Therefore is it meet and right that the soul of the philosopher
alone should recover her wings, for she, so far as may be, is ever near
in memory to those things a god's nearness whereunto makes him
truly god. Wherefore if a man makes right use of such means of
remembrance, and ever approaches to the full vision of the perfect
mysteries, he and he alone becomes truly perfect. Standing aside from
the busy doings of mankind, and drawing nigh to the divine, he is
rebuked by the multitude as being out of his wits, for they know not
that he is possessed by a deity.

Mark therefore the sum and substance of all our discourse touching
the fourth sort of madness—to wit, that this is the best of all forms
of divine possession, both in itself and in its sources, both for him
that has it and for him that shares therein—and when he that loves
beauty is touched by such madness he is called a lover. Such a one,
as soon as he beholds the beauty of this world, is reminded of true

beauty, and his wings begin to grow; then is he fain to lift his wings and fly upward; yet he has not the power, but inasmuch as he gazes upward like a bird, and cares nothing for the world beneath, men charge it upon him that he is demented.

Now, as we have said, every human soul has, by reason of her nature, had contemplation of true being; else would she never have entered into this human creature; but to be put in mind thereof by things here is not easy for every soul. Some, when they had the vision, had it but for a moment; some when they had fallen to earth consorted unhappily with such as led them to deeds of unrighteousness, wherefore they forgot the holy objects of their vision. Few indeed are left that can still remember much, but when these discern some likeness of the things yonder, they are amazed, and no longer masters of themselves, and know not what is come upon them by reason of their perception being dim.

Now in the earthly likenesses of justice and temperance and all other prized possessions of the soul there dwells no luster; nay, so dull are the organs wherewith men approach their images that hardly can a few behold that which is imaged, but with beauty it is otherwise. Beauty it was ours to see in all its brightness in those days when, amidst that happy company, we beheld with our eyes that blessed vision, ourselves in the train of Zeus, others following some other god; then were we all initiated into that mystery which is rightly accounted blessed beyond all others; whole and unblemished were we that did celebrate it, untouched by the evils that awaited us in days to come; whole and unblemished likewise, free from all alloy, steadfast and blissful were the spectacles on which we gazed in the moment of final revelation; pure was the light that shone around us, and pure were we, without taint of that prison house which now we are encompassed withal, and call a body, fast bound therein as an oyster in its shell.

There let it rest then, our tribute to a memory that has stirred us to linger awhile on those former joys for which we yearn. Now beauty, as we said, shone bright amidst these visions, and in this world below we apprehend it through the clearest of our senses, clear and resplendent. For sight is the keenest mode of perception vouchsafed us through the body; wisdom, indeed, we cannot see thereby—how passionate had been our desire for her, if she had granted us so clear an image of herself to gaze upon—nor yet any other of those beloved objects, save only beauty; for beauty alone this has been ordained, to be most manifest to sense and most lovely of them all.

Now he whose vision of the mystery is long past, or whose purity has been sullied, cannot pass swiftly hence to see beauty's self yonder, when he beholds that which is called beautiful here; wherefore he looks upon it with no reverence, and surrendering to pleasure he essays to go after the fashion of a four-footed beast, and to beget offspring of the flesh, or consorting with wantonness he has no fear nor shame in running after unnatural pleasure. But when one who is fresh from the mystery, and saw much of the vision, beholds a godlike face or bodily form that truly expresses beauty, first there come upon him a shuddering and a measure of that awe which the vision inspired, and then reverence as at the sight of god, and but for fear of being deemed a very madman he would offer sacrifice to his beloved, as to a holy image of deity. Next, with the passing of the shudder, a strange sweating and fever seizes him. For by reason of the stream of beauty entering in through his eyes there comes a warmth, whereby his soul's plumage is fostered, and with that warmth the roots of the wings are melted, which for long had been so hardened and closed up that nothing could grow; then as the nourishment is poured in, the stump of the wing swells and hastens to grow from the root over the whole substance of the soul, for aforetime the whole soul was furnished with wings. Meanwhile she throbs with ferment in every part, and even as a teething child feels an aching and pain in its gums when a tooth has just come through, so does the soul of him who is beginning to grow his wings feel a ferment and painful irritation. Wherefore as she gazes upon the boy's beauty, she admits a flood of particles streaming therefrom—that is why we speak of a 'flood of passion'—whereby she is warmed and fostered; then has she respite from her anguish, and is filled with joy. But when she has been parted from him and become parched, the openings of those outlets at which the wings are sprouting dry up likewise and are closed, so that the wing's germ is barred off. And behind its bars, together with the flood aforesaid, it throbs like a fevered pulse, and pricks at its proper outlet, and thereat the whole soul round about is stung and goaded into anguish; howbeit she remembers the beauty of her beloved, and rejoices again. So between joy and anguish she is distraught at being in such strange case, perplexed and frenzied; with madness upon her she can neither sleep by night nor keep still by day, but runs hither and thither, yearning for him in whom beauty dwells, if haply she may behold him. At last she does behold him, and lets the flood pour in upon her, releasing the imprisoned waters; then has she refreshment and respite from her stings and sufferings, and at that moment tastes a pleasure that is sweet beyond compare. Nor will she willingly give it up. Above all others does she esteem her beloved in his beauty; mother, brother, friends, she forgets them all. Nought does she reck of losing worldly possessions through neglect. All the rules of conduct, all the graces of life, of which aforetime she was proud, she now disdains, welcoming a slave's estate and any couch where she may be suffered to lie down close beside her darling, for besides her reverence for the possessor of beauty she has found in him the only physician for her grievous suffering.

Hearken, fair boy to whom I speak. This is the experience that men term love (ἔρως), but when you hear what the gods call it, you will probably smile at its strangeness. There are a couple of verses on love quoted by certain Homeric scholars from the unpublished works, the second of which is remarkably bold and a trifle astray in its quantities. They run as follows:

> Eros, cleaver of air, in mortals' speech is he named,
> But, since he must grow wings, Pteros the celestials call him.

You may believe that or not, as you please; at all events the cause and the nature of the lover's experience are in fact what I have said.

Now if he whom Love has caught be among the followers of Zeus, he is able to bear the burden of the winged one with some constancy, but they that attend upon Ares, and did range the heavens in his train, when they are caught by Love and fancy that their beloved is doing them some injury, will shed blood and not scruple to offer both themselves and their loved ones in sacrifice. And so does each lover live, after the manner of the god in whose company he once was, honoring him and copying him so far as may be, so long as he remains uncorrupt and is still living in his first earthly period, and in like manner does he comport himself toward his beloved and all his other associates. And so each selects a fair one for his love after his disposition, and even as if the beloved himself were a god he fashions for himself as it were an image, and adorns it to be the object of his veneration and worship.

Thus the followers of Zeus seek a beloved who is Zeuslike in soul; wherefore they look for one who is by nature disposed to the love of wisdom and the leading of men, and when they have found him and come to love him they do all in their power to foster that disposition. And if they have not aforetime trodden this path, they now set out upon it, learning the way from any source that may offer or finding it for themselves, and as they follow up the trace within themselves of the nature of their own god their task is made easier, inasmuch as they are constrained to fix their gaze upon him, and reaching out after him in memory they are possessed by him, and from him they take their ways and manners of life, in so far as a man can partake of a god. But all this, mark you, they attribute to the beloved, and the draughts which they draw from Zeus they pour out, like bacchants, into the soul of the beloved, thus creating in him the closest possible likeness to the god they worship.

Those who were in the train of Hera look for a royal nature, and when they have found him they do unto him all things in like fashion. And so it is with the followers of Apollo and each other god. Every lover is fain that his beloved should be of a nature like to his own god, and when he has won him, he leads him on to walk in the ways of their god, and after his likeness, patterning himself thereupon and giving counsel and discipline to the boy. There is no jealousy nor petty spitefulness in his dealings, but his every act is aimed at bringing the beloved to be every whit like unto himself and unto the god of their worship.

So therefore glorious and blissful is the endeavor of true lovers in that mystery rite, if they accomplish that which they endeavor after the fashion of which I speak, when mutual affection arises through the madness inspired by love. But the beloved must needs be captured, and the manner of that capture I will now tell.

In the beginning of our story we divided each soul into three parts, two being like steeds and the third like a charioteer. Well and good. Now of the steeds, so we declare, one is good and the other is not, but we have not described the excellence of the one nor the badness of the other, and that is what must now be done. He that is on the more honorable side is upright and clean-limbed, carrying his neck high, with something of a hooked nose; in color he is white, with black eyes; a lover of glory, but with temperance and modesty; one that consorts with genuine renown, and needs no whip, being driven by the word of command alone. The other is crooked of frame, a massive jumble of a creature, with thick short neck, snub nose, black skin, and gray eyes; hot-blooded, consorting with wantonness and vainglory; shaggy of ear, deaf, and hard to control with whip and goad.

Now when the driver beholds the person of the beloved, and causes a sensation of warmth to suffuse the whole soul, he begins to experience a tickling or pricking of desire, and the obedient steed, constrained now as always by modesty, refrains from leaping upon the beloved. But his fellow, heeding no more the driver's goad or whip, leaps and dashes on, sorely troubling his companion and his driver, and forcing them to approach the loved one and remind him of the delights of love's commerce. For a while they struggle, indignant that he should force them to a monstrous and forbidden act, but at last, finding no end to their evil plight, they yield and agree to do his bidding. And so he draws them on, and now they are quite close and behold the spectacle of the beloved flashing upon them. At that sight the driver's memory goes back to that form of beauty, and he sees her once again enthroned by the side of temperance upon her holy seat; then in awe and reverence he falls upon his back, and therewith is compelled to pull the reins so violently that he brings both steeds down on their haunches, the good one willing and unresistant, but the wanton sore against his will. Now that they are a little way off, the good horse in shame and horror drenches the whole soul with sweat, while the other, contriving to recover his wind after the pain of the bit and his fall, bursts into angry abuse, railing at the charioteer and his yokefellow as cowardly treacherous deserters. Once again he tries to force them to advance, and when they beg him to delay awhile he grudgingly consents. But when the time appointed is come, and they feign to have forgotten, he reminds them of it—struggling and neighing and pulling until he compels them a second time to approach the beloved and renew their offer—and when they have come close, with head down and tail stretched out he takes the bit between his teeth and shamelessly plunges on. But the driver, with resentment even stronger than before, like a racer recoiling from the starting rope, jerks back the bit in the mouth of the wanton horse with an even stronger pull, bespatters his railing tongue and his jaws with blood, and forcing him down on legs and haunches delivers him over to anguish.

And so it happens time and again, until the evil steed casts off his wantonness; humbled in the end, he obeys the counsel of his driver, and when he sees the fair beloved is like to die of fear. Wherefore at long last the soul of the lover follows after the beloved with reverence and awe.

Thus the loved one receives all manner of service, as peer of the gods, from a lover that is no pretender but loves in all sincerity; of his own nature, too, he is kindly disposed to him who pays such service. Now it may be that in time past he has been misled, by his schoolfellows or others, who told him that it is shameful to have commerce with a lover, and by reason of this he may repel his advances. Nevertheless as time goes on ripening age and the ordinance of destiny together lead him to welcome the other's society, for assuredly fate does not suffer one evil man to be friend to another, nor yet one good man to lack the friendship of another.

And now that he has come to welcome his lover and to take pleasure in his company and converse, it comes home to him what a depth of kindliness he has found, and he is filled with amazement, for he perceives that all his other friends and kinsmen have nothing to offer in comparison with this friend in whom there dwells a god. So as he continues in this converse and society, and comes close to his lover in the gymnasium and elsewhere, that flowing stream which Zeus, as the lover of Ganymede, called the 'flood of passion,' pours in upon the lover. And part of it is absorbed within him, but when he can contain no more the rest flows away outside him, and as a breath of wind or an echo, rebounding from a smooth hard surface, goes back to its place of origin, even so the stream of beauty turns back and reenters the eyes of the fair beloved. And so by the natural channel it reaches his soul and gives it fresh vigor, watering the roots of the wings and quickening them to growth, whereby the soul of the beloved, in its turn, is filled with love. So he loves, yet knows not what he loves; he does not understand, he cannot tell what has come upon him; like one that has caught a disease of the eye from another, he cannot account for it, not realizing that his lover is as it were a mirror in which he beholds himself. And when the other is beside him, he shares his respite from anguish; when he is absent, he likewise shares his longing and being longed for, since he possesses that counterlove which is the image of love, though he supposes it to be friendship rather than love, and calls it by that name. He feels a desire—like the lover's, yet not so strong—to behold, to touch, to kiss him, to share his couch, and now ere long the desire, as one might guess, leads to the act.

So when they lie side by side, the wanton horse of the lover's soul would have a word with the charioteer, claiming a little guerdon for all his trouble. The like steed in the soul of the beloved has no word to say, but, swelling with desire for he knows not what, embraces and kisses the lover, in grateful acknowledgment of all his kindness. And when they lie by one another, he is minded not to refuse to do his part in gratifying his lover's entreaties; yet his yokefellow in turn, being moved by reverence and heedfulness, joins with the driver in resisting. And so, if the victory be won by the higher elements of mind guiding them into the ordered rule of the philosophical life, their days on earth will be blessed with happiness and concord, for the power of evil in the soul has been subjected, and the power of goodness liberated; they have won self-mastery and inward peace. And when life is over, with burden shed and wings recovered they stand victorious in the first of the three rounds in that truly Olympic struggle; nor can any nobler prize be secured whether by the wisdom that is of man or by the madness that is of god.

But if they turn to a way of life more ignoble and unphilosophical, yet covetous of honor, then mayhap in a careless hour, or when the wine is flowing, the wanton horses in their two souls will catch them off their guard, bring the pair together, and choosing that part which the multitude account blissful achieve their full desire. And this once done, they continue therein, albeit but rarely, seeing that their minds are not wholly set thereupon. Such a pair as this also are dear friends, but not so dear as that other pair, one to another, both in the time of their love and when love is past, for they feel that they have exchanged the most binding pledges, which it were a sin to break by becoming enemies. When death comes they quit the body wingless indeed, yet eager to be winged, and therefore they carry off no mean reward for their lovers' madness, for it is ordained that all such as have taken the first steps on the celestial highway shall no more return to the dark pathways beneath the earth, but shall walk together in a life of shining bliss, and be furnished in due time with like plumage the one to the other, because of their love.

These then, my boy, are the blessings great and glorious which will come to you from the friendship of a lover. He who is not a lover can offer a mere acquaintance flavored with worldly wisdom, dispensing a niggardly measure of worldly goods; in the soul to which he is attached he will engender an ignoble quality extolled by the multitude as virtue, and condemn it to float for nine thousand years hither and thither, around the earth and beneath it, bereft of understanding.

Thus then, dear god of love, I have offered the fairest recantation and fullest atonement that my powers could compass; some of its language, in particular, was perforce poetical, to please Phaedrus. Grant me thy pardon for what went before, and thy favor for what ensued; be merciful and gracious, and take not from me the lover's talent wherewith thou hast blessed me; neither let it wither by reasson of thy displeasure, but grant me still to increase in the esteem of the fair. And if anything that Phaedrus and I said earlier sounded discordant to thy ear, set it down to Lysias, the only begetter of that discourse, and staying him from discourses after this fashion turn him toward the love of wisdom, even as his brother Polemarchus has been turned. Then will his loving disciple here present no longer halt between two opinions, as now he does, but live for Love in singleness of purpose with the aid of philosophical discourse.

PHAEDRUS If that be for our good, Socrates, I join in your prayer for it. And I have this long while been filled with admiration for your speech as a far finer achievement than the one you made before. It makes me afraid that I shall find Lysias cutting a poor figure, if he proves to be willing to compete with another speech of his own. The fact is that only the other day, my dear good sir, one of our politicians was railing at him and reproaching him on this very score, constantly dubbing him a 'speech writer'; so possibly we shall find him desisting from further composition to preserve his reputation.

SOCRATES What a ridiculous line to take, young man! And how utterly you misjudge our friend, if you suppose him to be such a timid creature! Am I to believe you really do think that the person you speak of meant his raillery as a reproach?

PHAEDRUS He gave me that impression, Socrates, and of course you know as well as I do that the men of greatest influence and dignity in political life are reluctant to write speeches and bequeath to posterity compositions of their own, for fear of the verdict of later ages, which might pronounce them Sophists.

SOCRATES Phaedrus, you are unaware that the expression 'Pleasant Bend' comes from the long bend in the Nile, and besides the matter of the Bend you are unaware that the proudest of politicians have the strongest desire to write speeches and bequeath compositions; why, whenever they write a speech, they are so pleased to have admirers that they put in a special clause at the beginning with the names of the persons who admire the speech in question.

PHAEDRUS What do you mean? I don't understand.

SOCRATES You don't understand that when a politician begins a composition the first thing he writes is the name of his admirer.

PHAEDRUS Is it?

SOCRATES Yes, he says maybe, 'Resolved by the Council' or 'by the people' or by both, and then 'Proposed by so-and-so'—a pompous piece of self-advertisement on the part of the author—after which he proceeds with what he has to say, showing off his own wisdom to his admirers, sometimes in a very lengthy composition. This sort of thing amounts, don't you think, to composing a speech?

PHAEDRUS Yes, I think it does.

SOCRATES Then if the speech holds its ground, the author quits the scene rejoicing, but if it is blotted out, and he loses his status as a recognized speech writer, he goes into mourning, and his friends with him.

PHAEDRUS Quite so.

SOCRATES Which clearly implies that their attitude to the profession is not one of disdain, but of admiration.

PHAEDRUS To be sure.

SOCRATES Tell me then, when an orator, or a king, succeeds in acquiring the power of a Lycurgus, a Solon, or a Darius, and so winning immortality among his people as a speech writer, doesn't he deem himself a peer of the gods while still living, and do not people of later ages hold the same opinion of him when they contemplate his writings?

PHAEDRUS Yes, indeed.

SOCRATES Then do you suppose that anyone of that type, whoever he might be, and whatever his animosity toward Lysias, could reproach him simply on the ground that he writes?

PHAEDRUS What you say certainly makes that improbable, for apparently he would be reproaching what he wanted to do himself.

SOCRATES Then the conclusion is obvious, that there is nothing shameful in the mere writing of speeches.

PHAEDRUS Of course.

SOCRATES But in speaking and writing shamefully and badly, instead of as one should, that is where the shame comes in, I take it.

PHAEDRUS Clearly.

SOCRATES Then what is the nature of good writing and bad? Is it incumbent on us, Phaedrus, to examine Lysias on this point, and all such as have written or mean to write anything at all, whether in the field of public affairs or private, whether in the verse of the poet or the plain speech of prose?

PHAEDRUS Is it incumbent! Why, life itself would hardly be worth living save for pleasure like this—certainly not for those pleasures that involve previous pain, as do almost all concerned with the body, which for that reason are rightly called slavish.

SOCRATES Well, I suppose we can spare the time, and I think too that the cicadas overhead, singing after their wont in the hot sun and conversing with one another, don't fail to observe us as well. So if they were to see us two behaving like ordinary folk at midday, not conversing but dozing lazy-minded under their spell, they would very properly have the laugh of us, taking us for a pair of slaves that had invaded their retreat like sheep, to have their midday sleep beside the spring. If however they see us conversing and steering clear of their bewitching Siren song, they might feel respect for us and grant us that boon which heaven permits them to confer upon mortals.

PHAEDRUS Oh, what is that? I don't think I have heard of it.

SOCRATES Surely it is unbecoming in a devotee of the Muses not to have heard of a thing like that! The story is that once upon a time these creatures were men—men of an age before there were any Muses—and that when the latter came into the world, and music made its appearance, some of the people of those days were so thrilled with pleasure that they went on singing, and quite forgot to eat and drink until they actually died without noticing it. From them in due course sprang the race of cicadas, to which the Muses have granted the boon of needing no sustenance right from their birth, but of singing from the very first, without food or drink, until the day of their death, after which they go and report to the Muses how they severally are paid honor among mankind, and by whom. So for those whom they report as having honored Terpsichore in the dance they win that Muse's favor, for those that have worshiped in the rites of love the favor of Erato, and so with all the others, according to the nature of the worship paid to each. To the eldest, Calliope, and to her next sister, Urania, they tell of those who live a life of philosophy and so do honor to the music of those twain whose theme is the heavens and all the story of gods and men, and whose song is the noblest of them all.

Thus there is every reason for us not to yield to slumber in the noontide, but to pursue our talk.

PHAEDRUS Of course we must pursue it.

SOCRATES Well, the subject we proposed for inquiry just now was the nature of good and bad speaking and writing; so we are to inquire into that.

PHAEDRUS Plainly.

SOCRATES Then does not a good and successful discourse presuppose a knowledge in the mind of the speaker of the truth about his subject?

PHAEDRUS As to that, dear Socrates, what I have heard is that the intending orator is under no necessity of understanding what is truly just, but only what is likely to be thought just by the body of men who are to give judgment; nor need he know what is truly good or noble, but what will be thought so, since it is on the latter, not the former, that persuasion depends.

SOCRATES 'Not to be lightly rejected,' Phaedrus, is any word of the wise. Perhaps they are right; one has to see. And in particular this present assertion must not be dismissed.

PHAEDRUS I agree.

SOCRATES Well, here is my suggestion for discussion.

PHAEDRUS Yes?

SOCRATES Suppose I tried to persuade you to acquire a horse to use in battle against the enemy, and suppose that neither of us knew what a horse was, but I knew this much about you, that Phaedrus believes a horse to be that tame animal which possesses the largest ears.

PHAEDRUS A ridiculous thing to suppose, Socrates.

SOCRATES Wait a moment. Suppose I continued to urge upon you in all seriousness, with a studied encomium of a donkey, that it was what I called it, a horse, that it was highly important for you to possess the creature, both at home and in the field, that it was just the animal to ride on into battle, and that it was handy, into the bargain, for carrying your equipment and so forth.

PHAEDRUS To go to that length would be utterly ridiculous.

SOCRATES Well, isn't it better to be a ridiculous friend than a clever enemy?

PHAEDRUS I suppose it is.

SOCRATES Then when a master of oratory, who is ignorant of good and evil, employs his power of persuasion on a community as ignorant as himself, not by extolling a miserable donkey as being really a horse, but by extolling evil as being really good, and when by studying the beliefs of the masses he persuades them to do evil instead of good, what kind of crop do you think his oratory is likely to reap from the seed thus sown?

PHAEDRUS A pretty poor one.

SOCRATES Well now, my good friend, have we been too scurrilous in our abuse of the art of speech? Might it not retort, 'Why do you extraordinary people talk such nonsense? I never insist on ignorance of the truth on the part of one who would learn to speak; on the contrary, if my advice goes for anything, it is that he should only resort to me after he has come into possession of truth; what I do however pride myself on is that without my aid knowledge of what is true will get a man no nearer to mastering the art of persuasion.'

PHAEDRUS   And will not such a retort be just?

SOCRATES   Yes, if the arguments advanced against oratory sustain its claim to be an art. In point of fact, I fancy I can hear certain arguments advancing, and protesting that the claim is false, that it is no art, but a knack that has nothing to do with art, inasmuch as there is, as the Spartans put it, no 'soothfast' art of speech, nor assuredly will there ever be one, without a grasp of truth.

PHAEDRUS   We must have these arguments, Socrates. Come, bring them up before us, and examine their support.

SOCRATES   Come hither then, you worthy creatures, and impress upon Phaedrus, who is so blessed in his offspring, that unless he gets on with his philosophy he will never get on as a speaker on any subject, and let Phaedrus be your respondent.

PHAEDRUS   I await their questions.

SOCRATES   Must not the art of rhetoric, taken as a whole, be a kind of influencing of the mind by means of words, not only in courts of law and other public gatherings, but in private places also? And must it not be the same art that is concerned with great issues and small, its right employment commanding no more respect when dealing with important matters than with unimportant? Is that what you have been told about it?

PHAEDRUS   No indeed, not exactly that. It is principally, I should say, to lawsuits that an art of speaking and writing is applied—and of course to public harangues also. I know of no wider application.

SOCRATES   What? Are you acquainted only with the 'Arts' or manuals of oratory by Nestor and Odysseus, which they composed in their leisure hours at Troy? Have you never heard of the work of Palamedes?

PHAEDRUS   No, upon my word, nor of Nestor either, unless you are casting Gorgias for the role of Nestor, with Odysseus played by Thrasymachus, or maybe Theodorus.

SOCRATES   Perhaps I am. But anyway we may let them be, and do you tell me, what is it that the contending parties in law courts do? Do they not in fact contend with words, or how else should we put it?

PHAEDRUS   That is just what they do.

SOCRATES   About what is just and unjust?

PHAEDRUS   Yes.

SOCRATES   And he who possesses the art of doing this can make the same thing appear to the same people now just, now unjust, at will?

PHAEDRUS   To be sure.

SOCRATES   And in public harangues, no doubt, he can make the same things seem to the community now good, and now the reverse of good?

PHAEDRUS   Just so.

SOCRATES   Then can we fail to see that the Palamedes of Elea has an art of speaking, such that he can make the same things appear to his audience like and unlike, or one and many, or again at rest and in motion?

PHAEDRUS   Indeed he can.

SOCRATES   So contending with words is a practice found not only in lawsuits and public harangues but, it seems, wherever men speak we find this single art, if indeed it is an art, which enables people to make out everything to be like everything else, within the limits of possible comparison, and to expose the corresponding attempts of others who disguise what they are doing.

PHAEDRUS   How so, pray?

SOCRATES   I think that will become clear if we put the following question. Are we misled when the difference between two things is wide, or narrow?

PHAEDRUS   When it is narrow.

SOCRATES   Well then, if you shift your ground little by little, you are more likely to pass undetected from so-and-so to its opposite than if you do so at one bound.

PHAEDRUS   Of course.

SOCRATES   It follows that anyone who intends to mislead another, without being misled himself, must discern precisely the degree of resemblance and dissimilarity between this and that.

PHAEDRUS   Yes, that is essential.

SOCRATES   Then if he does not know the truth about a given thing, how is he going to discern the degree of resemblance between that unknown thing and other things?

PHAEDRUS   It will be impossible.

SOCRATES   Well now, when people hold beliefs contrary to fact, and are misled, it is plain that the error has crept into their minds through the suggestion of some similarity or other.

PHAEDRUS   That certainly does happen.

SOCRATES   But can anyone possibly master the art of using similarities for the purpose of bringing people round, and leading them away from the truth about this or that to the opposite of the truth, or again can anyone possibly avoid this happening to himself, unless he has knowledge of what the thing in question really is?

PHAEDRUS   No, never.

SOCRATES   It would seem to follow, my friend, that the art of speech displayed by one who has gone chasing after beliefs, instead of knowing the truth, will be a comical sort of art, in fact no art at all.

PHAEDRUS   I dare say.

SOCRATES Then would you like to observe some instances of what I call the presence and absence of art in that speech of Lysias which you are carrying, and in those which I have delivered?

PHAEDRUS Yes, by all means. At present our discussion is somewhat abstract, for want of adequate illustrations.

SOCRATES Why, as to that it seems a stroke of luck that in the two speeches we have a sort of illustration of the way in which one who knows the truth can mislead his audience by playing an oratorical joke on them. I myself, Phaedrus, put that down to the local deities, or perhaps those mouthpieces of the Muses that are chirping over our heads have vouchsafed us their inspiration, for of course I don't lay claim to any oratorical skill myself.

PHAEDRUS I dare say that is so, but please explain your point.

SOCRATES Well, come along, read the beginning of Lysias' speech.

PHAEDRUS 'You know how I am situated, and I have told you that I think it to our advantage that the thing should be done. Now I claim that I should not be refused what I ask simply because I am not your lover. Lovers repent when ...'

SOCRATES Stop. Our business is to indicate where the speaker is at fault, and shows absence of art, isn't it?

PHAEDRUS Yes.

SOCRATES Well now, is not the following assertion obviously true—that there are some words about which we all agree, and others about which we are at variance?

PHAEDRUS I think I grasp your meaning, but you might make it still plainer.

SOCRATES When someone utters the word 'iron' or 'silver,' we all have the same object before our minds, haven't we?

PHAEDRUS Certainly.

SOCRATES But what about the words 'just' and 'good'? Don't we diverge, and dispute not only with one another but with our own selves?

PHAEDRUS Yes indeed.

SOCRATES So in some cases we agree, and in others we don't.

PHAEDRUS Quite so.

SOCRATES Now in which of the cases are we more apt to be misled, and in which is rhetoric more effective?

PHAEDRUS Plainly in the case where we fluctuate.

SOCRATES Then the intending student of the art of rhetoric ought, in the first place, to make a systematic division of words, and get hold of some mark distinguishing the two kinds of words, those namely in the use of which the multitude are bound to fluctuate, and those in which they are not.

PHAEDRUS To grasp that, Socrates, would certainly be an excellent piece of discernment.

SOCRATES   And secondly, I take it, when he comes across a particular word he must realize what it is, and be swift to perceive which of the two kinds the thing he proposes to discuss really belongs to.

PHAEDRUS   To be sure.

SOCRATES   Well then, shall we reckon love as one of the disputed terms, or as one of the other sort?

PHAEDRUS   As a disputed term, surely. Otherwise can you suppose it would have been possible for you to say of it what you said just now, namely that it is harmful both to the beloved and the lover, and then to turn round and say that it is really the greatest of goods?

SOCRATES   An excellent point. But now tell me this, for thanks to my inspired condition I can't quite remember. Did I define love at the beginning of my speech?

PHAEDRUS   Yes indeed, and immensely thorough you were about it.

SOCRATES   Upon my word, you rate the nymphs of Achelous and Pan, son of Hermes, much higher as artists in oratory than Lysias, son of Cephalus. Or am I quite wrong? Did Lysias at the beginning of his discourse on love compel us to conceive of it as a certain definite entity, with a meaning he had himself decided upon? And did he proceed to bring all his subsequent remarks, from first to last, into line with that meaning? Shall we read his first words once again?

PHAEDRUS   If you like, but what you are looking for isn't there.

SOCRATES   Read it out, so that I can listen to the author himself.

PHAEDRUS   'You know how I am situated, and I have told you that I think it to our advantage that the thing should be done. Now I claim that I should not be refused what I ask simply because I am not your lover. Lovers, when their craving is at an end, repent of such benefits as they have conferred.'

SOCRATES   No, he doesn't seem to get anywhere near what we are looking for; he goes about it like a man swimming on his back, in reverse, and starts from the end instead of the beginning; his opening words are what the lover would naturally say to his boy only when he had finished. Or am I quite wrong, dear Phaedrus?

PHAEDRUS   I grant you, Socrates, that the substance of his address is really a peroration.

SOCRATES   And to pass to other points, doesn't his matter strike you as thrown out at haphazard? Do you find any cogent reason for his next remark, or indeed any of his remarks, occupying the place it does? I myself, in my ignorance, thought that the writer, with a fine abandon, put down just what came into his head. Can you find any cogent principle of composition which he observed in setting down his observations in this particular order?

PHAEDRUS   You flatter me in supposing that I am competent to see into his mind with all that accuracy.

Plato

SOCRATES   Well, there is one point at least which I think you will admit, namely that any discourse ought to be constructed like a living creature, with its own body, as it were; it must not lack either head or feet; it must have a middle and extremities so composed as to suit each other and the whole work.

PHAEDRUS   Of course.

SOCRATES   Then ask yourself whether that is or is not the case with your friend's speech. You will find that it is just like the epitaph said to have been carved on the tomb of Midas the Phrygian.

PHAEDRUS   What is that, and what's wrong with it?

SOCRATES   It runs like this:

> A maid of bronze I stand on Midas' tomb,
> So long as waters flow and trees grow tall,
> Abiding here on his lamented grave,
> I tell the traveler Midas here is laid.

I expect you notice that it makes no difference what order the lines come in.

PHAEDRUS   Socrates, you are making a joke of our speech!

SOCRATES   Well, to avoid distressing you, let us say no more of that—though indeed I think it provides many examples which it would be profitable to notice, provided one were chary of imitating them—and let us pass to the other speeches, for they, I think, presented a certain feature which everyone desirous of examining oratory would do well to observe.

PHAEDRUS   To what do you refer?

SOCRATES   They were of opposite purport, one maintaining that the lover should be favored, the other the nonlover.

PHAEDRUS   Yes, they did so very manfully.

SOCRATES   I thought you were going to say—and with truth—madly, but that reminds me of what I was about to ask. We said, did we not, that love is a sort of madness?

PHAEDRUS   Yes.

SOCRATES   And that there are two kinds of madness, one resulting from human ailments, the other from a divine disturbance of our conventions of conduct.

PHAEDRUS   Quite so.

SOCRATES   And in the divine kind we distinguished four types, ascribing them to four gods: the inspiration of the prophet to Apollo, that of the mystic to Dionysus, that of the poet to the Muses, and a fourth type which we declared to be the highest, the madness of the lover, to Aphrodite and Eros. Moreover we painted, after a fashion, a picture of the lover's experience, in which perhaps we attained some degree of truth, though we may well have sometimes gone astray—the blend resulting in a discourse which had some claim to plausibility, or shall we say a mythical hymn of praise, in due religious language, a festal celebration of my master and yours too, Phaedrus, that god of love who watches over the young and fair.

PHAEDRUS   It certainly gave me great pleasure to listen to it.

SOCRATES   Then let us take one feature of it, the way in which the discourse contrived to pass from censure to encomium.

PHAEDRUS   Well now, what do you make of that?

SOCRATES   For the most part I think our festal hymn has really been just a festive entertainment, but we did casually allude to a certain pair of procedures, and it would be very agreeable if we could seize their significance in a scientific fashion.

PHAEDRUS   What procedures do you mean?

SOCRATES   The first is that in which we bring a dispersed plurality under a single form, seeing it all together—the purpose being to define so-and-so, and thus to make plain whatever may be chosen as the topic for exposition. For example, take the definition given just now of love. Whether it was right or wrong, at all events it was that which enabled our discourse to achieve lucidity and consistency.

PHAEDRUS   And what is the second procedure you speak of, Socrates?

SOCRATES   The reverse of the other, whereby we are enabled to divide into forms, following the objective articulation; we are not to attempt to hack off parts like a clumsy butcher, but to take example from our two recent speeches. The single general form which they postulated was irrationality; next, on the analogy of a single natural body with its pairs of like-named members, right arm or leg, as we say, and left, they conceived of madness as a single objective form existing in human beings. Wherefore the first speech divided off a part on the left, and continued to make divisions, never desisting until it discovered one particular part bearing the name of 'sinister' love, on which it very properly poured abuse. The other speech conducted us to the forms of madness which lay on the right-hand side, and upon discovering a type of love that shared its name with the other but was divine, displayed it to our view and extolled it as the source of the greatest goods that can befall us.

PHAEDRUS   That is perfectly true.

SOCRATES   Believe me, Phaedrus, I am myself a lover of these divisions and collections, that I may gain the power to speak and to think, and whenever I deem another man able to discern an objective unity and plurality, I follow 'in his footsteps where he leadeth as a god.' Furthermore—whether I am right or wrong in doing so, God alone knows —it is those that have this ability whom for the present I call dialecticians.

Plato   377

But now tell me what we ought to call them if we take instruction from Lysias and yourself. Or is what I have been describing precisely that art of oratory thanks to which Thrasymachus and the rest of them have not only made themselves masterly orators, but can do the same for anyone else who cares to bring offerings to these princes among men?

PHAEDRUS   Doubtless they behave like princes, but assuredly they do not possess the kind of knowledge to which you refer. No, I think you are right in calling the procedure that you have described dialectic, but we still seem to be in the dark about rhetoric.

SOCRATES   What? Can there really be anything of value that admits of scientific acquisition despite the lack of that procedure? If so, you and I should certainly not disdain it, but should explain what this residuum of rhetoric actually consists in.

PHAEDRUS   Well, Socrates, of course there is plenty of matter in the rhetorical manuals.

SOCRATES   Thank you for the reminder. The first point, I suppose, is that a speech must begin with a preamble. You are referring, are you not, to such niceties of the art?

PHAEDRUS   Yes.

SOCRATES   And next comes exposition accompanied by direct evidence; thirdly, indirect evidence; fourthly, probabilities; besides which there are the proof and supplementary proof mentioned by the Byzantine master of rhetorical artifice.

PHAEDRUS   You mean the worthy Theodorus?

SOCRATES   Of course. And we are to have a refutation and supplementary refutation both for prosecution and defense. And can we leave the admirable Evenus of Paros out of the picture, the inventor of covert allusion and indirect compliment and, according to some accounts, of the indirect censure in mnemonic verse? A real master, that. But we won't disturb the rest of Tisias and Gorgias, who realized that probability deserves more respect than truth, who could make trifles seem important and important points trifles by the force of their language, who dressed up novelties as antiques and vice versa, and found out how to argue concisely or at interminable length about anything and everything. This last accomplishment provoked Prodicus once to mirth when he heard me mention it; he remarked that he and he alone had discovered what sort of speeches the art demands—to wit, neither long ones nor short, but of fitting length.

PHAEDRUS   Masterly, Prodicus!

SOCRATES   Are we forgetting Hippias? I think Prodicus' view would be supported by the man of Elis.

PHAEDRUS   No doubt.

SOCRATES And then Polus. What are we to say of his *Muses' Treasury of Phrases* with its reduplications and maxims and similes, and of words à la Licymnius which that master made him a present of as a contribution to his fine writing?

PHAEDRUS But didn't Protagoras in point of fact produce some such works, Socrates?

SOCRATES Yes, my young friend, there is his *Correct Diction,* and many other excellent works. But to pass now to the application of pathetic language to the poor and aged, the master in that style seems to me to be the mighty man of Chalcedon, who was also expert at rousing a crowd to anger and then soothing them down again with his spells, to quote his own saying, while at casting aspersions and dissipating them, whatever their source, he was unbeatable.

But to resume, on the way to conclude a speech there seems to be general agreement, though some call it recapitulation and others by some other name.

PHAEDRUS You mean the practice of reminding the audience toward the end of a speech of its main points?

SOCRATES Yes. And now if you have anything further to add about the art of rhetoric ...

PHAEDRUS Only a few unimportant points.

SOCRATES If they are unimportant, we may pass them over. But let us look at what we have got in a clearer light, to see what power the art possesses, and when.

PHAEDRUS A very substantial power, Socrates, at all events in large assemblies.

SOCRATES Yes indeed, But have a look at it, my good sir, and see whether you discern some holes in the fabric, as I do.

PHAEDRUS Do show them me.

SOCRATES Well, look here. Suppose someone went up to your friend Eryximachus, or his father Acumenus, and said, 'I know how to apply such treatment to a patient's body as will induce warmth or coolness, as I choose; I can make him vomit, if I see fit, or go to stool, and so on and so forth. And on the strength of this knowledge I claim to be a competent physician, and to make a competent physician of anyone to whom I communicate this knowledge.' What do you imagine they would have to say to that?

PHAEDRUS They would ask him, of course, whether he also knew which patients ought to be given the various treatments, and when, and for how long.

SOCRATES Then what if he said, 'Oh, no, but I expect my pupils to manage what you refer to by themselves'?

PHAEDRUS I expect they would say, 'The man is mad; he thinks he has made himself a doctor by picking up something out of a book, or coming across some common drug or other, without any real knowledge of medicine.'

SOCRATES Now suppose someone went up to Sophocles or Euripides and said he knew how to compose lengthy dramatic speeches about a trifling matter, and quite short ones about a matter of moment, that he could write pathetic passages when he chose, or again passages of intimidation and menace, and so forth, and that he considered that by teaching these accomplishments he could turn a pupil into a tragic poet.

PHAEDRUS I imagine that they too would laugh at anyone who supposed that you could make a tragedy otherwise than by so arranging such passages as to exhibit a proper relation to one another and to the whole of which they are parts.

SOCRATES Still I don't think they would abuse him rudely, but rather treat him as a musician would treat a man who fancied himself to be a master of harmony simply because he knew how to produce the highest possible note and the lowest possible on his strings. The musician would not be so rude as to say, 'You miserable fellow, you're off your head,' but rather, in the gentler language befitting his profession, 'My good sir, it is true that one who proposes to become a master of harmony must know the things you speak of, but it is perfectly possible for one who has got as far as yourself to have not the slightest real knowledge of harmony. You are acquainted with what has to be learned before studying harmony, but of harmony itself you know nothing.'

PHAEDRUS Perfectly true.

SOCRATES Similarly then Sophocles would tell the man who sought to show off to himself and Euripides that what he knew was not tragic composition but its antecedents, and Acumenus would make the same distinction between medicine and the antecedents of medicine.

PHAEDRUS I entirely agree.

SOCRATES And if 'mellifluous' Adrastus, or shall we say Pericles, were to hear of those admirable artifices that we were referring to just now— the brachylogies and imageries and all the rest of them, which we enumerated and deemed it necessary to examine in a clear light—are we to suppose that they would address those who practice and teach this sort of thing, under the name of the art of rhetoric, with the severity you and I displayed, and in rude, coarse language? Or would they, in their ampler wisdom, actually reproach us and say, 'Phaedrus and Socrates, you ought not to get angry, but to make allowances for such people; it is because they are ignorant of dialectic that they are incapable of properly defining rhetoric, and that in turn leads them to imagine that by possessing themselves of the requisite ante-

The Theory of Rhetoric

cedent learning they have discovered the art itself. And so they teach these antecedents to their pupils, and believe that that constitutes a complete instruction in rhetoric; they don't bother about employing the various artifices in such a way that they will be effective, or about organizing a work as a whole; that is for the pupils to see to for themselves when they come to make speeches.'

PHAEDRUS   Well yes, Socrates, I dare say that does more or less describe what the teachers and writers in question regard as the art of rhetoric; personally I think what you say is true. But now by what means and from what source can one attain the art of the true rhetorician, the real master of persuasion?

SOCRATES   If you mean how can one become a finished performer, then probably—indeed I might say undoubtedly—it is the same as with anything else. If you have an innate capacity for rhetoric, you will become a famous rhetorician, provided you also acquire knowledge and practice, but if you lack any of these three you will be correspondingly unfinished. As regards the art itself, as distinct from the artist, I fancy that the line of approach adopted by Lysias and Thrasymachus is not the one I have in view.

PHAEDRUS   Then what is?

SOCRATES   I am inclined to think, my good friend, that it was not surprising that Pericles became the most finished exponent of rhetoric there has ever been.

PHAEDRUS   Why so?

SOCRATES   All the great arts need supplementing by a study of nature; your artist must cultivate garrulity and high-flown speculation; from that source alone can come the mental elevation and thoroughly finished execution of which you are thinking, and that is what Pericles acquired to supplement his inborn capacity. He came across the right sort of man, I fancy, in Anaxagoras, and by enriching himself with high speculation and coming to recognize the nature of wisdom and folly—on which topics of course Anaxagoras was always discoursing— he drew from that source and applied to the art of rhetoric what was suitable thereto.

PHAEDRUS   How do you mean?

SOCRATES   Rhetoric is in the same case as medicine, don't you think?

PHAEDRUS   How so?

SOCRATES   In both cases there is a nature that we have to determine, the nature of body in the one, and of soul in the other, if we mean to be scientific and not content with mere empirical routine when we apply medicine and diet to induce health and strength, or words and rules of conduct to implant such convictions and virtues as we desire.

PHAEDRUS   You are probably right, Socrates.

Plato

SOCRATES   Then do you think it possible to understand the nature of the soul satisfactorily without taking it as a whole?

PHAEDRUS   If we are to believe Hippocrates, the Asclepiad, we can't understand even the body without such a procedure.

SOCRATES   No, my friend, and he is right. But we must not just rely on Hippocrates; we must examine the assertion and see whether it accords with the truth.

PHAEDRUS   Yes.

SOCRATES   Then what is it that Hippocrates and the truth have to say on this matter of nature? I suggest that the way to reflect about the nature of anything is as follows: first, to decide whether the object in respect of which we desire to have scientific knowledge, and to be able to impart it to others, is simple or complex; secondly, if it is simple, to inquire what natural capacity it has of acting upon another thing, and through what means; or by what other thing, and through what means, it can be acted upon; or, if it is complex, to enumerate its parts and observe in respect of each what we observe in the case of the simple object, to wit what its natural capacity, active or passive, consists in.

PHAEDRUS   Perhaps so, Socrates.

SOCRATES   Well, at all events, to pursue an inquiry without doing so would be like a blind man's progress. Surely we mustn't make out that any sort of scientific inquirer resembles a blind or deaf person. No, it is plain that if we are to address people scientifically, we shall show them precisely what is the real and true nature of that object on which our discourse is brought to bear. And that object, I take it, is the soul.

PHAEDRUS   To be sure.

SOCRATES   Hence the speaker's whole effort is concentrated on that, for it is there that he is attempting to implant conviction. Isn't that so?

PHAEDRUS   Yes.

SOCRATES   Then it is plain that Thrasymachus, or anyone else who seriously proffers a scientific rhetoric, will, in the first place, describe the soul very precisely, and let us see whether it is single and uniform in nature or, analogously to the body, complex. For to do that is, we maintain, to show a thing's nature.

PHAEDRUS   Yes, undoubtedly.

SOCRATES   And secondly he will describe what natural capacity it has to act upon what, and through what means, or by what it can be acted upon.

PHAEDRUS   Quite so.

SOCRATES   Thirdly, he will classify the types of discourse and the types of soul, and the various ways in which souls are affected, explaining the reasons in each case, suggesting the type of speech appropriate to each type of soul, and showing what kind of speech can be relied on to create belief in one soul and disbelief in another, and why.

PHAEDRUS   I certainly think that would be an excellent procedure.

SOCRATES   Yes, in fact I can assure you, my friend, that no other scientific method of treating either our present subject or any other will ever be found, whether in the models of the schools or in speeches actually delivered. But the present-day authors of manuals of rhetoric, of whom you have heard, are cunning folk who know all about the soul but keep their knowledge out of sight. So don't let us admit their claim to write scientifically until they compose their speeches and writings in the way we have indicated.

PHAEDRUS   And what way is that?

SOCRATES   To give the actual words would be troublesome, but I am quite ready to say how one ought to compose if he means to be as scientific as possible.

PHAEDRUS   Then please do.

SOCRATES   Since the function of oratory is in fact to influence men's souls, the intending orator must know what types of soul there are. Now these are of a determinate number, and their variety results in a variety of individuals. To the types of soul thus discriminated there corresponds a determinate number of types of discourse. Hence a certain type of hearer will be easy to persuade by a certain type of speech to take such and such action for such and such reason, while another type will be hard to persuade. All this the orator must fully understand, and next he must watch it actually occurring, exemplified in men's conduct, and must cultivate a keenness of perception in following it, if he is going to get any advantage out of the previous instruction that he was given in the school. And when he is competent to say what type of man is susceptible to what kind of discourse; when, further, he can, on catching sight of so-and-so, tell himself, 'That is the man, that character now actually before me is the one I heard about in school, and in order to persuade him of so-and-so I have to apply *these* arguments in *this* fashion'; and when, on top of all this, he has further grasped the right occasions for speaking and for keeping quiet, and has come to recognize the right and the wrong time for the brachylogy, the pathetic passage, the exacerbation, and all the rest of his accomplishments—then and not till then has he well and truly achieved the art. But if in his speaking or teaching or writing he fails in any of these requirements, he may tell you that he has the art of speech, but one mustn't believe all one is told.

And now maybe our author will say, 'Well, what of it, Phaedrus and Socrates? Do you agree with me, or should we accept some other account of the art of speech?'

PHAEDRUS Surely we can't accept any other, Socrates; still it does seem a considerable business.

SOCRATES You are right, and that makes it necessary thoroughly to overhaul all our arguments, and see whether there is some easier and shorter way of arriving at the art; we don't want to waste effort in going off on a long rough road, when we might take a short smooth one. But if you can help us at all through what you have heard from Lysias or anyone else, do try to recall it.

PHAEDRUS As far as trying goes, I might, but I can suggest nothing on the spur of the moment.

SOCRATES Then would you like me to tell you something I have heard from those concerned with these matters?

PHAEDRUS Why, yes.

SOCRATES Anyhow, Phaedrus, we are told that even the devil's advocate ought to be heard.

PHAEDRUS Then you can put his case.

SOCRATES Well, they tell us that there is no need to make such a solemn business of it, or fetch such a long compass on an uphill road. As we remarked at the beginning of this discussion, there is, they maintain, absolutely no need for the budding orator to concern himself with the truth about what is just or good conduct, nor indeed about who are just and good men whether by nature or education. In the law courts nobody cares a rap for the truth about these matters, but only about what is plausible. And that is the same as what is probable, and is what must occupy the attention of the would-be master of the art of speech. Even actual facts ought sometimes not be stated, if they don't tally with probability; they should be replaced by what is probable, whether in prosecution or defense; whatever you say, you simply must pursue this probability they talk of, and can say good-by to the truth forever. Stick to that all through your speech, and you are equipped with the art complete.

PHAEDRUS Your account, Socrates, precisely reproduces what is said by those who claim to be experts in the art of speech. I remember that we did touch briefly on this sort of contention a while ago, and the professionals regard it as a highly important point.

SOCRATES Very well then, take Tisias himself; you have thumbed him carefully, so let Tisias tell us this. Does he maintain that the probable is anything other than that which commends itself to the multitude?

PHAEDRUS How could it be anything else?

SOCRATES Then in consequence, it would seem, of that profound scientific discovery he laid down that if a weak but brave man is arrested for assaulting a strong but cowardly one, whom he has robbed of his cloak or some other garment, neither of them ought to state the true facts; the coward should say that the brave man didn't assault him

The Theory of Rhetoric

singlehanded, and the brave man should contend that there were only the two of them, and then have recourse to the famous plea. 'How could a little fellow like me have attacked a big fellow like him?' Upon which the big fellow will not avow his own poltroonery but will try to invent some fresh lie which will probably supply his opponent with a means of refuting him. And similar 'scientific' rules are given for other cases of the kind. Isn't that so, Phaedrus?

PHAEDRUS To be sure.

SOCRATES Bless my soul! It appears that he made a brilliant discovery of a buried art, your Tisias, or whoever it really was and whatever he is pleased to be called after. But, my friend, shall we or shall we not say to him . . .

PHAEDRUS Say what?

SOCRATES This. 'In point of fact, Tisias, we have for some time before you came on the scene been saying that the multitude get their notion of probability as the result of a likeness to truth, and we explained just now that these likenesses can always be best discovered by one who knows the truth. Therefore if you have anything else to say about the art of speech, we should be glad to hear it, but if not we shall adhere to the point we made just now, namely that unless the aspirant to oratory can on the one hand list the various natures among his prospective audiences, and on the other divide things into their kinds and embrace each individual thing under a single form, he will never attain such success as is within the grasp of mankind. Yet he will assuredly never acquire such competence without considerable diligence, which the wise man should exert not for the sake of speaking to and dealing with his fellow men, but that he may be able to speak what is pleasing to the gods, and in all his dealings to do their pleasure to the best of his ability. For you see, Tisias, what we are told by those wiser than ourselves is true, that a man of sense ought never to study the gratification of his fellow slaves, save as a minor consideration, but that of his most excellent masters. So don't be surprised that we have to make a long detour; it is because the goal is glorious, though not the goal you think of.' Not but what those lesser objects also, if you would have them, can best be attained, so our argument assures us, as a consequence of the greater.

PHAEDRUS Your project seems to be excellent, Socrates, if only one could carry it out.

SOCRATES Well, when a man sets his hand to something good, it is good that he should take what comes to him.

PHAEDRUS Yes, of course.

SOCRATES Then we may feel that we have said enough about the art of speech, both the true art and the false?

PHAEDRUS Certainly.

Plato

SOCRATES But there remains the question of propriety and impropriety in writing, that is to say the conditions which make it proper or improper. Isn't that so?

PHAEDRUS Yes.

SOCRATES Now do you know how we may best please God, in practice and in theory, in this matter of words?

PHAEDRUS No indeed. Do you?

SOCRATES I can tell you the tradition that has come down from our forefathers, but they alone know the truth of it. However, if we could discover that for ourselves, should we still be concerned with the fancies of mankind?

PHAEDRUS What a ridiculous question! But tell me the tradition you speak of.

SOCRATES Very well. The story is that in the region of Naucratis in Egypt there dwelt one of the old gods of the country, the god to whom the bird called Ibis is sacred, his own name being Theuth. He it was that invented number and calculation, geometry and astronomy, not to speak of draughts and dice, and above all writing. Now the king of the whole country at that time was Thamus, who dwelt in the great city of Upper Egypt which the Greeks call Egyptian Thebes, while Thamus they call Ammon. To him came Theuth, and revealed his arts, saying that they ought to be passed on to the Egyptians in general. Thamus asked what was the use of them all, and when Theuth explained, he condemned what he thought the bad points and praised what he thought the good. On each art, we are told, Thamus had plenty of views both for and against; it would take too long to give them in detail. But when it came to writing Theuth said, 'Here, O king, is a branch of learning that will make the people of Egypt wiser and improve their memories; my discovery provides a recipe for memory and wisdom.' But the king answered and said, 'O man full of arts, to one it is given to create the things of art, and to another to judge what measure of harm and of profit they have for those that shall employ them. And so it is that you, by reason of your tender regard for the writing that is your offspring, have declared the very opposite of its true effect. If men learn this, it will implant forgetfulness in their souls; they will cease to exercise memory because they rely on that which is written, calling things to remembrance no longer from within themselves, but by means of external marks. What you have discovered is a recipe not for memory, but for reminder. And it is no true wisdom that you offer your disciples, but only its semblance, for by telling them of many things without teaching them you will make them seem to know much, while for the most part they know nothing, and as men filled, not with wisdom, but with a conceit of wisdom, they will be a burden to their fellows.'

PHAEDRUS It is easy for you, Socrates, to make up tales from Egypt or anywhere else you fancy.

SOCRATES Oh, but the authorities of the temple of Zeus at Dodona, my friend, said that the first prophetic utterances came from an oak tree. In fact the people of those days, lacking the wisdom of you young people, were content in their simplicity to listen to trees or rocks, provided these told the truth. For you apparently it makes a difference who the speaker is, and what country he comes from; you don't merely ask whether what he says is true or false.

PHAEDRUS I deserve your rebuke, and I agree that the man of Thebes is right in what he said about writing.

SOCRATES Then anyone who leaves behind him a written manual, and likewise anyone who takes it over from him, on the supposition that such writing will provide something reliable and permanent, must be exceedingly simple-minded; he must really be ignorant of Ammon's utterance, if he imagines that written words can do anything more than remind one who knows that which the writing is concerned with.

PHAEDRUS Very true.

SOCRATES You know, Phaedrus, that's the strange thing about writing, which makes it truly analogous to painting. The painter's products stand before us as though they were alive, but if you question them, they maintain a most majestic silence. It is the same with written words; they seem to talk to you as though they were intelligent, but if you ask them anything about what they say, from a desire to be instructed, they go on telling you just the same thing forever. And once a thing is put in writing, the composition, whatever it may be, drifts all over the place, getting into the hands not only of those who understand it, but equally of those who have no business with it; it doesn't know how to address the right people, and not address the wrong. And when it is ill-treated and unfairly abused it always needs its parent to come to its help, being unable to defend or help itself.

PHAEDRUS Once again you are perfectly right.

SOCRATES But now tell me, is there another sort of discourse, that is brother to the written speech, but of unquestioned legitimacy? Can we see how it originates, and how much better and more effective it is than the other?

PHAEDRUS What sort of discourse have you now in mind, and what is its origin?

SOCRATES The sort that goes together with knowledge, and is written in the soul of the learner, that can defend itself, and knows to whom it should speak and to whom it should say nothing.

PHAEDRUS You mean no dead discourse, but the living speech, the original of which the written discourse may fairly be called a kind of image.

SOCRATES Precisely. And now tell me this. If a sensible farmer had some seeds to look after and wanted them to bear fruit, would he with serious intent plant them during the summer in a garden of Adonis, and enjoy watching it producing fine fruit within eight days? If he did so at all, wouldn't it be in a holiday spirit, just by way of pastime? For serious purposes wouldn't he behave like a scientific farmer, sow his seeds in suitable soil, and be well content if they came to maturity within eight months?

PHAEDRUS I think we may distinguish as you say, Socrates, between what the farmer would do seriously and what he would do in a different spirit.

SOCRATES And are we to maintain that he who has knowledge of what is just, honorable, and good has less sense than the farmer in dealing with his seeds?

PHAEDRUS Of course not.

SOCRATES Then it won't be with serious intent that he 'writes them in water' or that black fluid we call ink, using his pen to sow words that can't either speak in their own defense or present the truth adequately.

PHAEDRUS It certainly isn't likely.

SOCRATES No, it is not. He will sow his seed in literary gardens, I take it, and write when he does write by way of pastime, collecting a store of refreshment both for his own memory, against the day 'when age oblivious comes,' and for all such as tread in his footsteps, and he will take pleasure in watching the tender plants grow up. And when other men resort to other pastimes, regaling themselves with drinking parties and suchlike, he will doubtless prefer to indulge in the recreation I refer to.

PHAEDRUS And what an excellent one it is, Socrates! How far superior to the other sort is the recreation that a man finds in words when he discourses about justice and the other topics you speak of.

SOCRATES Yes indeed, dear Phaedrus. But far more excellent, I think, is the serious treatment of them, which employs the art of dialectic. The dialectician selects a soul of the right type, and in it he plants and sows his words founded on knowledge, words which can defend both themselves and him who planted them, words which instead of remaining barren contain a seed whence new words grow up in new characters, whereby the seed is vouchsafed immortality, and its possessor the fullest measure of blessedness that man can attain unto.

PHAEDRUS Yes, that is a far more excellent way.

SOCRATES Then now that that has been settled, Phaedrus, we can proceed to the other point.

PHAEDRUS What is that?

SOCRATES The point that we wanted to look into before we arrived at our present conclusion. Our intention was to examine the reproach leveled against Lysias on the score of speech writing, and therewith the general question of speech writing and what does and does not make it an art. Now I think we have pretty well cleared up the question of art.

PHAEDRUS Yes, we did think so, but please remind me how we did it.

SOCRATES The conditions to be fulfilled are these. First, you must know the truth about the subject that you speak or write about; that is to say, you must be able to isolate it in definition, and having so defined it you must next understand how to divide it into kinds, until you reach the limit of division; secondly, you must have a corresponding discernment of the nature of the soul, discover the type of speech appropriate to each nature, and order and arrange your discourse accordingly, addressing a variegated soul in a variegated style that ranges over the whole gamut of tones, and a simple soul in a simple style. All this must be done if you are to become competent, within human limits, as a scientific practitioner of speech, whether you propose to expound or to persuade. Such is the clear purport of all our foregoing discussion.

PHAEDRUS Yes, that was undoubtedly how we came to see the matter.

SOCRATES And now to revert to our other question, whether the delivery and composition of speeches is honorable or base, and in what circumstances they may properly become a matter of reproach, our earlier conclusions have, I think, shown . . .

PHAEDRUS Which conclusions?

SOCRATES They have shown that any work, in the past or in the future, whether by Lysias or anyone else, whether composed in a private capacity or in the role of a public man who by proposing a law becomes the author of a political composition, is a matter of reproach to its author—whether or no the reproach is actually voiced—if he regards it as containing important truth of permanent validity. For ignorance of what is a waking vision and what is a mere dream image of justice and injustice, good and evil, cannot truly be acquitted of involving reproach, even if the mass of men extol it.

PHAEDRUS No indeed.

SOCRATES On the other hand, if a man believes that a written discourse on any subject is bound to contain much that is fanciful, that nothing that has ever been written whether in verse or prose merits much serious attention—and for that matter nothing that has ever been spoken in the declamatory fashion which aims at mere persuasion without any questioning or exposition—that in reality such compositions are, at the best, a means of reminding those who know the truth, that lucidity and completeness and serious importance belong only to those lessons on justice and honor and goodness that are expounded and set forth for the sake of instruction, and are veritably written in the soul of the listener, and that such discourses as these ought to be accounted a man's own legitimate children—a title to be applied primarily to such as originate within the man himself, and secondarily to such of their sons and brothers as have grown up aright in the souls of other men—the man, I say, who believes this, and disdains all manner of discourse other than this, is, I would venture to affirm, the man whose example you and I would pray that we might follow.

PHAEDRUS   My own wishes and prayers are most certainly to that effect.

SOCRATES   Then we may regard our literary pastime as having reached a satisfactory conclusion. Do you now go and tell Lysias that we two went down to the stream where is the holy place of the nymphs, and there listened to words which charge us to deliver a message, first to Lysias and all other composers of discourses, secondly to Homer and all others who have written poetry whether to be read or sung, and thirdly to Solon and all such as are authors of political compositions under the name of laws—to wit, that if any of them has done his work with a knowledge of the truth, can defend his statements when challenged, and can demonstrate the inferiority of his writings out of his own mouth, he ought not to be designated by a name drawn from those writings, but by one that indicates his serious pursuit.

PHAEDRUS   Then what names would you assign him?

SOCRATES   To call him wise, Phaedrus, would, I think be going too far; the epithet is proper only to a god. A name that would fit him better, and have more seemliness, would be 'lover of wisdom,' or something similar.

PHAEDRUS   Yes, that would be quite in keeping.

SOCRATES   On the other hand, one who has nothing to show of more value than the literary works on whose phrases he spends hours, twisting them this way and that, pasting them together and pulling them apart, will rightly, I suggest, be called a poet or speech writer or law writer.

PHAEDRUS   Of course.

SOCRATES   Then that is what you must tell your friend.

PHAEDRUS   But what about yourself? What are you going to do? You too have a friend who should not be passed over.

SOCRATES   Who is that?

PHAEDRUS   The fair Isocrates. What will be your message to him, Socrates, and what shall we call him?

SOCRATES   Isocrates is still young, Phaedrus, but I don't mind telling you the future I prophesy for him.

PHAEDRUS   Oh, what is that?

SOCRATES   It seems to me that his natural powers give him a superiority over anything that Lysias has achieved in literature, and also that in point of character he is of a nobler composition; hence it would not surprise me if with advancing years he made all his literary predecessors look like very small-fry—that is, supposing him to persist in the actual type of writing in which he engages at present—still more so, if he should become dissatisfied with such work, and a sublimer impulse lead him to do greater things. For that mind of his, Phaedrus, contains an innate tincture of philosophy.

Well then, there's the report I convey from the gods of this place to Isocrates my beloved, and there's yours for your beloved Lysias.

PHAEDRUS So be it. But let us be going, now that it has become less oppressively hot.

SOCRATES. Oughtn't we first to offer a prayer to the divinities here?

PHAEDRUS To be sure.

SOCRATES Dear Pan, and all ye other gods that dwell in this place, grant that I may become fair within, and that such outward things as I have may not war against the spirit within me. May I count him rich who is wise, and as for gold, may I possess so much of it as only a temperate man might bear and carry with him.

Is there anything more we can ask for, Phaedrus? The prayer contents me.

PHAEDRUS Make it a prayer for me too, since friends have all things in common.

SOCRATES Let us be going.

TOPICS FOR DISCUSSION

1. Why is the speech of Lysias thought a marvel? Is its aim to persuade the auditor of a truth sincerely held by the speaker? Are the points made in any order? For instance, is one point thought to be more clever than another?

2. What does Socrates seem to think the aim of the speech is? Why does Socrates say that he was thrilled by it? What seems to be his measure of a good speech? How does this measure differ initially from that of the young Phaedrus?

3. What is Socrates' aim in his own defense of the nonlover? Why does he not provide arguments for the nonlover, as Lysias did? Does he consider his speech more convincing?

4. How do the mood and construction of Socrates' second speech differ from those of the first? Are points enumerated? Does Socrates try harder in the second speech to involve Phaedrus in the argument? Would you say that the speech is emotional in appeal?

5. The speaker of Socrates' first speech is a rational man. Is the speaker of the second more than this? What differing views do they take of madness in love?

6. What popular conception of rhetoric does Socrates criticize, following his second speech? What does he mean by the "right employment" of rhetoric?

7. Why are comparisons important in rhetoric? How are they related to the conception of truth developed in the second speech?

8. Does Socrates' second speech have a beginning, a middle, and an end? Does it meet his measure of a good speech? Do his comments in any way qualify the second speech—that is, affect our interpretation and acceptance of it?

9. Are we to take seriously Socrates' statement that he was in too much ecstasy to remember his own speech? Or is he poking fun at Phaedrus?

10. Socrates analyzes the difference in his speeches in the following words:

> on the analogy of a single natural body with its pairs of like-named members, right arm or leg, as we say, and left, they conceived of madness as a single objective form existing in human beings. Wherefore the first speech divided off a part on the left, and continued to make divisions, never desisting until it discovered one particular part bearing the name of 'sinister' love, on which it very properly poured abuse. The other speech conducted us to the forms of madness which lay on the right-hand side, and upon discovering a type of love that shared its name with the other but was divine, displayed it to our view and extolled it as the source of the greatest goods that can befall us.

Explain the analogies in your own words.

11. Does Socrates consider the art of present and past rhetoricians specious or incomplete—or possibly both? What is the point of his analogies with medicine and the writing of tragedies? Why is it necessary to distinguish kinds of soul?

12. What is the application of the story Socrates tells about Theuth? What has this criticism of writing to do with rhetoric?

13. What is the difference between speech and writing?

14. According to Socrates' final comments, is a simple speech directed to the simple man less profound and further from the truth than a speech directed to the man more sophisticated or astute?

TOPICS FOR COMPOSITION

1. Write an analysis of the structure of *Phaedrus*. Indicate the relationship between the speeches of Lysias and Socrates and the discussion on rhetoric that follows.

2. Summarize the ideas on the soul developed by Socrates in his second speech. Explain the metaphors in your own words.

3. Discuss the implications of Plato's theory of knowledge—particularly his statement that intelligence is actually recollection—for a theory of education.

4. Summarize Plato's conception of true rhetoric.

ARISTOTLE

FROM
Rhetoric

PLATO refuses to admit that truth must be fitted to a particular audience; he measures rhetoric by absolute truth itself. Aristotle, by contrast, is less rigorous in his demands. Aristotle's assumption emerges in his comment, "Most of the things about which we make decisions, and into which therefore we inquire, present us with alternative possibilities. For it is about our actions that we deliberate and inquire, and all our actions have a contingent character; hardly any of them are determined by necessity." For Plato, dialectic is the means of discovering logically necessary truths. At the highest level it is related to the method of deduction, in which premises provide conclusive evidence for logical inferences; on this level recollection makes it possible to discourse about absolute ideas or forms without returning to sense experience. Though Aristotle believes that ideas exist, he does not think they exist in a realm wholly separate from sense experience; hence his approach to the question of dialectic is different from that of Plato. For Aristotle, dialectic takes the form of convincing, highly consistent inquiry; it is the technique of deliberative sciences like politics. Rhetoric is the counterpart of dialectic in persuasive discourse. The good rhetorician is devoted to the truth, though he may succeed only in approximating it. Thus Aristotle states in *Rhetoric:* "The true and the approximately true are apprehended by the same faculty; it may also be noted that men have a sufficient natural instinct for what is true, and usually do arrive at the truth. Hence the man who makes a good guess at truth is likely to make a good guess at probabilities."

The following excerpts from *Rhetoric,* Books One and Two, concern the nature of rhetoric and the topics or commonplaces, which in this translation are referred to as lines of proof or argument; in a section not included here Aristotle discusses the topics of specious enthymemes. The skilled rhetorician, Aristotle says, must be in control of these topics; his chief concern is the discovery of "artistic" proofs. The distinction between "artistic" and "nonartistic" proofs—as these are popularly known—is particularly revealing of Aristotle's conception of rhetoric. In this translation, these proofs are referred to as either belonging strictly to the art of rhetoric or not strictly belonging. Aristotle indicates that "nonartistic" proofs are far more subject to precise formulation than are the topics or lines of proof, though both are fitted to a particular audience. Because "nonartistic" proofs come to the rhetorician ready-made and do not depend on his practical determination, they are not "artistic"—that is, intrinsic to the art of rhetoric.

The relationship between dialectic and rhetoric is of great importance. R. H. McKeon explains this relationship in these words:

> The common-places of dialectic ... are used to set up or test definitions of terms, their genera, the properties asserted of them, and the accidents that may be connected with them. Dialectic explores defensible relations among terms as such; and in this function it may be a preliminary to, or even a part of, scientific inquiry. The common-places of rhetoric ... serve to arrange subject matters as they might be presented and to prepare arguments as they might be effective, preliminary to inquiring into the styles and organizations of speeches appropriate to arguments chosen with reference to the circumstances and tendencies of particular kinds of hearers.[1]

Rhetoric is the counterpart of Dialectic. Both alike are concerned with such things as come, more or less, within the general ken of all men and belong to no definite science. Accordingly all men make use, more or less, of both; for to a certain extent all men attempt to discuss statements and to maintain them, to defend themselves and to attack others. Ordinary people do this either at random or through practice and from acquired habit. Both ways being possible, the subject can plainly be handled systematically, for it is possible to inquire the reason why some speakers succeed through practice and others spontaneously; and every one will at once agree that such an inquiry is the function of an art.

Now, the framers of the current treatises on rhetoric have constructed but a small portion of that art. The modes of persuasion are the only true constituents of the art: everything else is merely accessory. These writers, however, say nothing about Enthymemes, which are the substance of rhetorical persuasion, but deal mainly with non-essentials. The arousing of prejudice, pity, anger, and similar emotions has nothing to do with the essential facts, but is merely a personal appeal to the man who is judging the case. Consequently if the rules for trials which are now laid down in some states—especially in well-governed states—were applied everywhere, such people would have nothing to say. All men, no doubt, *think* that the

---

[1]"Aristotle's Conception of Language," *Critics and Criticism*, ed. Ronald S. Crane (Chicago: Univ. of Chicago Press, 1952), p. 220.

RHETORIC From *Rhetorica*, W. Rhys Roberts (trans.), in *The Works of Aristotle*, W. D. Ross (ed.). Reprinted by permission of Clarendon Press, Oxford.

The Theory of Rhetoric

laws should prescribe such rules, but some, as in the court of Areopagus, give practical effect to their thoughts and forbid talk about non-essentials. This is sound law and custom. It is not right to pervert the judge by moving him to anger or envy or pity—one might as well warp a carpenters' rule before using it. Again, a litigant has clearly nothing to do but to show that the alleged fact is so or is not so, that it has or has not happened. As to whether a thing is important or unimportant, just or unjust, the judge must surely refuse to take his instructions from the litigants: he must decide for himself all such points as the law-giver has not already defined for him.

Now, it is of great moment that well-drawn laws should themselves define all the points they possibly can and leave as few as may be to the decision of the judges; and this for several reasons. First, to find one man, or a few men, who are sensible persons and capable of legislating and administering justice is easier than to find a large number. Next, laws are made after long consideration, whereas decisions in the courts are given at short notice, which makes it hard for those who try the case to satisfy the claims of justice and expediency. The weightiest reason of all is that the decision of the lawgiver is not particular but prospective and general, whereas members of the assembly and the jury find it *their* duty to decide on definite cases brought before them. They will often have allowed themselves to be so much influenced by feelings of friendship or hatred or self-interest that they lose any clear vision of the truth and have their judgement obscured by considerations of personal pleasure or pain. In general, then, the judge should, we say, be allowed to decide as few things as possible. But questions as to whether something has happened or has not happened, will be or will not be, is or is not, must of necessity be left to the judge, since the lawgiver cannot foresee them. If this is so, it is evident that any one who lays down rules about other matters, such as what must be the contents of the 'introduction' or the 'narration' or any of the other divisions of a speech, is theorizing about non-essentials as if they belonged to the art. The only question with which these writers here deal is how to put the judge into a given frame of mind. About the orator's proper modes of persuasion[1] they have nothing to tell us; nothing, that is, about how to gain skill in Enthymemes.

Hence it comes that, although the same systematic principles apply to political as to forensic oratory, and although the former is a nobler business, and fitter for a citizen, than that which concerns the relations of private individuals, these authors say nothing about political oratory, but try,

[1] That is, artistic proofs—those basic to the art of rhetoric, such as enthymeme and example—rather than nonartistic proofs—those external to the art of rhetoric, such as laws, eye-witness accounts, confessions obtained under torture and duress. In this translation, the reference to modes of persuasion belonging strictly to the art of rhetoric is to artistic proofs.

one and all, to write treatises on the way to plead in court. The reason for this is that in political oratory there is less inducement to talk about non-essentials. Political oratory is less given to unscrupulous practices than forensic, because it treats of wider issues. In a political debate the man who is forming a judgement is making a decision about his own vital interests. There is no need, therefore, to prove anything except that the facts are what the supporter of a measure maintains they are. In forensic oratory this is not enough; to conciliate the listener is what pays here. It is other people's affairs that are to be decided, so that the judges, intent on their own satisfaction and listening with partiality, surrender themselves to the disputants instead of judging between them. Hence in many places, as we have said already, irrelevant speaking is forbidden in the law-courts: in the public assembly those who have to form a judgment are themselves well able to guard against that.

It is clear, then, that rhetorical study, in its strict sense, is concerned with the modes of persuasion. Persuasion is clearly a sort of demonstration, since we are most fully persuaded when we consider a thing to have been demonstrated. The orator's demonstration is an Enthymeme, and this is, in general, the most effective of the modes of persuasion. The Enthymeme is a sort of syllogism, and the consideration of syllogisms of all kinds, without distinction, is the business of dialectic, either of dialectic as a whole or of one of its branches. It follows plainly, therefore, that he who is best able to see how and from what elements a syllogism is produced will also be best skilled in the Enthymeme, when he has further learnt what its subject-matter is and in what respects it differs from the syllogism of strict logic. The true and the approximately true are apprehended by the same faculty; it may also be noted that men have a sufficient natural instinct for what is true, and usually do arrive at the truth. Hence the man who makes a good guess at truth is likely to make a good guess at probabilities.

It has now been shown that the ordinary writers on rhetoric treat of non-essentials; it has also been shown why they have inclined more towards the forensic branch of oratory.

Rhetoric is useful (1) because things that are true and things that are just have a natural tendency to prevail over their opposites, so that if the decisions of judges are not what they ought to be, the defeat must be due to the speakers themselves, and they must be blamed accordingly. Moreover, (2) before some audiences not even the possession of the exactest knowledge will make it easy for what we say to produce conviction. For argument based on knowledge implies instruction, and there are people whom one cannot instruct. Here, then, we must use, as our modes of persuasion and argument, notions possessed by everybody, as we observed in the *Topics* when dealing with the way to handle a popular audience. Further, (3) we must be able to employ persuasion, just as strict reasoning can be employed, on opposite sides of a question, not in order that we may

The Theory of Rhetoric

in practice employ it in both ways (for we must not make people believe what is wrong), but in order that we may see clearly what the facts are, and that, if another man argues unfairly, we on our part may be able to confute him. No other of the arts draws opposite conclusions: dialectic and rhetoric alone do this. Both these arts draw opposite conclusions impartially. Nevertheless, the underlying facts do not lend themselves equally well to the contrary views. No; things that are true and things that are better are, by their nature, practically always easier to prove and easier to believe in. Again, (4) it is absurd to hold that a man ought to be ashamed of being unable to defend himself with his limbs, but not of being unable to defend himself with speech and reason, when the use of rational speech is more distinctive of a human being than the use of his limbs. And if it be objected that one who uses such power of speech unjustly might do great harm, *that* is a charge which may be made in common against all good things except virtue, and above all against the things that are most useful, as strength, health, wealth, generalship. A man can confer the greatest of benefits by a right use of these, and inflict the greatest of injuries by using them wrongly.

It is clear, then, that rhetoric is not bound up with a single definite class of subjects, but is as universal as dialectic; it is clear, also, that it is useful. It is clear, further, that its function is not simply to succeed in persuading, but rather to discover the means of coming as near such success as the circumstances of each particular case allow. In this it resembles all other arts. For example, it is not the function of medicine simply to make a man quite healthy, but to put him as far as may be on the road to health; it is possible to give excellent treatment even to those who can never enjoy sound health. Furthermore, it is plain that it is the function of one and the same art to discern the real and the apparent means of persuasion, just as it is the function of dialectic to discern the real and the apparent syllogism. What makes a man a 'sophist' is not his faculty, but his moral purpose. In rhetoric, however, the term 'rhetorician' may describe either the speaker's knowledge of the art, or his moral purpose. In dialectic it is different: a man is a 'sophist' because he has a certain kind of moral purpose, a 'dialectician' in respect, not of his moral purpose, but of his faculty.

Let us now try to give some account of the systematic principles of Rhetoric itself—of the right method and means of succeeding in the object we set before us. We must make as it were a fresh start, and before going further define what rhetoric is.

Rhetoric may be defined as the faculty of observing in any given case the available means of persuasion. This is not a function of any other art. Every other art can instruct or persuade about its own particular subject-matter; for instance, medicine about what is healthy and unhealthy, geometry about the properties of magnitudes, arithmetic about numbers, and the same is true of the other arts and sciences. But rhetoric we look upon as the power of observing the means of persuasion on almost any subject presented to us; and that is why we say that, in its technical character, it is not concerned with any special or definite class of subjects.

Of the modes of persuasion some belong strictly to the art of rhetoric and some do not. By the latter I mean such things as are not supplied by the speaker but are there at the outset—witnesses, evidence given under torture, written contracts, and so on. By the former I mean such as we can ourselves construct by means of the principles of rhetoric. The one kind has merely to be used, the other has to be invented.

Of the modes of persuasion furnished by the spoken word there are three kinds. The first kind depends on the personal character of the speaker; the second on putting the audience into a certain frame of mind; the third on the proof, or apparent proof, provided by the words of the speech itself. Persuasion is achieved by the speaker's personal character when the speech is so spoken as to make us think him credible. We believe good men more fully and more readily than others: this is true generally whatever the question is, and absolutely true where exact certainty is impossible and opinions are divided. This kind of persuasion, like the others, should be achieved by what the speaker says, not by what people think of his character before he begins to speak. It is not true, as some writers assume in their treatises on rhetoric, that the personal goodness revealed by the speaker contributes nothing to his power of persuasion; on the contrary, his character may almost be called the most effective means of persuasion he possesses. Secondly, persuasion may come through the hearers when the speech stirs their emotions. Our judgements when we are pleased and friendly are not the same as when we are pained and hostile. It is towards producing these effects, as we maintain, that present-day writers on rhetoric direct the whole of their efforts. This subject shall be treated in detail when we come to speak of the emotions. Thirdly, persuasion is effected through the speech itself when we have proved a truth or an apparent truth by means of the persuasive arguments suitable to the case in question.

There are, then, these three means of effecting persuasion. The man who is to be in command of them must, it is clear, be able (1) to reason logically, (2) to understand human character and goodness in their various forms, and (3) to understand the emotions—that is, to name them and describe them, to know their causes and the way in which they are excited. It thus appears that rhetoric is an offshoot of dialectic and also of ethical studies. Ethical studies may fairly be called political; and for this reason rhetoric masquerades as political science, and the professors of it as political experts—sometimes from want of education, sometimes from ostentation, sometimes owing to other human failings. As a matter of fact, it is a branch of dialectic and similar to it, as we said at the outset. Neither rhetoric nor dialectic is the scientific study of any one separate subject: both are faculties for providing arguments. This is perhaps a sufficient account of their scope and of how they are related to each other.

With regard to the persuasion achieved by proof or apparent proof: just as in dialectic there is induction on the one hand and syllogism or apparent syllogism on the other, so it is in rhetoric. The example is an induction, the Enthymeme is a syllogism, and the apparent Enthymeme is an apparent syllogism. I call the Enthymeme a rhetorical syllogism, and the example a rhetorical induction. Every one who effects persuasion through proof does in fact use either Enthymemes or examples; there is no other way. And since every one who proves anything at all is bound to use either syllogisms or inductions (and this is clear to us from the *Analytics*), it must follow that Enthymemes are syllogisms and examples are inductions. The difference between example and Enthymeme is made plain by the passages in the *Topics* where induction and syllogism have already been discussed. When we base the proof of a proposition on a number of similar cases, this is induction in dialectic, example in rhetoric; when it is shown that, certain propositions being true, a further and quite distinct proposition must also be true in consequence, whether invariably or usually, this is called syllogism in dialectic, Enthymeme in rhetoric. It is plain also that each of these types of oratory has its advantages. Types of oratory, I say: for what has been said in the *Methodics* applies equally well here; in some oratorical styles examples prevail, in others Enthymemes; and in like manner, some orators are better at the former and some at the latter. Speeches that rely on examples are as persuasive as the other kind, but those which rely on Enthymemes excite the louder applause. The sources of examples and Enthymemes, and their proper uses, we will discuss later. Our next step is to define the processes themselves more clearly.

A statement is persuasive and credible either because it is directly self-evident or because it appears to be proved from other statements that are so. In either case it is persuasive because there is somebody whom it persuades. But none of the arts theorize about individual cases. Medicine, for instance, does not theorize about what will help to cure Socrates or Callias, but only about what will help to cure any or all of a given class of patients: this alone is its business: individual cases are so infinitely various that no systematic knowledge of them is possible. In the same way the theory of rhetoric is concerned not with what seems probable to a given individual like Socrates or Hippias, but with what seems probable to men of a given type; and this is true of dialectic also. Dialectic does not construct its syllogisms out of any haphazard materials, such as the fancies of crazy people, but out of materials that call for discussion; and rhetoric, too, draws upon the regular subjects of debate. The duty of rhetoric is to deal with such matters as we deliberate upon without arts or systems to guide us, in the hearing of persons who cannot take in at a glance a complicated argument, or follow a long chain of reasoning. The subjects of our deliberation are such as seem to present us with alternative possibilities: about things that could not have been, and cannot now or in the future be, other than they are, nobody who takes them to be of this nature wastes his time in deliberation.

It is possible to form syllogisms and draw conclusions from the results of previous syllogisms; or, on the other hand, from premisses which have not been thus proved, and at the same time are so little accepted that they call for proof. Reasonings of the former kind will necessarily be hard to follow owing to their length, for we assume an audience of untrained thinkers; those of the latter kind will fail to win assent, because they are based on premisses that are not generally admitted or believed.

The Enthymeme and the example must, then, deal with what is in the main contingent, the example being an induction, and the Enthymeme a syllogism, about such matters. The Enthymeme must consist of few propositions, fewer often than those which make up the normal syllogism. For if any of these propositions is a familiar fact, there is no need even to mention it; the hearer adds it himself. Thus, to show that Dorieus has been victor in a contest for which the prize is a crown, it is enough to say 'For he has been victor in the Olympic games,' without adding 'And in the Olympic games the prize is a crown,' a fact which everybody knows.

There are few facts of the 'necessary' type that can form the basis of rhetorical syllogisms. Most of the things about which we make decisions, and into which therefore we inquire, present us with alternative possibilities. For it is about our actions that we deliberate and inquire, and all our actions have a contingent character; hardly any of them are determined by necessity. Again, conclusions that state what is merely usual or possible must be drawn from premisses that do the same, just as 'necessary' conclusions must be drawn from 'necessary' premisses; this too is clear to us from the *Analytics*. It is evident, therefore, that the propositions forming the basis of Enthymemes, though some of them may be 'necessary,' will most of them be only usually true. Now the materials of Enthymemes are Probabilities and Signs, which we can see must correspond respectively with the propositions that are generally and those that are necessarily true. A Probability is a thing that usually happens; not, however, as some definitions would suggest, anything whatever that usually happens; but only if it belongs to the class of the 'contingent' or 'variable.' It bears the same relation to that in respect of which it is probable as the universal bears to the particular. Of Signs, one kind bears the same relation to the statement it supports as the particular bears to the universal, the other the same as the universal bears to the particular. The infallible kind is a 'complete proof'; the fallible kind has no specific name. By infallible signs I mean those on which syllogisms proper may be based: and this shows us why this kind of Sign is called 'complete proof': when people think that what they have said cannot be refuted, they then think that they are bringing forward a 'complete proof,' meaning that the matter has now been demonstrated and completed; for the word *peras* has the same meaning (of 'end' or 'boundary') as the word *tekmar* in the ancient tongue. Now the one kind of Sign (that which bears to the proposition it supports the relation of particular to universal) may be illustrated thus. Suppose it were said, 'The fact that Socrates was wise and just is a sign that the wise are just.' Here we certainly have a Sign; but even though the proposition be true, the argument is refutable, since it does not form a syllogism. Suppose, on the other hand, it were said, 'The fact that he has a fever is a sign that he is ill,' or 'The fact that she is giving milk is a sign that she has lately borne a child.' Here we have the infallible kind of Sign, the only kind that constitutes a complete proof, since it is the only kind that, if the particular statement is true, is irrefutable. The other kind of Sign, that which bears to the proposition it supports the relation of universal to particular, might be illustrated by saying, 'The fact that he breathes fast is sign that he has a fever.' This argument also is refutable, even if the statement about the fast breathing be true, since a man may breathe hard without having a fever.

It has, then, been stated above what is the nature of a Probability, of a Sign, and of a complete proof, and what are the differences between them. In the *Analytics* a more explicit description has been given of these points; it is there shown why some of these reasonings can be put into syllogisms and some cannot.

The 'example' has already been described as one kind of induction; and the special nature of the subject-matter that distinguishes it from the other kinds has also been stated above. Its relation to the proposition it supports is not that of part to whole, nor whole to part, nor whole to whole, but of part to part, or like to like. When two statements are of the same order, but one is more familiar than the other, the former is an 'example.' The argument may, for instance, be that Dionysius, in asking as he does for a bodyguard, is scheming to make himself a despot. For in the past Peisistratus kept asking for a bodyguard in order to carry out such a scheme, and did make himself a despot as soon as he got it; and so did Theagenes at Megara; and in the same way all other instances known to the speaker are made into examples, in order to show what is not yet known, that Dionysius has the same purpose in making the same request: all these being instances of the one general principle, that a man who asks for a bodyguard is scheming to make himself a despot. We have now described the sources of those means of persuasion which are popularly supposed to be demonstrative.

There is an important distinction between two sorts of Enthymemes that has been wholly overlooked by almost everybody—one that also subsists between the syllogisms treated of in dialectic. One sort of Enthymeme really belongs to rhetoric, as one sort of syllogism really belongs to dialectic; but the other sort really belongs to other arts and faculties, whether to those we already exercise or to those we have not yet acquired. Missing this distinction, people fail to notice that the more correctly they handle their particular subject the further they are getting away from pure rhetoric or dialectic. This statement will be clearer if expressed more fully. I mean that the proper subjects of dialectical and rhetorical syllogisms are the things with which we say the regular or universal Lines of Argument are concerned, that is to say those lines of argument that apply equally to questions of right conduct, natural science, politics, and many other things that have nothing to do with one another. Take, for instance, the line of argument concerned with 'the more or less.' On this line of argument it is equally easy to base a syllogism or Enthymeme about any of what nevertheless are essentially disconnected subjects—right conduct, natural science, or anything else whatever. But there are also those special Lines of Argument which are based on such propositions as apply only to particular groups or classes of things. Thus there are propositions about natural science on which it is impossible to base any Enthymeme or syllogism about ethics, and other propositions about ethics on which nothing can be based about natural science. The same principle applies throughout. The general Lines of Argument have no special subject-matter, and therefore will not increase our understanding of any particular class of things. On the other hand, the better the selection one makes of propositions suitable for special Lines of Argument, the nearer one comes, unconsciously, to setting up a science that is distinct from dialectic and rhetoric. One may succeed in stating the required principles, but one's science will be no longer dialectic or rhetoric, but the science to which the principles thus discovered belong. Most Enthymemes are in fact based upon these particular or special Lines of Argument; comparatively few on the common or general kind. As in the *Topics*, therefore, so in this work, we must distinguish, in dealing with Enthymemes, the special and the general Lines of Argument on which they are to be founded. By special Lines of Argument I mean the propositions peculiar to each several class of things, by general those common to all classes alike. We may begin with the special Lines of Argument. But, first of all, let us classify rhetoric into its varieties. Having distinguished these we may deal with them one by one, and try to discover the elements of which each is composed, and the propositions each must employ.

Rhetoric falls into three divisions, determined by the three classes of listeners to speeches. For of the three elements in speech-making—speaker, subject, and person addressed—it is the last one, the hearer, that determines the speech's end and object. The hearer must be either a judge, with a

The Theory of Rhetoric

decision to make about things past or future, or an observer. A member of the assembly decides about future events, a juryman about past events: while those who merely decide on the orator's skill are observers. From this it follows that there are three divisions of oratory—(1) political, (2) forensic, and (3) the ceremonial oratory of display.[2]

Political speaking urges us either to do or not to do something: one of these two courses is always taken by private counsellors, as well as by men who address public assemblies. Forensic speaking either attacks or defends somebody: one or other of these two things must always be done by the parties in a case. The ceremonial oratory of display either praises or censures somebody. These three kinds of rhetoric refer to three different kinds of time. The political orator is concerned with the future: it is about things to be done hereafter that he advises, for or against. The party in a case at law is concerned with the past; one man accuses the other, the other defends himself, with reference to things already done. The ceremonial orator is, properly speaking, concerned with the present, since all men praise or blame in view of the state of things existing at the time, though they often find it useful also to recall the past and to make guesses at the future.

Rhetoric has three distinct ends in view, one for each of its three kinds. The political orator aims at establishing the expediency or the harmfulness of a proposed course of action; if he urges its acceptance, he does so on the ground that it will do good; if he urges its rejection, he does so on the ground that it will do harm; and all other points, such as whether the proposal is just or unjust, honourable or dishonourable, he brings in as subsidiary and relative to this main consideration. Parties in a law-case aim at establishing the justice or injustice of some action, and they too bring in all other points as subsidiary and relative to this one. Those who praise or attack a man aim at proving him worthy of honour or the reverse, and they too treat all other considerations with reference to this one.

That the three kinds of rhetoric do aim respectively at the three ends we have mentioned is shown by the fact that speakers will sometimes not try to establish anything else. Thus, the litigant will sometimes not deny that a thing has happened or that he has done harm. But that he is guilty of injustice he will never admit; otherwise there would be no need of a trial. So too, political orators often make any concession short of admitting that they are recommending their hearers to take an inexpedient course or not to take an expedient one. The question whether it is not *unjust* for a city to enslave its innocent neighbours often does not trouble them at all. In like manner those who praise or censure a man do not consider whether his acts have been expedient or not, but often make it a

---

[2]That is, deliberative, judicial, and epideictic—the oratory of legislative bodies, courts of law, and ceremonial assemblies.

ground of actual praise that he has neglected his own interest to do what was honourable. Thus, they praise Achilles because he championed his fallen friend Patroclus, though he knew that this meant death, and that otherwise he need not die: yet while to die thus was the nobler thing for him to do, the expedient thing was to live on.

It is evident from what has been said that it is these three subjects, more than any others, about which the orator must be able to have propositions at his command. Now the propositions of Rhetoric are Complete Proofs, Probabilities, and Signs. Every kind of syllogism is composed of propositions, and the enthymeme is a particular kind of syllogism composed of the aforesaid propositions.

Since only possible actions, and not impossible ones, can ever have been done in the past or the present, and since things which have not occurred, or will not occur, also cannot have been done or be going to be done, it is necessary for the political, the forensic, and the ceremonial speaker alike to be able to have at their command propositions about the possible and the impossible, and about whether a thing has or has not occurred, will or will not occur. Further, all men, in giving praise or blame, in urging us to accept or reject proposals for action, in accusing others or defending themselves, attempt not only to prove the points mentioned but also to show that the good or the harm, the honour or disgrace, the justice or injustice, is great or small, either absolutely or relatively; and therefore it is plain that we must also have at our command propositions about greatness or smallness and the greater or the lesser—propositions both universal and particular. Thus, we must be able to say which is the greater or lesser good, the greater or lesser act of justice or injustice; and so on.

Such, then, are the subjects regarding which we are inevitably bound to master the propositions relevant to them. We must now discuss each particular class of these subjects in turn, namely those dealt with in political, in ceremonial, and lastly in legal, oratory.

. . .

1. One line of positive proof is based upon consideration of the opposite of the thing in question. Observe whether that opposite has the opposite quality. If it has not, you refute the original proposition; if it has, you establish it. E.g. 'Temperance is beneficial; for licentiousness is hurtful.' Or, as in the Messenian speech, 'If war is the cause of our present troubles, peace is what we need to put things right again.' Or—

> For if not even evil-doers should
> Anger us if they meant not what they did,
> Then can we owe no gratitude to such
> As were constrained to do the good they did us.

Or—

> Since in this world liars may win belief,
> Be sure of the opposite likewise—that this world
> Hears many a true word and believes it not.[3]

2. Another line of proof is got by considering some modification of the key-word, and arguing that what can or cannot be said of the one, can or cannot be said of the other: e.g. 'just' does not always mean 'beneficial,' or 'justly' would always mean 'beneficially,' whereas it is *not* desirable to be justly put to death.

3. Another line of proof is based upon correlative ideas. If it is true that one man *gave* noble or just treatment to another, you argue that the other must have *received* noble or just treatment; or that where it is right to command obedience, it must have been right to obey the command. Thus Diomedon, the tax-farmer, said of the taxes: 'If it is no disgrace for you to sell them, it is no disgrace for us to buy them.' Further, if 'well' or 'justly' is true of the person to whom a thing is done, you argue that it is true of the doer. But it is possible to draw a false conclusion here. It may be just that A should be treated in a certain way, and yet *not* just that he should be so treated by B. Hence you must ask yourself two distinct questions: (1) Is it right that A should be thus treated? (2) Is it right that B should thus treat him? and apply your results properly, according as your answers are Yes or No. Sometimes in such a case the two answers differ: you may quite easily have a position like in the *Alcmaeon* of Theodectes:

> And was there none to loathe thy mother's crime?

to which question Alcmaeon in reply says,

> Why, there are two things to examine here.

And when Alphesiboea asks what he means, he rejoins:

> They judged *her* fit to die, not *me* to slay her.

Again there is the lawsuit about Demosthenes and the men who killed Nicanor; as they were judged to have killed him justly, it was thought that he was killed justly. And in the case of the man who was killed at Thebes, the judges were requested to decide whether it was unjust that he should be killed, since if it was not, it was argued that it could not have been unjust to kill him.

4. Another line of proof is the *a fortiori*. Thus it may be argued that if

[3]From the fragmentary *Thyestes* of Euripides.

even the gods are not omniscient, certainly human beings are not. The principle here is that, if a quality does not in fact exist where it is *more* likely to exist, it clearly does not exist where it is *less* likely. Again, the argument that a man who strikes his father also strikes his neighbours follows from the principle that, if the less likely thing is true, the more likely thing is true also; for a man is less likely to strike his father than to strike his neighbours. The argument, then, may run thus. Or it may be urged that, if a thing is not true where it is more likely, it is not true where it is less likely; or that, if it is true where it is less likely, it is true where it is more likely: according as we have to show that a thing *is* or is *not* true. This argument might also be used in a case of parity, as in the lines:

Thou hast pity for *thy* sire, who has lost his sons:
Hast none for Oeneus, whose brave son is dead?

And, again, 'if Theseus did no wrong, neither did Paris'; or 'if the sons of Tyndareus did no wrong, neither did Paris'; or 'if Hector did well to slay Patroclus, Paris did well to slay Achilles.' And 'if other followers of an art are not bad men, neither are philosophers.' And 'if generals are not bad men because it often happens that they are condemned to death, neither are sophists.' And the remark that 'if each individual among you ought to think of his own city's reputation, you ought all to think of the reputation of Greece as a whole.'

5. Another line of argument is based on considerations of time. Thus Iphicrates, in the case against Harmodius, said, 'if before doing the deed I had bargained that, if I did it, I should have a statue, you would have given me one. Will you not give me one now that I *have* done the deed? You must not make promises when you are expecting a thing to be done for you, and refuse to fulfil them when the thing has been done.' And, again, to induce the Thebans to let Philip pass through their territory into Attica, it was argued that 'if he had insisted on this before he helped them against the Phocians, they would have promised to do it. It is monstrous, therefore, that just because he threw away his advantage then, and trusted their honour, they should not let him pass through now.'

6. Another line is to apply to the other speaker what he has said against yourself. It is an excellent turn to give to a debate, as may be seen in the *Teucer*.[4] It was employed by Iphicrates in his reply to Aristophon. 'Would *you*,' he asked, 'take a bribe to betray the fleet?' 'No,' said Aristophon; and Iphicrates replied, 'Very good: if you, who are Aristophon, would not betray the fleet, would I, who am Iphicrates? Only, it must be recognized beforehand that the other man is more likely than you are to commit the crime in question. Otherwise you will make yourself ridiculous; if it is

[4]A work by Sophocles.

Aristeides who is prosecuting, you cannot say that sort of thing to him. The purpose is to discredit the prosecutor, who as a rule would have it appear that his character is better than that of the defendant, a pretension which it is desirable to upset. But the use of such an argument is in all cases ridiculous if you are attacking others for what you do or would do yourself, or are urging others to do what you neither do nor would do yourself.

7. Another line of proof is secured by defining your terms. Thus, 'What is the supernatural? Surely it is either a god or the work of a god. Well, anyone who believes that the work of a god exists, cannot help also believing that gods exist.' Or take the argument of Iphicrates, 'Goodness is true nobility; neither Harmodius nor Aristogeiton had any nobility before they did a noble deed.' He also argued that he himself was more akin to Harmodius and Aristogeiton than his opponent was. 'At any rate, my deeds are more akin to those of Harmodius and Aristogeiton than yours are.' Another example may be found in the *Alexander*. 'Every one will agree that by incontinent people we mean those who are not satisfied with the enjoyment of one love.' A further example is to be found in the reason given by Socrates for not going to the court of Archelaus. He said that 'one is *insulted* by being unable to requite benefits, as well as by being unable to requite injuries.' All the persons mentioned define their term and get at its essential meaning, and then use the result when reasoning on the point at issue.

8. Another line of argument is founded upon the various senses of a word. Such a word is 'rightly,' as has been explained in the *Topics*.

9. Another line is based upon logical division. Thus, 'All men do wrong from one fo three motives, A, B, or C: in my case A and B are out of the question, and even the accusers do not allege C.'

10. Another line is based upon induction. Thus from the case of the woman of Peparethus it might be argued that women everywhere can settle correctly the facts about their children. Another example of this occurred at Athens in the case between the orator Mantias and his son, when the boy's mother revealed the true facts: and yet another at Thebes, in the case between Ismenias and Stilbon, when Dodonis proved that it was Ismenias who was the father of her son Thettaliscus, and he was in consequence always regarded as being so. A further instance of induction may be taken from the *Law* of Theodectes: 'If we do not hand over our horses to the care of men who have mishandled other people's horses, nor ships to those who have wrecked other people's ships, and if this is true of everything else alike, then men who have failed to secure other people's safety are not to be employed to secure our own.' Another instance is the argument of Alcidamas: 'Every one honours the wise. Thus the Parians have honoured Archilochus, in spite of his bitter tongue; the Chians Homer, though he was not their countryman; the Mytilenaeans Sappho, though she was a

woman; the Lacedaemonians actually made Chilon a member of their senate, though they are the least literary of men; the Italian Greeks honoured Pythagoras; the inhabitants of Lampsacus gave public burial to Anaxagoras, though he was an alien, and honour him even to this day. [It may be argued that peoples for whom philosophers legislate are always prosperous] on the ground that the Athenians became prosperous under Solon's laws and the Lacedaemonians under those of Lycurgus, while at Thebes no sooner did the leading men become philosophers than the country began to prosper.

11. Another line of argument is founded upon some decision already pronounced, whether on the same subject or on one like it or contrary to it. Such a proof is most effective if every one has always decided thus; but if not every one, then at any rate most people; or if all, or most, wise or good men have thus decided, or the actual judges of the present question, or those whose authority they accept, or any one whose decision they cannot gainsay because he has complete control over them, or those whom it is not seemly to gainsay, as the gods, or one's father, or one's teachers. Thus Autocles said, when attacking Mixidemides, that it was a strange thing that the Dread Goddesses could without loss of dignity submit to the judgement of the Areopagus, and yet Mixidemides could not. Or as Sappho said, 'Death is an evil thing; the gods have so judged it, or they would die.' Or again as Aristippus said in reply to Plato when he spoke somewhat too dogmatically, as Aristippus thought: 'Well, anyhow, our *friend*,' meaning Socrates, 'never spoke like that.' And Hegesippus, having previously consulted Zeus at Olympia, asked Apollo at Delphi 'whether his opinion was the same as his father's,' implying that it would be shameful for him to contradict his father. Thus too Isocrates argued that Helen must have been a good woman, because Theseus decided that she was; and Paris a good man, because the goddesses chose him before all others; and Evagoras also, says Isocrates, was good, since when Conon met with his misfortune he betook himself to Evagoras without trying any one else on the way.[5]

12. Another line of argument consists in taking separately the parts of a subject. Such is that given in the *Topics:* 'What *sort* of motion is the soul? for it must be this or that.' The *Socrates* of Theodectes provides an example: 'What temple has he profaned? What gods recognized by the state has he not honoured?'

13. Since it happens that any given thing usually has both good and bad consequences, another line of argument consists in using those consequences as a reason for urging that a thing should or should not be done, for prosecuting or defending any one, for eulogy or censure. E.g. education leads both to unpopularity, which is bad, and to wisdom, which is good. Hence you either argue, 'It is therefore not well to be educated, since it is not well to be unpopular': or you answer, 'No, it is well to be educated, since it is well

[5]Aristotle is referring to the encomiums *Helen* and *Evagorus* of Isocrates.

The Theory of Rhetoric

to be wise.' The *Art of Rhetoric* of Callippus is made up of this line of argument, with the addition of those of Possibility and the others of that kind already described.

14. Another line of argument is used when we have to urge or discourage a course of action that may be done in either of two opposite ways, and have to apply the method just mentioned to both. The difference between this one and the last is that, whereas in the last any two things are contrasted, here the things contrasted are opposites. For instance, the priestess enjoined upon her son not to take to public speaking: 'For,' she said, 'if you say what is right, men will hate you; if you say what is wrong, the gods will hate you.' The reply might be, 'On the contrary, you *ought* to take to public speaking: for if you say what is right, the gods will love you; if you say what is wrong, men will love you.' This amounts to the proverbial 'buying the marsh with the salt.' It is just this situation, viz. when each of two opposites has both a good and a bad consequence opposite respectively to each other, that has been termed *divarication*.

15. Another line of argument is this: The things people approve of openly are not those which they approve of secretly: openly, their chief praise is given to justice and nobleness; but in their hearts they prefer their own advantage. Try, in face of this, to establish the point of view which your opponent has not adopted. This is the most effective of the forms of argument that contradict common opinion.

16. Another line is that of rational correspondence. E.g. Iphicrates, when they were trying to compel his son, a youth under the prescribed age, to perform one of the state duties because he was tall, said 'If you count tall boys men, you will next be voting short men boys.' And Theodectes in his *Law* said, 'You make citizens of such mercenaries as Strabax and Charidemus, as a reward of their merits; will you not make exiles of such citizens as those who have done irreparable harm among the mercenaries?'

17. Another line is the argument that if two results are the same their antecedents are also the same. For instance, it was a saying of Xenophanes that to assert that the gods had birth is as impious as to say that they die; the consequence of both statements is that there is a time when the gods do not exist. This line of proof assumes generally that the result of any given thing is always the same: e.g. 'you are going to decide not about Isocrates, but about the value of the whole profession of philosophy.' Or, 'to give earth and water' means slavery; or, 'to share in the Common Peace' means obeying orders. We are to make either such assumptions or their opposite, as suits us best.

18. Another line of argument is based on the fact that men do not always make the same choice on a later as on an earlier occasion, but reverse their previous choice. E.g. the following Enthymeme: 'When we were exiles, we fought in order to return; now we have returned, it would be strange to choose exile in order not to have to fight.' On one occasion, that is, they

chose to be true to their homes at the cost of fighting, and on the other to avoid fighting at the cost of deserting their homes.

19. Another line of argument is the assertion that some *possible* motive for an event or state of things is the *real* one: e.g. that a gift was given in order to cause pain by its withdrawal. This notion underlies the lines:

> God gives to many great prosperity,
> Not of good will towards them, but to make
> The ruin of them more conspicuous.

Or take the passage from the *Meleager* of Antiphon:

> To slay no boar, but to be witnesses
> Of Meleager's prowess unto Greece.

Or the argument in the *Ajax* of Theodectes, that Diomede chose out Odysseus not to do him honour, but in order that his companion might be a lesser man than himself—such a motive for doing so is quite possible.

20. Another line of argument is common to forensic and deliberative oratory, namely, to consider inducements and deterrents, and the motives people have for doing or avoiding the actions in question. These are the conditions which make us bound to act if they are for us, and to refrain from action if they are against us: that is, we are bound to act if the action is possible, easy, and useful to ourselves or our friends or hurtful to our enemies; this is true even if the action entails loss, provided the loss is outweighed by the solid advantage. A speaker will urge action by pointing to such conditions, and discourage it by pointing to the opposite. These same arguments also form the materials for accusation or defence—the deterrents being pointed out by the defence, and the inducements by the prosecution. As for the defence . . . this topic forms the whole *Art of Rhetoric* both of Pamphilus and of Callippus.

21. Another line of argument refers to things which are supposed to happen and yet seem incredible. We may argue that people could not have believed them, if they had not been true or nearly true: even that they are the more likely to be true because they are incredible. For the things which men believe are either facts or probabilities: if, therefore, a thing that *is* believed is improbable and even incredible, it must be true, since it is certainly not believed because it is at all probable or credible. An example is what Androcles of the deme Pitthus said in his well-known arraignment of the law. The audience tried to shout him down when he observed that the laws required a law to set them right. 'Why,' he went on, 'fish need salt, improbable and incredible as this might seem for creatures reared in salt water; and olive-cakes need oil, incredible as it is that what produces oil should need it.'

22. Another line of argument is to refute our opponent's case by noting any contrasts or contradictions of dates, acts, or words that it anywhere displays; and this in any of the three following connexions. (1) Referring to our opponent's conduct, e.g. 'He says he is devoted to you, yet he conspired with the Thirty.' (2) Referring to our own conduct, e.g. 'He says I am litigious, and yet he cannot prove that I have been engaged in a single lawsuit.' (3) Referring to both of us together, e.g. '*He* has never even *lent* any one a penny, but *I* have *ransomed* quite a number of you.'

23. Another line that is useful for men and causes that have been really or seemingly slandered, is to show why the facts are not as supposed; pointing out that there is a reason for the false impression given. Thus a woman, who had palmed off her son on another woman, was thought to be the lad's mistress because she embraced him; but when her action was explained the charge was shown to be groundless. Another example is from the *Ajax* of Theodectes, where Odysseus tells Ajax the reason why, though he is really braver than Ajax, he is not thought so.

24. Another line of argument is to show that if the *cause* is present, the *effect* is present, and if absent, absent. For by proving the cause you at once prove the effect, and conversely nothing can exist without its cause. Thus Thrasybulus accused Leodamas of having had his name recorded as a criminal on the slab in the Acropolis, and of erasing the record in the time of the Thirty Tyrants: to which Leodamas replied, 'Impossible: for the Thirty would have trusted me all the more if my quarrel with the commons had been inscribed on the slab.'

25. Another line is to consider whether the accused person can take or could have taken a better course than that which he is recommending or taking, or has taken. If he has *not* taken this better course, it is clear that he is not guilty, since no one deliberately and consciously chooses what is bad. This argument is, however, fallacious, for it often becomes clear after the event how the action could have been done better, though before the event this was far from clear.

26. Another line is, when a contemplated action is inconsistent with any past action, to examine them both together. Thus, when the people of Elea asked Xenophanes if they should or should not sacrifice to Leucothea and mourn for her, he advised them not to mourn for her if they thought her a goddess, and not to sacrifice to her if they thought her a mortal woman.

27. Another line is to make previous mistakes the grounds of accusation or defence. Thus, in the *Medea* of Carcinus the accusers allege that Medea has slain her children; 'at all events,' they say, 'they are not to be seen'— Medea having made the mistake of sending her children away. In defence she argues that it is not her children, but Jason, whom she would have slain; for it would have been a mistake on her part not to do this if she *had* done the other. This special line of argument for enthymeme forms the whole of the *Art of Rhetoric* in use before Theodorus.

28. Another line is to draw meanings from names. Sophocles, for instance, says,

O steel in heart as thou art steel in name.

This line of argument is common in praises of the gods. Thus, too, Conon called Thrasybulus *rash in counsel*. And Herodicus said of Thrasymachus, 'You are always *bold in battle*'; of Polus, 'you are always *a colt*'; and of the legislator Draco that his laws were those not of a human being but of a *dragon*, so savage were they. And, in Euripides, Hecuba says of Aphrodite,

Her name and Folly's rightly begin alike,[6]

and Chaeremon writes

Pentheus—a name foreshadowing grief to come.

The Refutative Enthymeme has a greater reputation than the Demonstrative, because within a small space it works out two opposing arguments, and arguments put side by side are clearer to the audience. But of all syllogisms, whether refutative or demonstrative, those are most applauded of which we foresee the conclusions from the beginning, so long as they are not obvious at first sight—for part of the pleasure we feel is at our own intelligent anticipation; or those which we follow well enough to see the point of them as soon as the last word has been uttered.

TOPICS FOR DISCUSSION

1. How does the opening discussion of judges and justice illustrate the difference between rhetoric and dialectic?
2. Why do writers of handbooks concern themselves with proofs not strictly belonging to the art of rhetoric? Why are they not intrinsic to the art? Why is deliberative or political rhetoric a nobler art than forensic or judicial rhetoric?
3. Why is proper rhetoric chiefly directed to the reason, particularly when both judges and auditors are shown to be susceptible to emotional appeals? Is Aristotle's conception of proper rhetoric wholly concerned with the ethical and ideal, or is it practical in conception also? Note pages 396–97, "It has now been shown . . . what rhetoric is."
4. Does Aristotle discuss the problem of proper rhetoric in the way Plato

[6]From the *Troades* of Euripides.

discusses it? Can you determine Aristotle's theory of truth from this discussion?

5. Why is it no violation of proper rhetoric to be able to argue both sides of a question? What is the point of the analogy with medicine on page 397?

6. How are rhetoric and dialectic similar and how do they differ? How are both shaped by the needs to which they are put?

7. Why is the character of the speaker the most powerful means of persuasion?

8. Why are only some of the premises in rhetorical deductions granted as necessary? What limits do circumstances enforce in such proofs?

9. How are the three kinds of rhetoric distinguished according to audience? Could the audiences overlap in these instances? What is the relation between the audience and the end of each kind of rhetoric?

10. What is the purpose of the lines of proof (given on pages 404–13) in relation to the enthymemes of rhetoric? How are these lines of proof to be defined?

11. Given Aristotle's distinction between proofs strictly and not strictly belonging to the art of rhetoric, could any of the proofs or topics cited on pages 404–13 be considered not strictly belonging? What about number 11 (page 408)—for a "decision already pronounced"?

12. Which topics are derived from the circumstances of the speech— including the opponent and audience?

TOPICS FOR COMPOSITION

1. Summarize the differences in Plato's and Aristotle's conceptions of rhetoric. Distinguish both the problems each is most interested in discussing and the assumptions about truth that underlie these discussions.

2. Provide an example of your own for each of the lines of proof— excluding numbers 20–23 and 25–28. If possible, choose these examples for a common subject so that they can be organized into a discourse.

3. Write a defense or an attack on the Vietnam war or on the preservation of the California redwoods—drawing on at least five of the lines of proof. Arrange your arguments so that they move from the less to the more convincing.

4. Examine the *Congressional Record* or *Vital Speeches* for examples of lines of proof and analyze their use in one or two instances.

❀ Modern
Theorists

RICHARD WEAVER

The "Phaedrus" and the Nature of Rhetoric

RICHARD WEAVER'S concern is not only with the structure of *Phaedrus*—with the theory of language it develops in relation to the speech being discussed—but with the nature of rhetoric itself. Weaver wishes to clarify even more than Plato does in the dialogue the essential relationship of dialectic to rhetoric. Dialectic is defined here with respect to the structure of *Phaedrus*. Weaver builds to his thesis, stated in one passage in the following words: "there is no honest rhetoric without a preceding dialectic." He reaches this idea by exploring the implicit assumptions about language underlying the three discourses of *Phaedrus*; he shows that each discourse implicitly argues for one such assumption and that the discourse itself, in its form and its ideas, illuminates the assumption. Then he moves to the general theory of rhetoric he derives from the dialogue as a whole. Basic to this theory is the idea that since dialectic is concerned with terms of policy, it is concerned with the soul itself; for terms of policy are terms of motion, and motion is an essential quality of soul. Socrates states, in explaining the myth of the charioteer, that whatever moves is immortal. Weaver states: "Rhetoric appears, finally, as a means by which the impulse of the soul to be ever moving is redeemed." The reason is that the virtuous rhetorician "has a soul of such movement that its dialectical perceptions are consonant with those of a divine mind." Weaver is using *Phaedrus* to develop a complete theory of rhetoric—that is, a theory that relates the nature of language to the nature of man. This key idea Weaver states on the title page of his complete book, in a quotation from the dialogue: "Thus it happens that rhetoric is an offshoot of dialectic and also of ethical studies."

Our subject begins with the threshold difficulty of defining the question which Plato's *Phaedrus* was meant to answer. Students of this justly celebrated dialogue have felt uncertain of its unity of theme, and the tendency has been to designate it broadly as a discussion of the ethical and the beautiful. The explicit topics of the dialogue are, in order: love, the soul, speechmaking, and the spoken and written word, or what is generally termed by us "composition." The development looks random, and some

THE PHAEDRUS AND THE NATURE OF RHETORIC From *The Ethics of Rhetoric* by Richard Weaver. Reprinted by permission of the publisher, Henry Regnery Company.

of the most interesting passages appear *jeux d'esprit*. The richness of the literary art diverts attention from the substance of the argument.

But a work of art which touches on many profound problems justifies more than one kind of reading. Our difficulty with the *Phaedrus* may be that our interpretation has been too literal and too topical. If we will bring to the reading of it even a portion of that imagination which Plato habitually exercised, we should perceive surely enough that it is consistently, and from beginning to end, about one thing, which is the nature of rhetoric.[1] Again, that point may have been missed because most readers conceive rhetoric to be a system of artifice rather than an idea,[2] and the *Phaedrus,* for all its apparent divagation, keeps very close to a single idea. A study of its rhetorical structure, especially, may give us the insight which has been withheld, while making us feel anew that Plato possessed the deepest divining rod among the ancients.

For the imaginative interpretation which we shall now undertake, we have both general and specific warrant. First, it scarcely needs pointing out that a Socratic dialogue is in itself an example of transcendence. Beginning with something simple and topical, it passes to more general levels of application; and not infrequently, it must make the leap into allegory for the final utterance. This means, of course, that a Socratic dialogue may be about its subject implicitly as well as explicitly. The implicit rendering is usually through some kind of figuration because it is the nature of this meaning to be ineffable in any other way. It is necessary, therefore, to be alert for what takes place through the analogical mode.

Second, it is a matter of curious interest that a warning against literal reading occurs at an early stage of the *Phaedrus.* Here in the opening pages, appearing as if to set the key of the theme, comes an allusion to the myth of Boreas and Oreithyia. On the very spot where the dialogue begins, Boreas is said to have carried off the maiden. Does Socrates believe that this tale is really true? Or is he in favor of a scientific explanation of what the myth alleges? Athens had scientific experts, and the scientific explanation was that the north wind had pushed her off some rocks where she was playing with a companion. In this way the poetical story is provided with a factual basis. The answer of Socrates is that many tales are open to this kind of rationalization, but that the result is tedious and actually irrelevant. It is irrelevant because our chief concern is with the nature of the man, and it is beside the point to probe into such matters while we are yet ignorant of ourselves. The scientific criticism of Greek mythology, which may be likened to the scientific criticism of the myths of the Bible in our own day, produces at best "a boorish sort of wisdom

[1]Cf. A. E. Taylor, *Plato: the Man and his Work* (New York, 1963), p. 300. [Weaver's notes throughout.]
[2]Cf. P. Albert Duhamel, "The Concept of Rhetoric as Effective Expression," *Journal of the History of Ideas,* X, No. 3 (June 1949), 344–56 *passim.*

The Theory of Rhetoric

($\dot{\alpha}\gamma\rho o i\kappa\omega$ $\tau\iota\nu\iota$ $\sigma o\phi i\dot{\alpha}$)." It is a limitation to suppose that the truth of the story lies in its historicity. The "boorish sort of wisdom" seeks to supplant poetic allegation with fact, just as an archaeologist might look for the foundations of the Garden of Eden. But while this sort of search goes on the truth flies off, on wings of imagination, and is not recoverable until the searcher attains a higher level of pursuit. Socrates is satisfied with the parable, and we infer from numerous other passages that he believed that some things are best told by parable and some perhaps discoverable only by parable. Real investigation goes forward with the help of analogy. "Freud without Sophocles is unthinkable," a modern writer has said.[3]

With these precepts in mind, we turn to that part of the *Phaedrus* which has proved most puzzling: why is so much said about the absurd relationship of the lover and the nonlover? Socrates encounters Phaedrus outside the city wall. The latter has just come from hearing a discourse by Lysias which enchanted him with its eloquence. He is prevailed upon to repeat this discourse, and the two seek out a shady spot on the banks of the Ilissus. Now the discourse is remarkable because although it was "in a way, a love speech," its argument was that people should grant favors to non-lovers rather than to lovers. "This is just the clever thing about it," Phaedrus remarks. People are in the habit of preferring their lovers, but it is much more intelligent, as the argument of Lysias runs, to prefer a non-lover. Accordingly, the first major topic of the dialogue is a eulogy of the non-lover. The speech provides good subject matter for jesting on the part of Socrates, and looks like another exhibition of the childlike ingeniousness which gives the Greeks their charm. Is it merely a piece of literary trifling? Rather, it is Plato's dramatistic presentation of a major thesis. Beneath the surface of repartee and mock seriousness, he is asking whether we ought to prefer a neuter form of speech to the kind which is ever getting us aroused over things and provoking an expense of spirit.

Sophistications of theory cannot obscure the truth that there are but three ways for language to affect us. It can move us toward what is good; it can move us toward what is evil; or it can, in hypothetical third place, fail to move us at all.[4] Of course there are numberless degrees of effect under the first two heads, and the third, as will be shown, is an approximate rather than an absolute zero of effect. But any utterance is a major assumption of responsibility, and the assumption that one can avoid that responsibility by doing something to language itself is one of the chief considerations of the *Phaedrus*, just as it is of contemporary semantic theory. What Plato has succeeded in doing in this dialogue, whether by a remarkably effaced design, or unconsciously through the formal pressure

---

[3]James Blish, "Rituals on Ezra Pound," *Sewanee Review*, LVIII (Spring, 1950), 223.
[4]The various aesthetic approaches to language offer refinements of perception, but all of them can be finally subsumed under the first head above.

Richard Weaver

of his conception, is to give us embodiments of the three types of discourse. These are respectively the non-lover, the evil lover, and the noble lover. We shall take up these figures in their sequence and show their relevance to the problem of language.

The eulogy of the non-lover in the speech of Lysias, as we hear it repeated to Socrates, stresses the fact that the non-lover follows a policy of enlightened self-interest. First of all, the non-lover does not neglect his affairs or commit extreme acts under the influence of passion. Since he acts from calculation, he never has occasion for remorse. No one ever says of him that he is not in his right mind, because all of his acts are within prudential bounds. The first point is, in sum, that the non-lover never sacrifices himself and therefore never feels the vexation which overtakes lovers when they recover from their passion and try to balance their pains with their profit. And the non-lover is constant whereas the lover is inconstant. The first argument then is that the non-lover demonstrates his superiority through prudence and objectivity. The second point of superiority found in non-lovers is that there are many more of them. If one is limited in one's choice to one's lovers, the range is small; but as there are always more non-lovers than lovers, one has a better chance in choosing among many of finding something worthy of one's affection. A third point of superiority is that association with the non-lover does not excite public comment. If one is seen going about with the object of one's love, one is likely to provoke gossip; but when one is seen conversing with the non-lover, people merely realize that "everybody must converse with somebody." Therefore this kind of relationship does not affect one's public standing, and one is not disturbed by what the neighbors are saying. Finally, non-lovers are not jealous of one's associates. Accordingly they do not try to keep one from companions of intellect or wealth for fear that they may be outshone themselves. The lover, by contrast, tries to draw his beloved away from such companionship and so deprives him of improving associations. The argument is concluded with a generalization that one ought to grant favors not to the needy or the importunate, but to those who are able to repay. Such is the favorable account of the non-lover given by Lysias.

We must now observe how these points of superiority correspond to those of "semantically purified" speech. By "semantically purified speech" we mean the kind of speech approaching pure notation in the respect that it communicates abstract intelligence without impulsion. It is a simple instrumentality, showing no affection for the object of its symbolizing and incapable of inducing bias in the hearer. In its ideal conception, it would have less power to move than $2 + 2 = 4$, since it is generally admitted that mathematical equations may have the beauty of elegance, and hence are not above suspicion where beauty is suspect. But this neuter language will be an unqualified medium of transmission of meanings from mind to mind, and by virtue of its minds can remain in an unprejudiced relationship to the world and also to other minds.

Since the characteristic of this language is absence of anything like affection, it exhibits toward the thing being represented merely a sober fidelity, like that of the non-lover toward his companion. Instead of passion, it offers the serviceability of objectivity. Its "enlightened self-interest" takes the form of an unvarying accuracy and regularity in its symbolic references, most, if not all of which will be to verifiable data in the extramental world. Like a thrifty burgher, it has no romanticism about it; and it distrusts any departure from the literal and prosaic. The burgher has his feet on the ground; and similarly the language of pure notation has its point-by-point contact with objective reality. As Stuart Chase, one of its modern proponents, says in *The Tyranny of Words: "If we wish to understand the world and ourselves, it follows that we should use a language whose structure corresponds to physical structure"* [5] (italics his). So this language is married to the world, and its marital fidelity contrasts with the extravagances of other languages.

In the second place, this language is far more "available." Whereas rhetorical language, or language which would persuade, must always be particularized to suit the occasion, drawing its effectiveness from many small nuances, a "utility" language is very general and one has no difficulty putting his meaning into it if he is satisfied with a paraphrase of that meaning. The 850 words recommended for Basic English, for example, are highly available in the sense that all native users of English have them instantly ready and learners of English can quickly acquire them. It soon becomes apparent, however, that the availability is a heavy tax upon all other qualities. Most of what we admire as energy and fullness tends to disappear when mere verbal counters are used. The conventional or public aspect of language can encroach upon the suggestive or symbolical aspect, until the naming is vague or blurred. In proportion as the medium is conventional in the widest sense and avoids all individualizing, personalizing, and heightening terms, it is common, and the commonness constitutes the negative virtue ascribed to the non-lover.

Finally, with reference to the third qualification of the non-lover, it is true that neuter language does not excite public opinion. This fact follows

[5]*The Tyranny of Words* (New York, 1938), p. 80. T. H. Huxley in *Lay Sermons* (New York, 1883), p. 112, outlined a noticeably similar ideal of scientific communication: "Therefore, the great business of the scientific teacher is, to imprint the fundamental, irrefragable facts of his science, not only by words upon the mind, but by sensible impressions upon the eye, and ear, and touch of the student in so complete a manner, that every term used, or law enunciated should afterwards call up vivid images of the particular structural, or other, facts which furnished the demonstration of the law, or illustration of the term."

from its character outlined above. Rhetorical language on the other hand, for whatever purpose used, excites interest and with it either pleasure or alarm. People listen instinctively to the man whose speech betrays inclination. It does not matter what the inclination is toward, but we may say that the greater the degree of inclination, the greater the curiosity or response. Hence a "style" in speech always causes one to be a marked man, and the public may not be so much impressed—at least initially—by what the man is for or against as by the fact that he has a style. The way therefore to avoid public comment is to avoid the speech of affection and to use that of business, since, to echo the original proposition of Lysias, everybody knows that one must do business with others. From another standpoint, then, this is the language of prudence. These are the features which give neuter discourse an appeal to those who expect a scientific solution of human problems.

In summing up the trend of meaning, we note that Lysias has been praising a disinterested kind of relationship which avoids all excesses and irrationalities, all the dementia of love. It is a circumspect kind of relationship, which is preferred by all men who wish to do well in the world and avoid tempestuous courses. We have compared its detachment with the kind of abstraction to be found in scientific notation. But as an earnest of what is to come let us note, in taking leave of this part, that Phaedrus expresses admiration for the eloquence, especially of diction, with which the suit of the non-lover has been urged. This is our warning of the dilemma of the non-lover.

Now we turn to the second major speech of the dialogue, which is made by Socrates. Notwithstanding Phaedrus' enthusiastic praise, Socrates is dissatisfied with the speech of the non-lover. He remembers having heard wiser things on the subject and feels that he can make a speech on the same theme "different from this and quite as good." After some playful exchange, Socrates launches upon his own abuse of love, which centers on the point that the lover is an exploiter. Love ($\check{\epsilon}\rho\omega\varsigma$) is defined as the kind of desire which overcomes rational opinion and moves toward the enjoyment of personal or bodily beauty. The lover wishes to make the object of his passion as pleasing to himself as possible; but to those possessed by this frenzy, only that which is subject to their will is pleasant. Accordingly, everything which is opposed, or is equal or better, the lover views with hostility. He naturally therefore tries to make the beloved inferior to himself in every respect. He is pleased if the beloved has intellectual limitations because they have the effect of making him manageable. For a similar reason he tries to keep him away from all influences which might "make a man of him," and of course the greatest of these is divine philosophy. While he is working to keep him intellectually immature, he works also to keep him weak and effeminate, with such harmful result that the beloved is unable to play a man's part in crises. The lover is, moreover, jealous of the possession of property because this gives the beloved an independence which he does not wish him to have. Thus the lover in exercising an unremitting compulsion over the beloved deprives him of all praiseworthy qualities, and this is the price the beloved pays for accepting a lover who is "necessarily without reason." In brief, the lover is not motivated by benevolence toward the beloved, but by selfish appetite; and Socrates can aptly close with the quotation: "As wolves love lambs, so lovers love their loves." The speech is on the single theme of exploitation. It is important for us to keep in mind the object of love as here described, because another kind of love with a different object is later introduced into the dialogue, and we shall discuss the counterpart of each.

As we look now for the parallel in language, we find ourselves confronting the second of the three alternatives: speech which influences us in the direction of what is evil. This we shall call base rhetoric because its end is the exploitation which Socrates has been condemning. We find that base rhetoric hates that which is opposed, or is equal or better because all such things are impediments to its will, and in the last analysis it knows only its will. Truth is the stubborn, objective restraint which this will endeavors to overcome. Base rhetoric is therefore always trying to keep its objects from the support which personal courage, noble associations, and divine philosophy provide a man.

The base rhetorician, we may say, is a man who has yielded to the wrong aspects of existence. He has allowed himself to succumb to the sights and shows, to the physical pleasures which conspire against noble life. He knows that the only way he can get a following in his pursuits (and a following seems necessary to maximum enjoyment of the pursuits) is to work against the true understanding of his followers. Consequently the things which would elevate he keeps out of sight, and the things with which he surrounds his "beloved" are those which minister immediately to desire. The beloved is thus emasculated in understanding in order that the lover may have his way. Or as Socrates expresses it, the selfish lover contrives things so that the beloved will be "most agreeable to him and most harmful to himself."

Examples of this kind of contrivance occur on every hand in the impassioned language of journalism and political pleading. In the world of affairs which these seek to influence, the many are kept in a state of pupillage so that they will be most docile to their "lovers." The techniques of the base lover, especially as exemplified in modern journalism, would make a long catalogue, but in general it is accurate to say that he seeks to keep the understanding in a passive state by never permitting an honest examination of alternatives. Nothing is more feared by him than a true dialectic, for this not only endangers his favored alternative, but also gives the "beloved"—how clearly here are these the "lambs" of Socrates' figure —some training in intellectual independence. What he does therefore is dress up one alternative in all the cheap finery of immediate hopes and fears, knowing that if he can thus prevent a masculine exercise of imagination and will, he can have his way. By discussing only one side of an issue, by mentioning cause without consequence or consequence without cause, acts without agents or agents without agency,[6] he often successfully blocks definition and cause-and-effect reasoning. In this way his choices are arrayed in such meretricious images that one can quickly infer the juvenile mind which they would attract. Of course the base rhetorician today, with his vastly augmented power of propagation, has means of deluding which no ancient rhetor in forum or market place could have imagined.

Because Socrates has now made a speech against love, representing it as an evil, the non-lover seems to survive in estimation. We observe, however, that the non-lover, instead of being celebrated, is disposed of dialectically. "So, in a word, I say that the non-lover possesses all the advantages that are opposed to the disadvantages we found in the lover." This is not without bearing upon the subject matter of the important third speech, to which we now turn.

At this point in the dialogue, Socrates is warned by his monitory spirit that he has been engaging in a defamation of love despite the fact that love is a divinity. "If love is, as indeed he is, a god or something divine, he can be nothing evil; but the two speeches just now said that he was evil." These discourses were then an impiety—one representing non-love as admirable and the other attacking love as base. Socrates resolves to make amends, and the recantation which follows is one of the most elaborate developments in the Platonic system. The account of love which emerges from this new position may be summarized as follows.

Love is often censured as a form of madness, yet not all madness is evil. There is a madness which is simple degeneracy, but on the other ·hand there are kinds of madness which are really forms of inspiration, from which come the greatest gifts conferred on man. Prophecy is a kind of madness, and so too is poetry. "The poetry of the sane man vanishes into nothingness before that of the inspired madman." Mere sanity, which is of human origin, is inferior to that madness which is inspired by the gods and which is a condition for the highest kind of achievement. In this category goes the madness of the true lover. His is a generous state which confers blessings to the ignoring of self, whereas the conduct of the non-lover displays all the selfishness of business: "the affection of the non-lover, which is alloyed with mortal prudence and follows mortal and parsimonious rules of conduct will beget in the beloved soul the narrowness which common folk praise as virtue; it will cause the soul to be a wanderer upon the earth for nine thousand years and a fool below the

[6]That is, by mentioning only parts of the total situation.

earth at last." It is the vulgar who do not realize that the madness of the noble lover is an inspired madness because he has his thoughts turned toward a beauty of divine origin.

Now the attitude of the noble lover toward the beloved is in direct contrast with that of the evil lover, who, as we have seen, strives to possess and victimize the object of his affections. For once the noble lover has mastered the conflict within his own soul by conquering appetite and fixing his attention upon the intelligible and the divine, he conceives an exalted attitude toward the beloved. The noble lover now "follows the beloved in reverence and awe." So those who are filled with this kind of love "exhibit no jealousy or meanness toward the loved one, but endeavor by every means in their power to lead him to the likeness of the god whom they honor." Such is the conversion by which love turns from the exploitative to the creative.

Here it becomes necessary to bring our concepts together and to think of all speech having persuasive power as a kind of "love." [7] Thus, rhetorical speech is madness to the extent that it departs from the line which mere sanity lays down. There is always in its statement a kind of excess or deficiency which is immediately discernible when the test of simple realism is applied. Simple realism operates on a principle of equation or correspondence; one thing must match another, or, representation must tally with thing represented, like items in a tradesman's account. Any excess or deficiency on the part of the representation invokes the existence of the world of symbolism, which simple realism must deny. This explains why there is an immortal feud between men of business and the users of metaphor and metonymy, the poets and the rhetoricians.[8] The man of business, the narrow and parsimonious soul in the allusion of Socrates, desires a world which is a reliable materiality. But this the poet and rhetorician will never let him have, for each, with his own purpose, is trying to advance the borders of the imaginative world. A primrose by the river's brim will not remain that in the poet's account, but is promptly turned into something very much larger and something highly implicative. He who is accustomed to record the world with an abacus cannot follow these transfigurations; and indeed the very occurrence of them subtly undermines the premise of his business. It is the historic tendency of the tradesman, therefore, to confine passion to quite narrow channels so that it will not upset the decent business arrangements of the world. But if the poet, as the chief transformer of our picture of the world, is the peculiar enemy of

---

[7] It is worth recalling that in the Christian New Testament, with its heavy Platonic influence, God is identified both with *logos*, "word, speech" (John 1:1), and with *agape*, "love" (2 John 4:8).

[8] The users of metaphor and metonymy who are in the hire of businessmen of course constitute a special case.

Richard Weaver

this mentality, the rhetorician is also hostile when practising the kind of love proper to him. The "passion" in his speech is revolutionary, and it has a practical end.

We have now indicated the significance of the three types of lovers; but the remainder of the *Phaedrus* has much more to say about the nature of rhetoric, and we must return to one or more points to place our subject in a wider context. The problem of rhetoric which occupied Plato persistently, not only in the *Phaedrus* but also in other dialogues where this art is reviewed, may be best stated as a question: if truth alone is not sufficient to persuade men, what else remains that can be legitimately added? In one of the exchanges with Phaedrus, Socrates puts the question in the mouth of a personified Rhetoric: "I do not compel anyone to learn to speak without knowing the truth, but if my advice is of any value, he learns that first and then acquires me. So what I claim is this, that without my help the knowledge of the truth does not give the art of persuasion."

Now rhetoric as we have discussed it in relation to the lovers consists of truth plus its artful presentation, and for this reason it becomes necessary to say something more about the natural order of dialectic and rhetoric. In any general characterization rhetoric will include dialectic,[9] but for the study of method it is necessary to separate the two. Dialectic is a method of investigation whose object is the establishment of truth about doubtful propositions. Aristotle in the *Topics* gives a concise statement of its nature. "A dialectical problem is a subject of inquiry that contributes either to choice or avoidance, or to truth and knowledge, and that either by itself, or as a help to the solution of some other such problem. It must, moreover, be something on which either people hold no opinion either way, or the masses hold a contrary opinion to the philosophers, or the philosophers to the masses, or each of them among themselves."[10] Plato is not perfectly clear about the distinction between positive and dialectical terms. In one passage[11] he contrasts the "positive" terms "iron" and "silver" with the "dialectical" terms "justice" and "goodness"; yet in other passages his "dialectical" terms seem to include categorizations of the external world. Thus Socrates indicates that distinguishing the horse from the ass is a dialectical operation;[12] and he tells us later that a good dialectician is able to divide things by classes "where the natural joints are" and will

---

[9]Cf. 277 b: "A man must know the truth about all the particular things of which he speaks or writes, and must be able to define everything separately; then when he has defined them, he must know how to divide them by classes until further division is impossible; and in the same way he must understand the nature of the soul, must find out the class of speech adapted to each nature, and must arrange and adorn his discourse accordingly, offering to the complex soul elaborate and harmonious discourses, and simple talks to the simple soul." [See p. 382.]

[10]104 b.

[11]263 a. [See p. 374.]

[12]260 b. [See p. 371.]

The Theory of Rhetoric

avoid breaking any part "after the manner of a bad carver." [13] Such, perhaps, is Aristotle's dialectic which contributes to truth and knowledge.

But there is a branch of dialectic which contributes to "choice or avoidance," and it is with this that rhetoric is regularly found joined. Generally
speaking, this is a rhetoric involving questions of policy, and the dialectic
which precedes it will determine not the application of positive terms but
that of terms which are subject to the contingency of evaluation. Here
dialectical inquiry will concern itself not with what is "iron" but with
what is "good." It seeks to establish what belongs in the category of the
"just" rather than what belongs in the genus *Canis*. As a general rule,
simple object words such as "iron" and "house" have no connotations of
policy, although it is frequently possible to give them these through speech
situations in which there is added to their referential function a kind of
impulse. We should have to interpret in this way "Fire!" or "Gold!" because these terms acquire something through intonation and relationship
which places them in the class of evaluative expressions.

Any piece of persuasion, therefore, will contain as its first process a
dialectic establishing terms which have to do with policy. Now a term of
policy is essentially a term of motion, and here begins the congruence of
rhetoric with the soul which underlies the speculation of the *Phaedrus*.
In his myth of the charioteer, Socrates declares that every soul is immortal because "that which is ever moving is immortal." Motion, it would
appear from this definition, is part of the soul's essence. And just because
the soul is ever tending, positive or indifferent terms cannot partake of
this congruence. But terms of tendency—goodness, justice, divinity, and
the like—are terms of motion and therefore may be said to comport with
the soul's essence. The soul's perception of goodness, justice, and divinity
will depend upon its proper tendency, while at the same time contacts with
these in discourse confirm and direct that tendency. The education of the
soul is not a process of bringing it into correspondence with a physical
structure like the external world, but rather a process of rightly affecting
its motion. By this conception, a soul which is rightly affected calls that
good which is good; but a soul which is wrongly turned calls that good
which is evil. What Plato has prepared us to see is that the virtuous rhetorician, who is a lover of truth, has a soul of such movement that its
dialectical perceptions are consonant with those of a divine mind. Or, in
the language of more technical philosophy, this soul is aware of axiological
systems which have ontic status. The good soul, consequently, will not
urge a perversion of justice as justice in order to impose upon the commonwealth. Insofar as the soul has its impulse in the right direction, its definitions will agree with the true nature of intelligible things.

There is, then, no true rhetoric without dialectic, for the dialectic pro-

[13]265 a. [See p. 377.]

Richard Weaver

vides that basis of "high speculation about nature" without which rhetoric in the narrower sense has nothing to work upon. Yet, when the disputed terms have been established, we are at the limit of dialectic. How does the noble rhetorician proceed from this point on? That the clearest demonstration in terms of logical inclusion and exclusion often fails to win assent we hardly need state; therefore, to what does the rhetorician resort at this critical passage? It is the stage at which he passes from the logical to the analogical, or it is where figuration comes into rhetoric.

To look at this for a moment through a practical illustration, let us suppose that a speaker has convinced his listeners that his position is "true" as far as dialectical inquiry may be pushed. Now he sets about moving the listeners toward that position, but there is no way to move them except through the operation of analogy. The analogy proceeds by showing that the position being urged resembles or partakes of something greater and finer. It will be represented, in sum, as one of the steps leading toward ultimate good. Let us further suppose our speaker to be arguing for the payment of a just debt. The payment of the just debt is not itself justice, but the payment of this particular debt is one of the many things which would have to be done before this could be a completely just world. It is just, then, because it partakes of the ideal justice, or it is a small analogue of all justice (in practice it will be found that the rhetorician makes extensive use of synecdoche, whereby the small part is used as a vivid suggestion of the grandeur of the whole). It is by bringing out these resemblances that the good rhetorician leads those who listen in the direction of what is good. In effect, he performs a cure of souls by giving impulse, chiefly through figuration, toward an ideal good.

We now see the true rhetorician as a noble lover of the good, who works through dialectic and through poetic or analogical association. However he is compelled to modulate by the peculiar features of an occasion, this is his method.

It may not be superfluous to draw attention to the fact that what we have here outlined is the method of the *Phaedrus* itself. The dialectic appears in the dispute about love. The current thesis that love is praiseworthy is countered by the antithesis that love is blameworthy. This position is fully developed in the speech of Lysias and in the first speech of Socrates. But this position is countered by a new thesis that after all love is praiseworthy because it is a divine thing. Of course, this is love on a higher level, or love re-defined. This is the regular process of transcendence which we have noted before. Now, having rescued love from the imputation of evil by excluding certain things from its definition, what does Socrates do? Quite in accordance with our analysis, he turns rhetorician. He tries to make this love as attractive as possible by bringing in the

[14]In the passage extending from 246 a to 256 d. [See p. 358.]

The Theory of Rhetoric

splendid figure of the charioteer.[14] In the narrower conception of this art, the allegory is the rhetoric, for it excites and fills us with desire for this kind of love, depicted with many terms having tendency toward the good. But in the broader conception the art must include also the dialectic, which succeeded in placing love in the category of divine things before filling our imaginations with attributes of divinity.[15] It is so regularly the method of Plato to follow a subtle analysis with a striking myth that it is not unreasonable to call him the master rhetorician. This goes far to explain why those who reject his philosophy sometimes remark his literary art with mingled admiration and annoyance.

The objection sometimes made that rhetoric cannot be used by a lover of truth because it indulges in "exaggerations" can be answered as follows. There is an exaggeration which is mere wantonness, and with this the true rhetorician has nothing to do. Such exaggeration is purely impressionistic in aim. Like caricature, whose only object is to amuse, it seizes upon any trait or aspect which could produce titillation and exploits this without conscience. If all rhetoric were like this, we should have to grant that rhetoricians are persons of very low responsibility and their art a disreputable one. But the rhetorician we have now defined is not interested in sensationalism.

The exaggeration which this rhetorician employs is not caricature but prophecy; and it would be a fair formulation to say that true rhetoric is concerned with the potency of things. The literalist, like the anti-poet described earlier, is troubled by its failure to conform to a present reality. What he fails to appreciate is that potentiality is a mode of existence, and that all prophecy is about the tendency of things. The discourse of the noble rhetorician, accordingly, will be about real potentiality or possible actuality, whereas that of the mere exaggerator is about unreal potentiality. Naturally this distinction rests upon a supposal that the rhetorician has insight, and we could not defend him in the absence of that condition. But given insight, he has the duty to represent to us the as yet unactualized future. It would be, for example, a misrepresentation of current facts but not of potential ones to talk about the joys of peace in a time of war. During the Second World War, at the depth of Britain's political and military disaster, Winston Churchill likened the future of Europe to "broad sunlit uplands." Now if one had regard only for the hour, this was a piece of mendacity such as the worst charlatans are found committing; but if one took Churchill's premises and then considered the potentiality, the picture was within bounds of actualization. His "exaggeration" was that the defeat of the enemy would place Europe in a position for long and peaceful progress. At the time the surface trends ran the other way; the actuality was a valley of humiliation. Yet the hope which transfigured this

[15]Cf. 263 d ff. [See p. 375.]

Richard Weaver 427

to "broad sunlit uplands" was not irresponsible, and we conclude by saying that the rhetorician talks about both what exists simply and what exists by favor of human imagination and effort.[16]

This interest in actualization is a further distinction between pure dialectic and rhetoric. With its forecast of the actual possibility, rhetoric passes from mere scientific demonstration of an idea to its relation to prudential conduct. A dialectic must take place *in vacuo,* and the fact alone that it contains contraries leaves it an intellectual thing. Rhetoric, on the other hand, always espouses one of the contraries. This espousal is followed by some attempt at impingement upon actuality. That is why rhetoric, with its passion for the actual, is more complete than mere dialectic with its dry understanding. It is more complete on the premise that man is a creature of passion who must live out that passion in the world. Pure contemplation does not suffice for this end. As Jacques Maritain has expressed it: "love . . . is not directed at possibilities or pure essences; it is directed at what exists; one does not love possibilities, one loves that which exists or is destined to exist." [17] The complete man, then, is the "lover" added to the scientist; the rhetorician to the dialectician. Understanding followed by actualization seems to be the order of creation, and there is no need for the role of rhetoric to be misconceived.

The pure dialectician is left in the theoretical position of the non-lover, who can attain understanding but who cannot add impulse to truth. We are compelled to say "theoretical position" because it is by no means certain that in the world of actual speech the non-lover has more than a putative existence. We have seen previously that his speech would consist of strictly referential words which would serve only as designata. Now the question arises: at what point is motive to come into such language? Kenneth Burke in *A Grammar of Motives* has pointed to "the pattern of embarrassment behind the contemporary ideal of a language that will best promote good action by entirely eliminating the element of exhorta-

---

[16]Indeed, in this particular rhetorical duel we see the two types of lovers opposed as clearly as illustration could desire. More than this, we see the third type, the non-lover, committing his ignominious failure. Britain and France had come to prefer as leaders the rhetoricless businessman type. And while they had thus emasculated themselves, there appeared an evil lover to whom Europe all but succumbed before the mistake was seen and rectified. For while the world must move, evil rhetoric is of more force than no rhetoric at all; and Herr Hitler, employing images which rested on no true dialectic, had persuaded multitudes that his order was the "new order," *i.e.,* the true potentiality. Britain was losing and could only lose until, reaching back in her traditional past, she found a voice which could match his accents with a truer grasp of the potentiality of things. Thus two men conspicuous for passion fought a contest for souls, which the nobler won. But the contest could have been lost by default.

[17]"Action: the Perfection of Human Life," *Sewanee Review,* LVI (Winter, 1948), 3.

tion or command. Insofar as such a project succeeded, its terms would involve a narrowing of circumference to a point where the principle of personal action is eliminated from language, so that an act would follow from it only as a non sequitur, a kind of humanitarian after-thought." [18]

The fault of this conception of language is that scientific intention turns out to be enclosed in artistic intention and not *vice versa*. Let us test this by taking as an example one of these "fact-finding committees" so favored by modern representative governments. A language in which all else is suppressed in favor of nuclear meanings would be an ideal instrumentality for the report of such a committee. But this committee, if it lived up to the ideal of its conception, would have to be followed by an "attitude-finding committee" to tell us what its explorations really mean. In real practice the fact-finding committee understands well enough that it is also an attitude-finding committee, and where it cannot show inclination through language of tendency, it usually manages to do so through selection and arrangement of the otherwise inarticulate facts. To recur here to the original situation in the dialogue, we recall that the eloquent Lysias, posing as a non-lover, had concealed designs upon Phaedrus, so that his fine speech was really a sheep's clothing. Socrates discerned in him a "peculiar craftiness." One must suspect the same today of many who ask us to place our faith in the neutrality of their discourse. We cannot deny that there are degrees of objectivity in the reference of speech. But this is not the same as an assurance that a vocabulary of reduced meanings will solve the problems of mankind. Many of those problems will have to be handled, as Socrates well knew, by the student of souls, who must primarily make use of the language of tendency. The soul is impulse, not simply cognition; and finally one's interest in rhetoric depends on how much poignancy one senses in existence.[19]

Rhetoric moves the soul with a movement which cannot finally be justified logically. It can only be valued analogically with reference to some supreme image. Therefore when the rhetorician encounters some soul "sinking beneath the double load of forgetfulness and vice" he seeks to

---

[18]*A Grammar of Motives* (New York, 1945), p. 90.

[19]Without rhetoric there seems no possibility of tragedy, and in turn, without the sense of tragedy, no possibility of taking an elevated view of life. The role of tragedy is to keep the human lot from being rendered as history. The cultivation of tragedy and a deep interest in the value-conferring power of language always occur together. The *Phaedrus*, the *Gorgias*, and the *Cratylus*, not to mention the works of many teachers of rhetoric, appear at the close of the great age of Greek tragedy. The Elizabethan age teemed with treatises on the use of language. The essentially tragic Christian view of life begins the long tradition of homiletics. Tragedy and the practice of rhetoric seem to find common sustenance in preoccupation with value, and then rhetoric follows as an analyzed art.

re-animate it by holding up to its sight the order of presumptive goods. This order is necessarily a hierarchy leading up to the ultimate good. All of the terms in a rhetorical vocabulary are like links in a chain stretching up to some master link which transmits its influence down through the linkages. It is impossible to talk about rhetoric as effective expression without having as a term giving intelligibility to the whole discourse, the Good. Of course, inferior concepts of the Good may be and often are placed in this ultimate position; and there is nothing to keep a base lover from inverting the proper order and saying, "Evil, be thou my good." Yet the fact remains that in any piece of rhetorical discourse, one rhetorical term overcomes another rhetorical term only by being nearer to the term which stands ultimate. There is some ground for calling a rhetorical education necessarily an aristocratic education in that the rhetorician has to deal with an aristocracy of notions, to say nothing of supplementing his logical and pathetic proofs with an ethical proof.

All things considered, rhetoric, noble or base, is a great power in the world; and we note accordingly that at the center of the public life of every people there is a fierce struggle over who shall control the means of rhetorical propagation. Today we set up "offices of information," which like the sly lover in the dialogue, pose as non-lovers while pushing their suits. But there is no reason to despair over the fact that men will never give up seeking to influence one another. We would not desire it to be otherwise; neuter discourse is a false idol, to worship which is to commit the very offense for which Socrates made expiation in his second speech.

Since we want not emancipation from impulse but clarification of impulse, the duty of rhetoric is to bring together action and understanding into a whole that is greater than scientific perception.[20] The realization that just as no action is really indifferent, so no utterance is without its responsibility introduces, it is true, a certain strenuosity into life, produced by a consciousness that "nothing is lost." Yet this is preferable to that desolation which proceeds from an infinite dispersion or feeling of unaccountability. Even so, the choice between them is hardly ours to make;

---

[20]Cf. Maritain, op. cit., pp. 3–4: "The truth of practical intellect is understood not as conformity to an extramental being but as conformity to a right desire; the end is no longer to know what is, but to bring into existence that which is not yet; further, the act of moral choice is so individualized both by the singularity of the person from which it proceeds and the context of the contingent circumstances in which it takes place, that the practical judgment in which it is expressed and by which I declare to myself: this is what I must do, can be right only if, hic et nunc, the dynamism of my will is right, and tends towards the true goods of human life.

"That is why practical wisdom, prudentia, is a virtue indivisibly moral and intellectual at the same time, and why, like the judgment of the conscience itself, it cannot be replaced by any sort of theoretical knowledge or science."

we did not create the order of things, but being accountable for our impulses, we wish these to be just.

Thus when we finally divest rhetoric of all the notions of artifice which have grown up around it, we are left with something very much like Spinoza's "intellectual love of God." This is its essence and the *fons et origo* of its power. It is "intellectual" because, as we have previously seen, there is no honest rhetoric without a preceding dialectic. The kind of rhetoric which is justly condemned is utterance in support of a position before that position has been adjudicated with reference to the whole universe of discourse[21]—and of such the world always produces more than enough. It is "love" because it is something in addition to bare theoretical truth. That element in addition is a desire to bring truth into a kind of existence, or to give it an actuality to which theory is indifferent. Now what is to be said about our last expression, "of God"? Echoes of theological warfare will cause many to desire a substitute for this, and we should not object. As long as we have in ultimate place the highest good man can intuit, the relationship is made perfect. We shall be content with "intellectual love of the Good." It is still the intellectual love of good which causes the noble lover to desire not to devour his beloved but to shape him according to the gods as far as mortal power allows. So rhetoric at its truest seeks to perfect men by showing them better versions of themselves, links in that chain extending up toward the ideal, which only the intellect can apprehend and only the soul have affection for. This is the justified affection of which no one can be ashamed, and he who feels no influence of it is truly outside the communion of minds. Rhetoric appears, finally, as a means by which the impulse of the soul to be ever moving is redeemed.

It may be granted that in this essay we have gone some distance from the banks of the Ilissus. What began as a simple account of passion becomes by transcendence an allegory of all speech. No one would think of suggesting that Plato had in mind every application which has here been made, but that need not arise as an issue. The structure of the dialogue, the way in which the judgments about speech concentre, and especially the close association of the true, the beautiful, and the good, constitute a unity of implication. The central idea is that all speech, which is the means the gods have given man to express his soul, is a form of eros, in the proper interpretation of the word. With that truth the rhetorician will always be brought face to face as soon as he ventures beyond the consideration of mere artifice and device.

[21]Socrates' criticism of the speech of Lysias (263 d ff.) is that the latter defended a position without having submitted it to the discipline of dialectic. [See p. 375.]

Richard Weaver

TOPICS FOR DISCUSSION

1. What does Weaver mean by "a Socratic dialogue is in itself an example of transcendence"? Look up *transcendence* and *dialectic* in a dictionary. What relationship do you find between these ideas? Where in *Phaedrus* is there a passing to "more general levels of application"?

2. Look up *parable* and *allegory* in a dictionary. What does Weaver mean on page 417 by "some things are best told by parable and some perhaps discoverable only by parable. Real investigation goes forward with the help of analogy"? How has Weaver interpreted the speech of Lysias and the first speech of Socrates?

3. In the discussion of the theory of language exemplified by the second speech (page 421), how does the context of the discussion help to define "a true dialectic"? How is the nonlover "disposed of dialectically" (page 422)?

4. What are the means of deluding that the "base rhetorician today" (pages 421–22) has at his command?

5. Why is there "an immortal feud between men of business and the users of metaphor and metonymy, the poets and the rhetoricians" (page 423)? How do the poet and the rhetorician each "advance the borders of the imaginative world"?

6. How does Weaver define "policy"? Why is the dialectic related to policy usually connected with rhetoric?

7. How is "a term of policy . . . essentially a term of motion" (page 425)? How is the Platonic idea that virtue is knowledge related to the idea of good rhetoric?

8. How may the rhetorician use synecdoche?

9. What is the difference between exaggeration and prophecy in rhetoric? Under what circumstances would Churchill's statement about the future of Europe have been a lie?

10. In what sense is rhetoric more complete than "mere dialectic"? What is its relationship to "prudential conduct"? What is the relationship between "actualization" and love?

11. What is Weaver's criticism of the language in which "all else is suppressed in favor of nuclear meanings"?

12. In what sense is no utterance without its responsibility? What does the context reveal about the meaning of "a certain strenuosity"?

13. Why can there be no "honest rhetoric without a preceding dialectic"?

14. In the concluding paragraph, Weaver deals by implication with the discussion in *Phaedrus* between the written and the spoken word. How does he do this, and what would be his interpretation of that discussion in relation to the whole dialogue?

15. Would Weaver agree with the distinction Aristotle makes between rhetoric and dialectic? Where do you think he would differ from Aristotle in his conception of the uses of rhetoric? Would he agree with Aristotle's conception of dialectic?

TOPICS FOR COMPOSITION

1. Summarize in your own words Weaver's conception of good rhetoric.
2. On the basis of his remarks in this essay discuss what you think Weaver's attitude would be toward Aristotle's conception of rhetoric. Compare carefully their various distinctions.
3. Analyze a piece of writing to indicate which of the three kinds of language you find. Give specific reasons for your judgments.
4. Summarize Weaver's analysis of the structure of *Phaedrus*.

WAYNE C. BOOTH

The Rhetorical Stance

WAYNE BOOTH'S chief concern here is with the problems both students and teachers face in composition courses and writing assignments. He believes that dull writing results when the writer fails to take what Booth calls a rhetorical stance—the balancing of three elements present in every writing and speaking situation. The nature of this stance is the subject of the essay. Booth originally directed this essay to teachers of English; his choice of examples reveals how carefully he has observed his own advice. Had he been writing to scholars chiefly concerned with producing the kind of articles he refers to in his discussion of the "pedant's stance," his management of tone—the management of language as a reflection of attitudes and values—his choice of examples, and his organization would have been different. He probably would have shown how greater attention to the audience might increase the interest of scholarly articles and perhaps even enliven them. Had Booth been writing to advertisers, he might have shown why many advertisements undervalue the subject and "overvalue pure effect." He would at the beginning have gauged the interests and particular qualities of his audience as we all do in any conversation in which we are interested in making a convincing point rather than in just hearing ourselves talk. Indeed the importance of Plato's distinction between writing and speech is revealed in Booth's remarks. A student who had discussed More's *Utopia* with his teacher or his class would not have produced a vacuous discussion because from the beginning he would have been aware of a purpose to which the discussion would be naturally fitted. This kind of determination is enforced by the speaking situation in a way that does not hold for the writing situation.

Last fall I had an advanced graduate student, bright, energetic, well-informed, whose papers were almost unreadable. He managed to be pretentious, dull, and disorganized in his paper on *Emma*, and pretentious, dull, and disorganized on *Madame Bovary*. On *The Golden Bowl* he was all these and obscure as well. Then one day, toward the end of term, he cornered me after class and said, "You know, I think you were all wrong about Robbe-Grillet's *Jealousy* today." We didn't have time to discuss it,

THE RHETORICAL STANCE From *College Composition and Communication*, Vol. 14, No. 3 (October 1963). Reprinted with the permission of the National Council of Teachers of English and Wayne C. Booth.

The Theory of Rhetoric

so I suggested that he write me a note about it. Five hours later I found in my faculty box a four-page polemic, unpretentious, stimulating, organized, convincing. Here was a man who had taught freshman composition for several years and who was incapable of committing any of the more obvious errors that we think of as characteristic of bad writing. Yet he could not write a decent sentence, paragraph, or paper until his rhetorical problem was solved—until, that is, he had found a definition of his audience, his argument, and his own proper tone of voice.

The word "rhetoric" is one of those catch-all terms that can easily raise trouble when our backs are turned. As it regains a popularity that it once seemed permanently to have lost, its meanings seem to range all the way from something like "the whole art of writing on any subject," as in Kenneth Burke's *The Rhetoric of Religion*, through "the special arts of persuasion," on down to fairly narrow notions about rhetorical figures and devices. And of course we still have with us the meaning of "empty bombast," as in the phrase "merely rhetorical."

I suppose that the question of the role of rhetoric in the English course is meaningless if we think of rhetoric in either its broadest or its narrowest meanings. No English course could avoid dealing with rhetoric in Burke's sense, under whatever name, and on the other hand nobody would ever advocate anything so questionable as teaching "mere rhetoric." But if we settle on the following, traditional, definition, some real questions are raised: "Rhetoric is the art of finding and employing the most effective means of persuasion on any subject, considered independently of intellectual mastery of that subject." As the students say, "Prof. X knows his stuff but he doesn't know how to put it across." If rhetoric is thought of as the art of "putting it across," considered as quite distinct from mastering an "it" in the first place, we are immediately landed in a bramble bush of controversy. Is there such an art? If so, what does it consist of? Does it have a content of its own? Can it be taught? Should it be taught? If it should, how do we go about it, head on or obliquely?

Obviously it would be foolish to try to deal with many of these issues in twenty minutes. But I wish that there were more signs of our taking all of them seriously. I wish that along with our new passion for structural linguistics, for example, we could point to the development of a rhetorical theory that would show just how knowledge of structural linguistics can be useful to anyone interested in the art of persuasion. I wish there were more freshman texts that related every principle and every rule to functional principles of rhetoric, or, where this proves impossible, I wish one found more systematic discussion of why it is impossible. But for today, I must content myself with a brief look at the charge that there is nothing distinctive and teachable about the art of rhetoric.

The case against the isolability and teachability of rhetoric may look at first like a good one. Nobody writes rhetoric, just as nobody ever writes writing. What we write and speak is always *this* discussion of the decline of railroading and *that* discussion of Pope's couplets and the other argument for abolishing the poll-tax or for getting rhetoric back into English studies.

We can also admit that like all the arts, the art of rhetoric is at best very chancy, only partly amenable to systematic teaching; as we are all painfully aware when our 1:00 section goes miserably and our 2:00 section of the same course is a delight, our own rhetoric is not entirely under control. Successful rhetoricians are to some extent like poets, born, not made. They are also dependent on years of practice and experience. And we can finally admit that even the firmest of principles about writing cannot be taught in the same sense that elementary logic or arithmetic or French can be taught. In my first year of teaching, I had a student who started his first two essays with a swear word. When I suggested that perhaps the third paper ought to start with something else, he protested that his high school teacher had taught him always to catch the reader's attention. Now the teacher was right, but the application of even such a firm principle requires reserves of tact that were somewhat beyond my freshman.

But with all of the reservations made, surely the charge that the art of persuasion cannot in any sense be taught is baseless. I cannot think that anyone who has ever read Aristotle's *Rhetoric* or, say, Whateley's *Elements of Rhetoric* could seriously make the charge. There is more than enough in these and the other traditional rhetorics to provide structure and content for a year-long course. I believe that such a course, when planned and carried through with intelligence and flexibility, can be one of the most important of all educational experiences. But it seems obvious that the arts of persuasion cannot be learned in one year, that a good teacher will continue to teach them regardless of his subject matter, and that we as English teachers have a special responsibility at all levels to get certain basic rhetorical principles into all of our writing assignments. When I think back over the experiences which have had any actual effect on my writing, I find the great good fortune of a splendid freshman course, taught by a man who believed in what he was doing, but I also find a collection of other experiences quite unconnected with a specific writing course. I remember the instructor in psychology who pencilled one word after a peculiarly pretentious paper of mine: *bull.* I remember the day when P. A. Christensen talked with me about my Chaucer paper, and made me understand that my failure to use effective transitions was not simply a technical fault but a fundamental block in my effort to get him to see my meaning. His off-the-cuff pronouncement that I should never let myself write a sentence that was not in some way explicitly attached to preceding and following sentences meant far more to me at that moment, when I had something I wanted to say, than it could have meant as part of a pattern of such rules offered in a writing course. Similarly, I can remember the devastating lessons about my bad writing that Ronald Crane could teach with a simple question mark on a graduate seminar paper, or a pencilled "Evidence for this?" or "Why this section here?" or "Everybody says so. Is it true?"

Such experiences are not, I like to think, simply the result of my being a late bloomer. At least I find my colleagues saying such things as "I didn't learn to write until I became a newspaper reporter," or "The most important training in writing I had was doing a dissertation under old *Blank*." Sometimes they go on to say that the freshman course was useless; sometimes they say that it was an indispensable preparation for the later experience. The diversity of such replies is so great as to suggest that before we try to reorganize the freshman course, with or without explicit confrontations with rhetorical categories, we ought to look for whatever there is in common among our experiences, both of good writing and of good writing instruction. Whatever we discover in such an enterprise ought to be useful to us at any level of our teaching. It will not, presumably, decide once and for all what should be the content of the freshman course, if there should be such a course. But it might serve as a guideline for the development of widely different programs in the widely differing institutional circumstances in which we must work.

The common ingredient that I find in all of the writing I admire—excluding for now novels, plays and poems—is something that I shall reluctantly call the rhetorical stance, a stance which depends on discovering and maintaining in any writing situation a proper balance among the three elements that are at work in any communicative effort: the available arguments about the subject itself, the interests and peculiarities of the audience and the voice, the implied character, of the speaker. I should like to suggest that it is this balance, this rhetorical stance, difficult as it is to describe, that is our main goal as teachers of rhetoric. Our ideal graduate will strike this balance automatically in any writing that he considers finished. Though he may never come to the point of finding the balance easily, he will know that it is what makes the difference between effective communication and mere wasted effort.

What I mean by the true rhetorician's stance can perhaps best be seen by contrasting it with two or three corruptions, unbalanced stances often assumed by people who think they are practicing the arts of persuasion.

The first I'll call the pedant's stance; it consists of ignoring or underplaying the personal relationship of speaker and audience and depending entirely on statements about a subject—that is, the notion of a job to be done for a particular audience is left out. It is a virtue, of course, to respect the bare truth of one's subject, and there may even be some subjects which in their very nature define an audience and a rhetorical purpose so that adequacy to the subject can be the whole art of presentation. For example, an article on "The relation of the ontological and teleological proofs," in a recent *Journal of Religion*, requires a minimum of adaptation of argument to audience. But most subjects do not in themselves imply in any necessary way a purpose and an audience and hence a speaker's tone. The writer who assumes that it is enough merely to write an exposition of what he happens to know on the subject will produce the kind of essay that soils our scholarly journals, written not for readers but for bibliographies.

In my first year of teaching I taught a whole unit on "exposition" without ever suggesting, so far as I can remember, that the students ask themselves what their expositions were *for*. So they wrote expositions like this one— I've saved it, to teach me toleration of my colleagues: the title is "Family relations in More's *Utopia*." "In this theme I would like to discuss some of the relationships with the family which Thomas More elaborates and sets forth in his book, *Utopia*. The first thing that I would like to discuss about family relations is that overpopulation, according to More, is a just cause of war." And so on. Can you hear that student sneering at me, in this opening? What he is saying is something like "you ask for a meaningless paper, I give you a meaningless paper." He knows that he has no audience except me. He knows that I don't want to read his summary of family relations in *Utopia*, and he knows that I know that he therefore has no rhetorical purpose. Because he has not been led to see a question which he considers worth answering, or an audience that could possibly care one way or the other, the paper is worse than no paper at all, even though it has no grammatical or spelling errors and is organized right down the line, one, two, three.

An extreme case, you may say. Most of us would never allow ourselves that kind of empty fencing? Perhaps. But if some carefree foundation is willing to finance a statistical study, I'm willing to wager a month's salary that we'd find at least half of the suggested topics in our freshman texts as pointless as mine was. And we'd find a good deal more than half of the discussions of grammar, punctuation, spelling, and style totally divorced from any notion that rhetorical purpose to some degree controls all such matters. We can offer objective descriptions of levels of usage from now until graduation, but unless the student discovers a desire to say something to somebody and learns to control his diction for a purpose, we've gained very little. I once gave an assignment asking students to describe the same classroom in three different statements, one for each level of usage. They were obedient, but the only ones who got anything from the assignment were those who intuitively imported the rhetorical instructions I had overlooked—such purposes as "Make fun of your scholarly surroundings by describing this classroom in extremely elevated style," or "Imagine a kid from the slums accidentally trapped in these surroundings and forced to write a description of this room." A little thought might have shown me how to give the whole assignment some human point, and therefore some educative value.

The Theory of Rhetoric

Just how confused we can allow ourselves to be about such matters is shown in a recent publication of the Educational Testing Service, called "Factors in Judgments of Writing Ability." In order to isolate those factors which affect differences in grading standards, ETS set six groups of readers—business men, writers and editors, lawyers, and teachers of English, social science and natural science—to reading the same batch of papers. Then ETS did a hundred-page "factor analysis" of the amount of agreement and disagreement, and of the elements which different kinds of graders emphasized. The authors of the report express a certain amount of shock at the discovery that the median correlation was only .31 and that 94% of the papers received either 7, 8, or 9 of the 9 possible grades.

But what *could* they have expected? In the first place, the students were given no purpose and no audience when the essays were assigned. And then all these editors and business men and academics were asked to judge the papers in a complete vacuum, using only whatever intuitive standards they cared to use. I'm surprised that there was any correlation at all. Lacking instructions, some of the students undoubtedly wrote polemical essays, suitable for the popular press; others no doubt imagined an audience, say, of *Reader's Digest* readers, and others wrote with the English teachers as implied audience; an occasional student with real philosophical bent would no doubt do a careful analysis of the pros and cons of the case. This would be graded low, of course, by the magazine editors, even though they would have graded it high if asked to judge it as a speculative contribution to the analysis of the problem. Similarly, a creative student who has been getting A's for his personal essays will write an amusing colorful piece, failed by all the social scientists present, though they would have graded it high if asked to judge it for what it was. I find it shocking that tens of thousands of dollars and endless hours should have been spent by students, graders, and professional testers analyzing essays and grading results totally abstracted from any notion of purposeful human communication. Did nobody protest? One might as well assemble a group of citizens to judge students' capacity to throw balls, say, without telling the students or the graders whether altitude, speed, accuracy or form was to be judged. The judges would be drawn from football coaches, hai-lai experts, lawyers, and English teachers, and asked to apply whatever standards they intuitively apply to ball throwing. Then we could express astonishment that the judgments did not correlate very well, and we could do a factor analysis to discover, lo and behold, that some readers concentrated on altitude, some on speed, some on accuracy, some on form—and the English teachers were simply confused.

One effective way to combat the pedantic stance is to arrange for weekly confrontations of groups of students over their own papers. We have done far too little experimenting with arrangements for providing a genuine audience in this way. Short of such developments, it remains true that a good teacher can convince his students that he is a true audience, if his comments on the papers show that some sort of dialogue is taking place. As Jacques Barzun says in *Teacher in America,* students should be made to feel that unless they have said something to someone, they have failed; to bore the teacher is a worse form of failure than to anger him. From this point of view we can see that the charts of grading symbols that mar even the best freshman texts are not the innocent time savers that we pretend. Plausible as it may seem to arrange for more corrections with less time, they inevitably reduce the student's sense of purpose in writing. When he sees innumerable W13's and P19's in the margin, he cannot possibly feel that the art of persuasion is as important to his instructor as when he reads personal comments, however few.

This first perversion, then, springs from ignoring the audience or over-reliance on the pure subject. The second which might be called the advertiser's stance, comes from *under*valuing the subject and overvaluing pure effect: how to win friends and influence people.

Some of our best freshman texts—Sheridan Baker's *The Practical Stylist,* for example—allow themselves on occasion to suggest that to be controversial or argumentative, to stir up an audience is an end in itself. Sharpen the controversial edge, one of them says, and the clear implication is that one should do so even if the truth of the subject is honed off in the process. This perversion is probably in the long run a more serious threat in our society than the danger of ignoring the audience. In the time of audience-reaction meters and pre-tested plays and novels, it is not easy to convince students of the old Platonic truth that good persuasion is honest persuasion, or even of the old Aristotelian truth that the good rhetorician must be master of his subject, no matter how dishonest he may decide ultimately to be. Having told them that good writers always to some degree accommodate their arguments to the audience, it is hard to explain the difference between justified accommodation—say changing *point one* to the final position—and the kind of accommodation that fills our popular magazines, in which the very substance of what is said is accommodated to some preconception of what will sell. "The publication of *Eros* [magazine] represents a major breakthrough in the battle for the liberation of the human spirit."

At a dinner about a month ago I sat between the wife of a famous civil rights lawyer and an advertising consultant. "I saw the article on your book yesterday in the Daily News," she said, "but I didn't even finish it. The title of your book scared me off. Why did you ever choose such a terrible title? Nobody would buy a book with a title like that." The man on my right, whom I'll call Mr. Kinches, overhearing my feeble reply, plunged into a conversation with her, over my torn and bleeding corpse. "Now with my *last* book," he said, "I listed 20 possible titles and then tested them out on 400 business men. The one I chose was voted for by

90 percent of the businessmen." "That's what I was just saying to Mr. Booth," she said. "A book title ought to grab you, and *rhetoric* is not going to grab anybody." "Right," he said. "My *last* book sold 50,000 copies already; I don't know how this one will do, but I polled 200 businessmen on the table of contents, and ..."

At one point I did manage to ask him whether the title he chose really fit the book. "Not quite as well as one or two of the others," he admitted, "but that doesn't matter, you know. If the book is designed right, so that the first chapter pulls them in, and you *keep* 'em in, who's going to gripe about a little inaccuracy in the title?"

Well, rhetoric is the art of persuading, not the art of seeming to persuade by giving everything away at the start. It presupposes that one has a purpose concerning a subject which itself cannot be fundamentally modified by the desire to persuade. If Edmund Burke had decided that he could win more votes in Parliament by choosing the other side—as he most certainly could have done—we would hardly hail this party-switch as a master stroke of rhetoric. If Churchill had offered the British "peace in our time," with some laughs thrown in, because opinion polls had shown that more Britishers were "grabbed" by these than by blood, sweat, and tears, we could hardly call his decision a sign of rhetorical skill.

One could easily discover other perversions of the rhetorician's balance —most obviously what might be called the entertainer's stance—the willingness to sacrifice substance to personality and charm. I admire Walker Gibson's efforts to startle us out of dry pedantry, but I know from experience that his exhortations to find and develop the speaker's voice can lead to empty colorfulness. A student once said to me, complaining about a colleague, "I soon learned that all I had to do to get an A was imitate Thurber."

But perhaps this is more than enough about the perversions of the rhetorical stance. Balance itself is always harder to describe than the clumsy poses that result when it is destroyed. But we all experience the balance whenever we find an author who succeeds in changing our minds. He can do so only if he knows more about the subject than we do, and if he then engages us in the process of thinking—and feeling—it through. What makes the rhetoric of Milton and Burke and Churchill great is that each presents us with the spectacle of a man passionately involved in thinking an important question through, in the company of an audience. Though each of them did everything in his power to make his point persuasive, including a pervasive use of the many emotional appeals that have been falsely scorned by many a freshman composition text, none would have allowed himself the advertiser's stance; none would have polled the audience in advance to discover which position would get the votes. Nor is the highly individual personality that springs out at us from their speeches and essays present for the sake of selling itself. The rhetorical balance among speakers, audience, and argument is with all three men habitual, as we see if we look at their non-political writings. Burke's work on the Sublime and Beautiful is a relatively unimpassioned philosophical treatise, but one finds there again a delicate balance: though the implied author of this work is a far different person, far less obtrusive, far more objective, than the man who later cried *sursum corda* to the British Parliament, he permeates with his philosophical personality his philosophical work. And though the signs of his awareness of his audience are far more subdued, they are still here: every effort is made to involve the *proper* audience, the audience of philosophical minds, in a fundamentally interesting inquiry, and to lead them through to the end. In short, because he was a man engaged with men in the effort to solve a human problem, one could never call what he wrote dull, however difficult or abstruse.

Now obviously the habit of seeking this balance is not the only thing we have to teach under the heading of rhetoric. But I think that everything worth teaching under that heading finds its justification finally in that balance. Much of what is now considered irrelevant or dull can, in fact, be brought to life when teachers and students know what they are seeking. Churchill reports that the most valuable training he ever received in rhetoric was in the diagramming of sentences. Think of it! Yet the diagramming of a sentence, regardless of the grammatical system, can be a live subject as soon as one asks not simply "How is this sentence put together," but rather "Why is it put together in this way?" or "Could the rhetorical balance and hence the desired persuasion be better achieved by writing it differently?"

As a nation we are reputed to write very badly. As a nation, I would say, we are more inclined to the perversions of rhetoric than to the rhetorical balance. Regardless of what we do about this or that course in the curriculum, our mandate would seem to be, then, to lead more of our students than we now do to care about and practice the true arts of persuasion.

TOPICS FOR DISCUSSION

1. How does the opening example show what Booth means by the "rhetorical problem"? How is this problem further clarified?
2. According to Booth's discussion, what appears to be the nature or role of rhetoric in teaching? What chief point is he making about the comments of his teachers on his writing?
3. Why is a "balance" necessary among the three elements of the writing situation? Why does Booth call this balance a "stance"?
4. Look up *pedant* in a dictionary. Why does Booth choose this word to describe the first unbalanced stance that he discusses? What kind of

subject is likely to define a pedant's purpose and audience? What does the example show?

5. How might the topic drawn from More's *Utopia* have been handled through a clear rhetorical purpose? If you were the teacher, how would you have made the assignment?

6. What does Booth mean by "some human point" in his discussion of the writing assignment on the classroom?

7. What defect does Booth find in the ETS "factor analysis"? What does this discussion suggest about the rhetorical stance?

8. Why is the advertiser's stance a more serious threat to our society than the pedant's?

9. What does Booth mean by "feeling" a subject through?

10. How could sentence diagramming be taught from a rhetorical point of view?

TOPICS FOR COMPOSITION

1. In his book *The Rhetoric of Fiction* (1961), Booth defines the "implied author" as "an implied version of 'himself,'" embodying normative values—the values we are to adopt in our identifying with or at least understanding the characters and action. The implied author speaks to us in some kind of voice, perhaps through the voice of a dramatic narrator or the voice of a present but undramatized narrator, or even the indirect voice of symbolism or plot construction. The implied author, furthermore, will most likely differ from work to work, as in each of his novels, we meet a different Charles Dickens, altered by circumstance and experience, representing a different or somewhat modified series of norms. In his essay Booth calls attention to Edmund Burke's implied image in his treatise on esthetics; he comments: "one finds there again a delicate balance: though the implied author of this work is a far different person, far less obtrusive, far more objective, than the man who later cried *sursum corda* to the British Parliament, he permeates with his philosophical personality his philosophical work." Analyze two essays, stories, or novels to distinguish the personality and values, such as you can determine them, of the implied author of each.

2. Analyze a signed newspaper or magazine article for the three elements Booth distinguishes in the rhetorical stance. Then discuss how aware you think the writer was of these elements; cite evidence of any such awareness.

3. Analyze a piece of writing you would point to as failing in one or all of the ways Booth cites. Be precise about your criteria.

4. Rewrite one paragraph of your analysis of a piece of bad writing and direct it to a member of your family or a friend who has not read Booth's essay.

5. Compare three advertisements for the same product to see how closely they adopt the "advertiser's stance," as Booth defines it.

**KENNETH
BURKE**

**Rhetoric—
Old and New**

EARLY in this essay Burke distinguishes the new rhetoric from the old rhetoric—the application of new scientific findings to the older considerations of persuasion. His essay is designed to reveal the nature of this application through a few of the stratagems or tactics he has distinguished in his other writings on the rhetoric of motives. In several books on this subject—among them are *Counter-Statement* (1953), *A Rhetoric of Motives* (1949), and *A Grammar of Motives* (1945) —Burke has worked out ideas that are relevant to our understanding of this essay.

Of chief importance is the idea of hierarchy, which Burke refers to in the course of the discussion. Men, says Burke, seek to identify themselves with various groups and people; yet, because these groups may differ in basic attitudes, men are bound to be aware of conflicts of many sorts that need to be reconciled. The interrelations both within and between groups or, to be more precise, the pattern of these interrelations is what Burke means by hierarchy. Rhetoric not only helps to maintain hierarchy but works also to relieve conflict and reconcile differences. For the individual this rhetoric may take the form of dialectic. Burke has stated: "Ideally, all the various 'voices' are partisan rhetoricians whose partial voices 'competitively cooperate' to form the position of the dialogue as a whole (a position that transcends all the partial voices of the participants, though there may be a Socratic voice that is *primus inter pares)."* [1] The essence of the new rhetoric, Burke states in this essay, is a concern with identification—at its simplest, a calculation by which the politician tries to become one with his audience, at its most complex, an end in itself: "In such identification there is a partially dreamlike, idealistic motive, somewhat compensatory to real differences or divisions, which the rhetoric of identification would transcend." Through this concern with transcendence, dialectic becomes related to rhetoric. In the concluding paragraph, Burke suggests that transcendence may be related to Spiritualization, "vibrant with the gestures of unification, promise, freedom." Rhetoric as a means of transcendence becomes the means to reconciliation.

---

[1] Quoted by Daniel Fogarty in his *Roots for a New Rhetoric* (New York: Teachers College, Columbia Univ., Bureau of Publications, 1959), p. 61.

On the assumption that writing and the criticism of writing have an area in common, this statement is offered in the hopes that, though presented from the standpoint of literary criticism, it may be found relevant to the teaching of communication.

Let us, as a conceit, imagine a dialogue between two characters: "Studiosus" and "Neurosis." Studiosus would be somewhat of a misnomer for the first figure, who represents a not very interested member of a freshman class taking a required course in composition; and Neurosis would be his teacher. Studiosus has complained bitterly of the work which the course requires of him, whereupon Neurosis delivers a passionate oration in defense of his subject (naturally without mention of a flitting fantasy he sometimes entertains, according to which he has been granted some *other* cross to bear).

Imagining his apology, we found it falling into three stages, that corresponded roughly to an Inferno, a Purgatorio, and a Paradiso. First would be an account of the abysmal problems that beset the use of language. Next would come a movement of transition, whereby the very sources of lamentation could, if beheld from a different angle, be transformed into the promissory. This would be the purgatorial stage. And, despite the mournfulness of our times, a glorious paradisiac ending seemed feasible, if we did a certain amount of contriving—but let us put off for a bit the description of this third stage, while we prepare for it by first giving the broad outlines of the other two.

The first stage would stress the great deceptions of speech. As with Baudelaire's sonnet on "Correspondences," it would note how men wander through "forests of symbols." Man a symbol-using animal. Expatiate on the fog of words through which we stumble, perhaps adding an image (the dog and the waterfall heard enigmatically beyond the mist). Here we would consider the problems of news: the *necessary* inadequacy of the report, even in the case of the *best* reporting; the bungling nature of the medium; the great bureaucratic dinosaurs of news-collecting; the added risks that arise from the *dramatic* aspects of news. (And to get a glimpse of what sinister practices we do accept as the norm, where international relations are concerned, imagine a prize fight reported in the style regularly used for news of international disputes: one fighter's blows would be reported as threats and provocations, while the other's were mentioned in the tonalities proper to long-suffering and calm retaliation regrettably made necessary by the outlandish aggressiveness of the opponent.)

We hoped next to work in a reference to what we like to call the "scene-act" ratio. That is, a situation may be so described that one particular kind of act or attitude is implicit in it (described not falsely, but with "honest

RHETORIC—OLD AND NEW   From *The Journal of General Education*, Vol. 5, No. 3 (1951). Reprinted by permission.

selectivity"). For a complex situation may without untruth be so reported that exclusively pugnacious rather than friendly or meditative attitudes are evoked; or the exact opposite may be as true—a rhetorical function thus lurking beneath the level of the report's "factuality." And when each day's "reality" is "dramatically" put together for us by enterprises that comb the entire world for calamities, conflicts, and dire forebodings, such a documentary replica of the arena confuses us as to the actual *recipe* of motives on which the world is operating. The most critical consideration of all is thus drastically slighted, namely, the *proportions* of the ingredients in a motivational cluster.

Given the conditions of our talk, we should pass over this stage rapidly. But before going into the second or purgatorial stage, I'd like to pause for an aside. I submit that this is the situation, as regards the present state of literary criticism: When aesthetic criticism came in, there was a corresponding demotion of rhetoric. Rhetoric was exiled. And, emigrating, it received a home among various so-called "new sciences." (Anthropology, social psychology, sociology, psychoanalysis, semantics, and the like all took over portions of it. I would also include here psychosomatic medicine, concerned as it is with ways in which our very physiques are led to take on attitudes in keeping with the rhetorical or persuasive aspects of ideas— attitudes of such conviction that they are worked into the very set of nerves, muscles, and organs.)

I shall cite one example of the way in which the "new sciences" took over: Anthropology now considers, under the heading of "magic," many symbolic devices for the establishing of social cohesion. Under the earlier dispensation, these would have been considered as aspects of *rhetoric*. But here is the paradox: After these topics were exiled and renamed "magic," literary critics who borrowed the new terms were accused by purists of importing alien perspectives into their special discipline. Accordingly, by a "new" rhetoric, we mean one designed to restore structures maimed by the vandalism of the exclusively aesthetic (an aesthetic stress, by the way, that had also made positive gains, though they are not our concern at the moment).

If I had to sum up in one word the difference between the "old" rhetoric and a "new" (a rhetoric reinvigorated by fresh insights which the "new sciences" contributed to the subject), I would reduce it to this: The key term for the old rhetoric was "persuasion" and its stress was upon deliberate design. The key term for the "new" rhetoric would be "identification," which can include a partially "unconscious" factor in appeal. "Identification" at its simplest is also a deliberate device, as when the politician seeks to identify himself with his audience. In this respect, its equivalents are plentiful in Aristotle's *Rhetoric*. But identification can also be an end, as when people earnestly yearn to identify themselves with some group or other. Here they are not necessarily being acted upon by a conscious external agent, but may be acting upon themselves to this end. In such identification there is a partially dreamlike, idealistic motive, somewhat compensatory to real differences or divisions, which the rhetoric of identification would transcend.

But we are now ready for our second stage. For, if identification includes the realm of transcendence, it has, by the same token, brought us into the realm of transformation, or dialectic. A rhetorician, I take it, is like one voice in a dialogue. Put several such voices together, with each voicing its own special assertion, let them act upon one another in co-operative competition, and you get a dialectic that, properly developed, can lead to views transcending the limitations of each. At which point, to signalize his change of heart, poor Neurosis might now be renamed "Socraticus."

Socraticus could point out how the very lostness of men in their symbolic quandaries has led to the invention of miraculously ingenious symbolic structures—whereat the very aspects of language we might otherwise fear can become engrossing objects of study and appreciation; and works once designed to play upon an audience's passions, to "move" them rhetorically toward practical decisions beyond the work, can now be enjoyed for their ability to move us in the purely poetic sense, as when, hearing a lyric or seeing a sunrise, we might say, "How moving!" (We here touch upon the kind of heightened or elevated diction discussed in Longinus' *On the Sublime.*)

Considering the relation between rhetoric and dialectic, we come with Socraticus upon the Platonic concern with the Upward Way (linguistic devices whereby we may move from a world of disparate particulars to a principle of one-ness, an "ascent" got, as the semanticists might say, by a movement toward progressively "higher levels of generalization"). Whereat there could be a descent, a Downward Way, back into the world of particulars, all of which would now be "identified" with the genius of the unitary principle discovered en route. (All would be thus made consubstantial by participation in a common essence, as with objects bathed in the light of the one sun, that shines down upon them as from the apex of a pyramid. And the absence of such dialectic journeys on the grand scale should not be allowed to conceal from us the fact that we are continually encountering fragmentary variants of them. For instance, you may look upon a world of disparate human beings; you can next "rise to a higher level of generalization" by arriving at some such abstraction as "economic man"; and, finally, you can look upon these unique human beings simply in terms of this one attribute, thus "identifying" them with a unitary term got by a tiny rise toward generalization and a descent again from it.)

Kenneth Burke

But the mention of the pyramid can lead us nicely into the third state, our Paradiso. Socraticus might now even change his name to "Hierarchicus"—and we might dwell upon the double nature of hierarchy. Thus there is the purely verbal ascent, with corresponding resources of identification (our notion being that a rhetorical structure is most persuasive when it possesses full dialectical symmetry—or, otherwise put, dialectical symmetry is at once the perfecting and transcending of rhetoric). But there is also another line of ascent; and this involves the relation between the dialectics of identification and hierarchic structure in the social, or sociological, sense (society conceived as, roughly, a ladder, or pyramid, of interrelated roles).

Here we would consider how matters of prestige (in the old style, "wonder," or in the terminology of Corneille, "admiration") figure in the ultimate resources of "identification." Here we would note how our ideas of "beauty," and even "nature," are "fabulous," concealing within themselves a social pageantry. Here would be the ultimate step in the discussion of the ways in which man walks among "forests of symbols."

Then, for the localizing of our thesis, we might have Neurosis-Socraticus-Hierarchicus cite Castiglione's *Book of the Courtier* as a neat instance of the merger of the two dialectical series: the verbal and the social pyramids. For it deals with questions of courtly ascent, while rising through four successive stages from the mere quest of personal advancement, to a concern with the insignia of the courtier as expert or specialist, thence to the cult of courtly sexual relations, and on to the vision of an *ultimate* courtship. In this fourth stage we move into a sacrificial order of motives, fittingly introduced in the dialogues by talk of death, so that, in contrast with the earlier analysis of laughter, there is now a solemn note. This fourth section deals, first, with the Socratic erotic, the love of truth, beauty, goodness, as seen in terms of the courtier who is now in a pedagogic role, aiming not at his own advantage but at the education of the prince in ways that will be beneficial to mankind as a whole.

After the pages on the courtier as educator of the prince, you will recall, through appropriate transitions the work rises to its exhilarating close, the oration by Cardinal Bembo, on Beauty as "an influence of the heavenly bountifulness." Here is, to perfection, the device of *spiritualization*. So, by the time the Cardinal is finished, we have gone from the *image* of beauty to the pure *idea* of beauty—we have united with ideal beauty: the courtly, truth, utility, goodness—finally we arrive at talk of the soul, which is given "to the beholding of its own substance," a substance angelic (the soul kindled by the desire to partake of the heavenly nature), whereat, with images of mounting and burning and coupling, we end on a prayer to "the father of true pleasures, of grace, peace, lowliness, and goodwill," and on talk of hopes to "smell those spiritual savors"—and lo! after the

The Theory of Rhetoric

Cardinal has paused, "ravished and beside himself," we discover that the discussion has continued until dawn, so that the company, edified,

> saw already in the East a fair morning like unto the color of roses, and all stars voided, saving only the sweet Governess of Heaven, Venus which keepeth the bounds of night and day, from which appeared to blow a sweet blast, that filling the air with a biting cold, began to quicken the tunable notes of the pretty birds, among the hushing woods of the hills.

Since this work is so exalted in its closing pages, like the final rejoicing of a symphonic finale, we thought we should contrive to end our apology on that. For it would be something that even Studiosus might readily applaud; and in applauding the citation, he might seem to be applauding the speaker.

But at that stage, we grew uneasy. Even suppose our ruse had succeeded. What of the morrow? What had we considered, as regards particular, practical problems?

To meet that question, we should go back to a hint introduced, in passing, when we mentioned the earlier stages of Castiglione's book. For there the author considers at great length the approved devices whereby the courtier can translate his aptitudes into schemes, stratagems, advantage-seeking actions. Can we not, when looking at the resources of words, seek to categorize and describe in that spirit the kinds of role which, while they impinge upon the rhetorical devices considered in Books vii, viii, and ix of Quintilian, have also a more personalized dimension? These would fall across all the three levels we have considered in our little Human Comedy.

Aristotle treated rhetoric as purely verbal. But there are also areas of overlap (making for a kind of "administrative" rhetoric). Consider, for instance, Machiavelli's *Prince*, as seen in this light:

> Machiavelli's *The Prince* can be treated as a rhetoric insofar as it deals with the *producing of effects upon an audience*. Sometimes the prince's subjects are his audience, sometimes the rulers or inhabitants of foreign states are the audience, sometimes particular factions within the State. If you have a political public in mind, Machiavelli says in effect, here is the sort of thing you must do to move them for your purposes. And he considers such principles of persuasion as these: either treat well or crush; defend weak neighbors and weaken the strong; where you foresee trouble, provoke war; don't make others powerful; be like the prince who appointed a harsh governor to establish order (after this governor had become an object of public hatred in carrying out the prince's wishes, the prince got popular acclaim by putting him to death for his cruelties); do necessary evils at one stroke, pay out benefits little by little; sometimes assure the citizens that the evil days will soon be over, at other times goad

them to fear the cruelties of the enemy; be sparing of your own and your subjects' wealth, but be liberal with the wealth of others; be a combination of strength and stealth (lion and fox); *appear* merciful, dependable, humane, devout, upright, but be the opposite in actuality, whenever the circumstances require it; yet always do lip-service to the virtues, since most people judge by appearances; provoke resistance, to make an impression by crushing it; use religion as a pretext for conquest, since it permits of "pious cruelty"; leave "affairs of reproach" to the management of others, but keep those "of grace" in your hands; be the patron of all talent, proclaim festivals, give spectacles, show deference to local organizations; but always retain the distance of your rank (he could have called this the "mystery" of rule); in order that you may get the advantage of good advice without losing people's respect, give experts permission to speak frankly, but only when asked to speak; have a few intimates who are encouraged to be completely frank, and who are well plied with rewards.[1]

As an instance of more purely literary tactics, we might cite this passage from Demetrius *On Style:*[2]

In fine, it is with language as with a lump of wax, out of which one man will mould a dog, another an ox, another a horse. One will deal with his subject in the way of exposition and asseveration, saying (for example) that "men leave property to their children, but they do not therewith leave the knowledge which will rightly use the legacy." [This he calls the method of Aristippus of Cyrene.]...Another will (as Xenophon commonly does) express the same thought in the way of precept, as "men ought to leave not only money to their children, but also the knowledge which will use the money rightly."

What is specifically called the "Socratic" manner...would recast the foregoing proposition in an interrogative form, somewhat as follows. "My dear lad, how much property has your father left you? Is it considerable and not easily assessed? It is considerable, Socrates. Well now, has he also left you the knowledge which will use it rightly?"

For some years, in tentative ways, somewhat on the side, I have been trying to decide on terms for categorizing various literary strategies, as seen in the light of these borrowings from Machiavelli and Demetrius. This is no place to display the lot. But I might cite a few brief illustrations. Here, for instance, are some cullings from my notes on what I tentatively call the "bland strategy":

At one point in *The Idiot*, Ippolit accuses Mishkin of learning how to "make use of his illness." Mishkin, he says, has managed to offer friend-

---

[1]See the author's *Rhetoric of Motives* (New York: Prentice-Hall, 1949), p. 158. [Burke's notes throughout.]

[2]v. 296–97, Loeb ed., trans. W. Rhys Roberts (Cambridge: Harvard University Press, 1946), p. 481.

The Theory of Rhetoric

ship and money "in such an ingenious way that now it's impossible to accept under any circumstances." Mishkin's behavior has been "either too innocent or too clever." Ippolit is here in effect giving the formula for blandness. Blandness is ironic, in that the underlying meaning is the opposite of the one that shows on its face, while there is always the invitation to assume that the surface meaning is the true one.

Diplomats often use it, when sending warships abroad in times of peace. Though the warships may be dispatched purely for purposes of threat, the enterprise can be blandly put forward as a "goodwill mission." Or a government may use troop movements as a threat, and blandly call attention to the troop movements by announcing that they are but part of a "routine action" and are not intended as a threat.

A friend said: "I once had an uncle who was gentle enough, but enjoyed watching fist fights among children. Each Saturday he would get a dollar of his pay changed into pennies; and calling the children of the neighborhood, he would toss the pennies one by one, while explaining unctuously: 'Just scramble for the pennies, and each of you can keep as many as he gets. But no pushing, no shoving, boys, and above all, no fighting.' While thus setting up conditions of the Scramble that almost automatically made for a fight, he could blandly call for peace, confident that war would come before he had tossed a dozen pennies."

Or there was the case of Joseph, who, without funds, had married a rich Josephine. At first, in all simplicity, he paid for his keep by being assiduously attentive. Then slowly over the years, a perverse, and even morbid blandness emerged in his treatment of her, unbeknownst to them both. Joseph began to plague Josephine with his worries for her welfare. He did not let her live a moment without the feel of a doctor's hand on her pulse. He was so attentive that no one could fail to comment on his devotion. And in her unexpressed and inexpressible desire to poison him, she felt so guilty that each day she became more sickly. Here was a situation worthy of the André Gide who wrote *The Immoralist*. Blandness could go no further.

Soon after our occupation of Japan in the last war, Japanese officials exploited a blandness of this sort. They confounded the victors by being painfully meticulous in their desire to co-operate. They never tired of asking for "clarifications" of military orders, so that they might obey to the last letter. They were even "scrupulous" in reporting their own violations and misunderstandings of any order. They were so assiduously anxious to please, that they made the conqueror sick of his own commands. For instead of resisting the regulations, they tirelessly brought up bothersome questions supposedly intended to "help put the regulations into effect."

An ironically bland kind of co-operation is said to have taken place during the German invasion of Czecho-Slovakia. The Nazis had been sending

Kenneth Burke

spies among the Czechs. These spies would spot anti-Nazi patriots by going to Czech cafes and talking "confidentially" against Hitler. Soon the Czechs learned of the ruse. Hence, next phase: Nazi spy comes to cafe where Czech patriots are gathered. In the role of *agent provocateur*, the spy talks against Hitler. Whereupon the Czechs virtuously pummel him "for saying such things against the Führer."

Given blandness enough, one person might co-operate another off the map.

Such stratagems, instances of which I have been collecting (still using a somewhat experimental terminology of placement, not logically schematized—at least not yet) sometimes apply to a rhetoric of human relations in general; sometimes they are confined to purely literary tactics. Many taken from the press fall halfway between a purely "verbal" and an "administrative" rhetoric. And many taken from books (thus from the realm of literature) at the same time have social relevance generally.

I might cite a few more places where concerns of this sort are observable.

In *The Making of Americans* Gertrude Stein came close to a systematic study of rhetorical devices in personal relations. Toward the end, for instance, when discussing how sensitiveness becomes transformed into suspicion, making a "simple thing" look like a "complicated thing," she writes:

> These then I am now describing who are completely for themselves suspicious ones, who have it in them to have emotion in them become suspicious before it is a real emotion of anything for anything about anything in them, these have it completely to be certain that every one is doing feeling seeing the thing that one is feeling doing seeing believing when such a one is not agreeing with them, when such a one is feeling thinking believing doing anything that such a one is doing that thing for a mean or wicked or jealous or stupid or obstinate or cursed or religious reason, it is not a real feeling believing seeing realizing, that this one having suspicion in him is certain.

She then gives the paradigm of an anecdote:

> One of such a kind of one once liked very well some one and then that one forgot to give this one five cents that this one had paid for that one and then this one hated that one, had no trust in that one for this one was certain that that one knowing that this one was too sensitive to be asking did not think it necessary to pay that one, he never could believe that any one forgot such a thing. This is an extreme thing of a way of feeling that is common to all of these of them.

The stress here moves rather toward the agent than the act (that is, in our terms, it is idealistic); but underlying it is clearly the concern with social tactics (which, one notes, her style is well adapted for stating in *generalized* form).

In a satiric epigram leveled at Cato the Censor, who had walked out of the theater in righteous indignation, Martial asks rhetorically: "Why did you come to the theater? That you might leave?"

In Aristotle's *Rhetoric* a similar pattern is considered when he notes,[3] as a "topic," that one person may make a present of something to another, in order to cause him pain by depriving him of it. Then Aristotle goes on to show how the device may be given cosmological proportions; he cites from an unknown author: "It is not from benevolence that the deity bestows great blessings upon many, but in order that they may suffer heavier calamities"—and whether or not this be a favorite device of the gods, it is certainly a device of a sort that should properly be fitted into a collection of strategies for characterizing the antics of the Human Comedy.

Proust's work is full of such concerns. The kind of closely interwoven relationships he deals with makes for tiny replicas of the stratagems used in the manipulating of mighty empires. Thus Proust notes that the servant Françoise and Aunt Eulalie are related as quarry to hunter, so that "they could never cease from trying to forestall each other's devices." And after describing the nature of their sparring, he concludes:

> a middle-aged lady in a small country town, by doing no more than yield wholehearted obedience to her own irresistible eccentricities, and to a spirit of mischief engendered by the utter idleness of her existence, could see, without ever having given a thought to Louis XIV, the most trivial occupations of her daily life, her morning toilet, her luncheon, her afternoon nap, assume, by virtue of their despotic singularity, something of the interest that was to be found in what Saint Simon used to call the "machinery" of life at Versailles; and was able, too, to persuade herself that her silence, a shade of good humour or of arrogance on her features, would provide Françoise with matter for a mental commentary as tense with passion and terror, as did the silence, the good humour or the arrogance of the King when a courtier, or even his greatest nobles, had presented a petition to him, at the turning of an avenue, at Versailles.

Nor was Françoise lacking in ability to wage the same kinds of warfare against underlings who were, in turn, subject to *her* jurisdiction. After referring to Fabre's descriptions of a wasp that paralyzes an insect and deposits its eggs in the victim, Proust continues:

> in the same way Françoise had adopted, to minister to her permanent and unfaltering resolution to render the house uninhabitable to any other servant, a series of crafty and pitiless stratagems. Many years later we discov-

3 2. 23. [See p. 410.]

ered that, if we had been fed on asparagus day after day, throughout that whole season, it was because the smell of the plants gave the poor kitchen-maid, who had to prepare them, such violent attacks of asthma that she was finally obliged to leave my aunt's service.

We could well cite Mark Twain as a source for a rhetoric of such devices. His concern with ruses, stratagems, with the lore of gamblers, swindlers, and the like, is not so much *moralistic* as *appreciative*. His roving enterprisers are not merely salesmen; they are rogues and spellbinders, preferably given to selling poor stuff grandiloquently.

Typically, Twain quotes this example of spiritualization, from a "now forgotten book," about a "big operator":

> He appears to have been a most dexterous as well as consummate villain. When he traveled, his usual disguise was that of an itinerant preacher; and it is said that his discourses were very "soul-moving"—interesting the hearers so much that they forgot to look after their horses, which were carried away by his confederates while he was preaching.

Deflection is a particularly important device. In a sense any slight bias or even unintended error in our vocabulary for describing reality serves as a deflection. Since even the most imaginative, intelligent, virtuous, and fortunate of men must err in their attempts to characterize reality, some measure of deflection is natural, inevitable. Deflection is so perennially effective when deliberately used, because it arises so spontaneously. The Freudian notion of "displacement" in dreams indicates how close it is to the roots of natural human evasiveness.

Thus a child, provoked when made to give his brother something that he wanted to keep, began crying bitterly because his brother hadn't said "Thank you." His brother promptly said "Thank you," whereupon the child cried all the louder, "because he didn't say it soon enough."

A variant of deflection is used constantly in jokes, where two infractions are involved, one important, one trivial, and laughter is elicited by shifting the stress to the trivial one when the important one was, of course, the real issue.

A typical kind of spontaneous deflection arises thus: Wherever there is control along with disorder, the control can be blamed for the disorder. But if controls are relaxed and there is disorder, the blame can be laid to the absence of controls. Since both the controls and the relaxed controls are matters of government, it follows that government can be blamed for everything.

There is no time now for us to consider the various formulations we have tentatively used in classifying the devices. But we would like to say a few words on one of these, already mentioned in passing. And it will

The Theory of Rhetoric

bring our discussion to a close. This is the device of "spiritualization," or the *nostrum* (which transcends the conflicts of the *mine* and the *thine*, the *meum* and *tuum*, by raising them to resonant terms of *ours*, the *nostrum*). Here is a grand device, central to polemic, which is forever translating back and forth between materialist and idealist terms for motives.

Are things disunited in "body"? Then unite them in "spirit." Would a nation extend its physical dominion? Let it talk of spreading its "ideals." Do you encounter contradictions? Call them "balances." Is an organization in disarray? Talk of its common *purpose*. Are there struggles over means? Celebrate agreement on ends. Sanction the troublously manifest, the incarnate, in terms of the ideally, perfectly invisible and intangible, the divine.

In a society beset by many conflicts of interests and aiming with the help of verbal tactics to transcend those conflicts, the uses of spiritualization as a device are endless. Spiritualization is the device par excellence of the Upward Way—vibrant with the gestures of unification, promise, freedom. And so, ending upon it (by recalling snatches, fragments, of Castiglione's symphonic finale):

> ... beauty ... truth ... utility ... goodness ... [all grandly united] ... spiritual savors ... in the East a fair morning like unto the color of roses ... the sweet Governess of Heaven, Venus which keepeth the bounds of night and day ... the tunable notes of the pretty birds, among the hushing woods of the hills. ...

TOPICS FOR DISCUSSION

1. What, specifically, is Neurosis apologizing for? Why would the three stages of his apology correspond to an Inferno, a Purgatorio, and a Paradiso?
2. Why is the first stage "the deceptions of speech"? What does the reporting of the prize fight in the style of international reporting show?
3. What does Burke mean by " 'scene-act' ratio" and "the *proportions* of the ingredients in a motivational cluster"? How are these connected?
4. Why, given the conditions of the talk, would the first stage be quickly passed over?
5. Under what circumstances did rhetoric reenter criticism after having been vandalized by exclusively esthetic interests?
6. What is the difference between "persuasion" and "identification"?
7. How does Burke define *dialectic*? To whose definition is he closer—Plato's or Aristotle's?
8. What is the double nature of hierarchy?

9. How does Castiglione's book illustrate the two dialectical series? Why would Neurosis cite this book in the third stage?
10. What practical problems are considered in the latter part of the essay?
11. How do the series of examples define what Burke means by blandness? What is the "bland strategy"?
12. What does the passage from Gertrude Stein reveal? In what sense does the stress move toward the agent?
13. What is "deflection"? How is it related to Freudian "displacement"? What does the example of the two brothers show?
14. What does the context of the concluding paragraph suggest about the meaning of "spiritualization"?

TOPICS FOR COMPOSITION

1. Summarize the relationship between rhetoric and dialectic as Burke conceives it. Then compare his conception with Booth's.
2. Drawing examples from the materials of this book, illustrate the difference between the old and the new rhetoric, as Burke distinguishes it.
3. Analyze the structure of Burke's essay, showing how the examples and organization are fitted to a particular audience. Discuss also the contribution of tone to the development of the argument.
4. Illustrate the stratagems Burke discusses in the latter part of the essay.

APPENDIX

Biographical Notes

ARISTOTLE (384–322 B.C.) was the son of Nicomachus, the physician to Amyntas II of Macedonia, a kingdom north of Athens. He acquired the name "the Stagirite" because he was born in Stagira in Thrace. Following a long course of study in Athens under Plato, he became tutor to young Alexander, the son of Philip of Macedonia. On the accession of Alexander in 335, Aristotle returned to Athens and founded his own school, the Lyceum. Because he and his students walked through the gardens of the school as they philosophized, the school came to be known as the Peripatetic. The curriculum covered every important field of knowledge but specialized in natural science (as Plato's Academy specialized in mathematics and metaphysics as well as politics). Following the death of Alexander, Aristotle came under the suspicion of the authorities and, like Socrates, was charged with impiety. Reputedly expressing the thought that one Socrates was enough, he left Athens for Chalcis where he died. The exhaustiveness as well as the acuteness of Aristotle's ideas—in particular, his emphasis on the *why* or the essential qualities of things—led philosophers of the Middle Ages, who discovered Aristotle chiefly through Arabic commentators, to refer to him as "the Philosopher." Aristotle was known to the ancient world largely through about twenty-seven dialogues, now lost, which Cicero and Quintilian considered worthy of Plato. His extant works seem to have been preserved in the form of systematic lecture notes, collected in his later years.

SAUL BELLOW (b. 1915), widely regarded as one of the outstanding novelists of this generation, was born of Jewish immigrant parents in Lachine, Quebec, Canada, but moved to Chicago during his childhood. He attended the University of Chicago and Northwestern, receiving a B.S. degree in 1937 from the latter. He taught at the Pestalozzi-Froebel Teachers College in Chicago until 1942. At the same time, his writing began to appear in national magazines and in anthologies. From 1943 to 1946, he was a member of the editorial department of the *Encyclopaedia Britannica*. In 1944, his first novel, *Dangling Man*, was published. *Dangling Man* is an introspective story about a sad young man who, after receiving his draft notice, quits his job and then has to wait a year before being called up. In 1946, Bellow joined the English faculty of the University of Minnesota as an assistant professor. While he was a Guggenheim Fellow, he published his second novel, *The Victim* (1947), a study of the guilt feelings of a Jew who is falsely accused by a Gentile of ruining his career. During his residence (1952–53) at Princeton University as Creative Writing Fellow, Bellow received both the National Institute of Arts and Letters Award and the National Book Award, the latter for his *The Adventures of Augie March* (1953), which tells the comic experiences of Augie March in the world of business and love.

During 1953–54, Bellow taught creative writing at Bard College. A second Guggenheim Fellowship was granted to him during 1955–56. In 1956, he published *Seize the Day*, which contained a novella as well as a play and several short stories. In 1959, Bellow published another novel, *Henderson, the Rainmaker*. Henderson, a giant both physically and morally, is dissatisfied with his humdrum life and fulfills his wish for real experience in Africa where he becomes the rainmaker, or headman, of a primitive tribe.

In 1961, an early version of *Herzog* was presented as a work in progress. It was clearly autobiographical in tone yet fraternally related to Bellow's earlier fiction in its stress on the moral and emotional aspects of experience. *Herzog* appeared in 1964.

Bellow's method in general is to begin not with a well-ordered plot but "with disorder and disharmony" and then to work "towards order by an unknown process of the imagination." He offers no ready interpretations of his stories, leaving the reader to decide their meaning and their relevance for himself.

VIOLET BONHAM CARTER (b. 1887) is the elder daughter of H. H. Asquith (1858–1928), first earl of Oxford and Asquith and Liberal Prime Minister of Great Britain from April 1908 to December 1916. Throughout much of his life she assisted her father and became a leader in the Liberal Party organization, serving as president from 1944 to 1945. In recognition of her many services to the British nation she was made a life peer in 1964.

WAYNE C. BOOTH (b. 1921) was educated at Brigham Young University and the University of Chicago. He taught at Haverford College, the University of Chicago, and Earlham College and is at present Dean of the Undergraduate College of the University of Chicago. He has written the influential *The Rhetoric of Fiction* (1961), for which he won in 1966 the David H. Russell Award for Distinguished Research given by the National Council of Teachers of English, as well as many articles in literary criticism and rhetoric. His ideas owe much to the Chicago neo-Aristotelian critics, a group led by R. M. McKeon and Ronald S. Crane.

EDMUND BURKE (1729–97) was born in Dublin and educated at Trinity College. In 1750, he migrated to London where he began the study of law at the Middle Temple. Although he admired the law and became one of its great scholars, Burke abandoned it for a literary career that brought him to great prominence in his early thirties. A secretaryship to Sir William Hamilton, then Secretary for Ireland, and later to the Marquis of Rockingham, the leader of a Whig faction, led Burke into politics where he served as a Member of Parliament from 1765 to 1794. Besides his interest in American affairs, Burke addressed himself to the problems of the British Empire in Ireland, India, and France. His tract on the Popery Laws (1765), a speech on Fox's East India Bill (1783), his speeches during the trial of

Warren Hastings (1788–94), and above all, his *Reflections on the French Revolution* (1790) contain some of his most powerful and representative thinking. Burke was a vigorous exponent of balanced views. Because he was for reform but against revolution he offended extremists of all kinds and rarely succeeded in winning his immediate arguments. History, however, has rendered a favorable verdict by frequently adopting Burke's wisdom.

KENNETH BURKE (b. 1897) was educated at Ohio State and Columbia universities. He has taught at many schools, among them the University of Chicago, Syracuse University, and Bennington College. He has devoted himself to many fields of knowledge, drawing upon the new social sciences, psychology, and biology for his contributions to a new theory of rhetoric. Among his works are *Counter-Statement* (1953), *Permanence and Change* (1935), *The Philosophy of Literary Form* (1941), *A Grammar of Motives* (1945), *A Rhetoric of Motives* (1949), and *A Rhetoric of Religion* (1961).

ABRAHAM COWLEY (1618–67) was born in London and received his education at Westminister School and Trinity College, Cambridge. Extremely precocious, he published his first volume of poetry when he was fifteen. A Latin play, *Naufragium Joculare,* and a pastoral drama, *Love's Riddle,* were both produced while he was an undergraduate. An ardent royalist during the Civil War, he fled to France with the royal family, where he acted as secretary to Queen Henrietta Maria and composed the poetry that appeared in *The Mistress* (1647) and *Miscellanies* (1656). He was arrested as a royalist spy by the Cromwell government in 1655 but was released after agreeing to submit to the Commonwealth. He then studied medicine at Oxford, from which he received an M.D. degree in 1657. Cowley's service to the crown, his genuine poetic talent, and his contributions to the advancement of science received high praise but little reward from his own generation. Although Charles II was not pleased at Cowley's agreement with the Cromwell government, Cowley did, after the Restoration, receive a small pension. He spent his last seven years in a small leasehold in Surrey, where he wrote Latin poems on flowers and plants and composed philosophic essays on the pleasures of retirement.

DANIEL DEFOE (1660–1731), the son of a butcher, was born in London and rose to become one of England's greatest journalists, pamphleteers, and novelists. A nonconformist in religion, he participated in the rebellion against James II and supported William of Orange. He was—sometimes simultaneously—a hosier, a merchant, an accountant, a government spy, and the prolific author of over four hundred books and pamphlets. Faithful to his middle-class origins, he wrote innumerable tracts aimed at the moral and economic improvement of his readers. His imaginative journalism frequently bordered on fiction, as in *A Journal of the Plague Year*, and crossed that border in realistic adventure novels like *Robinson Crusoe* (1719), *The Memories of a Cavalier* (1720), *Moll Flanders* (1722), and *Roxanna* (1724). Since his histories, journals, and tracts never lacked a touch of fiction, nor his fiction the touch of fact, literary historians sometimes dispute whether he is the founding father of the newspaper or of the novel. However, they do not dispute the fact that, because of the vigor and ease of his style, he is one of the founding fathers of modern English prose.

T. S. ELIOT (1888–1964) was born in St. Louis, Missouri, and educated at Harvard University, Oxford University, and the Sorbonne. He settled in London in 1915 and became a British citizen in 1927. Successively a school master, a book clerk, a magazine editor, he became known as a poet in 1917 with the publication of *Prufrock and Other Observations*. His sensitive essays contained in *The Sacred Wood* (1920) and in other collections, together with his bleak portrayals of the modern scene in poems like *The Wasteland* (1922) and "The Hollow Men" (1925), marked a revolution in the theory and practice of modern poetry. Gradually, however, Eliot turned to religious themes, in "Ash Wednesday" (1930) and *Murder in the Cathedral* (1935). The play *Murder in the Cathedral* tells of the martyrdom of Thomas à Becket in a manner that reflects medieval and Elizabethan drama as well as the problems of the contemporary struggle between church and state. One of the most successful parts of the play is the ironic portrayal of the Four Knights, whose modern colloquial prose reminds us of the contemporary relevance of the play. After receiving the Nobel Prize for Literature in 1948, Eliot devoted himself chiefly to the theater and to the essay. At the time of his death he was widely regarded as the most prominent English poet.

HENRY FIELDING (1707–54) was born near Glastonbury in Somerset, England, the son of a general. He was a high-spirited youth whose only early formal education was at Eton, although after producing his first play in London in 1728 he studied at the University of Leyden. He then returned to an active life in the theater, where twenty-one successful plays in seven years made him England's most popular playwright. His satires provoked the Licensing Act of 1737, which drove him from the stage. He turned to law and journalism, served with notable success as a justice of the peace, and instituted many reforms in criminal law. His career as a novelist began with *Joseph Andrews* (1742), which was a parody of Samuel Richardson's *Pamela*, and a mock-epic *Jonathan Wild, the Great* (1743), the fictitious life of a criminal, which ironically reversed the scale of human values. With *Tom Jones* (1749), Fielding achieved his greatest success. This "comic epic in prose" is notable for its elaborate plot, its illustration of Fielding's philosophy of benevolence, its range of social history, and its incidental

462

literary essays on the theory and technique of fiction. *Amelia* (1751), which depicted the evil effects of a husband's weakness and the saving quality of a wife's virtue, is less vigorous than *Tom Jones* but is an important revelation of the serious side of Fielding's personality. Fielding died in Lisbon where he had gone for his health.

E. M. FORSTER (b. 1879) was born in London and educated at Tonbridge School and King's College, Cambridge. He was a young man during the heyday of the Art for Art's Sake Movement. Five short novels, *Where Angels Fear to Tread* (1905), *The Longest Journey* (1907), *A Room with a View* (1908), *Howards End* (1916) and *A Passage to India* (1924), account chiefly for his extensive literary reputation. Forster, however, has also written memorable short stories, essays, biographies, and a notable study of fiction, *Aspects of the Novel* (1927), as well as several volumes of history and travel. Although *A Passage to India,* a study of the misunderstandings that baffle the gestures of good will by Indians and Englishmen, is his most widely known novel, his most characteristic work is probably *Howards End*. This novel contrasts lives dedicated to art, represented by the Schlegels, and lives dedicated to political and social life, represented by the Wilcoxes. Forster's main virtues are his subtle use of irony, his sustained contrasts between illusion and reality, and his adroitness in presenting various points of view.

JOHN HERSEY (b. 1914) was born in Tientsin, China, of missionary parents. After graduation from Yale, he served briefly as secretary to Sinclair Lewis, then became a correspondent for *Time, Life* and *The New Yorker*. His early works, *Men on Bataan* (1942) and *Into the Valley* (1943), were vivid reports of military actions in the Pacific during World War II. *A Bell for Adano* (1944), a blend of fiction and journalism, won the Pulitzer Prize in 1945. *Hiroshima* (1946) combined vivid reporting with imaginative techniques of psychological portraiture usually associated with fiction. By the same token, his major fiction *The Wall* (1950), a story of Jewish resistance to Hitler in the Warsaw ghetto, employs journalistic techniques to create realistic effects. While recent novels, *A Single Pebble* (1956), *The War Lover* (1959), and *The Child Buyer* (1960), are more inventive in design, they still reflect Hersey's commitment to the novel of contemporary history. In 1965, Hersey accepted an appointment as Master of Pearson College at Yale University.

SHIRLEY JACKSON (1919–65) was one of the most versatile American writers. In addition to her two family chronicles, *Life Among the Savages* (1953) and *Raising Demons* (1957), she wrote short stories, some of which may be found in *The Lottery* (1949), and several novels. Each new work gave her readers a fresh display of her originality. Her special ability, il-

Biographical Notes   **463**

lustrated in novels like *The Road Through the Wall* (1948), *Hangsaman* (1951), *The Bird's Nest* (1954), *Sundial* (1958), and *The Haunting of Hill House* (1959), was the fusion of psychological mystery with a realistic setting.

SAMUEL JOHNSON (1709–84) was born at Lichfield, where he obtained a precocious knowledge of books in his father's bookstore. After attending Pembroke College, Oxford, he served briefly as a schoolmaster, then, in 1737, he went to London where, in addition to working as "a Grub street Hack," he composed poetry and plays and worked as a translator and journalist. Publication of his *Dictionary* in 1755 earned him an enormous reputation. His essays in *The Rambler* (1750–52) and in the *Universal Chronicle* (1758–60) under the title of "The Idler," his novel *Rasselas* (1759), his edition of *The Plays of William Shakespeare* (1765), his travel account, *Journey to the Western Islands of Scotland* (1775), and his *Lives of the Poets* (1779–81) confirmed and extended his popularity as a man of letters. James Boswell's *Life* depicted him as a supreme conversationalist and dramatic personality as well as a critic, scholar, and moralist.

HOWARD MUMFORD JONES (b. 1892) was born in Saginaw, Michigan, and was educated at Wisconsin, Chicago, and Harvard. He has taught at the University of North Carolina, the University of Michigan and Harvard University, where he also served as Dean of the Graduate School of Arts and Sciences. Some of his best known books are *America and French Culture* (1927), *The Theory of American Literature* (1948), and *Guide to American Literature and Its Background Since 1890* (1953). Since 1955 he has served as chairman of the American Council of Learned Societies. Currently Professor Emeritus at Harvard, Mr. Jones is a prominent spokesman for the humanities.

JOHN FITZGERALD KENNEDY (1917–63) was born in Brookline, Massachusetts, and was educated at Choate and Harvard University. He served at the U.S. Embassy in London during the ambassadorship of his father, where he completed his senior thesis, *While England Slept* (1938). In 1956 his *Profiles in Courage,* stories of political heroism, received the Pulitzer Prize. During World War II, his service as a torpedo boat commander in the Pacific won him both the Navy Medal and the Purple Heart. Elected to the House of Representatives in 1947 and to the Senate in 1952, Mr. Kennedy overcame many physical handicaps to become a leading candidate for the Democratic nomination for the presidency. When he was elected in 1960, he was the youngest President in the history of the United States, the first Catholic to hold the office, and the President elected with the smallest popular majority. He was assassinated during a presidential visit to Dallas, Texas, on November 22, 1963.

C. S. LEWIS (1898–1963) was born in Belfast, Ireland, and taught medieval and Renaissance literature at Oxford and Cambridge. During his active career, he became a master of three distinct but interrelated kinds of writing. As a professional literary scholar he made important studies of Spenser, Milton, and medieval allegory. *The Allegory of Love* (1936) won the Hawthornden Prize and is widely regarded as a major work in medieval studies. As a Christian apologist, Lewis wrote more than a dozen books on various aspects of Christian theology, the most famous of which is *The Screwtape Letters* (1942). He was also a distinguished novelist both in theological fantasy, with such works as *Out of the Silent Planet* (1938), and in children's literature, such as *The Last Battle* (1957), which was awarded the Carnegie Prize. His autobiography *Surprised by Joy* (1955) is at once a candid account of his life and a revelation of the sources of his inspiration.

ABRAHAM LINCOLN (1809–65) was born in Kentucky and spent his early years as a farm boy in Kentucky, Indiana, and Illinois. He became a river boatman, a store keeper, a lawyer, a member of the Illinois legislature, a member of Congress, and finally President. Although he did not attend school, he acquired an extraordinary literary education by intense study of the Bible and John Bunyan, by the constant practice of debate, and by a profound knowledge of the oral literature of the frontier. Lincoln's strong convictions, his deep capacity to share in common feeling, his terse, vivid style, often combined, as in the *Gettysburg Address,* the letter to Mrs. Bixby, and the *Second Inaugural Address,* to communicate the most intensely personal and the most widely public emotions. Lincoln died just about a month after delivering the *Second Inaugural Address,* and many people regard it as his last testament to the nation.

SAMUEL ELIOT MORISON (b. 1887) was educated at St. Paul's School and at Harvard and Oxford universities. After teaching history for a year at the University of California, he returned to Harvard in 1915, where he began his notable career as a historian. In addition to his work on Massachusetts history, Morison has completed *Admiral of the Ocean Sea* (1942), a biography of Christopher Columbus, a fifteen-volume *History of the United States Naval Operations in World War II* (1947), *The Oxford History of the American People* (1965), and most recently *Old Bruin,* a biography of Commodore Matthew Perry. Besides numerous professional awards, Morison holds the rank of admiral in the U.S. Navy.

JOHN HENRY CARDINAL NEWMAN (1801–90) was educated at Ealing and Trinity College, Oxford. His undergraduate years at Oxford were marked by the extremes of disappointment and success: he failed to take honors but won the coveted Oriel Fellowship. While at Oriel he was active both as a preacher in the University Church and as an educational reformer. From 1833 to 1841, Newman, with Keble, Pusey, and others, was a leader in the Oxford Movement. He entered the Catholic church in 1845. Newman's career as a Catholic was notable for his pioneer work in the founding of the Catholic University of Dublin and his lectures on a wide variety of philosophical, historical, and religious themes. His major books, in addition to *The Idea of a University*, are his *Apologia pro Vita Sua* (1864), *A Grammar of Assent* (1870), and *Letter to the Duke of Norfolk* (1875).

WALTER PATER (1839–94) was born at Shadwell in East London. Pater's early years were marked by intense piety. During his residence at Queen's College, Oxford, however, he became a disciple of Jowett and the German school of philosophy. A trip to Italy in 1865 stimulated his love for the Renaissance and confirmed him in his tendency toward relativism. An early devotee of the Art for Art's Sake Movement, Pater pursued his esthetic themes with religious intensity in *Studies in the History of the Renaissance* (1873), *Appreciations* (1889), and in his remarkable novel *Marius the Epicurean* (1885). Although Pater's prose is much too complex to permit a single classification, he is justly called an esthetic critic. In *Renaissance*, he describes such a critic as one who regarded works of art "as powers or forces producing pleasurable sensations, each of a more or less peculiar or unique kind." Despite his life-long preoccupation with philosophy, Pater's chief concern was with experience itself, particularly those experiences that were the focus of the greatest number of vital forces. "To burn always with this hard, gem-like flame, to maintain this ecstasy, is success in life. . . . Not to discriminate every moment some passionate attitude in those about us . . . is . . . to sleep before evening." Thus philosophy was not so much knowledge as it was a special kind of awareness. Nevertheless, Pater admitted that all great art depended on its matter rather than its form.

PLATO (427?–347 B.C.), one of the most influential of all philosophers, was the son of aristocrats; his father reputedly traced his ancestry to the earliest rulers of Athens. In his youth, Plato excelled in every study, even in wrestling, from which he took the epithet *Platon*, meaning broad or robust. As he was deciding between a career in politics and in poetry, he came under the influence of Socrates, who directed his interest to philosophy. The oligarchic revolution in Athens in 404 B.C. headed by his relatives and the later trial and execution of Socrates on charges of subverting the youth of Athens and teaching impious ideas forced Plato into exile. Though he returned to the city in 395 B.C.—four years after the death of Socrates in 399 B.C.—he traveled widely throughout his life, studying mathematics and philosophy in different countries. Following one of his visits to Sicily, he was reputedly sold into slavery and ransomed by his friends. On his return to Athens, he founded the Academy, technically a religious association dedicated to the Muses. The students, who paid no tuition but whose parents supported the institution, studied philosophy and mathematics. Over the entrance was the inscription, "No one without geometry may enter." In his later years, Plato developed and refined the ideas of his early dialogues; his later dialogues make it difficult to ascribe to him any fixed ideas on the important questions he discussed. Certain ideas and attitudes recur but are not always formulated or stated in the same way. Though many of these ideas have profoundly influenced the course of Western civilization, Plato is perhaps most important because of the ways he asked these important questions and indicated how they might be discussed.

WILLIAM H. PRESCOTT (1796–1859) was born in Salem, Massachusetts, and educated at Harvard University. He originally intended to follow his father's profession of the law, but an injury to his eye in a schoolboy accident forced him into private scholarship. Prescott's heroic dedication to his profession resulted in four major historical works, all of them vivid accounts of heroic figures. His detailed biography appears in Samuel Eliot Morison's *Prescott, the American Thucydides.*

J. B. PRIESTLEY (b. 1894) was born at Bradford, Yorkshire. He joined the army in World War I, became an officer, was wounded and invalided from the service. Priestley wrote for the *Yorkshire Post* before entering Trinity Hall, Cambridge in 1919. He became known first for his magazine essays and literary studies, such as *The English Comic Characters* (1925), and his critical biographies, *Meredith* (1926) and *Peacock* (1927). After the great popular success of his novel *The Good Companions* (1929), Priestley divided his writing time among fiction, playwriting, and essays. Although he is best known for his novels, many of which have been filmed, and for plays of suspense like *Dangerous Corner* (1932) and *Time and the Conways* (1937), Priestley has always retained a special audience for his brilliant and sometimes prophetic essays on the nature of man and of contemporary society. *Midnight on the Desert* (1937) is a provocative study of time, and *Thoughts in the Wilderness* (1957) contains stimulating analyses of social problems.

GEORGE SAINTSBURY (1845–1933), one of the most prominent critics and literary historians of his time, was born at Southampton, England. After graduation from Merton College, Oxford, he taught at various public schools until 1895, when he became professor of English literature at the University of Edinburgh. A prolific writer of articles for magazines and encyclopedias as well as of books on literature, Saintsbury is best remembered for his *History of Criticism* (1900–04), *History of English Prosody* (1906–10), and his surveys of English and French literature. Saintsbury's command of logic enabled him to communicate his wide learning in various languages and literatures to the common reader as well as to academicians.

RICHARD STEELE (1672–1729) was born in Dublin, and was orphaned in his childhood. He was educated at Charterhouse School, where he met Joseph Addison, and at Merton College, Oxford. In 1694 he left Oxford to serve as a cadet in the Life Guards; he transferred to another regiment and rose to the rank of captain by 1700. His regimental friendships, associations with worldly Restoration wits like Sedley, Vanbrugh, and Congreve, and his own ebullient disposition led him to youthful excesses that greatly disturbed his conscience. In 1701 he wrote *The Christian Hero,* in which he argued that the spirit of the gentleman was the outgrowth of Christian virtues. In three comic plays, *The Funeral* (1701), *The Lying Lover* (1703), and *The Tender Husband* (1705), he repudiated the hitherto dominant tendency to exalt amoral wit over sincere piety. Although these plays, together with *The Conscious Lovers* (1722), marked a revolution in the English theater, Steele is best remembered for his contributions to the essay. In *The Tatler* (1709–10), whose three issues a week coincided with the mail schedule, and *The Spectator* (1711–12), a daily paper, Steele wrote "Talk of the Town" papers on virtually every phase of London life. His favorite topics were moral in tone: he attacked dueling, pedantry, artificial manners, in short "the false arts of life," and recommended "rational conduct." Steele's zest, geniality, and charm survived financial distress and the loss of personal, political, and literary friendships, including even that with Addison, his close collaborator on *The Spectator*. When Steele died in Carmathen, Wales, in 1729, he had achieved many of his aims: the reformation of the theater, elevation of the moral tone of English society, and the improvement of public taste.

JONATHAN SWIFT (1667–1745) was born in Dublin, Ireland. His career at Kilkenny Grammar School and Trinity College was marked by a more than usual resistance to the curriculum. His intellectual interests were stirred, however, by his life at Moor Park, the English estate of his relative, Sir William Temple, a prominent Whig lord and man of letters, for whom Swift acted as secretary for some ten years. Swift's experience of chicanery in high places, his disappointed ambitions, his life-long ill health, and his literary associations with Alexander Pope, John Arbuthnot and John Gay all fostered his own temperamental inclination to satire. In due course, he attacked literary folly in *The Battle of the Books,* religious discussion in *The Tale of a Tub* (both published in 1704), political stupidity in *On the Conduct of the Allies* (1713). After his appointment as Dean of St. Patrick's in Dublin, he began to identify himself with the cause of the Irish people. In his *Drapier's Letters* he attacked England's restrictions on Irish trade and attempted debasement of the coinage and in "A Modest Proposal" the culpable indifference of the landlords to the poverty of their tenants. All these themes, and others besides, are worked into *Gulliver's Travels* (1726), undoubtedly his masterpiece.

PIERRE TEILHARD DE CHARDIN (1881–1955) was educated by the Jesuits and became a member of their Society. After teaching in Cairo and serving as a chaplain in World War I, he devoted himself to science, first as a professor of geology at the *Institut Catholique* in Paris, then as a research scientist in China and elsewhere. Although honored by many fellow scientists and inducted into the Legion of Honor in 1943, Teilhard did not become widely known until after his death, when many of his books excited the attention of men of the humanities and science. Among the titles published in English are *The Phenomenon of Man* (1959), *The Divine Milieu* (1960), *The Future of Man* (1964), and *Hymn of the Universe* (1965). Karl Stern summed up the reason for this attention when he wrote: "It happens so rarely that science and wisdom are blended as they were in the person of Teilhard de Chardin."

WILLIAM D. TEMPLEMAN (b. 1903) was born in Princeton, Kentucky, and was educated at Western Reserve and Harvard Universities. Since 1945, he has been a professor at the University of Southern California where he has also served as chairman of the English department. A life-long student of Victorian literature, Mr. Templeman has written *Eight Essays on Victorian Literature* (1950), edited with Charles Harrold *The Prose of the Victorian Era* (1938), and contributed numerous articles and bibliographies in his special field to various journals.

RICHARD WEAVER (1910–63) was born in Asheville, North Carolina, and was educated at the University of Kentucky, Vanderbilt University, and Louisiana State University. He taught at Vanderbilt, Louisiana State, and the University of Chicago. Among his books are *Ideas Have Consequences* (1948), *The Ethics of Rhetoric* (1953), *Composition: A Course in Writing and Rhetoric* (1957), and *Life Without Prejudice and Other Essays* (1964).

E. B. WHITE (b. 1899) was born in Mount Vernon, New York, and was educated at Cornell University where he studied rhetoric under William Strunk, Jr., whose textbook *The Elements of Style* he subsequently revised and made famous. After a brief career in advertising, White joined the staff of *The New Yorker*, where he wrote brilliant brief essays on the editorial page under the title "Notes and Comment." He published these and other longer essays, many on political topics, in books like *One Man's Meat* (1942), *The Wild Flag* (1946), *Here is New York* (1949), *The Second Tree from the Corner* (1953), and *The Points of My Compass* (1962). Although White also writes verse and children's books, his essays, chiefly those interpreting contemporary life, are currently regarded as his most successful literary achievements.

Selected Bibliography of Modern Works on Rhetoric

Atkins, J. W. H. *English Literary Criticism: The Medieval Phase.* Cambridge: Cambridge Univ. Press, 1943.

———. *English Literary Criticism: The Renascence.* London: Methuen, 1947.

———. *English Literary Criticism: The Seventeenth and Eighteenth Centuries.* London: Methuen, 1951.

Baldwin, Charles Sears. *Ancient Rhetoric and Poetic.* New York: Macmillan, 1924.

———. *Medieval Rhetoric and Poetic.* New York: Macmillan, 1928.

———. *Renaissance Literary Theory and Practice.* New York: Columbia Univ. Press, 1939.

Baldwin, T. W. *William Shakspere's Small Latine and Lesse Greeke.* 2 vols. Urbana: Univ. of Illinois Press, 1944.

Brooks, Cleanth, and Wimsatt, William K., Jr. *Literary Criticism: A Short History.* New York: Knopf, 1957.

Burke, Kenneth. *A Rhetoric of Motives.* Englewood Cliffs, N.J.: Prentice-Hall, 1949.

Clark, Donald L. *Rhetoric and Poetry in the Renaissance.* New York: Columbia Univ. Press, 1922.

———. *Rhetoric in Greco-Roman Education.* New York: Columbia Univ. Press, 1957.

Cochrane, C. N. *Christianity and Classical Culture.* New York: Oxford Univ. Press, 1944.

Crane, William G. *Wit and Rhetoric in the Renaissance.* New York: Columbia Univ. Press, 1937.

Duhamel, P. A., "The Logic and Rhetoric of Peter Ramus," *Modern Philology.* Vol. 46 (February 1949), pp. 163–71.

Fogarty, Daniel. *Roots for a New Rhetoric.* New York: Teachers College of Columbia University, Bureau of Publications, 1959.

471

Grant, Michael (ed.). *Selected Works of Cicero.* Baltimore: Penguin Books, 1960.

Grierson, Herbert J. C. *Rhetoric and English Composition,* 2d ed. Edinburgh: Oliver and Boyd, 1945.

Herrick, Marvin T. *The Poetics of Aristotle in England.* New Haven, Conn.: Yale Univ. Press, 1930.

Howell, Wilbur S. *Logic and Rhetoric in England, 1500–1700.* Princeton: Princeton Univ. Press, 1956.

Howes, Raymond F. (ed.). *Historical Studies of Rhetoric and Rhetoricians.* Ithaca, N.Y.: Cornell Univ. Press, 1961.

Joseph, Sister Miriam. *Shakespeare's Use of the Arts of Language.* New York: Columbia Univ. Press, 1947.

Kennedy, George. *The Art of Persuasion in Greece.* Princeton: Princeton Univ. Press, 1963.

Kennedy, Milton B. *The Oration in Shakespeare.* Chapel Hill: Univ. of North Carolina Press, 1942.

McKeon, Richard. "Aristotle's Conception of Language and the Arts of Language," "Rhetoric in the Middle Ages," "Poetry and Philosophy in the Twelfth Century: The Renaissance of Rhetoric," in *Critics and Criticism.* Ronald S. Crane (ed.). Chicago: Univ. of Chicago Press, 1952.

Newman, John Henry. "Personal and Literary Character of Cicero," *Historical Sketches.* Vol. 1. London: Longmans, Green, 1948.

Roberts, W. Rhys. *Greek Rhetoric and Literary Theory.* London: Longmans, Green, 1928.

Schilling, Bernard N. (ed.). *Essential Articles for the Study of English Augustan Backgrounds.* Hamden, Conn.: Shoe String Press, 1961.

Solmsen, Friedrich. *Aristotle's System of the Physical World.* Ithaca, N.Y.: Cornell Univ. Press, 1960.

Weaver, Richard M. *The Ethics of Rhetoric.* Chicago: Regnery, 1953.

Wellek, René. *A History of Modern Criticism: 1750–1950.* 2 vols. New Haven, Conn.: Yale Univ. Press, 1955.

Williamson, George. *The Senecan Amble.* Chicago: Univ. of Chicago Press, 1951.

AUTHOR-
TITLE INDEX

Weaver, Richard

White, E. B.